W9-CJQ-208

EVERYMAN, I will go with thee,

and be thy guide,

In thy most need to go by thy side

DISCARDED

BEN JONSON

Believed to have been born in Westminster in 1573. Fought against the Spaniards in Flanders, returning in 1592, and took to the stage. Trial for murder, 1598; became a Roman Catholic for twelve years. Journey to France, 1613; to Scotland, 1618. Died in 1637.

DISCARDED

Ben Jonson's Plays

IN TWO VOLUMES · VOLUME TWO

INTRODUCTION BY
FELIX E. SCHELLING

DENT: LONDON
EVERYMAN'S LIBRARY
DUTTON: NEW YORK

All rights reserved
Made in Great Britain
at the
Aldine Press · Letchworth · Herts
for

J. M. DENT & SONS LTD
Aldine House · Bedford Street · London
First included in Everyman's Library 1910
Last reprinted 1966

NO. 490

CONTENTS

THE ALCHEMIST

TO THE LADY MOST DESERVING HER NAME AND BLOOD
LADY MARY WROTH

MADAM,—In the age of sacrifices, the truth of religion was not in the greatness and fat of the offerings, but in the devotion and zeal of the sacrificers: else what could a handful of gums have done in the sight of a hecatomb? or how might I appear at this altar, except with those affections that no less love the light and witness, than they have the conscience of your virtue? If what I offer bear an acceptable odour, and hold the first strength, it is your value of it, which remembers where, when, and to whom it was kindled. Otherwise, as the times are, there comes rarely forth that thing so full of authority or example, but by assiduity and custom grows less, and loses. This, yet, safe in your judgment (which is a SIDNEY'S) is forbidden to speak more, lest it talk or look like one of the ambitious faces of the time, who, the more they paint, are the less themselves. Your ladyship's true honourer,
BEN JONSON.

TO THE READER

IF thou beest more, thou art an understander, and then I trust thee. If thou art one that takest up, and but a pretender, beware of what hands thou receivest thy commodity; for thou wert never more fair in the way to be cozened, than in this age, in poetry, especially in plays: wherein, now the concupiscence of dances and of antics so reigneth, as to run away from nature, and be afraid of her, is the only point of art that tickles the spectators. But how out of purpose, and place, do I name art? When the professors are grown so obstinate contemners of it, and presumers on their own naturals, as they are deriders of all diligence that way, and, by simple mocking at the terms, when they understand not the things, think to get off wittily with their ignorance. Nay, they are esteemed the more learned, and sufficient for this, by the many, through their excellent vice of judgment. For they commend writers, as they do fencers or wrestlers; who if they come in robustuously, and put for it with a great deal of violence, are received for the braver fellows: when many times their own rudeness is the cause of their disgrace, and a little touch of their adversary gives all that boisterous force the foil. I deny not, but that these men, who always seek to do more than enough, may some time happen on some thing that is good, and great; but very seldom; and when it comes it doth not recompense the rest of their ill. It sticks out, perhaps, and is more eminent, because all is sordid and vile about it: as lights are more discerned in a thick darkness, than a faint shadow. I speak not this, out of a hope to do good to any man against his will; for I know, if it were put to the question of theirs and mine, the worse would find more suffrages: because the most favour common errors. But I give thee this warning, that there is a great difference between those, that, to gain the opinion of copy, utter all they can, however unfitly; and those that use election and a mean. For it is only the disease of the unskilful, to think rude things greater than polished; or scattered more numerous than composed.

DRAMATIS PERSONÆ

SUBTLE, *the Alchemist.*
FACE, *the Housekeeper.*
DOL COMMON, *their Colleague.*
DAPPER, *a Lawyer's Clerk.*
DRUGGER, *a Tobacco Man.*
LOVEWIT, *Master of the House.*
SIR EPICURE MAMMON, *a Knight.*
PERTINAX SURLY, *a Gamester.*

TRIBULATION WHOLESOME, *a Pastor of Amsterdam.*
ANANIAS, *a Deacon there.*
KASTRIL, *the angry Boy.*
DAME PLIANT, *his Sister, a Widow.*
Neighbours.

Officers, Attendants, *etc.*

SCENE,—LONDON

ARGUMENT

T *he sickness hot, a master quit, for fear,*
H *is house in town, and left one servant there;*
E *ase him corrupted, and gave means to know*

A *Cheater, and his punk; who now brought low,*
L *eaving their narrow practice, were become*
C *ozeners at large; and only wanting some*
H *ouse to set up, with him they here contract,*
E *ach for a share, and all begin to act.*
M *uch company they draw, and much abuse,*
I *n casting figures, telling fortunes, news,*
S *elling of flies, flat bawdry with the stone,*
T *ill it, and they, and all in fume are gone.*

PROLOGUE.

Fortune, that favours fools, these two short hours,
    We wish away, both for your sakes and ours,
Judging spectators; and desire, in place,
    To the author justice, to ourselves but grace.
Our scene is London, 'cause we would make known,
No country's mirth is better than our own:
No clime breeds better matter for your whore,
    Bawd, squire, impostor, many persons more,
Whose manners, now call'd humours, feed the stage;
    And which have still been subject for the rage
Or spleen of comic writers. Though this pen
    Did never aim to grieve, but better men;
Howe'er the age he lives in doth endure
    The vices that she breeds, above their cure.
But when the wholesome remedies are sweet,
    And in their working gain and profit meet,

He hopes to find no spirit so much diseased,
  But will with such fair correctives be pleased:
For here he doth not fear who can apply.
If there be any that will sit so nigh
Unto the stream, to look what it doth run,
  They shall find things, they'd think or wish were done;
They are so natural follies, but so shewn,
  As even the doers may see, and yet not own.

ACT I

SCENE I.—*A Room in* LOVEWIT's *House.*

Enter FACE, *in a captain's uniform, with his sword drawn, and* SUBTLE *with a vial, quarrelling, and followed by* DOL COMMON.

Face. Believe 't, I will.

Sub. Thy worst. I fart at thee.

Dol. Have you your wits? why, gentlemen! for love—

Face. Sirrah, I'll strip you—

Sub. What to do? lick figs
Out at my—

Face. Rogue, rogue!—out of all your sleights.

Dol. Nay, look ye, sovereign, general, are you madmen?

Sub. O, let the wild sheep loose. I'll gum your silks
With good strong water, an you come.

Dol. Will you have
The neighbours hear you? will you betray all?
Hark! I hear somebody.

Face. Sirrah—

Sub. I shall mar
All that the tailor has made, if you approach.

Face. You most notorious whelp, you insolent slave,
Dare you do this?

Sub. Yes, faith; yes, faith.

Face. Why, who
Am I, my mungrel? who am I?

Sub. I'll tell you,
Since you know not yourself.

Face. Speak lower, rogue.

Sub. Yes, you were once (time's not long past) the good,
Honest, plain, livery-three-pound-thrum, that kept
Your master's worship's house here in the Friars,
For the vacations—

Face. Will you be so loud?

Sub. Since, by my means, translated suburb-captain.

Face. By your means, doctor dog!

Sub. Within man's memory,
All this I speak of.

Face. Why, I pray you, have I
Been countenanced by you, or you by me?
Do but collect, sir, where I met you first.

Sub. I do not hear well.

Face. Not of this, I think it.
But I shall put you in mind, sir;—at Pie-corner,
Taking your meal of steam in, from cooks' stalls,
Where, like the father of hunger, you did walk
Piteously costive, with your pinch'd-horn-nose,
And your complexion of the Roman wash,
Stuck full of black and melancholic worms,
Like powder corns shot at the artillery-yard.

Sub. I wish you could advance your voice a little.

Face. When you went pinn'd up in the several rags
You had raked and pick'd from dunghills, before day;
Your feet in mouldy slippers, for your kibes;
A felt of rug, and a thin threaden cloke,
That scarce would cover your no buttocks—

Sub. So, sir!

Face. When all your alchemy, and your algebra,
Your minerals, vegetals, and animals,
Your conjuring, cozening, and your dozen of trades,
Could not relieve your corps with so much linen
Would make you tinder, but to see a fire;
I gave you countenance, credit for your coals,
Your stills, your glasses, your materials;
Built you a furnace, drew you customers,
Advanced all your black arts; lent you, beside,
A house to practise in—

Sub. Your master's house!

Face. Where you have studied the more thriving skill
Of bawdry since.

Sub. Yes, in your master's house.
You and the rats here kept possession.
Make it not strange. I know you were one could keep
The buttery-hatch still lock'd, and save the chippings,
Sell the dole beer to aqua-vitæ men,
The which, together with your Christmas vails
At post-and-pair, your letting out of counters,
Made you a pretty stock, some twenty marks,
And gave you credit to converse with cobwebs,
Here, since your mistress' death hath broke up house.

Face. You might talk softlier, rascal.

Sub. No, you scarab,
I'll thunder you in pieces: I will teach you
How to beware to tempt a Fury again,
That carries tempest in his hand and voice.

Face. The place has made you valiant.

Sub. No, your clothes.—

Thou vermin, have I ta'en thee out of dung,
So poor, so wretched, when no living thing
Would keep thee company, but a spider, or worse?
Rais'd thee from brooms, and dust, and watering-pots,
Sublimed thee, and exalted thee, and fix'd thee
In the third region, call'd our state of grace?
Wrought thee to spirit, to quintessence, with pains
Would twice have won me the philosopher's work?
Put thee in words and fashion, made thee fit
For more than ordinary fellowships?
Giv'n thee thy oaths, thy quarrelling dimensions,
Thy rules to cheat at horse-race, cock-pit, cards,
Dice, or whatever gallant tincture else?
Made thee a second in mine own great art?
And have I this for thanks! Do you rebel,
Do you fly out in the projection?
Would you be gone now?

  Dol. Gentlemen, what mean you?
Will you mar all?

  Sub. Slave, thou hadst had no name—

  Dol. Will you undo yourselves with civil war?

  Sub. Never been known, past *equi clibanum*,
The heat of horse-dung, under ground, in cellars,
Or an ale-house darker than deaf John's; been lost
To all mankind, but laundresses and tapsters,
Had not I been.

  Dol. Do you know who hears you, sovereign?

  Face. Sirrah—

  Dol. Nay, general, I thought you were civil.

  Face. I shall turn desperate, if you grow thus loud.

  Sub. And hang thyself, I care not.

  Face. Hang thee, collier,
And all thy pots, and pans, in picture, I will,
Since thou hast moved me—

  Dol. O, this will o'erthrow all.

  Face. Write thee up bawd in Paul's, have all thy tricks
Of cozening with a hollow cole, dust, scrapings,
Searching for things lost, with a sieve and sheers,
Erecting figures in your rows of houses,
And taking in of shadows with a glass,
Told in red letters; and a face cut for thee,
Worse than Gamaliel Ratsey's.

  Dol. Are you sound?
Have you your senses, masters?

  Face. I will have
A book, but barely reckoning thy impostures,
Shall prove a true philosopher's stone to printers.

  Sub. Away, you trencher-rascal!

  Face. Out, you dog-leach!

The vomit of all prisons—
   Dol. Will you be
Your own destructions, gentlemen?
   Face. Still spew'd out
For lying too heavy on the basket.
   Sub. Cheater!
   Face. Bawd!
   Sub. Cow-herd!
   Face. Conjurer!
   Sub. Cut-purse!
   Face. Witch!
   Dol. O me!
We are ruin'd, lost! have you no more regard
To your reputations? where's your judgment? 'slight,
Have yet some care of me, of your republic—
   Face. Away, this brach! I'll bring thee, rogue, within
The statute of sorcery, tricesimo tertio
Of Harry the Eighth: ay, and perhaps, thy neck
Within a noose, for laundring gold and barbing it.
   Dol. [*snatches Face's sword.*] You'll bring your head within
     a cockscomb, will you?
And you, sir, with your menstrue—
               [*Dashes Subtle's vial out of his hand.*
              Gather it up.—
'Sdeath, you abominable pair of stinkards,
Leave off your barking, and grow one again,
Or, by the light that shines, I'll cut your throats.
I'll not be made a prey unto the marshal,
For ne'er a snarling dog-bolt of you both.
Have you together cozen'd all this while,
And all the world, and shall it now be said,
You've made most courteous shift to cozen yourselves?
You will accuse him! you will *bring him in*   [*To Face.*
Within the statute! Who shall take your word?
A whoreson, upstart, apocryphal captain,
Whom not a Puritan in Blackfriars will trust
So much as for a feather: and you, too,   [*To Subtle.*
Will give the cause, forsooth! you will insult,
And claim a primacy in the divisions!
You must be chief! as if you only had
The powder to project with, and the work
Were not begun out of equality?
The venture tripartite? all things in common?
Without priority? 'Sdeath! you perpetual curs,
Fall to your couples again, and cozen kindly,
And heartily, and lovingly, as you should,
And lose not the beginning of a term,
Or, by this hand, I shall grow factious too,
And take my part, and quit you.

Face. 'Tis his fault;
He ever murmurs, and objects his pains,
And says, the weight of all lies upon him.

  Sub. Why, so it does.

  Dol. How does it? do not we
Sustain our parts?

  Sub. Yes, but they are not equal.

  Dol. Why, if your part exceed to-day, I hope
Ours may, to-morrow, match it.

  Sub. Ay, they *may.*

  Dol. May, murmuring mastiff! ay, and do. Death on me!
Help me to throttle him.   [*Seizes Sub. by the throat.*

  Sub. Dorothy! mistress Dorothy!
'Ods precious, I'll do any thing. What do you mean?

  Dol. Because o' your fermentation and cibation?

  Sub. Not I, by heaven—

  Dol. Your Sol and Luna——help me.   [*To Face.*

  Sub. Would I were hang'd then! I'll conform myself.

  Dol. Will you, sir? do so then, and quickly: swear.

  Sub. What should I swear?

  Dol. To leave your faction, sir,
And labour kindly in the common work.

  Sub. Let me not breathe if I meant aught beside.
I only used those speeches as a spur
To him.

  Dol. I hope we need no spurs, sir. Do we?

  Face. 'Slid, prove to-day, who shall shark best.

  Sub. Agreed.

  Dol. Yes, and work close and friendly.

  Sub. 'Slight, the knot
Shall grow the stronger for this breach, with me.

                       [*They shake hands.*

  Dol. Why, so, my good baboons! Shall we go make
A sort of sober, scurvy, precise neighbours,
That scarce have smiled twice since the king came in,
A feast of laughter at our follies? Rascals,
Would run themselves from breath, to see me ride,
Or you t' have but a hole to thrust your heads in,
For which you should pay ear-rent? No, agree.
And may don Provost ride a feasting long,
In his old velvet jerkin and stain'd scarfs,
My noble sovereign, and worthy general,
Ere we contribute a new crewel garter
To his most worsted worship.

  Sub. Royal Dol!
Spoken like Claridiana, and thyself.

  Face. For which at supper, thou shalt sit in triumph,
And not be styled Dol Common, but Dol Proper,
Dol Singular: the longest cut at night,

Shall draw thee for his Doll Particular.   *[Bell rings without.*

  Sub. Who's that? one rings. To the window, Dol: *[Exit Dol.]*
   —pray heaven,
The master do not trouble us this quarter.
  Face. O, fear not him. While there dies one a week
O' the plague, he's safe, from thinking toward London:
Beside, he's busy at his hop-yards now;
I had a letter from him. If he do,
He'll send such word, for airing of the house,
As you shall have sufficient time to quit it:
Though we break up a fortnight, 'tis no matter.

Re-enter DOL.

  Sub. Who is it, Dol?
  Dol. A fine young quodling.
  Face. O,
My lawyer's clerk, I lighted on last night,
In Holborn, at the Dagger. He would have
(I told you of him) a familiar,
To rifle with at horses, and win cups.
  Dol. O, let him in.
  Sub. Stay. Who shall do't?
  Face. Get you
Your robes on: I will meet him as going out.
  Dol. And what shall I do?
  Face. Not be seen; away!   *[Exit Dol.*
Seem you very reserv'd.   *[Exit.*
  Sub. Enough.
  Face. [aloud and retiring.] God be wi' you, sir,
I pray you let him know that I was here:
His name is Dapper. I would gladly have staid, but—
  Dap. [within.] Captain, I am here.
  Face. Who's that?—He's come, I think, doctor.

Enter DAPPER.

Good faith, sir, I was going away.
  Dap. In truth,
I am very sorry, captain.
  Face. But I thought
Sure I should meet you.
  Dap. Ay, I am very glad.
I had a scurvy writ or two to make,
And I had lent my watch last night to one
That dines to-day at the sheriff's, and so was robb'd
Of my past-time.

Re-enter SUBTLE, in his velvet Cap and Gown.

Is this the cunning-man?
  Face. This is his worship.

Dap. Is he a doctor?

Face. Yes.

Dap. And you have broke with him, captain?

Face. Ay.

Dap. And how?

Face. Faith, he does make the matter, sir, so dainty
I know not what to say.

Dap. Not so, good captain.

Face. Would I were fairly rid of it, believe me.

Dap. Nay, now you grieve me, sir. Why should you wish so?
I dare assure you, I'll not be ungrateful.

Face. I cannot think you will, sir. But the law
Is such a thing——and then he says, Read's matter
Falling so lately.

Dap. Read! he was an ass,
And dealt, sir, with a fool.

Face. It was a clerk, sir.

Dap. A clerk!

Face. Nay, hear me, sir, you know the law
Better, I think—

Dap. I should, sir, and the danger:
You know, I shew'd the statute to you.

Face. You did so.

Dap. And will I tell then! By this hand of flesh,
Would it might never write good court-hand more,
If I discover. What do you think of me,
That I am a chiaus?

Face. What's that?

Dap. The Turk was here.
As one would say, do you think I am a Turk?

Face. I'll tell the doctor so.

Dap. Do, good sweet captain.

Face. Come, noble doctor, pray thee let's prevail;
This is the gentleman, and he is no chiaus.

Sub. Captain, I have return'd you all my answer.
I would do much, sir, for your love——But this
I neither may, nor can.

Face. Tut, do not say so.
You deal now with a noble fellow, doctor,
One that will thank you richly; and he is no chiaus:
Let that, sir, move you.

Sub. Pray you, forbear—

Face. He has
Four angels here.

Sub. You do me wrong, good sir.

Face. Doctor, wherein? to tempt you with these spirits?

Sub. To tempt my art and love, sir, to my peril.
Fore heaven, I scarce can think you are my friend,
That so would draw me to apparent danger.

Face. I draw you! a horse draw you, and a halter,
You, and your flies together—

Dap. Nay, good captain.

Face. That know no difference of men.

Sub. Good words, sir.

Face. Good deeds, sir, doctor dogs-meat.   'Slight, I bring you
No cheating Clim o' the Cloughs, or Claribels,
That look as big as five-and-fifty, and flush;
And spit out secrets like hot custard—

Dap. Captain!

Face. Nor any melancholic under-scribe,
Shall tell the vicar; but a special gentle,
That is the heir to forty marks a year,
Consorts with the small poets of the time,
Is the sole hope of his old grandmother;
That knows the law, and writes you six fair hands,
Is a fine clerk, and has his cyphering perfect,
Will take his oath o' the Greek Testament,
If need be, in his pocket; and can court
His mistress out of Ovid.

Dap. Nay, dear captain—

Face. Did you not tell me so?

Dap. Yes; but I'd have you
Use master doctor with some more respect.

Face. Hang him, proud stag, with his broad velvet head!—
But for your sake, I'd choak, ere I would change
An article of breath with such a puckfist:
Come, let's be gone.   [*Going.*

Sub. Pray you let me speak with you.

Dap. His worship calls you, captain.

Face. I am sorry
I e'er embark'd myself in such a business.

Dap. Nay, good sir; he did call you.

Face. Will he take then?

Sub. First, hear me—

Face. Not a syllable, 'less you take.

Sub. Pray you, sir—

Face. Upon no terms, but an *assumpsit.*

Sub. Your humour must be law.   [*He takes the four angels.*

Face. Why now, sir, talk.
Now I dare hear you with mine honour.   Speak.
So may this gentleman too.

Sub. Why, sir—   [*Offering to whisper Face.*

Face. No whispering.

Sub. Fore heaven, you do not apprehend the loss
You do yourself in this.

Face. Wherein? for what?

Sub. Marry, to be so importunate for one,
That, when he has it, will undo you all:

He'll win up all the money in the town.

   Face. How!

   Sub. Yes, and blow up gamester after gamester,
As they do crackers in a puppet play.
If I do give him a familiar,
Give you him all you play for; never set him:
For he will have it.

   Face. You are mistaken, doctor.
Why he does ask one but for cups and horses,
A rifling fly; none of your great familiars.

   Dap. Yes, captain, I would have it for all games.

   Sub. I told you so.

   Face. [*taking Dap. aside.*] 'Slight, that is a new business!
I understood you, a tame bird, to fly
Twice in a term, or so, on Friday nights,
When you had left the office, for a nag
Of forty or fifty shillings.

   Dap. Ay, 'tis true, sir;
But I do think now I shall leave the law,
And therefore—

   Face. Why, this changes quite the case.
Do you think that I dare move him?

   Dap. If you please, sir;
All's one to him, I see.

   Face. What! for that money?
I cannot with my conscience; nor should you
Make the request, methinks.

   Dap. No, sir, I mean
To add consideration.

   Face. Why then, sir,
I'll try.—[*Goes to Subtle.*] Say that it were for all games, doctor?

   Sub. I say then, not a mouth shall eat for him
At any ordinary, but on the score,
That is a gaming mouth, conceive me.

   Face. Indeed!

   Sub. He'll draw you all the treasure of the realm,
If it be set him.

   Face. Speak you this from art?

   Sub. Ay, sir, and reason too, the ground of art.
He is of the only best complexion,
The queen of Fairy loves.

   Face. What! is he?

   Sub. Peace.
He'll overhear you. Sir, should she but see him—

   Face. What?

   Sub. Do not you tell him.

   Face. Will he win at cards too?

   Sub. The spirits of dead Holland, living Isaac,
You'd swear were in him; such a vigorous luck

As cannot be resisted. 'Slight, he'll put
Six of your gallants to a cloke, indeed.

Face. A strange success, that some man shall be born to!

Sub. He hears you, man—

Dap. Sir, I'll not be ingrateful.

Face. Faith, I have confidence in his good nature:
You hear, he says he will not be ingrateful.

Sub. Why, as you please; my venture follows yours.

Face. Troth, do it, doctor; think him trusty, and make him.
He may make us both happy in an hour;
Win some five thousand pound, and send us two on't.

Dap. Believe it, and I will, sir.

Face. And you shall, sir.   [*Takes him aside.*
You have heard all?

Dap. No, what was't? Nothing, I, sir.

Face. Nothing!

Dap. A little, sir.

Face. Well, a rare star
Reign'd at your birth.

Dap. At mine, sir! No.

Face. The doctor
Swears that you are—

Sub. Nay, captain, you'll tell all now.

Face. Allied to the queen of Fairy.

Dap. Who? that I am?
Believe it, no such matter—

Face. Yes, and that
You were born with a cawl on your head.

Dap. Who says so?

Face. Come,
You know it well enough, though you dissemble it.

Dap. I'fac, I do not: you are mistaken.

Face. How!
Swear by your fac, and in a thing so known
Unto the doctor? How shall we, sir, trust you
In the other matter? can we ever think,
When you have won five or six thousand pound,
You'll send us shares in't, by this rate?

Dap. By Jove, sir,
I'll win ten thousand pound, and send you half.
I'fac's no oath.

Sub. No, no, he did but jest.

Face. Go to. Go thank the doctor: he's your friend,
To take it so.

Dap. I thank his worship.

Face. So!
Another angel.

Dap. Must I?

Face. Must you! 'slight,

What else is thanks? will you be trivial?—Doctor,

[Dapper gives him the money.

When must he come for his familiar?

    Dap. Shall I not have it with me?

    Sub. O, good sir!

There must a world of ceremonies pass;
You must be bath'd and fumigated first:
Besides the queen of Fairy does not rise
Till it be noon.

    Face. Not, if she danced, to-night.

    Sub. And she must bless it.

    Face. Did you never see
Her royal grace yet?

    Dap. Whom?

    Face. Your aunt of Fairy?

    Sub. Not since she kist him in the cradle, captain;
I can resolve you that.

    Face. Well, see her grace,
Whate'er it cost you, for a thing that I know.
It will be somewhat hard to compass; but
However, see her. You are made, believe it,
If you can see her. Her grace is a lone woman,
And very rich; and if she take a fancy,
She will do strange things. See her, at any hand.
'Slid, she may hap to leave you all she has:
It is the doctor's fear.

    Dap. How will't be done, then?

    Face. Let me alone, take you no thought. Do you
But say to me, captain, I'll see her grace.

    Dap. Captain, I'll see her grace.

    Face. Enough.

                            [Knocking within.

    Sub. Who's there?

Anon.—Conduct him forth by the back way.—   *[Aside to Face.*
Sir, against one o'clock prepare yourself;
Till when you must be fasting; only take
Three drops of vinegar in at your nose,
Two at your mouth, and one at either ear;
Then bathe your fingers' ends and wash your eyes,
To sharpen your five senses, and cry *hum*
Thrice, and then *buz* as often; and then come.   *[Exit.*

    Face. Can you remember this?

    Dap. I warrant you.

    Face. Well then, away. It is but your bestowing
Some twenty nobles 'mong her grace's servants,
And put on a clean shirt: you do not know
What grace her grace may do you in clean linen.

                         [Exeunt Face and Dapper.

    Sub. [within.] Come in! Good wives, I pray you forbear me now;
Troth I can do you no good till afternoon—

Re-enters, followed by DRUGGER.

What is your name, say you, Abel Drugger?

 Drug. Yes, sir.

 Sub. A seller of tobacco?

 Drug. Yes, sir.

 Sub. Umph!

Free of the grocers?

 Drug. Ay, an't please you.

 Sub. Well—

Your business, Abel?

 Drug. This, an't please your worship;

I am a young beginner, and am building

Of a new shop, an't like your worship, just

At corner of a street:—Here is the plot on't—

And I would know by art, sir, of your worship,

Which way I should make my door, by necromancy,

And where my shelves; and which should be for boxes,

And which for pots. I would be glad to thrive, sir:

And I was wish'd to your worship by a gentleman,

One captain Face, that says you know men's planets,

And their good angels, and their bad.

 Sub. I do,

If I do see them—

Re-enter FACE.

 Face. What! my honest Abel?

Thou art well met here.

 Drug. Troth, sir, I was speaking,

Just as your worship came here, of your worship:

I pray you speak for me to master doctor.

 Face. He shall do any thing.—Doctor, do you hear!

This is my friend, Abel, an honest fellow;

He lets me have good tobacco, and he does not

Sophisticate it with sack-lees or oil,

Nor washes it in muscadel and grains,

Nor buries it in gravel, under ground,

Wrapp'd up in greasy leather, or piss'd clouts;

But keeps it in fine lily pots, that, open'd,

Smell like conserve of roses, or French beans.

He has his maple block, his silver tongs,

Winchester pipes, and fire of Juniper:

A neat, spruce, honest fellow, and no goldsmith.

 Sub. He is a fortunate fellow, that I am sure on.

 Face. Already, sir, have you found it? Lo thee, Abel!

 Sub. And in right way toward riches—

 Face. Sir!

 Sub. This summer

He will be of the clothing of his company,

And next spring call'd to the scarlet; spend what he can.

Face. What, and so little beard?

Sub. Sir, you must think,
He may have a receipt to make hair come:
But he'll be wise, preserve his youth, and fine for't;
His fortune looks for him another way.

Face. 'Slid, doctor, how canst thou know this so soon?
I am amused at that!

Sub. By a rule, captain,
In metoposcopy, which I do work by;
A certain star in the forehead, which you see not.
Your chestnut or your olive-colour'd face
Does never fail: and your long ear doth promise.
I knew't by certain spots, too, in his teeth,
And on the nail of his mercurial finger.

Face. Which finger's that?

Sub. His little finger. Look.
You were born upon a Wednesday?

Drug. Yes, indeed, sir.

Sub. The thumb, in chiromancy, we give Venus;
The fore-finger, to Jove; the midst, to Saturn;
The ring, to Sol; the least, to Mercury,
Who was the lord, sir, of his horoscope,
His house of life being Libra; which fore-shew'd,
He should be a merchant, and should trade with balance.

Face. Why, this is strange! Is it not, honest Nab?

Sub. There is a ship now, coming from Ormus,
That shall yield him such a commodity
Of drugs——This is the west, and this the south?

                          [Pointing to the plan.

Drug. Yes, sir.

Sub. And those are your two sides?

Drug. Ay, sir.

Sub. Make me your door, then, south; your broad side, west:
And on the east side of your shop, aloft,
Write Mathlai, Tarmiel, and Baraborat;
Upon the north part, Rael, Velel, Thiel.
They are the names of those mercurial spirits,
That do fright flies from boxes.

Drug. Yes, sir.

Sub. And
Beneath your threshold, bury me a load-stone
To draw in gallants that wear spurs: the rest,
They'll seem to follow.

Face. That's a secret, Nab!

Sub. And, on your stall, a puppet, with a vice
And a court-fucus to call city-dames:
You shall deal much with minerals.

Drug. Sir, I have
At home, already—

Sub. Ay, I know you have arsenic,
Vitriol, sal-tartar, argaile, alkali,
Cinoper: I know all.—This fellow, captain,
Will come, in time, to be a great distiller,
And give a say—I will not say directly,
But very fair—at the philosopher's stone.

Face. Why, how now, Abel! is this true?

Drug. Good captain,   *[Aside to Face.*
What must I give?

Face. Nay, I'll not counsel thee.
Thou hear'st what wealth (he says, spend what thou canst,)
Thou'rt like to come to.

Drug. I would gi' him a crown.

Face. A crown! and toward such a fortune? heart,
Thou shalt rather gi' him thy shop. No gold about thee?

Drug. Yes, I have a portague, I have kept this half year.

Face. Out on thee, Nab! 'Slight, there was such an offer—
Shalt keep't no longer, I'll give't him for thee. Doctor,
Nab prays your worship to drink this, and swears
He will appear more grateful, as your skill
Does raise him in the world.

Drug. I would entreat
Another favour of his worship.

Face. What is't, Nab?

Drug. But to look over, sir, my almanack,
And cross out my ill days, that I may neither
Bargain, nor trust upon them.

Face. That he shall, Nab;
Leave it, it shall be done, 'gainst afternoon.

Sub. And a direction for his shelves.

Face. Now, Nab,
Art thou well pleased, Nab?

Drug. 'Thank, sir, both your worships.

Face. Away.—   *[Exit Drugger.*
Why, now, you smoaky persecutor of nature!
Now do you see, that something's to be done,
Beside your beech-coal, and your corsive waters,
Your crosslets, crucibels, and cucurbites?
You must have stuff brought home to you, to work on:
And yet you think, I am at no expense
In searching out these veins, then following them,
Then trying them out. 'Fore God, my intelligence
Costs me more money, than my share oft comes to,
In these rare works.

Sub. You are pleasant, sir.—

Re-enter DOL.

How now!

What says my dainty Dolkin?

Dol. Yonder fish-wife
Will not away.   And there's your giantess,
The bawd of Lambeth.
    Sub. Heart, I cannot speak with them.
    Dol. Not afore night, I have told them in a voice,
Thorough the trunk, like one of your familiars.
— But I have spied sir Epicure Mammon—
    Sub. Where?
    Dol. Coming along, at far end of the lane,
Slow of his feet, but earnest of his tongue
To one that's with him.
    Sub. Face, go you, and shift.
Dol, you must presently make ready, too.   [*Exit Face.*
    Dol. Why, what's the matter?
    Sub. O, I did look for him
With the sun's rising: 'marvel he could sleep,
This is the day I am to perfect for him
The magisterium, our great work, the stone;
And yield it, made, into his hands: of which
He has, this month, talk'd as he were possess'd.
And now he's dealing pieces on't away.—
Methinks I see him entering ordinaries,
Dispensing for the pox, and plaguy houses,
Reaching his dose, walking Moorfields for lepers,
And offering citizens' wives pomander-bracelets,
As his preservative, made of the elixir;
Searching the spittal, to make old bawds young;
And the highways, for beggars, to make rich:
I see no end of his labours.   He will make
Nature asham'd of her long sleep: when art,
Who's but a step-dame, shall do more than she,
In her best love to mankind, ever could:
If his dream lasts, he'll turn the age to gold.   [*Exeunt.*

ACT II

SCENE I.—*An Outer Room in* LOVEWIT's *House.*

Enter Sir EPICURE MAMMON *and* SURLY.

    Mam. Come on, sir.   Now, you set your foot on shore
In *Novo Orbe;* here's the rich Peru:
And there within, sir, are the golden mines,
Great Solomon's Ophir! he was sailing to't,
Three years, but we have reach'd it in ten months.
This is the day, wherein, to all my friends,
I will pronounce the happy word, BE RICH;
THIS DAY YOU SHALL BE SPECTATISSIMI.
You shall no more deal with the hollow dye,

Or the frail card.   No more be at charge of keeping
The livery-punk for the young heir, that must
Seal, at all hours, in his shirt: no more,
If he deny, have him beaten to't, as he is
That brings him the commodity.   No more
Shall thirst of satin, or the covetous hunger
Of velvet entrails for a rude-spun cloke,
To be display'd at madam Augusta's, make
The sons of Sword and Hazard fall before
The golden calf, and on their knees, whole nights
Commit idolatry with wine and trumpets:
Or go a feasting after drum and ensign.
No more of this.   You shall start up young viceroys,
And have your punks, and punketees, my Surly.
And unto thee I speak it first, BE RICH.
Where is my Subtle, there?   Within, ho!

    Face. [*within.*] Sir, he'll come to you by and by.

    Mam. That is his fire-drake,
His Lungs, his Zephyrus, he that puffs his coals,
Till he firk nature up, in her own centre.
You are not faithful, sir.   This night, I'll change
All that is metal, in my house, to gold:
And, early in the morning, will I send
To all the plumbers and the pewterers,
And buy their tin and lead up; and to Lothbury
For all the copper.

    Sur. What, and turn that too?

    Mam. Yes, and I'll purchase Devonshire and Cornwall,
And make them perfect Indies! you admire now?

    Sur. No, faith.

    Mam. But when you see th' effects of the Great Medicine,
Of which one part projected on a hundred
Of Mercury, or Venus, or the moon,
Shall turn it to as many of the sun;
Nay, to a thousand, so ad infinitum:
You will believe me.

    Sur. Yes, when I see't, I will.
But if my eyes do cozen me so, and I
Giving them no occasion, sure I'll have
A whore, shall piss them out next day.

    Mam. Ha! why?
Do you think I fable with you? I assure you,
He that has once the flower of the sun,
The perfect ruby, which we call elixir,
Not only can do that, but, by its virtue,
Can confer honour, love, respect, long life;
Give safety, valour, yea, and victory,
To whom he will.   In eight and twenty days,
I'll make an old man of fourscore, a child.

Sur. No doubt; he's that already.

Mam. Nay, I mean,
Restore his years, renew him, like an eagle,
To the fifth age; make him get sons and daughters,
Young giants; as our philosophers have done,
The ancient patriarchs, afore the flood,
But taking, once a week, on a knife's point,
The quantity of a grain of mustard of it;
Become stout Marses, and beget young Cupids.

Sur. The decay'd vestals of Pict-hatch would thank you,
That keep the fire alive, there.

Mam. 'Tis the secret
Of nature naturis'd 'gainst all infections,
Cures all diseases coming of all causes;
A month's grief in a day, a year's in twelve;
And, of what age soever, in a month:
Past all the doses of your drugging doctors.
I'll undertake, withal, to fright the plague
Out of the kingdom in three months.

Sur. And I'll
Be bound, the players shall sing your praises, then,
Without their poets.

Mam. Sir, I'll do't. Mean time,
I'll give away so much unto my man,
Shall serve the whole city, with preservative,
Weekly; each house his dose, and at the rate—

Sur. As he that built the Water-work, does with water?

Mam. You are incredulous.

Sur. Faith I have a humour,
I would not willingly be gull'd. Your stone
Cannot transmute me.

Mam. Pertinax, [my] Surly,
Will you believe antiquity? records?
I'll shew you a book where Moses and his sister,
And Solomon have written of the art;
Ay, and a treatise penn'd by Adam—

Sur. How!

Mam. Of the philosopher's stone, and in High Dutch.

Sur. Did Adam write, sir, in High Dutch?

Mam. He did;
Which proves it was the primitive tongue.

Sur. What paper?

Mam. On cedar board.

Sur. O that, indeed, they say,
Will last 'gainst worms.

Mam. 'Tis like your Irish wood,
'Gainst cob-webs. I have a piece of Jason's fleece, too,
Which was no other than a book of alchemy,
Writ in large sheep-skin, a good fat ram-vellum.

Such was Pythagoras' thigh, Pandora's tub,
And, all that fable of Medea's charms,
The manner of our work; the bulls, our furnace,
Still breathing fire; our argent-vive, the dragon:
The dragon's teeth, mercury sublimate,
That keeps the whiteness, hardness, and the biting:
And they are gather'd into Jason's helm,
The alembic, and then sow'd in Mars his field,
And thence sublimed so often, till they're fixed.
Both this, the Hesperian garden, Cadmus' story,
Jove's shower, the boon of Midas, Argus' eyes,
Boccace his Demogorgon, thousands more,
All abstract riddles of our stone.—

Enter FACE, *as a Servant.*

　　　　　　　　　　　　　How now!
Do we succeed? Is our day come? and holds it?
　　Face. The evening will set red upon you, sir;
You have colour for it, crimson: the red ferment
Has done his office; three hours hence prepare you
To see projection.
　　Mam. Pertinax, my Surly,
Again I say to thee, aloud, Be rich.
This day, thou shalt have ingots; and, to-morrow,
Give lords th' affront.—Is it, my Zephyrus, right?
Blushes the bolt's-head?
　　Face. Like a wench with child, sir,
That were but now discover'd to her master
　　Mam. Excellent witty Lungs!—my only care
Where to get stuff enough now, to project on;
This town will not half serve me.
　　Face. No, sir! buy
The covering off o' churches.
　　Mam. That's true.
　　Face. Yes.
Let them stand bare, as do their auditory;
Or cap them, new, with shingles.
　　Mam. No, good thatch:
Thatch will lie light open the rafters, Lungs.—
Lungs, I will manumit thee from the furnace;
I will restore thee thy complexion, Puffe,
Lost in the embers; and repair this brain.
Hurt with the fume o' the metals.
　　Face. I have blown, sir,
Hard for your worship; thrown by many a coal,
When 'twas not beech; weigh'd those I put in, just,
To keep your heat still even; these blear'd eyes
Have wak'd to read your several colours, sir,
Of the pale citron, the green lion, the crow,

The peacock's tail, the plumed swan.
Mam. And, lastly,
Thou hast descry'd the flower, the sanguis agni?
Face. Yes, sir.
Mam. Where's master?
Face. At his prayers, sir, he;
Good man, he's doing his devotions
For the success.
Mam. Lungs, I will set a period
To all thy labours; thou shalt be the master
Of my seraglio.
Face. Good, sir.
Mam. But do you hear?
I'll geld you, Lungs.
Face. Yes, sir.
Mam. For I do mean
To have a list of wives and concubines,
Equal with Solomon, who had the stone
Alike with me; and I will make me a back
With the elixir, that shall be as tough
As Hercules, to encounter fifty a night.—
Thou art sure thou saw'st it blood?
Face. Both blood and spirit, sir.
Mam. I will have all my beds blown up, not stuft:
Down is too hard: and then, mine oval room
Fill'd with such pictures as Tiberius took
From Elephantis, and dull Aretine
But coldly imitated. Then, my glasses
Cut in more subtle angles, to disperse
And multiply the figures, as I walk
Naked between my succubæ. My mists
I'll have of perfume, vapour'd 'bout the room,
To lose ourselves in; and my baths, like pits
To fall into; from whence we will come forth,
And roll us dry in gossamer and roses.—
Is it arrived at ruby?—Where I spy
A wealthy citizen, or [a] rich lawyer,
Have a sublimed pure wife, unto that fellow
I'll send a thousand pound to be my cuckold.
Face. And I shall carry it?
Mam. No. I'll have no bawds,
But fathers and mothers: they will do it best,
Best of all others. And my flatterers
Shall be the pure and gravest of divines,
That I can get for money. My mere fools,
Eloquent burgesses, and then my poets
The same that writ so subtly of the fart,
Whom I will entertain still for that subject.
The few that would give out themselves to be

Court and town-stallions, and, each-where, bely
Ladies who are known most innocent for them;
Those will I beg, to make me eunuchs of:
And they shall fan me with ten estrich tails
A-piece, made in a plume to gather wind.
We will be brave, Puffe, now we have the med'cine.
My meat shall all come in, in Indian shells,
Dishes of agat set in gold, and studded
With emeralds, sapphires, hyacinths, and rubies.
The tongues of carps, dormice, and camels' heels,
Boil'd in the spirit of sol, and dissolv'd pearl,
Apicius' diet, 'gainst the epilepsy:
And I will eat these broths with spoons of amber,
Headed with diamond and carbuncle.
My foot-boy shall eat pheasants, calver'd salmons,
Knots, godwits, lampreys: I myself will have
The beards of barbels served, instead of sallads;
Oil'd mushrooms; and the swelling unctuous paps
Of a fat pregnant sow, newly cut off,
Drest with an exquisite, and poignant sauce;
For which, I'll say unto my cook, *There's gold,
Go forth, and be a knight.*
    Face. Sir, I'll go look
A little, how it heightens.   [*Exit.*
    Mam. Do.—My shirts
I'll have of taffeta-sarsnet, soft and light
As cobwebs; and for all my other raiment,
It shall be such as might provoke the Persian,
Were he to teach the world riot anew.
My gloves of fishes' and birds' skins, perfumed
With gums of paradise, and eastern air—
    Sur. And do you think to have the stone with this?
    Mam. No, I do think t' have all this with the stone.
    Sur. Why, I have heard, he must be *homo frugi*,
A pious, holy, and religious man,
One free from mortal sin, a very virgin.
    Mam. That makes it, sir; he is so: but I buy it;
My venture brings it me. He, honest wretch,
A notable, superstitious, good soul,
Has worn his knees bare, and his slippers bald,
With prayer and fasting for it: and sir, let him
Do it alone, for me, still. Here he comes.
Not a profane word afore him: 'tis poison.—

Enter SUBTLE.

Good morrow, father.
    Sub. Gentle son, good morrow.
And to your friend there. What is he, is with you?
    Mam. An heretic, that I did bring along,

The Alchemist

In hope, sir, to convert him.
  Sub. Son, I doubt
You are covetous, that thus you meet your time
In the just point: prevent your day at morning.
This argues something, worthy of a fear
Of importune and carnal appetite.
Take heed you do not cause the blessing leave you,
With your ungovern'd haste. I should be sorry
To see my labours, now even at perfection,
Got by long watching and large patience,
Not prosper where my love and zeal hath placed them.
Which (heaven I call to witness, with your self,
To whom I have pour'd my thoughts) in all my ends,
Have look'd no way, but unto public good,
To pious uses, and dear charity
Now grown a prodigy with men. Wherein
If you, my son, should now prevaricate,
And, to your own particular lusts employ
So great and catholic a bliss, be sure
A curse will follow, yea, and overtake
Your subtle and most secret ways.
  Mam. I know, sir;
You shall not need to fear me: I but come,
To have you confute this gentleman.
  Sur. Who is,
Indeed, sir, somewhat costive of belief
Toward your stone; would not be gull'd.
  Sub. Well, son,
All that I can convince him in, is this,
The WORK IS DONE, bright sol is in his robe.
We have a medicine of the triple soul,
The glorified spirit. Thanks be to heaven,
And make us worthy of it!—Ulen Spiegel!
  Face. [*within.*] Anon, sir.
  Sub. Look well to the register.
And let your heat still lessen by degrees,
To the aludels.
  Face. [*within.*] Yes, sir.
  Sub. Did you look
On the bolt's-head yet?
  Face. [*within.*] Which? on D, sir?
  Sub. Ay;
What's the complexion?
  Face. [*within.*] Whitish.
  Sub. Infuse vinegar,
To draw his volatile substance and his tincture:
And let the water in glass E be filter'd,
And put into the gripe's egg. Lute him well;
And leave him closed in balneo.

Face. [within.] I will, sir.

Sur. What a brave language here is! next to canting.

Sub. I have another work, you never saw, son,
That three days since past the philosopher's wheel
In the lent heat of Athanor; and's become
Sulphur of Nature.

Mam. But 'tis for me?

Sub. What need you?
You have enough in that is perfect.

Mam. O but—

Sub. Why, this is covetise!

Mam. No, I assure you,
I shall employ it all in pious uses,
Founding of colleges and grammar schools,
Marrying young virgins, building hospitals,
And now and then a church.

Re-enter FACE.

Sub. How now!

Face. Sir, please you,
Shall I not change the filter?

Sub. Marry, yes;
And bring me the complexion of glass B.   [*Exit Face.*

Mam. Have you another?

Sub. Yes, son; were I assured—
Your piety were firm, we would not want
The means to glorify it: but I hope the best.—
I mean to tinct C in sand-heat to-morrow,
And give him imbibition.

Mam. Of white oil?

Sub. No, sir, of red.   F is come over the helm too,
I thank my Maker, in S. Mary's bath,
And shews *lac virginis.*   Blessed be heaven!
I sent you of his fæces there calcined:
Out of that calx, I have won the salt of mercury.

Mam. By pouring on your rectified water?

Sub. Yes, and reverberating in Athanor.

Re-enter FACE.

How now! what colour says it?

Face. The ground black, sir.

Mam. That's your crow's head?

Sur. Your cock's-comb's, is it not?

Sub. No, 'tis not perfect.   Would it were the crow!
That work wants something.

Sur. O, I look'd for this.
The hay's a pitching.   [*Aside.*

Sub. Are you sure you loosed them
In their own menstrue?

The Alchemist

5

Face. Yes, sir, and then married them,
And put them in a bolt's-head nipp'd to digestion,
According as you bade me, when I set
The liquor of Mars to circulation
In the same heat.

Sub. The process then was right.

Face. Yes, by the token, sir, the retort brake,
And what was saved was put into the pelican,
And sign'd with Hermes' seal.

Sub. I think 'twas so.
We should have a new amalgama.

Sur. O, this ferret
Is rank as any pole-cat.   *[Aside.*

Sub. But I care not:
Let him e'en die; we have enough beside,
In embrion. H has his white shirt on?

Face. Yes, sir,
He's ripe for inceration, he stands warm,
In his ash-fire. I would not you should let
Any die now, if I might counsel, sir,
For luck's sake to the rest: it is not good.

Mam. He says right.

Sur. Ay, are you bolted?   *[Aside.*

Face. Nay, I know't, sir,
I have seen the ill fortune. What is some three ounces
Of fresh materials?

Mam. Is't no more?

Face. No more, sir,
Of gold, t'amalgame with some six of mercury.

Mam. Away, here's money. What will serve?

Face. Ask him, sir.

Mam. How much?

Sub. Give him nine pound:—you may give him ten.

Sur. Yes, twenty, and be cozen'd, do.

Mam. There 'tis.   *[Gives Face the money.*

Sub. This needs not; but that you will have it so,
To see conclusions of all: for two
Of our inferior works are at fixation,
A third is in ascension. Go your ways.
Have you set the oil of luna in kemia?

Face. Yes, sir.

Sub. And the philosopher's vinegar?

Face. Ay.

Sur. We shall have a sallad!   *[Exit.*

Mam. When do you make projection?

Sub. Son, be not hasty, I exalt our med'cine,
By hanging him *in balneo vaporoso,*
And giving him solution; then congeal him;
And then dissolve him; then again congeal him:

For look, how oft I iterate the work,
So many times I add unto his virtue.
As, if at first one ounce convert a hundred,
After his second loose, he'll turn a thousand;
His third solution, ten; his fourth, a hundred:
After his fifth, a thousand thousand ounces
Of any imperfect metal, into pure
Silver or gold, in all examinations,
As good as any of the natural mine.
Get you your stuff here against afternoon,
Your brass, your pewter, and your andirons.

   Mam. Not those of iron?

   Sub. Yes, you may bring them too:
We'll change all metals.

   Sur. I believe you in that.

   Mam. Then I may send my spits?

   Sub. Yes, and your racks.

   Sur. And dripping pans, and pot-hangers, and hooks,
Shall he not?

   Sub. If he please.

   Sur. —To be an ass.

   Sub. How, sir!

   Mam. This gentleman you must bear withal:
I told you he had no faith.

   Sur. And little hope, sir;
But much less charity, should I gull myself.

   Sub. Why, what have you observ'd, sir, in our art,
Seems so impossible?

   Sur. But your whole work, no more.
That you should hatch gold in a furnace, sir,
As they do eggs in Egypt!

   Sub. Sir, do you
Believe that eggs are hatch'd so?

   Sur. If I should?

   Sub. Why, I think that the greater miracle.
No egg but differs from a chicken more
Than metals in themselves.

   Sur. That cannot be.
The egg's ordain'd by nature to that end,
And is a chicken *in potentia*.

   Sub. The same we say of lead and other metals,
Which would be gold, if they had time.

   Mam. And that
Our art doth further.

   Sub. Ay, for 'twere absurd
To think that nature in the earth bred gold
Perfect in the instant: something went before.
There must be remote matter.

   Sur. Ay, what is that?

Sub. Marry, we say—
Mam. Ay, now it heats: stand, father,
Pound him to dust.
    Sub. It is, of the one part,
A humid exhalation, which we call
Materia liquida, or the unctuous water;
On the other part, a certain crass and vicious
Portion of earth; both which, concorporate,
Do make the elementary matter of gold;
Which is not yet *propria materia,*
But common to all metals and all stones;
For, where it is forsaken of that moisture,
And hath more driness, it becomes a stone:
Where it retains more of the humid fatness,
It turns to sulphur, or to quicksilver,
Who are the parents of all other metals.
Nor can this remote matter suddenly
Progress so from extreme unto extreme,
As to grow gold, and leap o'er all the means.
Nature doth first beget the imperfect, then
Proceeds she to the perfect. Of that airy
And oily water, mercury is engender'd;
Sulphur of the fat and earthy part; the one,
Which is the last, supplying the place of male.
The other of the female, in all metals.
Some do believe hermaphrodeity,
That both do act and suffer. But these two
Make the rest ductile, malleable, extensive.
And even in gold they are; for we do find
Seeds of them, by our fire, and gold in them;
And can produce the species of each metal
More perfect thence, than nature doth in earth.
Beside, who doth not see in daily practice
Art can beget bees, hornets, beetles, wasps,
Out of the carcasses and dung of creatures;
Yea, scorpions of an herb, being rightly placed?
And these are living creatures, far more perfect
And excellent than metals.
    Mam. Well said, father!
Nay, if he take you in hand, sir, with an argument,
He'll bray you in a mortar.
    Sur. Pray you, sir, stay.
Rather than I'll be bray'd, sir, I'll believe
That Alchemy is a pretty kind of game,
Somewhat like tricks o' the cards, to cheat a man
With charming.
    Sub. Sir?
    Sur. What else are all your terms,
Whereon no one of your writers 'grees with other?

Of your elixir, your *lac virginis*,
Your stone, your med'cine, and your chrysosperme,
Your sal, your sulphur, and your mercury,
Your oil of height, your tree of life, your blood,
Your marchesite, your tutie, your magnesia,
Your toad, your crow, your dragon, and your panther;
Your sun, your moon, your firmament, your adrop,
Your lato, azoch, zernich, chibrit, heautarit,
And then your red man, and your white woman,
With all your broths, your menstrues, and materials,
Of piss and egg-shells, women's terms, man's blood,
Hair o' the head, burnt clouts, chalk, merds, and clay,
Powder of bones, scalings of iron, glass,
And worlds of other strange ingredients,
Would burst a man to name?

Sub. And all these named,
Intending but one thing: which art our writers
Used to obscure their art.

Mam. Sir, so I told him—
Because the simple idiot should not learn it,
And make it vulgar.

Sub. Was not all the knowledge
Of the Ægyptians writ in mystic symbols?
Speak not the scriptures oft in parables?
Are not the choicest fables of the poets,
That were the fountains and first springs of wisdom,
Wrapp'd in perplexed allegories?

Mam. I urg'd that,
And clear'd to him, that Sysiphus was damn'd
To roll the ceaseless stone, only because
He would have made Ours common. [*Dol appears at the door.*]—
          Who is this?

Sub. 'Sprecious!—What do you mean? go in, good lady,
Let me entreat you. [*Dol retires.*]—Where's this varlet?

Re-enter FACE.

Face. Sir.

Sub. You very knave! do you use me thus?

Face. Wherein, sir?

Sub. Go in and see, you traitor. Go!   [*Exit Face.*

Mam. Who is it, sir?

Sub. Nothing, sir; nothing.

Mam. What's the matter, good sir?
I have not seen you thus distemper'd: who is't?

Sub. All arts have still had, sir, their adversaries,
But ours the most ignorant.—

Re-enter FACE.

What now?

Face. 'Twas not my fault, sir; she would speak with you.

Sub. Would she, sir! Follow me. [*Exit.*
Mam. [*stopping him.*] Stay, Lungs.
Face. I dare not, sir.
Mam. Stay, man; what is she?
Face. A lord's sister, sir.
Mam. How! pray thee, stay.
Face. She's mad, sir, and sent hither—
He'll be mad too—
Mam. I warrant thee.—
Why sent hither?
Face. Sir, to be cured.
Sub. [*within.*] Why, rascal!
Face. Lo you!—Here, sir! [*Exit.*
Mam. 'Fore God, a Bradamante, a brave piece.
Sur. Heart, this is a bawdy-house! I will be burnt else.
Mam. O, by this light, no: do not wrong him. He's
Too scrupulous that way: it is his vice.
No, he's a rare physician, do him right,
An excellent Paracelsian, and has done
Strange cures with mineral physic. He deals all
With spirits, he; he will not hear a word
Of Galen, or his tedious recipes—

Re-enter FACE.

How now, Lungs!
Face. Softly, sir; speak softly. I meant
To have told your worship all. This must not hear.
Mam. No, he will not be " gull'd: " let him alone.
Face. You are very right, sir, she is a most rare scholar,
And is gone mad with studying Broughton's works.
If you but name a word touching the Hebrew,
She falls into her fit, and will discourse
So learnedly of genealogies,
As you would run mad too, to hear her, sir.
Mam. How might one do t' have conference with her, Lungs?
Face. O divers have run mad upon the conference:
I do not know, sir. I am sent in haste,
To fetch a vial.
Sur. Be not gull'd, sir Mammon.
Mam. Wherein? pray ye, be patient.
Sur. Yes, as you are,
And trust confederate knaves and bawds and whores.
Mam. You are too foul, believe it.—Come here, Ulen,
One word.
Face. I dare not, in good faith. [*Going.*
Mam. Stay, knave.
Face. He is extreme angry that you saw her, sir.
Mam. Drink that. [*Gives him money.*] What is she when
      she's out of her fit?

Face. O, the most affablest creature, sir! so merry!
So pleasant! she'll mount you up, like quicksilver,
Over the helm; and circulate like oil,
A very vegetal: discourse of state,
Of mathematics, bawdry, any thing—

Mam. Is she no way accessible? no means,
No trick to give a man a taste of her—wit—
Or so?

Sub. [*within.*] Ulen!

Face. I'll come to you again, sir.   [*Exit.*

Mam. Surly, I did not think one of your breeding
Would traduce personages of worth.

Sur. Sir Epicure,
Your friend to use; yet still loth to be gull'd:
I do not like your philosophical bawds.
Their stone is letchery enough to pay for,
Without this bait.

Mam. 'Heart, you abuse yourself.
I know the lady, and her friends, and means,
The original of this disaster.   Her brother
Has told me all.

Sur. And yet you never saw her
Till now!

Mam. O yes, but I forgot.   I have, believe it,
One of the treacherousest memories, I do think,
Of all mankind.

Sur. What call you her brother?

Mam. My lord—
He will not have his name known, now I think on't.

Sur. A very treacherous memory!

Mam. On my faith—

Sur. Tut, if you have it not about you, pass it,
Till we meet next.

Mam. Nay, by this hand, 'tis true.
He's one I honour, and my noble friend;
And I respect his house.

Sur. Heart! can it be,
That a grave sir, a rich, that has no need,
A wise sir, too, at other times, should thus,
With his own oaths, and arguments, make hard means
To gull himself?   An this be your elixir,
Your *lapis mineralis*, and your lunary,
Give me your honest trick yet at primero,
Or gleek; and take your *lutum sapientis*,
Your *menstruum simplex!*   I'll have gold before you,
And with less danger of the quicksilver,
Or the hot sulphur.

Re-enter FACE.

Face. Here's one from captain Face, sir, [*to Surly.*]

Desires you meet him in the Temple-church,
Some half hour hence, and upon earnest business.
Sir, [*whispers Mammon.*] if you please to quit us, now; and come
Again within two hours, you shall have
My master busy examining o' the works;
And I will steal you in, unto the party,
That you may see her converse.—Sir, shall I say,
You'll meet the captain's worship?

  Sur. Sir, I will.—   [*Walks aside.*
But, by attorney, and to a second purpose.
Now, I am sure it is a bawdy-house;
I'll swear it, were the marshal here to thank me:
The naming this commander doth confirm it.
Don Face! why he's the most authentic dealer
In these commodities, the superintendant
To all the quainter traffickers in town!
He is the visitor, and does appoint,
Who lies with whom, and at what hour; what price;
Which gown, and in what smock; what fall; what tire.
Him will I prove, by a third person, to find
The subtleties of this dark labyrinth:
Which if I do discover, dear sir Mammon,
You'll give your poor friend leave, though no philosopher,
To laugh: for you that are, 'tis thought, shall weep.

  Face. Sir, he does pray, you'll not forget.

  Sur. I will not, sir.
Sir Epicure, I shall leave you.   [*Exit.*

  Mam. I follow you, straight.

  Face. But do so, good sir, to avoid suspicion.
This gentleman has a parlous head.

  Mam. But wilt thou, Ulen,
Be constant to thy promise?

  Face. As my life, sir.

  Mam. And wilt thou insinuate what I am, and praise me,
And say, I am a noble fellow?

  Face. O, what else, sir?
And that you'll make her royal with the stone,
An empress; and yourself, king of Bantam.

  Mam. Wilt thou do this?

  Face. Will I, sir!

  Mam. Lungs, my Lungs!
I love thee.

  Face. Send your stuff, sir, that my master
May busy himself about projection.

  Mam. Thou hast witch'd me, rogue: take, go.
                              [*Gives him money.*

  Face. Your jack, and all, sir.

  Mam. Thou art a villain—I will send my jack,
And the weights too. Slave, I could bite thine ear.

Away, thou dost not care for me.

   Face. Not I, sir!

   Mam. Come, I was born to make thee, my good weasel,
Set thee on a bench, and have thee twirl a chain
With the best lord's vermin of 'em all.

   Face. Away, sir.

   Mam. A count, nay, a count palatine—

   Face. Good, sir, go.

   Mam. Shall not advance thee better: no, nor faster.   [*Exit.*

Re-enter Subtle and Dol.

   Sub. Has he bit? has he bit?

   Face. And swallowed too, my Subtle.
I have given him line, and now he plays, i'faith.

   Sub. And shall we twitch him?

   Face. Thorough both the gills.
A wench is a rare bait, with which a man
No sooner's taken, but he straight firks mad.

   Sub. Dol, my lord What'ts'hums sister, you must now
Bear yourself *statelich.*

   Dol. O let me alone.
I'll not forget my race, I warrant you.
I'll keep my distance, laugh and talk aloud;
Have all the tricks of a proud scurvy lady,
And be as rude as her woman.

   Face. Well said, sanguine!

   Sub. But will he send his andirons?

   Face. His jack too,
And's iron shoeing horn; I have spoke to him.   Well,
I must not lose my wary gamester yonder.

   Sub. O monsieur Caution, that *will not be gull'd.*

   Face. Ay,
If I can strike a fine hook into him, now!
The Temple-church, there I have cast mine angle.
Well, pray for me.   I'll about it.   [*Knocking without.*

   Sub. What, more gudgeons!
Dol, scout, scout! [*Dol goes to the window.*] Stay, Face, you must
    go to the door,
'Pray God it be my anabaptist.—Who is't, Dol?

   Dol. I know him not: he looks like a gold-endman.

   Sub. Ods so! 'tis he, he said he would send what call you him?
The sanctified elder, that should deal
For Mammon's jack and andirons. Let him in.
Stay, help me off, first, with my gown. [*Exit Face with the gown.*]
    Away,
Madam, to your withdrawing chamber. [*Exit Dol.*] Now,
In a new tune, new gesture, but old language.—
This fellow is sent from one negociates with me
About the stone too; for the holy brethren

Of Amsterdam, the exiled saints; that hope
To raise their discipline by it. I must use him
In some strange fashion, now, to make him admire me.—

Enter ANANIAS.

Where is my drudge? [*Aloud.*

Re-enter FACE.

  Face. Sir!
  Sub. Take away the recipient,
And rectify your menstrue from the phlegma.
Then pour it on the Sol, in the cucurbite,
And let them macerate together.
  Face. Yes, sir.
And save the ground?
  Sub. No: *terra damnata*
Must not have entrance in the work.—Who are you?
  Ana. A faithful brother, if it please you.
  Sub. What's that?
A Lullianist? a Ripley? *Filius artis?*
Can you sublime and dulcify? calcine?
Know you the sapor pontic? sapor stiptic?
Or what is homogene, or heterogene?
  Ana. I understand no heathen language, truly.
  Sub. Heathen! you Knipper-doling? is Ars sacra,
Or chrysopœia, or spagyrica,
Or the pamphysic, or panarchic knowledge,
A heathen language?
  Ana. Heathen Greek, I take it.
  Sub. How! heathen Greek?
  Ana. All's heathen but the Hebrew.
  Sub. Sirrah, my varlet, stand you forth and speak to him,
Like a philosopher: answer in the language.
Name the vexations, and the martyrisations
Of metals in the work.
  Face. Sir, putrefaction,
Solution, ablution, sublimation,
Cohobation, calcination, ceration, and
Fixation.
  Sub. This is heathen Greek to you, now!—
And when comes vivification?
  Face. After mortification.
  Sub. What's cohobation?
  Face. 'Tis the pouring on
Your aqua regis, and then drawing him off,
To the trine circle of the seven spheres.
  Sub. What's the proper passion of metals?
  Face. Malleation.
  Sub. What's your *ultimum supplicium auri?*
  Face. Antimonium.

Sub. This is heathen Greek to you!—And what's your mercury?

Face. A very fugitive, he will be gone, sir.

Sub. How know you him?

Face. By his viscosity,
His oleosity, and his suscitability.

Sub. How do you sublime him?

Face. With the calce of egg-shells,
White marble, talc.

Sub. Your magisterium, now,
What's that?

Face. Shifting, sir, your elements,
Dry into cold, cold into moist, moist into hot,
Hot into dry.

Sub. This is heathen Greek to you still!
Your *lapis philosophicus?*

Face. 'Tis a stone,
And not a stone; a spirit, a soul, and a body:
Which if you do dissolve, it is dissolved;
If you coagulate, it is coagulated;
If you make it to fly, it flieth.

Sub. Enough.   [*Exit Face.*
This is heathen Greek to you! What are you, sir?

Ana. Please you, a servant of the exiled brethren,
That deal with widows' and with orphans' goods;
And make a just account unto the saints:
A deacon.

Sub. O, you are sent from master Wholesome,
Your teacher?

Ana. From Tribulation Wholesome,
Our very zealous pastor.

Sub. Good! I have
Some orphans' goods to come here.

Ana. Of what kind, sir?

Sub. Pewter and brass, andirons and kitchen-ware,
Metals, that we must use our medicine on:
Wherein the brethren may have a pennyworth,
For ready money.

Ana. Were the orphans' parents
Sincere professors?

Sub. Why do you ask?

Ana. Because
We then are to deal justly, and give, in truth,
Their utmost value.

Sub. 'Slid, you'd cozen else,
And if their parents were not of the faithful!—
I will not trust you, now I think on it,
'Till I have talk'd with your pastor. Have you brought money
To buy more coals?

Ana. No, surely.

Sub. No! how so?

Ana. The brethren bid me say unto you, sir,
Surely, they will not venture any more,
Till they may see projection.

Sub. How!

Ana. You have had,
For the instruments, as bricks, and lome, and glasses,
Already thirty pound; and for materials,
They say, some ninety more: and they have heard since,
That one at Heidelberg, made it of an egg,
And a small paper of pin-dust.

Sub. What's your name?

Ana. My name is Ananias.

Sub. Out, the varlet
That cozen'd the apostles! Hence, away!
Flee, mischief! had your holy consistory
No name to send me, of another sound,
Than wicked Ananias? send your elders
Hither to make atonement for you quickly,
And give me satisfaction; or out goes
The fire; and down th' alembics, and the furnace,
Piger Henricus, or what not. Thou wretch!
Both sericon and bufo shall be lost,
Tell them. All hope of rooting out the bishops,
Or the antichristian hierarchy, shall perish,
If they stay threescore minutes: the aqueity,
Terreity, and sulphureity
Shall run together again, and all be annull'd,
Thou wicked Ananias! [*Exit Ananias.*] This will fetch 'em,
And make them haste towards their gulling more.
A man must deal like a rough nurse, and fright
Those that are froward, to an appetite.

Re-enter FACE *in his uniform, followed by* DRUGGER.

Face. He is busy with his spirits, but we'll upon him.

Sub. How now! what mates, what Baiards have we here?

Face. I told you, he would be furious.—Sir, here's Nab,
Has brought you another piece of gold to look on:
—We must appease him. Give it me,—and prays you,
You would devise—what is it, Nab?

Drug. A sign, sir.

Face. Ay, a good lucky one, a thriving sign, doctor.

Sub. I was devising now.

Face. 'Slight, do not say so,
He will repent he gave you any more—
What say you to his constellation, doctor,
The Balance?

Sub. No, that way is stale, and common.
A townsman born in Taurus, gives the bull,

Or the bull's-head: in Aries, the ram,
A poor device! No, I will have his name
Form'd in some mystic character; whose radii,
Striking the senses of the passers by,
Shall, by a virtual influence, breed affections,
That may result upon the party owns it:
As thus—
    Face. Nab!
    Sub. He shall have *a bel*, that's *Abel;*
And by it standing one whose name is *Dee,*
In a *rug* gown, there's *D*, and *Rug*, that's *drug:*
And right anenst him a dog snarling *er;*
There's *Drugger*, Abel Drugger. That's his sign.
And here's now mystery and hieroglyphic!
    Face. Abel, thou art made.
    Drug. Sir, I do thank his worship.
    Face. Six o' thy legs more will not do it, Nab.
He has brought you a pipe of tobacco, doctor.
    Drug. Yes, sir:
I have another thing I would impart—
    Face. Out with it, Nab.
    Drug. Sir, there is lodged, hard by me,
A rich young widow—
    Face. Good! a bona roba?
    Drug. But nineteen, at the most.
    Face. Very good, Abel.
    Drug. Marry, she's not in fashion yet; she wears
A hood, but it stands a cop.
    Face. No matter, Abel.
    Drug. And I do now and then give her a fucus—
    Face. What! dost thou deal, Nab?
    Sub. I did tell you, captain.
    Drug. And physic too, sometime, sir; for which she trusts me
With all her mind. She's come up here of purpose
To learn the fashion.
    Face. Good (his match too!)—On, Nab.
    Drug. And she does strangely long to know her fortune.
    Face. Ods lid, Nab, send her to the doctor, hither.
    Drug. Yes, I have spoke to her of his worship already;
But she's afraid it will be blown abroad,
And hurt her marriage.
    Face. Hurt it! 'tis the way
To heal it, if 'twere hurt; to make it more
Follow'd and sought: Nab, thou shalt tell her this.
She'll be more known, more talk'd of; and your widows
Are ne'er of any price till they be famous;
Their honour is their multitude of suitors:
Send her, it may be thy good fortune. What!
Thou dost not know.

Drug. No, sir, she'll never marry
Under a knight: her brother has made a vow.

Face. What! and dost thou despair, my little Nab,
Knowing what the doctor has set down for thee,
And seeing so many of the city dubb'd?
One glass o' thy water, with a madam I know,
Will have it done, Nab: what's her brother, a knight?

Drug. No, sir, a gentleman newly warm in his land, sir,
Scarce cold in his one and twenty, that does govern
His sister here; and is a man himself
Of some three thousand a year, and is come up
To learn to quarrel, and to live by his wits,
And will go down again, and die in the country.

Face. How! to quarrel?

Drug. Yes, sir, to carry quarrels,
As gallants do; to manage them by line.

Face. 'Slid, Nab, the doctor is the only man
In Christendom for him. He has made a table,
With mathematical demonstrations,
Touching the art of quarrels: he will give him
An instrument to quarrel by. Go, bring them both,
Him and his sister. And, for thee, with her
The doctor happ'ly may persuade. Go to:
'Shalt give his worship a new damask suit
Upon the premises.

Sub. O, good captain!

Face. He shall;
He is the honestest fellow, doctor.—Stay not,
No offers; bring the damask, and the parties.

Drug. I'll try my power, sir,

Face. And thy will too, Nab.

Sub. 'Tis good tobacco, this! what is't an ounce?

Face. He'll send you a pound, doctor.

Sub. O no.

Face. He will do't.
It is the goodest soul!—Abel, about it.
Thou shalt know more anon. Away, be gone.— [*Exit Abel.*
A miserable rogue, and lives with cheese,
And has the worms. That was the cause, indeed,
Why he came now: he dealt with me in private,
To get a med'cine for them.

Sub. And shall, sir. This works.

Face. A wife, a wife for one of us, my dear Subtle!
We'll e'en draw lots, and he that fails, shall have
The more in goods, the other has in tail.

Sub. Rather the less: for she may be so light
She may want grains.

Face. Ay, or be such a burden,
A man would scarce endure her for the whole. ——

Sub. Faith, best let's see her first, and then determine.
Face. Content: but Dol must have no breath on't.
Sub. Mum.
Away you, to your Surly yonder, catch him.
    Face. 'Pray God I have not staid too long.
    Sub. I fear it.   [*Exeunt.*

ACT III

SCENE I.—*The Lane before* LOVEWIT'S *House.*

Enter TRIBULATION WHOLESOME *and* ANANIAS.

Tri. These chastisements are common to the saints,
And such rebukes, we of the separation
Must bear with willing shoulders, as the trials
Sent forth to tempt our frailties.
    Ana. In pure zeal,
I do not like the man, he is a heathen,
And speaks the language of Canaan, truly.
    Tri. I think him a profane person indeed.
    Ana. He bears
The visible mark of the beast in his forehead.
And for his stone, it is a work of darkness,
And with philosophy blinds the eyes of man.
    Tri. Good brother, we must bend unto all means
That may give furtherance to the holy cause.
    Ana. Which his cannot: the sanctified cause
Should have a sanctified course.
    Tri. Not always necessary:
The children of perdition are oft-times
Made instruments even of the greatest works:
Beside, we should give somewhat to man's nature,
The place he lives in, still about the fire,
And fume of metals, that intoxicate
The brain of man, and make him prone to passion.
Where have you greater atheists than your cooks?
Or more profane, or choleric, than your glass-men?
More antichristian than your bell-founders?
What makes the devil so devilish, I would ask you,
Sathan, our common enemy, but his being
Perpetually about the fire, and boiling
Brimstone and arsenic? We must give, I say,
Unto the motives, and the stirrers up
Of humours in the blood. It may be so,
When as the work is done, the stone is made,
This heat of his may turn into a zeal,
And stand up for the beauteous discipline,
Against the menstruous cloth and rag of Rome.

We must await his calling, and the coming
Of the good spirit. You did fault, t' upbraid him
With the brethren's blessing of Heidelberg, weighing
What need we have to hasten on the work,
For the restoring of the silenced saints,
Which ne'er will be, but by the philosopher's stone.
And so a learned elder, one of Scotland,
Assured me; *aurum potabile* being
The only med'cine, for the civil magistrate,
T' incline him to a feeling of the cause;
And must be daily used in the disease.

    Ana. I have not edified more, truly, by man;
Not since the beautiful light first shone on me:
And I am sad my zeal hath so offended.

    Tri. Let us call on him then.

    Ana. The motion's good,
And of the spirit; I will knock first. [*Knocks.*] Peace be within!
               [*The door is opened, and they enter.*

SCENE II.—*A Room in* LOVEWIT'S *House.*

Enter SUBTLE, *followed by* TRIBULATION *and* ANANIAS.

    Sub. O, are you come? 'twas time. Your threescore minutes
Were at last thread, you see: and down had gone
Furnus acediæ, turris circulatorius:
Lembec, bolt's-head, retort and pelican
Had all been cinders.—Wicked Ananias!
Art thou return'd? nay then, it goes down yet.

    Tri. Sir, be appeased; he is come to humble
Himself in spirit, and to ask your patience,
If too much zeal hath carried him aside
From the due path.

    Sub. Why, this doth qualify!

    Tri. The brethren had no purpose, verily,
To give you the least grievance: but are ready
To lend their willing hands to any project
The spirit and you direct.

    Sub. This qualifies more!

    Tri. And for the orphan's goods, let them be valued,
Or what is needful else to the holy work,
It shall be numbered; here, by me, the saints,
Throw down their purse before you.

    Sub. This qualifies most!
Why, thus it should be, now you understand.
Have I discours'd so unto you of our stone,
And of the good that it shall bring your cause?
Shew'd you (beside the main of hiring forces
Abroad, drawing the Hollanders, your friends,
From the Indies, to serve you, with all their fleet)

That even the med'cinal use shall make you a faction,
And party in the realm? As, put the case,
That some great man in state, he have the gout,
Why, you but send three drops of your elixir,
You help him straight: there you have made a friend.
Another has the palsy or the dropsy,
He takes of your incombustible stuff,
He's young again: there you have made a friend,
A lady that is past the feat of body,
Though not of mind, and hath her face decay'd
Beyond all cure of paintings, you restore,
With the oil of talc: there you have made a friend;
And all her friends. A lord that is a leper,
A knight that has the bone-ache, or a squire
That hath both these, you make them smooth and sound,
With a bare fricace of your med'cine: still
You increase your friends.
    Tri. Ay, it is very pregnant.
    Sub. And then the turning of this lawyer's pewter
To plate at Christmas.—
    Ana. Christ-tide, I pray you.
    Sub. Yet, Ananias!
    Ana. I have done.
    Sub. Or changing
His parcel gilt to massy gold. You cannot
But raise you friends. Withal, to be of power
To pay an army in the field, to buy
The king of France out of his realms, or Spain
Out of his Indies. What can you not do
Against lords spiritual or temporal,
That shall oppone you?
    Tri. Verily, 'tis true.
We may be temporal lords ourselves, I take it.
    Sub. You may be any thing, and leave off to make
Long-winded exercises; or suck up
Your *ha!* and *hum!* in a tune. I not deny,
But such as are not graced in a state,
May, for their ends, be adverse in religion,
And get a tune to call the flock together:
For, to say sooth, a tune does much with women,
And other phlegmatic people; it is your bell.
    Ana. Bells are profane; a tune may be religious.
    Sub. No warning with you! then farewell my patience.
'Slight, it shall down: I will not be thus tortured.
    Tri. I pray you, sir.
    Sub. All shall perish. I have spoken it.
    Tri. Let me find grace, sir, in your eyes; the man
He stands corrected: neither did his zeal,
But as your self, allow a tune somewhere.

Which now, being tow'rd the stone, we shall not need.
 Sub. No, nor your holy vizard, to win widows
To give you legacies; or make zealous wives
To rob their husbands for the common cause:
Nor take the start of bonds broke but one day,
And say, they were forfeited by providence.
Nor shall you need o'er night to eat huge meals,
To celebrate your next day's fast the better;
The whilst the brethren and the sisters humbled,
Abate the stiffness of the flesh.   Nor cast
Before your hungry hearers scrupulous bones;
As whether a Christian may hawk or hunt,
Or whether matrons of the holy assembly
May lay their hair out, or wear doublets,
Or have that idol starch about their linen.
 Ana. It is indeed an idol.
 Tri. Mind him not, sir.
I do command thee, spirit of zeal, but trouble,
To peace within him!   Pray, you, sir, go on.
 Sub. Nor shall you need to libel 'gainst the prelates,
And shorten so your ears against the hearing
Of the next wire-drawn grace.   Nor of necessity
Rail against plays, to please the alderman
Whose daily custard you devour: nor lie
With zealous rage till you are hoarse.   Not one
Of these so singular arts.   Nor call your selves
By names of Tribulation, Persecution,
Restraint, Long-patience, and such-like, affected
By the whole family or wood of you,
Only for glory, and to catch the ear
Of the disciple.
 Tri. Truly, sir, they are
Ways that the godly brethren have invented,
For propagation of the glorious cause,
As very notable means, and whereby also
Themselves grow soon, and profitably, famous.
 Sub. O, but the stone, all's idle to it! nothing!
The art of angels' nature's miracle,
The divine secret that doth fly in clouds
From east to west; and whose tradition
Is not from men, but spirits.
 Ana. I hate traditions;
I do not trust them.—
 Tri. Peace!
 Ana. They are popish all.
I will not peace: I will not—
 Tri. Ananias!
 Ana. Please the profane, to grieve the godly; I may not.
 Sub. Well, Ananias, thou shalt overcome.

Tri. It is an ignorant zeal that haunts him, sir;
But truly, else, a very faithful brother,
A botcher, and a man, by revelation,
That hath a competent knowledge of the truth.

Sub. Has he a competent sum there in the bag
To buy the goods within? I am made guardian,
And must, for charity, and conscience sake,
Now see the most be made for my poor orphan;
Though I desire the brethren too good gainers:
There they are within. When you have view'd, and bought 'em,
And ta'en the inventory of what they are,
They are ready for projection; there's no more
To do: cast on the med'cine, so much silver
As there is tin there, so much gold as brass,
I'll give't you in by weight.

Tri. But how long time,
Sir, must the saints expect yet?

Sub. Let me see,
How's the moon now? Eight, nine, ten days hence,
He will be silver potate; then three days
Before he citronise: Some fifteen days,
The magisterium will be perfected.

Ana. About the second day of the third week,
In the ninth month?

Sub. Yes, my good Ananias.

Tri. What will the orphan's goods arise to, think you?

Sub. Some hundred marks, as much as fill'd three cars,
Unladed now: you'll make six millions of them.—
But I must have more coals laid in.

Tri. How!

Sub. Another load,
And then we have finish'd. We must now increase
Our fire to *ignis ardens*, we are past
Fimus equinus, balnei, cineris,
And all those lenter heats. If the holy purse
Should with this draught fall low, and that the saints
Do need a present sum, I have a trick
To melt the pewter, you shall buy now, instantly,
And with a tincture make you as good Dutch dollars
As any are in Holland.

Tri. Can you so?

Sub. Ay, and shall 'bide the third examination.

Ana. It will be joyful tidings to the brethren.

Sub. But you must carry it secret.

Tri. Ay; but stay,
This act of coining, is it lawful?

Ana. Lawful!
We know no magistrate; or, if we did,
This is foreign coin.

Sub. It is no coining, sir.
It is but casting.

Tri. Ha! you distinguish well:
Casting of money may be lawful.

Ana. 'Tis, sir.

Tri. Truly, I take it so.

Sub. There is no scruple,
Sir, to be made of it; believe Ananias:
This case of conscience he is studied in.

Tri. I'll make a question of it to the brethren.

Ana. The brethren shall approve it lawful, doubt not.
Where shall it be done?   *[Knocking without.*

Sub. For that we'll talk anon.
There's some to speak with me. Go in, I pray you,
And view the parcels. That's the inventory.
I'll come to you straight. *[Exeunt Trib. and Ana.]* Who is
    it?—Face! appear.
        Enter FACE, *in his uniform.*
How now! good prize?

Face. Good pox! yond' costive cheater
Never came on.

Sub. How then?

Face. I have walk'd the round
Till now, and no such thing.

Sub. And have you quit him?

Face. Quit him! an hell would quit him too, he were happy.
'Slight! would you have me stalk like a mill-jade,
All day, for one that will not yield us grains?
I know him of old.

Sub. O, but to have gull'd him,
Had been a mastery.

Face. Let him go, black boy!
And turn thee, that some fresh news may possess thee.
A noble count, a don of Spain, my dear
Delicious compeer, and my party-bawd,
Who is come hither private for his conscience,
And brought munition with him, six great slops,
Bigger than three Dutch hoys, beside round trunks,
Furnish'd with pistolets, and pieces of eight,
Will straight be here, my rogue, to have thy bath,
(That is the colour,) and to make his battery
Upon our Dol, our castle, our cinque-port,
Our Dover pier, our what thou wilt. Where is she?
She must prepare perfumes, delicate linen,
The bath in chief, a banquet, and her wit,
For she must milk his epididimis.
Where is the doxy?

Sub. I'll send her to thee:
And but dispatch my brace of little John Leydens,

And come again my self.

    Face. Are they within then?

    Sub. Numbering the sum.

    Face. How much?

    Sub. A hundred marks, boy.   [*Exit.*

    Face. Why, this is a lucky day.   Ten pounds of Mammon!
Three of my clerk! a portague of my grocer!
This of the brethren! beside reversions,
And states to come in the widow, and my count!
My share to-day will not be bought for forty—

Enter DOL.

    Dol. What?

    Face. Pounds, dainty Dorothy! art thou so near?

    Dol. Yes; say, lord general, how fares our camp?

    Face. As with the few that had entrench'd themselves
Safe, by their discipline, against a world, Dol,
And laugh'd within those trenches, and grew fat
With thinking on the booties, Dol, brought in
Daily by their small parties.   This dear hour,
A doughty don is taken with my Dol;
And thou mayst make his ransom what thou wilt,
My Dousabel; he shall be brought here fetter'd
With thy fair looks, before he sees thee; and thrown
In a down-bed, as dark as any dungeon;
Where thou shalt keep him waking with thy drum;
Thy drum, my Dol, thy drum; till he be tame
As the poor black-birds were in the great frost,
Or bees are with a bason; and so hive him
In the swan-skin coverlid, and cambric sheets,
Till he work honey and wax, my little God's-gift.

    Dol. What is he, general?

    Face. An adalantado,
A grandee, girl.   Was not my Dapper here yet?

    Dol. No.

    Face. Nor my Drugger?

    Dol. Neither.

    Face. A pox on 'em,
They are so long a furnishing! such stinkards
Would not be seen upon these festival days.—

Re-enter SUBTLE.

How now! have you done?

    Sub. Done.   They are gone: the sum
Is here in bank, my Face.   I would we knew
Another chapman now would buy 'em outright.

    Face. 'Slid, Nab shall do't against he have the widow,
To furnish household.

    Sub. Excellent, well thought on:

Pray God he come!
  Face. I pray he keep away
Till our new business be o'erpast.
  Sub. But, Face,
How cam'st thou by this secret don?
  Face. A spirit
Brought me th' intelligence in a paper here,
As I was conjuring yonder in my circle
For Surly; I have my flies abroad. Your bath
Is famous, Subtle, by my means. Sweet Dol,
You must go tune your virginal, no losing
O' the least time: and, do you hear? good action.
Firk, like a flounder; kiss, like a scallop, close;
And tickle him with thy mother-tongue. His great
Verdugoship has not a jot of language;
So much the easier to be cozen'd, my Dolly.
He will come here in a hired coach, obscure,
And our own coachman, whom I have sent as guide,
No creature else. [*Knocking without.*] Who's that?   [*Exit Dol.*
  Sub. It is not he?
  Face. O no, not yet this hour.

Re-enter DOL.

  Sub. Who is't?
  Dol. Dapper,
Your clerk.
  Face. God's will then, queen of Fairy,
On with your tire; [*Exit Dol.*] and, doctor, with your robes.
Let's dispatch him for God's sake.
  Sub. 'Twill be long.
  Face. I warrant you, take but the cues I give you,
It shall be brief enough. [*Goes to the window.*] 'Slight, here are more!
Abel, and I think the angry boy, the heir,
That fain would quarrel.
  Sub. And the widow?
  Face. No,
Not that I see. Away!   [*Exit Sub.*

Enter DAPPER.

          —O sir, you are welcome.
The doctor is within a moving for you;
I have had the most ado to win him to it!—
He swears you'll be the darling of the dice:
He never heard her highness dote till now.
Your aunt has given you the most gracious words
That can be thought on.
  Dap. Shall I see her grace?
  Face. See her, and kiss her too.—

Enter ABEL, *followed by* KASTRIL.

What, honest Nab!

Hast brought the damask?

Drug. No, sir; here's tobacco.

Face. 'Tis well done, Nab: thou'lt bring the damask too?

Drug. Yes: here's the gentleman, captain, master Kastril,
I have brought to see the doctor.

Face. Where's the widow?

Drug. Sir, as he likes, his sister, he says, shall come.

Face. O, is it so? good time.   Is your name Kastril, sir?

Kas. Ay, and the best of the Kastrils, I'd be sorry else,
By fifteen hundred a year.   Where is the doctor?
My mad tobacco-boy, here, tells me of one
That can do things: has he any skill?

Face. Wherein, sir?

Kas. To carry a business, manage a quarrel fairly,
Upon fit terms.

Face. It seems, sir, you are but young
About the town, that can make that a question.

Kas. Sir, not so young, but I have heard some speech
Of the angry boys, and seen them take tobacco;
And in his shop; and I can take it too.
And I would fain be one of 'em, and go down
And practise in the country.

Face. Sir, for the duello,
The doctor, I assure you, shall inform you,
To the least shadow of a hair; and shew you
An instrument he has of his own making,
Wherewith no sooner shall you make report
Of any quarrel, but he will take the height on't
Most instantly, and tell in what degree
Of safety it lies in, or mortality.
And how it may be borne, whether in a right line,
Or a half circle; or may else be cast
Into an angle blunt, if not acute:
All this he will demonstrate.   And then, rules
To give and take the lie by.

Kas. How! to take it?

Face. Yes, in oblique he'll shew you, or in circle;
But never in diameter.   The whole town
Study his theorems, and dispute them ordinarily
At the eating academies.

Kas. But does he teach
Living by the wits too?

Face. Anything whatever.
You cannot think that subtlety, but he reads it.
He made me a captain.   I was a stark pimp,
Just of your standing, 'fore I met with him;

It is not two months since. I'll tell you his method:
First, he will enter you at some ordinary.

    Kas. No, I'll not come there: you shall pardon me.

    Face. For why, sir?

    Kas. There's gaming there, and tricks.

    Face. Why, would you be
A gallant, and not game?

    Kas. Ay, 'twill spend a man.

    Face. Spend you! it will repair you when you are spent:
How do they live by their wits there, that have vented
Six times your fortunes?

    Kas. What, three thousand a-year!

    Face. Ay, forty thousand.

    Kas. Are there such?

    Face. Ay, sir,
And gallants yet. Here's a young gentleman
Is born to nothing,—[*Points to Dapper.*] forty marks a-year,
Which I count nothing:—he is to be initiated,
And have a fly of the doctor. He will win you,
By unresistible luck, within this fortnight,
Enough to buy a barony. They will set him
Upmost, at the groom porters, all the Christmas:
And for the whole year through, at every place,
Where there is play, present him with the chair;
The best attendance, the best drink; sometimes
Two glasses of Canary, and pay nothing;
The purest linen, and the sharpest knife,
The partridge next his trencher: and somewhere
The dainty bed, in private, with the dainty.
You shall have your ordinaries bid for him,
As play-houses for a poet; and the master
Pray him aloud to name what dish he affects,
Which must be butter'd shrimps: and those that drink
To no mouth else, will drink to his, as being
The goodly president mouth of all the board.

    Kas. Do you not gull one?

    Face. 'Ods my life! do you think it?
You shall have a cast commander, (can but get
In credit with a glover, or a spurrier,
For some two pair of either's ware aforehand,)
Will, by most swift posts, dealing [but] with him,
Arrive at competent means to keep himself,
His punk and naked boy, in excellent fashion,
And be admired for't.

    Kas. Will the doctor teach this?

    Face. He will do more, sir: when your land is gone,
As men of spirit hate to keep earth long,
In a vacation, when small money is stirring,
And ordinaries suspended till the term,

He'll shew a perspective, where on one side
You shall behold the faces and the persons
Of all sufficient young heirs in town,
Whose bonds are current for commodity;
On th' other side, the merchants' forms, and others,
That without help of any second broker,
Who would expect a share, will trust such parcels:
In the third square, the very street and sign
Where the commodity dwells, and does but wait
To be deliver'd, be it pepper, soap,
Hops, or tobacco, oatmeal, woad, or cheeses.
All which you may so handle, to enjoy
To your own use, and never stand obliged.
    Kas. I'faith! is he such a fellow?
    Face. Why, Nab here knows him.
And then for making matches for rich widows,
Young gentlewomen, heirs, the fortunat'st man!
He's sent to, far and near, all over England,
To have his counsel, and to know their fortunes.
    Kas. God's will, my suster shall see him.
    Face. I'll tell you, sir,
What he did tell me of Nab. It's a strange thing:—
By the way, you must eat no cheese, Nab, it breeds melancholy,
And that same melancholy breeds worms; but pass it:—
He told me, honest Nab here was ne'er at tavern
But once in's life!
    Drug. Truth, and no more I was not.
    Face. And then he was so sick—
    Drug. Could he tell you that too?
    Face. How should I know it?
    Drug. In troth we had been a shooting,
And had a piece of fat ram-mutton to supper,
That lay so heavy o' my stomach—
    Face. And he has no head
To bear any wine; for what with the noise of the fidlers,
And care of his shop, for he dares keep no servants—
    Drug. My head did so ach—
    Face. As he was fain to be brought home,
The doctor told me: and then a good old woman—
    Drug. Yes, faith, she dwells in Sea-coal-lane,—did cure me,
With sodden ale, and pellitory of the wall;
Cost me but two-pence. I had another sickness
Was worse than that.
    Face. Ay, that was with the grief
Thou took'st for being cess'd at eighteen-pence,
For the water-work.
    Drug. In truth, and it was like
T' have cost me almost my life.
    Face. Thy hair went off?

Drug. Yes, sir; 'twas done for spight.

Face. Nay, so says the doctor.

Kas. Pray thee, tobacco-boy, go fetch my suster;
I'll see this learned boy before I go;
And so shall she.

Face. Sir, he is busy now:
But if you have a sister to fetch hither,
Perhaps your own pains may command her sooner;
And he by that time will be free.

Kas. I go.   [*Exit.*

Face. Drugger, she's thine: the damask!—[*Exit Abel.*]
     Subtle and I
Must wrestle for her. [*Aside.*]—Come on, master Dapper,
You see how I turn clients here away,
To give your cause dispatch; have you perform'd
The ceremonies were enjoin'd you?

Dap. Yes, of the vinegar,
And the clean shirt.

Face. 'Tis well: that shirt may do you
More worship than you think. Your aunt's a-fire,
But that she will not shew it, t' have a sight of you.
Have you provided for her grace's servants?

Dap. Yes, here are six score Edward shillings.

Face. Good!

Dap. And an old Harry's sovereign.

Face. Very good!

Dap. And three James shillings, and an Elizabeth groat,
Just twenty nobles.

Face. O, you are too just.
I would you had had the other noble in Maries.

Dap. I have some Philip and Maries.

Face. Ay, those same
Are best of all: where are they? Hark, the doctor.

Enter SUBTLE, *disguised like a priest of Fairy, with a stripe
of cloth.*

Sub. [*in a feigned voice.*] Is yet her grace's cousin come?

Face. He is come.

Sub. And is he fasting?

Face. Yes.

Sub. And hath cried hum?

Face. Thrice, you must answer.

Dap. Thrice.

Sub. And as oft buz?

Face. If you have, say.

Dap. I have.

Sub. Then, to her cuz,
Hoping that he hath vinegar'd his senses,
As he was bid, the Fairy queen dispenses,

By me, this robe, the petticoat of fortune;
Which that he straight put on, she doth importune.
And though to fortune near be her petticoat,
Yet nearer is her smock, the queen doth note:
And therefore, ev'n of that a piece she hath sent
Which, being a child, to wrap him in was rent;
And prays him for a scarf he now will wear it,
With as much love as then her grace did tear it,
About his eyes, [*They blind him with the rag,*] to shew he is fortunate.
And, trusting unto her to make his state,
He'll throw away all worldly pelf about him;
Which that he will perform, she doth not doubt him.

   Face. She need not doubt him, sir.   Alas, he has nothing,
But what he will part withal as willingly,
Upon her grace's word—throw away your purse—
As she would ask it;—handkerchiefs and all—
                            [*He throws away, as they bid him.*
She cannot bid that thing, but he'll obey.—
If you have a ring about you, cast it off,
Or a silver seal at your wrist; her grace will send
Her fairies here to search you, therefore deal
Directly with her highness: if they find
That you conceal a mite, you are undone.

   Dap. Truly, there's all.
   Face. All what?
   Dap. My money; truly.
   Face. Keep nothing that is transitory about you.
Bid Dol play music.   [*Aside to Subtle.*]—Look, the elves are come
                    [*Dol plays on the cittern within.*
To pinch you, if you tell not truth.   Advise you.   [*They pinch him.*
   Dap. O! I have a paper with a spur-ryal in't.
   Face. *Ti, ti.*
They knew't, they say.
   Sub. *Ti, ti, ti, ti.*   He has more yet.
   Face. *Ti, ti-ti-ti.*   In the other pocket.   [*Aside to Sub.*
   Sub. *Titi, titi, titi, titi, titi.*
They must pinch him or he will never confess, they say.
                    [*They pinch him again.*

   Dap. O, O!
   Face. Nay, pray you hold: he is her grace's nephew.
Ti, ti, ti?   What care you? good faith, you shall care.—
Deal plainly, sir, and shame the fairies.   Shew
You are innocent.
   Dap. By this good light, I have nothing.
   Sub. *Ti, ti, ti, ti, to, ta.*   He does equivocate, she says:
Ti, ti do ti, ti ti do, ti da; and swears by the *light* when he is blinded.
   Dap. By this good *dark*, I have nothing but a half-crown
Of gold about my wrist, that my love gave me;
And a leaden heart I wore since she forsook me.

Face. I thought 'twas something.   And would you incur
Your aunt's displeasure for these trifles?   Come,
I had rather you had thrown away twenty half-crowns. [*Takes it off.*
You may wear your leaden heart still.—

Enter DOL, *hastily.*

How now!

Sub. What news, Dol?
Dol. Yonder's your knight, sir Mammon.
Face. 'Ods lid, we never thought of him till now!
Where is he?
Dol. Here hard by: he is at the door.
Sub. And you are not ready, now!   Dol, get his suit.   [*Exit Dol.*
He must not be sent back.
Face. O by no means.
What shall we do with this same puffin here,
Now he's on the spit?
Sub. Why, lay him back awhile,
With some device.

Re-enter DOL, *with* FACE's *clothes.*

—*Ti, ti, ti, ti, ti, ti,* Would her grace speak with me?
I come.—Help, Dol!   [*Knocking without.*
Face. [*speaks through the key-hole.*] Who's there?   sir Epicure,
My master's in the way.   Please you to walk
Three or four turns, but till his back be turn'd,
And I am for you.—Quickly, Dol!
Sub. Her grace
Commends her kindly to you, master Dapper.
Dap. I long to see her grace.
Sub. She now is set
At dinner in her bed, and she has sent you
From her own private trencher, a dead mouse,
And a piece of gingerbread, to be merry withal,
And stay your stomach, lest you faint with fasting;
Yet if you could hold out till she saw you, she says,
It would be better for you.
Face. Sir, he shall
Hold out, an 'twere this two hours, for her highness;
I can assure you that.   We will not lose
All we have done.—
Sub. He must not see, nor speak
To any body, till then.
Face. For that we'll put, sir,
A stay in's mouth.
Sub. Of what?
Face. Of gingerbread.
Make you it fit.   He that hath pleas'd her grace
Thus far, shall not now crincle for a little.—

Gape, sir, and let him fit you.

              [They thrust a gag of gingerbread in his mouth.

  Sub. Where shall we now

Bestow him?

  Dol. In the privy.

  Sub. Come along, sir,

I now must shew you Fortune's privy lodgings.

  Face. Are they perfum'd, and his bath ready?

  Sub. All:

Only the fumigation's somewhat strong.

  Face. [*speaking through the key-hole.*] Sir Epicure, I am yours,

      sir, by and by.   *[Exeunt with Dapper.*

ACT IV

SCENE I.—*A Room in* LOVEWIT's *House.*

Enter FACE *and* MAMMON.

Face. O sir, you are come in the only finest time.—

Mam. Where's master?

Face. Now preparing for projection, sir.

Your stuff will be all changed shortly.

  Mam. Into gold?

Face. To gold and silver, sir.

Mam. Silver I care not for.

Face. Yes, sir, a little to give beggars.

Mam. Where's the lady?

Face. At hand here. I have told her such brave things of you,

Touching your bounty, and your noble spirit—

  Mam. Hast thou?

Face. As she is almost in her fit to see you.

But, good sir, no divinity in your conference,

For fear of putting her in rage.—

  Mam. I warrant thee.

Face. Six men [sir] will not hold her down: and then,

If the old man should hear or see you—

  Mam. Fear not.

Face. The very house, sir, would run mad. You know it,

How scrupulous he is, and violent,

'Gainst the least act of sin. Physic, or mathematics,

Poetry, state, or bawdry, as I told you,

She will endure, and never startle; but

No word of controversy.

  Mam. I am school'd, good Ulen.

Face. And you must praise her house, remember that,

And her nobility.

  Mam. Let me alone:

No herald, no, nor antiquary, Lungs,

Shall do it better.   Go.
   Face. Why, this is yet
A kind of modern happiness, to have
Dol Common for a great lady.   [*Aside and exit.*
   Mam. Now, Epicure,
Heighten thyself, talk to her all in gold;
Rain her as many showers as Jove did drops
Unto his Danäe; shew the god a miser,
Compared with Mammon.   What! the stone will do't.
She shall feel gold, taste gold, hear gold, sleep gold;
Nay, we will *concumbere* gold: I will be puissant,
And mighty in my talk to her.—

     Re-enter FACE, *with* DOL *richly dressed.*

                Here she comes.
   Face. To him, Dol, suckle him.—This is the noble knight,
I told your ladyship—
   Mam. Madam, with your pardon,
I kiss your vesture.
   Dol. Sir, I were uncivil
If I would suffer that; my lip to you, sir.
   Mam. I hope my lord your brother be in health, lady.
   Dol. My lord, my brother is, though I no lady, sir.
   Face. Well said, my Guinea bird.   [*Aside.*
   Mam. Right noble madam—
   Face. O, we shall have most fierce idolatry.   [*Aside.*
   Mam. 'Tis your prerogative.
   Dol. Rather your courtesy.
   Mam. Were there nought else to enlarge your virtues to me,
These answers speak your breeding and your blood.
   Dol. Blood we boast none, sir, a poor baron's daughter.
   Mam. Poor! and gat you? profane not.   Had your father
Slept all the happy remnant of his life
After that act, lien but there still, and panted,
He had done enough to make himself, his issue,
And his posterity noble.
   Dol. Sir, although
We may be said to want the gilt and trappings,
The dress of honour, yet we strive to keep
The seeds and the materials.
   Mam. I do see
The old ingredient, virtue, was not lost,
Nor the drug money used to make your compound.
There is a strange nobility in your eye,
This lip, that chin! methinks you do resemble
One of the Austriac princes.
   Face. Very like!
Her father was an Irish costarmonger.   [*Aside.*
   Mam. The house of Valois just had such a nose,

And such a forehead yet the Medici
Of Florence boast.
　　Dol. Troth, and I have been liken'd
To all these princes.
　　Face. I'll be sworn, I heard it.
　　Mam. I know not how! it is not any one,
But e'en the very choice of all their features.
　　Face. I'll in, and laugh.　　　　[*Aside and exit.*
　　Mam. A certain touch, or air,
That sparkles a divinity, beyond
An earthly beauty!
　　Dol. O, you play the courtier.
　　Mam. Good lady, give me leave—
　　Dol. In faith, I may not,
To mock me, sir.
　　Mam. To burn in this sweet flame;
The phœnix never knew a nobler death.
　　Dol. Nay, now you court the courtier, and destroy
What you would build: this art, sir, in your words,
Calls your whole faith in question.
　　Mam. By my soul—
　　Dol. Nay, oaths are made of the same air, sir.
　　Mam. Nature
Never bestow'd upon mortality
A more unblamed, a more harmonious feature;
She play'd the step-dame in all faces else:
Sweet Madam, let me be particular—
　　Dol. Particular, sir!　I pray you know your distance.
　　Mam. In no ill sense, sweet lady; but to ask
How your fair graces pass the hours?　I see
You are lodg'd here, in the house of a rare man,
An excellent artist; but what's that to you?
　　Dol. Yes, sir; I study here the mathematics,
And distillation.
　　Mam. O, I cry your pardon.
He's a divine instructor! can extract
The souls of all things by his art; call all
The virtues, and the miracles of the sun,
Into a temperate furnace; teach dull nature
What her own forces are.　A man, the emperor
Has courted above Kelly; sent his medals
And chains, to invite him.
　　Dol. Ay, and for his physic, sir—
　　Mam. Above the art of Æsculapius,
That drew the envy of the thunderer!
I know all this, and more.
　　Dol. Troth, I am taken, sir,
Whole with these studies, that contemplate nature.
　　Mam. It is a noble humour; but this form

Was not intended to so dark a use.
Had you been crooked, foul, of some coarse mould
A cloister had done well; but such a feature
That might stand up the glory of a kingdom,
To live recluse! is a mere solœcism,
Though in a nunnery. It must not be.
I muse, my lord your brother will permit it:
You should spend half my land first, were I he.
Does not this diamond better on my finger,
Than in the quarry?
 Dol. Yes.
 Mam. Why, you are like it.
You were created, lady, for the light.
Here, you shall wear it; take it, the first pledge
Of what I speak, to bind you to believe me.
 Dol. In chains of adamant?
 Mam. Yes, the strongest bands.
And take a secret too—here, by your side,
Doth stand this hour, the happiest man in Europe.
 Dol. You are contented, sir!
 Mam. Nay, in true being,
The envy of princes and the fear of states.
 Dol. Say you so, sir Epicure?
 Mam. Yes, and thou shalt prove it,
Daughter of honour. I have cast mine eye
Upon thy form, and I will rear this beauty
Above all styles.
 Dol. You mean no treason, sir?
 Mam. No, I will take away that jealousy.
I am the lord of the philosopher's stone,
And thou the lady.
 Dol. How, sir! have you that?
 Mam. I am the master of the mystery.
This day the good old wretch here o' the house
Has made it for us; now he's at projection.
Think therefore thy first wish now, let me hear it,
And it shall rain into thy lap, no shower,
But floods of gold, whole cataracts, a deluge,
To get a nation on thee.
 Dol. You are pleased, sir,
To work on the ambition of our sex.
 Mam. I am pleased the glory of her sex should know,
This nook, here, of the Friers is no climate
For her to live obscurely in, to learn
Physic and surgery, for the constable's wife
Of some odd hundred in Essex; but come forth,
And taste the air of palaces; eat, drink
The toils of empirics, and their boasted practice;
Tincture of pearl, and coral, gold and amber;

Be seen at feasts and triumphs; have it ask'd,
What miracle she is? set all the eyes
Of court a-fire, like a burning glass,
And work them into cinders, when the jewels
Of twenty states adorn thee, and the light
Strikes out the stars! that when thy name is mention'd,
Queens may look pale; and we but shewing our love,
Nero's Poppæa may be lost in story!
Thus will we have it.

   Dol. I could well consent, sir. .
But, in a monarchy, how will this be?
The prince will soon take notice, and both seize
You and your stone, it being a wealth unfit
For any private subject.

   Mam. If he knew it.

   Dol. Yourself do boast it, sir.

   Mam. To thee, my life.

   Dol. O, but beware, sir! you may come to end
The remnants of your days in a loth'd prison,
By speaking of it.

   Mam. 'Tis no idle fear:
We'll therefore go withal, my girl, and live
In a free state, where we will eat our mullets,
Soused in high-country wines, sup pheasants' eggs,
And have our cockles boil'd in silver shells;
Our shrimps to swim again, as when they liv'd,
In a rare butter made of dolphin's milk,
Whose cream does look like opals; and with these
Delicate meats set ourselves high for pleasure,
And take us down again, and then renew
Our youth and strength with drinking the elixir,
And so enjoy a perpetuity
Of life and lust! And thou shalt have thy wardrobe
Richer than nature's, still to change thy self,
And vary oftener, for thy pride, than she,
Or art, her wise and almost-equal servant.

Re-enter FACE.

   Face. Sir, you are too loud. I hear you every word
Into the laboratory. Some fitter place;
The garden, or great chamber above. How like you her?

   Mam. Excellent! Lungs. There's for thee. [*Gives him money.*

   Face. But do you hear?
Good sir, beware, no mention of the rabbins.

   Mam. We think not on 'em.   [*Exeunt Mam. and Dol.*

   Face. O, it is well, sir.—Subtle!

Enter SUBTLE.

Dost thou not laugh?

   Sub. Yes; are they gone?

Face. All's clear.

Sub. The widow is come.

Face. And your quarrelling disciple?

Sub. Ay.

Face. I must to my captainship again then.

Sub. Stay, bring them in first.

Face. So I meant. What is she?
A bonnibel?

Sub. I know not.

Face. We'll draw lots:
You'll stand to that?

Sub. What else?

Face. O, for a suit,
To fall now like a curtain, flap!

Sub. To the door, man.

Face. You'll have the first kiss, 'cause I am not ready.   [*Exit.*

Sub. Yes, and perhaps hit you through both the nostrils.

Face. [*within.*] Who would you speak with?

Kas. [*within.*] Where's the captain?

Face. [*within.*] Gone, sir,
About some business.

Kas. [*within.*] Gone!

Face. [*within.*] He'll return straight.
But master doctor, his lieutenant, is here.

Enter KASTRIL, *followed by* Dame PLIANT.

Sub. Come near, my worshipful boy, my *terræ fili*,
That is, my boy of land; make thy approaches:
Welcome; I know thy lusts, and thy desires,
And I will serve and satisfy them. Begin,
Charge me from thence, or thence, or in this line;
Here is my centre: ground thy quarrel.

Kas. You lie.

Sub. How, child of wrath and anger! the loud lie?
For what, my sudden boy?

Kas. Nay, that look you to,
I am afore-hand.

Sub. O, this is no true grammar,
And as ill logic! You must render causes, child,
Your first and second intentions, know your canons
And your divisions, moods, degrees, and differences,
Your predicaments, substance, and accident,
Series, extern and intern, with their causes,
Efficient, material, formal, final,
And have your elements perfect.

Kas. What is this!
The angry tongue he talks in?   [*Aside.*

Sub. That false precept,
Of being afore-hand, has deceived a number,

And made them enter quarrels, often-times,
Before they were aware; and afterward,
Against their wills.
    Kas. How must I do then, sir?
    Sub. I cry this lady mercy: she should first
Have been saluted. [*Kisses her.*] I do call you lady,
Because you are to be one, ere't be long,
My soft and buxom widow.
    Kas. Is she, i'faith?
    Sub. Yes, or my art is an egregious liar.
    Kas. How know you?
    Sub. By inspection on her forehead,
And subtlety of her lip, which must be tasted
Often, to make a judgment. [*Kisses her again.*] 'Slight, she melts
Like a myrobolane:—here is yet a line,
In *rivo frontis*, tells me he is no knight.
    Dame P. What is he then, sir?
    Sub. Let me see your hand.
O, your *linea fortunæ* makes it plain;
And stella here *in monte Veneris*.
But, most of all, *junctura annularis*.
He is a soldier, or a man of art, lady,
But shall have some great honour shortly.
    Dame P. Brother,
He's a rare man, believe me!

Re-enter Face, in his uniform.

    Kas. Hold your peace.
Here comes the t'other rare man.—'Save you, captain.
    Face. Good master Kastril! Is this your sister?
    Kas. Ay, sir.
Please you to kuss her, and be proud to know her.
    Face. I shall be proud to know you, lady.   [*Kisses her.*
    Dame P. Brother,
He calls me lady too.   [*Takes her aside.*
    Kas. Ay, peace: I heard it.
    Face. The count is come.
    Sub. Where is he?
    Face. At the door.
    Sub. Why, you must entertain him.
    Face. What will you do
With these the while?
    Sub. Why, have them up, and shew them
Some fustian book, or the dark glass.
    Face. 'Fore God,
She is a delicate dab-chick! I must have her.   [*Exit.*
    Sub. Must you! ay, if your fortune will, you must.—
Come, sir, the captain will come to us presently:
I'll have you to my chamber of demonstrations,

Where I will shew you both the grammar, and logic,
And rhetoric of quarrelling; my whole method
Drawn out in tables; and my instrument,
That hath the several scales upon't, shall make you
Able to quarrel at a straw's-breadth by moon-light.
And, lady, I'll have you look in a glass,
Some half an hour, but to clear your eye-sight,
Against you see your fortune; which is greater,
Than I may judge upon the sudden, trust me.

[*Exit, followed by* Kast. *and Dame P.*

Re-enter FACE.

Face. Where are you, doctor?
Sub. [*within.*] I'll come to you presently.
Face. I will have this same widow, now I have seen her,
On any composition.

Re-enter SUBTLE.

Sub. What do you say?
Face. Have you disposed of them?
Sub. I have sent them up.
Face. Subtle, in troth, I needs must have this widow.
Sub. Is that the matter?
Face. Nay, but hear me.
Sub. Go to.
If you rebel once, Dol shall know it all:
Therefore be quiet, and obey your chance.
Face. Nay, thou art so violent now—Do but conceive,
Thou art old, and canst not serve—
Sub. Who cannot? I?
'Slight, I will serve her with thee, for a—
Face. Nay,
But understand: I'll give you composition.
Sub. I will not treat with thee; what! sell my fortune?
'Tis better than my birth-right. Do not murmur:
Win her, and carry her. If you grumble, Dol
Knows it directly.
Face. Well, sir, I am silent.
Will you go help to fetch in Don in state? [*Exit.*
Sub. I follow you, sir: we must keep Face in awe,
Or he will over-look us like a tyrant.

Re-enter FACE, *introducing* SURLY *disguised as a Spaniard.*

Brain of a tailor! who comes here? Don John!
Sur. Señores, beso las manos a vuestras mercedes.
Sub. Would you had stoop'd a little, and kist our anos!
Face. Peace, Subtle.
Sub. Stab me; I shall never hold, man.
He looks in that deep ruff like a head in a platter,

Serv'd in by a short cloke upon two trestles.

Face. Or, what do you say to a collar of brawn, cut down
Beneath the souse, and wriggled with a knife?

Sub. 'Slud, he does look too fat to be a Spaniard.

Face. Perhaps some Fleming or some Hollander got him
In d'Alva's time; count Egmont's bastard.

Sub. Don,
Your scurvy, yellow, Madrid face is welcome.

Sur. Gratia.

Sub. He speaks out of a fortification.
Pray God he have no squibs in those deep sets.

Sur. Por dios, señores, muy linda casa!

Sub. What says he?

Face. Praises the house, I think;
I know no more but's action.

Sub. Yes, the *casa,*
My precious Diego, will prove fair enough
To cozen you in. Do you mark? you shall
Be cozen'd, Diego.

Face. Cozen'd, do you see,
My worthy Donzel, cozen'd.

Sur. Entiendo.

Sub. Do you intend it? so do we, dear Don.
Have you brought pistolets, or portagues,
My solemn Don?—Dost thou feel any?

Face. [*feels his pockets.*] Full.

Sub. You shall be emptied, Don, pumped and drawn
Dry, as they say.

Face. Milked, in troth, sweet Don.

Sub. See all the monsters; the great lion of all, Don.

Sur. Con licencia, se puede ver a esta señora?

Sub. What talks he now?

Face. Of the sennora.

Sub. O, Don,
That is the lioness, which you shall see
Also, my Don.

Face. 'Slid, Subtle, how shall we do?

Sub. For what?

Face. Why Dol's employ'd, you know.

Sub. That's true.
'Fore heaven, I know not: he must stay, that's all.

Face. Stay! that he must not by no means.

Sub. No! why?

Face. Unless you'll mar all. 'Slight, he will suspect it:
And then he will not pay, not half so well.
This is a travelled punk-master, and does know
All the delays; a notable hot rascal,
And looks already rampant.

Sub. 'Sdeath, and Mammon

Must not be troubled.

Face. Mammon! in no case.

Sub. What shall we do then?

Face. Think: you must be sudden.

Sur. *Entiendo que la señora es tan hermosa, que codicio tan verla, como la bien aventuranza de mi vida.*

Face. *Mi vida!* 'Slid, Subtle, he puts me in mind o' the widow.
What dost thou say to draw her to it, ha!
And tell her 'tis her fortune? all our venture
Now lies upon't. It is but one man more,
Which of us chance to have her: and beside,
There is no maidenhead to be fear'd or lost.
What dost thou think on't, Subtle?

Sub. Who, I? why—

Face. The credit of our house too is engaged.

Sub. You made me an offer for my share erewhile.
What wilt thou give me, i'faith?

Face. O, by that light
I'll not buy now: You know your doom to me.
E'en take your lot, obey your chance, sir; win her,
And wear her out, for me.

Sub. 'Slight, I'll not work her then.

Face. It is the common cause; therefore bethink you.
Dol else must know it, as you said.

Sub. I care not.

Sur. *Señores, porque se tarda tanto?*

Sub. Faith, I am not fit, I am old.

Face. That's now no reason, sir.

Sur. *Puede ser de hazer burla de mi amor?*

Face. You hear the Don too? by this air, I call,
And loose the hinges: Dol!

Sub. A plague of hell—

Face. Will you then do?

Sub. You are a terrible rogue!
I'll think of this: will you, sir, call the widow?

Face. Yes, and I'll take her too with all her faults,
Now I do think on't better.

Sub. With all my heart, sir;
Am I discharged o' the lot?

Face. As you please.

Sub. Hands.   [*They take hands.*

Face. Remember now, that upon any change,
You never claim her.

Sub. Much good joy, and health to you, sir.
Marry a whore! fate, let me wed a witch first.

Sur. *Por estas honradas barbas—*

Sub. He swears by his beard.
Dispatch, and call the brother too.   [*Exit Face.*

Sur. *Tengo duda, señores, que no me hagan alguna traycion.*

Sub. How, issue on? yes, præsto, sennor. Please you
Enthratha the *chambrata*, worthy don:
Where if you please the fates, in your *bathada*,
You shall be soked, and stroked, and tubb'd, and rubb'd,
And scrubb'd, and fubb'd, dear don, before you go.
You shall in faith, my scurvy baboon don.
Be curried, claw'd and flaw'd, and taw'd, indeed.
I will the heartlier go about it now,
And make the widow a punk so much the sooner,
To be revenged on this impetuous Face:
The quickly doing of it, is the grace.   [*Exeunt Sub. and Surly.*

SCENE II.—*Another Room in the same.*

Enter FACE, KASTRIL, *and* Dame PLIANT.

Face. Come, lady: I knew the Doctor would not leave,
Till he had found the very nick of her fortune.
    Kas. To be a countess, say you, a Spanish countess, sir?
    Dame P. Why, is that better than an English countess?
    Face. Better! 'Slight, make you that a question, lady?
    Kas. Nay, she is a fool, captain, you must pardon her.
    Face. Ask from your courtier, to your inns-of-court-man,
To your mere milliner; they will tell you all,
Your Spanish gennet is the best horse; your Spanish
Stoup is the best garb: your Spanish beard
Is the best cut; your Spanish ruffs are the best
Wear; your Spanish pavin the best dance;
Your Spanish titillation in a glove
The best perfume: and for your Spanish pike,
And Spanish blade, let your poor captain speak—
Here comes the doctor.

Enter SUBTLE, *with a paper.*

Sub. My most honour'd lady,
For so I am now to style you, having found
By this my scheme, you are to undergo
An honourable fortune, very shortly.
What will you say now, if some—
    Face. I have told her all, sir;
And her right worshipful brother here, that she shall be
A countess; do not delay them, sir: a Spanish countess.
    Sub. Still, my scarce-worshipful captain, you can keep
No secret! Well, since he has told you, madam,
Do you forgive him, and I do.
    Kas. She shall do that, sir;
I'll look to't, 'tis my charge.
    Sub. Well then: nought rests
But that she fit her love now to her fortune.
    Dame P. Truly I shall never brook a Spaniard.

Sub. No!

Dame P. Never since eighty-eight could I abide them,
And that was some three year afore I was born, in truth.

Sub. Come, you must love him, or be miserable,
Choose which you will.

Face. By this good rush, persuade her,
She will cry strawberries else within this twelvemonth.

Sub. Nay, shads and mackarel, which is worse.

Face. Indeed, sir!

Kas. Ods lid, you shall love him, or I'll kick you.

Dame P. Why,
I'll do as you will have me, brother.

Kas. Do,
Or by this hand I'll maul you.

Face. Nay, good sir,
Be not so fierce.

Sub. No, my enraged child;
She will be ruled. What, when she comes to taste
The pleasures of a countess! to be courted—

Face. And kiss'd, and ruffled!

Sub. Ay, behind the hangings.

Face. And then come forth in pomp!

Sub. And know her state!

Face. Of keeping all the idolators of the chamber
Barer to her, than at their prayers!

Sub. Is serv'd
Upon the knee!

Face. And has her pages, ushers,
Footmen, and coaches—

Sub. Her six mares—

Face. Nay, eight!

Sub. To hurry her through London, to the Exchange,
Bethlem, the china-houses—

Face. Yes, and have
The citizens gape at her, and praise her tires,
And my lord's goose-turd bands, that ride with her.

Kas. Most brave! By this hand, you are not my suster,
If you refuse.

Dame P. I will not refuse, brother.

Enter SURLY.

Sur. *Que es esto, señores, que no venga ? Esta tardanza me mata !*

Face. It is the count come:
The doctor knew he would be here, by his art.

Sub. *En gallanta madama, Don ! gallantissima !*

Sur. *Por todos los dioses, la mas acabada hermosura, que he visto en mi vida !*

Face. Is't not a gallant language that they speak?

Kas. An admirable language! Is't not French?

Face. No, Spanish, sir.

Kas. It goes like law-French,
And that, they say, is the courtliest language.

Face. List, sir.

Sur. *El sol ha perdido su lumbre, con el esplandor que trae esta
dama ! Valgame dios !*

Face. He admires your sister.

Kas. Must not she make curt'sy?

Sub. Ods will, she must go to him, man, and kiss him!
It is the Spanish fashion, for the women
To make first court.

Face. 'Tis true he tells you, sir:
His art knows all.

Sur. *Porque no se acude ?*

Kas. He speaks to her, I think.

Face. That he does, sir.

Sur. *Por el amor de dios, que es esto que se tarda ?*

Kas. Nay, see: she will not understand him! gull,
Noddy.

Dame P. What say you, brother?

Kas. Ass, my suster.
Go kuss him, as the cunning man would have you;
I'll thrust a pin in your buttocks else.

Face. O no, sir.

Sur. *Señora mia, mi persona esta muy indigna de allegar a tanta
hermosura.*

Face. Does he not use her bravely?

Kas. Bravely, i'faith!

Face. Nay, he will use her better.

Kas. Do you think so?

Sur. *Señora, si sera servida, entremonos.* [*Exit with Dame Pliant.*

Kas. Where does he carry her?

Face. Into the garden, sir;
Take you no thought: I must interpret for her.

Sub. Give Dol the word. [*Aside to Face, who goes out.*]—Come,
my fierce child, advance,
We'll to our quarrelling lesson again.

Kas. Agreed.
I love a Spanish boy with all my heart.

Sub. Nay, and by this means, sir, you shall be brother
To a great count.

Kas. Ay, I knew that at first.
This match will advance the house of the Kastrils.

Sub. 'Pray God your sister prove but pliant!

Kas. Why,
Her name is so, by her other husband.

Sub. How!

Kas. The widow Pliant. Knew you not that?

Sub. No faith, sir;

Yet, by erection of her figure, I guest it.
Come, let's go practise.
    Kas. Yes, but do you think, doctor,
I e'er shall quarrel well?
    Sub. I warrant you.   *[Exeunt.*

        SCENE III.—*Another Room in the same.*

    Enter DOL *in her fit of raving, followed by* MAMMON.

    Dol. For after Alexander's death—
    Mam. Good lady—
    Dol. That Perdiccas and Antigonus, were slain,
The two that stood, Seleuc', and Ptolomee—
    Mam. Madam.
    Dol. Made up the two legs, and the fourth beast,
That was Gog-north, and Egypt-south: which after
Was call'd Gog-iron-leg, and South-iron-leg—
    Mam. Lady—
    Dol. And then Gog-horned. So was Egypt, too:
Then Egypt-clay-leg, and Gog-clay-leg—
    Mam. Sweet madam.
    Dol. And last Gog-dust, and Egypt-dust, which fall
In the last link of the fourth chain. And these
Be stars in story, which none see, or look at—
    Mam. What shall I do?
    Dol. For, as he says, except
We call the rabbins, and the heathen Greeks—
    Mam. Dear lady.
    Dol. To come from Salem, and from Athens,
And teach the people of Great Britain—

    Enter FACE, *hastily, in his Servant's Dress.*

    Face. What's the matter, sir?
    Dol. To speak the tongue of Eber, and Javan—
    Mam. O,
She's in her fit.
    Dol. We shall know nothing—
    Face. Death, sir,
We are undone!
    Dol. Where then a learned linguist
Shall see the ancient used communion
Of vowels and consonants—
    Face. My master will hear!
    Dol. A wisdom, which Pythagoras held most high—
    Mam. Sweet honorable lady!
    Dol. To comprise
All sounds of voices, in few marks of letters—
    Face. Nay, you must never hope to lay her now,
                           [They all speak together.

Dol. And so we may arrive by Talmud skill,
And profane Greek, to raise the building up
Of Helen's house against the Ismaelite,
King of Thogarma, and his habergions
Brimstony, blue, and fiery; and the force
Of king Abaddon, and the beast of Cittim:
Which rabbi David Kimchi, Onkelos,
And Aben Ezra do interpret Rome.

 Face. How did you put her into't?

 Mam. Alas! I talk'd
Of a fifth monarchy I would erect,
With the philosopher's stone, by chance, and she
Falls on the other four straight.

 Face. Out of Broughton!
I told you so. 'Slid, stop her mouth.

 Mam. Is't best?

 Face. She'll never leave else. If the old man hear her,
We are but fæces, ashes.

 Sub. [*within.*] What's to do there?

 Face. O, we are lost! Now she hears him, she is quiet.

   Enter SUBTLE, *they run different ways.*

 Mam. Where shall I hide me!

 Sub. How! what sight is here?
Close deeds of darkness, and that shun the light!
Bring him again. Who is he? What, my son!
O, I have lived too long.

 Mam. Nay, good, dear father,
There was no unchaste purpose.

 Sub. Not! and flee me,
When I come in?

 Mam. That was my error.

 Sub. Error!
Guilt, guilt, my son: give it the right name. No marvel,
If I found check in our great work within,
When such affairs as these were managing!

 Mam. Why, have you so?

 Sub. It has stood still this half hour:
And all the rest of our less works gone back.
Where is the instrument of wickedness,
My lewd false drudge?

 Mam. Nay, good sir, blame not him;
Believe me, 'twas against his will or knowledge:
I saw her by chance.

 Sub. Will you commit more sin,
To excuse a varlet?

 Mam. By my hope, 'tis true, sir.

 Sub. Nay, then I wonder less, if you, for whom
The blessing was prepared, would so tempt heaven.

And lose your fortunes.
   Mam. Why, sir?
   Sub. This will retard
The work, a month at least.
   Mam. Why, if it do,
What remedy? But think it not, good father:
Our purposes were honest.
   Sub. As they were,
So the reward will prove.—[*A loud explosion within.*] How now!
     ah me!
God, and all saints be good to us.—

Re-enter FACE.

                      What's that?
   Face. O, sir, we are defeated! all the works
Are flown *in fumo*, every glass is burst:
Furnace, and all rent down! as if a bolt
Of thunder had been driven through the house.
Retorts, receivers, pelicans, bolt-heads,
All struck in shivers!   [*Subtle falls down as in a swoon.*
           Help, good sir! alas,
Coldness, and death invades him. Nay, sir Mammon,
Do the fair offices of a man! you stand,
As you were readier to depart than he.   [*Knocking within.*
Who's there? my lord her brother is come.
   Mam. Ha, Lungs!
   Face. His coach is at the door. Avoid his sight,
For he's as furious as his sister's mad.
   Mam. Alas!
   Face. My brain is quite undone with the fume, sir,
I ne'er must hope to be mine own man again.
   Mam. Is all lost, Lungs? will nothing be preserv'd
Of all our cost?
   Face. Faith, very little, sir;
A peck of coals or so, which is cold comfort, sir.
   Mam. O my voluptuous mind! I am justly punish'd.
   Face. And so am I, sir.
   Mam. Cast from all my hopes—
   Face. Nay, certainties, sir.
   Mam. By mine own base affections.
   Sub. [*seeming to come to himself.*] O, the curst fruits of vice and
     lust!
   Mam. Good father,
It was my sin. Forgive it.
   Sub. Hangs my roof
Over us still, and will not fall, O justice,
Upon us, for this wicked man!
   Face. Nay, look, sir,

You grieve him now with staying in his sight:
Good sir, the nobleman will come too, and take you,
And that may breed a tragedy.

 Mam. I'll go.

 Face. Ay, and repent at home, sir. It may be,
For some good penance you may have it yet;
A hundred pound to the box at Bethlem—

 Mam. Yes.

 Face. For the restoring such as—have their wits.

 Mam. I'll do't.

 Face. I'll send one to you to receive it.

 Mam. Do.

Is no projection left?

 Face. All flown, or stinks, sir.

 Mam. Will nought be sav'd that's good for med'cine, think'st
  thou?

 Face. I cannot tell, sir. There will be perhaps,
Something about the scraping of the shards,
Will cure the itch,—though not your itch of mind, sir. [*Aside.*
It shall be saved for you, and sent home. Good sir,
This way, for fear the lord should meet you. [*Exit Mammon.*

 Sub. [*raising his head.*] Face!

 Face. Ay.

 Sub. Is he gone?

 Face. Yes, and as heavily
As all the gold he hoped for were in's blood.
Let us be light though.

 Sub. [*leaping up.*] Ay, as balls, and bound
And hit our heads against the roof for joy:
There's so much of our care now cast away.

 Face. Now to our don.

 Sub. Yes, your young widow by this time
Is made a countess, Face; she has been in travail
Of a young heir for you.

 Face. Good sir.

 Sub. Off with your case,
And greet her kindly, as a bridegroom should,
After these common hazards.

 Face. Very well, sir.
Will you go fetch don Diego off, the while?

 Sub. And fetch him over too, if you'll be pleased, sir:
Would Dol were in her place, to pick his pockets now!

 Face. Why, you can do't as well, if you would set to't.
I pray you prove your virtue.

 Sub. For your sake, sir.   [*Exeunt.*

SCENE IV.—*Another Room in the same.*

Enter SURLY *and* Dame PLIANT.

Sur. Lady, you see into what hands you are fall'n;
'Mongst what a nest of villains! and how near
Your honour was t' have catch'd a certain clap,
Through your credulity, had I but been
So punctually forward, as place, time,
And other circumstances would have made a man;
For you're a handsome woman: would you were wise too!
I am a gentleman come here disguised,
Only to find the knaveries of this citadel;
And where I might have wrong'd your honour and have not,
I claim some interest in your love.   You are,
They say, a widow, rich: and I'm a batchelor,
Worth nought: your fortunes may make me a man,
As mine have preserv'd you a woman.   Think upon it,
And whether I have deserv'd you or no.
    Dame P. I will, sir.
    Sur. And for these household-rogues, let me alone
To treat with them.

Enter SUBTLE.

    Sub. How doth my noble Diego,
And my dear madam countess? hath the count
Been courteous, lady? liberal, and open?
Donzel, methinks you look melancholic,
After your coitum, and scurvy: truly,
I do not like the dulness of your eye;
It hath a heavy cast, 'tis upsee Dutch,
And says you are a lumpish whore-master.
Be lighter, I will make your pockets so.   [*Attempts to pick them.*
    Sur. [*throws open his cloak.*] Will you, don bawd and pick-
        purse? [*strikes him down.*] how now! reel you?
Stand up, sir, you shall find, since I am so heavy,
I'll give you equal weight.
    Sub. Help! murder!
    Sur. No, sir,
There's no such thing intended: a good cart,
And a clean whip shall ease you of that fear.
I am the Spanish don *that should be cozen'd,*
Do you see, cozen'd!   Where's your captain Face,
That parcel broker, and whole-bawd, all rascal!

Enter FACE, *in his uniform.*

    Face. How, Surly!
    Sur. O, make your approach, good captain.
I have found from whence your copper rings and spoons

Come, now, wherewith you cheat abroad in taverns.
'Twas here you learn'd t' anoint your boot with brimstone,
Then rub men's gold on't for a kind of touch,
And say 'twas naught, when you had changed the colour,
That you might have't for nothing. And this doctor,
Your sooty, smoky-bearded compeer, he
Will close you so much gold, in a bolt's-head,
And, on a turn, convey in the stead another
With sublimed mercury, that shall burst in the heat,
And fly out all *in fumo !* Then weeps Mammon;
Then swoons his worship. [*Face slips out.*] Or, he is the Faustus,
That casteth figures and can conjure, cures
Plagues, piles, and pox, by the ephemerides,
And holds intelligence with all the bawds
And midwives of three shires: while you send in—
Captain—what! is he gone?—damsels with child,
Wives that are barren, or the waiting-maid
With the green sickness. [*Seizes Subtle as he is retiring.*
               Nay, sir, you must tarry,
Though he be scaped; and answer by the ears, sir.

Re-enter FACE, *with* KASTRIL.

Face. Why, now's the time, if ever you will quarrel
Well, as they say, and be a true-born child:
The doctor and your sister both are abused.
Kas. Where is he? which is he? he is a slave,
Whate'er he is, and the son of a whore.—Are you
The man, sir, I would know?
Sur. I should be loth, sir,
To confess so much.
Kas. Then you lie in your throat.
Sur. How!
Face. [*to Kastril.*] A very errant rogue, sir, and a cheater,
Employ'd here by another conjurer
That does not love the doctor, and would cross him,
If he knew how.
Sur. Sir, you are abused.
Kas. You lie:
And 'tis no matter.
Face. Well said, sir! He is
The impudent'st rascal—
Sur. You are indeed: Will you hear me, sir?
Face. By no means: bid him be gone.
Kas. Begone, sir, quickly.
Sur. This 's strange!—Lady, do you inform your brother.
Face. There is not such a foist in all the town,
The doctor had him presently; and finds yet,
The Spanish count will come here.—Bear up, Subtle. [*Aside.*
Sub. Yes, sir, he must appear within this hour.

Face. And yet this rogue would come in a disguise,
By the temptation of another spirit,
To trouble our art, though he could not hurt it!
    Kas. Ay,
I know—Away, [*to his sister,*] you talk like a foolish mauther.
    Sur. Sir, all is truth she says.
    Face. Do not believe him, sir.
He is the lying'st swabber!   Come your ways, sir.
    Sur. You are valiant out of company!
    Kas. Yes, how then, sir?

Enter DRUGGER, *with a piece of damask.*

    Face. Nay, here's an honest fellow, too, that knows him,
And all his tricks.   Make good what I say, Abel,
This cheater would have cozen'd thee o' the widow.—
                                          [*Aside to Drug.*
He owes this honest Drugger here, seven pound,
He has had on him, in two-penny'orths of tobacco.
    Drug. Yes, sir.
And he has damn'd himself three terms to pay me.
    Face. And what does he owe for lotium?
    Drug. Thirty shillings, sir;
And for six syringes.
    Sur. Hydra of villainy!
    Face. Nay, sir, you must quarrel him out o' the house.
    Kas. I will:
—Sir, if you get not out o' doors, you lie;
And you are a pimp.
    Sur. Why, this is madness, sir,
Not valour in you; I must laugh at this.
    Kas. It is my humour: you are a pimp and a trig,
And an *Amadis de Gaul,* or a Don Quixote.
    Drug. Or a knight o' the curious coxcomb, do you see?

Enter ANANIAS.

    Ana. Peace to the household!
    Kas. I'll keep peace for no man.
    Ana. Casting of dollars is concluded lawful.
    Kas. Is he the constable?
    Sub. Peace, Ananias.
    Face. No, sir.
    Kas. Then you are an otter, and a shad, a whit,
A very tim.
    Sur. You'll hear me, sir?
    Kas. I will not.
    Ana. What is the motive?
    Sub. Zeal in the young gentleman,
Against his Spanish slops.
    Ana. They are profane,

Lewd, superstitious, and idolatrous breeches.

Sur. New rascals!

Kas. Will you begone, sir?

Ana. Avoid, Sathan!
Thou art not of the light: That ruff of pride
About thy neck, betrays thee; and is the same
With that which the unclean birds, in seventy-seven,
Were seen to prank it with on divers coasts:
Thou look'st like antichrist, in that lewd hat.

Sur. I must give way.

Kas. Be gone, sir.

Sur. But I'll take
A course with you—

Ana. Depart, proud Spanish fiend!

Sur. Captain and Doctor.

Ana. Child of perdition!

Kas. Hence, sir!   [*Exit Surly.*
Did I not quarrel bravely?

Face. Yes, indeed, sir.

Kas. Nay, an I give my mind to't, I shall do't.

Face. O, you must follow, sir, and threaten him tame:
He'll turn again else.

Kas. I'll re-turn him then.   [*Exit.*
                      [*Subtle takes Ananias aside.*

Face. Drugger, this rogue prevented us for thee:
We had determin'd that thou should'st have come
In a Spanish suit, and have carried her so; and he,
A brokerly slave! goes, puts it on himself.
Hast brought the damask?

Drug. Yes, sir.

Face. Thou must borrow
A Spanish suit: hast thou no credit with the players?

Drug. Yes, sir; did you never see me play the Fool?

Face. I know not, Nab:—Thou shalt, if I can help it.—   [*Aside.*
Hieronimo's old cloak, ruff, and hat will serve;
I'll tell thee more when thou bring'st 'em.   [*Exit Drugger.*

Ana. Sir, I know
The Spaniard hates the brethren, and hath spies
Upon their actions: and that this was one
I make no scruple.—But the holy synod
Have been in prayer and meditation for it;
And 'tis reveal'd no less to them than me,
That casting of money is most lawful.

Sub. True,
But here I cannot do it; if the house
Shou'd chance to be suspected, all would out,
And we be lock'd up in the Tower for ever,
To make gold there for the state, never come out;
And then are you defeated.

Ana. I will tell
This to the elders and the weaker brethren,
That the whole company of the separation
May join in humble prayer again.

Sub. And fasting.

Ana. Yea, for some fitter place. The peace of mind
Rest with these walls!   *[Exit.*

Sub. Thanks, courteous Ananias.

Face. What did he come for?

Sub. About casting dollars,
Presently out of hand. And so I told him,
A Spanish minister came here to spy,
Against the faithful—

Face. I conceive. Come, Subtle,
Thou art so down upon the least disaster!
How wouldst thou ha' done, if I had not help't thee out?

Sub. I thank thee, Face, for the angry boy, i'faith.

Face. Who would have look'd it should have been that rascal,
Surly? he had dyed his beard and all. Well, sir,
Here's damask come to make you a suit.

Sub. Where's Drugger?

Face. He is gone to borrow me a Spanish habit;
I'll be the count, now.

Sub. But where's the widow?

Face. Within, with my lord's sister: madam Dol
Is entertaining her.

Sub. By your favour, Face,
Now she is honest, I will stand again.

Face. You will not offer it.

Sub. Why?

Face. Stand to your word,
Or——here comes Dol, she knows—

Sub. You are tyrannous still.

Enter DOL, *hastily.*

Face. Strict for my right.—How now, Dol? Hast [thou] told her,
The Spanish count will come?

Dol. Yes; but another is come,
You little look'd for!

Face. Who is that?

Dol. Your master;
The master of the house.

Sub. How, Dol!

Face. She lies,
This is some trick. Come, leave your quiblins, Dorothy.

Dol. Look out, and see.   *[Face goes to the window.*

Sub. Art thou in earnest?

Dol. 'Slight,
Forty o' the neighbours are about him, talking.

Face. 'Tis he, by this good day.

Dol. 'Twill prove ill day

For some on us.

Face. We are undone, and taken.

Dol. Lost, I'm afraid.

Sub. You said he would not come,

While there died one a week within the liberties.

Face. No: 'twas within the walls.

Sub. Was't so! cry you mercy.

I thought the liberties. What shall we do now, Face?

Face. Be silent: not a word, if he call or knock.

I'll into mine old shape again and meet him,

Of Jeremy, the butler. In the mean time,

Do you two pack up all the goods and purchase,

That we can carry in the two trunks. I'll keep him

Off for to-day, if I cannot longer: and then

At night, I'll ship you both away to Ratcliff,

Where we will meet to-morrow, and there we'll share.

Let Mammon's brass and pewter keep the cellar;

We'll have another time for that. But, Dol,

'Prythee go heat a little water quickly;

Subtle must shave me: all my captain's beard

Must off, to make me appear smooth Jeremy.

You'll do it?

Sub. Yes, I'll shave you, as well as I can.

Face. And not cut my throat, but trim me?

Sub. You shall see, sir.　　　　　　　　　[*Exeunt.*

ACT V

SCENE I.—*Before* LOVEWIT's *Door.*

Enter LOVEWIT, *with several of the* Neighbours.

Love. Has there been such resort, say you?

1 *Nei.* Daily, sir.

2 *Nei.* And nightly, too.

3 *Nei.* Ay, some as brave as lords.

4 *Nei.* Ladies and gentlewomen.

5 *Nei.* Citizens' wives.

1 *Nei.* And knights.

6 *Nei.* In coaches.

2 *Nei.* Yes, and oyster women.

1 *Nei.* Beside other gallants.

3 *Nei.* Sailors' wives.

4 *Nei.* Tobacco men.

5 *Nei.* Another Pimlico!

Love. What should my knave advance,

To draw this company? he hung out no banners
Of a strange calf with five legs to be seen,
Or a huge lobster with six claws?
   6 *Nei.* No, sir.
   3 *Nei.* We had gone in then, sir.
   Love. He has no gift
Of teaching in the nose that e'er I knew of.
You saw no bills set up that promised cure
Of agues, or the tooth-ach?
   2 *Nei.* No such thing, sir.
   Love. Nor heard a drum struck for baboons or puppets?
   5 *Nei.* Neither, sir.
   Love. What device should he bring forth now?
I love a teeming wit as I love my nourishment:
'Pray God he have not kept such open house,
That he hath sold my hangings, and my bedding!
I left him nothing else. If he have eat them,
A plague o' the moth, say I! Sure he has got
Some bawdy pictures to call all this ging!
The friar and the nun; or the new motion
Of the knight's courser covering the parson's mare;
The boy of six year old with the great thing:
Or 't may be, he has the fleas that run at tilt
Upon a table, or some dog to dance.
When saw you him?
   1 *Nei.* Who, sir, Jeremy?
   2 *Nei.* Jeremy butler?
We saw him not this month.
   Love. How!
   4 *Nei.* Not these five weeks, sir.
   6 *Nei.* These six weeks at the least.
   Love. You amaze me, neighbours!
   5 *Nei.* Sure, if your worship know not where he is,
He's slipt away.
   6 *Nei.* Pray God, he be not made away.
   Love. Ha! it's no time to question, then.   [*Knocks at the door.*
   6 *Nei.* About
Some three weeks since, I heard a doleful cry,
As I sat up a mending my wife's stockings.
   Love. 'Tis strange that none will answer! Didst thou hear
A cry, sayst thou?
   6 *Nei.* Yes, sir, like unto a man
That had been strangled an hour, and could not speak.
   2 *Nei.* I heard it too, just this day three weeks, at two o'clock
Next morning.
   Love. These be miracles, or you make them so!
A man an hour strangled, and could not speak,
And both you heard him cry?
   3 *Nei.* Yes, downward, sir.

Love. Thou art a wise fellow.   Give me thy hand, I pray thee,
What trade art thou on?

3 Nei. A smith, an't please your worship.

Love. A smith! then lend me thy help to get this door open.

3 Nei. That I will presently, sir, but fetch my tools— [*Exit.*

1 Nei. Sir, best to knock again, afore you break it.

Love. [*knocks again.*] I will.

Enter FACE, *in his butler's livery.*

Face. What mean you, sir?

1, 2, 4 Nei. O, here's Jeremy!

Face. Good sir, come from the door.

Love. Why, what's the matter?

Face. Yet farther, you are too near yet.

Love. In the name of wonder,
What means the fellow!

Face. The house, sir, has been visited.

Love. What, with the plague? stand thou then farther.

Face. No, sir,
I had it not.

Love. Who had it then? I left
None else but thee in the house.

Face. Yes, sir, my fellow,
The cat that kept the buttery, had it on her
A week before I spied it; but I got her
Convey'd away in the night: and so I shut
The house up for a month—

Love. How!

Face. Purposing then, sir,
T' have burnt rose-vinegar, treacle, and tar,
And have made it sweet, that you shou'd ne'er have known it;
Because I knew the news would but afflict you, sir.

Love. Breathe less, and farther off! Why this is stranger:
The neighbours tell me all here that the doors
Have still been open—

Face. How, sir!

Love. Gallants, men and women,
And of all sorts, tag-rag, been seen to flock here
In threaves, these ten weeks, as to a second Hogsden,
In days of Pimlico and Eye-bright.

Face. Sir,
Their wisdoms will not say so.

Love. To-day they speak
Of coaches, and gallants; one in a French hood
Went in, they tell me; and another was seen
In a velvet gown at the window: divers more
Pass in and out.

Face. They did pass through the doors then,
Or walls, I assure their eye-sights, and their spectacles;

For here, sir, are the keys, and here have been,
In this my pocket, now above twenty days:
And for before, I kept the fort alone there.
But that 'tis yet not deep in the afternoon,
I should believe my neighbours had seen double
Through the black pot, and made these apparitions!
For, on my faith to your worship, for these three weeks
And upwards the door has not been open'd.

Love. Strange!

1 Nei. Good faith, I think I saw a coach.

2 Nei. And I too,
I'd have been sworn.

Love. Do you but think it now?
And but one coach?

4 Nei. We cannot tell, sir: Jeremy
Is a very honest fellow.

Face. Did you see me at all?

1 Nei. No; that we are sure on.

2 Nei. I'll be sworn o' that.

Love. Fine rogues to have your testimonies built on!

Re-enter Third Neighbour, *with his Tools.*

3 Nei. Is Jeremy come!

1 Nei. O yes; you may leave your tools;
We were deceived, he says.

2 Nei. He has had the keys;
And the door has been shut these three weeks.

3 Nei. Like enough.

Love. Peace and get hence, you changelings.

Enter Surly *and* Mammon.

Face. Surly come!
And Mammon made acquainted! they'll tell all.
How shall I beat them off? what shall I do?
Nothing's more wretched than a guilty conscience.   [*Aside.*

Sur. No, sir, he was a great physician. This,
It was no bawdy house, but a mere chancel!
You knew the lord and his sister.

Mam. Nay, good Surly—

Sur. The happy word, BE RICH—

Mam. Play not the tyrant.—

Sur. Should be to-day pronounced to all your friends.
And where be your andirons now? and your brass pots,
That should have been golden flagons, and great wedges?

Mam. Let me but breathe. What, they have shut their doors,
Methinks!

Sur. Ay, now 'tis holiday with them.

Mam. Rogues,
Cozeners, impostors, bawds!   [*He and Surly knock.*

Face. What mean you, sir?

Mam. To enter if we can.

Face. Another man's house!
Here is the owner, sir: turn you to him,
And speak your business.

Mam. Are you, sir, the owner?

Love. Yes, sir.

Mam. And are those knaves within your cheaters?

Love. What knaves, what cheaters?

Mam. Subtle and his Lungs.

Face. The gentleman is distracted, sir! No lungs,
Nor lights have been seen here these three weeks, sir,
Within these doors, upon my word.

Sur. Your word,
Groom arrogant!

Face. Yes, sir, I am the housekeeper,
And know the keys have not been out of my hands.

Sur. This is a new Face.

Face. You do mistake the house, sir:
What sign was't at?

Sur. You rascal! this is one
Of the confederacy. Come, let's get officers,
And force the door.

Love. 'Pray you stay, gentlemen.

Sur. No, sir, we'll come with warrant.

Mam. Ay, and then
We shall have your doors open.   [*Exeunt Mam. and Sur.*

Love. What means this?

Face. I cannot tell, sir.

1 Nei. These are two of the gallants
That we do think we saw.

Face. Two of the fools!
You talk as idly as they. Good faith, sir,
I think the moon has crazed 'em all.—O me,

Enter KASTRIL.

The angry boy come too! He'll make a noise,
And ne'er away till he have betray'd us all.   [*Aside.*

Kas. [*knocking.*] What rogues, bawds, slaves, you'll open the
    door, anon!
Punk, cockatrice, my suster! By this light
I'll fetch the marshal to you. You are a whore
To keep your castle—

Face. Who would you speak with, sir?

Kas. The bawdy doctor, and the cozening captain,
And puss my suster.

Love. This is something, sure.

Face. Upon my trust, the doors were never open, sir.

Kas. I have heard all their tricks told me twice over,

By the fat knight and the lean gentleman.

   Love. Here comes another.

Enter ANANIAS *and* TRIBULATION.

   Face. Ananias too!

And his pastor!

   Tri. [*beating at the door.*] The doors are shut against us.

   Ana. Come forth, you seed of sulphur, sons of fire!

Your stench it is broke forth; abomination

Is in the house.

   Kas. Ay, my suster's there.

   Ana. The place,

It is become a cage of unclean birds.

   Kas. Yes, I will fetch the scavenger, and the constable.

   Tri. You shall do well.

   Ana. We'll join to weed them out.

   Kas. You will not come then, punk devise, my sister!

   Ana. Call her not sister; she's a harlot verily.

   Kas. I'll raise the street.

   Love. Good gentleman, a word.

   Ana. Satan avoid, and hinder not our zeal!

[Exeunt Ana., Trib., and Kast.

   Love. The world's turn'd Bethlem.

   Face. These are all broke loose,

Out of St. Katherine's, where they use to keep

The better sort of mad-folks.

   1 *Nei.* All these persons

We saw go in and out here.

   2 *Nei.* Yes, indeed, sir.

   3 *Nei.* These were the parties.

   Face. Peace, you drunkards! Sir,

I wonder at it: please you to give me leave

To touch the door, I'll try an the lock be chang'd.

   Love. It mazes me!

   Face. [*goes to the door.*] Good faith, sir, I believe

There's no such thing: 'tis all *deceptio visus*—

Would I could get him away.   [*Aside.*

   Dap. [*within.*] Master captain! master doctor!

   Love. Who's that?

   Face. Our clerk within, that I forgot! [*Aside.*] I know not, sir.

   Dap. [*within.*] For God's sake, when will her grace be at leisure?

   Face. Ha!

Illusions, some spirit o' the air!—His gag is melted,

And now he sets out the throat.   [*Aside.*

   Dap. [*within.*] I am almost stifled—

   Face. Would you were altogether.   [*Aside.*

   Love. 'Tis in the house.

Ha! list.

   Face. Believe it, sir, in the air.

   Love. Peace, you.

Dap. [*within.*] Mine aunt's grace does not use me well.

Sub. [*within.*] You fool,
Peace, you'll mar all.

Face. [*speaks through the key-hole, while Lovewit advances to the
     door unobserved.*] Or you will else, you rogue.

Love. O, is it so? then you converse with spirits!—
Come, sir. No more of your tricks, good Jeremy,
The truth, the shortest way.

Face. Dismiss this rabble, sir.—
What shall I do? I am catch'd.   [*Aside.*

Love. Good neighbours,
I thank you all. You may depart. [*Exeunt Neighbours.*]—Come, sir,
You know that I am an indulgent master;
And therefore conceal nothing. What's your medicine,
To draw so many several sorts of wild fowl?

Face. Sir, you were wont to affect mirth and wit—
But here's no place to talk on't in the street.
Give me but leave to make the best of my fortune,
And only pardon me the abuse of your house:
It's all I beg. I'll help you to a widow,
In recompence, that you shall give me thanks for,
Will make you seven years younger, and a rich one.
'Tis but your putting on a Spanish cloak:
I have her within. You need not fear the house;
It was not visited.

Love. But by me, who came
Sooner than you expected.

Face. It is true, sir.
'Pray you forgive me.

Love. Well: let's see your widow.   [*Exeunt.*

SCENE II.—*A Room in the same.*

Enter SUBTLE, *leading in* DAPPER, *with his eyes bound as before.*

Sub. How! have you eaten your gag?

Dap. Yes faith, it crumbled
Away in my mouth.

Sub. You have spoil'd all then.

Dap. No!
I hope my aunt of Fairy will forgive me.

Sub. Your aunt's a gracious lady; but in troth
You were to blame.

Dap. The fume did overcome me,
And I did do't to stay my stomach. 'Pray you
So satisfy her grace.

Enter FACE, *in his uniform.*

Here comes the captain.

Face. How now! is his mouth down?

Sub. Ay, he has spoken!

Face. A pox, I heard him, and you too.—He's undone then.—
I have been fain to say, the house is haunted
With spirits, to keep churl back.

Sub. And hast thou done it?

Face. Sure, for this night.

Sub. Why, then triumph and sing
Of Face so famous, the precious king
Of present wits.

Face. Did you not hear the coil
About the door?

Sub. Yes, and I dwindled with it.

Face. Shew him his aunt, and let him be dispatch'd:
I'll send her to you.   [*Exit Face.*

Sub. Well, sir, your aunt her grace
Will give you audience presently, on my suit,
And the captain's word that you did not eat your gag
In any contempt of her highness.   [*Unbinds his eyes.*

Dap. Not I, in troth, sir.

Enter DOL, *like the Queen of Fairy.*

Sub. Here she is come.   Down o' your knees and wriggle:
She has a stately presence. [*Dapper kneels, and shuffles towards her.*]
         Good!   Yet nearer,
And bid, God save you!

Dap. Madam!

Sub. And your aunt.

Dap. And my most gracious aunt, God save your grace.

Dol. Nephew, we thought to have been angry with you;
But that sweet face of yours hath turn'd the tide,
And made it flow with joy, that ebb'd of love.
Arise, and touch our velvet gown.

Sub. The skirts,
And kiss 'em.   So!

Dol. Let me now stroak that head.
Much, nephew, shalt thou win, much shalt thou spend,
Much shalt thou give away, much shalt thou lend.

Sub. Ay, much! indeed. [*Aside.*] Why do you not thank her
    grace?

Dap. I cannot speak for joy.

Sub. See the kind wretch!
Your grace's kinsman right.

Dol. Give me the bird.
Here is your fly in a purse, about your neck, cousin;
Wear it, and feed it about this day sev'n-night,
On your right wrist—

Sub. Open a vein with a pin.
And let it suck but once a week; till then,
You must not look on't.

Dol. No: and kinsman,
Bear yourself worthy of the blood you come on.

Sub. Her grace would have you eat no more Woolsack pies,
Nor Dagger frumety.

Dol. Nor break his fast
In Heaven and Hell.

Sub. She's with you every where!
Nor play with costarmongers, at mum-chance, tray-trip,
God make you rich; (when as your aunt has done it;)
But keep
The gallant'st company, and the best games—

Dap. Yes, sir.

Sub. Gleek and primero: and what you get, be true to us.

Dap. By this hand, I will.

Sub. You may bring's a thousand pound
Before to-morrow night, if but three thousand
Be stirring, an you will.

Dap. I swear I will then.

Sub. Your fly will learn you all games.

Face. [*within.*] Have you done there?

Sub. Your grace will command him no more duties?

Dol. No:
But come, and see me often.   I may chance
To leave him three or four hundred chests of treasure,
And some twelve thousand acres of fairy land,
If he game well and comely with good gamesters.

Sub. There's a kind aunt! kiss her departing part.—
But you must sell your forty mark a year, now.

Dap. Ay, sir, I mean.

Sub. Or, give't away; pox on't!

Dap. I'll give't mine aunt: I'll go and fetch the writings. [*Exit.*

Sub. 'Tis well—away!

Re-enter FACE.

Face. Where's Subtle?

Sub. Here: what news?

Face. Drugger is at the door, go take his suit,
And bid him fetch a parson, presently;
Say, he shall marry the widow.   Thou shalt spend
A hundred pound by the service! [*Exit Subtle.*]   Now, queen Dol,
Have you pack'd up all?

Dol. Yes.

Face. And how do you like
The lady Pliant?

Dol. A good dull innocent.

Re-enter SUBTLE.

Sub. Here's your Hieronimo's cloak and hat.

Face. Give me them.

Sub. And the ruff too?

Face. Yes; I'll come to you presently.   [*Exit.*

Sub. Now he is gone about his project, Dol,
I told you of, for the widow.

Dol. 'Tis direct
Against our articles.

Sub. Well, we will fit him, wench.
Hast thou gull'd her of her jewels or her bracelets?

Dol. No; but I will do't.

Sub. Soon at night, my Dolly,
When we are shipp'd, and all our goods aboard,
Eastward for Ratcliff; we will turn our course
To Brainford, westward, if thou sayst the word,
And take our leaves of this o'er-weening rascal,
This peremptory Face.

Dol. Content, I'm weary of him.

Sub. Thou'st cause, when the slave will run a wiving, Dol,
Against the instrument that was drawn between us.

Dol. I'll pluck his bird as bare as I can.

Sub. Yes, tell her,
She must by any means address some present
To the cunning man, make him amends for wronging
His art with her suspicion; send a ring
Or chain of pearl; she will be tortured else
Extremely in her sleep, say, and have strange things
Come to her. Wilt thou?

Dol. Yes.

Sub. My fine flitter-mouse,
My bird o' the night! we'll tickle it at the Pigeons,
When we have all, and may unlock the trunks,
And say, this's mine, and thine; and thine, and mine. [*They kiss.*

Re-enter FACE.

Face. What now! a billing?

Sub. Yes, a little exalted
In the good passage of our stock-affairs.

Face. Drugger has brought his parson; take him in, Subtle,
And send Nab back again to wash his face.

Sub. I will: and shave himself.   [*Exit.*

Face. If you can get him.

Dol. You are hot upon it, Face, whate'er it is!

Face. A trick that Dol shall spend ten pound a month by.

Re-enter SUBTLE.

Is he gone?

Sub. The chaplain waits you in the hall, sir.

Face. I'll go bestow him.   [*Exit.*

Dol. He'll now marry her, instantly.

Sub. He cannot yet, he is not ready. Dear Dol,

Cozen her of all thou canst.   To deceive him
Is no deceit, but justice, that would break
Such an inextricable tie as ours was.
    Dol. Let me alone to fit him.

Re-enter FACE.

    Face. Come, my venturers,
You have pack'd up all? where be the trunks? bring forth.
    Sub. Here.
    Face. Let us see them.   Where's the money?
    Sub. Here,
In this.
    Face. Mammon's ten pound; eight score before:
The brethren's money, this.   Drugger's and Dapper's.
What paper's that?
    Dol. The jewel of the waiting-maid's,
That stole it from her lady, to know certain—
    Face. If she should have precedence of her mistress?
    Dol. Yes.
    Face. What box is that?
    Sub. The fish-wives' rings, I think,
And the ale-wives' single money.   Is't not, Dol?
    Dol. Yes; and the whistle that the sailor's wife
Brought you to know an her husband were with Ward.
    Face. We'll wet it to-morrow; and our silver-beakers
And tavern cups.   Where be the French petticoats,
And girdles and hangers?
    Sub. Here, in the trunk,
And the bolts of lawn.
    Face. Is Drugger's damask there,
And the tobacco?
    Sub. Yes.
    Face. Give me the keys.
    Dol. Why you the keys?
    Sub. No matter, Dol; because
We shall not open them before he comes.
    Face. 'Tis true, you shall not open them, indeed;
Nor have them forth, do you see? not forth, Dol.
    Dol. No!
    Face. No, my smock rampant.   The right is, my master
Knows all, has pardon'd me, and he will keep them;
Doctor, 'tis true—you look—for all your figures:
I sent for him indeed.   Wherefore, good partners,
Both he and she be satisfied; for here
Determines the indenture tripartite
'Twixt Subtle, Dol, and Face.   All I can do
Is to help you over the wall, o' the back-side,
Or lend you a sheet to save your velvet gown, Dol.
Here will be officers presently, bethink you

Of some course suddenly to 'scape the dock:
For thither you will come else. [*Loud knocking.*] Hark
$\qquad$ you, thunder.
   Sub. You are a precious fiend!
   Offi. [*without.*] Open the door.
   Face. Dol, I am sorry for thee, i'faith; but hear'st thou?
It shall go hard but I will place thee somewhere:
Thou shalt have my letter to mistress Amo—
   Dol. Hang you!
   Face. Or madam Cæsarean.
   Dol. Pox upon you, rogue,
Would I had but time to beat thee!
   Face. Subtle,
Let's know where you set up next; I will send you
A customer now and then, for old acquaintance:
What new course have you?
   Sub. Rogue, I'll hang myself;
That I may walk a greater devil than thou,
And haunt thee in the flock-bed and the buttery.   [*Exeunt.*

SCENE III.—*An outer Room in the same.*

Enter LOVEWIT *in the Spanish dress, with the Parson.*

[*Loud knocking at the door.*]

   Love. What do you mean, my masters?
   Mam. [*without.*] Open your door,
Cheaters, bawds, conjurers.
   Offi. [*without.*] Or we will break it open.
   Love. What warrant have you?
   Offi. [*without.*] Warrant enough, sir, doubt not,
If you'll not open it.
   Love. Is there an officer, there?
   Offi. [*without.*] Yes, two or three for failing.
   Love. Have but patience,
And I will open it straight.

Enter FACE, *as butler.*

   Face. Sir, have you done?
Is it a marriage? perfect?
   Love. Yes, my brain.
   Face. Off with your ruff and cloak then; be yourself, sir.
   Sur. [*without.*] Down with the door.
   Kas. [*without.*] 'Slight, ding it open.
   Love. [*opening the door.*] Hold,
Hold, gentlemen, what means this violence?

MAMMON, SURLY, KASTRIL, ANANIAS, TRIBULATION, *and*
$\qquad$ Officers, *rush in.*

   Mam. Where is this collier?
   Sur. And my captain Face?

Mam. These day owls.

Sur. That are birding in men's purses.

Mam. Madam suppository.

Kas. Doxy, my suster.

Ana. Locusts

Of the foul pit.

Tri. Profane as Bel and the dragon.

Ana. Worse than the grasshoppers, or the lice of Egypt.

Love. Good gentlemen, hear me. Are you officers,

And cannot stay this violence?

1 *Offi.* Keep the peace.

Love. Gentlemen, what is the matter? whom do you seek?

Mam. The chemical cozener.

Sur. And the captain pander.

Kas. The nun my suster.

Mam. Madam Rabbi.

Ana. Scorpions,

And caterpillars.

Love. Fewer at once, I pray you.

2 *Offi.* One after another, gentlemen, I charge you,

By virtue of my staff.

Ana. They are the vessels

Of pride, lust, and the cart.

Love. Good zeal, lie still

A little while.

Tri. Peace, deacon Ananias.

Love. The house is mine here, and the doors are open;

If there be any such persons as you seek for,

Use your authority, search on o' God's name.

I am but newly come to town, and finding

This tumult 'bout my door, to tell you true,

It somewhat mazed me; till my man, here, fearing

My more displeasure, told me he had done

Somewhat an insolent part, let out my house

(Belike, presuming on my known aversion

From any air o' the town while there was sickness,)

To a doctor and a captain: who, what they are

Or where they be, he knows not.

Mam. Are they gone?

Love. You may go in and search, sir. [*Mammon, Ana., and Trib.*
     go in.] Here, I find

The empty walls worse than I left them, smoak'd,

A few crack'd pots, and glasses, and a furnace:

The ceiling fill'd with poesies of the candle,

And madam with a dildo writ o' the walls:

Only one gentlewoman, I met here,

That is within, that said she was a widow—

Kas. Ay, that's my suster; I'll go thump her. Where is she?

                                   [*Goes in.*

Love. And should have married a Spanish count, but he,
When he came to't, neglected her so grossly,
That I, a widower, am gone through with her.

  Sur. How! have I lost her then?

  Love. Were you the don, sir?
Good faith, now, she does blame you extremely, and says
You swore, and told her you had taken the pains
To dye your beard, and umbre o'er your face,
Borrowed a suit, and ruff, all for her love;
And then did nothing. What an oversight,
And want of putting forward, sir, was this!
Well fare an old harquebuzier, yet,
Could prime his powder, and give fire, and hit,
All in a twinkling!

Re-enter MAMMON.

  Mam. The whole nest are fled!

  Love. What sort of birds were they?

  Mam. A kind of choughs,
Or thievish daws, sir, that have pick'd my purse
Of eight score and ten pounds within these five weeks,
Beside my first materials; and my goods,
That lie in the cellar, which I am glad they have left,
I may have home yet.

  Love. Think you so, sir?

  Mam. Ay.

  Love. By order of law, sir, but not otherwise.

  Mam. Not mine own stuff!

  Love. Sir, I can take no knowledge
That they are yours, but by public means.
If you can bring certificate that you were gull'd of them,
Or any formal writ out of a court,
That you did cozen your self, I will not hold them.

  Mam. I'll rather lose them.

  Love. That you shall not, sir,
By me, in troth: upon these terms, they are yours.
What! should they have been, sir, turn'd into gold, all?

  Mam. No,
I cannot tell—It may be they should—What then?

  Love. What a great loss in hope have you sustain'd!

  Mam. Not I, the commonwealth has.

  Face. Ay, he would have built
The city new; and made a ditch about it
Of silver, should have run with cream from Hogsden;
That, every Sunday, in Moorfields, the younkers,
And tits and tom-boys should have fed on, gratis.

  Mam. I will go mount a turnip-cart, and preach
The end of the world, within these two months. Surly,
What! in a dream?

Sur. Must I needs cheat myself,
With that same foolish vice of honesty!
Come, let us go and hearken out the rogues:
That Face I'll mark for mine, if e'er I meet him.

Face. If I can hear of him, sir, I'll bring you word,
Unto your lodging; for in troth, they were strangers
To me, I thought them honest as my self, sir.

[*Exeunt Mam. and Sur.*

Re-enter ANANIAS *and* TRIBULATION.

Tri. 'Tis well, the saints shall not lose all yet. Go,
And get some carts—

Love. For what, my zealous friends?

Ana. To bear away the portion of the righteous
Out of this den of thieves.

Love. What is that portion?

Ana. The goods sometimes the orphan's, that the brethren
Bought with their silver pence.

Love. What, those in the cellar,
The knight sir Mammon claims?

Ana. I do defy
The wicked Mammon, so do all the brethren,
Thou profane man! I ask thee with what conscience
Thou canst advance that idol against us,
That have the seal? were not the shillings number'd,
That made the pounds; were not the pounds told out,
Upon the second day of the fourth week,
In the eighth month, upon the table dormant,
The year of the last patience of the saints,
Six hundred and ten?

Love. Mine earnest vehement botcher,
And deacon also, I cannot dispute with you:
But if you get you not away the sooner,
I shall confute you with a cudgel.

Ana. Sir!

Tri. Be patient, Ananias.

Ana. I am strong,
And will stand up, well girt, against an host
That threaten Gad in exile.

Love. I shall send you
To Amsterdam, to your cellar.

Ana. I will pray there,
Against thy house: may dogs defile thy walls,
And wasps and hornets breed beneath thy roof,
This seat of falsehood, and this cave of cozenage!

[*Exeunt Ana. and Trib.*

Enter DRUGGER.

Love. Another too?

Drug. Not I, sir, I am no brother.

Love. [*beats him.*] Away, you Harry Nicholas! do you talk?
　　　　　　　　　　　　　　　　　　　　[*Exit Drug.*
　　Face. No, this was Abel Drugger.　Good sir, go. [*To the Parson.*
And satisfy him; tell him all is done:
He staid too long a washing of his face.
The doctor, he shall hear of him at West-chester,
And of the captain, tell him, at Yarmouth, or
Some good port-town else, lying for a wind.　　　[*Exit Parson.*
If you can get off the angry child, now, sir—

　　　　　　Enter KASTRIL, *dragging in his sister.*

　　Kas. Come on, you ewe, you have match'd most sweetly, have
　　　　you not?
Did not I say, I would never have you tupp'd
But by a dubb'd boy, to make you a lady-tom?
'Slight, you are a mammet!　O, I could touse you, now.
Death, mun' you marry, with a pox!
　　Love. You lie, boy;
As sound as you; and I'm aforehand with you.
　　Kas. Anon!
　　Love. Come, will you quarrel?　I will feize you, sirrah;
Why do you not buckle to your tools?
　　Kas. Od's light,
This is a fine old boy as e'er I saw!
　　Love. What, do you change your copy now?　proceed,
Here stands my dove: stoop at her, if you dare.
　　Kas. 'Slight, I must love him!　I cannot choose, i'faith,
An I should be hang'd for't!　Suster, I protest,
I honour thee for this match.
　　Love. O, do you so, sir?
　　Kas. Yes, an thou canst take tobacco and drink, old boy,
I'll give her five hundred pound more to her marriage,
Than her own state.
　　Love. Fill a pipe full, Jeremy.
　　Face. Yes; but go in and take it, sir.
　　Love. We will—
I will be ruled by thee in any thing, Jeremy.
　　Kas. 'Slight, thou art not hide-bound, thou art a jovy boy!
Come, let us in, I pray thee, and take our whiffs.
　　Love. Whiff in with your sister, brother boy. [*Exeunt Kas. and
　　　　Dame P.*]　That master
That had received such happiness by a servant,
In such a widow, and with so much wealth,
Were very ungrateful, if he would not be
A little indulgent to that servant's wit,
And help his fortune, though with some small strain
Of his own candour. [*advancing.*]—*Therefore, gentlemen,*
And kind spectators, if I have outstript

An old man's gravity, or strict canon, think
What a young wife and a good brain may do;
Stretch age's truth sometimes, and crack it too.
Speak for thy self, knave.

    Face. *So I will, sir.* [advancing to the front of the stage.]
        Gentlemen,
My part a little fell in this last scene,
Yet 'twas decorum. And though I am clean
Got off from Subtle, Surly, Mammon, Dol,
Hot Ananias, Dapper, Drugger, all
With whom I traded: yet I put my self
On you, that are my country: and this pelf
Which I have got, if you do quit me, rests
To feast you often, and invite new guests.   [Exeunt.

CATILINE HIS CONSPIRACY

TO THE GREAT EXAMPLE OF HONOUR AND VIRTUE, THE MOST NOBLE

WILLIAM, EARL OF PEMBROKE,

LORD CHAMBERLAIN, ETC.

MY LORD,—In so thick and dark an ignorance, as now almost covers the age, I crave leave to stand near your light, and by that to be read. Posterity may pay your benefit the honour and thanks, when it shall know, that you dare, in these jig-given times, to countenance a legitimate *Poem*. I call it so, against all noise of opinion; from whose crude and airy reports, I appeal to the great and singular faculty of judgment in your lordship, able to vindicate truth from error. It is the first, of this race, that ever I dedicated to any person; and had I not thought it the best, it should have been taught a less ambition. Now it approacheth your censure cheerfully, and with the same assurance that innocency would appear before a magistrate. Your lordship's most faithful honourer,

BEN JONSON.

TO THE READER IN ORDINARY

THE muses forbid that I should restrain your meddling, whom I see already busy with the title, and tricking over the leaves: it is your own. I departed with my right, when I let it first abroad; and now, so secure an interpreter I am of my chance, that neither praise nor dispraise from you can affect me. Though you commend the two first acts, with the people, because they are the worst; and dislike the oration of Cicero, in regard you read some pieces of it at school, and understand them not yet: I shall find the way to forgive you. Be any thing you will be at your own charge. Would I had deserved but half so well of it in translation, as that ought to deserve of you in judgment, if you have any. I know you will pretend, whosoever you are, to have that, and more: but all pretensions are not just claims. The commendation of good things may fall within a many, the approbation but in a few; for the most commend out of affection, self-tickling, an easiness, or imitation: but men judge only out of knowledge. That is the trying faculty: and to those works that will bear a judge, nothing is more dangerous than a foolish praise. You will say, I shall not have yours therefore: but rather the contrary, all vexation of censure. If I were not above such molestations now, I had great cause to think unworthily of my studies, or they had so of me. But I leave you to your exercise. Begin.

TO THE READER EXTRAORDINARY

YOU I would understand to be the better man, though places in court go otherwise: to you I submit myself and work. Farewell. BEN JONSON.

DRAMATIS PERSONÆ

SYLLA'S GHOST.	CATULUS.
L. SERGIUS CATILINE.	CRASSUS.
PUBLIUS LENTULUS.	CÆSAR.
CAIUS CETHEGUS.	QU. CICERO.
AUTRONIUS.	SYLLANUS.
QUINTUS CURIUS.	FLACCUS.
VARGUNTEIUS.	POMTINIUS.
LUCIUS CASSIUS LONGINUS.	Q. FABIUS SANGA.
PORCIUS LECCA.	PETREIUS.
FULVIUS.	Senators.
LUCIUS BESTIA.	Allobroges.
GABINIUS CIMBER.	AURELIA ORESTILLA.
STATILIUS.	FULVIA.
CEPARIUS.	SEMPRONIA.
C. CORNELIUS.	GALLA.
VOLTURTIUS.	Soldiers, Porters, Lictors, Servants,
CICERO.	Pages, *etc.*
CAIUS ANTONIUS.	Chorus.
CATO.	

SCENE,—PARTLY AT ROME, AND PARTLY IN FESULÆ.

ACT I

SCENE I.—*A Room in* CATILINE'S *House.*

The Ghost of SYLLA *rises.*

Dost thou not feel me, Rome? not yet! is night
So heavy on thee, and my weight so light?
Can Sylla's ghost arise within thy walls,
Less threatening than an earthquake, the quick falls
Of thee and thine? Shake not the frighted heads
Of thy steep towers, or shrink to their first beds?
Or, as their ruin the large Tyber fills,
Make that swell up, and down thy seven proud hills?
What sleep is this doth seize thee so like death,
And is not it? wake, feel her in my breath:
Behold, I come, sent from the Stygian sound,
As a dire vapour that had cleft the ground,
To ingender with the night, and blast the day;
Or like a pestilence that should display
Infection through the world: which thus I do.—
      [The curtain draws, and Catiline is discovered in his study.
Pluto be at thy counsels, and into
Thy darker bosom enter Sylla's spirit!
All that was mine, and bad, thy breast inherit.
Alas, how weak is that for Catiline!
Did I but say—vain voice!—all that was mine?—
All that the Gracchi, Cinna, Marius would.
What now, had I a body again, I could,
Coming from hell, what fiends would wish should be,

And Hannibal could not have wish'd to see,
Think thou, and practise. Let the long-hid seeds
Of treason in thee, now shoot forth in deeds
Ranker than horror; and thy former facts
Not fall in mention, but to urge new acts.
Conscience of them provoke thee on to more:
Be still thy incests, murders, rapes, before
Thy sense; thy forcing first a vestal nun;
Thy parricide, late, on thine own only son,
After his mother, to make empty way
For thy last wicked nuptials; worse than they,
That blaze that act of thy incestuous life,
Which got thee at once a daughter and a wife.
I leave the slaughters that thou didst for me,
Of senators; for which, I hid for thee
Thy murder of thy brother, being so bribed,
And writ him in the list of my proscribed
After thy fact, to save thy little shame;
Thy incest with thy sister, I not name;
These are too light; fate will have thee pursue
Deeds, after which no mischief can be new;
The ruin of thy country: Thou wert built
For such a work, and born for no less guilt.
What though defeated once thou'st been, and known,
Tempt it again: That is thy act, or none.
What all the several ills that visit earth,
Brought forth by night with a sinister birth,
Plagues, famine, fire, could not reach unto,
The sword, nor surfeits; let thy fury do:
Make all past, present, future ill thine own;
And conquer all example in thy one.
Nor let thy thought find any vacant time
To hate an old, but still a fresher crime
Drown the remembrance; let not mischief cease,
But while it is in punishing, increase:
Conscience and care die in thee; and be free
Not heaven itself from thy impiety:
Let night grow blacker with thy plots, and day,
At shewing but thy head forth, start away
From this half-sphere; and leave Rome's blinded walls
To embrace lusts, hatreds, slaughters, funerals,
And not recover sight till their own flames
Do light them to their ruins! All the names
Of thy confederates too be no less great
In hell than here: that when we would repeat
Our strengths in muster, we may name you all,
And furies upon you for furies call!
Whilst what you do may strike them into fears,
Or make them grieve, and wish your mischief theirs.   [Sinks.

CATILINE *rises, and comes forward.*

Cat. It is decreed: nor shall thy fate, O Rome,
Resist my vow.   Though hills were set on hills,
And seas met seas to guard thee, I would through,
Ay, plough up rocks, steep as the Alps in dust,
And lave the Tyrrhene waters into clouds,
But I would reach thy head, thy head, proud city!
The ills that I have done cannot be safe
But by attempting greater; and I feel
A spirit within me chides my sluggish hands,
And says, they have been innocent too long.
Was I a man bred great as Rome herself,
One form'd for all her honours, all her glories,
Equal to all her titles; that could stand
Close up with Atlas, and sustain her name
As strong as he doth heaven! and was I,
Of all her brood, mark'd out for the repulse
By her no-voice, when I stood candidate
To be commander in the Pontic war!
I will hereafter call her step-dame ever.
If she can lose her nature, I can lose
My piety, and in her stony entrails
Dig me a seat; where I will live again,
The labour of her womb, and be a burden
Weightier than all the prodigies and monsters
That she hath teem'd with, since she first knew Mars—

Enter AURELIA ORESTILLA.

Who's there?
  Aur. 'Tis I.
  Cat. Aurelia?
  Aur. Yes.
  Cat. Appear,
And break like day, my beauty, to this circle:
Upbraid thy Phœbus, that he is so long
In mounting to that point, which should give thee
Thy proper splendour.   Wherefore frowns my sweet?
Have I too long been absent from these lips,
This cheek, these eyes? [*Kisses them.*] What is my trespass, speak?
  Aur. It seems you know, that can accuse yourself.
  Cat. I will redeem it.
  Aur. Still you say so.   When?
  Cat. When Orestilla, by her bearing well
These my retirements, and stol'n times for thought,
Shall give their effects leave to call her queen
Of all the world, in place of humbled Rome.
  Aur. You court me now.
  Cat. As I would always, love,
By this ambrosiac kiss, and this of nectar,

Wouldst thou but hear as gladly as I speak.
Could my Aurelia think I meant her less,
When, wooing her, I first removed a wife,
And then a son, to make my bed and house
Spacious and fit to embrace her? these were deeds
Not to have begun with, but to end with more
And greater: He that, building, stays at one
Floor, or the second, hath erected none.
'Twas how to raise thee I was meditating,
To make some act of mine answer thy love;
That love, that, when my state was now quite sunk,
Came with thy wealth and weigh'd it up again,
And made my emergent fortune once more look
Above the main; which now shall hit the stars,
And stick my Orestilla there amongst them,
If any tempest can but make the billow,
And any billow can but lift her greatness.
But I must pray my love, she will put on
Like habits with myself; I have to do
With many men, and many natures: Some
That must be blown and sooth'd; as Lentulus,
Whom I have heav'd with magnifying his blood,
And a vain dream out of the Sybil's books,
That a third man of that great family
Whereof he is descended, the Cornelii,
Should be a king in Rome: which I have hired
The flattering augurs to interpret Him,
Cinna and Sylla dead. Then bold Cethegus,
Whose valour I have turn'd into his poison,
And praised so into daring, as he would
Go on upon the gods, kiss lightning, wrest
The engine from the Cyclops, and give fire
At face of a full cloud, and stand his ire,
When I would bid him move. Others there are,
Whom envy to the state draws, and puts on
For contumelies received, (and such are sure ones,)
As Curius, and the forenamed Lentulus,
Both which have been degraded in the senate,
And must have their disgraces still new rubb'd,
To make them smart, and labour of revenge.
Others whom mere ambition fires, and dole
Of provinces abroad, which they have feign'd
To their crude hopes, and I as amply promised:
These, Lecca, Vargunteius, Bestia, Autronius.
Some whom their wants oppress, as the idle captains
Of Sylla's troops; and divers Roman knights,
The profuse wasters of their patrimonies,
So threaten'd with their debts, as they will now
Run any desperate fortune for a change.

These, for a time, we must relieve, Aurelia,
And make our house their safeguard: like for those
That fear the law, or stand within her gripe,
For any act past or to come; such will,
From their own crimes, be factious, as from ours.
Some more there be, slight airlings, will be won
With dogs and horses, or perhaps a whore;
Which must be had: and if they venture lives
For us, Aurelia, we must hazard honours
A little. Get thee store and change of women,
As I have boys; and give them time and place,
And all connivance: be thy self, too, courtly;
And entertain and feast, sit up, and revel;
Call all the great, the fair, and spirited dames
Of Rome about thee; and begin a fashion
Of freedom and community: some will thank thee,
Though the sour senate frown, whose heads must ache
In fear and feeling too. We must not spare
Or cost or modesty: It can but shew
Like one of Juno's or of Jove's disguises,
In either thee or me: and will as soon,
When things succeed, be thrown by, or let fall,
As is a veil put off, a visor changed,
Or the scene shifted in our theatres—   [*Noise within.*
Who's that? It is the voice of Lentulus.
  Aur. Or of Cethegus.
  Cat. In, my fair Aurelia,
And think upon these arts: they must not see
How far you're trusted with these privacies,
Though on their shoulders, necks and heads you rise. [*Exit Aurelia.*

Enter LENTULUS, *in discourse with* CETHEGUS.

  Len. It is, methinks, a morning full of fate!
It riseth slowly, as her sullen car
Had all the weights of sleep and death hung at it!
She is not rosy-finger'd, but swoll'n black;
Her face is like a water turn'd to blood,
And her sick head is bound about with clouds,
As if she threaten'd night ere noon of day!
It does not look as it would have a hail
Or health wish'd in it, as on other morns.
  Cet. Why, all the fitter, Lentulus; our coming
Is not for salutation, we have business.
  Cat. Said nobly, brave Cethegus! Where's Autronius?
  Cet. Is he not come?
  Cat. Not here.
  Cet. Nor Vargunteius?
  Cat. Neither.
  Cet. A fire in their beds and bosoms,

That so will serve their sloth rather than virtue!
They are no Romans,—and at such high need
As now!

Len. Both they, Longinus, Lecca, Curius,
Fulvius, Gabinius, gave me word, last night,
By Lucius Bestia, they would all be here,
And early.

Cet. Yes; as you, had I not call'd you.
Come, we all sleep, and are mere dormice; flies
A little less than dead: more dullness hangs
On us than on the morn. We are spirit-bound
In ribs of ice, our whole bloods are one stone,
And honour cannot thaw us, nor our wants,
Though they burn hot as fevers to our states.

Cat. I muse they would be tardy at an hour
Of so great purpose.

Cet. If the gods had call'd
Them to a purpose, they would just have come
With the same tortoise speed; that are thus slow
To such an action, which the gods will envy,
As asking no less means than all their powers,
Conjoin'd, to effect! I would have seen Rome burn
By this time, and her ashes in an urn;
The kingdom of the senate rent asunder,
And the degenerate talking gown run frighted
Out of the air of Italy.

Cat. Spirit of men!
Thou heart of our great enterprise! how much
I love these voices in thee!

Cet. O, the days
Of Sylla's sway, when the free sword took leave
To act all that it would!

Cat. And was familiar
With entrails, as our augurs.

Cet. Sons kill'd fathers,
Brothers their brothers.

Cat. And had price and praise.
All hate had license given it, all rage reins.

Cet. Slaughter bestrid the streets, and stretch'd himself
To seem more huge; whilst to his stained thighs
The gore he drew flow'd up, and carried down
Whole heaps of limbs and bodies through his arch.
No age was spared, no sex.

Cat. Nay, no degree.

Cet. Not infants in the porch of life were free.
The sick, the old, that could but hope a day
Longer by nature's bounty, not let stay.
Virgins, and widows, matrons, pregnant wives,
All died.

　　Cat. 'Twas crime enough, that they had lives:
To strike but only those that could do hurt,
Was dull and poor: some fell to make the number,
As some the prey.

　　Cet. The rugged Charon fainted,
And ask'd a navy, rather than a boat,
To ferry over the sad world that came:
The maws and dens of beasts could not receive
The bodies that those souls were frighted from;
And e'en the graves were fill'd with men yet living,
Whose flight and fear had mix'd them with the dead.

　　Cat. And this shall be again, and more, and more,
Now Lentulus, the third Cornelius,
Is to stand up in Rome.

　　Len. Nay, urge not that
Is so uncertain.

　　Cat. How!

　　Len. I mean, not clear'd,
And therefore not to be reflected on.

　　Cat. The Sybil's leaves uncertain! or the comments
Of our grave, deep, divining men not clear.

　　Len. All prophecies, you know, suffer the torture.

　　Cat. But this already hath confess'd, without:
And so been weigh'd, examined and compared,
As 'twere malicious ignorance in him
Would faint in the belief.

　　Len. Do you believe it?

　　Cat. Do I love Lentulus, or pray to see it?

　　Len. The augurs all are constant I am meant.

　　Cat. They had lost their science else.

　　Len. They count from Cinna.

　　Cat. And Sylla next, and so make you the third;
All that can say the sun is risen, must think it.

　　Len. Men mark me more of late, as I come forth.

　　Cat. Why, what can they do less? Cinna and Sylla
Are set and gone; and we must turn our eyes
On him that is, and shines. Noble Cethegus,
But view him with me here! he looks already
As if he shook a sceptre o'er the senate,
And the awed purple dropp'd their rods and axes:
The statues melt again, and household gods
In groans confess the travail of the city;
The very walls sweat blood before the change,
And stones start out to ruin ere it comes.

　　Cet. But he, and we, and all are idle still.

　　Len. I am your creature, Sergius; and whate'er
The great Cornelian name shall win to be,
It is not augury nor the Sybil's books,
But Catiline that makes it.

Cat. I am shadow
To honour'd Lentulus and Cethegus here,
Who are the heirs of Mars.
    Cet. By Mars himself,
Catiline is more my parent; for whose virtue
Earth cannot make a shadow great enough,
Though envy should come too.   *[Noise within.]*   O, here they are.
Now we shall talk more, though we yet do nothing.

Enter AUTRONIUS, VARGUNTEIUS, LONGINUS, CURIUS, LECCA,
    BESTIA, FULVIUS, GABINIUS, *etc., and* Servants.

    Aut. Hail, Lucius Catiline.
    Var. Hail, noble Sergius.
    Lon. Hail, Publius Lentulus.
    Cur. Hail, the third Cornelius.
    Lec. Caius Cethegus, hail.
    Cet. Hail, sloth and words,
Instead of men and spirits!
    Cat. Nay, dear Caius—
    Cet. Are your eyes yet unseel'd? dare they look day
In the dull face?
    Cat. He's zealous for the affair,
And blames your tardy coming, gentlemen.
    Cet. Unless we had sold ourselves to sleep and ease,
And would be our slaves' slaves—
    Cat. Pray you forbear.
    Cet. The north is not so stark and cold.
    Cat. Cethegus—
    Bes. We shall redeem all if your fire will let us.
    Cat. You are too full of lightning, noble Caius.
Boy, see all doors be shut, that none approach us
On this part of the house. *[Exit Servant.]* Go you, and bid
The priest, he kill the slave I mark'd last night,
And bring me of his blood, when I shall call him;
Till then, wait all without.   *[Exeunt Servants.*
    Var. How is't, Autronius?
    Aut. Longinus?
    Lon. Curius?
    Cur. Lecca?
    Var. Feel you nothing?
    Lon. A strange unwonted horror doth invade me,
I know not what it is.   *[A darkness comes over the place.*
    Lec. The day goes back,
Or else my senses!
    Cur. As at Atreus' feast!
    Ful. Darkness grows more and more!
    Len. The vestal flame,
I think, be out.   *[A groan of many people is heard under ground.*

    Gab. What groan was that?

    Cet. Our phant'sies:
Strike fire out of our selves, and force a day.   [*A second groan.*

    Aut. Again it sounds!

    Bes. As all the city gave it!

    Cet. We fear what our selves feign.   [*A fiery light appears.*

    Var. What light is this?

    Cur. Look forth.

    Len. It still grows greater!

    Lec. From whence comes it?

    Lon. A bloody arm it is that holds a pine
Lighted above the capitol! and now
It waves unto us!

    Cat. Brave, and ominous!
Our enterprise is seal'd.

    Cet. In spite of darkness,
That would discountenance it.   Look no more;
We lose time and our selves.   To what we came for,—
Speak, Lucius, we attend you.

    Cat. Noblest Romans,
If you were less, or that your faith and virtue
Did not hold good that title, with your blood,
I should not now unprofitably spend
My self in words, or catch at empty hopes,
By airy ways, for solid certainties;
But since in many, and the greatest dangers,
I still have known you no less true than valiant,
And that I taste in you the same affections,
To will or nil, to think things good or bad,
Alike with me, which argues your firm friendship;
I dare the boldlier with you set on foot,
Or lead unto this great and goodliest action.
What I have thought of it afore, you all
Have heard apart: I then express'd my zeal
Unto the glory; now, the need inflames me.
When I forethink the hard conditions
Our states must undergo, except in time
We do redeem our selves to liberty,
And break the iron yoke forged for our necks;
For what less can we call it, when we see,
The commonwealth engross'd so by a few,
The giants of the state, that do by turns
Enjoy her, and defile her! all the earth,
Her kings and tetrarchs, are their tributaries;
People and nations pay them hourly stipends;
The riches of the world flow to their coffers,
And not to Rome's.   While, (but those few,) the rest,
However great we are, honest, and valiant,
Are herded with the vulgar, and so kept,

As we were only bred to consume corn,
Or wear out wool; to drink the city's water;
Ungraced, without authority or mark,
Trembling beneath their rods; to whom, if all
Were well in Rome, we should come forth bright axes,
All places, honours, offices are theirs,
Or where they will confer them: they leave us
The dangers, the repulses, judgments, wants;
Which how long will you bear, most valiant spirits?
Were we not better to fall once with virtue,
Than draw a wretched and dishonour'd breath,
To lose with shame, when these men's pride will laugh?
I call the faith of Gods and men to question,
The power is in our hands, our bodies able,
Our minds as strong; o' the contrary, in them
All things grown aged, with their wealth and years:
There wants but only to begin the business,
The issue is certain.

    Cet. Lon. On! let us go on!
    Cur. Bes. Go on, brave Sergius!
    Cat. It doth strike my soul,
And who can scape the stroke, that hath a soul,
Or but the smallest air of man within him?
To see them swell with treasure, which they pour
Out in their riots, eating, drinking, building,
Ay, in the sea! planing of hills with valleys,
And raising valleys above hills! whilst we
Have not to give our bodies necessaries.
They have their change of houses, manors, lordships;
We scarce a fire, or a poor household Lar!
They buy rare Attic statues, Tyrian hangings,
Ephesian pictures, and Corinthian plate,
Attalic garments, and now new-found gems,
Since Pompey went for Asia, which they purchase
At price of provinces! the river Phasis
Cannot afford them fowl, nor Lucrine lake
Oysters enow: Circei too is search'd,
To please the witty gluttony of a meal!
Their ancient habitations they neglect,
And set up new; then, if the echo like not
In such a room, they pluck down those, build newer,
After them too; and by all frantic ways,
Vex their wild wealth, as they molest the people,
From whom they force it! Yet they cannot tame,
Or overcome their riches! not by making
Baths, orchards, fish-pools, letting in of seas
Here, and then there forcing them out again
With mountainous heaps, for which the earth hath lost
Most of her ribs, as entrails; being now

Wounded no less for marble, than for gold!
We, all this while, like calm benumb'd spectators,
Sit till our seats do crack, and do not hear
The thund'ring ruins; whilst at home our wants,
Abroad, our debts do urge us; our states daily
Bending to bad, our hopes to worse: and what
Is left but to be crush'd? Wake, wake, brave friends,
And meet the liberty you oft have wish'd for.
Behold, renown, riches, and glory court you!
Fortune holds out these to you, as rewards.
Methinks, though I were dumb, the affair itself,
The opportunity, your needs, and dangers,
With the brave spoil the war brings, should invite you.
Use me, your general, or soldier: neither
My mind nor body shall be wanting to you:
And, being consul, I not doubt to effect
All that you wish, if trust not flatter me,
And you'd not rather still be slaves, than free.

   Cet. Free, Free!

   Lon. 'Tis Freedom.

   Cur. Freedom we all stand for.

   Cat. Why these are noble voices! Nothing wants, then,
But that we take a solemn sacrament,
To strengthen our design.

   Cet. And most to act it:
Deferring hurts, where powers are so prepared.

   Aut. Yet, ere we enter into open act,
With favour, 'twere no loss, if't might be inquired,
What the condition of these arms would be.

   Var. Ay, and the means to carry us through.

   Cat. How, friends!
Think you that I would bid you grasp the wind
Or call you to th' embracing of a cloud?
Put your known valours on so dear a business,
And have no other second than the danger,
Nor other garland than the loss? Become
Your own assurances. And for the means,
Consider, first, the stark security
The commonwealth is in now; the whole senate
Sleepy, and dreaming no such violent blow;
Their forces all abroad; of which the greatest,
That might annoy us most, is farthest off,
In Asia, under Pompey; those near hand,
Commanded by our friends; one army in Spain,
By Cneus Piso; the other in Mauritania,
By Nucerinus; both which I have firm,
And fast unto our plot. My self, then, standing
Now to be consul, with my hoped colleague
Caius Antonius, one no less engaged

By his wants, than we; and whom I've power to melt,
And cast in any mould: beside, some others,
That will not yet be named, both sure, and great ones,
Who, when the time comes, shall declare themselves
Strong for our party; so that no resistance
In nature can be thought.   For our reward then,
First, all our debts are paid; dangers of law,
Actions, decrees, judgments against us quitted,
The rich men, as in Sylla's times, proscribed,
And publication made of all their goods:
That house is yours; that land is his; those waters,
Orchards, and walks, a third's; he has that honour,
And he that office: such a province falls
To Vargunteius; this to Autronius; that
To bold Cethegus; Rome to Lentulus.
You share the world, her magistracies, priesthoods,
Wealth and felicity, amongst you, friends;
And Catiline your servant.   Would you, Curius,
Revenge the contumely stuck upon you,
In being removed from the senate? now,
Now is your time.   Would Publius Lentulus
Strike for the like disgrace? now is his time.
Would stout Longinus walk the streets of Rome,
Facing the Prætor? now has he a time
To spurn and tread the fasces into dirt,
Made of the usurers' and the lictors' brains.
Is there a beauty here in Rome you love?
An enemy you would kill? what head's not your's?
Whose wife, which boy, whose daughter, of what race,
That the husband, or glad parents, shall not bring you,
And boasting of the office? only spare
Your selves, and you have all the earth beside,
A field to exercise your longings in.
I see you raised, and read your forward minds
High in your faces.   Bring the wine and blood
You have prepared there.

Enter Servants, *with a bowl.*

  Lon. How!
  Cat. I have kill'd a slave,
And of his blood caused to be mix'd with wine:
Fill every man his bowl.   There cannot be
A fitter drink to make this sanction in.
Here I begin the sacrament to all.
O for a clap of thunder now, as loud
As to be heard throughout the universe,
To tell the world the fact, and to applaud it!
Be firm, my hand, not shed a drop; but pour
Fierceness into me with it, and fell thirst

Of more and more, till Rome be left as bloodless
As ever her fears made her, or the sword.
And when I leave to wish this to thee, step-dame,
Or stop to affect it, with my powers fainting,
So may my blood be drawn, and so drunk up,
As is this slave's.   *[Drinks.*

   Lon. And so be mine.

   Len. And mine.

   Aut. And mine.

   Var. And mine.   *[They drink.*

   Cet. Swell me my bowl yet fuller.
Here, I do drink this, as I would do Cato's,
Or the new fellow Cicero's, with that vow
Which Catiline hath given.   *[Drinks.*

   Cur. So do I.

   Lec. And I.

   Bes. And I.

   Ful. And I.

   Gab. And all of us.   *[They drink.*

   Cat. Why now's the business safe, and each man strengthen'd—
Sirrah, what ail you?

   Page. Nothing.

   Bes. Somewhat modest.

   Cat. Slave, I will strike your soul out with my foot,
Let me but find you again with such a face:
You whelp—

   Bes. Nay, Lucius.

   Cat. Are you coying it,
When I command you to be free, and general
To all?

   Bes. You'll be observed.

   Cat. Arise! and shew
But any least aversion in your look
To him that bourds you next; and your throat opens.—
Noble confederates, thus far is perfect.
Only your suffrages I will expect
At the assembly for the choosing consuls,
And all the voices you can make by friends
To my election: then let me work out
Your fortunes and mine own. Meanwhile, all rest
Seal'd up and silent, as when rigid frosts
Have bound up brooks and rivers, forced wild beasts
Unto their caves, and birds into the woods,
Clowns to their houses, and the country sleeps:
That, when the sudden thaw comes, we may break
Upon them like a deluge, bearing down
Half Rome before us, and invade the rest
With cries, and noise, able to wake the urns
Of those are dead, and make their ashes fear.

The horrors that do strike the world, should come
Loud, and unlook'd for; till they strike, be dumb.
   Cet. Oraculous Sergius!
   Len. God-like Catiline!   [*Exeunt.*

CHORUS.

    Can nothing great, and at the height,
    Remain so long, but its own weight
    Will ruin it? or is't blind chance,
    That still desires new states to advance,
    And quit the old? else why must Rome
    Be by itself now overcome?
    Hath she not foes enow of those
    Whom she hath made such, and enclose
    Her round about? or are they none,
    Except she first become her own:
    O wretchedness of greatest states,
    To be obnoxious to these fates!
    That cannot keep what they do gain;
    And what they raise so ill sustain!
    Rome now is mistress of the whole
    World, sea and land, to either pole;
    And even that fortune will destroy
    The pow'r that made it: she doth joy
    So much in plenty, wealth, and ease,
    As now th' excess is her disease.

      She builds in gold, and to the stars,
    As if she threaten'd heav'n with wars;
    And seeks for hell in quarries deep,
    Giving the fiends, that there do keep,
    A hope of day. Her women wear
    The spoils of nations in an ear,
    Changed for the treasure of a shell;
    And in their loose attires do swell,
    More light than sails, when all winds play:
    Yet are the men more loose than they,
    More kemb'd, and bath'd, and rubb'd, and trimm'd,
    More sleek, more soft, and slacker limb'd;
    As prostitute; so much, that kind
    May seek itself there, and not find.
    They eat on beds of silk and gold,
    At ivory tables, or wood sold
    Dearer than it; and leaving plate,
    Do drink in stone of higher rate.
    They hunt all grounds, and draw all seas,
    Fowl every brook and bush, to please
    Their wanton taste; and in request
    Have new and rare things, not the best.

Hence comes that wild and vast expense,
That hath enforced Rome's virtue thence,
Which simple poverty first made:
And now ambition doth invade
Her state, with eating avarice,
Riot, and every other vice.
Decrees are bought, and laws are sold,
Honours, and offices, for gold;
The people's voices, and the free
Tongues in the senate, bribed be:
Such ruin of her manners Rome
Doth suffer now, as she's become
(Without the gods it soon gainsay)
Both her own spoiler, and own prey.
    So, Asia, art thou cru'lly even
With us, for all the blows thee given;
When we, whose virtue conquer'd thee,
Thus, by thy vices, ruin'd be.

ACT II

SCENE I.—*A Room in* FULVIA'S *House.*

Enter FULVIA, GALLA, *and* Servant.

Ful. Those rooms do smell extremely.   Bring my glass
And table hither.—Galla!
    Gal. Madam.
    Ful. Look
Within, in my blue cabinet, for the pearl
I had sent me last, and bring it.
    Gal. That from Clodius?
    Ful. From Caius Cæsar.   You are for Clodius still,
Or Curius.   [*Exit Galla.*]—Sirrah, if Quintus Curius come,
I am not in fit mood; I keep my chamber:
Give warning so without.   [*Exit Servant.*

Re-enter GALLA.

    Gal. Is this it, madam?
    Ful. Yes; help to hang it in mine ear.
    Gal. Believe me,
It is a rich one, madam.
    Ful. I hope so:
It should not be worn there else.   Make an end,
And bind my hair up.
    Gal. As 'twas yesterday?
    Ful. No, nor the t'other day: when knew you me

Appear two days together in one dressing?

Gal. Will you have't in the globe or spire?

Ful. How thou wilt;
Any way, so thou wilt do it, good impertinence.
Thy company, if I slept not very well
A-nights, would make me an arrant fool, with questions.

Gal. Alas, madam—

Ful. Nay, gentle half o' the dialogue, cease.

Gal. I do it indeed but for your exercise,
As your physician bids me.

Ful. How! does he bid you
To anger me for exercise?

Gal. Not to anger you,
But stir your blood a little; there is difference
Between lukewarm and boiling, madam.

Ful. Jove!
She means to cook me, I think. Pray you, have done.

Gal. I mean to dress you, madam.

Ful. O, my Juno,
Be friend to me! offering at wit too? why, Galla,
Where hast thou been?

Gal. Why, madam?

Ful. What hast thou done
With thy poor innocent self?

Gal. Wherefore, sweet madam?

Ful. Thus to come forth, so suddenly, a wit-worm?

Gal. It pleases you to flout one. I did dream
Of lady Sempronia—

Ful. O, the wonder's out!
That did infect thee: well, and how?

Gal. Methought
She did discourse the best—

Ful. That ever thou heard'st?

Gal. Yes.

Ful. In thy sleep! of what was her discourse?

Gal. Of the republic, madam, and the state,
And how she was in debt, and where she meant
To raise fresh sums: she's a great stateswoman!

Ful. Thou dream'st all this?

Gal. No, but you know she is, madam;
And both a mistress of the Latin tongue,
And of the Greek.

Ful. Ay, but I never dreamt it, Galla,
As thou hast done; and therefore you must pardon me.

Gal. Indeed you mock me, madam.

Ful. Indeed, no:
Forth with your learned lady. She has a wit too?

Gal. A very masculine one.

Ful. A she-critic, Galla?

And can compose in verse, and make quick jests,
Modest, or otherwise?
    Gal. Yes, madam.
    Ful. She can sing too?
And play on instruments?
    Gal. Of all kinds, they say.
    Ful. And doth dance rarely?
    Gal. Excellent! so well,
As a bald senator made a jest, and said,
'Twas better than an honest woman need.
    Ful. Tut, she may bear that: few wise women's honesties
Will do their courtship hurt.
    Gal. She's liberal too, madam.
    Ful. What, of her money or her honour, prithee?
    Gal. Of both; you know not which she doth spare least.
    Ful. A comely commendation!
    Gal. Troth, 'tis pity
She is in years.
    Ful. Why, Galla?
    Gal. For it is.
    Ful. O, is that all! I thought thou'dst had a reason.
    Gal. Why, so I have: she has been a fine lady,
And yet she dresses herself, except you, madam,
One of the best in Rome; and paints, and hides
Her decays very well.
    Ful. They say, it is
Rather a visor, than a face, she wears.
    Gal. They wrong her verily, madam; she doth sleek
With crumbs of bread and milk, and lies a-nights
In as neat gloves——But she is fain, of late,
To seek, more than she's sought to, the fame is,
And so spends that way.
    Ful. Thou know'st all! but, Galla,
What say you to Catiline's lady, Orestilla?
There is the gallant!
    Gal. She does well. She has
Very good suits, and very rich; but then
She cannot put them on; she knows not how
To wear a garment. You shall have her all
Jewels and gold sometimes, so that her self
Appears the least part of herself. No, in troth,
As I live, madam, you put them all down
With your mere strength of judgment, and do draw, too,
The world of Rome to follow you! You attire
Your self so diversely, and with that spirit,
Still to the noblest humours, they could make
Love to your dress, although your face were away, they say.
    Ful. And body too, and have the better match on't.
Say they not so too, Galla?

Re-enter Servant.

                    Now! what news
Travails your countenance with?
    Serv. If't please you, madam,
The lady Sempronia is lighted at the gate.
    Gal. Castor, my dream, my dream!
    Serv. And comes to see you.
    Gal. For Venus' sake, good madam, see her.   [*Exit Serv.*
    Ful. Peace,
The fool is wild, I think.
    Gal. And hear her talk,
Sweet madam, of state-matters and the senate.

Enter SEMPRONIA.

    Sem. Fulvia, good wench, how dost thou?
    Ful. Well, Sempronia.
Whither are you thus early addrest?
    Sem. To see
Aurelia Orestilla: she sent for me.
I came to call thee with me; wilt thou go?
    Ful. I cannot now, in troth; I have some letters
To write and send away.
    Sem. Alas, I pity thee.
I have been writing all this night, and am
So very weary, unto all the tribes,
And centuries, for their voices, to help Catiline
In his election. We shall make him consul,
I hope, amongst us. Crassus, I, and Cæsar
Will carry it for him.
    Ful. Does he stand for it?
    Sem. He's the chief candidate.
    Ful. Who stands beside?—
Give me some wine and powder for my teeth.
    Sem. Here's a good pearl, in troth.
    Ful. A pretty one.
    Sem. A very orient one!—there are competitors,
Caius Antonius, Publius Galba, Lucius
Cassius Longinus, Quintus Cornificius,
Caius Licinius, and that talker Cicero.
But Catiline and Antonius will be chosen;
For four of the other, Licinius, Longinus,
Galba and Cornificius, will give way:
And Cicero they will not choose.
    Ful. No! why?
    Sem. It will be cross'd by the nobility.
    Gal. How she does understand the common business! [*Aside.*
    Sem. Nor were it fit. He is but a new fellow,
An inmate here in Rome, as Catiline calls him,

And the patricians should do very ill
To let the consulship be so defiled
As't would be, if he obtain'd it! a mere upstart,
That has no pedigree, no house, no coat,
No ensigns of a family!

    Ful. He has virtue.

    Sem. Hang virtue! where there is no blood, 'tis vice,
And in him sauciness. Why should he presume
To be more learned or more eloquent
Than the nobility? or boast any quality
Worthy a nobleman, himself not noble?

    Ful. 'Twas virtue only, at first, made all men noble.

    Sem. I yield you, it might at first, in Rome's poor age,
When both her kings and consuls held the plough,
Or garden'd well; but now we have no need
To dig, or lose our sweat for't. We have wealth,
Fortune, and ease: and then their stock to spend on,
Of name, for virtue; which will bear us out
'Gainst all new comers, and can never fail us,
While the succession stays. And we must glorify
A mushroom! one of yesterday! a fine speaker!
'Cause he has suck'd at Athens! and advance him,
To our own loss! no, Fulvia; there are they
Can speak Greek too, if need were. Cæsar and I,
Have sat upon him; so hath Crassus too,
And others. We have all decreed his rest,
For rising farther.

    Gal. Excellent rare lady!

    Ful. Sempronia, you are beholden to my woman here,
She does admire you.

    Sem. O good Galla, how dost thou?

    Gal. The better for your learned ladyship.

    Sem. Is this grey powder a good dentifrice?

    Ful. You see I use it.

    Sem. I have one is whiter.

    Ful. It may be so.

    Sem. Yet this smells well.

    Gal. And cleanses
Very well, madam, and resists the crudities.

    Sem. Fulvia, I pray thee, who comes to thee now,
Which of our great patricians?

    Ful. Faith, I keep
No catalogue of them: sometimes I have one,
Sometimes another, as the toy takes their bloods.

    Sem. Thou hast them all. Faith, when was Quintus Curius,
Thy special servant, here?

    Ful. My special servant!

    Sem. Yes, thy idolater, I call him.

    Ful. He may be yours,

If you do like him.

 Sem. How!

 Ful. He comes not here;
I have forbid him hence.

 Sem. Venus forbid!

 Ful. Why?

 Sem. Your so constant lover!

 Ful. So much the rather.
I would have change; so would you too, I am sure:
And now you may have him.

 Sem. He's fresh yet, Fulvia;
Beware how you do tempt me.

 Ful. Faith, for me
He's somewhat too fresh indeed; the salt is gone,
That gave him season: his good gifts are done.
He does not yield the crop that he was wont:
And for the act, I can have secret fellows,
With backs worth ten of him, and they shall please me,
Now that the land is fled, a myriad better.

 Sem. And those one may command.

 Ful. 'Tis true: these lordlings,
Your noble Fauns, they are so imperious, saucy,
Rude, and as boisterous as centaurs, leaping
A lady at first sight.

 Sem. And must be borne
Both with and out, they think.

 Ful. Tut, I'll observe
None of them all, nor humour them a jot
Longer than they come laden in the hand,
And say, Here's one for t'other.

 Sem. Does Cæsar give well?

 Ful. They shall all give and pay well, that come here,
If they will have it; and that, jewels, pearl,
Plate, or round sums to buy these. I'm not taken
With a cob-swan, or a high-mounting bull,
As foolish Leda and Europa were;
But the bright gold, with Danäe. For such price
I would endure a rough, harsh Jupiter,
Or ten such thund'ring gamesters, and refrain
To laugh at 'em, till they are gone, with my much suffering.

 Sem. Thou'rt a most happy wench, that thus canst make
Use of thy youth and freshness, in the season;
And hast it to make use of.

 Ful. Which is the happiness.

 Sem. I am now fain to give to them, and keep music,
And a continual table to invite them.

 Ful. Yes, and they study your kitchen more than you.

 Sem. Eat myself out with usury, and my lord too,
And all my officers, and friends besides,

To procure money for the needful charge
I must be at, to have them; and yet scarce
Can I achieve them so.

    Ful. Why, that's because
You affect young faces only, and smooth chins,
Sempronia. If you'd love beards and bristles,
One with another, as others do, or wrinkles—   [*Knocking within.*
Who's that? look, Galla.

    Gal. 'Tis the party, madam.

    Ful. What party? has he no name?

    Gal. 'Tis Quintus Curius.

    Ful. Did I not bid them say, I kept my chamber?

    Gal. Why, so they do.

    Sem. I'll leave you, Fulvia.

    Ful. Nay, good Sempronia, stay.

    Sem. In faith, I will not.

    Ful. By Juno, I would not see him.

    Sem. I'll not hinder you.

    Gal. You know he will not be kept out, madam.

    Sem. No,
Nor shall not, careful Galla, by my means.

    Ful. As I do live, Sempronia—

    Sem. What needs this?

    Ful. Go, say I am asleep, and ill at ease.

    Sem. By Castor, no, I'll tell him, you are awake;
And very well: stay, Galla; farewell, Fulvia,
I know my manners. Why do you labour thus,
With action against purpose? Quintus Curius,
She is, i'faith, here, and in disposition.   [*Exit.*

    Ful. Spight with your courtesy! how shall I be tortured!

Enter CURIUS.

    Cur. Where are you, fair one, that conceal yourself,
And keep your beauty within locks and bars here,
Like a fool's treasure?

    Ful. True, she was a fool,
When first she shew'd it to a thief.

    Cur. How, pretty sullenness,
So harsh and short!

    Ful. The fool's artillery, sir.

    Cur. Then take my gown off for the encounter.
                      [*Takes off his gown.*

    Ful. Stay, sir,
I am not in the mood.

    Cur. I'll put you into 't.

    Ful. Best put yourself in your case again, and keep
Your furious appetite warm against you have place for't.

    Cur. What! do you coy it?

    Ful. No, sir; I am not proud.

Cur. I would you were! You think this state becomes you,
By Hercules, it does not. Look in your glass now,
And see how scurvily that countenance shews;
You would be loth to own it.

Ful. I shall not change it.

Cur. Faith, but you must, and slack this bended brow;
And shoot less scorn: there is a Fortune coming
Towards you, dainty, that will take thee thus,
And set thee aloft, to tread upon the head
Of her own statue here in Rome.

Ful. I wonder
Who let this promiser in! Did you, good diligence?
Give him his bribe again: or, if you had none,
Pray you demand him, why he is so venturous,
To press thus to my chamber, being forbidden,
Both by myself and servants?

Cur. How! this is handsome,
And somewhat a new strain!

Ful. 'Tis not strain'd, sir;
'Tis very natural.

Cur. I have known it otherwise
Between the parties, though.

Ful. For your foreknowledge,
Thank that which made it: It will not be so
Hereafter, I assure you.

Cur. No, my mistress!

Ful. No; though you bring the same materials.

Cur. Hear me,
You over-act when you should under-do.
A little call your self again, and think.
If you do this to practise on me, or find
At what forced distance you can hold your servant;
That it be an artificial trick to inflame,
And fire me more, fearing my love may need it,
As heretofore you have done, why, proceed.

Ful. As I have done heretofore!

Cur. Yes, when you'd feign
Your husband's jealousy, your servants' watches,
Speak softly, and run often to the door,
Or to the window, from strange fears that were not:
As if the pleasure were less acceptable,
That were secure.

Ful. You are an impudent fellow.

Cur. And, when you might better have done it at the gate,
To take me in at the casement.

Ful. I take you in!

Cur. Yes, you, my lady. And then, being a-bed with you,
To have your well-taught waiter here come running,
And cry, *her lord!* and hide me without cause,

Crush'd in a chest, or thrust up in a chimney:
When he, tame crow, was winking at his farm;
Or, had he been here, and present, would have kept
Both eyes and beak seel'd up, for six sesterces.

Ful. You have a slanderous, beastly, unwash'd tongue
In your rude mouth, and savouring yourself,
Unmanner'd lord.

Cur. How now!

Ful. It is your title, sir;
Who, since you've lost your own good name, and know not
What to lose more, care not whose honour you wound,
Or fame you poison with it.   You should go
And vent your self in the region where you live,
Among the suburb-brothels, bawds, and brokers,
Whither your broken fortunes have design'd you.

Cur. Nay, then I must stop your fury, I see; and pluck
The tragic visor off.   Come, lady Cypris,
Know your own virtues, quickly.   I'll not be
Put to the wooing of you thus, afresh,
At every turn, for all the Venus in you.
Yield, and be pliant, or by Pollux——[*Offers to force her, she
                 draws her knife.*]   How now!
Will Lais turn a Lucrece?

Ful. No, but by Castor,
Hold off your ravisher's hands, I pierce your heart else.
I'll not be put to kill myself, as she did,
For you, sweet Tarquin.   What! do you fall off?
Nay, it becomes you graciously!   Put not up.
You'll sooner draw your weapon on me, I think it,
Than on the senate, who have cast you forth
Disgracefully, to be the common tale
Of the whole city; base, infamous man!
For, were you other, you would there employ
Your desperate dagger.

Cur. Fulvia, you do know
The strengths you have upon me: do not use
Your power too like a tyrant; I can bear,
Almost until you break me.

Ful. I do know, sir.
So does the senate too know, you can bear.

Cur. By all the gods, that senate will smart deep
For your upbraidings.   I should be right sorry
To have the means so to be venged on you,
At least, the will, as I shall shortly on them.
But go you on still: fare you well, dear lady;
You could not still be fair, unless you were proud.
You will repent these moods, and ere't be long, too:
I shall have you come about again.

Ful. Do you think so?

Cur. Yes, and I know so.

Ful. By what augury?

Cur. By the fair entrails of the matron's chests,
Gold, pearl, and jewels here in Rome, which Fulvia
Will then, but late, say that she might have shared;
And grieving miss.

Ful. Tut, all your promised mountains,
And seas, I am so stalely acquainted with—

Cur. But, when you see the universal flood
Run by your coffers; that my lords, the senators,
Are sold for slaves, their wives for bondwomen,
Their houses, and fine gardens, given away,
And all their goods, under the spear at outcry,
And you have none of this, but are still Fulvia,
Or perhaps less, while you are thinking of it;
You will advise then, coyness with your cushion,
And look on your fingers; say, how you were wish'd—
And so he left you.   *[Exit.*

Ful. Call him again, Galla: *[Exit Galla.*
This is not usual.   Something hangs on this
That I must win out of him.

Re-enter CURIUS.

Cur. How now, melt you?

Ful. Come, you will laugh now, at my easiness:
But 'tis no miracle: doves, they say, will bill,
After their pecking and their murmuring.

Cur. Yes,
And then 'tis kindly.   I would have my love
Angry sometimes, to sweeten off the rest
Of her behaviour.

Ful. You do see, I study
How I may please you then.—But you think, Curius,
'Tis covetise hath wrought me; if you love me,
Change that unkind conceit.

Cur. By my loved soul,
I love thee, like to it; and 'tis my study,
More than mine own revenge, to make thee happy.

Ful. And 'tis that just revenge doth make me happy
To hear you prosecute; and which, indeed,
Hath won me to you, more than all the hope
Of what can else be promised.   I love valour
Better than any lady loves her face,
Or dressing—than my self does.   Let me grow
Still where I do embrace.   But what good means
Have you to effect it? shall I know your project?

Cur. Thou shalt, if thou'lt be gracious.

Ful. As I can be.

Cur. And wilt thou kiss me then?

Ful. As close as shells
Of cockles meet.
 Cur. And print them deep?
 Ful. Quite through
Our subtle lips.
 Cur. And often?
 Ful. I will sow them
Faster than you can reap. What is your plot?
 Cur. Why now my Fulvia looks like her bright name,
And is herself!
 Ful. Nay, answer me, your plot:
I pray thee tell me, Quintus.
 Cur. Ay, these sounds
Become a mistress. Here is harmony!
When you are harsh, I see the way to bend you
Is not with violence, but service. Cruel,
A lady is a fire; gentle, a light.
 Ful. Will you not tell me what I ask you?

       [*Kisses and flatters him along still.*

 Cur. All
That I can think, sweet love, or my breast holds,
I'll pour into thee.
 Ful. What is your design then?
 Cur. I'll tell thee; Catiline shall now be consul:
But you will hear more shortly.
 Ful. Nay, dear love—
 Cur. I'll speak it in thine arms; let us go in.
Rome will be sack'd, her wealth will be our prize;
By public ruin private spirits must rise.   [*Exeunt.*

CHORUS.

Great father Mars, and greater Jove,
 By whose high auspice Rome hath stood
 So long; and first was built in blood
Of your great nephew, that then strove
Not with his brother, but your rites:
 Be present to her now, as then,
 And let not proud and factious men
Against your wills oppose their mights.

Our consuls now are to be made;
 O, put it in the public voice
 To make a free and worthy choice;
Excluding such as would invade
The commonwealth. Let whom we name
 Have wisdom, foresight, fortitude,
 Be more with faith than face endued,
And study conscience above fame.

Such as not seek to get the start
   In state, by power, parts or bribes,
    Ambition's bawds; but move the tribes
By virtue, modesty, desart.
Such as to justice will adhere,
   Whatever great one it offend:
    And from th' embraced truth not bend
For envy, hatred, gifts or fear;
That by their deeds will make it known,
   Whose dignity they do sustain;
    And life, state, glory, all they gain,
Count the republic's, not their own.

Such the old Bruti, Decii were,
   The Cipi, Curtii, who did give
    Themselves for Rome, and would not live
As men, good only for a year.
Such were the great Camilli too;
   The Fabii, Scipios; that still thought
    No work at price enough was bought,
That for their country they could do.

And to her honour so did knit,
   As all their acts were understood
    The sinews of the public good;
And they themselves, one soul with it.
These men were truly magistrates,
   These neither practised force nor forms;
    Nor did they leave the helm in storms:
And such they are make happy states.

ACT III

SCENE I.—*The Field of Mars.*

Enter CICERO, CATO, CATULUS, ANTONIUS, CRASSUS, CÆSAR,
Lictors, *and* People.

Cic. Great honours are great burdens, but on whom
They are cast with envy, he doth bear two loads.
His cares must still be double to his joys,
In any dignity; where, if he err,
He finds no pardon: and for doing well
A most small praise, and that wrung out by force.
I speak this, Romans, knowing what the weight
Of the high charge, you have trusted to me, is:
Not that thereby I would with art decline
The good, or greatness of your benefit;
For I ascribe it to your singular grace,

And vow to owe it to no title else,
Except the gods, that Cicero is your consul.
I have no urns, no dusty monuments,
No broken images of ancestors,
Wanting an ear, or nose; no forged tables
Of long descents, to boast false honours from,
Or be my undertakers to your trust;
But a new man, as I am styled in Rome,
Whom you have dignified; and more, in whom
You have cut a way, and left it ope for virtue
Hereafter to that place: which our great men
Held, shut up with all ramparts, for themselves.
Nor have but few of them in time been made
Your consuls, so; new men, before me, none:
At my first suit, in my just year; preferr'd
To all competitors! and some the noblest—
    Cra. [*aside to Cæsar.*] Now the vein swells!
    Cæs. Up, glory.
    Cic. And to have
Your loud consents from your own utter'd voices,
Not silent books; nor from the meaner tribes,
But first and last, the universal concourse!
This is my joy, my gladness. But my care,
My industry and vigilance now must work,
That still your counsels of me be approved,
Both by yourselves, and those, to whom you have,
With grudge, preferr'd me. Two things I must labour,
That neither they upbraid, nor you repent you;
For every lapse of mine will now be call'd
Your error, if I make such: but my hope is,
So to bear through, and out, the consulship,
As spite shall ne'er wound you, though it may me.
And for myself, I have prepared this strength,
To do so well, as, if there happen ill
Unto me, it shall make the gods to blush;
And be their crime, not mine, that I am envied.
    Cæs. O confidence! more new than is the man.
    Cic. I know well in what terms I do receive
The commonwealth, how vexed, how perplex'd:
In which there's not that mischief, or ill fate,
That good men fear not, wicked men expect not.
I know, besides, some turbulent practices
Already on foot, and rumours of more dangers—
    Cras. Or you will make them, if there be none.   [*Aside.*
    Cic. Last,
I know 'twas this, which made the envy and pride
Of the great Roman blood bate, and give way
To my election.
    Cato. Marcus Tullius, true;

Our need made thee our consul, and thy virtue.
 Cæs. Cato, you will undo him with your praise.
 Cato. Cæsar will hurt himself with his own envy.
 People. The voice of Cato is the voice of Rome.
 Cato. The voice of Rome is the consent of heaven!
And that hath placed thee, Cicero, at the helm,
Where thou must render now thyself a man,
And master of thy art.   Each petty hand
Can steer a ship becalm'd; but he that will
Govern and carry her to her ends, must know
His tides, his currents; how to shift his sails;
What she will bear in foul, what in fair weathers;
Where her springs are, her leaks; and how to stop 'em;
What sands, what shelves, what rocks do threaten her;
The forces and the natures of all winds,
Gusts, storms, and tempests; when her keel ploughs hell,
And deck knocks heaven; then to manage her,
Becomes the name and office of a pilot.
 Cic. Which I'll perform with all the diligence
And fortitude I have; not for my year,
But for my life; except my life be less,
And that my year conclude it; if it must,
Your will, loved gods.   This heart shall yet employ
A day, an hour is left me, so for Rome,
As it shall spring a life out of my death,
To shine for ever glorious in my facts:
The vicious count their years, virtuous their acts.
 People. Most noble consul! let us wait him home.
      [Exeunt Cato, Cicero, Lictors, and People.
 Cæs. Most popular consul he is grown, methinks!
 Cras. How the rout cling to him!
 Cæs. And Cato leads them!
 Cras. You, his colleague Antonius, are not look'd on.
 Ant. Not I, nor do I care.
 Cæs. He enjoys rest,
And ease the while: let the other's spirit toil,
And wake it out, that was inspired for turmoil.
 Catu. If all reports be true yet, Caius Cæsar,
The time hath need of such a watch and spirit.
 Cæs. Reports! do you believe them, Catulus?
Why, he does make and breed 'em for the people,
To endear his service to them.   Do you not taste
An art that is so common?   Popular men,
They must create strange monsters, and then quell them,
To make their arts seem something.   Would you have
Such an Herculean actor in the scene,
And not his hydra? they must sweat no less
To fit their properties, than to express their parts.
 Cras. Treasons and guilty men are made in states,

Too oft, to dignify the magistrates.

Catu. Those states be wretched that are forced to buy
Their rulers' fame with their own infamy.

Cras. We therefore should provide that ours do not.

Cæs. That will Antonius make his care.

Ant. I shall.

Cæs. And watch the watcher.

Catu. Here comes Catiline.
How does he brook his late repulse?

Cæs. I know not,
But hardly sure.

Catu. Longinus too did stand?

Cæs. At first: but he gave way unto his friend.

Catu. Who's that come?   Lentulus?

Cæs. Yes; he is again
Taken into the senate.

Ant. And made prætor.

Catu. I know't; he had my suffrage, next the consuls.

Cæs. True, you were there, prince of the senate, then.

Enter CATILINE, LONGINUS, *and* LENTULUS.

Cat. Hail, noblest Romans!   The most worthy consul,
I gratulate your honour.

Ant. I could wish
It had been happier by your fellowship,
Most noble Sergius, had it pleased the people.

Cat. It did not please the Gods, who instruct the people:
And their unquestion'd pleasures must be serv'd.
They know what's fitter for us than ourselves;
And 'twere impiety to think against them.

Catu. You bear it rightly, Lucius; and it glads me,
To find your thoughts so even.

Cat. I shall still
Study to make them such to Rome, and heaven.
I would withdraw with you a little, Julius.   [*Aside to Cæsar.*

Cæs. I'll come home to you: Crassus would not have you
To speak to him 'fore Quintus Catulus.   [*Aside.*

Cat. I apprehend you.   No, when they shall judge
Honours convenient for me, I shall have them,
With a full hand; I know it.   In mean time,
They are no less part of the commonwealth,
That do obey, than those that do command.

Catu. O let me kiss your forehead, Lucius.
How are you wrong'd!

Cat. By whom?

Catu. Public report;
That gives you out to stomach your repulse,
And brook it deadly.

Cat. Sir, she brooks not me.

Believe me rather, and yourself, now of me:
It is a kind of slander to trust rumour.
 Catu. I know it: and I could be angry with it.
 Cat. So may not I: Where it concerns himself,
Who's angry at a slander makes it true.
 Catu. Most noble Sergius! this your temper melts me.
 Cras. Will you do office to the consul, Quintus?
 Cæs. Which Cato and the rout have done the other?
 Catu I wait when he will go. Be still yourself.
He wants no state, or honours, that hath virtue.
   [*Exeunt Catulus, Antonius, Cæsar, Crassus, Lictors, etc.*
 Cat. Did I appear so tame as this man thinks me!
Look'd I so poor? so dead? so like that nothing,
Which he calls virtuous? O my breast, break quickly;
And shew my friends my in-parts, lest they think
I have betray'd them.   [*Aside.*
 Lon. Where's Gabinius?
 Len. Gone.
 Lon. And Vargunteius?
 Len. Slipt away; all shrunk:
Now that he miss'd the consulship.
 Cat. I am
The scorn of bondmen, who are next to beasts.
What can I worse pronounce myself, that's fitter,
The owl of Rome, whom boys and girls will hoot!
That were I set up for that wooden god
That keeps our gardens, could not fright the crows,
Or the least bird, from muting on my head!   [*Aside.*
 Lon. 'Tis strange how he should miss it!
 Len. Is't not stranger,
The upstart Cicero should carry it so,
By all consents, from men so much his masters?
 Lon. 'Tis true.
 Cat. To what a shadow am I melted!   [*Aside.*
 Lon. Antonius won it but by some few voices.
 Cat. Struck through, like air, and feel it not! My wounds
Close faster than they're made.   [*Aside.*
 Len. The whole design
And enterprise is lost by it: all hands quit it,
Upon his fail.
 Cat. I grow mad at my patience:
It is a visor that hath poison'd me:
Would it had burnt me up, and I died inward,
My heart first turn'd to ashes!
 Lon. Here's Cethegus yet.

Enter CETHEGUS.

 Cat. Repulse upon repulse! an in-mate consul!—
That I could reach the axle, where the pins are

Which bolt this frame; that I might pull them out,
And pluck all into Chaos, with myself!

 Cet. What! are we wishing now?

 Cat. Yes, my Cethegus;
Who would not fall with all the world about him?

 Cet. Not I, that would stand on it, when it falls;
And force new nature out to make another.
These wishings taste of woman, not of Roman;
Let us seek other arms.

 Cat. What should we do?

 Cet. Do, and not wish; something that wishes take not:
So sudden, as the gods should not prevent,
Nor scarce have time to fear.

 Cat. O noble Caius!

 Cet. It likes me better that you are not consul.
I would not go through open doors, but break 'em;
Swim to my ends through blood; or build a bridge
Of carcasses; make on upon the heads
Of men struck down like piles, to reach the lives
Of those remain and stand: then is't a prey,
When danger stops, and ruin makes the way.

 Cat. How thou dost utter me, brave soul, that may not
At all times shew such as I am, but bend
Unto occasion! Lentulus, this man,
If all our fire were out, would fetch down new,
Out of the hand of Jove; and rivet him
To Caucasus, should he but frown; and let
His own gaunt eagle fly at him, to tire.

 Len. Peace, here comes Cato.

 Cat. Let him come, and hear;
I will no more dissemble. Quit us all;
I, and my loved Cethegus here, alone
Will undertake this giants' war, and carry it.

Re-enter CATO.

 Len. What needs this, Lucius?

 Lon. Sergius, be more wary.

 Cat. Now, Marcus Cato, our new consul's spy,
What is your sour austerity sent to explore?

 Cato. Nothing in thee, licentious Catiline;
Halters and racks cannot express from thee
More than thy deeds: 'tis only judgment waits thee.

 Cat. Whose? Cato's! shall he judge me?

 Cato. No, the gods,
Who ever follow those they go not with;
And senate, who with fire must purge sick Rome
Of noisome citizens, whereof thou art one.
Be gone, or else let me. 'Tis bane to draw
The same air with thee.

Cet. Strike him.

Len. Hold, good Caius.

Cet. Fear'st thou not, Cato?

Cato. Rash Cethegus, no.
'Twere wrong with Rome, when Catiline and thou
Do threat, if Cato fear'd.

Cat. The fire you speak of,
If any flame of it approach my fortunes,
I'll quench it not with water, but with ruin.

Cato. You hear this, Romans. [*Exit.*

Cat. Bear it to the consul.

Cet. I would have sent away his soul before him.
You are too heavy, Lentulus, and remiss;
It is for you we labour, and the kingdom
Promised you by the Sybils.

Cat. Which his prætorship,
And some small flattery of the senate more,
Will make him to forget.

Len. You wrong me, Lucius.

Lon. He will not need these spurs.

Cet. The action needs them;
These things, when they proceed not, they go backward.

Len. Let us consult then.

Cet. Let us first take arms:
They that deny us just things now, will give
All that we ask, if once they see our swords.

Cat. Our objects must be sought with wounds, not words.
[*Exeunt.*

SCENE II.—CICERO's *House.*

Enter CICERO *and* FULVIA.

Cic. Is there a heaven, and gods? and can it be
They should so slowly hear, so slowly see!
Hath Jove no thunder, or is Jove become
Stupid as thou art, O near-wretched Rome,
When both thy senate and thy gods do sleep,
And neither thine, nor their own states do keep!
What will awake thee, heaven? what can excite
Thine anger, if this practice be too light?
His former drifts partake of former times,
But this last plot was only Catiline's;
O, that it were his last! but he before
Hath safely done so much, he'll still dare more.
Ambition, like a torrent, ne'er looks back;
And is a swelling, and the last affection
A high mind can put off; being both a rebel
Unto the soul and reason, and enforceth
All laws, all conscience, treads upon religion,

And offereth violence to nature's self.
But here is that transcends it! A black purpose
To confound nature; and to ruin that,
Which never age nor mankind can repair!—
Sit down, good lady; Cicero is lost
In this your fable: for, to think it true
Tempteth my reason, it so far exceeds
All insolent fictions of the tragic scene!
The commonwealth yet panting underneath
The stripes and wounds of a late civil war,
Gasping for life, and scarce restored to hope;
To seek t' oppress her with new cruelty,
And utterly extinguish her long name,
With so prodigious and unheard of fierceness!
What sink of monsters, wretches of lost minds,
Mad after change, and desperate in their states,
Wearied and gall'd with their necessities,
For all this I allow them, durst have thought it?
Would not the barbarous deeds have been believed,
Of Marius and Sylla, by our children,
Without this fact had risse forth greater for them?
All that they did was piety to this!
They yet but murder'd kinsfolk, brothers, parents,
Ravish'd the virgins, and perhaps some matrons;
They left the city standing, and the temples:
The gods and majesty of Rome were safe yet!—
These purpose to fire it, to despoil them,
(Beyond the other evils) and lay waste
The far triumphed world: for, unto whom
Rome is too little, what can be enough?
   Ful. 'Tis true, my lord, I had the same discourse.
   Cic And then, to take a horrid sacrament
In human blood, for execution
Of this their dire design; which might be call'd
The height of wickedness: but that that was higher
For which they did it!
   Ful. I assure your lordship,
The extreme horror of it almost turn'd me
To air, when first I heard it; I was all
A vapour when 'twas told me, and I long'd
To vent it any where: 'twas such a secret,
I thought it would have burnt me up.
   Cic. Good Fulvia,
Fear not your act; and less repent you of it.
   Ful. I do not, my good lord; I know to whom
I've utter'd it.
   Cic. You have discharged it safely.
Should Rome, for whom you've done the happy service,
Turn most ingrate, yet were your virtue paid

In conscience of the fact: so much good deeds
Reward themselves!

 Ful. My lord, I did it not
To any other aim but for itself;
To no ambition.

 Cic. You have learn'd the difference
Of doing office to the public weal,
And private friendship: and have shewn it, lady.
Be still your self. I have sent for Quintus Curius,
And for your virtuous sake, if I can win him
Yet to the commonwealth, he shall be safe too.

 Ful. I'll undertake, my lord, he shall be won.

 Cic. Pray you join with me then, and help to work him.

Enter a Lictor.

 Cic. How now! Is he come?

 Lict. He's here, my lord.

 Cic. Go presently,
Pray my colleague Antonius I may speak with him,
About some present business of the state;
And, as you go, call on my brother Quintus,
And pray him, with the tribunes, to come to me.
Bid Curius enter. [*Exit Lict.*]—Fulvia, you will aid me?

 Ful. It is my duty.

Enter CURIUS.

 Cic. O, my noble lord!
I have to chide you, i'faith. Give me your hand,—
Nay, be not troubled; it shall be gently, Curius.
You look upon this lady? what! do you guess
My business yet? come, if you frown, I thunder;
Therefore put on your better looks and thoughts:
There's nought but fair and good intended to you;
And I would make those your complexion.
Would you, of whom the senate had that hope
As, on my knowledge, it was in their purpose,
Next sitting to restore you, as they had done
The stupid and ungrateful Lentulus,—
Excuse me, that I name you thus together,
For yet you are not such—would you, I say,
A person both of blood and honour, stock'd
In a long race of virtuous ancestors,
Embark your self for such a hellish action,
With parricides and traitors, men turn'd furies,
Out of the waste and ruin of their fortunes?
(For 'tis despair that is the mother of madness,)
Such as want that, which all conspirators,
But they, have first, mere colour for their mischief?
O, I must blush with you. Come, you shall not labour

To extenuate your guilt, but quit it clean:
Bad men excuse their faults, good men will leave them.
He acts the third crime that defends the first.
Here is a lady that hath got the start
In piety of us all, and for whose virtue
I could almost turn lover again, but that
Terentia would be jealous.   What an honour
Hath she achieved to herself! what voices,
Titles, and loud applauses will pursue her
Through every street! what windows will be fill'd,
To shoot eyes at her! what envy and grief in matrons,
They are not she, when this her act shall seem
Worthier a chariot, than if Pompey came
With Asia chain'd! all this is, while she lives;
But dead, her very name will be a statue,
Not wrought for time, but rooted in the minds
Of all posterity; when brass and marble,
Ay, and the Capitol itself is dust!
    Ful. Your honour thinks too highly of me.
    Cic. No;
I cannot think enough, and I would have
Him emulate you.   'Tis no shame to follow
The better precedent.   She shews you, Curius,
What claim your country lays to you, and what duty
You owe to it: be not afraid to break
With murderers and traitors, for the saving
A life so near and necessary to you,
As is your country's.   Think but on her right.
No child can be too natural to his parent:
She is our common mother, and doth challenge
The prime part of us;   do not stop, but give it.
He that is void of fear, may soon be just;
And no religion binds men to be traitors.
    Ful. My lord, he understands it, and will follow
Your saving counsel;   but his shame yet stays him.
I know that he is coming.
    Cur. Do you know it?
    Ful. Yes;   let me speak with you.   [*Takes him aside.*
    Cur. O, you are—
    Ful. What am I?
    Cur. Speak not so loud.
    Ful. I am what you should be.   [*Lowering her voice.*
Come, do you think I'd walk in any plot
Where madam Sempronia should take place of me,
And Fulvia come in the rear, or on the by?
That I would be her second in a business,
Though it might vantage me all the sun sees?
It was a silly phant'sy of yours.   Apply
Yourself to me and the consul, and be wise;

Follow the fortune I have put you into:
You may be something this way, and with safety.
  Cic. Nay, I must tolerate no whisperings, lady.
  Ful. Sir, you may hear: I tell him in the way
Wherein he was, how hazardous his course was.
  Cic. How hazardous! how certain to all ruin.
Did he, or do yet any of them imagine
The gods would sleep to such a Stygian practice,
Against that commonwealth which they have founded
With so much labour, and like care have kept,
Now near seven hundred years? It is a madness,
Wherewith heaven blinds them, when it would confound them,
That they should think it. Come, my Curius,
I see your nature's right; you shall no more
Be mention'd with them: I will call you mine,
And trouble this good shame no farther. Stand
Firm for your country, and become a man
Honour'd and loved: it were a noble life,
To be found dead, embracing her. Know you
What thanks, what titles, what rewards the senate
Will heap upon you, certain, for your service?
Let not a desperate action more engage you,
Than safety should; and wicked friendship force,
What honesty and virtue cannot work.
  Ful. He tells you right, sweet friend: 'tis saving counsel.
  Cur. Most noble consul, I am yours and hers,
I mean my country's; you have form'd me new,
Inspiring me with what I should be truly:
And I entreat, my faith may not seem cheaper
For springing out of penitence.
  Cic. Good Curius,
It shall be dearer rather; and because
I'd make it such, hear how I trust you more.
Keep still your former face, and mix again
With these lost spirits; run all their mazes with them;
For such are treasons: find their windings out,
And subtle turnings; watch their snaky ways,
Through brakes and hedges, into woods of darkness
Where they are fain to creep upon their breasts
In paths ne'er trod by men, but wolves and panthers.
Learn, beside Catiline, Lentulus, and those
Whose names I have, what new ones they draw in;
Who else are likely; what those great ones are
They do not name; what ways they mean to take·
And whether their hopes point to war, or ruin
By some surprise. Explore all their intents;
And what you find may profit the republic,
Acquaint me with it, either by your self,
Or this your virtuous friend, on whom I lay

The care of urging you: I'll see that Rome
Shall prove a thankful and a bounteous mother.
Be secret as the night.

   Cur. And constant, sir.

   Cic. I do not doubt it, though the time cut off
All vows: The dignity of truth is lost
With much protesting.　Who is there?

Enter a Servant.

                              This way,
Lest you be seen and met.　And when you come,
Be this your token [*whispers with him.*] to this fellow.　Light them.
                               [*Exit Servant with Cur. and Fulvia.*

O Rome, in what a sickness art thou fallen!
How dangerous and deadly, when thy head
Is drown'd in sleep, and all thy body fevery!
No noise, no pulling, no vexation wakes thee,
Thy lethargy is such: or if, by chance,
Thou heav'st thy eye-lids up, thou dost forget,
Sooner than thou wert told, thy proper danger.
I did unreverently to blame the gods,
Who wake for thee, though thou snore to thy self.
Is it not strange thou should'st be so diseased,
And so secure? but more, that the first symptoms
Of such a malady should not rise out
From any worthy member, but a base
And common strumpet, worthless to be named
A hair, or part of thee?　Think, think, hereafter,
What thy needs were, when thou must use such means;
And lay it to thy breast, how much the gods
Upbraid thy foul neglect of them, by making
So vile a thing the author of thy safety.
They could have wrought by nobler ways, have struck
Thy foes with forked lightning, or ramm'd thunder;
Thrown hills upon them in the act; have sent
Death, like a damp, to all their families;
Or caus'd their consciences to burst them: but
When they will shew thee what thou art, and make
A scornful difference 'twixt their power and thee,
They help thee by such aids as geese and harlots.

Re-enter Lictor.

How now, what answer? is he come?

   Lict. Your brother
Will straight be here, and your colleague, Antonius,
Said coldly he would follow me.　　　　　　　　　　　　[*Exit.*

   Cic. Ay, that
Troubles me somewhat, and is worth my fear.
He is a man 'gainst whom I must provide,

That, as he'll do no good, he do no harm.
He, though he be not of the plot, will like it,
And wish it should proceed; for, unto men
Prest with their wants, all change is ever welcome,
I must with offices and patience win him,
Make him by art that which he is not born,
A friend unto the public, and bestow
The province on him, which is by the senate
Decreed to me; that benefit will bind him:
'Tis well, if some men will do well for price;
So few are virtuous when the reward's away.
Nor must I be unmindful of my private;
For which I have call'd my brother and the tribunes,
My kinsfolks, and my clients, to be near me.
He that stands up 'gainst traitors, and their ends,
Shall need a double guard, of law, and friends,
Especially in such an envious state,
That sooner will accuse the magistrate,
Than the delinquent; and will rather grieve
The treason is not acted, than believe.   [*Exit.*

SCENE III.—*A Room in* CATILINE'S *House.*

Enter CÆSAR *and* CATILINE.

Cæs. The night grows on, and you are for your meeting;
I'll therefore end in few.   Be resolute,
And put your enterprise in act.   The more
Actions of depth and danger are consider'd,
The less assuredly they are perform'd:
And thence it happeneth, that the bravest plots,
Not executed straight, have been discover'd.
Say, you are constant, or another, a third,
Or more; there may be yet one wretched spirit,
With whom the fear of punishment shall work
'Bove all the thoughts of honour and revenge.
You are not now to think what's best to do,
As in beginnings, but what must be done,
Being thus enter'd; and slip no advantage
That may secure you.   Let them call it mischief;
When it is past, and prosper'd, 'twill be virtue.
They're petty crimes are punish'd, great rewarded.
Nor must you think of peril, since attempts
Begun with danger, still do end with glory;
And, when need spurs, despair will be call'd wisdom.
Less ought the care of men, or fame to fright you;
For they that win, do seldom receive shame
Of victory, howe'er it be achieved;
And vengeance, least: for who, besieged with wants,
Would stop at death, or anything beyond it?

Come, there was never any great thing yet
Aspired, but by violence or fraud:
And he that sticks for folly of a conscience
To reach it—
    Cat. Is a good religious fool.
    Cæs. A superstitious slave, and will die beast.
Good night.   You know what Crassus thinks, and I,
By this.   Prepare your wings as large as sails,
To cut through air, and leave no print behind you.
A serpent, ere he comes to be a dragon,
Does eat a bat; and so must you a consul,
That watches.   What you do, do quickly, Sergius.   [*Going.*
You shall not stir for me.
    Cat. Excuse me.—Lights there!
    Cæs. By no means.
    Cat. Stay then.   All good thoughts to Cæsar,
And like to Crassus.
    Cæs. Mind but your friends' counsels.   [*Exit.*
    Cat. Or I will bear no mind.—

Enter AURELIA.

How now, Aurelia!
Are your confederates come, the ladies?
    Aur. Yes.
    Cat. And is Sempronia there?
    Aur. She is.
    Cat. That's well.
She has a sulphurous spirit, and will take
Light at a spark.   Break with them, gentle love,
About the drawing as many of their husbands
Into the plot, as can; if not, to rid them:
That will be the easier practice unto some,
Who have been tired with them long.   Solicit
Their aids for money, and their servants' help,
In firing of the city at the time
Shall be design'd.   Promise them states and empires,
And men for lovers, made of better clay
Than ever the old potter Titan knew.

Enter LECCA.

Who's that?   O, Porcius Lecca!   Are they met?
    Lec. They are all here.
    Cat. Love, you have your instructions:
I'll trust you with the stuff you have to work on,
You'll form it! [*Exit Aurelia.*] Porcius, fetch the silver eagle
I gave you in charge; and pray 'em they will enter.   [*Exit Lecca.*

Enter CETHEGUS, CURIUS, LENTULUS, VARGUNTEIUS, LONGINUS,
GABINIUS, CEPARIUS, AUTRONIUS, etc.

    Cat. O friends, your faces glad me!   This will be
Our last, I hope, of consultation.

Cet. So it had need.

Cur. We lose occasion daily.

Cat. Ay, and our means; whereof one wounds me most
That was the fairest: Piso is dead in Spain.

Cet. As we are here.

Lon. And, as 'tis thought, by envy
Of Pompey's followers.

Len. He too's coming back,
Now, out of Asia.

Cat. Therefore, what we intend
We must be swift in. Take your seats, and hear.
I have already sent Septimius
Into the Picene territory, and Julius,
To raise force for us in Apulia;
Manlius, at Fesulæ is by this time up,
With the old needy troops that follow'd Sylla;
And all do but expect when we will give
The blow at home.

Re-enter P. LECCA *with the eagle.*

Behold this silver eagle,
'Twas Marius' standard in the Cimbrian war,
Fatal to Rome; and as our augurs tell me,
Shall still be so: for which one ominous cause,
I've kept it safe, and done it sacred rites,
As to a godhead, in a chapel built
Of purpose to it. Pledge then all your hands,
To follow it with vows of death and ruin,
Struck silently and home. So waters speak
When they run deepest. Now's the time, this year
The twentieth from the firing of the Capitol,
As fatal too to Rome, by all predictions;
And in which honour'd Lentulus must rise
A king, if he pursue it.

Cur. If he do not,
He is not worthy the great destiny.

Len. It is too great for me; but what the gods
And their great loves decree me, I must not
Seem careless of.

Cat. No, nor we envious,
We have enough beside; all Gallia, Belgia,
Greece, Spain and Africk.

Cur. Ay, and Asia too,
Now Pompey is returning.

Cat. Noblest Romans,
Methinks our looks are not so quick and high,
As they were wont.

Cur. No! whose is not?

Cat. We have

No anger in our eyes, no storm, no lightning:
Our hate is spent, and fumed away in vapour,
Before our hands be at work: I can accuse
Not any one, but all, of slackness.

    Cet. Yes,
And be yourself such, while you do it.

    Cat. Ha!
'Tis sharply answer'd, Caius.

    Cet. Truly, truly.

    Len. Come, let us each one know his part to do,
And then be accused. Leave these untimely quarrels.

    Cur. I would there were more Romes than one to ruin!

    Cet. More Romes! more worlds.

    Cur. Nay then, more gods and natures,
If they took part.

    Len. When shall the time be first?

    Cat. I think, the Saturnals!

    Cet. 'Twill be too long.

    Cat. They are not now far off, 'tis not a month.

    Cet. A week, a day, an hour is too far off:
Now were the fittest time.

    Cat. We have not laid
All things so safe and ready.

    Cet. While we are laying,
We shall all lie and grow to earth. Would I
Were nothing in it, if not now: these things,
They should be done, ere thought.

    Cat. Nay, now your reason
Forsakes you, Caius. Think but what commodity
That time will minister; the city's custom
Of being then in mirth and feast—

    Len. Loos'd whole
In pleasure and security—

    Aut. Each house
Resolved in freedom—

    Cur. Every slave a master—

    Lon. And they too no mean aids—

    Cur. Made from their hope
Of liberty—

    Len. Or hate unto their lords.

    Var. 'Tis sure, there cannot be a time found out
More apt and natural.

    Len. Nay, good Cethegus,
Why do your passions now disturb our hopes?

    Cet. Why do your hopes delude your certainties?

    Cat. You must lend him his way. [*Aside to Lentulus.*
Think for the order,
And process of it.

    Lon. Yes.

Len. I like not fire,
'Twill too much waste my city.

Cat. Were it embers,
There will be wealth enough raked out of them,
To spring a new.   It must be fire, or nothing.

Lon. What else should fright or terrify them?

Var. True.
In that confusion must be the chief slaughter.

Cur. Then we shall kill them bravest.

Cep. And in heaps.

Aut. Strew sacrifices.

Cur. Make the earth an altar.

Lon. And Rome the fire.

Lec. 'Twill be a noble night.

Var. And worth all Sylla's days.

Cur. When husbands, wives,
Grandsires, and nephews, servants, and their lords,
Virgins, and priests, the infant and the nurse,
Go all to hell together in a fleet.

Cat. I would have you, Longinus and Statilius,
To take the charge o' the firing, which must be,
At a sign given with a trumpet, done
In twelve chief places of the city at once.
The flax and sulphur are already laid
In, at Cethegus' house; so are the weapons.
Gabinius, you, with other force, shall stop
The pipes and conduits, and kill those that come
For water.

Cur. What shall I do?

Cat. All will have
Employment, fear not: ply the execution.

Cur. For that, trust me and Cethegus.

Cat. I will be
At hand with the army, to meet those that scape:
And, Lentulus, begirt you Pompey's house,
To seize his sons alive; for they are they
Must make our peace with him: all else cut off,
As Tarquin did the poppy-heads, or mowers
A field of thistles; or else, up, as ploughs
Do barren lands, and strike together flints
And clods, th' ungrateful senate and the people;
Till no rage gone before, or coming after,
May weigh with yours, though horror leap'd herself
Into the scale: but, in your violent acts,
The fall of torrents and the noise of tempests,
The boiling of Charybdis, the sea's wildness,
The eating force of flames, and wings of winds,
Be all out-wrought by your transcendant furies.
It had been done ere this, had I been consul;

We had had no stop, no let.

    Len. How find you Antonius?

    Cat. The other has won him,—lost: that Cicero
Was born to be my opposition,
And stands in all our ways.

    Cur. Remove him first.

    Cet. May that yet be done sooner?

    Cat. Would it were done.

    Cur. Var. I'll do't.

    Cet. It is my province; none usurp it.

    Len. What are your means?

    Cet. Enquire not. He shall die.
Shall, was too slowly said; he's dying: that
Is yet too slow; he's dead.

    Cat. Brave, only Roman,
Whose soul might be the world's soul, were that dying;
Refuse not yet the aids of these your friends.

    Len. Here's Vargunteius holds good quarter with him.

    Cat. And under the pretext of clientele
And visitation, with the morning hail,
Will be admitted.

    Cet. What is that to me?

    Var. Yes, we may kill him in his bed, and safely.

    Cet. Safe is your way then, take it: mine's mine own.   [*Exit.*

    Cat. Follow him, Vargunteius, and persuade,
The morning is the fittest time.

    Lon. The night
Will turn all into tumult.

    Len. And perhaps
Miss of him too.

    Cat. Entreat and conjure him
In all our names—

    Len. By all our vows and friendships.   [*Exit Vargunteius.*

       Enter SEMPRONIA, AURELIA, *and* FULVIA.

    Sem. What! is our council broke up first?

    Aur. You say,
Women are greatest talkers.

             [*Whispers with Cat. while Ful. takes Cur. aside.*

    Sem. We have done,
And are now fit for action.

    Lon. Which is passion;
There is your best activity, lady.

    Sem. How
Knows your wise fatness that?

    Lon. Your mother's daughter
Did teach me, madam.

    Cat. Come, Sempronia, leave him;
He is a giber, and our present business

Is of more serious consequence.   Aurelia
Tells me, you've done most masculinely within,
And play'd the orator.

    Sem. But we must hasten
To our design as well, and execute;
Not hang still in the fever of an accident.

    Cat. You say well, lady.

    Sem. I do like our plot
Exceeding well; 'tis sure, and we shall leave
Little to fortune in it.

    Cat. Your banquet stays.
Aurelia, take her in.   Where's Fulvia?

    Sem. O, the two lovers are coupling.

    Cur. In good faith,
She's very ill with sitting up.

    Sem. You'd have her
Laugh, and lie down.

    Ful. No, faith, Sempronia,
I am not well; I'll take my leave, it draws
Toward the morning.   Curius shall stay with you.
Madam, I pray you pardon me; my health
I must respect

    Aur. Farewell, good Fulvia.

    Cur. [*aside to Fulvia.*] Make haste, and bid him get his guards
        about him;
For Vargunteius and Cornelius
Have underta'en it, should Cethegus miss:
Their reason, that they think his open rashness
Will suffer easier discovery
Than their attempt, so veiled under friendship.
I'll bring you to your coach.   Tell him, beside,
Of Cæsar's coming forth here.

    Cat. My sweet madam,
Will you be gone?

    Ful. I am, my lord, in truth
In some indisposition.

    Cat. I do wish
You had all your health, sweet lady.   Lentulus,
You'll do her service.

    Len. To her coach,—and duty.   [*Exeunt all but Catiline.*

    Cat. What ministers men must for practice use,
The rash, the ambitious, needy, desperate,
Foolish and wretched, e'en the dregs of mankind,
To whores and women! still it must be so.
Each have their proper place, and in their rooms
They are the best.   Grooms fittest kindle fires,
Slaves carry burdens, butchers are for slaughters,
Apothecaries, butlers, cooks, for poisons;
As these for me: dull stupid Lentulus,

My stale, with whom I stalk; the rash Cethegus,
My executioner; and fat Longinus,
Statilius, Curius, Ceparius, Cimber,
My labourers, pioneers, and incendiaries:
With these domestic traitors, bosom thieves,
Whom custom hath call'd wives: the readiest helps
To strangle headstrong husbands, rob the easy,
And lend the moneys on returns of lust.
Shall Catiline not do now, with these aids,
So sought, so sorted, something shall be call'd
Their labour, but his profit? and make Cæsar
Repent his venturing counsels to a spirit
So much his lord in mischief? when all these
Shall, like the brethren sprung of dragons' teeth,
Ruin each other, and he fall amongst them,
With Crassus, Pompey, or who else appears
But like, or near a great one. May my brain
Resolve to water, and my blood turn phlegm,
My hands drop off unworthy of my sword,
And that be inspired of itself to rip
My breast for my lost entrails, when I leave
A soul that will not serve; and who will, are
The same with slaves, such clay I dare not fear.
The cruelty I mean to act, I wish
Should be call'd mine, and tarry in my name;
Whilst after-ages do toil out themselves
In thinking for the like, but do it less:
And were the power of all the fiends let loose,
With fate to boot, it should be still example,
When, what the Gaul or Moor could not effect,
Nor emulous Carthage, with their length of spight,
Shall be the work of one, and that MY night.   [*Exit.*

SCENE IV.—*A Room in* CICERO'S *House.*

Enter CICERO, FULVIA, *and* Attendant.

    Cic. I thank your vigilance. Where's my brother Quintus?
Call all my servants up!   [*Exit Attendant.*]   Tell noble Curius,
And say it to yourself, you are my savers:
But that's too little for you; you are Rome's.
What could I then hope less?

Enter QUINTUS CICERO.

                           O brother! now
The enginers I told you of are working,
The machine 'gins to move. Where are your weapons?
Arm all my household presently, and charge
The porter, he let no man in till day.
    Qui. Not clients, and your friends?

Cic. They wear those names,
That come to murder me. Yet send for Cato,
And Quintus Catulus; those I dare trust;
And Flaccus and Pomtinius, the prætors,
By the back way.

Qui. Take care, good brother Marcus,
Your fears be not form'd greater than they should;
And make your friends grieve, while your enemies laugh.

Cic. 'Tis brother's counsel, and worth thanks. But do
As I entreat you. [*Exit Quintus.*] I provide, not fear.—
Was Cæsar there, say you?

Ful. Curius says he met him
Coming from thence.

Cic. O, so. And had you a council
Of ladies too? who was your speaker, madam?

Ful. She that would be, had there been forty more;
Sempronia, who had both her Greek and figures,
And ever and anon would ask us, if
The witty consul could have mended that,
Or orator Cicero could have said it better?

Cic. She is my gentle enemy. Would Cethegus
Had no more danger in him! But my guards
Are you, great Powers, and the unbated strengths
Of a firm conscience, which shall arm each step
Ta'en for the state! and teach me slack no pace
For fear of malice.

Re-enter QUINTUS.

How now, brother?

Qui. Cato,
And Quintus Catulus were coming to you,
And Crassus with them. I have let them in
By the garden.

Cic. What would Crassus have?

Qui. I hear
Some whispering 'bout the gate, and making doubt
Whether it be not yet too early or no?
But I do think, they are your friends and clients,
Are fearful to disturb you.

Cic. You will change
To another thought anon. Have you given the porter
The charge I will'd you?

Qui. Yes.

Cic. Withdraw and hearken.   [*Exeunt.*

SCENE V.—*The Street before* CICERO'S *House.*

Enter VARGUNTEIUS *and* CORNELIUS, *with armed men.*

Var. The door's not open yet.
Cor. You were best to knock.

Var. Let them stand close then; and, when we are in,
Rush after us.

Cor. But where's Cethegus?

Var. He
Has left it, since he might not do't his way.   [*Knocks.*

Por. [*within.*] Who's there?

Var. A friend, or more.

Por. [*within.*] I may not let
Any man in, till day.

Var. No! why?

Cor. Thy reason?

Por. [*within.*] I am commanded so.

Var. By whom?

Cor. I hope
We are not discover'd.

Var. Yes, by revelation!—
Pray thee, good slave, who has commanded thee?

Por. [*within.*] He that may best, the consul.

Var. We are his friends.

Por. [*within.*] All's one.

Cor. Best give your name.

Var. Dost thou hear, fellow?
I have some instant business with the consul.
My name is Vargunteius.

Cic. [*appears at the window above, with Cato, Catulus, and Crassus.*]
      True he knows it,
And for what friendly office you are sent.
Cornelius too is there—

Var. We are betray'd.

Cic. And desperate Cethegus, is he not?

Var. Speak you, he knows my voice.

Cic. What say you to't?

Cor. You are deceived, sir.

Cic. No, 'tis you are so;
Poor misled men. Your states are yet worth pity,
If you would hear, and change your savage minds.
Leave to be mad; forsake your purposes
Of treason, rapine, murder, fire, and horror:
The commonwealth hath eyes that wake as sharply
Over her life, as yours do for her ruin.
Be not deceived, to think her lenity
Will be perpetual; or, if men be wanting,
The gods will be to such a calling cause.
Consider your attempts, and while there's time,
Repent you of them. It doth make me tremble,
There should those spirits yet breathe, that when they cannot
Live honestly, would rather perish basely.

Cato. You talk too much to 'em, Marcus; they are lost:
Go forth, and apprehend them.

Catu. If you prove
This practice, what should let the commonwealth
To take due vengeance?
    Var. Let us shift away!
The darkness hath conceal'd us yet. We'll say,
Some have abus'd our names.
    Cor. Deny it all.   *[Exeunt below.*
    Cato. Quintus, what guards have you? call the tribunes' aid,
And raise the city. Consul, you are too mild,
The foulness of some facts takes thence all mercy;
Report it to the senate. [*It thunders and lightens violently on a
      sudden.*] Hear! the gods
Grow angry with your patience. 'Tis their care,
And must be yours, that guilty men escape not:
As crimes do grow, justice should rouse itself.   *[Exeunt above.*

CHORUS.

What is it, heavens, you prepare
    With so much swiftness, and so sudden rising?
There are no sons of earth that dare,
    Again, rebellion? or the gods' surprising?

The world doth shake, and nature fears;
    Yet is the tumult and the horror greater
Within our minds, than in our ears:
    So much Rome's faults (now grown her fate) do threat her.

The priests and people run about,
    Each order, age, and sex amaz'd at other;
And at the ports all thronging out,
    As if their safety were to quit their mother:

Yet find they the same dangers there,
    From which they make such haste to be preserved:
For guilty states do ever bear
    The plagues about them which they have deserved.

And till those plagues do get above
    The mountain of our faults, and there do sit,
We see them not: thus still we love
    Th' evil we do, until we suffer it.

But most ambition, that near vice
    To virtue, hath the fate of Rome provoked;
And made that now Rome's self['s] no price
    To free her from the death wherewith she's yoked.

That restless ill that still doth build
    Upon success, and ends not in aspiring:
But there begins; and ne'er is fill'd
    While ought remains that seems but worth desiring,

Wherein the thought, unlike the eye,
   To which things far seem smaller than they are,
Deems all contentment placed on high;
   And thinks there's nothing great but what is far.

O, that in time Rome did not cast
   Her errors up this fortune to prevent!
To have seen her crimes ere they were past,
   And felt her faults before her punishment.

ACT IV

SCENE I.—*A Street at the foot of the Capitol.*

[The Storm continued.]

Enter the Allobrogian Ambassadors. *Divers* Senators *pass by them, quaking and trembling.*

1 *Am.* Can these men fear, who are not only ours,
But the world's masters! Then I see the Gods
Upbraid our suff'rings, or would humble them,
By sending these affrights while we are here;
That we might laugh at their ridiculous fear,
Whose names we trembled at beyond the Alps.
Of all that pass, I do not see a face
Worthy a man; that dares look up and stand
One thunder out: but downward all, like beasts,
Running away from every flash is made.
The falling world could not deserve such baseness.
Are we employed here by our miseries,
Like superstitious fools, or rather slaves,
To plain our griefs, wrongs, and oppressions,
To a mere clothed senate, whom our folly
Hath made, and still intends to keep, our tyrants?
It is our base petitionary breath
That blows them to this greatness; which this prick
                              [Points to his sword.
Would soon let out, if we were bold and wretched.
When they have taken all we have, our goods,
Crop, lands and houses, they will leave us this:
A weapon and an arm will still be found,
Though naked left, and lower than the ground.

Enter CATO, CATULUS, *and* CICERO.

Cato. Do; urge thine anger still, good heaven and just!
Tell guilty men what powers are above them.
In such a confidence of wickedness,
'Twas time they should know something fit to fear.
   Catu. I never saw a morn more full of horror.

Cato. To Catiline and his: but to just men,
Though heaven should speak with all his wrath at once,
That with his breath the hinges of the world
Did crack, we should stand upright and unfear'd.

Cic. Why so we do, good Cato. Who be these?

Catu. Ambassadors from the Allobroges,
I take them, by their habits.

1 Am. Ay, these men
Seem of another race; let's sue to these,
There's hope of justice with their fortitude.

Cic. Friends of the senate and of Rome, to-day
We pray you to forbear us: on the morrow,
What suit you have, let us, by Fabius Sanga,
Whose patronage your state doth use, but know it,
And on the consul's word, you shall receive
Dispatch, or else an answer worth your patience.

2 Am. We could not hope for more, most worthy consul.
                    [*Exeunt Cato, Catulus, and Cicero.*
This magistrate hath struck an awe into me,
And by his sweetness won a more regard
Unto his place, than all the boist'rous moods
That ignorant greatness practiseth, to fill
The large, unfit authority it wears.
How easy is a noble spirit discern'd
From harsh and sulphurous matter, that flies out
In contumelies, makes a noise, and stinks!
May we find good and great men: that know how
To stoop to wants and meet necessities,
And will not turn from any equal suits!
Such men, they do not succour more the cause
They undertake with favour and success,
Than by it their own judgments they do raise,
In turning just men's needs into their praise.   [*Exeunt.*

SCENE II.—*The Temple of Jupiter Stator.*

Enter CICERO, ANTONIUS, CATO, CATULUS, CÆSAR, CRASSUS,
and many other Senators, Prætor, Officers, *etc.*

Præ. Room for the consuls! Fathers, take your places.
Here in the house of Jupiter the Stayer,
By edict from the consul, Marcus Tullius,
You're met, a frequent senate. Hear him speak.

Cic. What may be happy and auspicious still
To Rome and hers!
        Honour'd and conscript fathers,
If I were silent, and that all the dangers
Threat'ning the state and you, were yet so hid
In night, or darkness thicker in their breasts,
That are the black contrivers, so that no

Beam of the light could pierce them; yet the voice
Of heaven, this morning hath spoke loud enough
T' instruct you with a feeling of the horror,
And wake you from a sleep as stark as death.
I have of late spoke often in this senate
Touching this argument, but still have wanted
Either your ears or faith; so incredible
Their plots have seem'd, or I so vain, to make
These things for mine own glory and false greatness,
As hath been given out.   But be it so.
When they break forth, and shall declare themselves
By their too foul effects, then, then the envy
Of my just cares will find another name.
For me, I am but one, and this poor life,
So lately aim'd at, not an hour yet since,
They cannot with more eagerness pursue,
Than I with gladness would lay down and lose
To buy Rome's peace, if that would purchase it.
But when I see they'd make it but the step
To more and greater; unto yours, Rome's, all;
I would with those preserve it, or then fall.

    Cæs. Ay, ay, let you alone, cunning artificer!
See how his gorget peers above his gown,
To tell the people in what danger he was.
It was absurdly done of Vargunteius,
To name himself before he was got in.   [*Aside to Crassus.*

    Cras. It matters not, so they deny it all:
And can but carry the lie constantly.
Will Catiline be here?

    Cæs. I have sent for him.

    Cras. And have you bid him to be confident?

    Cæs. To that his own necessity will prompt him.

    Cras. Seem to believe nothing at all that Cicero
Relates us.

    Cæs. It will mad him.

    Cras. O, and help
The other party.

    Enter Q. CICERO, *with the* Tribunes *and* Guards.

             Who is that, his brother?
What new intelligence has he brought him now?

    Cæs. Some cautions from his wife, how to behave him.

    Cic. Place some of them without, and some bring in.
Thank their kind loves: it is a comfort yet,
That all depart not from their country's cause.

    Cæs. How now, what means this muster, consul Antonius?

    Ant. I do not know; ask my colleague, he'll tell you.
There is some reason in state that I must yield to,
And I have promised him; indeed he has bought it,

With giving me the province.
    Cic. I profess,
It grieves me, fathers, that I am compell'd
To draw these arms, and aids for your defence;
And more, against a citizen of Rome,
Born here amongst you, a patrician,
A man, I must confess, of no mean house,
Nor no small virtue, if he had employ'd
Those excellent gifts of fortune and of nature,
Unto the good, not ruin of the state.
But being bred in his father's needy fortunes,
Brought up in his sister's prostitution,
Confirm'd in civil slaughter, entering first
The commonwealth with murder of the gentry;
Since, both by study and custom conversant
With all licentiousness, what could be hoped
In such a field of riot, but a course
Extreme pernicious? though I must protest,
I found his mischiefs sooner with mine eyes
Than with my thought; and with these hands of mine,
Before they touch'd at my suspicion.
    Cæs. What are his mischiefs, consul? you declaim
Against his manners, and corrupt your own:
No wise man should, for hate of guilty men,
Lose his own innocence.
    Cic. The noble Cæsar
Speaks god-like truth. But when he hears I can
Convince him, by his manners, of his mischiefs,
He might be silent; and not cast away
His sentences in vain, where they scarce look
Toward his subject.

    Enter CATILINE, *and sits down by* CATO, *who quits his place.*

    Cato. Here he comes himself.
If he be worthy any good man's voice,
That good man sit down by him: Cato will not.
    Catu. If Cato leave him, I'll not keep aside.   [*Rises.*
    Cat. What face is this the senate here puts on
Against me, fathers? give my modesty
Leave to demand the cause of so much strangeness.
    Cæs. It is reported here, you are the head
To a strange faction, Lucius.
    Cic. Ay, and will
Be proved against him.
    Cat. Let it be. Why, consul,
If in the commonwealth there be two bodies,
One lean, weak, rotten, and that hath a head,
The other strong and healthful, but hath none;
If I do give it one, do I offend?
Restore your selves unto your temper, fathers,

And, without perturbation, hear me speak.
Remember who I am, and of what place,
What petty fellow this is that opposes;
One that hath exercised his eloquence
Still to the bane of the nobility,
A boasting, insolent tongue-man!—
　　Cato. Peace, lewd traitor,
Or wash thy mouth.　He is an honest man,
And loves his country; would thou didst so too.
　　Cat. Cato, you are too zealous for him.
　　Cato. No;
Thou art too impudent.
　　Catu. Catiline, be silent.
　　Cat. Nay then, I easily fear my just defence
Will come too late to so much prejudice.
　　Cæs. Will he sit down?　　　　　　　　　[*Aside.*
　　Cat. Yet let the world forsake me,
My innocence must not.
　　Cato. Thou innocent!
So are the furies.
　　Cic. Yes, and Até too.
Dost thou not blush, pernicious Catiline,
Or hath the paleness of thy guilt drunk up
Thy blood, and drawn thy veins as dry of that,
As is thy heart of truth, thy breast of virtue?
Whither at length wilt thou abuse our patience?
Still shall thy fury mock us! to what license
Dares thy unbridled boldness run itself!
Do all the nightly guards kept on the palace,
The city's watches, with the people's fears,
The concourse of all good men, this so strong
And fortified seat here of the senate,
The present looks upon thee, strike thee nothing?
Dost thou not feel thy counsels all laid open,
And see thy wild conspiracy bound in
With each man's knowledge?　Which of all this order
Canst thou think ignorant, if they will but utter
Their conscience to the right, of what thou didst
Last night, what on the former, where thou wert,
Whom thou didst call together, what your plots were?
O age and manners! this the consul sees,
The senate understands, yet this man lives!—
Lives! ay, and comes here into council with us,
Partakes the public cares, and with his eye
Marks and points out each man of us to slaughter.
And we, good men, do satisfy the state,
If we can shun but this man's sword and madness.
There was that virtue once in Rome, when good men
Would, with more sharp coercion, have restrain'd

A wicked citizen, than the deadliest foe.
We have that law still, Catiline, for thee;
An act as grave as sharp: the state's not wanting,
Nor the authority of this senate; we,
We that are consuls, only fail ourselves.
This twenty days the edge of that decree
We have let dull and rust; kept it shut up,
As in a sheath, which drawn, should take thy head.
Yet still thou liv'st: and liv'st not to lay by
Thy wicked confidence, but to confirm it.
I could desire, grave fathers, to be found
Still merciful, to seem, in these main perils
Grasping the state, a man remiss and slack;
But then I should condemn myself of sloth,
And treachery. Their camp's in Italy,
Pitch'd in the jaws here of Hetruria;
Their numbers daily increasing, and their general
Within our walls; nay, in our council! plotting
Hourly some fatal mischief to the public.
If, Catiline, I should command thee now,
Here to be taken, kill'd; I make just doubt,
Whether all good men would not think it done
Rather too late, than any man too cruel.

    Cato. Except he were of the same meal and batch.

    Cic. But that which ought to have been done long since,
I will, and for good reason, yet forbear.
Then will I take thee, when no man is found
So lost, so wicked, nay, so like thyself,
But shall profess, 'tis done of need and right.
While there is one that dares defend thee, live;
Thou shalt have leave, but so as now thou liv'st;
Watch'd at a hand, besieged, and opprest
From working least commotion to the state.
I have those eyes and ears shall still keep guard,
And spial on thee, as they've ever done,
And thou not feel it. What then canst thou hope?
If neither night can with her darkness hide
Thy wicked meetings, nor a private house
Can, in her walls, contain the guilty whispers
Of thy conspiracy: if all break out,
All be discover'd, change thy mind at last,
And lose thy thoughts of ruin, flame, and slaughter.
Remember how I told here to the senate,
That such a day thy lictor, Caius Manlius,
Would be in arms. Was I deceived, Catiline,
Or in the fact, or in the time, the hour?
I told too in this senate, that thy purpose
Was, on the fifth o' the kalends of November,
To have slaughter'd this whole order: which my caution

Made many leave the city. Canst thou here
Deny, but this thy black design was hinder'd
That very day, by me? thy self closed in
Within my strengths, so that thou could'st not move
Against a public reed; when thou wert heard
To say upon the parting of the rest,
Thou would'st content thee with the murder of us
That did remain? Hadst thou not hope beside,
By a surprise by night to take Præneste?
Where when thou cam'st, didst thou not find the place
Made good against thee with my aids, my watches?
My garrisons fortified it. Thou dost nothing, Sergius,
Thou canst endeavour nothing, nay, not think,
But I both see and hear it; and am with thee,
By and before, about and in thee too.
Call but to mind thy last night's business—Come,
I'll use no circumstance—at Lecca's house,
The shop and mint of your conspiracy,
Among your sword-men, where so many associates
Both of thy mischief and thy madness met.
Dar'st thou deny this? wherefore art thou silent?
Speak, and this shall convince thee: here they are,
I see them in this senate, that were with thee.
O, ye immortal Gods! in what clime are we,
What region do we live in, in what air?
What commonwealth or state is this we have?
Here, here, amongst us, our own number, fathers,
In this most holy council of the world
They are, that seek the spoil of me, of you,
Of ours, of all; what I can name's too narrow:
Follow the sun, and find not their ambition.
These I behold, being consul: nay, I ask
Their counsels of the state, as from good patriots:
Whom it were fit the axe should hew in pieces,
I not so much as wound yet with my voice.
Thou wast last night with Lecca, Catiline,
Your shares of Italy you there divided;
Appointed who, and whither each should go;
What men should stay behind in Rome, were chosen;
Your offices set down; the parts mark'd out,
And places of the city, for the fire;
Thy self, thou affirm'dst, wast ready to depart,
Only a little let there was that stay'd thee,
That I yet lived. Upon the word, stepp'd forth
Three of thy crew, to rid thee of that care;
Two undertook this morning, before day,
To kill me in my bed. All this I knew,
Your convent scarce dismiss'd, arm'd all my servants,
Call'd both my brother and friends, shut out your clients

You sent to visit me; whose names I told
To some there of good place, before they came.
   Cato. Yes, I, and Quintus Catulus can affirm it.
   Cæs. He's lost and gone! His spirits have forsook him. [*Aside.*
   Cic. If this be so, why, Catiline, dost thou stay?
Go where thou mean'st. The ports are open; forth!
The camp abroad wants thee, their chief too long.
Lead with thee all thy troops out; purge the city.
Draw dry that noisome and pernicious sink,
Which, left behind thee, would infect the world.
Thou wilt free me of all my fears at once,
To see a wall between us. Dost thou stop
To do that, now commanded, which, before,
Of thine own choice, thou wert prone to? Go! the consul
Bids thee, an enemy, to depart the city:
Whither, thou'lt ask, to exile? I not bid
Thee that: but ask my counsel, I persuade it.
What is there here in Rome, that can delight thee?
Where not a soul, without thine own foul knot,
But fears and hates thee. What domestic note
Of private filthiness, but is burnt in
Into thy life, what close and secret shame,
But is grown one with thine own infamy?
What lust was ever absent from thine eyes,
What lewd fact from thy hands, what wickedness
From thy whole body? where's that youth drawn in
Within thy nets, or catch'd up with thy baits,
Before whose rage thou hast not borne a sword,
And to whose lusts thou hast not held a torch?
Thy latter nuptials I let pass in silence,
Where sins incredible on sins were heap'd;
Which I not name, lest in a civil state
So monstrous facts should either appear to be,
Or not to be revenged. Thy fortunes too
I glance not at, which hang but till next ides.
I come to that which is more known, more public;
The life and safety of us all, by thee
Threaten'd and sought. Stood'st thou not in the field,
When Lepidus and Tullus were our consuls,
Upon the day of choice, arm'd, and with forces,
To take their lives, and our chief citizens?
When not thy fear, nor conscience changed thy mind,
But the mere fortune of the commonwealth
Withstood thy active malice? Speak but right.
How often hast thou made attempt on me?
How many of thy assaults have I declined
With shifting but my body, as we'd say?
Wrested thy dagger from thy hand, how oft?
How often hath it fallen, or slipt, by chance?

Yet can thy side not want it: which, how vow'd,
Or with what rites 'tis sacred of thee, I know not,
That still thou mak'st it a necessity,
To fix it in the body of a consul.
But let me lose this way, and speak to thee,
Not as one moved with hatred, which I ought,
But pity, of which none is owing thee.

    Cato. No more than unto Tantalus or Tityus.

    Cic. Thou cam'st erewhile into this senate: Who
Of such a frequency, so many friends
And kindred thou hast here, saluted thee?
Were not the seats made bare upon thy entrance?
Risse not the consular men, and left their places,
So soon as thou sat'st down, and fled thy side,
Like to a plague or ruin, knowing how oft
They had by thee been mark'd out for the shambles?
How dost thou bear this? Surely, if my slaves
At home fear'd me with half the affright and horror
That here thy fellow-citizens do thee,
I should soon quit my house, and think it need too.
Yet thou dar'st tarry here! go forth at last,
Condemn thyself to flight and solitude.
Discharge the commonwealth of her deep fear.—
Go; into banishment, if thou wait'st the word:
Why dost thou look? they all consent unto it.
Dost thou expect the authority of their voices,
Whose silent wills condemn thee? while they sit,
They approve it; while they suffer it, they decree it;
And while they are silent to it, they proclaim it.
Prove thou there honest, I'll endure the envy.
But there's no thought thou shouldst be ever he,
Whom either shame should call from filthiness,
Terror from danger, or discourse from fury.
Go; I entreat thee: yet why do I so?
When I already know they are sent afore,
That tarry for thee in arms, and do expect thee
On the Aurelian way. I know the day
Set down 'twixt thee and Manlius, unto whom
The silver eagle too is sent before;
Which I do hope shall prove to thee as baneful
As thou conceiv'st it to the commonwealth.
But, may this wise and sacred senate say,
What mean'st thou, Marcus Tullius? if thou know'st
That Catiline be look'd for to be chief
Of an intestine war; that he's the author
Of such a wickedness: the caller out
Of men of mark in mischief, to an action
Of so much horror; prince of such a treason;
Why dost thou send him forth? why let him 'scape?

This is to give him liberty and power:
Rather thou should'st lay hold upon him, send him
To deserv'd death, and a just punishment.
To these so holy voices thus I answer:
If I did think it timely, conscript fathers,
To punish him with death, I would not give
The fencer use of one short hour to breathe;
But when there are in this grave order some,
Who, with soft censures, still do nurse his hopes;
Some that, with not believing, have confirm'd
His designs more, and whose authority
The weaker, as the worst men too, have follow'd,
I would now send him where they all should see
Clear as the light, his heart shine; where no man
Could be so wickedly or fondly stupid,
But should cry out, he saw, touch'd, felt, and grasp'd it.
Then, when he hath run out himself, led forth
His desperate party with him, blown together
Aids of all kinds, both shipwreck'd minds and fortunes;
Not only the grown evil that now is sprung
And sprouted forth, would be pluck'd up and weeded,
But the stock, root, and seed of all the mischiefs
Choking the commonwealth: where, should we take,
Of such a swarm of traitors, only him,
Our cares and fears might seem awhile relieved,
But the main peril would bide still inclosed
Deep in the veins and bowels of the state.
As human bodies labouring with fevers,
While they are tost with heat, if they do take
Cold water, seem for that short space much eased,
But afterward are ten times more afflicted.
Wherefore, I say, let all this wicked crew
Depart, divide themselves from good men, gather
Their forces to one head; as I said oft,
Let them be sever'd from us with a wall;
Let them leave off attempts upon the consul
In his own house; to circle in the prætor;
To gird the court with weapons; to prepare
Fire and balls, swords, torches, sulphur, brands;
In short, let it be writ in each man's forehead
What thoughts he bears the public. I here promise,
Fathers conscript, to you, and to myself,
That diligence in us consuls, for my honour'd
Colleague abroad, and for myself at home;
So great authority in you; so much
Virtue in these, the gentlemen of Rome,
Whom I could scarce restrain to-day in zeal
From seeking out the parricide, to slaughter;
So much consent in all good men and minds,

As on the going out of this one Catiline,
All shall be clear, made plain, oppress'd, reveng'd.
And with this omen go, pernicious plague!
Out of the city, to the wish'd destruction
Of thee and those, that, to the ruin of her,
Have ta'en that bloody and black sacrament.
Thou, Jupiter, whom we do call the STAYER
Both of this city and this empire, wilt,
With the same auspice thou didst raise it first,
Drive from thy altars, and all other temples,
And buildings of this city, from our walls,
Lives, states and fortunes of our citizens,
This fiend, this fury, with his complices.
And all th' offence of good men, these known traitors
Unto their country, thieves of Italy,
Join'd in so damn'd a league of mischief, thou
Wilt with perpetual plagues, alive and dead,
Punish for Rome, and save her innocent head.

    Cat. If an oration, or high language, fathers,
Could make me guilty, here is one hath done it:
He has strove to emulate this morning's thunder,
With his prodigious rhetoric. But I hope
This senate is more grave than to give credit
Rashly to all he vomits, 'gainst a man
Of your own order, a patrician,
And one whose ancestors have more deserv'd
Of Rome than this man's eloquence could utter,
Turn'd the best way; as still it is the worst.

    Cato. His eloquence hath more deserv'd to-day,
Speaking thy ill, than all thy ancestors
Did, in their good; and that the state will find,
Which he hath saved.

    Cat. How, he! were I that enemy
That he would make me, I'd not wish the state
More wretched than to need his preservation.
What do you make him, Cato, such a Hercules?
An Atlas? a poor petty inmate!

    Cato. Traitor!

    Cat. He save the state! a burgess' son of Arpinum.
The gods would rather twenty Romes should perish
Than have that contumely stuck upon them,
That he should share with them in the preserving
A shed, or sign-post.

    Cato. Peace, thou prodigy!

    Cat. They would be forced themselves again, and lost
In the first rude and indigested heap,
Ere such a wretched name as Cicero
Should sound with theirs.

    Catu. Away, thou impudent head.

Cat. Do you all back him? are you silent too?
Well, I will leave you, fathers, I will go.

                     [He turns suddenly on Cicero.

But—my fine dainty speaker—

Cic. What now, fury,
Wilt thou assault me here?

Omnes. Help, aid the consul.

Cat. See, fathers, laugh you not? who threaten'd him?
In vain thou dost conceive, ambitious orator,
Hope of so brave a death as by this hand.

Cato. Out of the court with the pernicious traitor!

Cat. There is no title that this flattering senate,
Nor honour the base multitude can give thee,
Shall make thee worthy Catiline's anger.

Cato. Stop,
Stop that portentous mouth.

Cat. Or when it shall,
I'll look thee dead.

Cato. Will none restrain the monster?

Catu. Parricide!

Qui. Butcher! traitor! leave the senate.

Cat. I am gone to banishment, to please you, fathers,
Thrust headlong forth!

Cato. Still dost thou murmur, monster?

Cat. Since I am thus put out, and made a—

Cic. What?

Catu. Not guiltier than thou art.

Cat. I will not burn
Without my funeral pile.

Cato. What says the fiend?

Cat. I will have matter, timber.

Cato. Sing out, screech-owl.

Cat. It shall be in—

Catu. Speak thy imperfect thoughts.

Cat. The common fire, rather than mine own:
For fall I will with all, ere fall alone.   *[Rushes out of the Senate.*

Cra. He's lost, there is no hope of him.   *[Aside to Cæsar.*

Cæs. Unless
He presently take arms, and give a blow
Before the consul's forces can be levied.

Cic. What is your pleasure, fathers, shall be done?

Catu. See, that the commonwealth receive no loss.

Cato. Commit the care thereof unto the consuls.

Cra. 'Tis time.

Cæs. And need.   *[Goes aside with Crassus.*

Cic. Thanks to this frequent senate.
But what decree they unto Curius,
And Fulvia?

Catu. What the consul shall think meet.

Cic. They must receive reward, though it be not known;
Lest when a state needs ministers, they've none.

Cato. Yet, Marcus Tullius, do not I believe,
But Crassus and this Cæsar here ring hollow.

Cic. And would appear so, if that we durst prove them.

Cato. Why dare we not? what honest act is that,
The Roman senate should not dare and do!

Cic. Not an unprofitable dangerous act,
To stir too many serpents up at once.
Cæsar and Crassus, if they be ill men,
Are mighty ones; and we must so provide,
That while we take one head from this foul hydra,
There spring not twenty more.

Cato. I approve your counsel.

Cic. They shall be watch'd and look'd to. Till they do
Declare themselves, I will not put them out
By any question. There they stand. I'll make
Myself no enemies, nor the state no traitors.   [*Exeunt*

SCENE III.—CATILINE'S *House.*

Enter CATILINE, LENTULUS, CETHEGUS, CURIUS, GABINIUS,
LONGINUS, *and* STATILIUS.

Cat. False to ourselves? all our designs discover'd
To this state-cat?

Cet. Ay; had I had my way,
He had mew'd in flames at home, not in the senate;
I had singed his furs by this time.

Cat. Well, there's now
No time of calling back, or standing still.
Friends, be yourselves; keep the same Roman hearts
And ready minds you had yester-night. Prepare
To execute what we resolv'd; and let not
Labour, or danger, or discovery fright you.
I'll to the army; you, the while, mature
Things here at home: draw to you any aids
That you think fit, of men of all conditions,
Of any fortunes, that may help a war.
I'll bleed a life, or win an empire for you.
Within these few days look to see my ensigns
Here, at the walls: be you but firm within.
Mean time, to draw an envy on the consul,
And give a less suspicion of our course,
Let it be given out here in the city,
That I am gone, an innocent man, to exile
Into Massilia; willing to give way
To fortune and the times; being unable
To stand so great a faction, without troubling

The commonwealth; whose peace I rather seek,
Than all the glory of contention,
Or the support of mine own innocence.
Farewell the noble Lentulus, Longinus,
Curius, the rest! and thou, my better genius,
The brave Cethegus: when we meet again,
We'll sacrifice to liberty.

 Cet. And revenge;
That we may praise our hands once.

 Len. O ye fates,
Give fortune now her eyes, to see with whom
She goes along, that she may ne'er forsake him.

 Cur. He needs not her nor them. Go but on, Sergius:
A valiant man is his own fate and fortune.

 Lon. The fate and fortune of us all go with him.

 Gab. Sta. And ever guard him!

 Cat. I am all your creature.   [*Exit.*

 Len. Now, friends, 'tis left with us. I have already
Dealt by Umbrenus with the Allobroges
Here resiant in Rome; whose state, I hear,
Is discontent with the great usuries
They are oppress'd with: and have made complaints
Divers unto the senate, but all vain.
These men I have thought (both for their own oppressions,
As also that by nature they're a people
Warlike and fierce, still watching after change,
And now in present hatred with our state,)
The fittest, and the easiest to be drawn
To our society, and to aid the war:
The rather for their seat; being next borderers
On Italy; and that they abound with horse,
Of which one want our camp doth only labour:
And I have found them coming. They will meet
Soon at Sempronia's house, where I would pray you
All to be present, to confirm them more.
The sight of such spirits hurts not, nor the store.

 Gab. I will not fail.

 Sta. Nor I.

 Cur. Nor I.

 Cet. Would I
Had somewhat by myself apart to do;
I have no genius to these many counsels:
Let me kill all the senate for my share,
I'll do it at next sitting.

 Len. Worthy Caius,
Your presence will add much.

 Cet. I shall mar more.

             [*Exeunt.*

SCENE IV.—*The House of* BRUTUS.

Enter CICERO *and* SANGA.

Cic. The state's beholden to you, Fabius Sanga,
For this great care: and those Allobroges
Are more than wretched, if they lend a listening
To such persuasion.
    San. They, most worthy consul,
As men employ'd here from a grieved state,
Groaning beneath a multitude of wrongs,
And being told there was small hope of ease
To be expected to their evils from hence,
Were willing at the first to give an ear
To anything that sounded liberty:
But since, on better thoughts, and my urg'd reasons,
They're come about, and won to the true side.
The fortune of the commonwealth has conquer'd.
    Cic. What is that same Umbrenus was the agent?
    San. One that hath had negociation
In Gallia oft, and known unto their state.
    Cic. Are the ambassadors come with you?
    San. Yes.
    Cic. Well, bring them in; if they be firm and honest,
Never had men the means so to deserve
Of Rome as they. [*Exit Sanga.*] A happy wish'd occasion,
And thrust into my hands for the discovery
And manifest conviction of these traitors:
Be thank'd, O Jupiter!

Re-enter SANGA, *with the* Allobrogian Ambassadors.

               My worthy lords,
Confederates of the senate, you are welcome!
I understand by Quintus Fabius Sanga,
Your careful patron here, you have been lately
Solicited against the commonwealth,
By one Umbrenus—take a seat, I pray you—
From Publius Lentulus, to be associates
In their intended war. I could advise,
That men whose fortunes are yet flourishing,
And are Rome's friends, would not without a cause
Become her enemies; and mix themselves
And their estates with the lost hopes of Catiline,
Or Lentulus, whose mere despair doth arm them:
That were to hazard certainties for air,
And undergo all danger for a voice.
Believe me, friends, loud tumults are not laid
With half the easiness that they are raised:
All may begin a war, but few can end it.

The senate have decreed that my colleague
Shall lead their army against Catiline,
And have declared both him and Manlius traitors:
Metellus Celer hath already given
Part of their troops defeat.   Honours are promised
To all will quit them; and rewards proposed
Even to slaves, that can detect their courses.
Here in the city, I have, by the prætors
And tribunes, placed my guards and watches so,
That not a foot can tread, a breath can whisper,
But I have knowledge.   And be sure, the senate
And people of Rome, of their accustom'd greatness,
Will sharply and severely vindicate
Not only any fact, but any practice
Or purpose 'gainst the state: therefore, my lords,
Consult of your own ways, and think which hand
Is best to take.   You now are present suitors
For some redress of wrongs: I'll undertake
Not only that shall be assured you; but
What grace, or privilege else, senate or people
Can cast upon you worthy such a service,
As you have now the way and means to do them,
If but your wills consent with my designs.

  1 *Amb.* We covet nothing more, most worthy consul.
And howsoe'er we have been tempted lately
To a defection, that not makes us guilty:
We are not yet so wretched in our fortunes,
Nor in our wills so lost, as to abandon
A friendship, prodigally, of that price,
As is the senate and the people of Rome's,
For hopes that do precipitate themselves.

  Cic. You then are wise and honest.   Do but this then—
When shall you speak with Lentulus and the rest?

  1 *Amb.* We are to meet anon at Brutus' house.

  Cic. Who, Decius Brutus? he is not in Rome.

  San. O, but his wife Sempronia.

  Cic. You instruct me,
She is a chief.   Well, fail not you to meet them,
And to express the best affection
You can put on, to all that they intend.
Like it, applaud it, give the commonwealth
And senate lost to 'em: promise any aids
By arms or counsel.   What they can desire,
I would have you prevent.   Only say this,
You have had dispatch in private by the consul,
Of your affairs; and for the many fears
The state's now in, you are will'd by him this evening
To depart Rome: which you, by all sought means,
Will do, of reason, to decline suspicion.

Now for the more authority of the business
They have trusted to you, and to give it credit
With your own state at home, you would desire
Their letters to your senate and your people,
Which shewn, you durst engage both life and honour,
The rest should every way answer their hopes.
Those had, pretend sudden departure, you,
And as you give me notice at what port
You will go out, I'll have you intercepted,
And all the letters taken with you: so
As you shall be redeem'd in all opinions,
And they convicted of their manifest treason.
Ill deeds are well turn'd back upon their authors:
And 'gainst an injurer the revenge is just.
This must be done now.

   1 Amb. Cheerfully and firmly,
We are they would rather haste to undertake it,
Than stay to say so.

   Cic. With that confidence, go:
Make yourselves happy while you make Rome so.
By Sanga let me have notice from you.

   1 Amb. Yes.

                               [Exeunt.

SCENE V.—*A Room in* Brutus' (Sempronia's) *House.*

Enter Sempronia *and* Lentulus.

   Sem. When come these creatures, the ambassadors?
I would fain see them.   Are they any scholars?

   Len. I think not, madam.

   Sem. Have they no Greek?

   Len. No surely.

   Sem. Fie, what do I here waiting on 'em then,
If they be nothing but mere statesmen?

   Len. Yes,
Your ladyship shall observe their gravity,
And their reservedness, their many cautions,
Fitting their persons.

   Sem. I do wonder much,
That states and commonwealths employ not women
To be ambassadors, sometimes; we should
Do as good public service, and could make
As honourable spies, for so Thucydides
Calls all ambassadors—

Enter Cethegus.

                Are they come, Cethegus?

   Cet. Do you ask me! am I your scout or bawd?

   Len. O, Caius, it is no such business.

   Cet. No!

What does a woman at it then?

Sem. Good sir,
There are of us can be as exquisite traitors,
As e'er a male-conspirator of you all.

Cet. Ay, at smock-treason, matron, I believe you;
And if I were your husband;—but when I
Trust to your cobweb-bosoms any other,
Let me there die a fly, and feast you, spider.

Len. You are too sour and harsh, Cethegus.

Cet. You
Are kind and courtly. I'd be torn in pieces,
With wild Hippolytus, nay prove the death
Every limb over, ere I'd trust a woman
With wind, could I retain it.

Sem. Sir, they'll be trusted
With as good secrets yet as you have any;
And carry them too as close and as conceal'd,
As you shall for your heart.

Cet. I'll not contend with you
Either in tongue or carriage, good Calypso.

Enter LONGINUS.

Lon. The ambassadors are come.

Cet. Thanks to thee, Mercury,
That so hast rescued me!

Enter VOLTURTIUS, STATILIUS, *and* GABINIUS, *with the*
Allobrogian Ambassadors.

Len. How now, Volturtius?

Vol. They do desire some speech with you in private.

Len. O! 'tis about the prophecy belike,
And promise of the Sibyls.   [*He takes them apart.*

Gab. It may be.

Sem. Shun they to treat with me too?

Gab. No, good lady,
You may partake; I have told them who you are.

Sem. I should be loth to be left out, and here too.

Cet. Can these, or such, be any aids to us?
Look they as they were built to shake the world,
Or be a moment to our enterprize?
A thousand such as they are, could not make
One atom of our souls.   They should be men
Worth heaven's fear, that looking up but thus,
Would make Jove stand upon his guard, and draw
Himself within his thunder; which, amazed,
He should discharge in vain, and they unhurt:
Or if they were like Capaneus at Thebes,
They should hang dead upon the highest spires,
And ask the second bolt to be thrown down.—

Why, Lentulus, talk you so long? this time
Had been enough to have scatter'd all the stars,
To have quench'd the sun and moon, and made the world
Despair of day, or any light but ours.

    Len. How do you like this spirit?   In such men
Mankind doth live: they are such souls as these,
That move the world.

    Sem. Ay, though he bear me hard,
I yet must do him right: he is a spirit
Of the right Martian breed.

    1 *Amb.* He is a Mars.
Would we had time to live here, and admire him!

    Len. Well, I do see you would prevent the consul,
And I commend your care; it was but reason,
To ask our letters, and we had prepared them:
Go in, and we will take an oath, and seal them.
You shall have letters too to Catiline,
To visit him i' the way, and to confirm
The association.   This our friend, Volturtius,
Shall go along with you.   Tell our great general
That we are ready here; that Lucius Bestia,
The tribune, is provided of a speech,
To lay the envy of the war on Cicero;
That all but long for his approach and person:
And then you are made freemen as ourselves.   [*Exeunt.*

SCENE VI.—*A Room in* CICERO's *House.*

Enter CICERO, FLACCUS, *and* POMTINIUS.

    Cic. I cannot fear the war but to succeed well,
Both for the honour of the cause, and worth
Of him that doth command: for my colleague,
Being so ill affected with the gout,
Will not be able to be there in person;
And then Petreius, his lieutenant, must
Of need take charge o' the army; who is much
The better soldier, having been a tribune,
Præfect, lieutenant, prætor in the war,
These thirty years, so conversant in the army,
As he knows all the soldiers by their names.

    Flac. They'll fight then bravely with him.

    Pom. Ay, and he
Will lead them on as bravely.

    Cic. They have a foe
Will ask their braveries, whose necessities
Will arm him like a fury: but, however,
I'll trust it to the manage and the fortune
Of good Petreius, who's a worthy patriot:

Metellus Celer, with three legions too,
Will stop their course for Gallia.

Enter FABIUS SANGA.

How now, Fabius?
San. The train hath taken. You must instantly
Dispose your guards upon the Milvian bridge,
For by that way they mean to come.
Cic. Then thither,
Pomtinius and Flaccus, I must pray you
To lead that force you have, and seize them all;
Let not a person 'scape: the ambassadors
Will yield themselves. If there be any tumult,
I'll send you aid. [*Exeunt Flaccus and Pomtinius.*] I, in mean
time, will call
Lentulus to me, Gabinius, and Cethegus,
Statilius, Ceparius, and all these,
By several messengers: who no doubt will come
Without sense or suspicion. Prodigal men
Feel not their own stock wasting. When I have them,
I'll place those guards upon them, that they start not.
San. But what will you do with Sempronia?
Cic. A state's anger
Should not take knowledge either of fools or women.
I do not know whether my joy or care
Ought to be greater, that I have discover'd
So foul a treason, or must undergo
The envy of so many great men's fate.
But happen what there can, I will be just;
My fortune may forsake me, not my virtue:
That shall go with me, and before me still,
And glad me doing well, though I hear ill.   [*Exeunt.*

SCENE VII.—*The Milvian Bridge.*

Enter FLACCUS *and* POMTINIUS, *with* Guards, *on one side, and*
VOLTURTIUS, *with the* Allobrogian Ambassadors, *on the other.*

Flac. Stand! who goes there?
1 *Amb.* We are the Allobroges,
And friends of Rome.
Pom. If you be so, then yield
Yourselves unto the prætors, who, in name
Of the whole senate, and the people of Rome,
Yet till you clear yourselves, charge you of practice
Against the state.
Vol. Die, friends; and be not taken.
Flac. What voice is that? down with them all.
1 *Amb.* We yield.
Pom. What's he stands out? Kill him there.

Vol. Hold, hold, hold.
I yield upon conditions.
　Flac. We give none
To traitors; strike him down.
　Vol. My name's Volturtius,
I know Pomtinius.
　Pom. But he knows not you,
While you stand out upon these traitorous terms.
　Vol. I'll yield upon the safety of my life.
　Pom. If it be forfeited, we cannot save it.
　Vol. Promise to do your best.　I'm not so guilty
As many others I can name, and will,
If you will grant me favour.
　Pom. All we can,
Is to deliver you to the consul.—Take him,
And thank the gods that thus have saved Rome.　　　*[Exeunt.*

CHORUS.

Now do our ears, before our eyes,
　Like men in mists,
Discover who'd the state surprise,
　And who resists?

And as these clouds do yield to light,
　Now do we see
Our thoughts of things, how they did fight,
　Which seem'd t' agree?

Of what strange pieces are we made,
　Who nothing know;
But as new airs our ears invade,
　Still censure so?

That now do hope and now do fear
　And now envy;
And then do hate and then love dear,
　But know not why:

Or if we do, it is so late,
　As our best mood,
Though true, is then thought out of date,
　And empty of good.

How have we changed and come about
　In every doom,
Since wicked Catiline went out,
　And quitted Rome?

One while we thought him innocent;
　And then we accused
The consul, for his malice spent,
　And power abused.

Since that we hear he is in arms,
  We think not so:
Yet charge the consul with our harms,
  That let him go.

So in our censure of the state,
  We still do wander;
And make the careful magistrate
  The mark of slander.

What age is this, where honest men,
  Placed at the helm,
A sea of some foul mouth or pen
  Shall overwhelm?

And call their diligence, deceit;
  Their virtue, vice;
Their watchfulness, but lying in wait;
  And blood, the price?

O, let us pluck this evil seed
  Out of our spirits:
And give to every noble deed
  The name it merits.

Lest we seem fallen, if this endures,
  Into those times,
To love disease, and brook the cures
  Worse than the crimes.

ACT V

SCENE I.—ETRURIA. *The Country near* FESULÆ.
Enter PETREIUS, *marching, at the head of his Army.*

  Pet. It is my fortune and my glory, soldiers,
This day, to lead you on; the worthy consul
Kept from the honour of it by disease:
And I am proud to have so brave a cause
To exercise your arms in. We not now
Fight for how long, how broad, how great, and large
Th' extent and bounds o' the people of Rome shall be;
But to retain what our great ancestors,
With all their labours, counsels, arts, and actions,
For us, were purchasing so many years.
The quarrel is not now of fame, of tribute,
Or of wrongs done unto confederates,
For which the army of the people of Rome
Was wont to move: but for your own republic,
For the raised temples of the immortal gods,

For all your fortunes, altars, and your fires,
For the dear souls of your loved wives and children,
Your parents' tombs, your rites, laws, liberty,
And, briefly, for the safety of the world;
Against such men, as only by their crimes
Are known; thrust out by riot, want, or rashness.
One sort, Sylla's old troops, left here in Fesulæ,
Who, suddenly made rich in those dire times,
Are since, by their unbounded, vast expense,
Grown needy and poor; and have but left to expect
From Catiline new bills, and new proscriptions.
These men, they say, are valiant: yet, I think them
Not worth your pause: for either their old virtue
Is in their sloth and pleasures lost; or, if
It tarry with them, so ill match to yours,
As they are short in number or in cause.
The second sort are of those city-beasts,
Rather than citizens, who, whilst they reach
After our fortunes, have let fly their own;
These whelm'd in wine, swell'd up with meats, and weaken'd
With hourly whoredoms, never left the side
Of Catiline in Rome; nor here are loosed
From his embraces: such as, trust me, never
In riding or in using well their arms,
Watching, or other military labour,
Did exercise their youth; but learn'd to love,
Drink, dance, and sing, make feasts, and be fine gamesters:
And these will wish more hurt to you than they bring you.
The rest are a mixt kind, all sorts of furies,
Adulterers, dicers, fencers, outlaws, thieves,
The murderers of their parents, all the sink
And plague of Italy met in one torrent,
To take, to-day, from us the punishment,
Due to their mischiefs, for so many years.
And who in such a cause, and 'gainst such fiends,
Would not now wish himself all arm and weapon,
To cut such poisons from the earth, and let
Their blood out to be drawn away in clouds,
And pour'd on some inhabitable place,
Where the hot sun and slime breeds nought but monsters?
Chiefly when this sure joy shall crown our side,
That the least man that falls upon our party
This day, (as some must give their happy names
To fate, and that eternal memory
Of the best death, writ with it, for their country,)
Shall walk at pleasure in the tents of rest;
And see far off, beneath him, all their host
Tormented after life; and Catiline there
Walking a wretched and less ghost than he.

I'll urge no more: move forward with your eagles,
And trust the senate's and Rome's cause to heaven.
   Omnes. To thee, great father Mars, and greater Jove! [*Exeunt.*

SCENE II.—ROME. *A Street near the Temple of Concord.*

Enter CÆSAR *and* CRASSUS.

Cæs. I ever look'd for this of Lentulus,
When Catiline was gone.
   Cras. I gave them lost,
Many days since.
   Cæs. But wherefore did you bear
Their letter to the consul, that they sent you
To warn you from the city?
   Cras. Did I know
Whether he made it? it might come from him,
For aught I could assure me: if they meant
I should be safe among so many, they might
Have come as well as writ.
   Cæs. There is no loss
In being secure: I have of late too plied him
Thick with intelligences, but they have been
Of things he knew before.
   Cras. A little serves
To keep a man upright on these state-bridges,
Although the passage were more dangerous:
Let us now take the standing part.
   Cæs. We must,
And be as zealous for't as Cato. Yet,
I would fain help these wretched men.
   Cras. You cannot:
Who would save them, that have betray'd themselves? [*Exeunt.*

SCENE III.—CICERO'S *House.*

Enter CICERO, Q. CICERO, *and* CATO.

Cic. I will not be wrought to it, brother Quintus.
There's no man's private enmity shall make
Me violate the dignity of another.
If there were proof 'gainst Cæsar, or whoever,
To speak him guilty, I would so declare him.
But Quintus Catulus and Piso both
Shall know, the consul will not, for their grudge,
Have any man accused or named falsely.
   Quin. Not falsely: but if any circumstance,
By the Allobroges, or from Volturtius,
Would carry it.
   Cic. That shall not be sought by me.
If it reveal itself, I would not spare

You, brother, if it pointed at you, trust me.
  Cato. *Good* Marcus Tullius, which is more than *great*,
Thou had'st thy education with the gods.
  Cic. Send Lentulus forth, and bring away the rest.
This office I am sorry, sir, to do you.   [*Exeunt.*

SCENE IV.—*The Temple of Concord.*

Enter Lictors, CICERO, (*with letters,*) CATO, Q. CICERO, CÆSAR,
            CRASSUS, SYLLANUS, *and other* Senators.

  Cic. What may be happy still and fortunate,
To Rome and to this senate! Please you, fathers,
To break these letters, and to view them round,
If that be not found in them which I fear,
I yet entreat, at such a time as this,
My diligence be not contemn'd.—   [*Gives the letters to the Senate.*

Enter (*the* Prætors) FLACCUS *and* POMTINIUS.

                              Have you brought
The weapons hither from Cethegus' house?
  Præ. They are without.
  Cic.   Be ready, with Volturtius,
To bring him when the senate calls; and see
None of the rest confer together.   [*Exeunt Prætors.*]—Fathers,
What do you read? Is it yet worth your care,
If not your fear, what you find practised there?
  Cæs. It hath a face of horror!
  Cras. I am amazed!
  Cato. Look there.
  Syl. Gods! can such men draw common air?
  Cic. Although the greatness of the mischief, fathers,
Hath often made my faith small in this senate,
Yet since my casting Catiline out, (for now
I do not fear the envy of the word,
Unless the deed be rather to be fear'd,
That he went hence alive, when those I meant
Should follow him did not,) I have spent both days
And nights in watching what their fury and rage
Was bent on, that so stay'd against my thought;
And that I might but take them in that light,
Where, when you met their treason with your eyes,
Your minds at length would think for your own safety:
And now 'tis done. There are their hands and seals.
Their persons too are safe, thanks to the gods!
Bring in Volturtius and the Allobroges.

Re-enter Prætors, *with* VOLTURTIUS *and the* Allobrogian
                        Ambassadors.

These be the men were trusted with their letters.
  Vol. Fathers, believe me, I knew nothing; I

Was travelling for Gallia, and am sorry—

Cic. Quake not, Volturtius; speak the truth, and hope
Well of this senate, on the consul's word.

Vol. Then, I knew all: but truly, I was drawn in
But t'other day.

Cæs. Say what thou know'st, and fear not,
Thou hast the senate's faith and consul's word,
To fortify thee.

Vol. [*speaks with fears and interruptions.*] I was sent with
letters—
And had a message too—from Lentulus—
To Catiline—that he should use all aids—
Servants or others—and come with his army,
As soon unto the city as he could—
For they were ready, and but stay'd for him—
To intercept those that should flee the fire:
These men, the Allobroges, did hear it too.

1 *Amb.* Yes, fathers, and they took an oath to us,
Besides their letters, that we should be free;
And urged us for some present aid of horse.

                         [*The weapons and arms are brought in.*

Cic. Nay, here be other testimonies, fathers,
Cethegus' armoury.

Cras. What, not all these?

Cic. Here's not the hundred part. Call in the fencer,
That we may know the arms to all these weapons.

               Enter CETHEGUS, *guarded.*

Come, my brave sword-player, to what active use
Was all this steel provided?

Cet. Had you ask'd
In Sylla's days, it had been to cut throats;
But now it was to look on only: I loved
To see good blades, and feel their edge and points,
To put a helm upon a block and cleave it,
And now and then to stab an armour through.

Cic. Know you that paper? that will stab you through.
Is it your hand? [*Cethegus tears the letters*] hold, save the pieces.
      Traitor,
Hath thy guilt waked thy fury?

Cet. I did write
I know not what, nor care not; that fool Lentulus
Did dictate, and I, t'other fool, did sign it.

Cic. Bring in Statilius: does he know his hand too?
And Lentulus.

     Enter STATILIUS *and* P. LENTULUS, *guarded.*

         Reach him that letter.

Stat. I
Confess it all.

Cic. Know you that seal yet, Publius?

Len. Yes, it is mine.

Cic. Whose image is that on it?

Len. My grandfather's.

Cic. What, that renown'd good man,
That did so only embrace his country, and loved
His fellow-citizens! Was not his picture,
Though mute, of power to call thee from a fact
So foul—

Len. As what, impetuous Cicero?

Cic. As thou art, for I do not know what's fouler.
Look upon these. [*Points to the Allobrogian Ambassadors.*] Do
      not these faces argue
Thy guilt and impudence?

Len. What are these to me?
I know them not.

1 *Amb.* No, Publius! we were with you
At Brutus' house.

Vol. Last night.

Len. What did you there?
Who sent for you?

1 *Amb.* Yourself did. We had letters
From you, Cethegus, this Statilius here,
Gabinius Cimber, all but from Longinus,
Who would not write, because he was to come
Shortly in person after us, he said,
To take the charge of the horse, which we should levy.

Cic. And he is fled to Catiline, I hear.

Len. Spies! spies!

1 *Amb.* You told us too o' the Sibyl's books,
And how you were to be a king this year,
The twentieth from the burning of the capitol;
That three Cornelii were to reign in Rome,
Of which you were the last: and praised Cethegus,
And the great spirits were with you in the action.

Cet. These are your honourable ambassadors,
My sovereign lord!

Cato. Peace, that too bold Cethegus.

1 *Amb.* Besides Gabinius, your agent, named
Autronius, Servius Sylla, Vargunteius,
And divers others.

Vol. I had letters from you
To Catiline, and a message, which I've told
Unto the senate truly word for word;
For which I hope they will be gracious to me.
I was drawn in by that same wicked Cimber,
And thought no hurt at all.

Cic. Volturtius, peace.—
Where is thy visor or thy voice now, Lentulus?

Art thou confounded? wherefore speak'st thou not?
Is all so clear, so plain, so manifest,
That both thy eloquence and impudence,
And thy ill nature too, have left thee at once?
Take him aside. There's yet one more, Gabinius,
The enginer of all. [*Gabinius Cimber is brought in.*] Shew him
    that paper,
If he do know it?
  Gab. I know nothing.
  Cic. No!
  Gab. No; neither will I know.
  Cato. Impudent head!
Stick it into his throat; were I the consul,
I'd make thee eat the mischief thou hast vented.
  Gab. Is there a law for't, Cato?
  Cato. Dost thou ask
After a law, that would'st have broke all laws
Of nature, manhood, conscience, and religion?
  Gab. Yes, I may ask for't.
  Cato. No, pernicious Cimber.
The inquiring after good does not belong
Unto a wicked person.
  Gab. Ay, but Cato
Does nothing but by law.
  Cras. Take him aside.
There's proof enough, though he confess not.
  Gab. Stay,
I will confess. All's true your spies have told you,
Make much of them.
  Cet. Yes, and reward them well,
For fear you get no more such. See they do not
Die in a ditch, and stink, now you have done with 'em;
Or beg o' the bridges here in Rome, whose arches
Their active industry hath saved.
  Cic. See, fathers,
What minds and spirits these are, that being convicted
Of such a treason, and by such a cloud
Of witnesses, dare yet retain their boldness!
What would their rage have done if they had conquer'd?
I thought when I had thrust out Catiline,
Neither the state nor I should need to have fear'd
Lentulus' sleep here, or Longinus' fat,
Or this Cethegus' rashness; it was he
I only watch'd, while he was in our walls,
As one that had the brain, the hand, the heart.
But now we find the contrary! where was there
A people grieved, or a state discontent,
Able to make or help a war 'gainst Rome,
But these, the Allobroges, and those they found?

Whom had not the just gods been pleased to make
More friends unto our safety than their own,
As it then seem'd, neglecting these men's offers,
Where had we been, or where the commonwealth?
When their great chief had been call'd home; this man,
Their absolute king, (whose noble grandfather,
Arm'd in pursuit of the seditious Gracchus,
Took a brave wound for dear defence of that
Which he would spoil,) had gather'd all his aids
Of ruffians, slaves, and other slaughtermen,
Given us up for murder to Cethegus,
The other rank of citizens to Gabinius,
The city to be fired by Cassius,
And Italy, nay the world, to be laid waste
By cursed Catiline and his complices.
Lay but the thought of it before you, fathers,
Think but with me you saw this glorious city,
The light of all the earth, tower of all nations,
Suddenly falling in one flame!   Imagine
You view'd your country buried with the heaps
Of slaughter'd citizens that had no grave;
This Lentulus here, reigning, as he dreamt,
And those his purple senate; Catiline come
With his fierce army; and the cries of matrons,
The flight of children, and the rape of virgins,
Shrieks of the living, with the dying groans,
On every side t' invade your sense; until
The blood of Rome were mixed with her ashes!
This was the spectacle these fiends intended
To please their malice.

 Cet. Ay, and it would
Have been a brave one, consul.   But your part
Had not then been so long as now it is:
I should have quite defeated your oration,
And slit that fine rhetorical pipe of yours,
In the first scene.

 Cato. Insolent monster!

 Cic. Fathers,
Is it your pleasures they shall be committed
Unto some safe, but a free custody,
Until the senate can determine farther?

 Omnes. It pleaseth well.

 Cic. Then, Marcus Crassus,
Take you charge of Gabinius; send him home
Unto your house.   You, Cæsar, of Statilius.
Cethegus shall be sent to Cornificius;
And Lentulus to Publius Lentulus Spinther,
Who now is ædile.

 Cato. It were best, the prætors

Carried them to their houses, and deliver'd 'em.
 Cic. Let it be so. Take them from hence.
 Cæs. But first
Let Lentulus put off his prætorship.
  Len. I do resign it here unto the senate.
   [*Exeunt Prætors and Guards, with Lentulus, Cethegus,
    Statilius, and Gabinius.*
  Cæs. So, now there's no offence done to religion.
  Cato. Cæsar, 'twas piously and timely urged.
  Cic. What do you decree to the Allobroges,
That were the lights to this discovery?
  Cras. A free grant from the state of all their suits.
  Cæs. And a reward out of the public treasure.
  Cato. Ay, and the title of honest men, to crown them.
  Cic. What to Volturtius?
  Cæs. Life and favour's well.
  Vol. I ask no more.
  Cato. Yes, yes, some money, thou need'st it:
'Twill keep thee honest; want made thee a knave.
  Syl. Let Flaccus and Pomtinius, the prætors,
Have public thanks, and Quintus Fabius Sanga,
For their good service.
  Cras. They deserve it all.
  Cato. But what do we decree unto the consul,
Whose virtue, counsel, watchfulness, and wisdom
Hath freed the commonwealth, and without tumult,
Slaughter, or blood, or scarce raising a force,
Rescued us all out of the jaws of fate?
  Cras. We owe our lives unto him, and our fortunes.
  Cæs. Our wives, our children, parents and our gods.
  Syl. We all are saved by his fortitude.
  Cato. The commonwealth owes him a civic garland:
He is the only father of his country.
  Cæs. Let there be public prayer to all the gods,
Made in that name for him.
  Cras. And in these words:
*For that he hath, by his vigilance, preserv'd
Rome from the flame, the senate from the sword,
And all her citizens from massacre.*
  Cic. How are my labours more than paid, grave fathers,
In these great titles, and decreed honours!
Such as to me, first of the civil robe,
Of any man since Rome was Rome, have happen'd;
And from this frequent senate: which more glads me,
That I now see you have sense of your own safety.
If those good days come no less grateful to us,
Wherein we are preserv'd from some great danger,
Than those wherein we're born and brought to light,
Because the gladness of our safety is certain,

But the condition of our birth not so;
And that we are sav'd with pleasure, but are born
Without the sense of joy: why should not then
This day, to us, and all posterity
Of ours, be had in equal fame and honour,
With that when Romulus first rear'd these walls,
When so much more is saved, than he built?
 Cæs. It ought.
 Cras. Let it be added to our Fasti.   [*Noise without.*
 Cic. What tumult's that?

Re-enter FLACCUS.

 Flac. Here's one Tarquinius taken,
Going to Catiline, and says he was sent
By Marcus Crassus, whom he names to be
Guilty of the conspiracy.
 Cic. Some lying varlet.
Take him away to prison.
 Cras. Bring him in,
And let me see him.
 Cic. He is not worth it, Crassus.
Keep him up close and hungry, till he tell
By whose pernicious counsel he doth slander
So great and good a citizen.
 Cras. By yours,
I fear, 'twill prove.   [*Aside.*
 Syl. Some of the traitors, sure
To give their action the more credit, bid him
Name you, or any man.
 Cic. I know myself,
By all the tracts and courses of this business,
Crassus is noble, just, and loves his country.
 Flac. Here is a libel too, accusing Cæsar,
From Lucius Vectius, and confirm'd by Curius.
 Cic. Away with all, throw it out o' the court.
 Cæs. A trick on me too!
 Cic. It is some men's malice.
I said to Curius I did not believe him.
 Cæs. Was not that Curius your spy, that had
Reward decreed unto him the last senate,
With Fulvia, upon your private motion?
 Cic. Yes.
 Cæs. But he has not that reward yet?
 Cic. No.
Let not this trouble you, Cæsar; none believes it.
 Cæs. It shall not, if that he have no reward:
But if he have, sure I shall think myself
Very untimely and unsafely honest,
Where such as he is may have pay to accuse me.

Cic. You shall have no wrong done you, noble Cæsar,
But all contentment.
  Cæs. Consul, I am silent.   [*Exeunt.*

SCENE V.—*The Country near* FESULÆ.

Enter CATILINE *with his Army.*

  Cat. I never yet knew, soldiers, that in fight
Words added virtue unto valiant men;
Or that a general's oration made
An army fall or stand: but how much prowess,
Habitual or natural, each man's breast
Was owner of, so much in act it shew'd.
Whom neither glory, or danger can excite,
'Tis vain to attempt with speech; for the mind's fear
Keeps all brave sounds from entering at that ear.
I yet would warn you some few things, my friends,
And give you reason of my present counsels.
You know, no less than I, what state, what point
Our affairs stand in; and you all have heard
What a calamitous misery the sloth
And sleepiness of Lentulus hath pluck'd
Both on himself, and us; how, whilst our aids
There, in the city, look'd for, are defeated,
Our entrance into Gallia too is stopt.
Two armies wait us; one from Rome, the other
From the Gaul provinces: and where we are,
Although I most desire it, the great want
Of corn and victuals forbids longer stay:
So that of need we must remove, but whither,
The sword must both direct, and cut the passage.
I only therefore wish you, when you strike,
To have your valours and your souls about you;
And think you carry in your labouring hands
The things you seek, glory, and liberty,
Your country, which you want now, with the fates,
That are to be instructed by our swords.
If we can give the blow, all will be safe to us,
We shall not want provision, nor supplies.
The colonies and free towns will lie open;
Where, if we yield to fear, expect no place,
Nor friend, to shelter those whom their own fortune,
And ill-used arms, have left without protection.
You might have lived in servitude, or exile,
Or safe at Rome, depending on the great ones;
But that you thought those things unfit for men;
And, in that thought, you then were valiant:
For no man ever yet changed peace for war,
But he that meant to conquer. Hold that purpose.

There's more necessity you should be such,
In fighting for yourselves, than they for others.
He's base that trusts his feet, whose hands are arm'd.
Methinks I see Death and the Furies waiting
What we will do, and all the heaven at leisure
For the great spectacle.   Draw then your swords;
And if our destiny envy our virtue
The honour of the day, yet let us care
To sell ourselves at such a price as may
Undo the world to buy us, and make Fate,
While she tempts ours, fear her own estate.   [*Exeunt marching.*

SCENE VI.—ROME.   *The Temple of Jupiter Stator.*

Enter Lictors, Prætors, (POMTINIUS *and* FLACCUS,) CICERO,
SYLLANUS, CÆSAR, CATO, CRASSUS, *and other* Senators.

1 Sen. What means this hasty calling of the senate?
2 Sen. We shall know straight: wait till the consul speaks.
Pom. Fathers conscript, bethink you of your safeties,
And what to do with these conspirators:
Some of their clients, their freed-men, and slaves,
'Gin to make head.   There's one of Lentulus' bawds
Runs up and down the shops, through every street,
With money to corrupt the poor artificers,
And needy tradesmen, to their aid; Cethegus
Hath sent too to his servants, who are many,
Chosen and exercised in bold attemptings,
That forthwith they should arm themselves and prove
His rescue: all will be in instant uproar,
If you prevent it not with present counsels.
We have done what we can to meet the fury,
And will do more: be you good to yourselves.
Cic. What is your pleasure, fathers, shall be done?
Syllanus, you are consul next design'd;
Your sentence of these men.
Syl. 'Tis short, and this.
Since they have sought to blot the name of Rome
Out of the world, and raze this glorious empire
With her own hands and arms turn'd on herself,
I think it fit they die: and could my breath
Now execute 'em, they should not enjoy
An article of time, or eye of light,
Longer to poison this our common air.
1 Sen. I think so too.
2 Sen. And I.
3 Sen. And I.
4 Sen. And I.
Cic. Your sentence, Caius Cæsar.
Cæs. Conscript fathers,

In great affairs, and doubtful, it behoves
Men that are ask'd their sentence, to be free
From either hate or love, anger or pity:
For where the least of these do hinder, there
The mind not easily discerns the truth.
I speak this to you in the name of Rome,
For whom you stand; and to the present cause:
That this foul fact of Lentulus, and the rest,
Weigh not more with you than your dignity;
And you be more indulgent to your passion,
Than to your honour.   If there could be found
A pain or punishment equal to their crimes,
I would devise and help: but if the greatness
Of what they have done exceed all man's invention,
I think it fit to stay where our laws do.
Poor petty states may alter upon humour,
Where, if they offend with anger, few do know it,
Because they are obscure; their fame and fortune
Is equal and the same: but they that are
Head of the world, and live in that seen height,
All mankind knows their actions.   So we see,
The greater fortune hath the lesser license.
They must not favour, hate, and least be angry;
For what with others is call'd anger, there
Is cruelty and pride.   I know Syllanus,
Who spoke before me, a just, valiant man,
A lover of the state, and one that would not,
In such a business, use or grace or hatred;
I know too, well, his manners and his modesty;
Nor do I think his sentence cruel, (for
'Gainst such delinquents what can be too bloody?)
But that it is abhorring from our state;
Since to a citizen of Rome offending,
Our laws give exile, and not death.   Why then
Decrees he that? 'twere vain to think, for fear;
When by the diligence of so worthy a consul,
All is made safe and certain.   Is't for punishment?
Why, death's the end of evils, and a rest
Rather than torment: it dissolves all griefs;
And beyond that, is neither care nor joy.
You hear my sentence would not have them die.
How then? set free, and increase Catiline's army?
So will they, being but banish'd.   No, grave fathers,
I judge them, first, to have their states confiscate;
Then, that their persons remain prisoners
In the free towns, far off from Rome, and sever'd;
Where they might neither have relation,
Hereafter, to the senate or the people.
Or, if they had, those towns then to be mulcted,

As enemies to the state, that had their guard.

Omnes. 'Tis good, and honourable, Cæsar hath utter'd.

Cic. Fathers, I see your faces and your eyes
All bent on me, to note, of these two censures,
Which I incline to.   Either of them are grave,
And answering the dignity of the speakers,
The greatness of the affair, and both severe.
One urgeth death; and he may well remember
This state hath punish'd wicked citizens so:
The other, bonds, and those perpetual, which
He thinks found out for the more singular plague.
Decree which you shall please: you have a consul,
Not readier to obey, than to defend,
Whatever you shall act for the republic;
And meet with willing shoulders any burden,
Or any fortune, with an even face,
Though it were death; which to a valiant man
Can never happen foul, nor to a consul
Be immature, nor to a wise man wretched.

Syl. Fathers, I spake but as I thought the needs
Of the commonwealth required.

Cato. Excuse it not.

Cic. Cato, speak you your sentence.

Cato. This it is.
You here dispute on kinds of punishment,
And stand consulting what you should decree
'Gainst those of whom you rather should beware:
This mischief is not like those common facts,
Which when they're done, the laws may prosecute;
But this, if you provide not ere it happen,
When it is happen'd, will not wait your judgment.
Good Caius Cæsar here hath very well,
And subtlely discours'd of life and death,
As if he thought those things a pretty fable
That are deliver'd us of hell and furies,
Or of the divers ways that ill men go
From good, to filthy, dark, and ugly places:
And therefore he would have these live, and long too;
But far from Rome, and in the small free towns,
Lest here they might have rescue: as if men
Fit for such acts were only in the city,
And not throughout all Italy; or, that boldness
Could not do more, where it found least resistance!
'Tis a vain counsel, if he think them dangerous:
Which if he do not, but that he alone,
In so great fear of all men, stand unfrighted,
He gives me cause, and you too, more to fear him.
I am plain, fathers.   Here you look about
One at another, doubting what to do,

With faces, as you trusted to the gods,
That still have saved you; and they can do it: but
They are not wishings, or base womanish pray'rs,
Can draw their aids; but vigilance, counsel, action;
Which they will be ashamed to forsake.
'Tis sloth they hate, and cowardice. Here you have
The traitors in your houses; yet you stand,
Fearing what to do with them; let them loose,
And send them hence with arms too, that your mercy
May turn your misery, as soon as't can!—
O, but they are great men, and have offended
But through ambition; we would spare their honour.
Ay, if themselves had spared it, or their fame,
Or modesty, or either god or man;
Then I would spare them. But as things now stand,
Fathers, to spare these men, were to commit
A greater wickedness than you would revenge.
If there had been but time and place for you
To have repair'd this fault, you should have made it;
It should have been your punishment, to have felt
Your tardy error: but necessity
Now bids me say, let them not live an hour,
If you mean Rome should live a day. I have done.

    Omnes. Cato hath spoken like an oracle.
    Cras. Let it be so decreed.
    Sen. We all were fearful.
    Syl. And had been base, had not his virtue raised us.
    Sen. Go forth, most worthy consul, we'll assist you.
    Cæs. I am not yet changed in my sentence, fathers.
    Cato. No matter.

Enter a Messenger *with letters.*

                What be those?
    1 Sen. Letters for Cæsar!
    Cato. From whom? let them be read in open senate.
Fathers, they come from the conspirators,
I crave to have them read, for the republic.
    Cæs. Cato, read you it. 'Tis a love-letter,
From your dear sister to me: though you hate me,
Do not discover it.   *[Aside to Cato.*
    Cato. Hold thee, drunkard.—Consul,
Go forth, and confidently.
    Cæs. You'll repent
This rashness, Cicero.
    Præ. Cæsar shall repent it.   *[The Prætors attempt to seize him.*
    Cic. Hold, friends!
    Præ. He's scarce a friend unto the public.
    Cic. No violence. Cæsar, be safe. *[They all rise.]*—Lead on.
Where are the public executioners?

Bid them wait on us.   On to Spinther's house.
Bring Lentulus forth.   [*He is brought out.*]—Here, you, the sad
    revengers
Of capital crimes against the public, take
This man unto your justice; strangle him.
    Len. Thou dost well, consul.   'Twas a cast at dice,
In fortune's hand, not long since, that thyself
Should'st have heard these, or other words as fatal.
                      [*Exit Len. guarded.*
    Cic. Lead on to Quintus Cornificius' house.
Bring forth Cethegus.   [*He is brought out.*]—Take him to the due
Death that he hath deserv'd, and let it be
Said, he was once.
    Cet. A beast, or what is worse,
A slave, Cethegus.   Let that be the name
For all that's base, hereafter; that would let
This worm pronounce on him, and not have trampled
His body into——Ha! art thou not moved?
    Cic. Justice is never angry.   Take him hence.
    Cet. O, the whore Fortune, and her bawds the Fates,
That put these tricks on men, which knew the way
To death by a sword! strangle me, I may sleep;
I shall grow angry with the gods else.   [*Exit, guarded.*
    Cic. Lead
To Caius Cæsar, for Statilius.
Bring him and rude Gabinius out.   [*They are brought out.*]—Here
    take them
To your cold hands, and let them feel death from you.
    Gab. I thank you, you do me a pleasure.
Stat. And me too.   [*Exeunt Gab. and Stat. guarded.*
    Cato. So, Marcus Tullius, thou may'st now stand up,
And call it happy Rome, thou being consul.
Great parent of thy country! go, and let
The old men of the city, ere they die,
Kiss thee, the matrons dwell about thy neck,
The youths and maids lay up, 'gainst they are old,
What kind of man thou wert, to tell their nephews,
When, such a year, they read, within our Fasti,
Thy consulship—

              Enter PETREIUS.

        Who's this?   Petreius!
    Cic. Welcome,
Welcome, renowned soldier.   What's the news?
This face can bring no ill with 't unto Rome.
How does the worthy consul, my colleague?
    Pet. As well as victory can make him, sir.
He greets the fathers, and to me hath trusted
The sad relation of the civil strife;

For, in such war, the conquest still is black.
  Cic. Shall we withdraw into the house of Concord?
  Cato. No, happy consul; here let all ears take
The benefit of this tale. If he had voice
To spread unto the poles, and strike it through
The centre to the antipodes, it would ask it.
  Pet. The straits and needs of Catiline being such,
As he must fight with one of the two armies,
That then had ne'er inclosed him; it pleased fate
To make us the object of his desperate choice,
Wherein the danger almost poised the honour:
And as he rose, the day grew black with him,
And Fate descended nearer to the earth,
As if she meant to hide the name of things
Under her wings, and make the world her quarry.
At this we roused, lest one small minute's stay
Had left it to be inquired, what Rome was;
And, as we ought, arm'd in the confidence
Of our great cause, in form of battle stood;
Whilst Catiline came on, not with the face
Of any man, but of a public ruin.
His countenance was a civil war itself,
And all his host had standing in their looks
The paleness of the death that was to come;
Yet cried they out like vultures, and urged on,
As if they would precipitate our fates.
Nor stay'd we longer for them: but himself
Struck the first stroke; and with it fled a life,
Which cut, it seem'd a narrow neck of land
Had broke between two mighty seas, and either
Flow'd into other; for so did the slaughter:
And whirl'd about, as when two violent tides
Meet, and not yield. The Furies stood on hills,
Circling the place, and trembling to see men
Do more than they; whilst Piety left the field,
Grieved for that side, that in so bad a cause
They knew not what a crime their valour was.
The sun stood still, and was, behind the cloud
The battle made, seen sweating, to drive up
His frighted horse, whom still the noise drove backward.
And now had fierce Enyo, like a flame,
Consumed all it could reach, and then itself,
Had not the fortune of the commonwealth
Come, Pallas-like, to every Roman thought:
Which Catiline seeing, and that now his troops
Cover'd that earth they had fought on, with their trunks,
Ambitious of great fame to crown his ill,
Collected all his fury, and ran in,
Arm'd with a glory high as his despair,

Into our battle, like a Libyan lion
Upon his hunters, scornful of our weapons,
Careless of wounds, plucking down lives about him,
Till he had circled in himself with death:
Then fell he too, t' embrace it where it lay.
And as in that rebellion 'gainst the gods,
Minerva holding forth Medusa's head,
One of the giant-brethren felt himself
Grow marble at the killing sight, and now
Almost made stone, began to inquire, what flint,
What rock it was, that crept through all his limbs,
And ere he could think more, was that he fear'd;
So Catiline, at the sight of Rome in us,
Became his tomb: yet did his look retain
Some of his fierceness, and his hands still moved,
As if he labour'd yet to grasp the state
With those rebellious parts.
   Cato. A brave bad death!
Had this been honest now, and for his country,
As 'twas against it, who had e'er fall'n greater?
   Cic. Honour'd Petreius, Rome, not I, must thank you.
How modestly has he spoken of himself!
   Cato. He did the more.
   Cic. Thanks to the immortal gods,
Romans, I now am paid for all my labours,
My watchings, and my dangers! here conclude
Your praises, triumphs, honours, and rewards,
Decreed to me: only the memory
Of this glad day, if I may know it live
Within your thoughts, shall much affect my conscience,
Which I must always study before fame.
Though both be good, the latter yet is worst,
And ever is ill got, without the first.   [*Exeunt.*

BARTHOLOMEW FAIR

DRAMATIS PERSONÆ

JOHN LITTLEWIT, *a Proctor.*
ZEAL-OF-THE-LAND BUSY, *Suitor to* Dame PURECRAFT, *a Banbury Man.*
WINWIFE, *his rival, a Gentleman.*
TOM QUARLOUS, *companion to* WINWIFE, *a Gamester.*
BARTHOLOMEW COKES, *an Esquire of Harrow.*
HUMPHREY WASPE, *his Man.*
ADAM OVERDO, *a Justice of Peace.*
LANTHORN LEATHERHEAD, *a Hobby-Horse Seller (Toyman).*
EZECHIEL EDGWORTH, *a Cutpurse.*
NIGHTINGALE, *a Ballad-Singer.*
MOONCALF, *Tapster to* URSULA.
DAN. JORDAN KNOCKEM, *a Horse-Courser, and a Ranger of Turnbull.*
VAL. CUTTING, *a Roarer, or Bully.*
CAPTAIN WHIT, *a Bawd.*
TROUBLE-ALL, *a Madman.*
BRISTLE, } *Watchmen.*
HAGGISE, }

POCHER, *a Beadle.*
FILCHER, } *Door-keepers to the*
SHARKWELL, } *Puppet-Show.*
SOLOMON, LITTLEWIT'S *Man.*
NORTHERN, *a Clothier (a Northern Man).*
PUPPY, *a Wrestler (a Western Man).*

WIN-THE-FIGHT LITTLEWIT.
DAME PURECRAFT, *her Mother, and a Widow.*
DAME OVERDO.
GRACE WELLBORN, *Ward to* Justice OVERDO.
JOAN TRASH, *a Gingerbread-Woman.*
URSULA, *a Pig-Woman.*
ALICE, *Mistress o' the game.*

Costard - Monger, Mousetrap - Man, Corn - Cutter, Watch, Porters, Puppets, Passengers, Mob, Boys, *etc.*

PROLOGUE.

TO THE KING'S MAJESTY.

Your Majesty is welcome to a Fair;
Such place, such men, such language, and such ware
You must expect: with these, the zealous noise
Of your land's faction, scandalised at toys,
As babies, hobby-horses, puppet-plays,
And such-like rage, whereof the petulant ways
Yourself have known, and have been vext with long.
These for your sport, without particular wrong,
Or just complaint of any private man,
Who of himself, or shall think well, or can,
The maker doth present: and hopes, to-night
To give you for a fairing, true delight.

THE INDUCTION.

THE STAGE.

Enter the Stage-keeper.

Stage. Gentlemen, have a little patience, they are e'en upon coming, instantly. He that should begin the play, master Littlewit, the proctor, has a stitch new fallen in his black silk stocking; 'twill be drawn up ere you can tell twenty: he plays one o' the Arches that dwells about the hospital, and he has a very pretty part. But for the whole play, will you have the truth on't?—I am looking, lest the poet hear me, or his man, master Brome, behind the arras—it is like to be a very conceited scurvy one, in plain English. When't comes to the Fair once, you were e'en as good go to Virginia, for any thing there is of Smithfield. He has not hit the humours, he does not know them; he has not conversed with the Bartholomew birds, as they say; he has ne'er a sword and buckler-man in his Fair; nor a little Davy, to take toll o' the bawds there, as in my time; nor a Kindheart, if any body's teeth should chance to ache in his play; nor a juggler with a well-educated ape, to come over the chain for a king of England, and back again for the prince, and sit still on his arse for the pope and the king of Spain. None of these fine sights! Nor has he the canvas-cut in the night, for a hobby-horse man to creep into his she-neighbour, and take his leap there. Nothing! No: an some writer that I know had had but the penning o' this matter, he would have made you such a jig-a-jog in the booths, you should have thought an earthquake had been in the Fair! But these master poets, they will have their own absurd courses; they will be informed of nothing. He has (sir reverence) kick'd me three or four times about the tiring-house, I thank him, for but offering to put in with my experience. I'll be judged by you, gentlemen, now, but for one conceit of mine: would not a fine pomp upon the stage have done well, for a property now? and a punk set under upon her head, with her stern upward, and have been soused by my witty young masters o' the Inns of Court? What think you of this for a show, now? he will not hear o' this! I am an ass! I! and yet I kept the stage in master Tarleton's time, I thank my stars. Ho! an that man had lived to have played in Bartholomew Fair, you should have seen him have come in, and have been cozen'd in the cloth-quarter, so finely! and Adams, the rogue, have leaped and capered upon him, and have dealt his vermin about, as though they had cost him nothing! and then a substantial watch to have stolen in upon them, and taken them away, with mistaking words, as the fashion is in the stage-practice.

Enter the Bookholder *with a* Scrivener.

Book. How now! what rare discourse are you fallen upon, ha? have you found any familiars here, that you are so free! what's the business?

Stage. Nothing, but the understanding gentlemen o' the ground here ask'd my judgment.

Book. Your judgment, rascal! for what? sweeping the stage, or gathering up the broken apples for the bears within? Away, rogue, it's come to a fine degree in these spectacles, when such a youth as you pretend to a judgment. [*Exit Stage-keeper.*]—And yet he may, in the most of this matter, i'faith: for the author has writ it just to his meridian, and the scale of the grounded judgments here, his play-fellows in wit.—Gentlemen, [*comes forward*] not for want of a prologue, but by way of a new one, I am sent out to you here, with a scrivener, and certain articles drawn out in haste between our author and you; which if you please to hear, and as they appear reasonable, to approve of; the play will follow presently.—Read, scribe; give me the counterpane.

Scriv. Articles of agreement, indented, between the spectators or hearers, at the Hope on the Bankside in the county of Surry, on the one party; and the author of Bartholomew Fair, in the said place and county, on the other party: the one and thirtieth day of October, 1614, and in the twelfth year of the reign of our sovereign lord JAMES, *by the grace of God, king of England, France, and Ireland, defender of the faith; and of Scotland the seven and fortieth.*

Imprimis. *It is covenanted and agreed, by and between the parties aforesaid, and the said spectators and hearers, as well the curious and envious, as the favouring and judicious, as also the grounded judgments and understandings, do for themselves severally covenant and agree to remain in the places their money or friends have put them in, with patience, for the space of two hours and an half, and somewhat more. In which time the author promiseth to present them by us, with a new sufficient play, called Bartholomew Fair, merry, and as full of noise, as sport: made to delight all, and to offend none; provided they have either the wit or the honesty to think well of themselves.*

It is further agreed, that every person here have his or their free-will of censure, to like or dislike at their own charge, the author having now departed with his right: it shall be lawful for any man to judge his sixpen'worth, his twelvepen'worth, so to his eighteen-pence, two shillings, half a crown, to the value of his place; provided always his place get not above his wit. And if he pay for half a dozen, he may censure for all them too, so that he will undertake that they shall be silent. He shall put in for censures here, as they do for lots at the lottery: marry, if he drop but six-pence at the door, and will censure a crown's-worth, it is thought there is no conscience or justice in that.

It is also agreed, that every man here exercise his own judgment, and not censure by contagion, or upon trust, from another's voice or face, that sits by him, be he never so first in the commission of wit; as also. that he be fixed and settled in his censure that what he approves or not approves to-day, he will do the same to-morrow; and if to-morrow, the next day, and so the next week, if need be: and not to be brought about by any that sits on the bench with him, though they indite and arraign plays daily. He that will swear, Jeronimo *or* Andronicus, *are the best plays yet, shall pass unexcepted at here, as a man whose judgment shews it is constant, and hath stood still these five and twenty or thirty years. Though it be an ignorance it is a virtuous and staid ignorance; and next to truth, a confirmed error does well; such a one the author knows where to find him.*

It is further covenanted, concluded, and agreed, That how great soever the expectation be, no person here is to expect more than he knows, or better ware than a fair will afford: neither to look back to the sword and buckler age of Smithfield, but content himself with the present. Instead of a little Davy to take toll o' the bawds, the author doth promise a strutting horse-courser, with a leer drunkard, two or three to attend him, in as good equipage as you would wish. And then for Kindheart the tooth-drawer, a fine oily pig-woman with her tapster, to bid you welcome, and a consort of roarers for musick. A wise justice of peace meditant, instead of a juggler with an ape. A civil cutpurse searchant. A sweet singer of new ballads allurant: and as fresh an hypocrite, as ever was broached, rampant. If there be never a servant-monster in the fair, who can help it, he says, nor a nest of antiques? he is loth to make nature afraid in his plays, like those that beget tales, tempests, and such-like drolleries, to mix his head with other men's heels; let the concupiscence of jigs and dances reign as strong as it will amongst you: yet if the puppets will please any body, they shall be intreated to come in.

In consideration of which, it is finally agreed, by the aforesaid hearers and spectators, That they neither in themselves conceal, nor suffer by them to be concealed, any state-decypherer, or politic pick-lock of the scene so solemnly ridiculous, as to search out, who was meant by the gingerbread-woman, who by the hobby-horse man, who by the costard-monger, nay, who by their wares. Or that will pretend to affirm on his own inspired ignorance, what Mirror of Magistrates is meant by the justice, what great lady by the pig-woman, what concealed statesman by the seller of mouse-traps, and so of the rest. But that such person, or persons, so found, be left discovered to the mercy of the author, as a forfeiture to the stage, and your laughter aforesaid. As also such as shall so desperately, or ambitiously play the fool by his place aforesaid, to challenge the author of scurrility, because the language somewhere savours of Smithfield, the booth, and the pigbroth, or of profaneness, because a madman cries, God quit you, or bless you! In witness whereof, as you have preposterously put to your seals already, which is your money, you will now add the other part of suffrage, your hands. The play shall presently begin. And though the Fair be not kept in the same region that some here, perhaps, would have it; yet think, that therein the author hath observed a special decorum, the place being as dirty as Smithfield, and as stinking every whit.

Howsoever, he prays you to believe, his ware is still the same, else you will make him justly suspect that he that is so loth to look on a baby or an hobby-horse here, would be glad to take up a commodity of them, at any laughter or loss in another place.   [Exeunt.

ACT I

SCENE I.—*A Room in* LITTLEWIT'S *House.*

Enter LITTLEWIT *with a license in his hand.*

Lit. A pretty conceit, and worth the finding! I have such luck to spin out these fine things still, and, like a silk-worm, out of my self. Here's master Bartholomew Cokes, of Harrow o' the Hill, in the county of Middlesex, esquire, takes forth his license to marry mistress Grace Wellborn, of the said place and county: and when does he take it forth? to-day! the four and twentieth of August! Bartholomew-day! Bartholomew upon Bartholomew! there's the device! who would have marked such a leap-frog chance now! A very . . . less than ames-ace, on two dice! Well, go thy ways, John Littlewit, proctor John Littlewit: one of the pretty wits of Paul's, the Littlewit of London, so thou art called, and something beside. When a quirk or a quiblin does 'scape thee, and thou dost not watch and apprehend it, and bring it afore the constable of conceit, (there now, I speak quib too,) let them carry thee out o' the archdeacon's court into his kitchen, and make a Jack of thee, instead of a John. There I am again la!—

Enter Mrs. LITTLEWIT.

Win, good-morrow, Win; ay, marry, Win, now you look finely indeed, Win! this cap does convince! You'd not have worn it, Win, nor have had it velvet, but a rough country beaver, with a copper band, like the coney-skin woman of Budge-row; sweet Win, let me kiss it! And her fine high shoes, like the Spanish lady! Good Win, go a little, I would fain see thee pace, pretty Win; by this fine cap, I could never leave kissing on't.

Mrs. Lit. Come indeed la, you are such a fool still!

Lit. No, but half a one, Win, you are the t'other half: man and wife make one fool, Win. Good! Is there the proctor, or doctor indeed, in the diocese, that ever had the fortune to win him such a Win! There I am again! I do feel conceits coming upon me, more than I am able to turn tongue to. A pox o' these pretenders to wit! your Three Cranes, Mitre and Mermaid men! not a corn of true salt, not a grain of right mustard amongst them all. They may stand for places, or so, again the next wit-fall, and pay two-pence in a quart more for their canary than other men. But give me the man can start up a justice of wit out of six shillings beer, and give the law to all the poets and poet-suckers in town:—because they are the player's gossips! 'Slid! other men have wives as fine as the players, and as well drest. Come hither, Win! [*Kisses her.*

Enter WINWIFE.

Winw. Why, how now, master Littlewit! measuring of lips, or moulding of kisses? which is it?

Lit. Troth, I am a little taken with my Win's dressing here: does it not fine, master Winwife? How do you apprehend, sir? she would not have worn this habit. I challenge all Cheapside to shew such another: Moorfields, Pimlico-path, or the Exchange, in a summer evening, with a lace to boot, as this has. Dear Win, let master Winwife kiss you. He comes a wooing to our mother, Win, and may be our father perhaps, Win. There's no harm in him, Win.

Winw. None in the earth, master Littlewit. [*Kisses her.*

Lit. I envy no man my delicates, sir.

Winw. Alas, you have the garden where they grow still! A wife here with a strawberry breath, cherry lips, apricot cheeks, and a soft velvet head, like a melicotton.

Lit. Good, i'faith! now dulness upon me, that I had not that before him, that I should not light on't as well as he! velvet head!

Winw. But my taste, master Littlewit, tends to fruit of a later kind; the sober matron, your wife's mother.

Lit. Ay, we know you are a suitor, sir; Win and I both wish you well: By this license here, would you had her, that your two names were as fast in it as here are a couple! Win would fain have a fine young father-i'-law, with a feather; that her mother might hood it and chain it with mistress Overdo. But you do not take the right course, master Winwife.

Winw. No, master Littlewit, why?

Lit. You are not mad enough.

Winw. How! is madness a right course?

Lit. I say nothing, but I wink upon Win. You have a friend, one master Quarlous, comes here sometimes.

Winw. Why, he makes no love to her, does he?

Lit. Not a tokenworth that ever I saw, I assure you: but—

Winw. What?

Lit. He is the more mad-cap of the two. You do not apprehend me.

Mrs. Lit. You have a hot coal in your mouth, now, you cannot hold.

Lit. Let me out with it, dear Win.

Mrs. Lit. I'll tell him myself.

Lit. Do, and take all the thanks, and much good do thy pretty heart, Win.

Mrs. Lit. Sir, my mother has had her nativity-water cast lately by the cunning-men in Cow-lane, and they have told her her fortune, and do ensure her, she shall never have happy hour, unless she marry within this sen'night; and when it is, it must be a madman, they say.

Lit. Ay, but it must be a gentleman madman.

Mrs. Lit. Yes, so the t'other man of Moorfields says.

Winw. But does she believe them?

Lit. Yes, and has been at Bedlam twice since every day, to inquire if any gentleman be there, or to come there mad.

Winw. Why, this is a confederacy, a mere piece of practice upon her by these impostors.

Lit. I tell her so; or else, say I, that they mean some young madcap gentleman; for the devil can equivocate as well as a shop keeper: and therefore would I advise you to be a little madder than master Quarlous hereafter.

Winw. Where is she, stirring yet?

Lit. Stirring! yes, and studying an old elder come from Banbury, a suitor that puts in here at meal tide, to praise the painful brethren, or pray that the sweet singers may be restored; says a grace as long as his breath lasts him! Some time the spirit is so strong with him, it gets quite out of him, and then my mother, or Win, are fain to fetch it again with malmsey or aqua cœlestis.

Mrs. Lit. Yes, indeed, we have such a tedious life with him for his diet, and his clothes too! he breaks his buttons, and cracks seams at every saying he sobs out.

Lit. He cannot abide my vocation, he says.

Mrs. Lit. No; he told my mother, a proctor was a claw of the beast, and that she had little less than committed abomination in marrying me so as she has done.

Lit. Every line, he says, that a proctor writes, when it comes to be read in the bishop's court, is a long black hair, kemb'd out of the tail of Antichrist.

Winw. When came this proselyte?

Lit. Some three days since.

Enter QUARLOUS.

Quar. O sir, have you ta'en soil here? It's well a man may reach you after three hours' running yet! What an unmerciful companion art thou, to quit thy lodging at such ungentlemanly hours! none but a scattered covey of fidlers, or one of these rag-rakers in dunghills, or some marrow-bone man at most, would have been up when thou wert gone abroad, by all description. I pray thee what ailest thou, thou canst not sleep? hast thou thorns in thy eye-lids, or thistles in thy bed?

Winw. I cannot tell: it seems you had neither in your feet, that took this pain to find me.

Quar. No, an I had, all the lime hounds o' the city should have drawn after you by the scent rather. Master John Littlewit! God save you, sir. 'Twas a hot night with some of us, last night, John: shall we pluck a hair of the same wolf to-day, proctor John?

Lit. Do you remember, master Quarlous, what we discoursed on last night?

Quar. Not I, John, nothing that I either discourse or do; at those times I forfeit all to forgetfulness.

Lit. No! not concerning Win? look you, there she is, and drest, as I told you she should be: hark you, sir, [*whispers him.*] had you forgot?

Quar. By this head I'll beware how I keep you company, John, when I [am] drunk, an you have this dangerous memory: that's certain.

Lit. Why, sir?

Quar. Why! we were all a little stained last night, sprinkled with a cup or two, and I agreed with proctor John here, to come and do somewhat with Win (I know not what 'twas) to-day; and he puts me in mind on't now; he says he was coming to fetch me. Before truth, if you have that fearful quality, John, to remember when you are sober, John, what you promise drunk, John; I shall take heed of you, John. For this once I am content to wink at you. Where's your wife? come hither, Win. [*Kisses her.*

Mrs. Lit. Why, John! do you see this, John? look you! help me, John.

Lit. O Win, fie, what do you mean, Win? be womanly, Win; make an outcry to your mother, Win! master Quarlous is an honest gentleman, and our worshipful good friend, Win; and he is master Winwife's friend too: and master Winwife comes a suitor to your mother, Win; as I told you before, Win, and may perhaps be our father, Win: they'll do you no harm, Win; they are both our worshipful good friends. Master Quarlous! you must know master Quarlous, Win; you must not quarrel with master Quarlous, Win.

Quar. No, we'll kiss again, and fall in. [*Kisses her again.*

Lit. Yes, do, good Win.

Mrs. Lit. In faith you are a fool, John.

Lit. A fool-John, she calls me; do you mark that, gentlemen? pretty Littlewit of velvet? a fool-John.

Quar. She may call you an apple-John, if you use this. [*Aside.* [*Kisses her again.*

Winw. Pray thee forbear, for my respect, somewhat.

Quar. Hoy-day! how respective you are become o' the sudden? I fear this family will turn you reformed too; pray you come about again. Because she is in possibility to be your daughter-in-law, and may ask you blessing hereafter, when she courts it to Totenham to eat cream! Well, I will forbear, sir; but i'faith, would thou wouldst leave thy exercise of widow-hunting once; this drawing after an old reverend smock by the splay-foot! There cannot be an ancient tripe or trillibub in the town, but thou art straight nosing it, and 'tis a fine occupation thou'lt confine thyself to, when thou hast got one; scrubbing a piece of buff, as if thou hadst the perpetuity of Pannier-ally to stink in; or perhaps worse, currying a carcass that thou hast bound thyself to alive. I'll be sworn, some of them that thou art, or hast been suitor to, are so old, as no chaste or married pleasure can ever become them; the honest instrument of procreation has forty years since left to belong to them; thou must visit them as thou wouldst do a tomb, with a torch or three handfuls of link, flaming hot, and so thou may'st hap to make them feel thee and after come to inherit according to thy inches. A sweet course for a man to waste the brand of life for, to be still raking himself a fortune in an old woman's embers! We shall have

thee, after thou hast been but a month married to one of them,
look like the quartan ague and the black jaundice met in a face,
and walk as if thou hadst borrow'd legs of a spinner, and voice of
a cricket. I would endure to hear fifteen sermons a week for her,
and such coarse and loud ones, as some of them must be! I would
e'en desire of fate, I might dwell in a drum, and take in my sus-
tenance with an old broken tobacco-pipe and a straw. Dost thou
ever think to bring thine ears or stomach to the patience of a dry
grace as long as thy table-cloth; and droned out by thy son here
(that might be thy father) till all the meat on thy board has forgot
it was that day in the kitchen? or to brook the noise made in a
question of predestination, by the good labourers and painful eaters
assembled together, put to them by the matron your spouse; who
moderates with a cup of wine, ever and anon, and a sentence out
of Knox between? Or the perpetual spitting before and after a
sober-drawn exhortation of six hours, whose better part was the
hum-ha-hum? or to hear prayers, groaned out over thy iron chests,
as if they were charms to break them? And all this for the hope
of two apostle-spoons, to suffer! and a cup to eat a caudle in! for
that will be thy legacy. She'll have convey'd her state safe enough
from thee, an she be a right widow.

Winw. Alas, I am quite off that scent now.

Quar. How so?

Winw. Put off by a brother of Banbury, one that, they say, is
come here, and governs all already.

Quar. What do you call him? I knew divers of those Banburians
when I was in Oxford.

Winw. Master Littlewit can tell us.

Lit. Sir!—Good Win go in, and if master Bartholomew Cokes,
his man, come for the license, (the little old fellow,) let him speak
with me. [*Exit Mrs. Littlewit.*]—What say you, gentlemen?

Winw. What call you the reverend elder you told me of, your
Banbury man?

Lit. Rabbi Busy, sir; he is more than an elder, he is a prophet,
sir.

Quar. O, I know him! a baker, is he not?

Lit. He was a baker, sir, but he does dream now, and see visions;
he has given over his trade.

Quar. I remember that too; out of a scruple he took, that, in
spiced conscience, those cakes he made, were served to bridals,
may-poles, morrices, and such profane feasts and meetings. His
christian-name is Zeal-of-the-land.

Lit. Yes, sir; Zeal-of-the-land Busy.

Winw. How! what a name's there!

Lit. O they have all such names, sir; he was witness for Win
here,—they will not be call'd godfathers—and named her Win-the-
fight: you thought her name had been Winnifred, did you not?

Winw. I did indeed.

Lit. He would have thought himself a stark reprobate, if it had.

Quar. Ay, for there was a blue-starch woman of the name at the same time. A notable hypocritical vermin it is; I know him. One that stands upon his face, more than his faith, at all times: ever in seditious motion, and reproving for vainglory; of a most lunatic conscience and spleen, and affects the violence of singularity in all he does: he has undone a grocer here, in Newgate-market, that broke with him, trusted him with currants, as arrant a zeal as he, that's by the way:—By his profession he will ever be in the state of innocence though, and childhood; derides all antiquity, defies any other learning than inspiration; and what discretion soever years should afford him, it is all prevented in his original ignorance: have not to do with him, for he is a fellow of a most arrogant and invincible dulness, I assure you.—Who is this?

Re-enter Mrs. LITTLEWIT *with* WASPE.

Waspe. By your leave, gentlemen, with all my heart to you; and God give you good morrow!—master Littlewit, my business is to you: is this license ready?

Lit. Here I have it for you in my hand, master Humphrey.

Waspe. That's well: nay, never open or read it to me, it's labour in vain, you know. I am no clerk, I scorn to be saved by my book, i'faith, I'll hang first; fold it up on your word, and give it me. What must you have for it?

Lit. We'll talk of that anon, master Humphrey.

Waspe. Now, or not at all, good master Proctor; I am for no anons, I assure you.

Lit. Sweet Win, bid Solomon send me the little black-box within in my study.

Waspe. Ay, quickly, good mistress, I pray you; for I have both eggs on the spit, and iron in the fire. [*Exit Mrs. Littlewit.*]—Say what you must have, good master Littlewit.

Lit. Why, you know the price, master Numps.

Waspe. I know! I know nothing, I: what tell you me of knowing? Now I am in haste, sir, I do not know, and I will not know, and I scorn to know, and yet, now I think on't, I will, and do know as well as another; you must have a mark for your thing here, and eight-pence for the box; I could have saved two-pence in that, an I had brought it myself; but here's fourteen shillings for you. Good Lord, how long your little wife stays! pray God, Solomon, your clerk, be not looking in the wrong box, master proctor.

Lit. Good i'faith! no, I warrant you Solomon is wiser than so, sir.

Waspe. Fie, fie, fie, by your leave, master Littlewit, this is scurvy, idle, foolish, and abominable, with all my heart; I do not like it.
[*Walks aside.*

Winw. Do you hear! Jack Littlewit, what business does thy pretty head think this fellow may have, that he keeps such a coil with?

Quar. More than buying of gingerbread in the cloister here, for that we allow him, or a gilt pouch in the fair?

Lit. Master Quarlous, do not mistake him; he is his master's both-hands, I assure you.

Quar. What! to pull on his boots a mornings, or his stockings, does he?

Lit. Sir, if you have a mind to mock him, mock him softly, and look t'other way: for if he apprehend you flout him once, he will fly at you presently. A terrible testy old fellow, and his name is Waspe too.

Quar. Pretty insect! make much on him.

Waspe. A plague o' this box, and the pox too, and on him that made it, and her that went for't, and all that should have sought it, sent it, or brought it! do you see, sir.

Lit. Nay, good master Waspe.

Waspe. Good master Hornet, t—in your teeth, hold you your tongue: do not I know you? your father was a 'pothecary, and sold clysters, more than he gave, I wusse: and t—in your little wife's teeth too—here she comes—

Re-enter Mrs. LITTLEWIT, *with the box.*

'twill make her spit, as fine as she is, for all her velvet custard on her head, sir.

Lit. O, be civil, master Numps.

Waspe. Why, say I have a humour not to be civil; how then? who shall compel me, you?

Lit. Here is the box now.

Waspe. Why, a pox o' your box, once again! let your little wife stale in it, an she will. Sir, I would have you to understand, and these gentlemen too, if they please—

Winw. With all our hearts, sir.

Waspe. That I have a charge, gentlemen.

Lit. They do apprehend, sir.

Waspe. Pardon me, sir, neither they nor you can apprehend me yet. You are an ass.—I have a young master, he is now upon his making and marring; the whole care of his well-doing is now mine. His foolish schoolmasters have done nothing but run up and down the country with him to beg puddings and cake-bread of his tenants, and almost spoil'd him; he has learn'd nothing but to sing catches, and repeat *Rattle bladder, rattle!* and *O Madge!* I dare not let him walk alone, for fear of learning of vile tunes, which he will sing at supper, and in the sermon-times! If he meet but a carman in the street, and I find him not talk to keep him off on him, he will whistle him and all his tunes over at night in his sleep! He has a head full of bees! I am fain now, for this little time I am absent, to leave him in charge with a gentlewoman: 'tis true she is a justice of peace his wife, and a gentlewoman of the hood, and his natural sister; but what may happen under a woman's government, there's the doubt. Gentlemen, you do not know him; he is another manner of piece than you think for: but nineteen years old, and yet he is taller than either of you by the head, God bless him!

Quar. Well, methinks this is a fine fellow.

Winw. He has made his master a finer by this description, I should think.

Quar. 'Faith, much about one, it is cross and pile, whether for a new farthing.

Waspe. I'll tell you, gentlemen—

Lit. Will't please you drink, master Waspe?

Waspe. Why, I have not talk'd so long to be dry, sir. You see no dust or cobwebs come out o' my mouth, do you? you'd have me gone, would you?

Lit. No, but you were in haste e'en now, master Numps.

Waspe. What an I were! so I am still, and yet I will stay too; meddle you with your match, your Win there, she has as little wit as her husband, it seems: I have others to talk to.

Lit. She's my match indeed, and as *little wit* as I, good!

Waspe. We have been but a day and a half in town, gentlemen, 'tis true; and yesterday in the afternoon we walked London to shew the city to the gentlewoman he shall marry, mistress Grace; but afore I will endure such another half day with him, I'll be drawn with a good gib-cat, through the great pond at home, as his uncle Hodge was. Why, we could not meet that heathen thing all the day, but staid him; he would name you all the signs over, as he went, aloud: and where he spied a parrot or a monkey, there he was pitched, with all the little long coats about him, male and female; no getting him away! I thought he would have run mad o' the black boy in Bucklersbury, that takes the scurvy, roguy tobacco there.

Lit. You say true, master Numps; there's such a one indeed.

Waspe. It's no matter whether there be or no, what's that to you?

Quar. He will not allow of John's reading at any hand.

Enter Cokes, Mistress Overdo, *and* Grace.

Cokes. O Numps! are you here, Numps? look where I am, Numps, and mistress Grace too! Nay, do not look angerly, Numps: my sister is here and all, I do not come without her.

Waspe. What the mischief do you come with her; or she with you?

Cokes. We came all to seek you, Numps.

Waspe. To seek me! why, did you all think I was lost, or run away with your fourteen shillings' worth of small ware here? or that I had changed it in the fair for hobby-horses? S'precious—to seek me!

Mrs. Over. Nay, good master Numps, do you shew discretion, though he be exorbitant, as master Overdo says, and it be but for conservation of the peace.

Waspe. Marry gip, goody She-justice, mistress Frenchhood! t—in your teeth, and t—in your Frenchhood's teeth too, to do you service, do you see! Must you quote your Adam to me! you think you are madam Regent still, mistress Overdo, when I am in place;

no such matter, I assure you, your reign is out, when I am in, dame.

Mrs. Over. I am content to be in abeyance, sir, and be governed by you; so should he too, if he did well; but 'twill be expected you should also govern your passions.

Waspe. Will it so, forsooth! good Lord, how sharp you are, with being at Bedlam yesterday! Whetstone has set an edge upon you, has he?

Mrs. Over. Nay, if you know not what belongs to your dignity, I do yet to mine.

Waspe. Very well then.

Cokes. Is this the license, Numps? for love's sake let me see't; I never saw a license.

Waspe. Did you not so? why, you shall not see't then.

Cokes. An you love me, good Numps.

Waspe. Sir, I love you, and yet I do not love you in these fooleries: set your heart at rest, there's nothing in it but hard words;—and what would you see it for?

Cokes. I would see the length and the breadth on't, that's all; and I will see it now, so I will.

Waspe. You shall not see it here.

Cokes. Then I'll see it at home, and I'll look upon the case here.

Waspe. Why, do so; a man must give way to him a little in trifles, gentlemen. These are errors, diseases of youth; which he will mend when he comes to judgment and knowledge of matters. I pray you conceive so, and I thank you: and I pray you pardon him, and I thank you again.

Quar. Well, this dry nurse, I say still, is a delicate man.

Mrs. Lit. And I am, for the cosset his charge: did you ever see a fellow's face more accuse him for an ass?

Quar. Accuse him! it confesses him one without accusing. What pity 'tis yonder wench should marry such a Cokes!

Winw. 'Tis true.

Quar. She seems to be discreet, and as sober as she is handsome.

Winw. Ay, and if you mark her, what a restrained scorn she casts upon all his behaviour and speeches!

Cokes. Well, Numps, I am now for another piece of business more, the Fair, Numps, and then—

Waspe. Bless me! deliver me! help, hold me! the Fair!

Cokes. Nay, never fidge up and down, Numps, and vex itself. I am resolute Bartholomew in this; I'll make no suit on't to you; 'twas all the end of my journey indeed, to shew mistress Grace my Fair. I call it my Fair, because of Bartholomew: you know my name is Bartholomew, and Bartholomew Fair.

Lit. That was mine afore, gentlemen; this morning. I had that, i'faith, upon his license, believe me, there he comes after me.

Quar. Come, John, this ambitious wit of yours, I am afraid, will do you no good in the end.

Lit. No! why, sir?

Quar. You grow so insolent with it, and over-doing, John, that if you look not to it, and tie it up, it will bring you to some obscure place in time, and there 'twill leave you.

Winw. Do not trust it too much, John, be more sparing, and use it but now and then; a wit is a dangerous thing in this age; do not over-buy it.

Lit. Think you so, gentlemen? I'll take heed on't hereafter.

Mrs. Lit. Yes, do, John.

Cokes. A pretty little soul, this same mistress Littlewit, would I might marry her!

Grace. So would I; or any body else, so I might 'scape you.
                                                            [*Aside.*

Cokes. Numps, I will see it, Numps, 'tis decreed: never be melancholy for the matter.

Waspe. Why, see it, sir, see it, do, see it: who hinders you? why do you not go see it? 'slid see it.

Cokes. The Fair, Numps, the Fair.

Waspe. Would the Fair, and all the drums and rattles in it, were in your belly for me! they are already in your brain. He that had the means to travel your head now, should meet finer sights than any are in the Fair, and make a finer voyage on't; to see it all hung with cockle shells, pebbles, fine wheat straws, and here and there a chicken's feather, and a cobweb.

Quar. Good faith, he looks, methinks, an you mark him, like one that were made to catch flies, with his sir Cranion-legs.

Winw. And his Numps, to flap them away.

Waspe. God be wi' you, sir, there's your bee in a box, and much good do't you.   [*Gives Cokes the box.*

Cokes. Why, your friend, and Bartholomew; an you be so contumacious.

Quar. What mean you, Numps?
                        [*Takes Waspe aside as he is going out.*

Waspe. I'll not be guilty, I, gentlemen.

Over. You will not let him go, brother, and lose him?

Cokes. Who can hold that will away? I had rather lose him than the Fair, I wusse.

Waspe. You do not know the inconvenience, gentlemen, you persuade to, nor what trouble I have with him in these humours. If he go to the Fair, he will buy of every thing to a baby there; and household stuff for that too. If a leg or an arm on him did not grow on, he would lose it in the press. Pray heaven I bring him off with one stone! And then he is such a ravener after fruit!—you will not believe what a coil I had t'other day to compound a business between a Cather'nepear woman, and him, about snatching: 'tis intolerable, gentlemen.

Winw. O, but you must not leave him now to these hazards, Numps.

Waspe. Nay, he knows too well I will not leave him, and that makes him presume: Well, sir, will you go now? if you have such

an itch in your feet, to foot it to the Fair, why do you stop, am I
[o'] your tarriers? go, will you go, sir? why do you not go?

Cokes. O Numps, have I brought you about? come, mistress
Grace, and sister, I am resolute Bat, i'faith, still.

Gra. Truly, I have no such fancy to the Fair, nor ambition to
see it: there's none goes thither of any quality or fashion.

Cokes. O Lord, sir! you shall pardon me, mistress Grace, we are
enow of ourselves to make it a fashion; and for qualities, let Numps
alone, he'll find qualities.

Quar. What a rogue in apprehension is this, to understand her
language no better!

Winw. Ay, and offer to marry her! Well, I will leave the chase
of my widow for to-day, and directly to the Fair. These flies
cannot, this hot season, but engender us excellent creeping sport.

Quar. A man that has but a spoonful of brain would think so.—
Farewell, John.   [*Exeunt Quarlous and Winwife.*

Lit. Win, you see 'tis in fashion to go to the Fair, Win; we must
to the Fair too, you and I, Win. I have an affair in the Fair, Win,
a puppet-play of mine own making, say nothing, that I writ for
the motion-man, which you must see, Win.

Mrs. Lit. I would I might, John; but my mother will never
consent to such a profane motion, she will call it.

Lit. Tut, we'll have a device, a dainty one: Now, Wit, help at a
pinch, good Wit, come, come, good Wit, an it be thy will! I have it,
Win, I have it i'faith, and 'tis a fine one. Win, long to eat of a pig,
sweet Win, in the Fair, do you see, in the heart of the Fair, not at
Pye-corner. Your mother will do any thing, Win, to satisfy your
longing, you know; pray thee long presently; and be sick o' the
sudden, good Win. I'll go in and tell her; cut thy lace in the
mean time, and play the hypocrite, sweet Win.

Mrs. Lit. No, I'll not make me unready for it: I can be hypo
crite enough, though I were never so strait-laced.

Lit. You say true, you have been bred in the family, and brought
up to't. Our mother is a most elect hypocrite, and has maintained
us all this seven year with it, like gentlefolks.

Mrs. Lit. Ay, let her alone, John, she is not a wise wilful widow
for nothing; nor a sanctified sister for a song. And let me alone
too, I have somewhat of the mother in me, you shall see: fetch her,
fetch her—[*Exit Littlewit.*] Ah! ah!   [*Seems to swoon.*

Re-enter LITTLEWIT *with* Dame PURECRAFT.

Pure. Now, the blaze of the beauteous discipline, fright away
this evil from our house! how now, Win-the-fight, child! how do
you? sweet child, speak to me.

Mrs. Lit. Yes, forsooth.

Pure. Look up, sweet Win-the-fight, and suffer not the enemy
to enter you at this door, remember that your education has been
with the purest: What polluted one was it, that named first the
unclean beast, pig, to you, child?

Mrs. Lit. Uh, uh!

Lit. Not I, on my sincerity, mother! she longed above three hours ere she would let me know it.—Who was it, Win?

Mrs. Lit. A profane black thing with a beard, John.

Pure. O, resist it, Win-the-fight, it is the tempter, the wicked tempter, you may know it by the fleshly motion of pig; be strong against it, and its foul temptations, in these assaults, whereby it broacheth flesh and blood, as it were on the weaker side; and pray against its carnal provocations; good child, sweet child, pray.

Lit. Good mother, I pray you, that she may eat some pig, and her belly full too; and do not you cast away your own child, and perhaps one of mine, with your tale of the tempter. How do you do, Win, are you not sick?

Mrs. Lit. Yes, a great deal, John, uh, uh!

Pure. What shall we do? Call our zealous brother Busy hither, for his faithful fortification in this charge of the adversary. [*Exit Littlewit.*] Child, my dear child, you shall eat pig; be comforted, my sweet child.

Mrs. Lit. Ay, but in the Fair, mother.

Pure. I mean in the Fair, if it can be any way made or found lawful.—

Re-enter LITTLEWIT.

Where is our brother Busy? will he not come? Look up, child.

Lit. Presently, mother, as soon as he has cleansed his beard. I found him fast by the teeth in the cold turkey-pie in the cupboard, with a great white loaf on his left hand, and a glass of malmsey on his right.

Pure. Slander not the brethren, wicked one.

Lit. Here he is now, purified, mother.

Enter ZEAL-OF-THE-LAND BUSY.

Pure. O brother Busy! your help here, to edify and raise us up in a scruple: my daughter Win-the-fight is visited with a natural disease of women, called a longing to eat pig.

Lit. Ay, sir, a Bartholomew pig; and in the Fair.

Pure. And I would be satisfied from you, religiously-wise, whether a widow of the sanctified assembly, or a widow's daughter, may commit the act without offence to the weaker sisters.

Busy. Verily, for the disease of longing, it is a disease, a carnal disease, or appetite, incident to women; and as it is carnal and incident, it is natural, very natural: now pig, it is a meat, and a meat that is nourishing and may be longed for, and so consequently eaten; it may be eaten; very exceeding well eaten; but in the Fair, and as a Bartholomew pig, it cannot be eaten; for the very calling it a Bartholomew pig, and to eat it so, is a spice of idolatry, and you make the Fair no better than one of the high-places. This, I take it, is the state of the question: a high-place.

Lit. Ay, but in state of necessity, place should give place, master Busy. I have a conceit left yet.

Pure. Good brother Zeal-of-the-land, think to make it as lawful as you can.

Lit. Yes, sir, and as soon as you can; for it must be, sir: you see the danger my little wife is in, sir.

Pure. Truly, I do love my child dearly, and I would not have her miscarry, or hazard her firstfruits, if it might be otherwise.

Bus. Surely, it may be otherwise, but it is subject to construction, subject, and hath a face of offence with the weak, a great face, a foul face; but that face may have a veil put over it, and be shadowed as it were; it may be eaten, and in the Fair, I take it, in a booth, the tents of the wicked: the place is not much, not very much, we may be religious in the midst of the profane, so it be eaten with a reformed mouth, with sobriety and humbleness; not gorged in with gluttony or greediness, there's the fear: for, should she go there, as taking pride in the place, or delight in the unclean dressing, to feed the vanity of the eye, or lust of the palate, it were not well, it were not fit, it were abominable, and not good.

Lit. Nay, I knew that afore, and told her on't; but courage, Win, we'll be humble enough, we'll seek out the homeliest booth in the Fair, that's certain; rather than fail, we'll eat it on the ground.

Pure. Ay, and I'll go with you myself, Win-the-fight, and my brother Zeal-of-the-land shall go with us too, for our better consolation.

Mrs. Lit. Uh, uh!

Lit. Ay, and Solomon too, Win, the more the merrier. Win, we'll leave Rabbi Busy in a booth. [*Aside to Mrs. Lit.*]—Solomon! my cloak.

Enter SOLOMON *with the cloak.*

Sol. Here, sir.

Bus. In the way of comfort to the weak, I will go and eat. I will eat exceedingly, and prophesy; there may be a good use made of it too, now I think on't: by the public eating of swine's flesh, to profess our hate and loathing of Judaism, whereof the brethren stand tax'd. I will therefore eat, yea, I will eat exceedingly.

Lit. Good, i'faith, I will eat heartily too, because I will be no Jew, I could never away with that stiff-necked generation: and truly, I hope my little one will be like me, that cries for pig so in the mother's belly.

Bus. Very likely, exceeding likely, very exceeding likely.

[*Exeunt.*

ACT II

SCENE I.—*The Fair.*

A number of Booths, Stalls, etc., set out.

LANTHORN LEATHERHEAD, JOAN TRASH, *and others, sitting by their wares.*

Enter JUSTICE OVERDO, *at a distance, in disguise.*

Over. Well, in justice name, and the king's, and for the common-wealth! defy all the world, Adam Overdo, for a disguise, and all story; for thou hast fitted thyself, I swear. Fain would I meet the Linceus now, that eagle's eye, that piercing Epidaurian serpent (as my Quintus Horace calls him) that could discover a justice of peace (and lately of the Quorum) under this covering. They may have seen many a fool in the habit of a justice; but never till now, a justice in the habit of a fool. Thus must we do though, that wake for the public good; and thus hath the wise magistrate done in all ages. There is a doing of right out of wrong, if the way be found. Never shall I enough commend a worthy worshipful man, sometime a capital member of this city, for his high wisdom in this point, who would take you now the habit of a porter, now of a carman, now of the dog-killer, in this month of August; and in the winter, of a seller of tinder-boxes. And what would he do in all these shapes? marry, go you into every alehouse, and down into every cellar; measure the length of puddings; take the gage of black pots and cans, ay, and custards, with a stick; and their cir-cumference with a thread; weigh the loaves of bread on his middle finger; then would he send for them home; give the puddings to the poor, the bread to the hungry, the custards to his children; break the pots, and burn the cans himself: he would not trust his corrupt officers, he would do it himself. Would all men in authority would follow this worthy precedent! for alas, as we are public persons, what do we know? nay, what can we know? we hear with other men's ears, we see with other men's eyes. A foolish constable or a sleepy watchman, is all our information; he slanders a gentle-man by the virtue of his place, as he calls it, and we, by the vice of ours, must believe him. As, a while agone, they made me, yea me, to mistake an honest zealous pursuivant for a seminary; and a proper young bachelor of musick, for a bawd. This we are subject to that live in high place; all our intelligence is idle, and most of our intelligencers knaves; and, by your leave, ourselves thought little better, if not arrant fools, for believing them. I, Adam Overdo, am resolved therefore to spare spy-money hereafter, and make mine own discoveries. Many are the yearly enormities of this Fair, in whose courts of Pie-poudres I have had the honour, during the three days, sometimes to sit as judge. But this is the special day for detection of those foresaid enormities. Here is my black book for the purpose; this the cloud that hides me; under this covert I shall see and not be seen. On, Junius Brutus. And as I began, so I'll end; in justice name, and the king's, and for the commonwealth! *[Advances to the booths, and stands aside.*

Leath. The Fair's pestilence dead methinks; people come not abroad to-day, whatever the matter is. Do you hear, sister Trash, lady of the basket? sit farther with your gingerbread progeny there, and hinder not the prospect of my shop, or I'll have it proclaimed in the Fair, what stuff they are made on.

Trash. Why, what stuff are they made on, brother Leatherhead? nothing but what's wholesome, I assure you.

Leath. Yes, stale bread, rotten eggs, musty ginger, and dead honey, you know.

Over. Ay! have I met with enormity so soon? *[Aside.*

Leath. I shall mar your market, old Joan.

Trash. Mar my market, thou too-proud pedlar! do thy worst, I defy thee, I, and thy stable of hobby-horses. I pay for my ground, as well as thou dost: an thou wrong'st me, for all thou art parcel-poet, and an inginer, I'll find a friend shall right me, and make a ballad of thee, and thy cattle all over. Are you puft up with the pride of your wares? your arsedine?

Leath. Go to, old Joan, I'll talk with you anon; and take you down too, afore justice Overdo: he is the man must charm you, I'll have you in the Pie-poudres.

Trash. Charm me! I'll meet thee face to face, afore his worship, when thou darest: and though I be a little crooked o' my body, I shall be found as upright in my dealing as any woman in Smithfield, I; charm me!

Over. I am glad to hear my name is their terror yet, this is doing of justice. *[Aside.]* *[A number of people pass over the stage.*

Leath. What do you lack? what is't you buy? what do you lack? rattles, drums, halberts, horses, babies o' the best, fiddles of the finest?

Enter Costard-monger, *followed by* NIGHTINGALE.

Cost. Buy any pears, pears, fine, very fine pears!
Trash. Buy any gingerbread, gilt gingerbread!
Night. Hey, *[Sings.*

> Now the Fair's a filling!
> O, for a tune to startle
> The birds o' the booths here billing,
> Yearly with old saint Bartle!
> The drunkards they are wading,
> The punks and chapmen trading;
> Who'd see the Fair without his lading?

Buy any ballads, new ballads?

Enter URSULA, *from her Booth.*

Urs. Fie upon't: who would wear out their youth and prime thus, in roasting of pigs, that had any cooler vocation? hell's a kind of cold cellar to't, a very fine vault, o' my conscience!—What, Mooncalf!

Moon. [*within.*] Here, mistress.

Night. How now, Ursula? in a heat, in a heat?

Urs. My chair, you false faucet you; and my morning's draught, quickly, a bottle of ale, to quench me, rascal. I am all fire and fat, Nightingale, I shall e'en melt away to the first woman, a rib again, I am afraid. I do water the ground in knots, as I go, like a great garden pot; you may follow me by the SS. I make.

Night. Alas, good Urse! was Zekiel here this morning?

Urs. Zekiel? what Zekiel?

Night. Zekiel Edgworth, the civil cutpurse, you know him well enough; he that talks bawdy to you still: I call him my secretary.

Urs. He promised to be here this morning, I remember.

Night. When he comes, bid him stay: I'll be back again presently.

Urs. Best take your morning dew in your belly, Nightingale.—

Enter MOONCALF, *with the Chair.*

Come, sir, set it here; did not I bid you should get a chair let out o' the sides for me, that my hips might play? you'll never think of any thing, till your dame be rump-gall'd; 'tis well, changeling: because it can take in your grasshopper's thighs, you care for no more. Now, you look as you had been in the corner of the booth, fleaing your breech with a candle's end, and set fire o' the Fair. Fill, Stote, fill.

Over. This pig-woman do I know, and I will put her in, for my second enormity; she hath been before me, punk, pinnace, and bawd, any time these two and twenty years upon record in the Pie-poudres.   [*Aside.*

Urs. Fill again, you unlucky vermin!

Moon. 'Pray you be not angry, mistress, I'll have it widen'd anon.

Urs. No, no, I shall e'en dwindle away to't, ere the Fair be done, you think, now you have heated me: a poor vex'd thing I am, I feel myself dropping already as fast as I can; two stone o' suet a day is my proportion. I can but hold life and soul together, with this, (here's to you, Nightingale,) and a whiff of tobacco at most. Where's my pipe now? not fill'd! thou arrant incubee.

Night. Nay, Ursula, thou'lt gall between the tongue and the teeth, with fretting, now.

Urs. How can I hope that ever he'll discharge his place of trust, tapster, a man of reckoning under me, that remembers nothing I say to him? [*Exit Night.*] but look to't, sirrah, you were best. Three-pence a pipe-full, I will have made, of all my whole half-pound of tobacco, and a quarter of pound of colt's-foot mixt with it too, to [eke] it out. I that have dealt so long in the fire, will not be to seek in smoke, now. Then six and twenty shillings a barrel I will advance on my beer, and fifty shillings a hundred on my bottle-ale; I have told you the ways how to raise it. Froth your cans well in the filling, at length, rogue, and jog your bottles o' the buttock, sirrah, then skink out the first glass ever, and drink with all companies, though you be sure to be drunk; you'll mis-reckon the better, and be less ashamed on't. But your true trick, rascal, must be, to be ever busy, and mistake away the bottles and cans, in haste, before they be half drunk off, and never hear any body call, (if they should chance to mark you,) till you have brought fresh, and be able to forswear them. Give me a drink of ale.

Over. This is the very womb and bed of enormity! gross as her-self! this must all down for enormity, all, every whit on't. [*Aside.*
[*Knocking within.*

Urs. Look who's there, sirrah: five shillings a pig is my price, at least; if it be a sow pig, sixpence more; if she be a great-bellied wife, and long for't, sixpence more for that.

Over. *O tempora! O mores!* I would not have lost my discovery of this one grievance, for my place, and worship o' the bench. How is the poor subject abused here! Well, I will fall in with her, and with her Mooncalf, and win out wonders of enormity. [*Comes forward.*]—By thy leave, goodly woman, and the fatness of the Fair, oily as the king's constable's lamp, and shining as his shooing-horn! hath thy ale virtue, or thy beer strength, that the tongue of man may be tickled, and his palate pleased in the morning? Let thy pretty nephew here go search and see.

Urs. What new roarer is this?

Moon. O Lord! do you not know him, mistress? 'tis mad Arthur of Bradley, that makes the orations.—Brave master, old Arthur of Bradley, how do you? welcome to the Fair! when shall we hear you again, to handle your matters, with your back against a booth, ha? I have been one of your little disciples, in my days.

Over. Let me drink, boy, with my love, thy aunt, here; that I may be eloquent: but of thy best, lest it be bitter in my mouth, and my words fall foul on the Fair.

Urs. Why dost thou not fetch him drink, and offer him to sit?

Moon. Is it ale or beer, master Arthur?

Over. Thy best, pretty stripling, thy best; the same thy dove drinketh, and thou drawest on holydays.

Urs. Bring him a sixpenny bottle of ale: they say, a fool's handsel is lucky.

Over. Bring both, child. [*Sits down in the booth.*] Ale for Arthur, and Beer for Bradley. Ale for thine aunt, boy. [*Exit Moon.*]—My disguise takes to the very wish and reach of it. I shall, by the benefit of this, discover enough, and more: and yet get off with the reputation of what I would be: a certain middling thing, between a fool and a madman. [*Aside.*

Enter KNOCKEM.

Knock. What! my little lean Ursula! my she-bear! art thou alive yet, with thy litter of pigs to grunt out another Bartholomew Fair? ha!

Urs. Yes, and to amble a foot, when the Fair is done, to hear you groan out of a cart, up the heavy hill—

Knock. Of Holbourn, Ursula, meanst thou so? for what, for what, pretty Urse?

Urs. For cutting halfpenny purses, or stealing little penny dogs out o' the Fair.

Knock. O! good words, good words, Urse.

Over. Another special enormity. A cut-purse of the sword, the boot, and the feather! those are his marks.　　　　[*Aside.*

Re-enter MOONCALF, *with the ale, etc.*

Urs. You are one of those horse-leeches that gave out I was dead, in Turnbull-street, of a surfeit of bottle-ale and tripes?

Knock. No, 'twas better meat, Urse: cow's udders, cow's udders!

Urs. Well, I shall be meet with your mumbling mouth one day.

Knock. What! thou'lt poison me with a newt in a bottle of ale, wilt thou? or a spider in a tobacco-pipe, Urse? Come, there's no malice in these fat folks, I never fear thee, an I can scape thy lean Mooncalf here. Let's drink it out, good Urse, and no vapours!

　　　　　　　　　　　　　　　　　　　　　[*Exit Ursula.*

Over. Dost thou hear, boy? There's for thy ale, and the remnant for thee.—Speak in thy faith of a faucet, now; is this goodly person before us here, this vapours, a knight of the knife?

Moon. What mean you by that, master Arthur?

Over. I mean a child of the horn-thumb, a babe of booty, boy, a cut-purse.

Moon. O Lord, sir! far from it. This is master Daniel Knockem Jordan: the ranger of Turnbull. He is a horse-courser, sir.

Over. Thy dainty dame, though, call'd him cut-purse.

Moon. Like enough, sir; she'll do forty such things in an hour (an you listen to her) for her recreation, if the toy take her in the greasy kerchief: it makes her fat, you see; she battens with it.

Over. Here I might have been deceived now, and have put a fool's blot upon myself, if I had not played an after game of discretion!　　　　[*Aside.*

Re-enter URSULA, *dropping.*

Knock. Alas, poor Urse! this is an ill season for thee.

Urs. Hang yourself, hackney-man!

Knock. How, how, Urse! vapours? motion breed vapours?

Urs. Vapours! never tusk, nor twirl your dibble, good Jordan, I know what you'll take to a very drop. Though you be captain of the roarers, and fight well at the case of piss-pots, you shall not fright me with your lion-chap, sir, nor your tusks; you angry!

you are hungry. Come, a pig's head will stop your mouth, and stay your stomach at all times.

Knock. Thou art such another mad, merry Urse, still! troth I do make conscience of vexing thee, now in the dog-days, this hot weather, for fear of foundering thee in the body, and melting down a pillar of the Fair. Pray thee take thy chair again, and keep state; and let's have a fresh bottle of ale, and a pipe of tobacco; and no vapours. I'll have this belly o' thine taken up, and thy grass scoured, wench.—

Enter EDGWORTH.

Look, here's Ezekiel Edgworth; a fine boy of his inches, as any is in the Fair! has still money in his purse, and will pay all, with a kind heart, and good vapours.

Edg. That I will indeed, willingly, master Knockem; fetch some ale and tobacco.   [*Exit Moon.—People cross the stage.*

Leath. What do you lack, gentlemen? maid, see a fine hobby-horse for your young master; cost you but a token a-week his provender.

Re-enter NIGHTINGALE, *with* Corn-cutter, *and* Mousetrap-man.

Corn. Have you any corns in your feet and toes?

Mouse. Buy a mousetrap, a mousetrap, or a tormentor for a flea?

Trash. Buy some gingerbread?

Night. Ballads, ballads! fine new ballads:

Hear for your love, and buy for your money.
A delicate ballad o' the ferret and the coney.
A preservative again' the punk's evil.
Another of goose-green starch, and the devil.
A dozen of divine points, and the godly garters:
The fairing of good counsel, of an ell and three-quarters.

What is't you buy?

The windmill blown down by the witch's fart.
Or saint George, that, O! did break the dragon's heart.

Re-enter MOONCALF, *with ale and tobacco.*

Edg. Master Nightingale, come hither, leave your mart a little.

Night. O my secretary! what says my secretary?
                                    [*They walk into the booth.*

Over. Child of the bottles, what's he? what's he?
                                    [*Points to Edgworth.*

Moon. A civil young gentleman, master Arthur, that keeps company with the roarers, and disburses all still. He has ever money in his purse; he pays for them, and they roar for him; one does good offices for another. They call him the secretary, but he serves nobody. A great friend of the ballad-man's, they are never asunder.

Over. What pity 'tis, so civil a young man should haunt this debauched company? here's the bane of the youth of our time apparent. A proper penman, I see't in his countenance, he has a good clerk's look with him, and I warrant him a quick hand.

Moon. A very quick hand, sir. [*Exit.*

Edg. [*whispering with Nightingale and Ursula.*] All the purses, and purchase, I give you to-day by conveyance, bring hither to Ursula's presently. Here we will meet at night in her lodge, and share. Look you choose good places for your standing in the Fair, when you sing, Nightingale.

Urs. Ay, near the fullest passages; and shift them often.

Edg. And in your singing, you must use your hawk's eye nimbly, and fly the purse to a mark still, where 'tis worn, and on which side; that you may give me the sign with your beak, or hang your head that way in the tune.

Urs. Enough, talk no more on't: your friendship, masters, is not now to begin. Drink your draught of indenture, your sup of covenant, and away: the Fair fills apace, company begins to come in, and I have ne'er a pig ready yet.

Knock. Well said! fill the cups, and light the tobacco: let's give fire in the works, and noble vapours.

Edg. And shall we have smocks, Ursula, and good whimsies, ha!

Urs. Come, you are in your bawdy vein!—the best the Fair will afford, Zekiel, if bawd Whit keep his word.—

Re-enter MOONCALF.

How do the pigs, Mooncalf?

Moon. Very passionate, mistress, one of 'em has wept out an eye. Master Arthur o' Bradley is melancholy here, nobody talks to him. Will you any tobacco, master Arthur?

Over. No, boy; let my meditations alone.

Moon. He's studying for an oration, now.

Over. If I can with this day's travail, and all my policy, but rescue this youth here out of the hands of the lewd man and the strange woman, I will sit down at night, and say with my friend Ovid,

Jamque opus exegi, quod nec Jovis ira, nec ignis, etc. [*Aside.*

Knock. Here, Zekiel, here's a health to Ursula, and a kind vapour; thou hast money in thy purse still, and store! how dost thou come by it? pray thee vapour thy friends some in a courteous vapour.

Edg. Half I have, master Dan. Knockem, is always at your service. [*Pulls out his purse.*

Over. Ha, sweet nature! what goshawk would prey upon such a lamb? [*Aside.*

Knock. Let's see what 'tis, Zekiel; count it, come, fill him to pledge me.

Enter WINWIFE *and* QUARLOUS.

Winw. We are here before them, methinks.

Quar. All the better, we shall see them come in now.

Leath. What do you lack, gentlemen, what is't you lack? a fine horse? a lion? a bull? a bear? a dog? or a cat? an excellent fine Bartholomew-bird? or an instrument? what is't you lack?

Quar. 'Slid! here's Orpheus among the beasts, with his fiddle and all!

Trash. Will you buy any comfortable bread, gentlemen?

Quar. And Ceres selling her daughter's picture, in ginger-work.

Winw. That these people should be so ignorant to think us chapmen for them! do we look as if we would buy gingerbread, or hobby-horses?

Quar. Why, they know no better ware than they have, nor better customers than come: and our very being here makes us fit to be demanded, as well as others. Would Cokes would come! there were a true customer for them.

Knock. [*to Edgworth.*] How much is't? thirty shillings? Who's yonder! Ned Winwife and Tom Quarlous, I think! yes: (give me it all, give it me all.)—Master Winwife! Master Quarlous! will you take a pipe of tobacco with us?—Do not discredit me now, Zekiel.
[*Edgworth gives him his purse.*

Winw. Do not see him: he is the roaring horse-courser, pray thee let's avoid him: turn down this way.

Quar. 'Slud, I'll see him, and roar with him too, an he roared as loud as Neptune; pray thee go with me.

Winw. You may draw me to as likely an inconvenience, when you please, as this.

Quar. Go to then, come along; we have nothing to do, man, but to see sights now. [*They advance to the booth.*

Knock. Welcome, master Quarlous, and master Winwife; will you take any froth and smoke with us?

Quar. Yes, sir; but you'll pardon us if we knew not of so much familiarity between us afore.

Knock. As what, sir?

Quar. To be so lightly invited to smoke and froth.

Knock. A good vapour! will you sit down, sir? this is old Ursula's mansion; how like you her bower? Here you may have your punk and your pig in state, sir, both piping hot.

Quar. I had rather have my punk cold, sir.

Over. There's for me: punk! and pig! [*Aside.*

Urs. [*within.*] What, Mooncalf, you rogue!

Moon. By and by, the bottle is almost off, mistress; here, master Arthur.

Urs. [*within.*] I'll part you and your play-fellow there, in the garded coat, an you sunder not the sooner.

Knock. Master Winwife, you are proud, methinks, you do not talk, nor drink; are you proud?

Winw. Not of the company I am in, sir, nor the place, I assure you.

Knock. You do not except at the company, do you! are you in vapours, sir?

Moon. Nay, good master Daniel Knockem, respect my mistress's bower, as you call it; for the honour of our booth, none o' your vapours here.

Enter URSULA *with a fire-brand.*

Urs. Why, you thin, lean polecat you, an they have a mind to be in their vapours must you hinder 'em? What did you know, vermin, if they would have lost a cloke, or such trifle? must you be drawing the air of pacification here, while I am tormented within i' the fire, you weasel?   [*Aside to Mooncalf.*

Moon. Good mistress, 'twas in behalf of your booth's credit that I spoke.

Urs. Why! would my booth have broke, if they had fallen out in't, sir? or would their heat have fired it? In, you rogue, and wipe the pigs, and mend the fire, that they fall not, or I'll both baste and roast you 'till your eyes drop out like them.—Leave the bottle behind you, and be curst awhile!   [*Exit Moon.*

Quar. Body o' the Fair! what's this? mother of the bawds?

Knock. No, she's mother of the pigs, sir, mother of the pigs.

Winw. Mother of the furies, I think, by her fire-brand.

Quar. Nay, she is too fat to be a fury, sure some walking sow of tallow!

Winw. An inspired vessel of kitchen stuff!

Quar. She'll make excellent geer for the coach-makers here in Smithfield, to anoint wheels and axletrees with.
                    [*She drinks this while.*

Urs. Ay, ay, gamesters, mock a plain plump soft wench of the suburbs, do, because she's juicy and wholesome; you must have your thin pinched ware, pent up in the compass of a dog-collar, (or 'twill not do) that looks like a long laced conger, set upright, and a green feather, like fennel in the joll on't.

Knock. Well said, Urse, my good Urse! to 'em, Urse!

Quar. Is she your quagmire, Daniel Knockem? is this your bog?

Night. We shall have a quarrel presently.

Knock. How! bog! quagmire? foul vapours! humph!

Quar. Yes, he that would venture for't, I assure him, might sink into her and be drown'd a week ere any friend he had could find where he were.

Winw. And then he would be a fortnight weighing up again.

Quar. 'Twere like falling into a whole shire of butter; they had need be a team of Dutchmen should draw him out.

Knock. Answer 'em, Urse: where's thy Bartholomew wit now, Urse, thy Bartholomew wit?

Urs. Hang 'em, rotten, roguy cheaters, I hope to see them plagued one day (pox'd they are already, I am sure) with lean playhouse poultry, that has the bony rump, sticking out like the ace of spades, or the point of a partizan, that every rib of them is like the tooth of a saw; and will so grate them with their hips and shoulders, as (take 'em altogether) they were as good lie with a hurdle.

Quar. Out upon her, how she drips! she's able to give a man the sweating sickness with looking on her.

Urs. Marry look off, with a patch on your face, and a dozen in your breech, though they be of scarlet, sir. I have seen as fine outsides as either of yours, bring lousy linings to the brokers, ere now, twice a week.

Quar. Do you think there may be a fine new cucking-stool in the Fair, to be purchased; one large enough, I mean? I know there is a pond of capacity for her.

Urs. For your mother, you rascal! Out, you rogue, you hedge-bird, you pimp, you pannier-man's bastard, you!

Quar. Ha, ha, ha!

Urs. Do you sneer, you dog's-head, you trendle-tail! you look as you were begotten a top of a cart in harvest time, when the whelp was hot and eager. Go, snuff after your brother's bitch, mistress Commodity; that's the livery you wear, 'twill be out at the elbows shortly. It's time you went to't for the t'other remnant.

Knock. Peace, Urse, peace, Urse;—they'll kill the poor whale, and make oil of her. Pray thee, go in.

Urs. I'll see them pox'd first, and piled, and double piled.

Winw. Let's away, her language grows greasier than her pigs.

Urs. Does it so, snotty-nose? good lord! are you snivelling? You were engendered on a she-beggar in a barn, when the bald thrasher, your sire, was scarce warm.

Winw. Pray thee let's go.

Quar. No, faith; I'll stay the end of her now; I know she cannot last long: I find by her smiles she wanes apace.

Urs. Does she so? I'll set you gone. Give me my pig-pan hither a little: I'll scald you hence, an you will not go.   [*Exit.*

Knock. Gentlemen, these are very strange vapours, and very idle vapours, I assure you.

Quar. You are a very serious ass, we assure you.

Knock. Humph, *ass!* and *serious!* nay, then pardon me my vapour. I have a foolish vapour, gentlemen: Any man that does vapour me the ass, master Quarlous—

Quar. What then, master Jordan?

Knock. I do vapour him the lie.

Quar. Faith, and to any man that vapours me the lie, I do vapour that.   [*Strikes him.*

Knock. Nay then, vapours upon vapours.   [*They fight.*

Re-enter URSULA, *with the dripping-pan.*

Edg. Night. 'Ware the pan, the pan, the pan! she comes with the pan, gentlemen! [*Ursula falls with the pan.*]—God bless the woman.

Urs. Oh!   [*Exeunt Quarlous and Winwife.*

Trash. [*runs in.*] What's the matter?

Over. Goodly woman!

Moon. Mistress!

Urs. Curse of hell! that ever I saw these fiends! oh! I have scalded my leg, my leg, my leg, my leg! I have lost a limb in the service! run for some cream and sallad-oil, quickly. Are you under-peering, you baboon? rip off my hose, an you be men, men, men.

Moon. Run you for some cream, good mother Joan. I'll look to your basket. [*Exit Trash.*

Leath. Best sit up in your chair, Ursula. Help, gentlemen.

Knock. Be of good cheer, Urse; thou hast hindered me the currying of a couple of stallions here, that abused the good race-bawd of Smithfield; 'twas time for them to go.

Night. I'faith, when the pan came,—they had made you run else. This had been a fine time for purchase, if you had ventured. [*Aside to Edgworth.*

Edg. Not a whit, these fellows were too fine to carry money.

Knock. Nightingale, get some help to carry her leg out of the air: take off her shoes. Body o' me! she has the mallanders, the scratches, the crown scab, and the quitter bone in the t'other leg.

Urs. Oh, the pox! why do you put me in mind of my leg thus, to make it prick and shoot? Would you have me in the hospital afore my time?

Knock. Patience, Urse, take a good heart, 'tis but a blister as big as a windgall. I'll take it away with the white of an egg, a little honey and hog's grease, have thy pasterns well roll'd, and thou shalt pace again by to-morrow. I'll tend thy booth, and look to thy affairs the while: thou shalt sit in thy chair, and give directions, and shine Ursa major.

[*Exeunt Knockem and Mooncalf, with Ursula in her chair.*

Over. These are the fruits of bottle-ale and tobacco! the foam of the one, and the fumes of the other! Stay, young man, and despise not the wisdom of these few hairs that are grown grey in care of thee.

Edg. Nightingale, stay a little. Indeed I'll hear some of this!

Enter COKES, *with his box,* WASPE, *Mistress* OVERDO, *and* GRACE.

Cokes. Come, Numps, come, where are you? Welcome into the Fair, mistress Grace.

Edg. 'Slight, he will call company, you shall see, and put us into doings presently.

Over. Thirst not after that frothy liquor, ale; for who knows when he openeth the stopple, what may be in the bottle? Hath not a snail, a spider, yea, a newt been found there? thirst not after it, youth; thirst not after it.

Cokes. This is a brave fellow, Numps, let's hear him.

Waspe. 'Sblood! how brave is he? in a garded coat! You were best truck with him; e'en strip, and truck presently, it will become you. Why will you hear him? because he is an ass. and may be a-kin to the Cokeses?

Cokes. O, good Numps.

Over. Neither do thou lust after that tawney weed tobacco.

Cokes. Brave words!

Over. Whose complexion is like the Indian's that vents it.

Cokes. Are they not brave words, sister?

Over. And who can tell, if before the gathering and making up thereof, the Alligarta hath not piss'd thereon?

Waspe. 'Heart! let 'em be brave words, as brave as they will! an they were all the brave words in a country, how then? Will you away yet, have you enough on him? Mistress Grace, come you away; I pray you, be not you accessary. If you do lose your license, or somewhat else, sir, with listening to his fables, say Numps is a witch, with all my heart, do, say so.

Cokes. Avoid in your satin doublet, Numps.

Over. The creeping venom of which subtle serpent, as some late writers affirm, neither the cutting of the perilous plant, nor the drying of it, nor the lighting or burning, can any way persway or assuage.

Cokes. Good, i'faith! is it not, sister?

Over. Hence it is that the lungs of the tobacconist are rotted, the liver spotted, the brain smoked like the backside of the pig-woman's booth here, and the whole body within, black as her pan you saw e'en now, without.

Cokes. A fine similitude that, sir! did you see the pan?

Edg. Yes, sir.

Over. Nay, the hole in the nose here of some tobacco-takers, or the third nostril, if I may so call it, which makes that they can vent the tobacco out, like the ace of clubs, or rather the flower-de-lis, is caused from the tobacco, the mere tobacco! when the poor innocent pox, having nothing to do there, is miserably and most unconscionably slandered.

Cokes. Who would have missed this, sister?

Mrs. Over. Not any body but Numps.

Cokes. He does not understand.

Edg. [*picks Cokes's pocket of his purse.*] Nor you feel.   [*Aside.*

Cokes. What would you have, sister, of a fellow that knows nothing but a basket-hilt, and an old fox in't? the best musick in the Fair will not move a log.

Edg. [*gives the purse aside to Night.*] In, to Ursula, Nightingale, and carry her comfort: see it told. This fellow was sent to us by Fortune, for our first fairing.   [*Exit Night.*

Over. But what speak I of the diseases of the body, children of the Fair?

Cokes. That's to us, sister. Brave, i'faith!

Over. Hark, O you sons and daughters of Smithfield! and hear what malady it doth the mind: it causeth swearing, it causeth swaggering, it causeth snuffling and snarling, and now and then a hurt.

Mrs. Over. He hath something of master Overdo, methinks, brother.

Cokes. So methought, sister, very much of my brother Overdo: and 'tis when he speaks.

Over. Look into any angle of the town, the Streights, or the Bermudas, where the quarrelling lesson is read, and how do they entertain the time, but with bottle-ale and tobacco? The lecturer is o' one side, and his pupils o' the other; but the seconds are still bottle-ale and tobacco, for which the lecturer reads, and the novices pay. Thirty pound a week in bottle-ale! forty in tobacco! and ten more in ale again. Then for a suit to drink in, so much, and, that being slaver'd, so much for another suit, and then a third suit, and a fourth suit! and still the bottle-ale slavereth, and the tobacco stinketh.

Waspe. Heart of a madman! are you rooted here? will you never away? what can any man find out in this bawling fellow, to grow here for? He is a full handful higher sin' he heard him. Will you fix here, and set up a booth, sir?

Over. I will conclude briefly—

Waspe. Hold your peace, you roaring rascal, I'll run my head in your chaps else. You were best build a booth, and entertain him; make your will, an you say the word, and him your heir! heart, I never knew one taken with a mouth of a peck afore. By this light, I'll carry you away on my back, an you will not come.

[*He gets Cokes up on pick-back.*

Cokes. Stay, Numps, stay, set me down: I have lost my purse, Numps. O my purse! One of my fine purses is gone!

Mrs. Over. Is it indeed, brother?

Cokes. Ay, as I am an honest man, would I were an arrant rogue else! a plague of all roguy damn'd cut-purses for me.

[*Examines his pockets.*

Waspe. Bless 'em with all my heart, with all my heart, do you see! now, as I am no infidel, that I know of, I am glad on't. Ay, I am, (here's my witness,) do you see, sir? I did not tell you of his fables, I! no, no, I am a dull malt horse, I, I know nothing. Are you not justly served, in your conscience, now, speak in your conscience? Much good do you with all my heart, and his good heart that has it, with all my heart again.

Edg. This fellow is very charitable, would he had a purse too! but I must not be too bold all at a time. [*Aside.*

Cokes. Nay, Numps, it is not my best purse.

Waspe. Not your best! death! why should it be your worst? why should it be any, indeed, at all? answer me to that, give me a reason from you, why it should be any?

Cokes. Nor my gold, Numps; I have that yet, look here else, sister. [*Shews the other purse.*

Waspe. Why so, there's all the feeling he has!

Mrs. Over. I pray you, have a better care of that, brother.

Cokes. Nay, so I will, I warrant you; let him catch this that catch can. I would fain see him get this, look you here.

Waspe. So, so, so, so, so, so, so, so! very good.

Cokes. I would have him come again now, and but offer at it. Sister, will you take notice of a good jest? I will put it just where the other was, and if we have good luck, you shall see a delicate fine trap to catch the cut-purse nibbling.

Edg. Faith, and he'll try ere you be out o' the Fair.   [*Aside.*

Cokes. Come, mistress Grace, prithee be not melancholy for my mischance; sorrow will not keep it, sweet-heart.

Grace. I do not think on't, sir.

Cokes. 'Twas but a little scurvy white money, hang it! it may hang the cut-purse one day. I have gold left to give thee a fairing yet, as hard as the world goes. Nothing angers me but that no body here look'd like a cut-purse, unless 'twere Numps.

Waspe. How! I, I look like a cut-purse? death! your sister's a cut-purse! and your mother and father, and all your kin were cut-purses! and here is a rogue is the bawd o' the cut-purses, whom I will beat to begin with.   [*Beats Overdo.*

Over. Hold thy hand, child of wrath, and heir of anger, make it not Childermass day in thy fury, or the feast of the French Bartholomew, parent of the massacre.

Cokes. Numps, Numps!

Mrs. Over. Good master Humphrey!

Waspe. You are the Patrico, are you? the patriarch of the cut-purses? You share, sir, they say; let them share this with you. Are you in your hot fit of preaching again? I'll cool you.

[*Beats him again.*
Over. Murther, murther, murther!   [*Exeunt.*

ACT III

SCENE I.—*The Fair.*

Lanthorn Leatherhead, Joan Trash, *and others, sitting by their wares, as before.*

Enter Val, Whit, Haggise, *and* Bristle.

Whit. Nay, tish all gone, now! dish tish, phen tou wilt not be phitin call, master offisher, phat ish a man te better to lishen out noyshes for tee, and tou art in an oder orld, being very shuffishient noyshes and gallantsh too? one o' their brabblesh would have fed ush all dish fortnight, but tou art so bushy about beggersh still, tou hast no leshure to intend shentlemen, and't be.

Hag. Why, I told you, Davy Bristle.

Bri. Come, come, you told me a pudding, Toby Haggise; a matter of nothing; I am sure it came to nothing. You said, let's go to Ursula's, indeed; but then you met the man with the monsters, and I could not get you from him. An old fool, not leave seeing yet!

Hag. Why, who would have thought any body would have quarrell'd so early; or that the ale o' the fair would have been up so soon?

Whit. Phy, phat a clock toest tou tink it ish, man?

Hag. I cannot tell.

Whit. Tou art a vish vatchman, i' te mean teem.

Had. Why, should the watch go by the clock, or the clock by the watch, I pray?

Bri. One should go by another, if they did well.

Whit. Tou art right now! phen didst tou ever know or hear of a shuffishient vatchment, but he did tell the clock, phat bushiness soever he had?

Bri. Nay, that's most true, a sufficient watchman knows what a clock it is.

Whit. Shleeping or vaking: ash well as te clock himshelf, or te Jack dat shtrikes him.

Bri. Let's enquire of master Leatherhead, or Joan Trash here.— Master Leatherhead, do you hear, master Leatherhead?

Whit. If it be a Ledderhead, tish a very tick Ledderhead, tat sho mush noish vill not piersh him.

Leath. I have a little business now, good friends, do not trouble me.

Whit. Phat, because o' ty wrought neet-cap, and ty phelvet sherkin, man? phy! I have sheene tee in ty ledder sherkin, ere now, mashter o' de hobby-horses, as bushy and stately as tou sheemest to be.

Trash. Why, what an you have, captain Whit? he has his choice of jerkins, you may see by that, and his caps too, I assure you, when he pleases to be either sick or employed.

Leath. God-a-mercy, Joan, answer for me.

Whit. Away, be not sheen in my company, here be shentlemen, and men of vorship.   [*Exeunt Haggise and Bristle.*

Enter QUARLOUS and WINWIFE.

Quar. We had wonderful ill luck, to miss this prologue o' the purse: but the best is, we shall have five acts of him ere night: he'll be spectacle enough, I'll answer for't.

Whit. O creesh, duke Quarlous, how dosht tou? tou dosht not know me, I fear: I am te vishesht man, but justish Overdo, in all Bartholomew Fair now. Give me twelve-pence from tee, I vill help tee to a vife vorth forty marks for't, and't be.

Quar. Away, rogue; pimp, away.

Whit. And she shall shew tee as fine cut orke for't in her shmock too as tou cansht vish i'faith; vilt tou have her, vorshipful Vinvife? I vill help tee to her here, be an't be, into pig-quarter, gi' me ty twelve-pence from tee.

Winw. Why, there's twelve-pence, pray thee wilt thou begone?

Whit. Tou art a vorthy man, and a vorshipful man still.

Quar. Get you gone, rascal.

Whit. I do mean it, man. Prinsh Quarlous, if tou hasht need on me, tou shalt find me here at Ursla's, I vill see phat ale and punque ish i' te pigsty for tee, bless ty good vorship.   [*Exit.*

Quar. Look! who comes here: John Littlewit!

Winw. And his wife, and my widow, her mother: the whole family.

Quar. 'Slight, you must give them all fairings now.

Winw. Not I, I'll not see them.

Quar. They are going a feasting. What schoolmaster's that is with 'em?

Winw. That's my rival, I believe, the baker.

Enter Rabbi BUSY, Dame PURECRAFT, JOHN LITTLEWIT, *and* Mrs. LITTLEWIT.

Busy. So, walk on in the middle way, fore-right, turn neither to the right hand nor to the left; let not your eyes be drawn aside with vanity, nor your ear with noises.

Quar. O, I know him by that start.

Leath. What do you lack, what do you buy, mistress? a fine hobby-horse, to make your son a tilter? a drum to make him a soldier? a fiddle to make him a reveller? what is't you lack? little dogs for your daughters? or babies, male or female?

Busy. Look not toward them, hearken not; the place is Smithfield, or the field of smiths, the grove of hobby-horses and trinkets, the wares are the wares of devils, and the whole Fair is the shop of Satan: they are hooks and baits, very baits, that are hung out on every side, to catch you, and to hold you, as it were, by the gills, and by the nostrils, as the fisher doth; therefore you must not look nor turn toward them.—The heathen man could stop his ears with wax against the harlot of the sea; do you the like with your fingers against the bells of the beast.

Winw. What flashes come from him!

Quar. O, he has those of his oven; a notable hot baker, 'twas when he plied the peel; he is leading his flock into the Fair now.

Winw. Rather driving them to the pens: for he will let them look upon nothing.

Enter KNOCKEM *and* WHIT *from* URSULA'S *booth.*

Knock. Gentlewomen, the weather's hot; whither walk you? have a care of your fine velvet caps, the Fair is dusty. Take a sweet delicate booth, with boughs, here in the way, and cool yourselves in the shade; you and your friends. The best pig and bottle-ale in the Fair, sir. Old Ursula is cook, there you may read; [*points to the sign, a pig's head, with a large writing under it.*] the pig's head speaks it. Poor soul, she has had a string-halt, the maryhinchco; but she's prettily amended.

Whit. A delicate show-pig, little mistress, with shweet sauce, and crackling, like de bay-leaf i' de fire, la! tou shalt ha' de clean side o' de table-clot, and di glass vash'd with phatersh of dame Annesh Cleare.

Lit. [*gazing at the inscription.*] This is fine verily. *Here be the best pigs, and she does roast them as well as ever she did,* the pig's head says.

Knock. Excellent, excellent, mistress; with fire o' juniper and rosemary branches! the oracle of the pig's head, that, sir.

Pure. Son, were you not warn'd of the vanity of the eye? have you forgot the wholesome admonition so soon?

Lit. Good mother, how shall we find a pig, if we do not look about for't: will it run off o' the spit, into our mouths, think you, as in Lubberland, and cry, *wee, wee!*

Busy. No, but your mother, religiously-wise, conceiveth it may offer itself by other means to the sense, as by way of steam, which I think it doth here in this place—huh, huh—yes, it doth. [*He scents after it like a hound.*] And it were a sin of obstinacy, great obstinacy, high and horrible obstinacy, to decline or resist the good titillation of the famelic sense, which is the smell. Therefore be bold—huh, huh, huh—follow the scent: enter the tents of the unclean, for once, and satisfy your wife's frailty. Let your frail wife be satisfied; your zealous mother, and my suffering self, will also be satisfied.

Lit. Come, Win, as good winny here as go farther, and see nothing.

Busy. We scape so much of the other vanities, by our early entering.

Pure. It is an edifying consideration.

Mrs. Lit. This is scurvy, that we must come into the Fair, and not look on't.

Lit. Win, have patience, Win, I'll tell you more anon.

[*Exeunt, into the booth, Littlewit, Mrs. Littlewit, Busy, and Purecraft.*

Knock. Mooncalf, entertain within there, the best pig in the booth, a pork-like pig. These are Banbury-bloods, o' the sincere stud, come a pig-hunting. Whit, wait, Whit, look to your charge.

[*Exit Whit.*

Busy. [*within.*] A pig prepare presently, let a pig be prepared to us.

Enter MOONCALF *and* URSULA.

Moon. 'Slight, who be these?

Urs. Is this the good service, Jordan, you'd do me?

Knock. Why, Urse, why, Urse? thou'lt have vapours i' thy leg again presently, pray thee go in, it may turn to the scratches else.

Urs. Hang your vapours, they are stale, and stink like you! Are these the guests o' the game you promised to fill my pit withal to-day?

Knock. Ay, what ail they, Urse?

Urs. Ail they! they are all sippers, sippers o' the city; they look as they would not drink off two pen'orth of bottle-ale amongst 'em.

Moon. A body may read that in their small printed ruffs.

Knock. Away, thou art a fool, Urse, and thy Mooncalf too: in your ignorant vapours now! hence! good guests, I say, right hypocrites, good gluttons. In, and set a couple o' pigs on the board, and half a dozen of the biggest bottles afore 'em, and call

Whit. [*Exit Mooncalf.*] I do not love to hear innocents abused; fine ambling hypocrites! and a stone puritan with a sorrel head and beard! good mouth'd gluttons; two to a pig, away.

Urs. Are you sure they are such?

Knock. O' the right breed, thou shalt try 'em by the teeth, Urse; where's this Whit?

Re-enter WHIT.

Whit. Behold, man, and see,
        What a worthy man am ee!
        With the fury of my sword,
        And the shaking of my beard,
        I will make ten thousand men afeard.

Knock. Well said, brave Whit! in, and *fear* the ale out o' the bottles into the bellies of the brethren, and . . . the sisters drink to the cause, and pure vapours. [*Exeunt Knockem, Whit, and Ursula.*

Quar. My roarer is turn'd tapster, methinks. Now were a fine time for thee, Winwife, to lay aboard thy widow, thou'lt never be master of a better season or place; she that will venture herself into the Fair and a pig-box, will admit any assault, be assured of that.

Winw. I love not enterprises of that suddenness though.

Quar. I'll warrant thee, then, no wife out of the widow's hundred: if I had but as much title to her, as to have breathed once on that straight stomacher of hers, I would now assure myself to carry her, yet, ere she went out of Smithfield; or she should carry me, which were the fitter sight, I confess. But you are a modest undertaker, by circumstances and degrees; come, 'tis disease in thee, not judgment; I should offer at all together.—

Enter OVERDO.

Look, here's the poor fool again, that was stung by the Waspe erewhile.

Over. I will make no more orations, shall draw on these tragical conclusions. And I begin now to think, that by a spice of collateral justice, Adam Overdo deserved this beating; for I, the said Adam, was one cause (a by-cause) why the purse was lost; and my wife's brother's purse too, which they know not of yet. But I shall make very good mirth with it at supper, that will be the sport, and put my little friend, master Humphrey Waspe's choler quite out of countenance: when, sitting at the upper end of my table, as I use, and drinking to my brother Cokes, and mistress Alice Overdo, as I will, my wife, for their good affection to old Bradley, I deliver to them, it was I that was cudgeled, and shew them the marks. To see what bad events may peep out o' the tail of good purposes! the care I had of that civil young man I took fancy to this morning, (and have not left it yet,) drew me to that exhortation, which drew the company indeed; which drew the cut-purse; which drew the money; which drew my brother Cokes his loss; which drew on

Waspe's anger; which drew on my beating: a pretty gradation! and they shall have it in their dish, i'faith, at night for fruit; I love to be merry at my table. I had thought once, at one special blow he gave me, to have revealed myself; but then (I thank thee, fortitude) I remembered that a wise man, and who is ever so great a part of the commonwealth in himself, for no particular disaster ought to abandon a public good design. The husbandman ought not, for one unthankful year, to forsake the plough; the shepherd ought not, for one scabbed sheep, to throw by his tar-box; the pilot ought not, for one leak in the poop, to quit the helm; nor the alderman ought not, for one custard more at a meal, to give up his cloke; the constable ought not to break his staff, and forswear the watch, for one roaring night; nor the piper of the parish, *ut parvis componere magna solebam*, to put up his pipes for one rainy Sunday. These are certain knocking conclusions; out of which, I am resolved, come what come can, come beating, come imprisonment, come infamy, come banishment, nay, come the rack, come the hurdle, (welcome all,) I will not discover who I am, till my due time; and yet still, all shall be, as I said ever, in justice name, and the king's, and for the commonwealth.

Winw. What does he talk to himself, and act so seriously, poor fool!

Quar. No matter what. Here's fresher argument, intend that.

Enter COKES, Mistress OVERDO, *and* GRACE WELLBORN, *followed by* WASPE, *loaded with toys.*

Cokes. Come, mistress Grace, come, sister, here's more fine sights yet, i'faith. Od's 'lid, where's Numps?

Leath. What do you lack, gentlemen? what is't you buy? fine rattles, drums, babies, little dogs, and birds for ladies? what do you lack?

Cokes. Good honest Numps, keep afore, I am so afraid thou'lt lose somewhat; my heart was at my mouth, when I mist thee.

Waspe. You were best buy a whip in your hand to drive me.

Cokes. Nay, do not mistake, Numps; thou art so apt to mistake! I would but watch the goods. Look you now, the treble fiddle was e'en almost like to be lost.

Waspe. Pray you take heed you lose not yourself; your best way were e'en get up and ride for more surety. Buy a token's worth of great pins, to fasten yourself to my shoulder.

Leath. What do you lack, gentlemen? fine purses, pouches, pincases, pipes? what is't you lack? a pair o' smiths to wake you in the morning? or a fine whistling bird?

Cokes. Numps, here be finer things than any we have bought by odds! and more delicate horses, a great deal; good Numps, stay, and come hither.

Waspe. Will you scourse with him? you are in Smithfield, you may fit yourself with a fine easy-going street-nag, for your saddle, again Michaelmas term, do: has he ne'er a little odd cart for you to make a caroch on, in the country, with four pied hobby-horses? Why the measles should you stand here, with your train, cheapning of dogs, birds, and babies? you have no children to bestow them on, have you?

Cokes. No, but again I have children. Numps, that's all one.

Waspe. Do, do, do, do; how many shall you have, think you? an I were as you, I'd buy for all my tenants too, they are a kind of civil savages, that will part with their children for rattles, pipes, and knives. You were best buy a hatchet or two, and truck with 'em.

Cokes. Good Numps, hold that little tongue o' thine, and save it a labour. I am resolute Bat, thou know'st.

Waspe. A resolute fool you are, I know, and a very sufficient coxcomb; with all my heart;—nay, you have it, sir, an you be angry, t—in your teeth, twice; if I said it not once afore, and much good do you.

Winw. Was there ever such a self-affliction, and so impertinent?

Quar. Alas, his care will go near to crack him; let's in and comfort him. [*They come forward.*

Waspe. Would I had been set in the ground, all but the head on me, and had my brains bowled at, or threshed out, when first I underwent this plague of a charge!

Quar. How now, Numps! almost tired in your protectorship? overparted, overparted?

Waspe. Why, I cannot tell, sir, it may be I am; does it grieve you?

Quar. No, I swear does't not, Numps; to satisfy you.

Waspe. Numps! 'sblood, you are fine and familiar: how long have we been acquainted, I pray you?

Quar. I think it may be remembered, Numps, that; 'twas since morning, sure.

Waspe. Why, I hope I know't well enough, sir; I did not ask to be told.

Quar. No! why, then?

Waspe. It's no matter why; you see with your eyes now, what I said to you to-day: you'll believe me another time?

Quar. Are you removing the Fair, Numps?

Waspe. A pretty question, and a civil one! yes faith, I have my lading, you see, or shall have anon; you may know whose beast I am by my burden. If the pannier-man's jack were ever better known by his loins of mutton, I'll be flayed, and feed dogs for him when his time comes.

Winw. How melancholic mistress Grace is yonder! pray thee let's go enter ourselves in grace with her.

Cokes. Those six horses, friend, I'll have—

Waspe. How!

Cokes. And the three Jew's-trumps; and half a dozen o' birds, and that drum, (I have one drum already) and your smiths; I like that device of your smiths, very pretty well; and four halberts—

and, let me see, that fine painted great lady, and her three women for state, I'll have.

Waspe. No, the shop; buy the whole shop, it will be best, the shop, the shop!

Leath. If his worship please.

Waspe. Yes, and keep it during the Fair, Bobchin.

Cokes. Peace, Numps.—Friend, do not meddle with him, an you be wise, and would shew your head above board; he will sting thorough your wrought night-cap, believe me. A set of these violins I would buy too, for a delicate young noise I have in the country, that are every one a size less than another, just like your fiddles. I would fain have a fine young masque at my marriage, now I think on't: But I do want such a number of things!—And Numps will not help me now, and I dare not speak to him.

Trash. Will your worship buy any gingerbread, very good bread, comfortable bread?

Cokes. Gingerbread! yes, let's see.   [*Runs to her shop.*

Waspe. There's the t'other springe.

Leath. Is this well, goody Joan, to interrupt my market in the midst, and call away my customers? can you answer this at the Pie-poudres?

Trash. Why, if his mastership has a mind to buy, I hope my ware lies as open as another's; I may shew my ware as well as you yours.

Cokes. Hold your peace; I'll content you both: I'll buy up his shop, and thy basket.

Waspe. Will you, i'faith?

Leath. Why should you put him from it, friend?

Waspe. Cry you mercy! you'd be sold too, would you? what's the price on you, jerkin and all, as you stand? have you any qualities?

Trash. Yes, good man, angry-man, you shall find he has qualities if you cheapen him.

Waspe. Od's so, you have the selling of him! What are they, will they be bought for love or money?

Trash. No indeed, sir.

Waspe. For what then, victuals?

Trash. He scorns victuals, sir; he has bread and butter at home, thanks be to God! and yet he will do more for a good meal, if the toy take him in the belly; marry then they must not set him at lower ends, if they do, he'll go away, though he fast; but put him a-top o' the table, where his place is, and he'll do you forty fine things. He has not been sent for, and sought out for nothing, at your great city-suppers, to put down Coriat and Cokely, and been laughed at for his labour; he'll play you all the puppets in the town over, and the players, every company, and his own company too; he spares nobody.

Cokes. I'faith?

Trash. He was the first, sir, that ever baited the fellow in the bear's skin, an't like your worship: no dog ever came near him since. And for fine motions!

Cokes. Is he good at those too? can he set out a masque, trow?

Trash. O lord, master! sought to far and near for his inventions; and he engrosses all, he makes all the puppets in the Fair.

Cokes. Dost thou, in troth, old velvet jerkin? give me thy hand.

Trash. Nay, sir, you shall see him in his velvet jerkin, and a scarf too at night, when you hear him interpret master Littlewit's motion.

Cokes. Speak no more, but shut up shop presently, friend, I'll buy both it and thee too, to carry down with me; and her hamper beside. Thy shop shall furnish out the masque, and her's the banquet: I cannot go less, to set out any thing with credit. What's the price, at a word, of thy whole shop, case and all as it stands?

Leath. Sir, it stands me in six and twenty shillings seven-pence halfpenny, besides three shillings for my ground.

Cokes. Well, thirty shillings will do all, then! and what comes yours to?

Trash. Four shillings and eleven-pence, sir, ground and all, an't like your worship.

Cokes. Yes, it does like my worship very well, poor woman; that's five shillings more: what a masque shall I furnish out, for forty shillings, twenty pound Scotch, and a banquet of gingerbread! there's a stately thing! Numps? sister?—and my wedding gloves too! that I never thought on afore! All my wedding gloves gingerbread? O me! what a device will there be, to make 'em eat their fingers' ends! and delicate brooches for the bridemen and all! and then I'll have this poesie put to them, *For the best grace,* meaning mistress Grace, my wedding poesie.

Grace. I am beholden to you, sir, and to your Bartholomew wit.

Waspe. You do not mean this, do you? Is this your first purchase?

Cokes. Yes, faith: and I do not think, Numps, but thou'lt say, it was the wisest act that ever I did in my wardship.

Waspe. Like enough! I shall say any thing, I!

Enter EDGWORTH, NIGHTINGALE *and People, followed, at a distance, by* OVERDO.

Over. I cannot beget a project, with all my political brain yet: my project is how to fetch off this proper young man from his debauched company. I have followed him all the Fair over, and still I find him with this songster, and I begin shrewdly to suspect their familiarity; and the young man of a terrible taint, poetry! with which idle disease if he be infected, there's no hope of him, in a state-course. *Actum est* of him for a commonwealth's-man, if he go to't in rhyme once. [*Aside.*

Edg. [*to Nightingale.*] Yonder he is buying of gingerbread; set in quickly, before he part with too much of his money.

Night. [advancing and singing.] *My masters, and friends, and good people, draw near—*

Cokes. [*runs to the ballad-man.*] Ballads! hark! hark! pray thee, fellow, stay a little; good Numps, look to the goods. What ballads hast thou? let me see, let me see myself.

Waspe. Why so! he's flown to another lime-bush, there he will flutter as long more; till he have ne'er a feather left. Is there a vexation like this, gentlemen? will you believe me now, hereafter, shall I have credit with you?

Quar. Yes, faith shalt thou, Numps, and thou art worthy on't, for thou sweatest for't. I never saw a young pimp-errant and his squire better match'd.

Winw. Faith, the sister comes after them well too.

Grace. Nay, if you saw the justice her husband, my guardian, you were fitted for the mess, he is such a wise one his way—

Winw. I wonder we see him not here.

Grace. O! he is too serious for this place, and yet better sport then than the other three, I assure you, gentlemen, wherever he is, though it be on the bench.

Cokes. How dost thou call it? *A caveat against cut-purses!* a good jest, i'faith, I would fain see that demon, your cut-purse you talk of, that delicate-handed devil; they say he walks hereabout; I would see him walk now. Look you, sister, here, here, [*he shews his purse boastingly*], let him come, sister, and welcome. Ballad-man, does any cut-purses haunt hereabout? pray thee raise me one or two; begin, and shew me one.

Night. Sir, this is a spell against them, spick and span new; and 'tis made as 'twere in mine own person, and I sing it in mine own defence. But 'twill cost a penny alone, if you buy it.

Cokes. No matter for the price; thou dost not know me, I see, I am an odd Bartholomew.

Mrs. Over. Has it a fine picture, brother?

Cokes. O, sister, do you remember the ballads over the nursery chimney at home o' my own pasting up? there be brave pictures, other manner of pictures than these, friend.

Waspe. Yet these will serve to pick the pictures out of your pockets, you shall see.

Cokes. *So I heard them say!* Pray thee mind him not, fellow; he'll have an oar in every thing.

Night. It was intended, sir, as if a purse should chance to be cut in my presence, now, I may be blameless though; as by the sequel will more plainly appear.

Cokes. We shall find that in the matter: pray thee begin.

Night. To the tune of Paggington's pound, sir.

Cokes. [sings.] *Fa, la la la, la la la, fa, la la la!* Nay, I'll put thee in tune and all; mine own country dance! Pray thee begin.

Night. It is a gentle admonition, you must know, sir, both to the purse-cutter and the purse-bearer.

Cokes. Not a word more out of the tune, an thou lov'st me;
Fa, la la la, la la la, fa, la la la. Come, when?

Night. [sings.] *My masters, and friends, and good people, draw near,
And look to your purses, for that I do say;*

Cokes. Ha, ha, this chimes! Good counsel at first dash.

*Night. And tho' little money in them you do bear,
It costs more to get, than to lose in a day.*

Cokes. Good!

*Night. You oft have been told,
     Both the young and the old,
And bidden beware of the cut-purse so bold;*

Cokes. Well said! he were to blame that would not, i'faith.

*Night. Then if you take heed not, free me from the curse,
Who both give you warning, for, and the cut-purse.
Youth, youth, thou had'st better been starv'd by thy nurse,
Than live to be hanged for cutting a purse.*

Cokes. Good, i'faith; how say you, Numps, is there any harm
in this?

*Night. It hath been upbraided to men of my trade,
That oftentimes we are the cause of this crime;*

Cokes. The more coxcombs they that did it, I wusse.

*Night. Alack and for pity, why should it be said?
As if they regarded or places or time !
     Examples have been
     Of some that were seen
In Westminster-hall, yea the pleaders between;
Then why should the judges be free from this curse,
More than my poor self, for cutting the purse ?*

Cokes. God a mercy for that! why should they be more free
indeed?

*Night. Youth, youth, thou had'st better been starv'd by thy nurse,
Than live to be hanged for cutting a purse.*

Cokes. That again, good ballad-man, that again. [*He sings the
burden with him.*] O rare! I would fain rub mine elbow now, but
I dare not pull out my hand.—On, I pray thee; he that made this
ballad shall be poet to my masque.

*Night. At Worc'ster, 'tis known well, and even in the jail,
A knight of good worship did there shew his face,
Against the foul sinners, in zeal for to rail,
And lost ipso facto his purse in the place.*

Cokes. Is it possible?

*Night. Nay, once from the seat
     Of judgment so great,
A judge there did lose a fair pouch of velvéte.*

Cokes. I'faith?

*Night. O Lord for thy mercy, how wicked or worse,
Are those that so venture their necks for a purse !
Youth, youth, thou had'st better been starv'd by thy nurse,
Than lived to be hanged for cutting a purse.*

Cokes. [sings after him.] *Youth, youth, etc.*—Pray thee, stay a little, friend. Yet o' thy conscience, Numps, speak, is there any harm in this?

Waspe. To tell you true, 'tis too good for you, less you had grace to follow it.

Over. It doth discover enormity, I'll mark it more: I have not liked a paltry piece of poetry so well a good while.   [*Aside.*

Cokes. *Youth, youth, etc.;* where's this youth now? a man must call upon him for his own good, and yet he will not appear. Look here, here's for him; [*shews his purse.*] handy dandy, which hand will he have? On, I pray thee, with the rest; I do hear of him, but I cannot see him, this master youth, the cut-purse.

Night. *At plays, and at sermons, and at the sessions,*
'Tis daily their practice such booty to make.
Yea under the gallows at executions,
They stick not the stare-abouts' purses to take.
        Nay one without grace,
        At a [far] better place,
At court, and in Christmas, before the king's face.

Cokes. That was a fine fellow! I would have him now.

Night. *Alack then for pity must I bear the curse,*
That only belongs to the cunning cut-purse?

Cokes. But where's their cunning now, when they should use it? they are all chain'd now, I warrant you. [*Sings.*] *Youth, youth, thou had'st better*—The rat-catchers' charms are all fools and asses to this: a pox on them, that they will not come! that a man should have such a desire to a thing, and want it!

Quar. 'Fore God I'd give half the Fair, an 'twere mine, for a cut-purse for him, to save his longing.

Cokes. Look you, sister [*shews his purse again*], here, here, where is't now? which pocket is't in, for a wager?

Waspe. I beseech you leave your wagers, and let him end his matter, an't may be.

Cokes. O, are you edified, Numps!

Over. Indeed he does interrupt him too much: there Numps spoke to purpose.   [*Aside.*

Cokes. Sister, I am an ass, I cannot keep my purse! [*Shews it again, and puts it up.*]—On, on, I pray thee, friend.

Night. *Youth, youth, thou had'st better been starv'd by thy nurse,*
Than live to be hanged for cutting a purse.

[*As Nightingale sings, Edgworth gets up to Cokes, and tickles him in the ear with a straw twice to draw his hand out of his pocket.*

Winw. Will you see sport? look, there's a fellow gathers up to him, mark.

Quar. Good, i'faith! O he has lighted on the wrong pocket.

Winw. He has it! 'fore God, he is a brave fellow: pity he should be detected.

Night. *But O, you vile nation of cut-purses all,*
Relent and repent, and amend and be sound,

And know that you ought not, by honest men's fall,
Advance your own fortunes, to die above ground;
   And though you go gay
    In silks, as you may,
It is not the highway to heaven (as they say).
Repent then, repent you, for better, for worse,
And kiss not the gallows for cutting a purse.
Youth, youth, thou had'st better been starv'd by thy nurse,
Than live to be hanged for cutting a purse.

All. An excellent ballad! an excellent ballad!

Edg. Friend, let me have the first, let me have the first, I pray you.

  [*As Nightingale reaches out the ballad, Edgworth slips the purse into his hand.*

Cokes. Pardon me, sir; first come first serv'd; and I'll buy the whole bundle too.

Winw. That conveyance was better than all, did you see't? he has given the purse to the ballad-singer.

Quar. Has he?

Edg. Sir, I cry you mercy, I'll not hinder the poor man's profit; pray you, mistake me not.

Cokes. Sir, I take you for an honest gentleman, if that be mistaking; I met you to-day afore: ha! humph! O Lord! my purse is gone, my purse, my purse, my purse!

Waspe. Come do not make a stir, and cry yourself an ass thorough the Fair afore your time.

Cokes. Why, hast thou it, Numps? good Numps, how came you by it, I marle?

Waspe. I pray you seek some other gamester to play the fool with; you may lose it time enough, for all your Fair wit.

Cokes. By this good hand, glove and all, I have lost it already if thou hast it not; feel else, and mistress Grace's handkerchief too, out of the t'other pocket.

Waspe. Why, 'tis well, very well, exceeding pretty and well.

Edg. Are you sure you have lost it, sir?

Cokes. O Lord! yes; as I am an honest man, I had it but e'en now, at *Youth, youth.*

Night. I hope you suspect not me, sir?

Edg. Thee! that were a jest indeed! dost thou think the gentleman is foolish? where hadst thou hands, I pray thee? Away, ass, away!   [*Exit Night.*

Over. I shall be beaten again, if I be spied.   [*Aside, retiring.*

Edg. Sir, I suspect an odd fellow, yonder, is stealing away.

Mrs. Over. Brother, it is the preaching fellow: you shall suspect him. He was at your t'other purse, you know! [*Seizes Overdo.*]— Nay, stay, sir, and view the work you have done; an you be beneficed at the gallows, and preach there, thank your own handywork.

Cokes. Sir, you shall take no pride in your preferment, you shall be silenced quickly.   [*They seize Overdo.*

Over. What do you mean, sweet buds of gentility?

Cokes. To have my pennyworths out on you, bud. No less than two purses a day serve you! I thought you a simple fellow, when my man Numps beat you in the morning, and pitied you.

Mrs. Over. So did I, I'll be sworn, brother; but now I see he is a lewd and pernicious enormity, as master Overdo calls him.

Over. Mine own words turn'd upon me like swords!   [*Aside.*

Cokes. Cannot a man's purse be at quiet for you in the master's pocket, but you must entice it forth, and debauch it!

[*Overdo is carried off.*

Waspe. Sir, sir, keep your debauch, and your fine Bartholomew terms to yourself, and make as much on 'em as you please. But give me this from you in the mean time; I beseech you, see if I can look to this.

Cokes. Why, Numps?

Waspe. Why! because you are an ass, sir, there's a reason the shortest way, an you will needs have it: now you have got the trick of losing, you'd lose your breech an 'twere loose. I know you, sir, come, deliver [*takes the box from him*], you'll go and crack the vermin you breed now, will you? 'tis very fine; will you have the truth on't? they are such retchless flies as you are, that blow cut-purses abroad in every corner; your foolish having of money makes them. An there were no wiser than I, sir, the trade should lie open for you, sir, it should, i'faith, sir. I would teach your wit to come to your head, sir, as well as your land to come into your hand, I assure you, sir.

Winw. Alack, good Numps!

Waspe. Nay, gentlemen, never pity me, I am not worth it: Lord send me at home once to Harrow o' the Hill, again, if I travel any more, call me Coriat with all my heart.

[*Exeunt Waspe, Cokes, and Mrs. Overdo, followed by Edgworth.*

Quar. [*stops Edgworth.*] Stay, sir, I must have a word with you in private. Do you hear?

Edg. With me, sir! what's your pleasure, good sir?

Quar. Do not deny it, you are a cut-purse, sir, this gentleman here and I saw you: nor do we mean to detect you, though we can sufficiently inform ourselves toward the danger of concealing you; but you must do us a piece of service.

Edg. Good gentlemen, do not undo me; I am a civil young man, and but a beginner indeed.

Quar. Sir, your beginning shall bring on your ending for us: we are no catchpoles nor constables. That you are to undertake is this: you saw the old fellow with the black box here?

Edg. The little old governor, sir?

Quar. That same: I see you have flown him to a mark already. I would have you get away that box from him, and bring it us.

Edg. Wou'd you have the box and all, sir, or only that that is in't? I'll get you that, and leave him the box to play with still, which will be the harder of the two, because I would gain your worship's good opinion of me.

Winw. He says well, 'tis the greater mastery, and 'twill make the more sport when 'tis mist.

Edg. Ay, and 'twill be the longer a missing, to draw on the sport.

Quar. But look you do it now, sirrah, and keep your word, or—

Edg. Sir, if ever I break my word with a gentleman, may I never read word at my need. Where shall I find you?

Quar. Somewhere i' the Fair, hereabouts: dispatch it quickly. [*Exit Edgworth.*] I would fain see the careful fool deluded! Of all beasts, I love the serious ass; he that takes pains to be one, and plays the fool with the greatest diligence that can be.

Grace. Then you would not choose, sir, but love my guardian, justice Overdo, who is answerable to that description in every hair of him.

Quar. So I have heard. But how came you, mistress Wellborn, to be his ward, or have relation to him at first?

Grace. Faith, through a common calamity, he bought me, sir; and now he will marry me to his wife's brother, this wise gentleman that you see; or else I must pay value o' my land.

Quar. 'Slid, is there no device of disparagement, or so? talk with some crafty fellow, some picklock of the law: would I had studied a year longer in the Inns of court, an't had been but in your case.

Winw. Ay, master Quarlous, are you proffering! [*Aside.*

Grace. You'd bring but little aid, sir.

Winw. I'll look to you, in faith, gamester.—[*Aside.*] An unfortunate foolish tribe you are fallen into, lady, I wonder you can endure them.

Grace. Sir, they that cannot work their fetters off must wear them.

Winw. You see what care they have on you, to leave you thus.

Grace. Faith, the same they have of themselves, sir. I cannot greatly complain, if this were all the plea I had against them.

Winw. 'Tis true: but will you please to withdraw with us a little, and make them think they have lost you. I hope our manners have been such hitherto, and our language, as will give you no cause to doubt yourself in our company.

Grace. Sir, I will give myself no cause; I am so secure of mine own manners, as I suspect not yours.

Quar. Look where John Littlewit comes.

Winw. Away, I'll not be seen by him.

Quar. No, you were not best, he'd tell his mother, the widow.

Winw. Heart! what do you mean?

Quar. Cry you mercy, is the wind there? must not the widow be named? [*Exeunt.*

Enter LITTLEWIT *from* URSULA'S *booth, followed by* Mrs. LITTLEWIT.

Lit. Do you hear, Win, Win?

Mrs. Lit. What say you, John?

Lit. While they are paying the reckoning, Win, I'll tell you a thing, Win; we shall never see any sights in the Fair, Win, except you long still, Win: good Win, sweet Win, long to see some hobby-horses, and some drums, and rattles, and dogs, and fine devices, Win. The bull with the five legs, Win; and the great hog. Now you have begun with pig, you may long for any thing, Win, and so for my motion, Win.

Mrs. Lit. But we shall not eat of the bull and the hog, John; how shall I long then?

Lit. O yes, Win: you may long to see, as well as to taste, Win: how did the pothecary's wife, Win, that longed to see the anatomy, Win? or the lady, Win, that desired to spit in the great lawyer's mouth, after an eloquent pleading? I assure you, they longed, Win; good Win, go in, and long.

[*Exeunt Littlewit and Mrs. Littlewit.*

Trash. I think we are rid of our new customer, brother Leather-head, we shall hear no more of him.

Leath. All the better; let's pack up all and begone, before he find us.

Trash. Stay a little, yonder comes a company; it may be we may take some more money.

Enter KNOCKEM and BUSY.

Knock. Sir, I will take your counsel, and cut my hair, and leave vapours: I see that tobacco, and bottle-ale, and pig, and Whit, and very Ursla herself, is all vanity.

Busy. Only pig was not comprehended in my admonition, the rest were: for long hair, it is an ensign of pride, a banner; and the world is full of those banners, very full of banners. And bottle-ale is a drink of Satan's, a diet-drink of Satan's, devised to puff us up, and make us swell in this latter age of vanity; as the smoke of tobacco, to keep us in mist and error: but the fleshly woman, which you call Ursla, is above all to be avoided, having the marks upon her of the three enemies of man; the world, as being in the Fair; the devil, as being in the fire; and the flesh, as being herself.

Enter Mrs. PURECRAFT.

Pure. Brother Zeal-of-the-land! what shall we do? my daughter Win-the-fight is fallen into her fit of longing again.

Busy. For more pig! there is no more, is there?

Pure. To see some sights in the Fair.

Busy. Sister, let her fly the impurity of the place swiftly, lest she partake of the pitch thereof. Thou art the seat of the beast, O Smithfield, and I will leave thee! Idolatry peepeth out on every side of thee. [*Goes forward.*

Knock. An excellent right hypocrite! now his belly is full, he falls a railing and kicking, the jade. A very good vapour! I'll in, and joy Ursla, with telling how her pig works; two and a half he eat to his share; and he has drunk a pailful. He eats with his eyes, as well as his teeth. [*Exit.*

Leath. What do you lack, gentlemen? what is't you buy? rattles, drums, babies—

Busy. Peace, with thy apocryphal wares, thou profane publican; thy bells, thy dragons, and thy Tobie's dogs. Thy hobby-horse is an idol, a very idol, a fierce and rank idol; and thou, the Nebuchadnezzar, the proud Nebuchadnezzar of the Fair, that sett'st it up, for children to fall down to, and worship.

Leath. Cry you mercy, sir; will you buy a fiddle to fill up your noise?

Re-enter LITTLEWIT *and his* Wife.

Lit. Look, Win, do, look a God's name, and save your longing. Here be fine sights.

Pure. Ay, child, so you hate them, as our brother Zeal does, you may look on them.

Leath. Or what do you say to a drum, sir?

Busy. It is the broken belly of the beast, and thy bellows there are his lungs, and these pipes are his throat, those feathers are of his tail, and thy rattles the gnashing of his teeth.

Trash. And what's my gingerbread, I pray you?

Busy. The provender that pricks him up. Hence with thy basket of popery, thy nest of images, and whole legend of ginger-work.

Leath. Sir, if you be not quiet the quicklier, I'll have you clapp'd fairly by the heels, for disturbing the Fair.

Busy. The sin of the Fair provokes me, I cannot be silent.

Pure. Good brother Zeal!

Leath. Sir, I'll make you silent, believe it.

Lit. I'd give a shilling you could, i'faith, friend.   *[Aside to Leatherhead.*

Leath. Sir, give me your shilling, I'll give you my shop, if I do not; and I'll leave it in pawn with you in the mean time.

Lit. A match, i'faith; but do it quickly then.

   [Exit Leatherhead.

Busy. [*to Mrs. Purecraft.*] Hinder me not, woman I was moved in spirit, to be here this day, in this Fair, this wicked and foul Fair; and fitter may it be called a Foul than a Fair; to protest against the abuses of it, the foul abuses of it, in regard of the afflicted saints, that are troubled, very much troubled, exceedingly troubled, with the opening of the merchandise of Babylon again, and the peeping of popery upon the stalls here, here, in the high places. See you not Goldylocks, the purple strumpet there, in her yellow gown and green sleeves? the profane pipes, the tinkling timbrels? a shop of relicks!   *[Attempts to seize the toys.*

Lit. Pray you forbear, I am put in trust with them.

Busy. And this idolatrous grove of images, this flasket of idols, which I will pull down—   *[Overthrows the gingerbread basket.*

Trash. O my ware, my ware! God bless it!

Busy. In my zeal and glory to be thus exercised.

Re-enter LEATHERHEAD, *with* BRISTLE, HAGGISE, *and other* Officers.

Leath. Here he is, pray you lay hold on his zeal; we cannot sell a whistle for him in tune. Stop his noise first.

Busy. Thou canst not; 'tis a sanctified noise: I will make a loud and most strong noise, till I have daunted the profane enemy. And for this cause—

Leath. Sir, here's no man afraid of you, or your cause. You shall swear it in the stocks, sir.

Busy. I will thrust myself into the stocks, upon the pikes of the land. [*They seize him.*

Leath. Carry him away.

Pure. What do you mean, wicked men?

Busy. Let them alone, I fear them not.

[*Exeunt Officers with Busy, followed by Dame Purecraft.*

Lit. Was not this shilling well ventured, Win, for our liberty? now we may go play, and see over the Fair, where we list ourselves: my mother is gone after him, and let her e'en go, and lose us.

Mrs. Lit. Yes, John; but I know not what to do.

Lit. For what, Win?

Mrs. Lit. For a thing I am ashamed to tell you, i'faith; and 'tis too far to go home.

Lit. I pray thee be not ashamed, Win. Come, i'faith, thou shalt not be ashamed: is it any thing about the hobby-horse man? an't be, speak freely.

Mrs. Lit. Hang him, base Bobchin, I scorn him; no, I have very great what sha' call 'um, John. [*Whispers him.*

Lit. O, is that all, Win? we'll go back to captain Jordan, to the pig-woman's, Win, he'll help us, or she, with a dripping-pan, or an old kettle, or something. The poor greasy soul loves you, Win; and after we'll visit the Fair all over, Win, and see my puppet-play, Win; you know it's a fine matter, Win.

[*Exeunt Littlewit and Mrs. Littlewit.*

Leath. Let's away; I counsell'd you to pack up afore, Joan.

Trash. A pox of his Bedlam purity! He has spoiled half my ware; but the best is, we lose nothing if we miss our first merchant.

Leath. It shall be hard for him to find or know us, when we are translated, Joan. [*Exeunt.*

ACT IV

SCENE I.—*The Fair.*

Booths, Stalls, a pair of Stocks, etc.

Enter COKES, BRISTLE, HAGGISE, *and* POCHER, *with* OVERDO, *followed by* TROUBLEALL.

Tro. My masters, I do make no doubt, but you are officers.
Bri. What then, sir?
Tro. And the king's loving and obedient subjects.
Bri. Obedient, friend! take heed what you speak, I advise you; Oliver Bristle advises you. His loving subjects, we grant you; but not his obedient, at this time, by your leave; we know ourselves a little better than so; we are to command, sir, and such as you are to be obedient. Here's one of his obedient subjects going to the stocks; and we'll make you such another, if you talk.
Tro. You are all wise enough in your places, I know.
Bri. If you know it, sir, why do you bring it in question?
Tro. I question nothing, pardon me. I do only hope you have warrant for what you do, and so quit you, and so multiply you.
[*Exit.*
Hag. What is he?—Bring him up to the stocks there. Why bring you him not up? [*Overdo is brought forward.*

Re-enter TROUBLEALL.

Tro. If you have justice Overdo's warrant, 'tis well; you are safe: that is the warrant of warrants. I'll not give this button for any man's warrant else.
Bri. Like enough, sir; but let me tell you, an you play away your buttons thus, you will want them ere night, for any store I see about you; you might keep them, and save pins, I wuss.
[*Exit Troubleall.*
Over. What should he be, that doth so esteem and advance my warrant? he seems a sober and discreet person: It is a comfort to a good conscience to be followed with a good fame in his sufferings. The world will have a pretty taste by this, how I can bear adversity; and it will beget a kind of reverence towards me hereafter, even from mine enemies, when they shall see, I carry my calamity nobly, and that it doth neither break me, nor bend me. [*Aside.*
Hag. Come, sir, here's a place for you to preach in. Will you put in your leg?
Over. That I will, cheerfully. [*They put him in the stocks.*
Bri. O' my conscience, a seminary! he kisses the stocks.
Cokes. Well, my masters, I'll leave him with you; now I see him bestowed, I'll go look for my goods, and Numps.
Hag. You may, sir, I warrant you; where's the t'other bawler? fetch him too, you shall find them both fast enough. [*Exit Cokes.*

Over. In the midst of this tumult, I will yet be the author of mine own rest, and not minding their fury, sit in the stocks in that calm as shall be able to trouble a triumph.　　　　　　[*Aside.*

Re-enter TROUBLEALL.

Tro. Do you assure me upon your words? May I undertake for you, if I be asked the question, that you have this warrant?

Hag. What's this fellow, for God's sake?

Tro. Do but shew me Adam Overdo, and I am satisfied.　[*Exit.*

Bri. He is a fellow that is distracted, they say; one Troubleall: he was an officer in the court of Pie-poudres here last year, and put out of his place by justice Overdo.

Over. Ha!　　　　　　　　　　　　　　　[*Aside.*

Bri. Upon which he took an idle conceit, and is run mad upon't: so that ever since he will do nothing but by justice Overdo's warrant; he will not eat a crust, nor drink a little, nor make him in his apparel ready. His wife, sir-reverence, cannot get him make his water, or shift his shirt, without his warrant.

Over. If this be true, this is my greatest disaster. How am I bound to satisfy this poor man, that is of so good a nature to me, out of his wits! where there is no room left for dissembling. [*Aside.*

Re-enter TROUBLEALL.

Tro. If you cannot shew me Adam Overdo, I am in doubt of you; I am afraid you cannot answer it.　　　　　　　　[*Exit.*

Hag. Before me, neighbour Bristle,—and now I think on't better, —justice Overdo is a very parantory person.

Bri. O, are you advised of that! and a severe justicer, by your leave.

Over. Do I hear ill o' that side too?　　　　　　　[*Aside.*

Bri. He will sit as upright on the bench, an you mark him, as a candle in the socket, and give light to the whole court in every business.

Hag. But he will burn blue, and swell like a boil, God bless us, an he be angry.

Bri. Ay, and he will be angry too, when he lists, that's more; and when he is angry, be it right or wrong, he has the law on's side ever; I mark that too.

Over. I will be more tender hereafter. I see compassion may become a justice, though it be a weakness, I confess, and nearer a vice than a virtue.　　　　　　　　　　　　　[*Aside.*

Hag. Well, take him out o' the stocks again; we'll go a sure way to work, we'll have the ace of hearts of our side, if we can.

[*They take Overdo out.*

Enter POCHER, *and* Officers *with* BUSY, *followed by*
Mrs. PURECRAFT.

Poch. Come, bring him away to his fellow there.—Master Busy, we shall rule your legs, I hope, though we cannot rule your tongue.

Busy. No, minister of darkness, no; thou canst not rule my tongue; my tongue it is mine own, and with it I will both knock and mock down your Bartholomew abominations, till you be made a hissing to the neighbouring parishes round about.

Hag. Let him alone, we have devised better upon't.

Pure. And shall he not into the stocks then?

Bri. No, mistress, we'll have them both to justice Overdo, and let him do over 'em as is fitting: then I, and my gossip Haggise, and my beadle Pocher, are discharged.

Pure. O, I thank you, blessed honest men!

Bri. Nay, never thank us; but thank this madman that comes here! he put it in our heads.

Re-enter TROUBLEALL.

Pure. Is he mad? now heaven increase his madness, and bless it, and thank it.—Sir, your poor handmaid thanks you.

Tro. Have you a warrant? an you have a warrant, shew it.

Pure. Yes, I have a warrant out of the word, to give thanks for removing any scorn intended to the brethren.

[Exeunt all but Troubleall.

Tro. It is justice Overdo's warrant that I look for; if you have not that, keep your word, I'll keep mine. Quit ye, and multiply ye.

Enter EDGWORTH *and* NIGHTINGALE.

Edg. Come away, Nightingale, I pray thee.

Tro. Whither go you? where's your warrant?

Edg. Warrant! for what, sir?

Tro. For what you go about, you know how fit it is; an you have no warrant, bless you, I'll pray for you, that's all I can do.

[Exit.

Edg. What means he?

Night. A madman that haunts the Fair; do you not know him? It's marvel he has not more followers after his ragged heels.

Edg. Beshrew him, he startled me: I thought he had known of our plot. Guilt's a terrible thing. Have you prepared the costard-monger?

Night. Yes, and agreed for his basket of pears; he is at the corner here, ready. And your prize, he comes down sailing that way all alone, without his protector; he is rid of him, it seems.

Edg. Ay, I know; I should have followed his protectorship, for a feat I am to do upon him: but this offered itself so in the way, I could not let scape: here he comes, whistle; be this sport call'd Dorring the Dotterel.

Re-enter COKES.

Night. Wh, wh, wh, wh, etc. *[Whistles.*

Cokes. By this light, I cannot find my gingerbread wife, nor my hobby-horse man, in all the Fair now, to have my money again: and I do not know the way out on't, to go home for more. Do you hear, friend, you that whistle? what tune is that you whistle?

Night. A new tune I am practising, sir.

Cokes. Dost thou know where I dwell, I pray thee? nay, on with thy tune; I have no such haste for an answer: I'll practise with thee.

Enter COSTARD-MONGER, *with a basket of Pears.*

Cos. Buy any pears, very fine pears, pears fine!

　　　[*Nightingale sets his foot afore him, and he falls with his basket.*

Cokes. Ods so! a muss, a muss, a muss, a muss!

　　　　　　　　　　　　[*Falls a scrambling for the pears.*

Cos. Good gentlemen, my ware, my ware; I am a poor man. Good sir, my ware.

Night. Let me hold your sword, sir, it troubles you.

Cokes. Do, and my cloke an thou wilt, and my hat too.

Edg. A delicate great boy! methinks he out-scrambles them all. I cannot persuade myself, but he goes to grammar-school yet, and plays the truant to-day.

Night. Would he had another purse to cut, Zekiel.

Edg. Purse! a man might cut out his kidneys, I think, and he never feel 'em, he is so earnest at the sport.

Night. His soul is half way out on's body at the game.

Edg. Away, Nightingale; that way.

　　　　　　[*Nightingale runs off with his sword, cloke, and hat.*

Cokes. I think I am furnish'd for cather'ne pears, for one under-meal: Give me my cloke.

Cos. Good gentleman, give me my ware.

Cokes. Where's the fellow I gave my cloke to? my cloke and my hat; ha! ods 'lid, is he gone? thieves, thieves! help me to cry, gentlemen.　　　　　　　　　　　　　　　　　　　[*Exit hastily.*

Edg. Away, costard-monger, come to us to Ursula's. [*Exit Cost.*] Talk of him to have a soul! 'heart, if he have any more than a thing given him instead of salt, only to keep him from stinking, I'll be hang'd afore my time, presently: where should it be, trow? in his blood? he has not so much toward it in his whole body as will maintain a good flea! and if he take this course, he will not have so much land left as to rear a calf, within this twelvemonth. Was there ever green plover so pull'd! that his little overseer had been here now, and been but tall enough to see him steal pears, in exchange for his beaver-hat and his cloke thus! I must go find him out next, for his black box, and his patent, it seems, he has of his place; which I think the gentleman would have a reversion of, that spoke to me for it so earnestly.　　　　　　　　　　　　　[*Exit.*

Re-enter COKES.

Cokes. Would I might lose my doublet, and hose, too, as I am an honest man, and never stir, if I think there be any thing but thieving and cozening in this whole Fair. Bartholomew Fair, quoth he! an ever any Bartholomew had that luck in't that I have had, I'll be martyr'd for him, and in Smithfield too. I have paid for my pears, a rot on 'em! I'll keep them no longer; [*throws away his pears.*] you were choke-pears to me: I had been better have gone to mum-chance for you, I wuss. Methinks the Fair should not have used me thus, an 'twere but for my name's-sake; I would not have used a dog o' the name so. O, Numps will triumph now!—

Enter TROUBLEALL.

Friend, do you know who I am, or where I lie? I do not myself, I'll be sworn. Do but carry me home, and I'll please thee; I have money enough there. I have lost myself, and my cloke, and my hat, and my fine sword, and my sister, and Numps, and mistress Grace, a gentlewoman that I should have married, and a cut-work handkerchief she gave me, and two purses, to-day; and my bargain of hobby-horses and gingerbread, which grieves me worst of all.

Tro. By whose warrant, sir, have you done all this?

Cokes. Warrant! thou art a wise fellow indeed: as if a man need a warrant to lose any thing with.

Tro. Yes, justice Overdo's warrant, a man may get and lose with, I'll stand to't.

Cokes. Justice Overdo! dost thou know him? I lie there, he is my brother-in-law, he married my sister: pray thee shew me the way; dost thou know the house?

Tro. Sir, shew me your warrant: I know nothing without a warrant, pardon me.

Cokes. Why, I warrant thee; come along: thou shalt see I have wrought pillows there, and cambric sheets, and sweet bags too. Pray thee guide me to the house.

Tro. Sir, I'll tell you; go you thither yourself first alone, tell your worshipful brother your mind, and but bring me three lines of his hand, or his clerk's, with Adam Overdo underneath, (here I'll stay you,) I'll obey you, and I'll guide you presently.

Cokes. 'Slid, this is an ass, I have found him: pox upon me, what do I talking to such a dull fool! farewell! you are a very coxcomb, do you hear?

Tro. I think I am; if justice Overdo sign to it, I am, and so we are all: he'll quit us all, multiply us all. [*Exeunt.*

SCENE II.—*Another part of the Fair.*

Enter GRACE, QUARLOUS, *and* WINWIFE, *with their swords drawn.*

Grace. Gentlemen, this is no way that you take; you do but breed one another trouble and offence, and give me no contentment at all. I am not she that affects to be quarrell'd for, or have my name or fortune made the question of men's swords.

Quar. 'Sblood, we love you.

Grace. If you both love me, as you pretend, your own reason will tell you, but one can enjoy me: and to that point there leads a directer line, than by my infamy, which must follow, if you fight. 'Tis true, I have profest it to you ingenuously, that rather than to be yoked with this bridegroom is appointed me, I would take up any husband almost upon any trust; though subtlety would say to me, I know, he is a fool, and has an estate, and I might govern him, and enjoy a friend beside: but these are not my aims; I must have a husband I must love, or I cannot live with him. I shall ill make one of these politic wives.

Winw. Why, if you can like either of us, lady, say, which is he, and the other shall swear instantly to desist.

Quar. Content, I accord to that willingly.

Grace. Sure you think me a woman of an extreme levity, gentlemen, or a strange fancy, that, meeting you by chance in such a place as this, both at one instant, and not yet of two hours' acquaintance, neither of you deserving afore the other of me, I should so forsake my modesty (though I might affect one more particularly) as to say, this is he, and name him.

Quar. Why, wherefore should you not? what should hinder you?

Grace. If you would not give it to my modesty, allow it yet to my wit; give me so much of woman and cunning, as not to betray myself impertinently. How can I judge of you, so far as to a choice, without knowing you more? You are both equal, and alike to me yet, and so indifferently affected by me, as each of you might be the man, if the other were away: for you are reasonable creatures, you have understanding and discourse; and if fate send me an understanding husband, I have no fear at all but mine own manners shall make him a good one.

Quar. Would I were put forth to making for you then.

Grace. It may be you are, you know not what is toward you: will you consent to a motion of mine, gentlemen?

·　*Winw.* Whatever it be, we'll presume reasonableness, coming from you.

Quar. And fitness too.

Grace. I saw one of you buy a pair of tables, e'en now.

Winw. Yes, here they be, and maiden ones too, unwritten in.

Grace. The fitter for what they may be employed in. You shall write either of you here a word or a name, what you like best, but of two or three syllables at most; and the next person that comes this way, because Destiny has a high hand in business of this nature, I'll demand which of the two words he or she doth approve, and, according to that sentence, fix my resolution and affection without change.

Quar. Agreed; my word is conceived already.

Winw. And mine shall not be long creating after.

Grace. But you shall promise, gentlemen, not to be curious to know which of you it is, taken; but give me leave to conceal that, till you have brought me either home, or where I may safely tender myself.

Winw. Why, that's but equal.

Quar. We are pleased.

Grace. Because I will bind both your endeavours to work together friendly and jointly each to the other's fortune, and have myself fitted with some means, to make him that is forsaken a part of amends.

Quar. These conditions are very courteous. Well, my word is out of the Arcadia, then; *Argalus.*

Winw. And mine out of the Play *Palemon.* [*They write.*

Enter TROUBLEALL.

Tro. Have you any warrant for this, gentlemen?

Quar. Winw. Ha!

Tro. There must be a warrant had, believe it.

Winw. For what?

Tro. For whatsoever it is, any thing indeed, no matter what.

Quar. 'Slight, here's a fine ragged prophet dropt down i' the nick!

Tro. Heaven quit you, gentlemen!

Quar. Nay, stay a little: good lady, put him to the question.

Grace. You are content then?

Winw. Quar. Yes, yes.

Grace. Sir, here are two names written—

Tro. Is justice Overdo one?

Grace. How, sir! I pray you read them to yourself; it is for a wager between these gentlemen; and with a stroke, or any difference, mark which you approve best.

Tro. They may be both worshipful names for aught I know, mistress; but Adam Overdo had been worth three of them, I assure you in this place, that's in plain English.

Grace. This man amazes me: I pray you like one of them, sir.

Tro. [*marks the book.*] I do like him there, that has the best warrant, mistress, to save your longing, and (multiply him) it may be this. But I am still for justice Overdo, that's my conscience; and quit you.

Winw. Is it done, lady?

Grace. Ay, and strangely, as ever I saw: what fellow is this, trow?

Quar. No matter what, a fortune-teller we have made him: which is it, which is it?

Grace. Nay, did you not promise not to inquire?

Enter EDGWORTH.

Quar. 'Slid, I forgot that, pray you pardon me.—Look, here's our Mercury come; the license arrives in the finest time too! 'tis but scraping out Cokes his name, and 'tis done.

Winw. How now, lime-twig, hast thou touch'd?

Edg. Not yet, sir; except you would go with me and see it, it is not worth speaking on. The act is nothing without a witness. Yonder he is, your man with the box, fallen into the finest company, and so transported with vapours! they have got in a northern clothier, and one Puppy, a western man, that's come to wrestle before my lord mayor anon, and captain Whit, and one Val. Cutting, that helps captain Jordan to roar, a circling boy; with whom your Numps is so taken, that you may strip him of his clothes, if you will. I'll undertake to geld him for you, if you had but a surgeon ready to sear him. And mistress Justice there, is the goodest woman! she does so love them all over in terms of justice and the style of authority, with her hood upright that—I beseech you come away, gentlemen, and see't.

Quar. 'Slight, I would not lose it for the Fair; what will you do, Ned?

Winw. Why, stay hereabout for you: mistress Wellborn must not be seen.

Quar. Do so, and find out a priest in the mean time; I'll bring the license.—Lead, which way is't?

Edg. Here, sir, you are on the back o' the booth already; you may hear the noise. [*Exeunt.*

SCENE III.—*Another part of the Fair.*

URSULA'S Booth as before.

KNOCKEM, WHIT, NORTHERN, PUPPY, CUTTING, WASPE, *and* Mrs. OVERDO, *discovered, all in a state of intoxication.*

Knock. Whit, bid Val. Cutting continue the vapours for a lift, Whit, for a lift. [*Aside to Whit.*

Nor. I'll ne mare, I'll ne mare; the eale's too meeghty.

Knock. How now! my galloway nag the staggers, ha! Whit, give him a slit in the forehead. Chear up, man; a needle and thread to stitch his ears. I'd cure him now, an I had it, with a little butter and garlick, long pepper and grains. Where's my horn? I'll give him a mash presently, shall take away this dizziness.

Pup. Why, where are you, zurs? do you vlinch, and leave us in the zuds now?

Nor. I'll ne mare, I is e'en as vull as a paiper's bag, by my troth, I.

Pup. Do my northern cloth zhrink i' the wetting, ha?

Knock. Why, well said, old flea-bitten; thou'lt never tire I see.
[*They fall to their vapours again.*

Cut. No, sir, but he may tire if it please him.

Whit. Who told dee sho, that he vuld never teer, man?

Cut. No matter who told him so, so long as he knows.

Knock. Nay, I know nothing, sir, pardon me there.

Enter behind, EDGWORTH *with* QUARLOUS.

Edg. They are at it still, sir; this they call vapours.

Whit. He shall not pardon dee, captain: dou shalt not be pardoned. Pre'dee, shweet-heart, do not pardon him.

Cut. 'Slight, I'll pardon him, an I list, whosoever says nay to't.

Quar. Where's Numps? I miss him.

Waspe. Why, I say nay to't.

Quar. O, there he is.

Knock. To what do you say nay, sir?

Waspe. To any thing, whatsoever it is, so long as I do not like it.

Whit. Pardon me, little man, dou musht like it a little.

Cut. No, he must not like it at all, sir: there you are i' the wrong.

Whit. I tink I bee; he musht not like it indeed.

Cut. Nay, then he both must and will like it, sir, for all you.

Knock. If he have reason, he may like it, sir.

Whit. By no meensh, captain, upon reason, he may like nothing upon reason.

Waspe. I have no reason, nor I will hear of no reason, nor I will look for no reason, and he is an ass that either knows any, or looks for't from me.

Cut. Yes, in some sense you may have reason, sir.

Waspe. Ay, in some sense, I care not if I grant you.

Whit. Pardon me, thou ougsht to grant him nothing in no shensh, if dou do love dyshelf, angry man.

Waspe. Why then, I do grant him nothing; and I have no sense.

Cut. 'Tis true, thou hast no sense indeed.

Waspe. 'Slid, but I have sense, now I think on't better, and I will grant him any thing, do you see.

Knock. He is in the right, and does utter a sufficient vapour.

Cut. Nay, it is no sufficient vapour neither, I deny that.

Knock. Then it is a sweet vapour.

Cut. It may be a sweet vapour.

Waspe. Nay, it is no sweet vapour neither, sir, it stinks, and I'll stand to it.

Whit. Yes, I tink it dosh shtink, captain: all vapour dosh shtink.

Waspe. Nay, then it does not stink, sir, and it shall not stink.

Cut. By your leave it may, sir.

Waspe. Ay, by my leave it may stink, I know that.

Whit. Pardon me, thou knowesht nothing, it cannot by thy leave, angry man.

Waspe. How can it not?

Knock. Nay, never question him, for he is in the right.

Whit. Yesh, I am in de right, I confesh it, so ish de little man too.

Waspe. I'll have nothing confest that concerns me. I am not in the right, nor never was in the right, nor never will be in the right, while I am in my right mind.

Cut. Mind! why, here's no man minds you, sir, nor any thing else.

[*They drink again.*

Pup. Vriend, will you mind this that we do?

[*Offering Northern the cup.*

Quar. Call you this vapours! this is such belching of quarrel as I never heard. Will you mind your business, sir?

Edg. You shall see, sir.   [*Goes up to Waspe.*

Nor. I'll ne mare, my waimb warkes too mickle with this aiready.

Edg. Will you take that, master Waspe, that nobody should mind you?

Waspe. Why, what have you to do? is't any matter to you?

Edg. No, but methinks you should not be unminded, though.

Waspe. Nor I wu' not be, now I think on't. Do you hear, new acquaintance? does no man mind me, say you?

Cut. Yes, sir, every man here minds you, but how?

Waspe. Nay, I care as little how as you do; that was not my question.

Whit. No, noting was ty question, tou art a learned man, and I am a valiant man, i'faith la, tou shalt speak for me, and I will fight for tee.

Knock. Fight for him, Whit! a gross vapour, he can fight for himself.

Waspe. It may be I can, but it may be I wu' not, how then?

Cut. Why then you may choose.

Waspe. Why, then I'll choose whether I choose or no.

Knock. I think you may, and 'tis true; and I allow it for a resolute vapour.

Waspe. Nay then, I do think you do not think, and it is no resolute vapour.

Cut. Yes, in some sort he may allow you.

Knock. In no sort, sir, pardon me, I can allow him nothing. You mistake the vapour.

Waspe. He mistakes nothing, sir, in no sort.

Whit. Yes I pre dee now, let him mistake.

Waspe. A t— in your teeth, never pre dee me, for I will have nothing mistaken.

Knock. T—! ha, t—? a noisome vapour: strike, Whit.

[*Aside to Whit.*

[*They fall together by the ears, while Edgworth steals the license out of the box, and exit.*

Mrs. Over. Why, gentlemen, why, gentlemen, I charge you upon my authority, conserve the peace. In the king's name, and my husband's, put up your weapons, I shall be driven to commit you myself, else.

Quar. Ha, ha, ha!

Waspe. Why do you laugh, sir?

Quar. Sir, you'll allow me my christian liberty; I may laugh, I hope.

Cut. In some sort you may, and in some sort you may not, sir.

Knock. Nay, in some sort, sir, he may neither laugh nor hope in this company.

Waspe. Yes, then he may both laugh and hope in any sort, an't please him.

Quar. Faith, and I will then, for it doth please me exceedingly.

Waspe. No exceedingly neither, sir.

Knock. No, that vapour is too lofty.

Quar. Gentlemen, I do not play well at your game of vapours, I am not very good at it, but—

Cut. [*draws a circle on the ground.*] Do you hear, sir? I would speak with you in circle.

Quar. In circle, sir! what would you with me in circle?

Cut. Can you lend me a piece, a Jacobus, in circle?

Quar. 'Slid, your circle will prove more costly than your vapours, then. Sir, no, I lend you none.

Cut. Your beard's not well turn'd up, sir.

Quar. How, rascal! are you playing with my beard? I'll break circle with you.   [*They all draw and fight.*

Pup. Nor. Gentlemen, gentlemen!

Knock. [*aside to Whit.*] Gather up, Whit, gather up, Whit, good vapours.

[*Exit, while Whit takes up the swords, clokes, etc., and conceals them.*

Mrs. Over. What mean you? are you rebels, gentlemen? shall I send out a serjeant at arms, or a writ of rebellion, against you? I'll commit you upon my woman-hood, for a riot, upon my justice-hood, if you persist.   [*Exeunt Quarlous and Cutting.*

Waspe. Upon my justice-hood! marry s— o' your hood: you'll commit! spoke like a true justice of peace's wife indeed, and a fine female lawyer! t— in your teeth for a fee, now.

Mrs. Over. Why, Numps, in master Overdo's name, I charge you.

Waspe. Good mistress Underdo, hold your tongue.

Mrs. Over. Alas, poor Numps!

Waspe. Alas! and why *alas* from you, I beseech you? or why *poor* Numps, goody Rich? Am I come to be pitied by your tuft-taffata now? Why, mistress, I knew Adam the clerk, your husband, when he was Adam Scrivener, and writ for two-pence a sheet, as high as he bears his head now, or you your hood, dame.—

Enter Bristle *and other* Watchmen.

What are you, sir?

Bri. We be men, and no infidels; what is the matter here, and the noises, can you tell?

Waspe. Heart, what ha' you to do? cannot a man quarrel in quietness, but he must be put out on't by you! what are you?

Bri. Why, we be his majesty's watch, sir.

Waspe. Watch! 'sblood, you are a sweet watch indeed. A body would think, an you watch'd well a nights, you should be contented to sleep at this time a day. Get you to your fleas and your flock-beds, you rogues, your kennels, and lie down close.

Bri. Down! yes, we will down, I warrant you: down with him, in his majesty's name, down, down with him, and carry him away to the pigeon-holes.

[*Some of the Watch seize Waspe, and carry him off.*

Mrs. Over. I thank you, honest friends, in the behalf o' the crown, and the peace, and in master Overdo's name, for suppressing enormities.

Whit. Stay, Bristle, here ish anoder brash of drunkards, but very quiet, special drunkards, will pay de five shillings very well. [*Points to Northern and Puppy, drunk, and asleep, on the bench.*] Take 'em to de, in de graish o' God: one of hem do's change cloth for ale in the Fair, here; te toder ish a strong man, a mighty man, my lord mayor's man, and a wrastler. He has wrashled so long with the bottle here, that the man with the beard hash almosht streek up hish heelsh.

Bri. 'Slid, the clerk o' the market has been to cry him all the Fair over here, for my lord's service.

Whit. Tere he ish, pre de taik him hensh, and make ty best on him. [*Exeunt Bristle and the rest of the Watch with Northern and Puppy.*]—How now, woman o' shilk, vat ailsh ty shweet faish? art tou melancholy?

Mrs. Over. A little distempered with these enormities. Shall I entreat a courtesy of you, captain?

Whit. Entreat a hundred, velvet voman, I vill do it, shpeak out.

Mrs. Over. I cannot with modesty speak it out, but—

[*Whispers him.*

Whit. I vill do it, and more and more, for de. What Ursla, an't be bitch, an't be bawd, an't be!

Enter URSULA.

Urs. How now, rascal! what roar you for, old pimp?

Whit. Here, put up de clokes, Ursh; de purchase. Pre de now, shweet Ursh, help dis good brave voman to a jordan, an't be.

Urs. 'Slid call your captain Jordan to her, can you not?

Whit. Nay, pre de leave dy consheits, and bring the velvet voman to de—

Urs. I bring her! hang her: heart, must I find a common pot for every punk in your purlieus?

Whit. O good voordsh, Ursh, it ish a guest o' velvet, i'fait la.

Urs. Let her sell her hood, and buy a spunge, with a pox to her! my vessel is employed, sir. I have but one, and 'tis the bottom of an old bottle. An honest proctor and his wife are at it within; if she'll stay her time, so.   [*Exit.*

Whit. As soon as tou cansht, shweet Ursh. Of a valiant man I tink I am te patientsh man i' the world, or in all Smithfield.

Re-enter KNOCKEM.

Knock. How now, Whit! close vapours, stealing your leaps! covering in corners, ha!

Whit. No, fait, captain, dough tou beesht a vishe man, dy vit is a mile hence now. I vas procuring a shmall courtesie for a woman of fashion here.

Mrs. Over. Yes, captain, though I am a justice of peace's wife, I do love men of war, and the sons of the sword, when they come before my husband.

Knock. Say'st thou so, filly? thou shalt have a leap presently, I'll horse thee myself, else.

Urs. [*within.*] Come, will you bring her in now, and let her take her turn?

Whit. Gramercy, good Ursh, I tank de.

Mrs. Over. Master Overdo shall thank her.   [*Exit.*

Re-enter URSULA, *followed by* LITTLEWIT, *and* Mrs. LITTLEWIT.

Lit. Good ga'mere Urse, Win and I are exceedingly beholden to you, and to captain Jordan, and captain Whit.—Win, I'll be bold to leave you, in this good company, Win; for half an hour or so, Win; while I go and see how my matter goes forward, and if the puppets be perfect; and then I'll come and fetch you, Win.

Mrs. Lit. Will you leave me alone with two men, John?

Lit. Ay, they are honest gentlemen, Win, captain Jordan and captain Whit; they'll use you very civilly, Win. God be wi' you, Win.   [*Exit.*

Urs. What, is her husband gone?

Knock. On his false gallop, Urse, away.

Urs. An you be right Bartholomew birds, now shew yourselves so: we are undone for want of fowl in the Fair, here. Here will be Zekiel Edgworth, and three or four gallants with him at night, and I have neither plover nor quail for them: persuade this between you two, to become a bird o' the game, while I work the velvet woman within, as you call her.

Knock. I conceive thee, Urse: go thy ways. [*Exit Ursula.*]— Dost thou hear, Whit? is't not pity, my delicate dark chestnut here, with the fine lean head, large forehead, round eyes, even mouth, sharp ears, long neck, thin crest, close withers, plain back, deep sides, short fillets, and full flanks; with a round belly, a plump buttock, large thighs, knit knees, strait legs, short pasterns, smooth hoofs, and short heels, should lead a dull honest woman's life, that might live the life of a lady?

Whit. Yes, by my fait and trot it is, captain; de honest woman's life is a scurvy dull life indeed, la.

Mrs. Lit. How, sir, is an honest woman's life a scurvy life?

Whit. Yes fait, shweet-heart, believe him, de leef of a bond-woman! but if dou vilt hearken to me, I vill make tee a free woman and a lady; dou shalt live like a lady, as te captain saish.

Knock. Ay, and be honest too sometimes; have her wires and her tires, her green gowns and velvet petticoats.

Whit. Ay, and ride to Ware and Rumford in dy coash, shee de players, be in love vit 'em: sup vit gallantsh, be drunk, and cost de noting.

Knock. Brave vapours!

Whit. And lie by twenty on 'em, if dou pleash, shweet-heart.

Mrs. Lit. What, and be honest still! that were fine sport.

Whit. Tish common, shweet-heart, tou may'st do it by my hand: it shall be justified to thy husband's faish, now: tou shalt be as honesht as the skin between his hornsh, la.

Knock. Yes, and wear a dressing, top and top-gallant, to compare with e'er a husband on 'em all, for a foretop: it is the vapour of spirit in the wife to cuckold now a days, as it is the vapour of fashion in the husband not to suspect. Your prying cat-eyed citizen is an abominable vapour.

Mrs. Lit. Lord, what a fool have I been!

Whit. Mend then, and do every ting like a lady hereafter; never know ty husband from another man.

Knock. Nor any one man from another, but in the dark.

Whit. Ay, and then it ish no disgrash to know any man.

Urs. [*within.*] Help, help here!

Knock. How now? what vapour's there?

Re-enter URSULA.

Urs. O, you are a sweet ranger, and look well to your walks! Yonder is your punk of Turnbull, ramping Alice, has fallen upon the poor gentlewoman within, and pull'd her hood over her ears, and her hair through it.

Enter ALICE, *beating and driving in* Mrs. OVERDO.

Mrs. Over. Help, help, in the king's name!

Alice. A mischief on you, they are such as you are that undo us and take our trade from us, with your tuft-taffata haunches.

Knock. How now, Alice!

Alice. The poor common whores can have no traffic for the privy rich ones; your caps and hoods of velvet call away our customers, and lick the fat from us.

Urs. Peace, you foul ramping jade, you—

Alice. Od's foot, you bawd in grease, are you talking?

Knock. Why, Alice, I say.

Alice. Thou sow of Smithfield, thou!

Urs. Thou tripe of Turnbull!

Knock. Cat-a-mountain vapours, ha!

Urs. You know where you were taw'd lately; both lash'd and slash'd you were in Bridewell.

Alice. Ay, by the same token you rid that week, and broke out the bottom of the cart, night-tub.

Knock. Why, lion face, ha! do you know who I am? shall I tear ruff, slit waistcoat, make rags of petticoat, ha! go to, vanish for fear of vapours. Whit, a kick, Whit, in the parting vapour. [*They kick out Alice.*] Come, brave woman, take a good heart, thou shalt be a lady too.

Whit. Yes fait, dey shall all both be ladies, and write madam: I vill do't myself for dem. Do is the word, and D is the middle letter of madam, D D, put 'em together, and make deeds, without which all words are alike, la.

Knock. 'Tis true: Ursula, take them in, open thy wardrobe, and fit them to their calling. Green gowns, crimson petticoats, green women, my lord mayor's green women! guests o' the game, true bred. I'll provide you a coach to take the air in.

Mrs. Lit. But do you think you can get one?

Knock. O, they are common as wheelbarrows where there are great dunghills. Every pettifogger's wife has 'em; for first he buys a coach that he may marry, and then he marries that he may be made cuckold in't: for if their wives ride not to their cuckolding, they do them no credit. [*Exeunt Ursula, Mrs. Littlewit, and Mrs. Overdo.*]—*Hide and be hidden, ride and be ridden,* says the vapour of experience.

Enter TROUBLEALL.

Tro. By what warrant does it say so?

Knock. Ha, mad child o' the Pie-poudres! art thou there? fill us a fresh can, Urse, we may drink together.

Tro. I may not drink without a warrant, captain.

Knock. 'Slood, thou'lt not stale without a warrant shortly. Whit, give me pen, ink, and paper, I'll draw him a warrant presently.

Tro. It must be justice Overdo's.

Knock. I know, man; fetch the drink, Whit.

Whit. I pre dee now, be very brief, captain, for de new ladies stay for dee.   [*Exit, and re-enters with a can.*

Knock. O, as brief as can be, here 'tis already. [*Gives Troubleall a paper.*] Adam Overdo.

Tro. Why now I'll pledge you, captain.

Knock. Drink it off, I'll come to thee anon again.   [*Exeunt.*

SCENE IV.—*The back of* URSULA'S *Booth.*

OVERDO *in the stocks, People, etc.*

Enter QUARLOUS *with the license, and* EDGWORTH.

Quar. Well, sir, you are now discharged; beware of being spied hereafter.

Edg. Sir, will it please you, enter in here at Ursula's, and take part of a silken gown, a velvet petticoat, or a wrought smock; I am promised such, and I can spare a gentleman a moiety.

Quar. Keep it for your companions in beastliness, I am none of them, sir. If I had not already forgiven you a greater trespass, or thought you yet worth my beating, I would instruct your manners, to whom you made your offers. But go your ways, talk not to me, the hangman is only fit to discourse with you; the hand of beadle is too merciful a punishment for your trade of life. [*Exit Edgworth.*] —I am sorry I employ'd this fellow, for he thinks me such; *facinus quos inquinat, æquat.* But it was for sport; and would I make it serious, the getting of this license is nothing to me, without other circumstances concur. I do think how impertinently I labour, if the word be not mine that the ragged fellow mark'd: and what advantage I have given Ned Winwife in this time now of working her, though it be mine. He'll go near to form to her what a debauched rascal I am, and fright her out of all good conceit of me: I should do so by him, I am sure, if I had the opportunity. But my hope is in her temper yet; and it must needs be next to despair, that is grounded on any part of a woman's discretion. I would give, by my troth now, all I could spare, to my clothes and my sword, to

meet my tatter'd soothsayer again, who was my judge in the
question, to know certainly whose word he has damn'd or saved;
for till then I live but under a reprieve. I must seek him. Who be
these?

Enter BRISTLE *and some of the* Watch, *with* WASPE.

Waspe. Sir, you are a Welsh cuckold, and a prating runt, and no
constable.

Bri. You say very well.—Come, put in his leg in the middle
roundel, and let him hole there.   *[They put him in the stocks.*

Waspe. You stink of leeks, metheglin, and cheese, you rogue.

Bri. Why, what is that to you, if you sit sweetly in the stocks
in the mean time? if you have a mind to stink too, your breeches
sit close enough to your bum.   Sit you merry, sir.

Quar. How now, Numps?

Waspe. It is no matter how; pray you look off.

Quar. Nay, I'll not offend you, Numps; I thought you had sat
there to be seen.

Waspe. And to be sold, did you not? pray you mind your business, an you have any.

Quar. Cry you mercy, Numps; does your leg lie high enough?

Enter HAGGISE.

Bri. How now, neighbour Haggise, what says justice Overdo's
worship to the other offenders?

Hag. Why, he says just nothing; what should he say, or where
should he say? He is not to be found, man; he has not been seen
in the Fair here all this live-long day, never since seven a clock i'
the morning. His clerks know not what to think on't. There is
no court of Pie-poudres yet. Here they be return'd.

Enter others of the Watch *with* BUSY.

Bri. What shall be done with them, then, in your discretion?

Hag. I think we were best put them in the stocks in discretion
(there they will be safe in discretion) for the valour of an hour, or
such a thing, till his worship come.

Bri. It is but a hole matter if we do, neighbour Haggise; come,
sir, [*to* Waspe.] here is company for you; heave up the stocks.

[*As they open the stocks, Waspe puts his shoe on his hand, and
slips it in for his leg.*

Waspe. I shall put a trick upon your Welsh diligence perhaps.
                                                [*Aside.*

Bri. Put in your leg, sir.   [*To* Busy.

Quar. What, rabbi Busy! is he come?

Busy. I do obey thee; the lion may roar, but he cannot bite. I
am glad to be thus separated from the heathen of the land, and put
apart in the stocks, for the holy cause.

Waspe. What are you, sir?

Busy. One that rejoiceth in his affliction, and sitteth here to prophesy the destruction of fairs and May-games, wakes and Whitson-ales, and doth sigh and groan for the reformation of these abuses.

Waspe. [*to Overdo.*] And do you sigh and groan too, or rejoice in your affliction?

Over. I do not feel it, I do not think of it, it is a thing without me: Adam, thou art above these batteries, these contumelies. *In te manca ruit fortuna,* as thy friend Horace says; thou art one, *Quem neque pauperies, neque mors, neque vincula, terrent.* And therefore, as another friend of thine says, I think it be thy friend Persius, *Non te quæsiveris extra.*

Quar. What's here! a stoic in the stocks? the fool is turn'd philosopher.

Busy. Friend, I will leave to communicate my spirit with you, if I hear any more of those superstitious relics, those lists of Latin, the very rags of Rome, and patches of popery.

Waspe. Nay, an you begin to quarrel, gentlemen, I'll leave you. I have paid for quarrelling too lately: look you, a device, but shifting in a hand for a foot. God be wi' you. [*Slips out his hand.*

Busy. Wilt thou then leave thy brethren in tribulation?

Waspe. For this once, sir. [*Exit, running.*

Busy. Thou art a halting neutral; stay him there, stop him, that will not endure the heat of persecution.

Bri. How now, what's the matter?

Busy. He is fled, he is fled, and dares not sit it out.

Bri. What, has he made an escape! which way? follow, neigh-bour Haggise. [*Exeunt Haggise and Watch.*

Enter Dame PURECRAFT.

Pure. O me, in the stocks! have the wicked prevail'd?

Busy. Peace, religious sister, it is my calling, comfort yourself; an extraordinary calling, and done for my better standing, my surer standing, hereafter.

Enter TROUBLEALL, *with a can.*

Tro. By whose warrant, by whose warrant, this?

Quar. O, here's my man dropt in I look'd for.

Over. Ha!

Pure. O, good sir, they have set the faithful here to be wonder'd at; and provided holes for the holy of the land.

Tro. Had they warrant for it? shew'd they justice Overdo's hand? if they had no warrant, they shall answer it.

Re-enter HAGGISE.

Bri. Sure you did not lock the stocks sufficiently, neighbour Toby.

Hag. No! see if you can lock them better.

Bri. They are very sufficiently lock'd, and truly; yet something is in the matter.

Tro. True, your warrant is the matter that is in question; by what warrant?

Bri. Madman, hold your peace, I will put you in his room else in the very same hold, do you see?

Quar. How, is he a madman?

Tro. Shew me justice Overdo's warrant, I obey you.

Hag. You are a mad fool, hold your tongue.

　　　　　　　　　　　　　　　　　[Exeunt Haggise and Bristle.

Tro. In justice Overdo's name, I drink to you, and here's my warrant.　　　　　　　　　　　　　　　　　　*[Shews his can.*

Over. Alas, poor wretch! how it yearns my heart for him! *[Aside.*

Quar. If he be mad, it is in vain to question him. I'll try him though.—Friend, there was a gentlewoman shew'd you two names some hours since, Argalus and Palemon, to mark in a book; which of them was it you mark'd?

Tro. I mark no name but Adam Overdo, that is the name of names, he only is the sufficient magistrate; and that name I reverence, shew it me.

Quar. This fellow's mad indeed: I am further off now than afore.

Over. I shall not breathe in peace till I have made him some amends.　　　　　　　　　　　　　　　　　　　　　*[Aside.*

Quar. Well, I will make another use of him is come in my head: I have a nest of beards in my trunk, one something like his.

　　　　　　　Re-enter BRISTLE *and* HAGGISE.

Bri. This mad fool has made me that I know not whether I have lock'd the stocks or no; I think I lock'd them.　　*[Tries the locks.*

Tro. Take Adam Overdo in your mind, and fear nothing.

Bri. 'Slid, madness itself! hold thy peace, and take that.

　　　　　　　　　　　　　　　　　　　　　　　[Strikes him.

Tro. Strikest thou without a warrant? take thou that.

　　　　　　　[They fight, and leave open the stocks in the scuffle.

Busy. We are delivered by miracle; fellow in fetters, let us not refuse the means; this madness was of the spirit: the malice of the enemy hath mock'd itself.　　　　　　　*[Exeunt Busy and Overdo.*

Pure. Mad do they call him! the world is mad in error, but he is mad in truth: I love him o' the sudden (the cunning man said all true) and shall love him more and more. How well it becomes a man to be mad in truth! O, that I might be his yoke-fellow, and be mad with him, what a many should we draw to madness in truth with us!　　　　　　　　　　　　　　　　　　*[Exit.*

Bri. How now, all 'scaped! where's the woman? it is witchcraft! her velvet hat is a witch, o' my conscience, or my key! the one.— The madman was a devil, and I am an ass; so bless me, my place, and mine office!　　　　　　　　　　　*[Exeunt, affrighted.*

ACT V

SCENE I.—*The Fair, as before.*

A Booth.

LANTHORN LEATHERHEAD, *dressed as a puppet-show man,* FILCHER, *and* SHARKWELL *with a flag.*

Leath. Well, luck and Saint Bartholomew! out with the sign of our invention, in the name of wit, and do you beat the drum the while: all the foul i' the Fair, I mean all the dirt in Smithfield,—that's one of master Littlewit's carwhitchets now—will be thrown at our banner to-day, if the matter does not please the people. O the motions that I Lanthorn Leatherhead have given light to, in my time, since my master Pod died! Jerusalem was a stately thing, and so was Nineveh, and the city of Norwich, and Sodom and Gomorrah, with the rising of the prentices, and pulling down the bawdy-houses there upon Shrove-Tuesday; but the Gun-powder plot, there was a get-penny! I have presented that to an eighteen or twenty pence audience, nine times in an afternoon. Your home-born projects prove ever the best, they are so easy and familiar; they put too much learning in their things now o' days: and that I fear will be the spoil of this. Littlewit! I say, Micklewit! if not too mickle! look to your gathering there, goodman Filcher.

Filch. I warrant you, sir.

Leath. An there come any gentlefolks, take two-pence apiece, Sharkwell.

Shark. I warrant you, sir, three-pence an we can. [*Exeunt.*

SCENE II.—*Another part of the Fair.*

Enter OVERDO, *disguised like a Porter.*

Over. This latter disguise, I have borrow'd of a porter, shall carry me out to all my great and good ends; which however interrupted, were never destroyed in me: neither is the hour of my severity yet come to reveal myself, wherein, cloud-like, I will break out in rain and hail, lightning and thunder, upon the head of enormity. Two main works I have to prosecute: first, one is to invent some satisfaction for the poor kind wretch, who is out of his wits for my sake, and yonder I see him coming, I will walk aside, and project for it.

Enter WINWIFE *and* GRACE.

Winw. I wonder where Tom Quarlous is, that he returns not: it may be he is struck in here to seek us.

Grace. See, here's our madman again.

Enter QUARLOUS, *in* TROUBLEALL'S *clothes, followed by*
Dame PURECRAFT.

Quar. I have made myself as like him, as his gown and cap will
give me leave.

Pure. Sir, I love you, and would be glad to be mad with you in
truth.

Winw. How! my widow in love with a madman?

Pure. Verily, I can be as mad in spirit as you.

Quar. By whose warrant? leave your canting. Gentlewoman,
have I found you? [*To mistress Grace.*] save ye, quit ye, and
multiply ye! Where's your book? 'twas a sufficient name I mark'd,
let me see't, be not afraid to shew't me.

Grace. What would you with it, sir?

Quar. Mark it again and again at your service.

Grace. Here it is, sir, this was it you mark'd.

Quar. Palemon! fare you well, fare you well.

Winw. How, Palemon!

Grace. Yes, faith, he has discovered it to you now, and therefore
'twere vain to disguise it longer; I am yours, sir, by the benefit of
your fortune.

Winw. And you have him, mistress, believe it, that shall never
give you cause to repent her benefit: but make you rather to think
that in this choice she had both her eyes.

Grace. I desire to put it to no danger of protestation.

[*Exeunt Grace and Winwife.*

Quar. Palemon the word, and Winwife the man!

Pure. Good sir, vouchsafe a yoke-fellow in your madness, shun
not one of the sanctified sisters, that would draw with you in
truth.

Quar. Away, you are a herd of hypocritical proud ignorants,
rather wild than mad; fitter for woods, and the society of beasts,
than houses, and the congregation of men. You are the second
part of the society of canters, outlaws to order and discipline,
and the only privileged church-robbers of Christendom. Let me
alone: *Palemon* the word, and Winwife the man!

Pure. I must uncover myself unto him, or I shall never enjoy
him, for all the cunning men's promises. [*Aside.*] Good sir, hear
me, I am worth six thousand pound, my love to you is become my
rack; I'll tell you all and the truth, since you hate the hypocrisy
of the party-coloured brotherhood. These seven years I have been
a wilful holy widow, only to draw feasts and gifts from my entangled
suitors: I am also by office an assisting sister of the deacons, and a
devourer, instead of a distributor of the alms. I am a special maker
of marriages for our decayed brethren with our rich widows, for a
third part of their wealth, when they are married, for the relief of
the poor elect: as also our poor handsome young virgins, with our
wealthy bachelors or widowers; to make them steal from their

husbands, when I have confirmed them in the faith, and got all put
into their custodies. And if I have not my bargain, they may sooner
turn a scolding drab into a silent minister, than make me leave
pronouncing reprobation and damnation unto them. Our elder,
Zeal-of-the-land, would have had me, but I know him to be the
capital knave of the land, making himself rich, by being made a
feoffee in trust to deceased brethren, and cozening their heirs, by
swearing the absolute gift of their inheritance. And thus having
eased my conscience, and utter'd my heart with the tongue of my
love; enjoy all my deceits together, I beseech you. I should not
have revealed this to you, but that in time I think you are mad,
and I hope you'll think me so too, sir?

Quar. Stand aside, I'll answer you presently. [*He walks by.*] Why
should I not marry this six thousand pound, now I think on't, and
a good trade too that she has beside, ha? The t'other wench
Winwife is sure of; there's no expectation for me there. Here I
may make myself some saver yet, if she continue mad, there's the
question. It is money that I want, why should not I marry the
money when 'tis offer'd me? I have a license and all, it is but
razing out one name, and putting in another. There's no playing
with a man's fortune! I am resolved: I were truly mad an I would
not!—Well, come your ways, follow me, an you will be mad, I'll
shew you a warrant! [*Takes her along with him.*

Pure. Most zealously, it is that I zealously desire.

Over. [*stopping him.*] Sir, let me speak with you.

Quar. By whose warrant?

Over. The warrant that you tender, and respect so; Justice
Overdo's. I am the man, friend Troubleall, though thus disguised
(as the careful magistrate ought) for the good of the republic in the
Fair, and the weeding out of enormity. Do you want a house, or
meat, or drink, or clothes? speak whatsoever it is, it shall be
supplied you; what want you?

Quar. Nothing but your warrant.

Over. My warrant! for what?

Quar. To be gone, sir.

Over. Nay, I pray thee stay; I am serious, and have not many
words, nor much time to exchange with thee. Think what may
do thee good.

Quar. Your hand and seal will do me a great deal of good; nothing
else in the whole Fair that I know.

Over. If it were to any end, thou shouldst have it willingly.

Quar. Why, it will satisfy me, that's end enough to look on; an
you will not give it me, let me go.

Over. Alas! thou shalt have it presently; I'll but step into the
scrivener's here by, and bring it. Do not go away. [*Exit.*

Quar. Why, this madman's shape will prove a very fortunate
one, I think. Can a ragged robe produce these effects? if this be
the wise justice, and he bring me his hand, I shall go near to make
some use on't.

Re-enter OVERDO.

He is come already!

Over. Look thee! here is my hand and seal, Adam Overdo; if there be any thing to be written above in that paper that thou want'st now, or at any time hereafter, think on't, it is my deed.   I deliver it so; can your friend write?

Quar. Her hand for a witness, and all is well.

Over. With all my heart.   [*He urges her to sign it.*

Quar. Why should not I have the conscience to make this a bond of a thousand pound now, or what I would else?   [*Aside.*

Over. Look you, there it is, and I deliver it as my deed again.

Quar. Let us now proceed in madness.

[*Exeunt Quarlous and Dame Purecraft.*

Over. Well, my conscience is much eased; I have done my part, though it doth him no good; yet Adam hath offered satisfaction. The sting is removed from hence! Poor man, he is much altered with his affliction, it has brought him low. Now for my other work, reducing the young man, I have follow'd so long in love, from the brink of his bane to the centre of safety. Here, or in some such-like vain place, I shall be sure to find him. I will wait the good time.   [*Exit.*

SCENE III.—*Another part of the Fair.*

The Puppet-show Booth, as before.

Enter SHARKWELL *and* FILCHER, *with bills, and* COKES *in his doublet and hose, followed by the Boys of the Fair.*

Cokes. How now! what's here to do, friend? art thou the master of the monuments?

Shark. 'Tis a motion, an't please your worship.

Enter OVERDO *behind.*

Over. My fantastical brother-in-law, master Bartholomew Cokes!

Cokes. A motion! what's that! [*Reads.*] *The ancient modern history of Hero and Leander, otherwise called the Touchstone of true Love, with as true a trial of friendship between Damon and Pythias, two faithful friends o' the Bank-side.*—Pretty, i'faith, what's the meaning on't? is't an interlude, or what is't?

Filch. Yes, sir, please you come near, we'll take your money within.

Cokes. Back with these children; they do so follow me up and down!

Enter LITTLEWIT.

Lit. By your leave, friend.

Filch. You must pay, sir, an you go in.

Lit. Who, I! I perceive thou know'st not me; call the master of the motion.

Shark. What, do you not know the author, fellow Filcher? You must take no money of him; he must come in gratis: master Littlewit is a voluntary; he is the author.

Lit. Peace, speak not too loud, I would not have any notice taken that I am the author, till we see how it passes.

Cokes. Master Littlewit, how dost thou?

Lit. Master Cokes! you are exceeding well met: what, in your doublet and hose, without a cloke or a hat?

Cokes. I would I might never stir, as I am an honest man, and by that fire; I have lost all in the Fair, and all my acquaintance too; didst thou meet any body that I know, master Littlewit? my man Numps, or my sister Overdo, or mistress Grace? Pray thee, master Littlewit, lend me some money to see the interlude here; I'll pay thee again, as I am a gentleman. If thou'lt but carry me home, I have money enough there.

Lit. O, sir, you shall command it; what, will a crown serve you?

Cokes. I think it will; what do we pay for coming in, fellows?

Filch. Two-pence, sir.

Cokes. Two-pence! there's twelve-pence, friend: nay, I am a gallant, as simple as I look now; if you see me with my man about me, and my artillery again.

Lit. Your man was in the stocks e'en now, sir.

Cokes. Who, Numps?

Lit. Yes, faith.

Cokes. For what, i'faith? I am glad o' that; remember to tell me on't anon; I have enough now. What manner of matter is this, master Littlewit? what kind of actors have you? are they good actors?

Lit. Pretty youths, sir, all children both old and young; here's the master of 'em—

Enter LEATHERHEAD.

Leath. [*aside to Littlewit.*] Call me not Leatherhead, but Lantern.

Lit. Master Lantern, that gives light to the business.

Cokes. In good time, sir! I would fain see them, I would be glad to drink with the young company; which is the tiring-house?

Leath. Troth, sir, our tiring-house is somewhat little; we are but beginners yet, pray pardon us; you cannot go upright in't.

Cokes. No! not now my hat is off? what would you have done with me, if you had had me feather and all, as I was once to-day? Have you none of your pretty impudent boys now, to bring stools, fill tobacco, fetch ale, and beg money, as they have at other houses? Let me see some of your actors.

Lit. Shew him them, shew him them. Master Lantern, this is a gentleman that is a favourer of the quality.   [*Exit Leatherhead.*

Over. Ay, the favouring of this licentious quality is the consumption of many a young gentleman; a pernicious enormity.

[*Aside.*

Re-enter LEATHERHEAD, *with a basket.*

Cokes. What! do they live in baskets?

Leath. They do lie in a basket, sir, they are o' the small players.

Cokes. These be players minors indeed. Do you call these players?

Leath. They are actors, sir, and as good as any, none dispraised, for dumb shows: indeed, I am the mouth of them all.

Cokes. Thy mouth will hold them all. I think one tailor would go near to beat all this company with a hand bound behind him.

Lit. Ay, and eat them all too, an they were in cake-bread.

Cokes. I thank you for that, master Littlewit; a good jest! Which is your Burbage now?

Leath. What mean you by that, sir?

Cokes. Your best actor, your Field?

Lit. Good, i'faith! you are even with me, sir.

Leath. This is he, that acts young Leander, sir: he is extremely beloved of the womenkind, they do so affect his action, the green gamesters, that come here! and this is lovely Hero; this with the beard, Damon; and this pretty Pythias: this is the ghost of king Dionysius in the habit of a scrivener; as you shall see anon at large.

Cokes. Well, they are a civil company, I like 'em for that; they offer not to fleer, nor jeer, nor break jests, as the great players do: and then, there goes not so much charge to the feasting of them, or making them drunk, as to the other, by reason of their littleness. Do they use to play perfect? are they never fluster'd?

Leath. No, sir, I thank my industry and policy for it; they are as well govern'd a company, though I say it——And here is young Leander, is as proper an actor of his inches, and shakes his head like an hostler.

Cokes. But do you play it according to the printed book? I have read that.

Leath. By no means, sir.

Cokes. No! how then?

Leath. A better way, sir; that is too learned and poetical for our audience: what do they know what *Hellespont* is, *guilty of true love's blood?* or what *Abydos* is? or *the other, Sestos hight?*

Cokes. Thou art in the right; I do not know myself.

Leath. No, I have entreated master Littlewit to take a little pains to reduce it to a more familiar strain for our people.

Cokes. How, I pray thee, good master Littlewit?

Lit. It pleases him to make a matter of it, sir; but there is no such matter, I assure you: I have only made it a little easy, and modern for the times, sir, that's all. As for the Hellespont, I imagine our Thames here; and then Leander I make a dyer's son about Puddle-wharf: and Hero a wench o' the Bank-side, who going over one morning to Old Fish-street, Leander spies her land at Trig-stairs, and falls in love with her. Now do I introduce Cupid, having metamorphosed himself into a drawer, and he strikes Hero in love with a pint of sherry; and other pretty passages there are of the friendship, that will delight you, sir, and please you of judgment.

Cokes. I'll be sworn they shall: I am in love with the actors already, and I'll be allied to them presently.—They respect gentlemen, these fellows: —Hero shall be my fairing: but which of my fairings?—let me see—i'faith, my fiddle; and Leander my fiddlestick: then Damon my drum, and Pythias my pipe, and the ghost of Dionysius my hobby-horse. All fitted.

Enter WINWIFE *and* GRACE.

Winw. Look, yonder's your Cokes gotten in among his playfellows; I thought we could not miss him at such a spectacle.

Grace. Let him alone, he is so busy he will never spy us.

Leath. Nay, good sir! [*To Cokes, who is handling the puppets.*

Cokes. I warrant thee I will not hurt her, fellow; what, dost thou think me uncivil? I pray thee be not jealous; I am toward a wife.

Lit. Well, good master Lantern, make ready to begin that I may fetch my wife; and look you be perfect, you undo me else, in my reputation.

Leath. I warrant you, sir, do not you breed too great an expectation of it among your friends; that's the hurter of these things.

Lit. No, no, no. [*Exit.*

Cokes. I'll stay here and see; pray thee let me see.

Winw. How diligent and troublesome he is!

Grace. The place becomes him, methinks.

Over. My ward, mistress Grace, in the company of a stranger! I doubt I shall be compell'd to discover myself before my time.

[*Aside.*

Enter KNOCKEM, EDGWORTH, *and* Mrs. LITTLEWIT, *followed by* WHIT *supporting* Mrs. OVERDO, *masked.*

Filch. Two-pence apiece, gentlemen, an excellent motion.

Knock. Shall we have fine fire-works, and good vapours?

Shark. Yes, captain, and water-works too.

Whit. I pree dee take care o' dy shmall lady there, Edgworth; I will look to dish tall lady myself.

Leath. Welcome, gentlemen, welcome, gentlemen.

Whit. Predee mashter o' the monshtersh, help a very sick lady here to a chair to shit in.

Leath. Presently, sir. [*A chair is brought in for Mrs. Overdo.*

Whit. Good fait now, Ursula's ale and acqua-vitæ ish to blame for't; shit down, shweet-heart, shit down and sleep a little.

Edg. [*to Mrs. Littlewit.*] Madam, you are very welcome hither.

Knock. Yes, and you shall see very good vapours.

Over. Here is my care come! I like to see him in so good company: and yet I wonder that persons of such fashion should resort hither. [*Aside.*

Edg. There is a very private house, madam.

Leath. Will it please your ladyship sit, madam?

Mrs. Lit. Yes, goodman. They do so all-to-be-madam me, I think they think me a very lady.

Edg. What else, madam?

Mrs. Lit. Must I put off my mask to him?

Edg. O, by no means.

Mrs. Lit. How should my husband know me then?

Knock. Husband! an idle vapour; he must not know you, nor you him: there's the true vapour.

Over. Yea! I will observe more of this. [*Aside.*] Is this a lady, friend?

Whit. Ay, and dat is anoder lady, shweet-heart; if dou hasht a mind to 'em, give me twelve-pence from tee, and dou shalt have eder oder on 'em.

Over. Ay, this will prove my chiefest enormity: I will follow this.   [*Aside.*

Edg. Is not this a finer life, lady, than to be clogg'd with a husband?

Mrs. Lit. Yes, a great deal. When will they begin, trow, in the name o' the motion?

Edg. By and by, madam; they stay but for company.

Knock. Do you hear, puppet-master, these are tedious vapours, when begin you?

Leath. We stay but for master Littlewit, the author, who is gone for his wife: and we begin presently.

Mrs. Lit. That's I, that's I.

Edg. That was you, lady; but now you are no such poor thing.

Knock. Hang the author's wife, a running vapour! here be ladies will stay for ne'er a Delia of them all.

Whit. But hear me now, here ish one o' de ladish ashleep, stay till shee but vake, man.

Enter WASPE.

Waspe. How now, friends! what's here to do?

Filch. Two-pence apiece, sir, the best motion in the Fair.

Waspe. I believe you lie; if you do, I'll have my money again, and beat you.

Mrs. Lit. Numps is come!

Waspe. Did you see a master of mine come in here, a tall young 'squire of Harrow o' the Hill, master Bartholomew Cokes?

Filch. I think there be such a one within.

Waspe. Look he be, you were best: but it is very likely: I wonder I found him not at all the rest. I have been at the Eagle, and the Black Wolf, and the Bull with the five legs and two pizzles:—he was a calf at Uxbridge fair two years agone—and at the dogs that dance the morrice, and the hare of the Tabor; and mist him at all these! Sure this must needs be some fine sight that holds him so, if it have him.

Cokes. Come, come, are you ready now?

Leath. Presently, sir.

Waspe. Hoyday, he's at work in his doublet and hose! do you hear, sir, are you employ'd, that you are bare-headed and so busy?

Cokes. Hold your peace, Numps; you have been in the stocks, I hear.

Waspe. Does he know that! nay, then the date of my authority is out; I must think no longer to reign, my government is at an end. He that will correct another must want fault in himself.

Winw. Sententious Numps! I never heard so much from him before.

Leath. Sure master Littlewit will not come; please you take your place, sir; we'll begin.

Cokes. I pray thee do, mine ears long to be at it, and my eyes too. O Numps, in the stocks, Numps! where's your sword, Numps!

Waspe. I pray you intend your game, sir, let me alone.

Cokes. Well then, we are quit for all. Come, sit down, Numps; I'll interpret to thee: did you see mistress Grace? It's no matter, neither, now I think on't, tell me anon.

Winw. A great deal of love and care he expresses!

Grace. Alas, would you have him to express more than he has? that were tyranny.

Cokes. Peace, ho! now, now.

Leath. *Gentles, that no longer your expectations may wander,*
Behold our chief actor, amorous Leander.
With a great deal of cloth, lapp'd about him like a scarf,
For he yet serves his father, a dyer at Puddle-wharf;
Which place we'll make bold with, to call it our Abydus,
As the Bank-side is our Sestos; and let it not be deny'd us.
Now as he is beating to make the dye take the fuller,
Who chances to come by, but fair Hero in a sculler;
And seeing Leander's naked leg and goodly calf,
Cast at him from the boat a sheep's eye and an half.
Now she is landed, and the sculler come back,
By and by you shall see what Leander doth lack.

Lean. Cole, Cole, old Cole!

Leath. *That is the sculler's name without controul.*

Lean. Cole, Cole, I say, Cole!

Leath. *We do hear you.*

Lean. Old Cole.

Leath. *Old Cole! is the dyer turn'd collier? how do you sell?*

Lean. *A pox o' your manners, kiss my hole here, and smell.*

Leath. *Kiss your hole and smell! there's manners indeed.*

Lean. *Why, Cole, I say, Cole!*

Leath. *Is't the sculler you need?*

Lean. *Ay, and be hang'd.*

Leath. *Be hang'd! look you yonder.*
Old Cole, you must go hang with master Leander.

Cole. Where is he?

Lean. *Here, Cole: what fairest of fairs,*
Was that fare that thou landedst but now at Trig-stairs:

Cokes. What was that, fellow? pray thee tell me, I scarce understand them.

Leath. Leander does ask, sir, what fairest of fairs,
Was the fare he landed but now at Trig-stairs?

Cole. *It is lovely Hero.*

Lean. *Nero?*

Cole. *No, Hero.*

Leath. *It is Hero*
Of the Bank-side, he saith, to tell you truth without erring,
Is come over into Fish-street to eat some fresh herring.
Leander says no more, but as fast as he can,
Gets on all his best clothes, and will after to the Swan.

Cokes. Most admirable good, is't not?

Leath. *Stay, sculler.*

Cole. *What say you?*

Leath. *You must stay for Leander,*
And carry him to the wench.

Cole. *You rogue, I am no pander.*

Cokes. He says he is no pander. 'Tis a fine language: I understand it now.

Leath. *Are you no pander, goodman Cole? here's no man says*
you are;
You'll grow a hot cole, it seems; pray you stay for your fare.

Cole. *Will he come away?*

Leath. *What do you say?*

Cole. *I'd have him come away.*

Leath. *Would you have Leander come away? why, pray, sir, stay.*
You are angry, goodman Cole; I believe the fair maid
Came over with you a' trust: tell us, sculler, are you paid?

Cole. *Yes, goodman Hogrubber of Pickthatch.*

Leath. *How, Hogrubber of Pickthatch.*

Cole. *Ay, Hogrubber of Pickthatch. Take you that.*

[*Strikes him over the pate.*

Leath. *O, my head!*

Cole. *Harm watch, harm catch!*

Cokes. Harm watch, harm catch, he says; very good, i'faith: the sculler had like to have knock'd you, sirrah.

Leath. Yes, but that his fare call'd him away.

Lean. *Row apace, row apace, row, row, row, row, row.*

Leath. *You are knavishly loaden, sculler, take heed where you go.*

Cole. *Knave in your face, goodman rogue.*

Lean. *Row, row, row, row, row.*

Cokes. He said, knave in your face, friend.

Leath. Ay, sir, I heard him; but there's no talking to these watermen, they will have the last word.

Cokes. Od's my life! I am not allied to the sculler yet; he shall be *Dauphin my boy.* But my fiddle-stick does fiddle in and out too much: I pray thee speak to him on't; tell him I would have him tarry in my sight more.

Leath. I pray you be content; you'll have enough on him, sir.
Now, gentles, I take it, here is none of you so stupid,
But that you have heard of a little god of love call'd Cupid;
Who out of kindness to Leander, hearing he but saw her,
This present day and hour doth turn himself to a drawer.
And because he would have their first meeting to be merry,
He strikes Hero in love to him with a pint of sherry;
Which he tells her from amorous Leander is sent her,
Who after him into the room of Hero doth venture.

> [Leander goes into Mistress Hero's room.

Jonas. A pint of sack, score a pint of sack in the Coney.

Cokes. Sack! you said but e'en now it should be sherry.

Jonas. Why, so it is; sherry, sherry, sherry.

Cokes. Sherry, sherry, sherry! By my troth he makes me merry. I must have a name for Cupid too. Let me see, thou might'st help me, now, an thou would'st, Numps, at a dead lift: but thou art dreaming of the stocks still.—Do not think on't, I have forgot it; 'tis but a nine days' wonder, man; let it not trouble thee.

Waspe. I would the stocks were about your neck, sir; condition I hung by the heels in them till the wonder were off from you, with all my heart.

Cokes. Well said, resolute Numps! but hark you, friend, where's the friendship all this while between my drum Damon, and my pipe Pythias?

Leath. You shall see by and by, sir.

Cokes. You think my hobby-horse is forgotten too; no, I'll see them all enact before I go; I shall not know which to love best else.

Knock. This gallant has interrupting vapours, troublesome vapours; Whit, puff with him.

Whit. No, I pree dee, captain, let him alone; he is a child, i'faith, la.

Leath. *Now, gentles, to the friends, who in number are two,*
And lodged in that ale-house in which fair Hero does do.
Damon, for some kindness done him the last week,
Is come, fair Hero, in Fish-street, this morning to seek
Pythias does smell the knavery of the meeting,
And now you shall see their true-friendly greeting.

Pythias. You whore-masterly slave, you.

Cokes. Whore-masterly slave you! very friendly and familiar, that.

Damon. Whore-master in thy face,
Thou hast lain with her thyself, I'll prove it in this place.

Cokes. Damon says, Pythias has lain with her himself, he'll prove't in this place.

Leath. *They are whore-masters both, sir, that's a plain case.*

Pythias. You lie like a rogue.

Leath. *Do I lie like a rogue?*

Pythias. A pimp and a scab.

Leath. *A pimp and a scab.*

I say, between you, you have both but one drab.

    Damon. *You lie again.*

    Leath. *Do I lie again?*

    Damon. *Like a rogue again.*

    Leath. *Like a rogue again?*

    Pythias. *And you are a pimp again.*

    Cokes. And you are a pimp again, he says.

    Damon. *And a scab again.*

    Cokes. And a scab again, he says.

    Leath. *And I say again, you are both whore-masters, again.*
And you have both but one drab again.

    Damon *and* Pythias. *Dost thou, dost thou, dost thou?*

                                   [They fall upon him.

    Leath. *What, both at once?*

    Pythias. *Down with him, Damon.*

    Damon. *Pink his guts, Pythias.*

    Leath. *What, so malicious?*
Will ye murder me, masters both, in my own house?

    Cokes. Ho! well acted, my drum, well acted, my pipe, well acted
still!

    Waspe. Well acted, with all my heart.

    Leath. *Hold, hold your hands.*

    Cokes. Ay, both your hands, for my sake! for you have both
done well.

    Damon. *Gramercy, pure Pythias.*

    Pythias. *Gramercy, dear Damon.*

    Cokes. Gramercy to you both, my pipe and my drum.

    Pythias *and* Damon. *Come, now we'll together to breakfast to Hero.*

    Leath. *'Tis well you can now go to breakfast to Hero.*
You have given me my breakfast, with a hone and honero.

    Cokes. How is't, friend, have they hurt thee?

    Leath. O no:
Between you and I, sir, we do but make show.—
Thus, gentles, you perceive, without any denial,
'Twixt Damon and Pythias here, friendship's true trial.
Though hourly they quarrel thus, and roar each with other,
They fight you no more than does brother with brother;
But friendly together, at the next man they meet,
They let fly their anger, as here you might see't.

    Cokes. Well, we have seen it, and thou hast felt it, whatsoe'er
thou sayest. What's next, what's next?

    Leath. *This while young Leander with fair Hero is drinking,*
And Hero grown drunk to any man's thinking!
Yet was it not three pints of sherry could flaw her,
Till Cupid distinguished like Jonas the drawer,
From under his apron, where his lechery lurks,
Put love in her sack. Now mark how it works.

    Hero. *O Leander, Leander, my dear, my dear Leander,*
I'll for ever be thy goose, so thou'lt be my gander.

Cokes. Excellently well said, Fiddle, she'll ever be his goose, so he'll be her gander; was't not so?

Leath. Yes, sir, but mark his answer now.

Lean. And sweetest of geese, before I go to bed,
I'll swim over the Thames, my goose, thee to tread.

Cokes. Brave! he will swim over the Thames, and tread his goose to-night, he says.

Leath. Ay, peace, sir, they'll be angry if they hear you eaves-dropping, now they are setting their match.

Lean. But lest the Thames should be dark, my goose, my dear friend,
Let thy window be provided of a candle's end.

Hero. Fear not, my gander, I protest I should handle
My matters very ill, if I had not a whole candle.

Lean. Well then, look to't, and kiss me to boot.

Leath. *Now here come the friends again, Pythias and Damon,*
And under their clokes they have of bacon a gammon.

Pythias. Drawer, fill some wine here.

Leath. How, some wine there!
There's company already, sir, pray forbear.

Damon. 'Tis Hero.

Leath. *Yes, but she will not to be taken,*
After sack and fresh herring, with your Dunmow-bacon.

Pythias. You lie, it's Westfabian.

Leath. *Westphalian* you should say.

Damon. If you hold not your peace, you are a coxcomb, I would say.
                                    [Leander and Hero kiss.

What's here, what's here? kiss, kiss, upon kiss!

Leath. *Ay, wherefore should they not? what harm is in this?*
'Tis mistress Hero.

Damon. Mistress Hero's a whore.

Leath. *Is she a whore? keep you quiet, or, sir, knave, out of door.*

Damon. Knave out of door?

Hero. Yes, knave out of door.

Damon. Whore out of door.   [They fall together by the ears.

Hero. I say, knave out of door.

Damon. I say, whore out of door.

Pythias. Yea, so say I too.

Hero. Kiss the whore o' the a—.

Leath. *Now you have something to do:*
You must kiss her o' the a—, she says.

Damon and Pythias. So we will, so we will.   [They kick her.

Hero. O my haunches, O my haunches, hold, hold.

Leath. *Stand'st thou still!*
Leander, where art thou? stand'st thou still like a sot,
And not offer'st to break both their heads with a pot?
See who's at thine elbow there! puppet Jonas and Cupid.

Jonas. Upon 'em, Leander, be not so stupid.

Lean. You goat-bearded slave!

Damon. You whore-master knave!   [They fight.

Lean. Thou art a whore-master.

Jonas. Whore-masters all.

Leath. See, Cupid with a word has tane up the brawl.

Knock. These be fine vapours!

Cokes. By this good day, they fight bravely; do they not, Numps?

Waspe. Yes, they lack'd but you to be their second all this while.

Leath. This tragical encounter falling out thus to busy us,
It raises up the ghost of their friend Dionysius;
Not like a monarch, but the master of a school,
In a scrivener's furr'd gown, which shews he is no fool:
For therein he hath wit enough to keep himself warm.
O Damon, he cries, and Pythias, what harm
Hath poor Dionysius done you in his grave,
That after his death you should fall out thus and rave,
And call amorous Leander whore-master knave?

Damon. I cannot, I will not, I promise you, endure it.

RABBI BUSY *rushes in.*

Busy. Down with Dagon! down with Dagon! 'tis I, I will no longer endure your profanations.

Leath. What mean you, sir?

Busy. I will remove Dagon there, I say, that idol, that heathenish idol, that remains, as I may say, a beam, a very beam,—not a beam of the sun, nor a beam of the moon, nor a beam of a balance, neither a house-beam, nor a weaver's beam, but a beam in the eye, in the eye of the brethren; a very great beam, an exceeding great beam; such as are your stage-players, rimers, and morrice-dancers, who have walked hand in hand, in contempt of the brethren, and the cause; and been born out by instruments of no mean countenance.

Leath. Sir, I present nothing but what is licensed by authority.

Busy. Thou art all license, even licentiousness itself, Shimei!

Leath. I have the master of the revels' hand for't, sir.

Busy. The master of the rebels' hand thou hast. Satan's! hold thy peace, thy scurrility, shut up thy mouth, thy profession is damnable, and in pleading for it thou dost plead for Baal. I have long opened my mouth wide, and gaped; I have gaped as the oyster for the tide, after thy destruction: but cannot compass it by suit or dispute; so that I look for a bickering, ere long, and then a battle.

Knock. Good Banbury vapours!

Cokes. Friend, you'd have an ill match on't, if you bicker with him here; though he be no man of the fist, he has friends that will to cuffs for him. Numps, will not you take our side?

Edg. Sir, it shall not need; in my mind he offers him a fairer course, to end it by disputation: hast thou nothing to say for thyself, in defence of thy quality?

Leath. Faith, sir, I am not well-studied in these controversies, between the hypocrites and us. But here's one of my motion, puppet Dionysius, shall undertake him, and I'll venture the cause on't.

Cokes. Who, my hobby-horse! will he dispute with him?

Leath. Yes, sir, and make a hobby-ass of him, I hope.

Cokes. That's excellent! indeed he looks like the best scholar of them all. Come, sir, you must be as good as your word now.

Busy. I will not fear to make my spirit and gifts known: assist me zeal, fill me, fill me, that is, make me full!

Winw. What a desperate, profane wretch is this! is there any ignorance or impudence like his, to call his zeal to fill him against a puppet?

Quar. I know no fitter match than a puppet to commit with an hypocrite!

Busy. First, I say unto thee, idol, thou hast no calling.

Dion. *You lie, I am call'd Dionysius.*

Leath. The motion says, you lie, he is call'd Dionysius in the matter, and to that calling he answers.

Busy. I mean no vocation, idol, no present lawful calling.

Dion. *Is yours a lawful calling?*

Leath. The motion asketh, if yours be a lawful calling.

Busy. Yes, mine is of the spirit.

Dion. *Then idol is a lawful calling.*

Leath. He says, then idol is a lawful calling; for you call'd him idol, and your calling is of the spirit.

Cokes. Well disputed, hobby-horse.

Busy. Take not part with the wicked, young gallant: he neigheth and hinnieth; all is but hinnying sophistry. I call him idol again; yet, I say, his calling, his profession is profane, it is profane, idol.

Dion. *It is not profane.*

Leath. It is not profane, he says.

Busy. It is profane.

Dion. *It is not profane.*

Busy. It is profane.

Dion. *It is not profane.*

Leath. Well said, confute him with *Not*, still. You cannot bear him down with your base noise, sir.

Busy. Nor he me, with his treble creeking, though he creek like the chariot wheels of Satan; I am zealous for the cause—

Leath. As a dog for a bone.

Busy. And I say, it is profane, as being the page of Pride, and the waiting-woman of Vanity.

Dion. *Yea! what say you to your tire-women, then?*

Leath. Good.

Dion. *Or feather-makers in the Friers, that are of your faction of faith? are not they with their perukes, and their puffs, their fans, and their huffs, as much pages of Pride, and waiters upon Vanity? What say you, what say you, what say you?*

Busy. I will not answer for them.

Dion. *Because you cannot, because you cannot. Is a bugle-maker a lawful calling? or the confect-makers? such you have there; or your French fashioner? you would have all the sin within yourselves, would you not, would you not?*

Busy. No, Dagon.

Dion. What then, Dagonet? is a puppet worse than these?

Busy. Yes, and my main argument against you is, that you are an abomination; for the male, among you, putteth on the apparel of the female, and the female of the male.

Dion. You lie, you lie, you lie abominably.

Cokes. Good, by my troth, he has given him the lie thrice.

Dion. It is your old stale argument against the players, but it will not hold against the puppets; for we have neither male nor female amongst us. And that thou may'st see, if thou wilt, like a malicious purblind zeal as thou art. [Takes up his garment.

Edg. By my faith, there he has answer'd you, friend, a plain demonstration.

Dion. Nay, I'll prove, against e'er a Rabbin of them all, that my standing is as lawful as his; that I speak by inspiration, as well as he; that I have as little to do with learning as he; and do scorn her helps as much as he.

Busy. I am confuted, the cause hath failed me.

Dion. Then be converted, be converted.

Leath. Be converted, I pray you, and let the play go on!

Busy. Let it go on; for I am changed, and will become a beholder with you.

Cokes. That's brave, i'faith, thou hast carried it away, hobby-horse; on with the play.

Over. [*discovering himself.*] Stay, now do I forbid; I am Adam Overdo! sit still, I charge you.

Cokes. What, my brother-in-law!

Grace. My wise guardian!

Edg. Justice Overdo!

Over. It is time to take enormity by the forehead, and brand it; for I have discovered enough.

Enter QUARLOUS *in* TROUBLEALL'S *clothes, as before, and* Dame PURECRAFT.

Quar. Nay, come, mistress bride; you must do as I do, now. You must be mad with me, in truth. I have here justice Overdo for it.

Over. Peace, good Troubleall; come hither, and you shall trouble none. I will take the charge of you, and your friend too; you also, young man [*to Edgeworth*] shall be my care; stand there.

Edg. Now, mercy upon me.

Knock. Would we were away, Whit, these are dangerous vapours; best fall off with our birds, for fear o' the cage.

[*They attempt to steal away.*

Over. Stay, is not my name your terror?

Whit. Yesh fait, man, and it ish for tat we would be gone, man.

Enter LITTLEWIT.

Lit. O, gentlemen! did you not see a wife of mine? I have lost my little wife, as I shall be trusted; my little pretty Win. I left her at the great woman's house in trust yonder, the pig-woman's, with captain Jordan, and captain Whit, very good men, and I cannot hear of her. Poor fool, I fear she's stepp'd aside. Mother, did you not see Win?

Over. If this grave matron be your mother, sir, stand by her, *et digito compesce labellum;* I may perhaps spring a wife for you anon. Brother Bartholomew, I am sadly sorry to see you so lightly given, and such a disciple of enormity, with your grave governor Humphrey: but stand you both there, in the middle place; I will reprehend you in your course. Mistress Grace, let me rescue you out of the hands of the stranger.

Winw. Pardon me, sir, I am a kinsman of hers.

Over. Are you so! of what name, sir?

Winw. Winwife, sir.

Over. Master Winwife! I hope you have won no wife of her, sir; if you have, I will examine the possibility of it, at fit leisure. Now, to my enormities: look upon me, O London! and see me, O Smithfield! the example of justice, and Mirrour of Magistrates; the true top of formality, and scourge of enormity. Hearken unto my labours, and but observe my discoveries; and compare Hercules with me, if thou dar'st, of old; or Columbus, Magellan, or our countryman Drake, of later times. Stand forth, you weeds of enormity, and spread. First, Rabbi Busy, thou superlunatical hypocrite;—[*to Leatherhead.*] Next thou other extremity, thou profane professor of puppetry, little better than poetry:—[*to Whit.*] Then thou strong debaucher and seducer of youth: witness this easy and honest young man, [*pointing to Edge*]—[*to Knock.*] Now, thou esquire of dames, madams, and twelve-penny ladies.—Now, my green madam herself of the price; let me unmask your ladyship.

                              [*Discovers Mrs. Lit.*

Lit. O my wife, my wife, my wife!

Over. Is she your wife? *redde te Harpocratem.*

Enter TROUBLEALL, *with a dripping-pan, followed by* URSULA *and* NIGHTINGALE.

Trou. By your leave, stand by, my masters, be uncover'd.

Urs. O stay him, stay him, help to cry, Nightingale; my pan, my pan!

Over. What's the matter?

Night. He has stolen gammar Ursula's pan.

Tro. Yes, and I fear no man but justice Overdo.

Over. Ursula! where is she? O the sow of enormity, this! welcome, stand you there; you, songster, there.

Urs. An't please your worship, I am in no fault: a gentleman stripped him in my booth, and borrowed his gown, and his hat; and he ran away with my goods here for it.

Over. [*to Quarlous.*] Then this is the true madman, and you are the enormity!

Quar. You are in the right: I am mad but from the gown outward.

Over. Stand you there.

Quar. Where you please, sir.

Mrs. Over. [*waking*] O, lend me a bason, I am sick, I am sick! where's master Overdo? Bridget, call hither my Adam.

Over. How! [*He is shamed and silenced.*

Whit. Dy very own wife, i'fait, worshipful Adam.

Mrs. Over. Will not my Adam come at me? shall I see him no more then?

Quar. Sir, why do you not go on with the enormity? are you oppressed with it? I'll help you: hark you, sir, in your ear— Your innocent young man, you have ta'en such care of all this day, is a cut-purse, that hath got all your brother Cokes' things, and helped you to your beating and the stocks; if you have a mind to hang him now, and shew him your magistrate's wit, you may: but I should think it were better recovering the goods, and to save your estimation in him. I thank you, sir, for the gift of your ward, mistress Grace; look you, here is your hand and seal, by the way. Master Winwife, give you joy, you are *Palemon,* you are possessed of the gentlewoman, but she must pay me value, here's warrant for it. And, honest madman, there's thy gown and cap again; I thank thee for my wife. Nay, I can be mad, sweet-heart, [*to Mrs. Pure*] when I please still; never fear me; and careful Numps, where's he? I thank him for my license.

Waspe. How!

Quar. 'Tis true, Numps.

Waspe. I'll be hang'd then.

Quar. Look in your box, Numps.—Nay, sir, [*to Overdo.*] stand not you fix'd here, like a stake in Finsbury, to be shot at, or the whipping-post in the Fair, but get your wife out o' the air, it will make her worse else; and remember you are but Adam, flesh and blood! you have your frailty, forget your other name of Overdo, and invite us all to supper. There you and I will compare our discoveries; and drown the memory of all enormity in your biggest bowl at home.

Cokes. How now, Numps, have you lost it? I warrant 'twas when thou wert in the stocks: Why dost not speak!

Waspe. I will never speak while I live again, for aught I know.

Over. Nay, Humphrey, if I be patient, you must be so too; this pleasant conceited gentleman hath wrought upon my judgment, and prevail'd: I pray you take care of your sick friend, mistress Alice, and my good friends all—

Quar. And no *enormities.*

Over. I invite you home with me to my house to supper: I will have none fear to go along, for my intents are *ad correctionem, non ad destructionem; ad œdificandum, non ad diruendum:* so lead on.

Cokes. Yes, and bring the actors along, we'll have the rest of the play at home. *[Exeunt.*

EPILOGUE.

*Your Majesty hath seen the play, and you
Can best allow it from your ear and view.
You know the scope of writers, and what store
Of leave is given them, if they take not more,
And turn it into license: you can tell
If we have us'd that leave you gave us well;
Or whether we to rage or license break,
Or be profane, or make profane men speak:
This is your power to judge, great sir, and not
The envy of a few. Which if we have got,
We value less what their dislike can bring,
If it so happy be, t' have pleased the King.*

THE DEVIL IS AN ASS

DRAMATIS PERSONÆ

SATAN, *the great Devil.*
PUG, *the less Devil.*
INIQUITY, *the Vice.*
FABIAN FITZDOTTREL, *a Squire of Norfolk.*
MEERCRAFT, *the Projector.*
EVERILL, *his Champion.*
WITTIPOL, *a young Gallant.*
EUSTACE MANLY, *his Friend.*
ENGINE, *a Broker.*
TRAINS, *the Projector's Man.*
THOMAS GILTHEAD, *a Goldsmith.*
PLUTARCHUS, *his Son.*
SIR PAUL EITHERSIDE, *a Lawyer, and Justice.*

AMBLER, *Gentleman-Usher to* Lady TAILBUSH.
SLEDGE, *a Smith, the Constable.*
SHACKLES, *Keeper of Newgate.*

MRS. FRANCES FITZDOTTREL.
LADY EITHERSIDE.
LADY TAILBUSH, *the Lady Projectress.*
PITFALL, *her Woman.*

Serjeants, Officers, Servants, Under-keepers, *etc.*

SCENE,—LONDON

PROLOGUE.

THE DEVIL IS AN ASS: *that is, to-day,*
The name of what you are met for, a new play.
Yet, grandees, would you were not come to grace
Our matter, with allowing us no place.
Though you presume Satan, a subtle thing,
And may have heard he's worn in a thumb-ring;
Do not on these presumptions force us act
In compass of a cheese-trencher. This tract
Will ne'er admit our Vice, because of yours.
Anon, who worse than you, the fault endures
That yourselves make? when you will thrust and spurn,
And knock us on the elbows; and bid, turn;
As if, when we had spoke, we must be gone,
Or, till we speak, must all run in, to one,
Like the young adders, at the old one's mouth!
Would we could stand due north, or had no south,
If that offend; or were Muscovy glass,
That you might look our scenes through as they pass.
We know not how to affect you. If you'll come
To see new plays, pray you afford us room,
And shew this but the same face you have done
Your dear delight, The Devil of Edmonton.
Or, if for want of room it must miscarry,
'Twill be but justice that your censure tarry,
Till you give some: and when six times you have seen't,
If this play do not like, the Devil is in't.

264

ACT I

SCENE I.

Enter SATAN *and* PUG.

Sat. Hoh, hoh, hoh, hoh, hoh, hoh, hoh, hoh!—
To earth! and why to earth, thou foolish spirit?
What wouldst thou do on earth?
  Pug. For that, great chief,
As time shall work. I do but ask my month,
Which every petty puisne devil has;
Within that term, the court of hell will hear
Something may gain a longer grant, perhaps.
  Sat. For what? the laming a poor cow or two,
Entering a sow, to make her cast her farrow,
Or crossing of a market-woman's mare
'Twixt this and Tottenham? these were wont to be
Your main achievements, Pug: You have some plot now,
Upon a tunning of ale, to stale the yeast,
Or keep the churn so, that the butter come not,
Spite of the housewife's cord, or her hot spit:
Or some good ribibe, about Kentish Town
Or Hogsden, you would hang now for a witch,
Because she will not let you play round Robin.
And you'll go sour the citizens' cream 'gainst Sunday,
That she may be accused for't, and condemn'd,
By a Middlesex jury, to the satisfaction
Of their offended friends, the Londoners' wives,
Whose teeth were set on edge with't. Foolish fiend,
Stay in your place, know your own strength, and put not
Beyond the sphere of your activity:
You are too dull a devil to be trusted
Forth in those parts, Pug, upon any affair
That may concern our name on earth. It is not
Every one's work. The state of hell must care
Whom it employs, in point of reputation,
Here about London. You would make, I think,
An agent to be sent for Lancashire,
Proper enough; or some parts of Northumberland,
So you had good instructions, Pug.
  Pug. O chief,
You do not know, dear chief, what there is in me!
Prove me but for a fortnight, for a week,
And lend me but a Vice, to carry with me,
To practise there with any play-fellow,
And you will see, there will come more upon't,
Than you'll imagine, precious chief.

Sat. What Vice?
What kind wouldst thou have it of?
Pug. Why any: Fraud,
Or Covetousness, or lady Vanity,
Or old Iniquity.
Sat. I'll call him hither.

Enter INIQUITY.

Iniq. What is he calls upon me, and would seem to lack a Vice?
Ere his words be half spoken, I am with him in a trice;
Here, there, and every where, as the cat is with the mice;
True *Vetus Iniquitas.* Lack'st thou cards, friend, or dice?
I will teach thee [to] cheat, child, to cog, lie and swagger,
And ever and anon to be drawing forth thy dagger:
To swear by Gogs-nowns, like a lusty Juventus,
In a cloak to thy heel, and a hat like a pent-house.
Thy breeches of three fingers, and thy doublet all belly,
With a wench that shall feed thee with cock-stones and jelly.
Pug. Is it not excellent, chief? how nimble he is!
Iniq. Child of hell, this is nothing! I will fetch thee a leap
From the top of Paul's steeple to the standard in Cheap:
And lead thee a dance thro' the streets without fail,
Like a needle of Spain, with a thread at my tail.
We will survey the suburbs, and make forth our sallies,
Down Petticoat-lane and up the Smock-alleys,
To Shoreditch, Whitechapel, and so to St. Kathern's,
To drink with the Dutch there, and take forth their patterns:
From thence, we will put in at Custom-house key there,
And see how the factors and prentices play there
False with their masters, and geld many a full pack,
To spend it in pies at the Dagger and the Woolsack.
Pug. Brave, brave Iniquity! will not this do, chief?
Iniq. Nay, boy, I will bring thee to the bawds and the roysters,
At Billingsgate, feasting with claret-wine and oysters;
From thence shoot the Bridge, child, to the Cranes in the Vintry,
And see there the gimblets, how they make their entry!
Or if thou hadst rather to the Strand down to fall,
'Gainst the lawyers come dabbled from Westminster-hall,
And mark how they cling, with their clients together,
Like ivy to oak, so velvet to leather:
Ha, boy, I wou'd shew thee—
Pug. Rare, rare!
Sat. Peace, dotard,
And thou, more ignorant thing, that so admir'st;
Art thou the spirit thou seem'st? so poor, to choose,
This for a Vice, to advance the cause of hell,
Now, as Vice stands this present year? Remember
What number it is, six hundred and sixteen.
Had it but been five hundred, though some sixty

Above; that's fifty years agone, and six,
When every great man had his Vice stand by him,
In his long coat, shaking his wooden dagger,
I could consent, that then this your grave choice
Might have done that, with his lord chief, the which
Most of his chamber can do now. But, Pug,
As the times are, who is it will receive you?
What company will you go to, or whom mix with?
Where canst thou carry him, except to taverns,
To mount upon a joint-stool, with a Jew's trump,
To put down Cokely, and that must be to citizens?
He ne'er will be admitted there, where Vennor comes.
He may perchance, in tail of a sheriff's dinner,
Skip with a rhyme on the table, from New-nothing
And take his Almain leap into a custard,
Shall make my lady mayoress and her sisters
Laugh all their hoods over their shoulders. But
This is not that will do, they are other things
That are received now upon earth, for Vices;
Stranger and newer: and changed every hour.
They ride them like their horses, off their legs,
And here they come to hell, whole legions of them,
Every week tired. We still strive to breed,
And rear up new ones; but they do not stand;
When they come there, they turn them on our hands.
And it is fear'd they have a stud o' their own
Will put down our's: both our breed and trade
Will suddenly decay, if we prevent not.
Unless it be a vice of quality,
Or fashion now, they take none from us. Carmen
Are got into the yellow starch, and chimney-sweepers
To their tobacco, and strong waters, Hum,
Meath and Obarni. We must therefore aim
At extraordinary subtle ones now,
When we do send to keep us up in credit:
Not old Iniquities. Get you e'en back, sir,
To making of your rope of sand again:
You are not for the manner, nor the times.
They have their vices there, most like to virtues:
You cannot know them apart by any difference:
They wear the same clothes, eat the same meat,
Sleep in the self-same beds, ride in those coaches,
Or very like, four horses in a coach,
As the best men and women. Tissue gowns,
Garters and roses, fourscore pound a pair,
Embroider'd stockings, cut-work smocks and shirts,
More certain marks of letchery now and pride,
Than e'er they were of true nobility!
But, Pug, since you do burn with such desire

[Exit Iniq.

To do the commonwealth of hell some service,
I am content, assuming of a body,
You go to earth, and visit men a day.
But you must take a body ready made, Pug;
I can create you none: nor shall you form
Yourself an airy one, but become subject
To all impression of the flesh you take,
So far as human frailty.   So, this morning,
There is a handsome cut-purse hang'd at Tyburn,
Whose spirit departed, you may enter his body:
For clothes, employ your credit with the hangman,
Or let our tribe of brokers furnish you.
And look how far your subtlety can work
Thorough those organs, with that body, spy
Amongst mankind, (you cannot there want vices,
And therefore the less need to carry them with you,)
But as you make your soon at night's relation,
And we shall find it merits from the state,
You shall have both trust from us, and employment.
   Pug. Most gracious chief!
   Sat. Only thus more I bind you,
To serve the first man that you meet; and him
I'll shew you now: observe him.   Yon' is he,
   [Shews him Fitzdottrel coming out of his house at a distance.
You shall see first after your clothing.   Follow him:
But once engaged, there you must stay and fix;
Not shift, until the midnight's cock do crow.
   Pug. Any conditions to be gone.
   Sat. Away then.   *[Exeunt severally.*

SCENE II.—*The Street before* FITZDOTTREL'S *House.*

Enter FITZDOTTREL.

   Fitz. Ay, they do now name Bretnor, as before
They talk'd of Gresham, and of doctor Foreman,
Franklin, and Fiske, and Savory, he was in too;
But there's not one of these that ever could
Yet shew a man the devil in true sort.
They have their crystals, I do know, and rings,
And virgin-parchment, and their dead men's sculls,
Their ravens'-wings, their lights, and pentacles,
With characters; I have seen all these.   But—
Would I might see the devil!   I would give
A hundred of these pictures to see him
Once out of picture.   May I prove a cuckold,
And that's the one main mortal thing I fear,
If I begin not now to think, the painters
Have only made him: 'slight, he would be seen

One time or other else; he would not let
An ancient gentleman, of [as] good a house
As most are now in England, the Fitzdottrels,
Run wild, and call upon him thus in vain,
As I have done this twelvemonth.   If he be not
At all, why are there conjurers? if they be not,
Why are there laws against them?   The best artists
Of Cambridge, Oxford, Middlesex and London,
Essex and Kent, I have had in pay to raise him,
These fifty weeks, and yet he appears not.   'Sdeath,
I shall suspect they can make circles only
Shortly, and know but his hard names.   They do say,
He will meet a man, of himself, that has a mind to him.
If he would so, I have a mind and a half for him:
He should not be long absent.   Prithee, come.
I long for thee:—an I were with child by him,
And my wife too, I could not more.   Come yet,
Good Beelzebub.   Were he a kind devil,
And had humanity in him, he would come, but
To save one's longing.   I should use him well,
I swear, and with respect; would he would try me!
Not as the conjurers do, when they have raised him,
Get him in bonds, and send him post on errands
A thousand miles; it is preposterous, that;
And, I believe, is the true cause he comes not:
And he has reason.   Who would be engaged,
That might live freely, as he may do?   I swear,
They are wrong all.   The burnt child dreads the fire,
They do not know to entertain the devil:
I would so welcome him, observe his diet,
Get him his chamber hung with arras, two of 'em,
In my own house, lend him my wife's wrought pillows;
And as I am an honest man, I think,
If he had a mind to her too, I should grant him,
To make our friendship perfect: so I would not
To every man.   If he but hear me now,
And should come to me in a brave young shape,
And take me at my word?—

Enter PUG, *handsomely shaped and apparelled.*

                        Ha! who is this?
Pug. Sir, your good pardon, that I thus presume
Upon your privacy.   I am born a gentleman,
A younger brother, but in some disgrace
Now with my friends; and want some little means
To keep me upright, while things be reconciled.
Please you to let my service be of use to you, sir.
   Fitz. Service! 'fore hell, my heart was at my mouth,

'Till I had view'd his shoes well: for those roses
Were big enough to hide a cloven foot.—   [*Aside.*
No, friend, my number's full.   I have one servant,
Who is my all, indeed; and from the broom
Unto the brush: for just so far I trust him.
He is my wardrobe-man, my cater, cook,
Butler, and steward: looks unto my horse;
And helps to watch my wife.   He has all the places
That I can think on, from the garret downward,
Even to the manger, and the curry-comb.

    Pug. Sir, I shall put your worship to no charge,
More than my meat, and that but very little;
I'll serve you for your love.

    Fitz. Ha! without wages?
I'd hearken o' that ear, were I at leisure;
But now I am busy.   Prithee, friend, forbear me—
An thou hadst been a devil, I should say
Somewhat more to thee: thou dost hinder now
My meditations.

    Pug. Sir, I am a devil.

    Fitz. How!

    Pug. A true devil, sir.

    Fitz. Nay, now you lie;
Under your favour, friend, for I'll not quarrel.
I look'd on your feet afore, you cannot cozen me,
Your shoe's not cloven, sir, you are whole hoof'd.

    Pug. Sir, that's a popular error, deceives many:
But I am that I tell you.

    Fitz. What's your name?

    Pug. My name is Devil, sir.

    Fitz. Say'st thou true?

    Pug. Indeed, sir.

    Fitz. 'Slid, there's some omen in this?   What countryman?

    Pug. Of Derbyshire, sir, about the Peak.

    Fitz. That hole
Belong'd to your ancestors?

    Pug. Yes, Devil's arse, sir.

    Fitz. I'll entertain him for the name sake.   Ha!
And turn away my t'other man, and save
Four pound a year by that! there's luck and thrift too!
The very Devil may come hereafter as well.   [*Aside.*
Friend, I receive you: but, withal, I acquaint you
Aforehand, if you offend me, I must beat you,
It is a kind of exercise I use;
And cannot be without.

    Pug. Yes, if I do not
Offend, you can, sure.

    Fitz. Faith, Devil, very hardly:
I'll call you by your surname, 'cause I love it.

Enter, behind, ENGINE, *with a cloke on his arm,* WITTIPOL, *and* MANLY.

Eng. Yonder he walks, sir, I'll go lift him for you.
Wit. To him, good Engine, raise him up by degrees,
Gently, and hold him there too, you can do it.
Shew yourself now a mathematical broker.
   Eng. I'll warrant you, for half a piece.
   Wit. 'Tis done, sir.
       [Engine goes to Fitzdottrel, and takes him aside.
   Man. Is't possible there should be such a man!
   Wit. You shall be your own witness; I'll not labour
To tempt you past your faith.
   Man. And is his wife
So very handsome, say you?
   Wit. I have not seen her
Since I came home from travel; and they say
She is not alter'd. Then, before I went,
I saw her once; but so, as she hath stuck
Still in my view, no object hath removed her.
   Man. 'Tis a fair guest, friend, beauty; and once lodged
Deep in the eyes, she hardly leaves the inn.
How does he keep her?
   Wit. Very brave; however
Himself be sordid, he is sensual that way:
In every dressing he does study her.
   Man. And furnish forth himself so from the brokers?
   Wit. Yes, that's a hired suit he now has on,
To see the DEVIL IS AN ASS, to-day, in.
This Engine gets three or four pound a week by him—
He dares not miss a new play or a feast,
What rate soever clothes be at; and thinks
Himself still new, in other men's old.
   Man. But stay,
Does he love meat so?
   Wit. Faith, he does not hate it.
But that's not it: his belly and his palate
Would be compounded with for reason. Marry,
A wit he has, of that strange credit with him,
'Gainst all mankind; as it doth make him do
Just what it list: it ravishes him forth
Whither it please, to any assembly or place,
And would conclude him ruin'd, should he scape
One public meeting, out of the belief
He has of his own great and catholic strengths,
In arguing and discourse. It takes, I see:
He has got the cloke upon him.
   Fitz. [*after saying on the cloke.*] A fair garment,
By my faith, Engine!

Eng. It was never made, sir,
For threescore pound, I assure you: 'twill yield thirty.
The plush, sir, cost three pound ten shillings a yard:
And then the lace and velvet!

Fitz. I shall, Engine,
Be look'd at prettily, in it: art thou sure
The play is play'd to-day?

Eng. O here's the bill, sir: [*He gives him the play-bill.*
I had forgot to give it you.

Fitz. Ha, the DEVIL!
I will not lose you, sirrah. But, Engine, think you
The gallant is so furious in his folly,
So mad upon the matter, that he'll part
With's cloke upon these terms?

Eng. Trust not your Engine,
Break me to pieces else, as you would do
A rotten crane, or an old rusty jack,
That has not one true wheel in him. Do but talk with him.

Fitz. I shall do that, to satisfy you, Engine,
And myself too. [*Comes forward.*]—With your leave, gentlemen,
Which of you is it, is so mere idolater
To my wife's beauty, and so very prodigal
Unto my patience, that, for the short parley
Of one swift hour's quarter, with my wife,
He will depart with (let me see) this cloke here,
The price of folly?—Sir, are you the man?

Wit. I am that venturer, sir.

Fitz. Good time! your name
Is Wittipol?

Wit. The same, sir.

Fitz. And 'tis told me
You have travell'd lately?

Wit. That I have, sir.

Fitz. Truly,
Your travels may have alter'd your complexion;
But sure your wit stood still.

Wit. It may well be, sir;
All heads have not like growth.

Fitz. The good man's gravity,
That left you land, your father, never taught you
These pleasant matches.

Wit. No, nor can his mirth,
With whom I make them, put me off.

Fitz. You are
Resolved then?

Wit. Yes, sir.

Fitz. Beauty is the saint,
You'll sacrifice yourself into the shirt to?

Wit. So I may still clothe and keep warm your wisdom.

Fitz. You lade me, sir!

Wit. I know what you will bear, sir.

Fitz. Well, to the point. 'Tis only, sir, you say,
To speak unto my wife?

Wit. Only to speak to her.

Fitz. And in my presence?

Wit. In your very presence.

Fitz. And in my hearing?

Wit. In your hearing; so
You interrupt us not.

Fitz. For the short space
You do demand, the fourth part of an hour,
I think I shall, with some convenient study,
And this good help to boot, [*shrugs himself up in the cloke*] bring
      myself to't.

Wit. I ask no more.

Fitz. Please you, walk toward my house,
Speak what you list; that time is yours; my right
I have departed with: but not beyond
A minute, or a second, look for. Length,
And drawing out may advance much to these matches.
And I except all kissing: kisses are
Silent petitions still with willing lovers.

Wit. Lovers! how falls that o' your phantasy?

Fitz. Sir,
I do know somewhat; I forbid all lip-work.

Wit. I am not eager at forbidden dainties:
Who covets unfit things, denies himself.

Fitz. You say well, sir; 'twas prettily said, that same:
He does indeed. I'll have no touches therefore,
Nor takings by the arms, nor tender circles
Cast 'bout the waist, but all be done at distance.
Love is brought up with those soft migniard handlings:
His pulse lies in his palm; and I defend
All melting joints and fingers, that's my bargain,
I do defend them any thing like action.
But talk, sir, what you will. Use all the tropes
And schemes, that prince Quintilian can afford you:
And much good do your rhetoric's heart. You are welcome, sir.
                    [*Opens the door of his house.*]
Engine, God be wi' you!

Wit. Sir, I must condition
To have this gentleman by, a witness.

Fitz. Well,
I am content, so he be silent.

Man. Yes, sir.

Fitz. Come, Devil, I'll make you room straight: but I'll shew you
First to your mistress, who's no common one,
You must conceive, that brings this gain to see her.

I hope thou'st brought me good luck.
  Pug. I shall do't, sir.   *[They all enter the house.*

SCENE III.—*A Room in* FITZDOTTREL'S *House.*

Enter WITTIPOL, MANLY, *and* ENGINE.

Wit. Engine, you hope of your half piece? 'tis there, sir.
Be gone. [*Exit Engine.*]—Friend Manly, who's within here? fixed!
                                 [Knocks him on the breast.
  Man. I am directly in a fit of wonder
What will be the issue of this conference.
  Wit. For that ne'er vex yourself till the event.
How like you him?
  Man. I would fain see more of him.
  Wit. What think you of this?
  Man. I am past degrees of thinking.
Old Afric, and the new America,
With all their fruit of monsters, cannot shew
So just a prodigy.
  Wit. Could you have believed,
Without your sight, a mind so sordid inward,
Should be so specious, and laid forth abroad,
To all the show that ever shop or ware was?
  Man. I believe any thing now, though I confess
His vices are the most extremities
I ever knew in nature.   But why loves he
The devil so?
  Wit. O, sir! for hidden treasure
He hopes to find; and has proposed himself
So infinite a mass, as to recover,
He cares not what he parts with, of the present,
To his men of art, who are the race may coin him.
Promise gold mountains, and the covetous
Are still most prodigal.
  Man. But have you faith,
That he will hold his bargain?
  Wit. O dear sir!
He will not off on't; fear him not: I know him.
One baseness still accompanies another.
See! he is here already, and his wife too.
  Man. A wondrous handsome creature, as I live!

Enter FITZDOTTREL, *with* Mrs. FRANCES, *his wife.*

  Fitz. Come, wife, this is the gentleman; nay, blush not.
  Mrs. Fitz. Why, what do you mean, sir, have you your reason?
  Fitz. Wife,
I do not know that I have lent it forth
To any one; at least, without a pawn, wife:

Or that I have eat or drunk the thing, of late,
That should corrupt it. Wherefore, gentle wife,
Obey, it is thy virtue; hold no acts
Of disputation.

    Mrs. Fitz. Are you not enough
The talk of feasts and meetings, but you'll still
Make argument for fresh?

    Fitz. Why, careful wedlock,
If I have a longing to have one tale more
Go of me, what is that to thee, dear heart?
Why shouldst thou envy my delight, or cross it,
By being solicitous, when it not concerns thee?

    Mrs. Fitz. Yes, I have share in this: the scorn will fall
As bitterly on me, where both are laugh'd at.

    Fitz. Laugh'd at, sweet bird! is that the scruple? come, come,
Thou art a niaise. Which of your great houses,
(I will not mean at home here, but abroad,)
Your families in France, wife, send not forth
Something within the seven year, may be laugh'd at?
I do not say seven months, nor seven weeks,
Nor seven days, nor hours; but seven year, wife:
I give them time. Once within seven year,
I think they may do something may be laugh'd at;
In France, I keep me there still. Wherefore, wife,
Let them that list laugh still, rather than weep
For me. Here is a cloke cost fifty pound, wife,
Which I can sell for thirty, when I have seen
All London in't, and London has seen me.
To-day I go to the Blackfriars play-house,
Sit in the view, salute all my acquaintance,
Rise up between the acts, let fall my cloke,
Publish a handsome man, and a rich suit,
As that's a special end why we go thither,
All that pretend to stand for't on the stage:
The ladies ask, who's that? for they do come
To see us, love, as we do to see them.
Now I shall lose all this, for the false fear
Of being laugh'd at? Yes, wusse. Let them laugh, wife.
Let me have such another cloke to-morrow,
And let them laugh again, wife, and again,
And then grow fat with laughing, and then fatter,
All my young gallants, let 'em bring their friends too;
Shall I forbid them? No, let heaven forbid them:
Or wit, if it have any charge on 'em. Come, thy ear, wife,
Is all I'll borrow of thee.—Set your watch, sir.—
Thou only art to hear, not speak a word, dove,
To aught he says: that I do give you in precept,
No less than counsel, on your wivehood, wife,
Not though he flatter you, or make court, or love,

As you must look for these, or say he rail;
Whate'er his arts be, wife, I will have thee
Delude them with a trick, thy obstinate silence.
I know advantages; and I love to hit
These pragmatic young men at their own weapons.
Is your watch ready? Here my sail bears for you:
Tack toward him, sweet pinnace. [*He disposes his wife to her place.*]
   Where's your watch?
 Wit. I'll set it, sir, with yours.
 Mrs. Fritz. I must obey.   [*Aside.*
 Man. Her modesty seems to suffer with her beauty.
And so, as if his folly were away,
It were worth pity.
 Fitz. Now they are right; begin, sir.
But first, let me repeat the contract briefly.
I am, sir, to enjoy this cloke I stand in,
Freely, and as your gift; upon condition
You may as freely speak here to my spouse,
Your quarter of an hour, always keeping
The measured distance of your yard or more,
From my said spouse; and in my sight and hearing.
This is your covenant?
 Wit. Yes, but you'll allow
For this time spent now?
 Fitz. Set them so much back.
 Wit. I think I shall not need it.
 Fitz. Well, begin, sir.
There is your bound, sir; not beyond that rush.
 Wit. If you interrupt me, sir, I shall discloke you.—
The time I have purchased, lady, is but short;
And therefore, if I employ it thriftily,
I hope I stand the nearer to my pardon.
I am not here to tell you, you are fair,
Or lovely, or how well you dress you, lady;
I'll save myself that eloquence of your glass,
Which can speak these things better to you than I.
And 'tis a knowledge wherein fools may be
As wise as a court-parliament.   Nor come I
With any prejudice or doubt, that you
Should, to the notice of your own worth, need
Least revelation. She's a simple woman,
Knows not her good, whoever knows her ill,
And at all caracts.   That you are the wife
To so much blasted flesh, as scarce hath soul,
Instead of salt, to keep it sweet; I think,
Will ask no witnesses to prove. The cold
Sheets that you lie in, with the watching candle,
That sees, how dull to any thaw of beauty
Pieces and quarters, half and whole nights sometimes,

The devil-given elfin squire, your husband,
Doth leave you, quitting here his proper circle,
For a much worse, in the walks of Lincoln's-inn,
Under the elms, t' expect the fiend in vain there,
Will confess for you.
   Fitz. I did look for this jeer.
   Wit. And what a daughter of darkness he does make you,
Lock'd up from all society, or object;
Your eye not let to look upon a face,
Under a conjurer's, or some mould for one,
Hollow and lean like his, but by great means,
As I now make; your own too sensible sufferings,
Without the extraordinary aids
Of spells, or spirits, may assure you, lady.
For my part, I protest 'gainst all such practice,
I work by no false arts, medicines, or charms
To be said forward and backward.
   Fitz. No, I except—
   Wit. Sir, I shall ease you.   [*He offers to discloke him.*
   Fitz. Mum.
   Wit. Nor have I ends, lady,
Upon you, more than this: to tell you how Love,
Beauty's good angel, he that waits upon her
At all occasions, and, no less than Fortune,
Helps the adventurous, in me makes that proffer,
Which never fair one was so fond to lose,
Who could but reach a hand forth to her freedom.
On the first sight I loved you, since which time,
Though I have travell'd, I have been in travail
More for this second blessing of your eyes,
Which now I've purchased, than for all aims else.
Think of it, lady, be your mind as active
As is your beauty: view your object well,
Examine both my fashion and my years;
Things that are like, are soon familiar:
And nature joys still in equality.
Let not the sign of the husband fright you, lady;
But ere your spring be gone, enjoy it. Flowers,
Though fair, are oft but of one morning; think,
All beauty doth not last until the autumn:
You grow old while I tell you this; and such
As cannot use the present, are not wise.
If Love and Fortune will take care of us,
Why should our will be wanting: This is all.
What do you answer, lady?
   Fitz. Now the sport comes.
Let him still wait, wait, wait; while the watch goes,
And the time runs, wife!
   Wit. How! not any word?

Nay, then I taste a trick in't.—Worthy lady,
I cannot be so false to my own thoughts
Of your presumed goodness, to conceive
This, as your rudeness, which I see's imposed.
Yet, since your cautelous jailer here stands by you,
And you are denied the liberty of the house,
Let me take warrant, lady, from your silence,
Which ever is interpreted consent,
To make your answer for you; which shall be
To as good purpose as I can imagine,
And what I think you'd speak.

    Fitz. No, no, no, no.

    Wit. I shall resume, sir.

    Man. Sir, what do you mean?

    Wit. One interruption more, sir, and you go
Into your hose and doublet, nothing saves you:
And therefore hearken. This is for your wife.

    Man. You must play fair, sir.

    Wit. Stand for me, good friend.—
               [*Sets Manly in his place, and speaks for the Lady.*
Troth, sir, 'tis more than true that you have utter'd
Of my unequal and so sordid match here,
With all the circumstances of my bondage.
I have a husband, and a two-legg'd one,
But such a moonling, as no wit of man,
Or roses can redeem from being an ass.
He's grown too much the story of men's mouths,
To scape his lading: should I make't my study,
And lay all ways, yea, call mankind to help
To take his burden off; why, this one act
Of his, to let his wife out to be courted,
And at a price, proclaims his asinine nature
So loud, as I am weary of my title to him.
But, sir, you seem a gentleman of virtue,
No less than blood; and one that every way
Looks as he were of too good quality,
To intrap a credulous woman, or betray her.
Since you have paid thus dear, sir, for a visit,
And made such venture on your wit and charge
Merely to see me, or at most, to speak to me,
I were too stupid, or, what's worse, ingrate
Not to return your venture. Think but how
I may with safety do it, I shall trust
My love and honour to you, and presume
You'll ever husband both, against this husband;
Who, if we chance to change his liberal ears
To other ensigns, and with labour make
A new beast of him, as he shall deserve,
Cannot complain he is unkindly dealt with.

This day he is to go to a new play, sir,
From whence no fear, no, nor authority,
Scarcely the king's command, sir, will restrain him,
Now you have fitted him with a stage-garment,
For the mere name's sake, were there nothing else;
And many more such journeys he will make;
Which, if they now, or any time hereafter,
Offer us opportunity, you hear, sir,
Who'll be as glad and forward to embrace,
Meet, and enjoy it cheerfully, as you.

                           [Shifts to his own place again.

I humbly thank you, lady—
   Fitz. Keep your ground, sir.
   Wit. Will you be lighten'd?
   Fitz. Mum.
   Wit. And but I am,
By the said contract, thus to take my leave of you
At this so envious distance, I had taught
Our lips ere this, to seal the happy mixture
Made of our souls: but we must both now yield,
To the necessity. Do not think yet, lady,
But I can kiss, and touch, and laugh, and whisper,
And do those crowning courtships too, for which
Day, and the public, have allow'd no name;
But now, my bargain binds me. 'Twere rude injury
To importune more, or urge a noble nature,
To what of its own bounty it is prone to:
Else I should speak——But, lady, I love so well,
As I will hope you'll do so too.—I have done, sir.
   Fitz. Well, then I have won?
   Wit. Sir, and I may win too.
   Fitz. O yes! no doubt on't. I'll take careful order,
That she shall hang forth ensigns at the window,
To tell you when I am absent! Or I'll keep
Three or four footmen, ready still of purpose,
To run and fetch you at her longings, sir!
I'll go bespeak me straight a gilt caroch,
For her and you to take the air in: yes,
Into Hyde-park, and thence into Blackfriars,
Visit the painters, where you may see pictures,
And note the properest limbs, and how to make them!
Or what do you say unto a middling gossip,
To bring you ay together, at her lodging,
Under pretext of teaching of my wife
Some rare receipt of drawing almond-milk, ha?
It shall be a part of my care. Good sir, God be wi' you!
I have kept the contract, and the cloke's mine own.
   Wit. Why, much good do't you, sir: it may fall out,
That you have bought it dear, though I've not sold it.   *[Exit.*

Fitz. A pretty riddle! fare you well, good sir.
Wife, your face this way; look on me, and think
You had a wicked dream, wife, and forget it.
     Man. This is the strangest motion I e'er saw.   [*Exit.*
     Fitz. Now, wife, sits this fair cloke the worse upon me
For my great sufferings, or your little patience, ha?
They laugh, you think?
     Mrs. Fitz. Why, sir, and you might see't.
What thought they have of you, may be soon collected
By the young gentleman's speech.
     Fitz. Young gentleman!
Death, you are in love with him, are you? could he not
Be named the gentleman, without the young?
Up to your cabin again.
     Mrs. Fitz. My cage, you were best
To call it.
     Fitz. Yes, sing there.   You'd fain be making
Blanc-manger with him at your mother's!   I know you.
Go, get you up.—   [*Exit Mrs. Fitz.*

Enter Pug.

How now! what say you, Devil?
     Pug. Here is one Engine, sir, desires to speak with you.
     Fitz. I thought he brought some news of a broker! well,
Let him come in, good Devil; fetch him else.   [*Exit Pug.*

Re-enter Engine.

O, my fine Engine! what's the affair, more cheats?
     Eng. No, sir, the wit, the brain, the great projector,
I told you of, is newly come to town.
     Fitz. Where, Engine?
     Eng. I have brought him (he's without)
Ere he pull'd off his boots, sir; but so follow'd
For businesses!
     Fitz. But what is a projector?
I would conceive.
     Eng. Why, one, sir, that projects
Ways to enrich men, or to make them great,
By suits, by marriages, by undertakings:
According as he sees they humour it.
     Fitz. Can he not conjure at all?
     Eng. I think he can, sir,
To tell you true.   But you do know, of late,
The state hath ta'en such note of 'em, and compell'd 'em
To enter such great bonds, they dare not practise.
     Fitz. 'Tis true, and I lie fallow for't the while!
     Eng. O, sir, you'll grow the richer for the rest.
     Fitz. I hope I shall: but, Engine, you do talk
Somewhat too much o' my courses: my cloke-customer

Could tell me strange particulars.
   Eng. By my means?
   Fitz. How should he have them else?
   Eng. You do not know, sir,
What he has; and by what arts: a money'd man, sir,
And is as great with your almanack-men as you are.
   Fitz. That gallant!
   Eng. You make the other wait too long here;
And he is extreme punctual.
   Fitz. Is he a gallant?
   Eng. Sir, you shall see: he's in his riding suit,
As he comes now from court: but hear him speak;
Minister matter to him, and then tell me.　　　　　*[Exeunt.*

ACT II

SCENE I.—*A Room in* FITZDOTTREL'S *House.*

Enter FITZDOTTREL, ENGINE, *and* MEERCRAFT, *followed by*
TRAINS, *with a bag, and three or four* Attendants.

   Meer. Sir, money is a whore, a bawd, a drudge;
Fit to run out on errands: let her go.
Via, pecunia! when she's run and gone,
And fled, and dead; then will I fetch her again
With *aqua vitæ,* out of an old hogshead!
While there are lees of wine, or dregs of beer,
I'll never want her! Coin her out of cobwebs,
Dust, but I'll have her! raise wool upon egg-shells,
Sir, and make grass grow out of marrow-bones,
To make her come.—Commend me to your mistress.
　　　　　　　　　　　　　　　　　[To 1 *Attendant.*
Say, let the thousand pound but be had ready,
And it is done. *[Exit* 1 *Atten.]*—I would but see the creature
Of flesh and blood, the man, the prince indeed,
That could employ so many millions
As I would help him to.
   Fitz. How talks he? millions!
   Meer. *[to* 2 *Atten.]* I'll give you an account of this to-morrow.
　　　　　　　　　　　　　　　　　[Exit 2 *Atten.*
—Yes, I will take no less, and do it too;
If they were myriads: and without the Devil,
By direct means, it shall be good in law.
   Eng. Sir.
   Meer. *[to* 3 *Atten.]* Tell master Woodcock I'll not fail to meet him
Upon the Exchange at night; pray him to have
The writings there, and we'll dispatch it. *[Exit* 3 *Atten.]*—Sir,
You are a gentleman of a good presence,
A handsome man; I have consider'd you

As a fit stock to graft honours upon:
I have a project to make you a duke now.
That you must be one, within so many months
As I set down, out of true reasons of state,
You shall not avoid it. But you must hearken, then.

Eng. Hearken! why, sir, do you doubt his ears? alas!
You do not know master Fitzdottrel.

Fitz. He does not know me indeed; I thank you, Engine,
For rectifying him.

Meer. Good! Why, Engine, then
I'll tell it you. (I see you have credit here,
And, that you can keep counsel, I'll not question.)
He shall but be an undertaker with me,
In a most feasible business. It shall cost him
Nothing.

Eng. Good, sir.

Meer. Except he please, but's countenance,
(That I will have) to appear in't, to great men,
For which I'll make him one. He shall not draw
A string of's purse. I'll drive his patent for him.
We'll take in citizens, commoners, and aldermen,
To bear the charge, and blow them off again,
Like so many dead flies, when it is carried.
The thing is for recovery of drown'd land,
Whereof the crown's to have a moiety,
If it be owner; else the crown and owners
To share that moiety, and the recoverers
To enjoy the t'other moiety for their charge.

Eng. Thoroughout England?

Meer. Yes, which will arise
To eighteen millions, seven the first year:
I have computed all, and made my survey
Unto my acre: I'll begin at the pan,
Not at the skirts; as some have done, and lost
All that they wrought, their timber-work, their trench,
Their banks, all borne away, or else fill'd up,
By the next winter. Tut, they never went
The way: I'll have it all.

Eng. A gallant tract
Of land it is!

Meer. 'Twill yield a pound an acre:
We must let cheap ever at first. But, sir,
This looks too large for you, I see. Come hither,
We'll have a less. Here's a plain fellow, [*points to Trains*] you
    see him,
Has his black bag of papers there, in buckram,
Will not be sold for the earldom of Pancridge: draw,
Give me out one by chance. [*Trains gives him a paper out of the bag.*]
    "*Project four: Dogs' skins.*"

Twelve thousand pound! the very worst at first.

Fitz. Pray you let's see it, sir.

Meer. 'Tis a toy, a trifle!

Fitz. Trifle! twelve thousand pound for dogs' skins?

Meer. Yes.

But, by my way of dressing, you must know, sir,
And med'cining the leather to a height
Of improved ware, like your borachio
Of Spain, sir, I can fetch nine thousand for't—

Eng. Of the king's glover?

Meer. Yes; how heard you that?

Eng. Sir, I do know you can.

Meer. Within this hour;
And reserve half my secret. Pluck another;
See if thou hast a happier hand; [*Trains draws out another.*] I
        thought so.
The very next worse to it! "*Bottle-ale.*"
Yet this is two and twenty thousand. Prithee
Pull out another, two or three.

Fitz. Good; stay, friend—
By bottle-ale two and twenty thousand pound?

Meer. Yes, sir, it's cast to penny-halfpenny farthing.
On the back-side, there you may see it, read,
I will not bate a Harrington of the sum.
I'll win it in my water, and my malt,
My furnaces, and hanging of my coppers,
The tonning, and the subtlety of my yest;
And, then the earth of my bottles, which I dig,
Turn up, and steep, and work, and neal, myself,
To a degree of porcelane. You will wonder
At my proportions, what I will put up
In seven years! for so long time I ask
For my invention. I will save in cork,
In my mere stop'ling, above three thousand pound,
Within that term; by googing of them out
Just to the size of my bottles, and not slicing:
There's infinite loss in that. [*Trains draws out another.*] What hast
        thou there?
O! "*Making wine of raisins:*" this is in hand now.

Eng. Is not that strange, sir, to make wine of raisins?

Meer. Yes, and as true a wine as the wines of France,
Or Spain, or Italy: look of what grape
My raisin is, that wine I'll render perfect,
As of the Muscatel grape, I'll render Muscatel;
Of the Canary, his; the Claret, his;
So of all kinds: and bate you of the prices
Of wine throughout the kingdom half in half.

Eng. But how, sir, if you raise the other commodity,
Raisins?

Meer. Why, then I'll make it out of blackberries,
And it shall do the same. 'Tis but more art,
And the charge less. Take out another.

Fitz. No, good sir,
Save you the trouble, I'll not look, nor hear
Of any but your first, there: the drown'd-land;
If't will do, as you say.

Meer. Sir, there's not place
To give you demonstration of these things,
They are a little too subtle. But I could shew you
Such a necessity in it, as you must be
But what you please; against the received heresy,
That England bears no dukes. Keep you the land, sir,
The greatness of the estate shall throw't upon you.
If you like better turning it to money,
What may not you, sir, purchase with that wealth?
Say you should part with two of your millions,
To be the thing you would, who would not do't?
As I protest I will, out of my dividend,
Lay for some pretty principality
In Italy, from the church: now you, perhaps,
Fancy the smoke of England rather? But—
Have you no private room, sir, to draw to.
To enlarge ourselves more upon?

Fitz. O yes.—Devil!

Meer. These, sir, are businesses ask to be carried
With caution, and in cloud.

Fitz. I apprehend
They do, sir.—

Enter Pug.

Devil, which way is your mistress?

Pug. Above, sir, in her chamber.

Fitz. O that's well:
Then this way, good sir.

Meer. I shall follow you. Trains,
Give me the bag, and go you presently,
Commend my service to my lady Tailbush.
Tell her I am come from court this morning; say,
I have got our business mov'd, and well: entreat her,
That she give you the fourscore angels, and see them
Disposed of to my counsel, sir Paul Eitherside.
Some time, to-day, I'll wait upon her ladyship,
With the relation. [*Exit Trains.*

Eng. Sir, of what dispatch
He is! do you mark? [*Aside to Fitz.*

Meer. Engine, when did you see
My cousin Everill? keeps he still your quarter
In the Bermudas?

Eng. Yes, sir, he was writing
This morning, very hard.
 Meer. Be not you known to him,
That I am come to town: I have effected
A business for him, but I would have it take him,
Before he thinks for't.
 Eng. Is it past?
 Meer. Not yet.
'Tis well o' the way.
 Eng. O sir! your worship takes
Infinite pains.
 Meer. I love friends to be active:
A sluggish nature puts off man, and kind.
 Eng. And such a blessing follows it.
 Meer. I thank
My fate—Pray you, let's be private, sir.
 Fitz. In, here.
 Meer. Where none may interrupt us.
        [Exeunt Meer. and Engine.

 Fitz. You hear, Devil,
Lock the street-doors fast, and let no one in,
Except they be this gentleman's followers,
To trouble me. Do you mark? You have heard and seen
Something to-day, and by it you may gather,
Your mistress is a fruit that's worth the stealing,
And therefore worth the watching. Be you sure, now,
You have all your eyes about you; and let in
No lace-woman, nor bawd, that brings French masks,
And cut-works; see you? nor old croans with wafers,
To convey letters: nor no youths, disguised
Like country wives, with cream and marrow puddings.
Much knavery may be vented in a pudding,
Much bawdy intelligence: they are shrewd cyphers.
Nor turn the key to any neighbours' need;
Be it but to kindle fire, or beg a little,
Put it out rather, all out to an ash,
That they may see no smoke. Or water, spill it;
Knock on the empty tubs, that by the sound
They may be forbid entry. Say, we are robb'd,
If any come to borrow a spoon or so:
I will not have Good Fortune, or God's Blessing
Let in, while I am busy.
 Pug. I'll take care, sir;
They shall not trouble you if they would.
 Fitz. Well, do so.   *[Exit.*
 Pug. I have no singular service of this now,
Nor no superlative master! I shall wish,
To be in hell again at leisure! bring
A Vice from thence! that had been such a subtlety,

As to bring broad-cloths hither, or transport
Fresh oranges into Spain.   I find it now;
My chief was in the right.   Can any fiend
Boast of a better Vice, than here by nature
And art they're owners of?   Hell never own me,
But I am taken! the fine tract of it
Pulls me along! to hear men such professors
Grown in our subtlest sciences!   My first act, now,
Shall be to make this master of mine, cuckold:
The primitive work of darkness I will practise.
I will deserve so well of my fair mistress
By my discoveries first, my counsels after,
And keeping counsel after that, as who
So ever is one, I will be another sure,
I'll have my share.   Most delicate damn'd flesh
She will be!   O, that I could stay time, now!
Midnight will come too fast upon me, I fear,
To cut my pleasure—

Enter Mrs. FITZDOTTREL.

   Mrs. Fitz. Look at the back-door,
One knocks, see who it is.
   Pug. Dainty she-Devil!   *[Aside and exit.*
   Mrs. Fitz. I cannot get this venture of the cloke
Out of my fancy, nor the gentleman's way
He took, which though't were strange, yet it was handsome,
And had a grace withal, beyond the newness.
Sure he will think me that dull stupid creature
He said, and may conclude it, if I find not
Some thought to thank the attempt.   He did presume
By all the carriage of it, on my brain,
For answer; and will swear 'tis very barren,
If it can yield him no return.—

Re-enter PUG.

Who is it?

   Pug. Mistress, it is—but first, let me assure
The excellence of mistresses, I am,
Although my master's man, my mistress' slave,
The servant of her secrets, and sweet turns,
And know what fitly will conduce to either.
   Mrs. Fitz. What's this?   I pray you come to yourself, and think
What your part is; to make an answer.   Tell,
Who is at the door?
   Pug. The gentleman, mistress,
Who was at the cloke-charge to speak with you
This morning; who expects only to take
Some small commandments from you, what you please,
Worthy your form, he says, and gentlest manners.

Mrs. Fitz. O! you'll anon prove his hired man, I fear;
What has he given you for this message? sir,
Bid him put off his hopes of straw, and leave
To spread his nets in view thus. Though they take
Master Fitzdottrel, I am no such foul
Nor fair one, tell him, will be had with stalking;
And wish him to forbear his acting to me,
At the gentleman's chamber-window in Lincoln's-inn there,
That opens to my gallery; else I swear
To acquaint my husband with his folly, and leave him
To the just rage of his offended jealousy.
Or if your master's sense be not so quick
To right me, tell him I shall find a friend
That will repair me. Say, I will be quiet
In mine own house. Pray you, in those words give it him.

   Pug. This is some fool turn'd!   *[Exit.*

   Mrs. Fitz. If he be the master,
Now, of that state and wit which I allow him,
Sure, he will understand me: I durst not
Be more direct; for this officious fellow,
My husband's new groom, is a spy upon me,
I find already. Yet, if he but tell him
This in my words, he cannot but conceive
Himself both apprehended and requited.
I would not have him think he met a statue,
Or spoke to one, not there, though I were silent.

Re-enter Pug.

How now? have you told him?
   Pug. Yes.
   Mrs. Fitz. And what says he?
   Pug. Says he!
That which myself would say to you, if I durst.
That you are proud, sweet mistress; and withal,
A little ignorant, to entertain
The good that's proffer'd; and, by your beauty's leave,
Not all so wise as some true politic wife
Would be; who having match'd with such a nupson
(I speak it with my master's peace) whose face
Hath left to accuse him, now, for it doth confess him,
What you can make him; will yet (out of scruple,
And a spiced conscience) defraud the poor gentleman,
At least delay him in the thing he longs for,
And makes it his whole study, how to compass
Only a title. Could but he write cuckold,
He had his ends: for, look you—
   Mrs. Fitz. This can be
None but my husband's wit.   *[Aside.*
   Pug. My precious mistress—

Mrs. Fitz. It creaks his engine: the groom never durst
Be else so saucy.   [*Aside.*

Pug. If it were not clearly
His worshipful ambition, and the top of it,
The very forked top too, why should he
Keep you thus mured up in a back-room, mistress,
Allow you ne'er a casement to the street,
Fear of engendering by the eyes, with gallants?
Forbid you paper, pen and ink, like rat's-bane;
Search your half pint of muscatel, lest a letter
Be sunk in the pot; and hold your new-laid egg
Against the fire, lest any charm be writ there?
Will you make benefit of truth, dear mistress,
If I do tell it you? I do't not often:
I am set over you, employ'd indeed
To watch your steps, your looks, your very breathings,
And to report them to him. Now, if you
Will be a true, right, delicate, sweet mistress,
Why, we will make a Cokes of this Wise Master,
We will, my mistress, an absolute fine Cokes.
And mock, to air, all the deep diligences
Of such a solemn and effectual ass,
An ass to so good purpose as we'll use him.
I will contrive it so, that you shall go
To plays, to masques, to meetings, and to feasts:
For, why is all this rigging and fine tackle, mistress,
If your neat handsome vessels, of good sail,
Put not forth ever and anon with your nets
Abroad into the world? It is your fishing.
There, you shall choose your friends, your servants, lady,
Your squires of honour; I'll convey your letters,
Fetch answers, do you all the offices
That can belong to your blood and beauty. And,
For the variety, at my times, although
I am not in due symmetry, the man
Of that proportion; or in rule
Of physic, of the just complexion;
Or of that truth of Picardil, in clothes,
To boast a sovereignty o'er ladies: yet
I know to do my turns, sweet mistress. Come, kiss—
    Mrs. Fitz. How now!
    Pug. Dear delicate mistress, I am your slave,
Your little worm, that loves you; your fine monkey,
Your dog, your Jack, your Pug, that longs to be
Styled, o' your pleasures.
    Mrs. Fitz. [*aloud.*] Hear you all this? Sir, pray you
Come from your standing, do, a little, spare
Yourself, sir, from your watch, t' applaud your squire,
That so well follows your instructions!

Enter FITZDOTTREL.

Fitz. How now, sweet-heart! what is the matter?
Mrs. Fitz. Good!
You are a stranger to the plot! you set not
Your saucy Devil here, to tempt your wife,
With all the insolent uncivil language,
Or action, he could vent!
Fitz. Did you so, Devil?
Mrs. Fitz. Not you!
You were not planted in your hole to hear him
Upon the stairs, or here behind the hangings!
I do not know your qualities! he durst do it
And you not give directions!
Fitz. You shall see, wife,
Whether he durst or no, and what it was,
I did direct. [*Exit.*
Pug. Sweet mistress, are you mad?

Re-enter FITZDOTTREL, *with a cudgel.*

Fitz. You most mere rogue! you open manifest villain!
You fiend apparent, you! you declared hell-hound!
Pug. Good sir.
Fitz. Good knave, good rascal, and good traitor,
Now, I do find you parcel Devil indeed.
Upon the point of trust! in your first charge,
The very day of your probation,
To tempt your mistress! [*Beats Pug.*] You do see, good wedlock,
How I directed him?
Mrs. Fitz. Why, where, sir, were you?
Fitz. Nay, there is one blow more for exercise:
[*Strikes him again.*
I told you, I should do it.
Pug. Would you had done, sir.
Fitz. O wife, the rarest man!—(yet there's another
To put you in mind o' the last)—[*beats him again*] such a brave
man, wife!
Within, he has his projects, and does vent them
The gallantest!—Were you tentiginous, ha?
Would you be acting of the incubus?
Did her silk's rustling move you?
Pug. Gentle sir!
Fitz. Out of my sight! If thy name were not Devil,
Thou should'st not stay a minute with me. In,
Go, yet stay, yet go too. I am resolv'd
What I will do, and you shall know't aforehand,
Soon as the gentleman is gone, do you hear?
I'll help your lisping. [*Exit Pug.*]—Wife, such a man, wife!
He has such plots! he will make me a duke!

No less, by heaven! six mares to your coach, wife!
That's your proportion! and your coachman bald,
Because he shall be bare enough.   Do not you laugh,
We are looking for a place, and all, in the map,
What to be of.   Have faith, be not an infidel.
You know I am not easy to be gull'd.
I swear, when I have my millions, else, I'll make
Another, dutchess; if you have not faith.

   Mrs. Fitz. You'll have too much, I fear, in these false spirits.

   Fitz. Spirits!   O, no such thing, wife; wit, mere wit.
This man defies the Devil and all his works,
He does't by engine, and devices, he!
He has his winged ploughs, that go with sails,
Will plough you forty acres at once! and mills
Will spout you water ten miles off!   All Crowland
Is ours, wife; and the fens, from us, in Norfolk,
To the utmost bounds in Lincolnshire! we have view'd it,
And measur'd it within all, by the scale:
The richest tract of land, love, in the kingdom!
There will be made seventeen or eighteen millions,
Or more, as't may be handled! wherefore think,
Sweet-heart, if thou hast a fancy to one place
More than another, to be dutchess of,
Now name it; I will have't, whate'er it cost,
(If 'twill be had for money) either here,
Or in France, or Italy.

   Mrs. Fitz. You have strangē phantasies!

Enter MEERCRAFT *and* ENGINE.

   Meer. Where are you, sir?

   Fitz. I see thou hast no talent
This way, wife.   Up to thy gallery, do, chuck,
Leave us to talk of it who understand it.   [*Exit Mrs. Fitz.*

   Meer. I think we have found a place to fit you now, sir.
Gloucester.

   Fitz. O no, I'll none.

   Meer. Why, sir?

   Fitz. 'Tis fatal.

   Meer. That you say right in.   Spenser, I think the younger,
Had his last honour thence.   But he was but earl.

   Fitz. I know not that, sir.   But Thomas of Woodstock,
I'm sure was duke, and he was made away
At Calice, as duke Humphrey was at Bury:
And Richard the Third, you know what end he came to.

   Meer. By my faith you are cunning in the chronicle, sir.

   Fitz. No, I confess I have it from the play-books,
And think they are more authentic.

   Eng. That is sure, sir.

   Meer. [*whispers him.*] What say you to this then?

Fitz. No, a noble house
Pretends to that. I will do no man wrong.

Meer. Then take one proposition more, and hear it
As past exception.

Fitz. What is that?

Meer. To be
Duke of those lands you shall recover: take
Your title thence, sir, DUKE OF THE DROWN'D LANDS,
Or, DROWN'D LAND.

Fitz. Ha! that last has a good sound:
I like it well. The duke of Drown'd-land?

Eng. Yes;
It goes like Groen-land, sir, if you mark it.

Meer. Ay;
And drawing thus your honour from the work,
You make the reputation of that greater,
And stay it the longer in your name.

Fitz. 'Tis true.
DROWN'D LANDS will live in drown'd-land!

Meer. Yes, when you
Have no foot left; as that must be, sir, one day.
And though it tarry in your heirs some forty,
Fifty descents, the longer liver at last, yet,
Must thrust them out on't, if no quirk in law,
Or odd vice of their own not do it first.
We see those changes daily: the fair lands
That were the client's, are the lawyer's now;
And those rich manors there of goodman Taylor's
Had once more wood upon them, than the yard
By which they were measured out for the last purchase.
Nature hath these vicissitudes. She makes
No man a state of perpetuity, sir.

Fitz. You are in the right. Let's in then, and conclude.—

Re-enter PUG.

In my sight again! I'll talk with you anon.

[*Exeunt Fitz, Meer., and Engine.*

Pug. Sure he will geld me if I stay, or worse,
Pluck out my tongue, one of the two. This fool,
There is no trusting of him; and to quit him,
Were a contempt against my chief past pardon.
It was a shrewd disheartening this, at first!
Who would have thought a woman so well harness'd,
Or rather well caparison'd, indeed,
That wears such petticoats, and lace to her smocks,
Broad seaming laces (as I see them hang there)
And garters which are lost, if she can shew them,
Could have done this? Hell! why is she so brave?
It cannot be to please duke Dottrel, sure,

Nor the dull pictures in her gallery,
Nor her own dear reflection in her glass;
Yet that may be: I have known many of them
Begin their pleasure, but none end it there:
(That I consider, as I go along with it)
They may, for want of better company,
Or that they think the better, spend an hour,
Two, three, or four, discoursing with their shadow;
But sure they have a farther speculation.
No woman drest with so much care and study,
Doth dress herself in vain.   I'll vex this problem
A little more, before I leave it sure.   [*Exit.*

SCENE II.—MANLY's *Chambers in Lincoln's Inn, opposite*
FITZDOTTREL's *House.*

Enter WITTIPOL *and* MANLY.

Wit. This was a fortune happy above thought,
That this should prove thy chamber; which I fear'd
Would be my greatest trouble! this must be
The very window and that the room.
   Man. It is.
I now remember, I have often seen there
A woman, but I never mark'd her much.
   Wit. Where was your soul, friend?
   Man. Faith, but now and then
Awake unto those objects.
   Wit. You pretend so.
Let me not live, if I am not in love
More with her wit, for this direction now,
Than with her form, though I have praised that prettily,
Since I saw her and you to-day.   Read those:
                    [*Gives him the copy of a song.*
They'll go unto the air you love so well.
Try them unto the note, may be the music
Will call her sooner; light, she's here! sing quickly.

Mrs. FITZDOTTREL *appears at a window of her house fronting
that of* MANLY's *Chambers.*

Mrs. Fitz. Either he understood him not; or else,
The fellow was not faithful in delivery
Of what I bade.   And, I am justly pay'd,
That might have made my profit of his service,
But by mistaking, have drawn on his envy,
And done the worse defeat upon myself.   [*Manly sings.*
How! music? then he may be there: and is sure.

Enter PUG *behind.*

Pug. O! is it so? is there the interview!
Have I drawn to you, at last, my cunning lady?

The Devil is an ass! fool'd off, and beaten!
Nay, made an instrument, and could not scent it.
Well, since you have shewn the malice of a woman,
No less than her true wit and learning, mistress,
I'll try, if little Pug have the malignity
To recompense it, and so save his danger.
'Tis not the pain, but the discredit of it,
The Devil should not keep a body entire.   [*Aside and exit.*

    Wit. Away, fall back, she comes.
    Man. I leave you, sir,
The master of my chamber: I have business.   [*Exit.*
    Wit. Mistress!
    Mrs. Fitz. [*advances to the window.*] You make me paint, sir.
    Wit. They are fair colours,
Lady, and natural! I did receive
Some commands from you, lately, gentle lady,
But so perplex'd, and wrapt in the delivery,
As I may fear to have misinterpreted:
But must make suit still, to be near your grace.
    Mrs. Fitz. Who is there with you, sir?
    Wit. None, but myself.
It falls out, lady, to be a dear friend's lodging;
Wherein there's some conspiracy of fortune
With your poor servant's blest affections.
    Mrs. Fitz. Who was it sung?
    Wit. He, lady, but he's gone
Upon my entreaty of him, seeing you
Approach the window. Neither need you doubt him,
If he were here; he is too much a gentleman.
    Mrs. Fitz. Sir, if you judge me by this simple action,
And by the outward habit, and complexion
Of easiness it hath, to your design;
You may with justice say, I am a woman;
And a strange woman. But when you shall please
To bring but that concurrence of my fortune
To memory, which to-day yourself did urge;
It may beget some favour like excuse,
Though none like reason.
    Wit. No, my tuneful mistress?
Then surely love hath none, nor beauty any;
Nor nature, violenced in both these:
With all whose gentle tongues you speak, at once.
I thought I had enough remov'd already
That scruple from your breast, and left you all reason;
When through my morning's perspective I shew'd you
A man so above excuse, as he's the cause,
Why any thing is to be done upon him;
And nothing call'd an injury, misplaced.
I rather now had hope, to shew you how love

By his accesses grows more natural:
And what was done this morning with such force,
Was but devised to serve the present, then.
That since Love hath the honour to approach
These sister-swelling breasts; and touch this soft
And rosy hand; he hath the skill to draw
Their nectar forth, with kissing; and could make
More wanton salts from this brave promontory,
Down to this valley, than the nimble roe;
Could play the hopping sparrow 'bout these nets;
And sporting squirrel in these crisped groves;
Bury himself in every silk-worm's kell,
Is here unravell'd; run into the snare,
Which every hair is, cast into a curl,
To catch a Cupid flying! bathe himself
In milk and roses here, and dry him there;
Warm his cold hands, to play with his smooth, round,
And well-torn'd chin, as with the billiard ball;
Roll on these lips, the banks of love, and there
At once both plant and gather kisses.   Lady,
Shall I, with what I have made to-day here, call
All sense to wonder, and all faith to sign
The mysteries revealed in your form?
And will Love pardon me the blasphemy
I utter'd when I said, a glass could speak
This beauty, or that fools had power to judge it?

> Do but look on her eyes, they do light
>   All that love's world compriseth,
> Do but look on her hair, it is bright
>   As love's star when it riseth!
> Do but mark, her forehead smoother
>   Than words that soothe her!
> And from her arched brows, such a grace
>   Sheds itself through the face;
> As alone, there triumphs to the life,
>   All the gain, all the good, of the elements' strife.
>
> Have you seen but a bright lily grow,
>   Before rude hands have touch'd it?
> Have you mark'd but the fall of the snow,
>   Before the soil hath smutch'd it?
> Have you felt the wool of the beaver?
>   Or swan's down ever?
> Or have smelt o' the bud of the brier?
>   Or the nard in the fire?
> Or have tasted the bag of the bee?
>   O, so white! O, so soft! O, so sweet is she!

FITZDOTTREL *appears at his Wife's back.*

Fitz. Is she so, sir? and I will keep her so,
If I know how, or can; that wit of man
Will do't, I'll go no farther. At this window
She shall no more be buzz'd at. Take your leave on't.
If you be sweetmeats, wedlock, or sweet flesh,
All's one: I do not love this hum about you,
A fly-blown wife is not so proper: in!—
For you, you, sir, look to hear from me.
    Wit. So I do, sir.
    Fitz. No, but in other terms. There's no man offers
This to my wife, but pays for't.
    Wit. That have I, sir.
    Fitz. Nay then, I tell you, you are—
    Wit. What am I, sir?
    Fitz. Why, that I'll think on, when I have cut your throat.
    Wit. Go, you are an ass.
    Fitz. I am resolv'd on't, sir.
    Wit. I think you are.
    Fitz. To call you to a reckoning.
    Wit. Away, you broker's block, you property!
    Fitz. 'Slight, if you strike me, I will strike your mistress.
                    [*Strikes Mrs. Fitz. and leads her out.*
    Wit. O! I could shoot mine eyes at him for that now,
Or leave my teeth in him, were they cuckold's bane,
Enough to kill him. What prodigious,
Blind, and most wicked change of fortune's this?
I have no air of patience: all my veins
Swell, and my sinews start at th' iniquity of it.
I shall break, break.   [*Exit.*

SCENE III.—*Another Room in* FITZDOTTREL'S *House.*

Enter PUG.

Pug. This for the malice of it,
And my revenge may pass! but now my conscience
Tells me, I have profited the cause of hell
But little, in the breaking off their loves.
Which, if some other act of mine repair not,
I shall hear ill of in my account!

Enter FITZDOTTREL *and his Wife.*

Fitz. O, bird,
Could you do this? 'gainst me! and at this time now!
When I was so employ'd, wholly for you,
Drown'd in my care (more than the land, I swear,
I have hope to win) to make you peerless, studying
For footmen for you, fine-paced huishers, pages,

To serve you on the knee; with what knight's wife
To bear your train, and sit with your four women
In council, and receive intelligences
From foreign parts, to dress you at all pieces!
You've almost turn'd my good affection to you;
Sour'd my sweet thoughts, all my pure purposes:
I could now find in my very heart to make
Another, lady dutchess; and depose you.
Well, go your ways in. [*Exit Mrs. Fitz.*]—Devil, you have redeem'd all;
I do forgive you: and I'll do you good.   [*Exit Pug.*

Enter MEERCRAFT *and* ENGINE.

Meer. Why have you these excursions! where have you been, sir?
Fitz. Where I have been vex'd a little with a toy.
Meer. O sir, no toys must trouble your grave head,
Now it is growing to be great.   You must
Be above all those things.
Fitz. Nay, nay, so I will.
Meer. Now you are toward the lord, you must put off
The man, sir.
Eng. He says true.
Meer. You must do nothing
As you have done it heretofore; not know,
Or salute any man.
Eng. That was your bedfellow
The other month.
Meer. The other month! the week.
Thou dost not know the privileges, Engine,
Follow that title; nor how swift: to-day,
When he has put on his lord's face once, then—
Fitz. Sir, for these things I shall do well enough,
There is no fear of me: but then my wife is
Such an untoward thing, she'll never learn
How to comport with it: I am out of all
Conceit, on her behalf.
Meer. Best have her taught, sir.
Fitz. Where! are there any schools for ladies? is there
An academy for women?   I do know
For men there was; I learn'd in it myself,
To make my legs, and do my postures.
Eng. [*whispers Meercraft.*] Sir,
Do you remember the conceit you had—
Of the Spanish gown at home?
Meer. Ha! I do thank thee
With all my heart, dear Engine.—Sir, there is
A certain lady, here about the town,
An English widow, who hath lately travell'd,
But she is call'd the Spaniard, 'cause she came

Latest from thence, and keeps the Spanish habit.
Such a rare woman! all our women here,
That are of spirit and fashion, flock unto her,
As to their president, their law, their canon;
More than they ever did to oracle Foreman,
Such rare receipts she has, sir, for the face,
Such oils, such tinctures, such pomatums,
Such perfumes, med'cines, quintessences, *et cœtera;*
And such a mistress of behaviour,
She knows from the duke's daughter to the doxy,
What is their due just, and no more!
   Fitz. O sir!
You please me in this, more than mine own greatness.
Where is she? Let us have her.
   Meer. By your patience,
We must use means, cast how to be acquainted—
   Fitz. Good, sir, about it.
   Meer. We must think how, first.
   Fitz. O!
I do not love to tarry for a thing,
When I have a mind to it. You do not know me,
If you do offer it.
   Meer. Your wife must send
Some pretty token to her, with a compliment,
And pray to be received in her good graces.
All the great ladies do it.
   Fitz. She shall, she shall.
What were it best to be?
   Meer. Some little toy,
I would not have it any great matter, sir:
A diamond ring of forty or fifty pound
Would do it handsomely, and be a gift
Fit for your wife to send, and her to take.
   Fitz. I'll go and tell my wife on't straight.   [*Exit.*
   Meer. Why, this
Is well! the clothes we have now, but where's this lady?
If we could get a witty boy now, Engine,
That were an excellent crack, I could instruct him
To the true height: for any thing takes this Dottrel.
   Eng. Why, sir, your best will be one of the players!
   Meer. No, there's no trusting them; they'll talk of it.
And tell their poets.
   Eng. What if they do! the jest
Will brook the stage. But there be some of them
Are very honest lads: there's Dickey Robinson,
A very pretty fellow, and comes often
To a gentleman's chamber, a friend of mine. We had
The merriest supper of it there, one night,
The gentleman's landlady invited him

To a gossip's feast: now he, sir, brought Dick Robinson,
Drest like a lawyer's wife, amongst them all:
I lent him clothes.—But to see him behave it,
And lay the law, and carve and drink unto them,
And then talk bawdy, and send frolics! O
It would have burst your buttons, or not left you
A seam.
 Meer. They say he's an ingenious youth.
 Eng. O sir! and dresses himself the best, beyond
Forty of your very ladies; did you never see him?
 Meer. No, I do seldom see those toys.   But think you
That we may have him?
 Eng. Sir, the young gentleman
I tell you of can command him: shall I attempt it?
 Meer. Yes, do it.

Re-enter FITZDOTTREL.

 Fitz. 'Slight, I cannot get my wife
To part with a ring on any terms, and yet
The sullen monkey has two.
 Meer. It were 'gainst reason
That you should urge it: sir, send to a goldsmith,
Let not her lose by it.
 Fitz. How does she lose by it?
Is it not for her?
 Meer. Make it your own bounty,
It will have the better success; what is a matter
Of fifty pound to you, sir?
 Fitz. I have but a hundred
Pieces to shew here; that I would not break—
 Meer. You shall have credit, sir.   I'll send a ticket
Unto my goldsmith.—

Enter TRAINS.

    Here my man comes too,
To carry it fitly.—How now, Trains! what birds?
 Trains. Your cousin Everill met me, and has beat me,
Because I would not tell him where you were:
I think he has dogg'd me to the house too.
 Meer. Well—
You shall go out at the back-door then, Trains.
You must get Gilthead hither by some means.
 Trains. It is impossible!
 Fitz. Tell him we have venison,
I'll give him a piece, and send his wife a pheasant.   [*Exit.*
 Trains. A forest moves not, 'till that forty pound
You had of him last be paid.   He keeps more stir
For that same petty sum, than for your bond
Of six, and statute of eight hundred.

Meer. Tell him
We'll hedge in that. Cry up Fitzdottrel to him,
Double his price: make him a man of metal.
   Trains. That will not need, his bond is current enough.

[*Exeunt.*

ACT III

SCENE I.—*A Room in* FITZDOTTREL's *House.*

Enter THOMAS GILTHEAD, *and* PLUTARCHUS.

Gilt. All this is to make you a gentleman!
I'll have you learn, son. Wherefore have I placed you
With sir Paul Eitherside, but to have so much law
To keep your own? Besides, he is a justice,
Here in the town; and dwelling, son, with him,
You shall learn that in a year, shall be worth twenty
Of having staid you at Oxford or at Cambridge,
Or sending you to the inns of court, or France.
I'm call'd for now in haste by master Meercraft,
To trust master Fitzdottrel, a good man,
I have enquired him, eighteen hundred a year,
(His name is current) for a diamond ring
Of forty, shall not be worth thirty; that's gained;
And this is to make you a gentleman!
   Plu. O, but, good father, you trust too much.
   Gilt. Boy, boy,
We live by finding fools out to be trusted.
Our shop-books are our pastures, our corn-grounds,
We lay 'em open, for them to come into;
And when we have them there, we drive them up
Into one of our two pounds, the compters, straight,
And this is to make you a gentleman!
We citizens never trust, but we do cozen:
For if our debtors pay, we cozen them;
And if they do not, then we cozen ourselves.
But that's a hazard every one must run,
That hopes to make his son a gentleman!
   Plu. I do not wish to be one, truly, father.
In a descent or two, we come to be,
Just in their state, fit to be cozen'd, like them:
And I had rather have tarried in your trade.
For, since the gentry scorn the city so much,
Methinks we should in time, holding together,
And matching in our own tribes, as they say,
Have got an act of common-council for it,
That we might cozen them out of *rerum natura.*
   Gilt. Ay, if we had an act first to forbid

The marrying of our wealthy heirs unto them,
And daughters with such lavish portions:
That confounds all.

    Plu. And makes a mongrel breed, father.
And when they have your money, then they laugh at you,
Or kick you down the stairs. I cannot abide them:
I would fain have them cozen'd, but not trusted.

Enter MEERCRAFT.

    Meer. O, is he come! I knew he would not fail me.—
Welcome, good Gilthead, I must have you do
A noble gentleman a courtesy here,
In a mere toy, some pretty ring or jewel,
Of fifty or threescore pound.—Make it a hundred,
And hedge in the last forty that I owe you,
And your own price for the ring.　[*Aside to Gilthead.*]　He's a good
    man, sir,
And you may hap see him a great one! he
Is likely to bestow hundreds and thousands
With you, if you can humour him. A great prince
He will be shortly. What do you say?

    Gilt. In truth, sir,
I cannot: 't has been a long vacation with us.

    Meer. Of what, I pray thee, of wit or honesty?
Those are your citizens' long vacations.

    Plu. Good father, do not trust them.

    Meer. Nay, Tom Gilthead,
He will not buy a courtesy and beg it;
He'll rather pay than pray. If you do for him,
You must do cheerfully: his credit, sir,
Is not yet prostitute. Who's this, thy son?
A pretty youth! what is his name?

    Plu. Plutarchus, sir.

    Meer. Plutarchus! how came that about?

    Gilt. That year, sir,
That I begot him, I bought Plutarch's lives,
And fell so in love with the book, as I call'd my son
By his name, in hope he should be like him,
And write the lives of our great men.—

    Meer. In the city!
And do you breed him there?

    Gilt. His mind, sir, lies
Much to that way.

    Meer. Why, then he's in the right way.

    Gilt. But now, I had rather get him a good wife,
And plant him in the country, there to use
The blessing I shall leave him.

    Meer. Out upon't!
And lose the laudable means thou hast at home here,

To advance and make him a young alderman?
Buy him a captain's place, for shame; and let him
Into the world early, and with his plume
And scarfs march through Cheapside, or along Cornhill,
And by the virtue of those, draw down a wife
There from a window, worth ten thousand pound!
Get him the posture-book and's leaden men
To set upon a table, 'gainst his mistress
Chance to come by, that he may draw her in,
And shew her Finsbury battles.
 Gilt. I have placed him
With justice Eitherside, to get so much law—
 Meer. As thou hast conscience. Come, come, thou dost wrong
Pretty Plutarchus, who had not his name
For nothing, but was born *to train the youth
Of London in the military truth*—
That way his genius lies.—

Enter Everill.

       My cousin Everill!
 Ever. O, are you here, sir! pray you let us whisper.
           [*Takes Meer. aside.*
 Plu. Father, dear father, trust him if you love me.
 Gilt. Why, I do mean it, boy, but what I do
Must not come easily from me: we must deal
With courtiers, boy, as courtiers deal with us.
If I have a business there with any of them,
Why, I must wait, I am sure on't, son; and though
My lord dispatch me, yet his worshipful man
Will keep me for his sport a month or two,
To shew me with my fellow-citizens
I must make his train long, and full, one quarter,
And help the spectacle of his greatness. There
Nothing is done at once but injuries, boy,
And they come headlong: all their good turns move not,
Or very slowly.
 Plu. Yet, sweet father, trust him.
 Gilt. Well, I will think.   [*They walk aside.*
 Ever. Come, you must do't, sir.
I am undone else, and your lady Tailbush
Has sent for me to dinner, and my clothes
Are all at pawn. I had sent out this morning,
Before I heard you were come to town, some twenty
Of my epistles, and no one return—
 Meer. Why, I have told you of this. This comes of wearing
Scarlet, gold lace, and cut-works! your fine gartering,
With your blown roses, cousin! and your eating
Pheasant, and godwit, here in London, haunting
The Globes and Mermaids, wedging in with lords

Still at the table, and affecting letchery
In velvet! where, could you have contented yourself
With cheese, salt butter, and a pickled herring,
In the Low Countries; there worn cloth and fustian,
Been satisfied with a leap o' your host's daughter,
In garrison, a wench of a storer, or
Your sutler's wife in the leaguer, of two blanks!
You never then had run upon this flat,
To write your letters missive, and send out
Your privy seals, that thus have frighted off
All your acquaintance, that they shun you at distance,
Worse than you do the bailiffs.

    Ever. Pox upon you!
I come not to you for counsel, I lack money.

    Meer. You do not think what you owe me already.

    Ever. I!
They owe you that mean to pay you: I'll be sworn
I never meant it.   Come, you will project,
I shall undo your practice, for this month, else;
You know me.

    Meer. Ay, you are a right sweet nature!

    Ever. Well, that's all one!

    Meer. You'll leave this empire one day;
You will not ever have this tribute paid
Your scepter of the sword!

    Ever. Tie up your wit,
Do, and provoke me not—

    Meer. Will you, sir, help
To what I shall provoke another for you?

    Ever. I cannot tell; try me: I think I am not
So utterly, of an ore un-to-be-melted,
But I can do myself good, on occasions.

Enter FITZDOTTREL.

    Meer. Strike in, then, for your part. [*They go up to Fitz.*]—
Master Fitzdottrel,
If I transgress in point of manners, afford me
Your best construction; I must beg my freedom
From your affairs, this day.

    Fitz. How, sir!

    Meer. It is
In succour of this gentleman's occasions,
My kinsman—

    Fitz. You'll not do me that affront, sir?

    Meer. I am sorry you should so interpret it.
But, sir, it stands upon his being invested
In a new office, he has stood for, long:
Master of the Dependences! a place
Of my projection too, sir, and hath met

Much opposition; but the state, now, sees
That great necessity of it, as after all
Their writing, and their speaking against duels
They have erected it.   His book is drawn—
For, since there will be differences daily
'Twixt gentlemen, and that the roaring manner
Is grown offensive; that those few, we call
The civil men of the sword, abhor the vapours;
They shall refer now, hither, for their process;
And such as trespass 'gainst the rule of court
Are to be fined.
   Fitz. In troth, a pretty place!
   Meer. A kind of arbitrary court 'twill be, sir.
   Fitz. I shall have matter for it, I believe,
Ere it be long; I had a distaste.
   Meer. But now, sir,
My learned counsel, they must have a feeling,
They'll part, sir, with no books, without the hand-gout
Be oil'd: and I must furnish.   If't be money,
To me straight; I am mine, mint, and exchequer,
To supply all.   What is't, a hundred pound?
   Ever. No, the harpy now stands on a hundred pieces.
   Meer. Why, he must have them, if he will.   To-morrow, sir,
Will equally serve your occasions—
And therefore, let me obtain, that you will yield
To timing a poor gentleman's distresses,
In terms of hazard.
   Fitz. By no means.
   Meer. I must
Get him this money, and will—
   Fitz. Sir, I protest,
I had rather stand engaged for it myself;
Than you should leave me.
   Meer. O good sir! do you think
So coarsely of our manners, that we would,
For any need of ours, be prest to take it
Though you be pleased to offer it?
   Fitz. Why, by heaven,
I mean it.
   Meer. I can never believe less;
But we, sir, must preserve our dignity,
As you do publish yours: by your fair leave, sir. [*Offers to be gone.*
   Fitz. As I am a gentleman, if you do offer
To leave me now, or if you do refuse me,
I will not think you love me.
   Meer. Sir, I honour you,
And with just reason, for these noble notes
Of the nobility you pretend to: but, sir,
I would know why? a motive (he a stranger)

You should do this?

Ever. [*aside to Meer.*] You'll mar all with your fineness.

Fitz. Why that's all one, if 'twere, sir, but my fancy.—
But I have a business, that perhaps I would have
Brought to his office.

Meer. O sir! I have done then;
If he can be made profitable to you.

Fitz. Yes, and it shall be one of my ambitions
To have it the first business: may I not?

Ever. So you do mean to make't a perfect business.

Fitz. Nay, I'll do that, assure you; shew me once.

Meer. Sir, it concerns, the first be a perfect business,
For his own honour.

Ever. Ay, and the reputation
Too, of my place.

Fitz. Why, why do I take this course, else?
I am not altogether an ass, good gentlemen.
Wherefore should I consult you, do you think?
To make a song on't? How's your manner? tell us.

Meer. Do, satisfy him; give him the whole course.

Ever. First, by request, or otherwise, you offer
Your business to the court; wherein you crave
The judgment of the master and the assistants.

Fitz. Well, that is done now; what do you upon it?

Ever. We straight, sir, have recourse to the spring-head:
Visit the ground, and so disclose the nature;
If it will carry, or no. If we do find,
By our proportions, it is like to prove
A sullen and black business; that it be
Incorrigible and out of treaty; then
We file it, a dependence!

Fitz. So, 'tis filed:
What follows? I do love the order of these things.

Ever. We then advise the party, if he be
A man of means and havings, that forthwith
He settle his estate; if not, at least
That he pretend it: for, by that, the world
Takes notice, that it now is a dependence:
And this we call, sir, publication.

Fitz. Very sufficient: after publication, now?

Ever. Then we grant out our process, which is diverse;
Either by chartel, sir, or ore-tenus,
Wherein the challenger and challengee,
Or, with your Spaniard, your provocador
And provocado, have their several courses—

Fitz. I have enough on't: for an hundred pieces,
Yes, for two hundred, under-write me, do.
Your man will take my bond?

Meer. That he will, sure:

But these same citizens, they are such sharks!
There's an old debt of forty, I gave my word   [*Aside to Fitz.*
For one has run away to the Bermudas,
And he will hook in that, or he'll not do.

  Fitz. Why, let him.   That and the ring, and a hundred pieces,
Will all but make two hundred.

  Meer. No, no more, sir.
What ready arithmetic you have!—Do you hear?

                                         [*Aside to Gilthead.*
A pretty morning's work for you, this! do it.
You shall have twenty pound on't.

  Gilt. Twenty pieces?

  Plu. Good father, do't.

  Meer. You will hook still? well,
Shew us your ring.   You could not have done this now,
With gentleness, at first, we might have thank'd you?
But groan, and have your courtesies come from you
Like a hard stool, and stink!   A man may draw
Your teeth out easier than your money.   Come,
Were little Gilthead here, no better a nature,
I should ne'er love him, that could pull his lips off now.

                                        [*Pulls him by the lips.*
Was not thy mother a gentlewoman?

  Plu. Yes, sir.

  Meer. And went to the court at Christmas, and St. George tide,
And lent the lords' men chains?

  Plu. Of gold and pearl, sir.

  Meer. I knew thou must take after somebody,
Thou could'st not be else.   This was no shop-look.
I'll have thee captain Gilthead, and march up,
And take in Pimlico, and kill the bush
At every tavern.   Thou shalt have a wife,
If smocks will mount, boy.   [*Turns to Gilthead.*]   How now; you
     have there now
Some Bristol stone or Cornish counterfeit
You'd put upon us!

  Gilt. No, sir, I assure you:
Look on his lustre, he will speak himself!
I'll give you leave to put him in the mill:
He is no great large stone, but a true paragon,
He has all his corners, view him well.

  Meer. He's yellow.

  Gilt. Upon my faith, sir, of the right black water,
And very deep! he's set without a foil, too.
Here's one of the yellow-water, I'll sell cheap.

  Meer. And what do you value this at, thirty pound?

  Gilt. No, sir, he cost me forty ere he was set.

  Meer. Turnings, you mean?   I know your equivokes:
You are grown the better fathers of 'em o' late.

Well, where it must go 'twill be judged, and therefore
Look you't be right.   You shall have fifty pound for't,
Not a denier more.—[*To Fitz.*] And because you would
Have things dispatch'd, sir, I'll go presently,
Inquire out this lady! If you think good, sir,
Having an hundred pieces ready, you may
Part with those now, to serve my kinsman's turns,
That he may wait upon you anon the freer;
And take them, when you have seal'd, again, of Gilthead.

Fitz. I care not if I do.

Meer. And dispatch all
Together.

Fitz. There, they are just a hundred pieces;
I have told them over twice a day these two months.

                                  [*Turns them out on the table.*

Meer. Well, go and seal then, sir; make your return
As speedy as you can.

                 [*Exeunt Fitzdottrel, Gilthead, and Plutarchus.*

Ever. Come, give me.   [*They fall to sharing.*

Meer. Soft, sir.

Ever. Marry, and fair too then; I'll no delaying, sir.

Meer. But you will hear?

Ever. Yes, when I have my dividend.

Meer. There's forty pieces for you.

Ever. What is this for?

Meer. Your half: you know that Gilthead must have twenty.

Ever. And what's your ring there?   Shall I have none o' that?

Meer. O, that is to be given to a lady.

Ever. Is it so?

Meer. By that good light, it is.

Ever. Come, give me
Ten pieces more, then.

Meer. Why?

Ever. For Gilthead, sir!
Do you think I'll allow him any such share?

Meer. You must.

Ever. Must I! do you your musts, sir, I'll do mine:
You will not part with the whole, sir, will you?   Go to,
Give me ten pieces!

Meer. By what law do you this?

Ever. Even lion-law, sir, I must roar else.

Meer. Good!

Ever. You have heard how the ass made his divisions wisely?

Meer. And I am he!—I thank you.

Ever. Much good do you, sir.

Meer. I shall be rid of this tyranny one day.

Ever. Not
While you do eat, and lie about the town here,
And cozen in your bullions; and I stand

Your name of credit, and compound your business,
Adjourn your beatings every term, and make
New parties for your projects. I have now
A pretty task of it, to hold you in
With your lady Tailbush: but the toy will be
How we shall both come off!
    Meer. Leave you your doubting,
And do your portion, what's assign'd you: I
Never fail'd yet.
    Ever. With reference to your aids!—
You'll still be unthankful. Where shall I meet you, anon?
You have some feat to do alone, now, I see;
You wish me gone; well, I will find you out,
And bring you after to the audit.   [*Exit.*
    Meer. 'Slight,
There's Engine's share, too, I had forgot! this reign
Is too-too-unsupportable; I must
Quit myself of this vassalage.—

      Enter ENGINE, *followed by* WITTIPOL.

                Engine! welcome.
How goes the cry?
    Eng. Excellent well.
    Meer. Will it do?
Where's Robinson?
    Eng. Here is the gentleman, sir,
Will undertake it himself. I have acquainted him.
    Meer. Why did you so?
    Eng. Why, Robinson would have told him,
You know: and he's a pleasant wit, will hurt
Nothing you purpose. Then he's of opinion,
That Robinson might want audacity,
She being such a gallant. Now, he has been
In Spain, and knows the fashions there; and can
Discourse; and being but mirth, he says, leave much
To his care.
    Meer. But he is too tall!
    Eng. For that,
He has the bravest device (you'll love him for't)
To say, he wears cioppinos; and they do so
In Spain: and Robinson's as tall as he.
    Meer. Is he so?
    Eng. Every jot.
    Meer. Nay, I had rather
To trust a gentleman with it, of the two.
    Eng. Pray you go to him then, sir, and salute him.
    Meer. Sir, my friend Engine has acquainted you
With a strange business here.
    Wit. A merry one, sir.

The duke of drown'd-land and his dutchess?

Meer. Yes, sir.

Now that the conjurors have laid him by,
I have made bold to borrow him a while.

Wit. With purpose, yet, to put him out, I hope,
To his best use.

Meer. Yes, sir.

Wit. For that small part
That I am trusted with, put off your care:
I would not lose to do it, for the mirth
Will follow of it; and well, I have a fancy.

Meer. Sir, that will make it well.

Wit. You will report it so.
Where must I have my dressing?

Eng. At my house, sir.

Meer. You shall have caution, sir, for what he yields,
To sixpence.

Wit. You shall pardon me: I will share, sir,
In your sports only, nothing in your purchase.
But you must furnish me with compliments,
To the manner of Spain; my coach, my guarda-duennas.

Meer. Engine's your provedoré.   But, sir, I must,
Now I have entered trust with you thus far,
Secure still in your quality, acquaint you
With somewhat beyond this.   The place design'd
To be the scene for this our merry matter,
Because it must have countenance of women
To draw discourse, and offer it, is here by,
At the lady Tailbush's.

Wit. I know her, sir,
And her gentleman-usher.

Meer. Master Ambler?

Wit. Yes, sir.

Meer. Sir, it shall be no shame to me, to confess,
To you, that we poor gentlemen that want acres,
Must for our needs turn fools up, and plough ladies
Sometimes, to try what glebe they are: and this
Is no unfruitful piece.   She and I now
Are on a project for the fact, and venting
Of a new kind of fucus, paint for ladies,
To serve the kingdom: wherein she herself
Hath travailed, specially, by way of service
Unto her sex, and hopes to get the monopoly
As the reward of her invention.

Wit. What is her end in this?

Meer. Merely ambition,
Sir, to grow great, and court it with the secret,
Though she pretend some other.   For she's dealing
Already upon caution for the shares;

And master Ambler he is named examiner
For the ingredients, and the register
Of what is vented, and shall keep the office.
Now, if she break with you of this, (as I
Must make the leading thread to your acquaintance,
That, how experience gotten in your being
Abroad, will help our business,) think of some
Pretty additions, but to keep her floating;
It may be she will offer you a part:
Any strange names of—

    Wit. Sir, I have my instructions.
Is it not high time to be making ready?

    Meer. Yes, sir.

    Eng. The fool's in sight, Dottrel.

    Meer. Away then.   *[Exeunt Engine and Wittipol.*

Re-enter Fitzdottrel.

    Meer. Return'd so soon!

    Fitz. Yes, here's the ring: I have seal'd.
But there's not so much gold in all the Row, he says—
Till it come from the mint: 'tis ta'en up for the gamesters.

    Meer. There's a shop-shift! plague on 'em!

    Fitz. He does swear it.

    Meer. He'll swear and forswear too, it is his trade;
You should not have left him.

    Fitz. 'Slid, I can go back,
And beat him yet.

    Meer. No, now let him alone.

    Fitz. I was so earnest after the main business,
To have this ring gone.

    Meer. True, and it is time.
I have learn'd, sir, since you went, her ladyship eats
With the lady Tailbush, here hard by.

    Fitz. In the lane here?

    Meer. Yes; if you had a servant now of presence,
Well clothed, and of an airy, voluble tongue,
Neither too big nor little for his mouth,
That could deliver your wife's compliment
To send along withal.

    Fitz. I have one, sir,
A very handsome gentleman-like fellow,
That I do mean to make my dutchess' usher—
I entertain'd him but this morning too:
I'll call him to you. The worst of him is his name.

    Meer. She'll take no note of that, but of his message.

    Fitz. Devil!—

Enter Pug.

How like you him, sir?—Pace, go a little,
Let's see you move.

Meer. He'll serve, sir; give it him,
And let him go along with me, I'll help
To present him and it.

Fitz. Look you do, sirrah,
Discharge this well, as you expect your place.
Do you hear? go on, come off with all your honours.
I would fain see him do it.

Meer. Trust him with it.

Fitz. Remember kissing of your hand, and answering
With the French time, and flexure of your body.
I could now so instruct him——and for his words—

Meer. I'll put them in his mouth.

Fitz. O, but I have them
Of the very academies.

Meer. Sir, you'll have use for them
Anon yourself, I warrant you, after dinner,
When you are call'd.

Fitz. 'Slight, that will be just play-time.
It cannot be, I must not lose the play!

Meer. Sir, but you must, if she appoint to sit,
And she is president.

Fitz. 'Slid, it is the Devil.

Meer. An 'twere his dam too, you must now apply
Yourself, sir, to this wholly, or lose all.

Fitz. If I could but see a piece—

Meer. Sir, never think on't.

Fitz. Come but to one act, and I did not care—
But to be seen to rise and go away,
To vex the players, and to punish their poet;
Keep him in awe—

Meer. But say that he be one
Will not be aw'd, but laugh at you; how then?

Fitz. Then he shall pay for's dinner himself.

Meer. Perhaps,
He would do that twice, rather than thank you.
Come get the devil out of your head, my lord,
(I'll call you so in private still,) and take
Your lordship in your mind.　You were, sweet lord,
In talk to bring a business to the office.

Fitz. Yes.

Meer. Why should not you, sir, carry it on yourself,
Before the office be up, and shew the world
You had no need of any man's direction,
In point, sir, of sufficiency?　I speak
Against a kinsman, but as one that tenders
Your grace's good.

Fitz. I thank you; to proceed—

Meer. To publication: have your deed drawn presently,
And leave a blank to put in your feoffees,

One, two, or more, as you see cause.

   Fitz. I thank you;
Heartily, I do thank you: not a word more,
I pray you, as you love me. Let me alone.
That I could not think of this as well as he!
O, I could beat my infinite blockhead.   [*Exeunt.*

SCENE II.—*The Lane near the* Lady TAILBUSH'S *House.*

Enter MEERCRAFT, *followed by* PUG.

   Meer. Come, we must this way.

   Pug. How far is't?

   Meer. Hard by here,
Over the way. [*They cross over.*]   Now, to achieve this ring
From this same fellow, that is, to assure it,
Before he give it. Though my Spanish lady
Be a young gentleman of means, and scorn
To share, as he doth say, I do not know
How such a toy may tempt his ladyship;
And therefore I think best it be assured.   {*Aside.*

   Pug. Sir, be the ladies brave we go unto?

   Meer. O, yes.

   Pug. And shall I see them, and speak to them?

   Meer. What else?

Enter TRAINS.

Have you your false beard about you, Trains?

   Trains. Yes.

   Meer. And is this one of your double clokes?

   Trains. The best of them.

   Meer. Be ready then.   [*Exeunt.*

SCENE III.—*A Hall in* Lady TAILBUSH'S *House.*

Enter MEERCRAFT *and* PUG, *met by* PITFALL.

   Meer. Sweet Pitfall!
Come, I must buss—   [*Offers to kiss her.*

   Pit. Away.

   Meer. I'll set thee up again.
Never fear that: canst thou get ne'er a bird?
No thrushes hungry! stay till cold weather come,
I'll help thee to an ousel or a fieldfare.
Who's within, with madam?

   Pit. I'll tell you straight.   [*Exit hastily.*

   Meer. Please you stay here a while, sir, I'll go in.   [*Exit.*

   Pug. I do so long to have a little venery
While I am in this body! I would taste
Of every sin a little, if it might be,
After the manner of man.—Sweet-heart!

Re-enter PITFALL.

Pit. What would you, sir?   [*Pug runs to her.*
    Pug. Nothing but fall in to you; be your black-bird,
My pretty Pit, as the gentleman said, your throstle,
Lie tame, and taken with you; here is gold,
To buy you so much new stuffs from the shop,
As I may take the old up—

Enter TRAINS, *in his false beard and cloke.*

Trains. You must send, sir,
The gentleman the ring.
    Pug. There 'tis. [*Exit Trains.*]—Nay look,
Will you be foolish, Pit?
    Pit. This is strange rudeness.
    Pug. Dear Pit.
    Pit. I'll call, I swear.

Enter MEERCRAFT.

Meer. Where are you, sir?
Is your ring ready! Go with me.
    Pug. I sent it you.
    Meer. Me! when? by whom?
    Pug. A fellow here, e'en now,
Came for it in your name.
    Meer. I sent none, sure.
My meaning ever was, you should deliver it
Yourself; so was your master's charge, you know.

Re-enter TRAINS, *dressed as at first.*

What fellow was it, do you know him?
    Pug. Here,
But now, he had it.
    Meer. Saw you any, Trains?
    Trains. Not I.
    Pug. The gentlewoman saw him.
    Meer. Enquire.
    Pug. I was so earnest upon her, I mark'd not.
My devilish chief has put me here in flesh,
To shame me! this dull body I am in,
I perceive nothing with, I offer at nothing
That will succeed!   [*Aside.*
    Trains. Sir, she saw none, she says.
    Pug. Satan himself has ta'en a shape to abuse me;
It could not be else!   [*Aside.*
    Meer. This is above strange.
That you should be so rechless! What will you do, sir,
How will you answer this, when you are question'd?
    Pug. Run from my flesh, if I could; put off mankind.

This is such a scorn, and will be a new exercise
For my arch-duke! Woe to the several cudgels
Must suffer on this back! [*Aside.*]—Can you no succours, sir?
   Meer. Alas! the use of it is so present.
   Pug. I ask,
Sir, credit for another but till to-morrow.
   Meer. There is not so much time, sir; but, however,
The lady is a noble lady, and will,
To save a gentleman from check, be entreated
To say, she has received it.
   Pug. Do you think so?
Will she be won?
   Meer. No doubt, to such an office,
It will be a lady's bravery and her pride.
   Pug. And not be known on't after, unto him?
   Meer. That were a treachery: Upon my word,
Be confident. Return unto your master,
My lady president sits this afternoon,
Has ta'en the ring, commends her services
Unto your lady dutchess. You may say
She is a civil lady, and does give her
All her respects already: bade you tell her,
She lives but to receive her wish'd commandments,
And have the honour here to kiss her hands,
For which she'll stay this hour yet. Hasten you
Your prince, away.
   Pug. And, sir, you will take care
The excuse be perfect?
   Meer. You confess your fears
Too much.
   Pug. The shame is more.
   Meer. I'll quit you of either.   *[Exeunt.*

ACT IV

SCENE I.—*A Room in* Lady TAILBUSH's *House.*

Enter Lady TAILBUSH *and* MEERCRAFT.

   Lady T. A pox upon referring to commissioners!
I had rather hear that it were past the seals:
You courtiers move so snail-like in your business.
Would I had not begun with you!
   Meer. We must move,
Madam, in order, by degrees; not jump.
   Lady T. Why, there was sir John Moneyman could jump
A business quickly.
   Meer. True, he had great friends;
But, because some, sweet madam, can leap ditches,

We must not all shun to go over bridges.
The harder parts, I make account, are done,
Now 'tis referr'd: you are infinitely bound
Unto the ladies, they have so cried it up!

Lady T. Do they like it then?

Meer. They have sent the Spanish lady
To gratulate with you.

Lady T. I must send them thanks,
And some remembrances.

Meer. That you must, and visit them.
Where's Ambler?

Lady T. Lost, to-day, we cannot hear of him.

Meer. Not, madam!

Lady T. No, in good faith: they say he lay not
At home to-night. And here has fallen a business
Between your cousin and master Manly, has
Unquieted us all.

Meer. So I hear, madam.
Pray you, how was it?

Lady T. Troth, it but appears
Ill on your kinsman's part. You may have heard,
That Manly is a suitor to me, I doubt not.

Meer. I guess'd it, madam.

Lady T. And it seems he trusted
Your cousin to let fall some fair reports
Of him unto me.

Meer. Which he did!

Lady T. So far
From it, as he came in, and took him railing
Against him.

Meer. How! And what said Manly to him?

Lady T. Enough, I do assure you; and with that scorn
Of him and the injury, as I do wonder
How Everill bore it; but that guilt undoes
Many men's valours.

Enter MANLY.

Meer. Here comes Manly.

Man. Madam, I'll take my leave—

Lady T. You shall not go, i'faith.
I'll have you stay and see this Spanish miracle,
Of our English lady.

Man. Let me pray your ladyship,
Lay your commands on me some other time.

Lady T. Now, I protest; and I will have all pieced,
And friends again.

Man. It will be but ill-solder'd!

Lady T. You are too much affected with it.

Man. I cannot,

Madam, but think on't for the injustice.

Lady T. Sir,
His kinsman here is sorry.

Meer. Not I, madam,
I am no kin to him, we but call cousins:
And if he were, sir, I have no relation
Unto his crimes.

Man. You are not urged with them.
I can accuse, sir, none but mine own judgment;
For though it were his crime so to betray me,
I am sure, 'twas more mine own, at all to trust him:
But he therein did use but his old manners,
And savour strongly what he was before.

Lady T. Come, he will change.

Man. Faith, I must never think it;
Nor were it reason in me to expect,
That, for my sake, he should put off a nature
He suck'd in with his milk. It may be, madam,
Deceiving trust is all he has to trust to:
If so, I shall be loth, that any hope
Of mine should bate him of his means.

Lady T. You are sharp, sir:
This act may make him honest.

Man. If he were
To be made honest by an act of parliament,
I should not alter in my faith of him.

Enter Lady EITHERSIDE.

Lady T. Eitherside!
Welcome, dear Eitherside; how hast thou done, good wench?
Thou hast been a stranger: I have not seen thee this week.

Lady E. Ever your servant, madam.

Lady T. Where hast thou been?
I did so long to see thee.

Lady E. Visiting, and so tired!
I protest, madam, 'tis a monstrous trouble.

Lady T. And so it is. I swear I must to-morrow
Begin my visits, would they were over, at court:
It tortures me to think on them.

Lady E. I do hear
You have cause, madam, your suit goes on.

Lady T. Who told thee?

Lady E. One that can tell; master Eitherside.

Lady T. O, thy husband.
Yes faith, there's life in't now; it is referr'd.
If we once see it under the seals, wench, then,
Have with them for the great caroch, six horses,
And the two coachmen, with my Ambler bare,
And my three women; we will live, i'faith,

The examples of the town, and govern it:
I'll lead the fashion still.

Lady E. You do that now,
Sweet madam.

Lady T. O but then, I'll every day
Bring up some new device.   Thou and I, Eitherside,
Will first be in it, I will give it thee;
And they shall follow us.   Thou shalt, I swear,
Wear every month a new gown out of it.

Lady E. Thank you, good madam.

Lady T. Pray thee call me Tailbush,
As I thee Eitherside; I love not this madam.

Lady E. Then I protest to you, Tailbush, I am glad
Your business so succeeds.

Lady T. Thank thee, good Eitherside.

Lady E. But master Eitherside tells me, that he likes
Your other business better.

Lady T. Which?

Lady E. Of the tooth-picks.

Lady T. I never heard of it.

Lady E. Ask master Meercraft.

Meer. Madam! [*Aside to Manly.*]—He is one, in a word, I'll trust
   his malice
With any man's credit, I would have abused.

Man. Sir, if you think you do please me in this,
You are deceived.

Meer. No, but because my lady
Named him my kinsman, I would satisfy you
What I think of him; and pray you upon it
To judge me.

Man. So I do; that ill men's friendship
Is as unfaithful as themselves.

Lady T. Do you hear?
Have you a business about tooth-picks?

Meer. Yes, madam;
Did I ne'er tell it you?   I meant to have offer'd it
Your ladyship, on the perfecting the patent.

Lady T. How is it?

Meer. For serving the whole state with tooth-picks;
Somewhat an intricate business to discourse: but
I shew how much the subject is abused,
First, in that one commodity; then what diseases
And putrefactions in the gums are bred,
By those are made of adulterate and false wood;
My plot for reformation of these, follows:
To have all tooth-picks brought unto an office,
There seal'd; and such as counterfeit them, mulcted.
And last, for venting them, to have a book
Printed, to teach their use, which every child

Shall have throughout the kingdom, that can read,
And learn to pick his teeth by: which beginning
Early to practise, with some other rules,
Of never sleeping with the mouth open, chewing
Some grains of mastick, will preserve the breath
Pure and so free from taint.—

Enter TRAINS, *and whispers him.*

                    Ha! what is't, say'st thou?
Lady T. Good faith, it sounds a very pretty business!
Lady E. So master Eitherside says, madam.
Meer. The lady is come.
Lady T. Is she! good, wait upon her in. [*Exit Meercraft.*]—My
    Ambler
Was never so ill absent. Eitherside,
How do I look to-day, am I not drest
Spruntly?   *Looks in her glass.*
Lady E. Yes verily, madam.
Lady T. Pox o' madam!
Will you not leave that?
Lady E. Yes, good Tailbush.
Lady T. So!
Sounds not that better? What vile fucus is this
Thou hast got on?
Lady E. 'Tis pearl.
Lady T. Pearl! oyster-shells;
As I breathe, Eitherside, I know't. Here comes,
They say, a wonder, sirrah, has been in Spain,
Will teach us all! she's sent to me from court,
To gratulate with me: prithee let's observe her,
What faults she has, that we may laugh at them,
When she is gone.
Lady E. That we will heartily, Tailbush.

Re-enter MEERCRAFT, *introducing* WITTIPOL *dressed as a*
Spanish lady.

Lady T. O me, the very infanta of the giants!
Meer. Here is a noble lady, madam, come
From your great friends at court, to see your ladyship,
And have the honour of your acquaintance.
Lady T. Sir,
She does us honour.
Wit. Pray you, say to her ladyship,
It is the manner of Spain to embrace only,
Never to kiss. She will excuse the custom.
Lady T. Your use of it is law. Please you, sweet madam,
To take a seat.
Wit. Yes, madam, I have had
The favour, through a world of fair report,

To know your virtues, madam; and in that
Name, have desired the happiness of presenting
My service to your ladyship.
    Lady T. Your love, madam;
I must not own it else.
    Wit. Both are due, madam,
To your great undertakings.
    Lady T. Great! In troth, madam,
They are my friends, that think them any thing:
If I can do my sex, by 'em, any service,
I have my ends, madam.
    Wit. And they are noble ones,
That make a multitude beholden, madam;
The commonwealth of ladies must acknowledge from you.
    Lady E. Except some envious, madam.
    Wit. You are right in that, madam,
Of which race, I encounter'd some but lately,
Who, it seems, have studied reasons to discredit
Your business.
    Lady T. How, sweet madam!
    Wit. Nay, the parties
Will not be worth your pause——most ruinous things, madam,
That have put off all hope of being recover'd
To a degree of handsomeness.
    Lady T. But their reasons, madam,
I would fain hear.
    Wit. Some, madam, I remember.
They say that painting quite destroys the face—
    Lady E. O, that's an old one, madam.
    Wit. There are new ones too.
Corrupts the breath; hath left so little sweetness
In kissing, as 'tis now used but for fashion;
And shortly will be taken for a punishment.
Decays the fore-teeth that should guard the tongue;
And suffers that run riot everlasting!
And, which is worse, some ladies when they meet
Cannot be merry and laugh, but they do spit
In one another's faces.
    Man. I should know
This voice and face too.   *[Aside.*
    Wit. Then, they say, 'tis dangerous
To all the fall'n, yet well-disposed mad-ams,
That are industrious, and desire to earn
Their living with their sweat: for any distemper
Of heat and motion may displace the colours;
And if the paint once run about their faces,
Twenty to one they will appear so ill-favour'd
Their servants run away too, and leave the pleasure
Imperfect, and the reckoning also unpaid.

Lady E. Pox! these are poets' reasons.

Lady T. Some old lady,
That keeps a poet, has devised these scandals.

Lady E. Faith, we must have the poets banish'd, madam,
As master Eitherside says.

Meer. Master Fitzdottrel,
And his wife!

Wit. Where?

Enter Mr. *and* Mrs. FITZDOTTREL, *followed by* PUG.

Meer. [*to Wit.*] Madam, the duke of Drown'd-land,
That will be shortly.

Wit. Is this my lord?

Meer. The same.

Fitz. Your servant, madam!

Wit. [*takes Manly aside.*] How now, friend! offended,
That I have found your haunt here?

Man. No, but wondering
At your strange-fashion'd venture hither.

Wit. It is
To shew you what they are you so pursue.

Man. I think 'twill prove a med'cine against marriage,
To know their manners.

Wit. Stay, and profit then.

Meer. The lady, madam, whose prince has brought her here
To be instructed.   [*Presents Mrs. Fitzdottrel.*

Wit. Please you sit with us, lady.

Meer. That's lady-president.

Fitz. A goodly woman!
I cannot see the ring, though.

Meer. Sir, she has it.

Lady T. But, madam, these are very feeble reasons.

Wit. So I urg'd, madam, that the new complexion
Now to come forth, in name of your ladyship's fucus,
Has no ingredient—

Lady T. But I durst eat, I assure you.

Wit. So do they in Spain.

Lady T. Sweet madam, be so liberal,
To give us some of your Spanish fucuses.

Wit. They are infinite, madam.

Lady T. So I hear.

Wit. They have
Water of gourds, of radish, the white beans,
Flowers of glass, of thistles, rose-marine,
Raw honey, mustard seed, and bread dough baked,
The crums of bread, goat's-milk, and whites of eggs
Camphire, and lily-roots, the fat of swans,
Marrow of veal, white pigeons, and pine-kernels
The seeds of nettles, purseline, and hare's-gall:

Lemons, thin-skinn'd—

    Lady E. How her ladyship has studied
All excellent things!

    Wit. But ordinary, madam:
No, the true rarities are the alvagada
And argentata of queen Isabella.

    Lady T. Ay, what are their ingredients, gentle madam?

    Wit. Your allum scagliola, or pol di pedra;
And zuccarino; turpentine of Abezzo,
Wash'd in nine waters: soda di levante,
Or your fern ashes; benjamin di gotta:
Grasso di serpe; porceletto marino;
Oils of lentisco; zucche mugia; make
The admirable varnish for the face,
Gives the right lustre; but two drops rubb'd on
With a piece of scarlet, makes a lady of sixty
Look as sixteen. But above all, the water
Of the white hen, of the lady Estifania's.

    Lady T. O, ay, that same, good madam, I have heard of:
How is it done?

    Wit. Madam, you take your hen,
Plume it, and skin it, cleanse it o' the inwards;
Then chop it, bones and all; add to four ounces
Of carravicins, pipitas, soap of Cyprus,
Make the decoction, strain it; then distil it,
And keep it in your gallipot well gliddered:
Three drops preserves from wrinkles, warts, spots, moles,
Blemish, or sun-burnings; and keeps the skin
In decimo sexto, ever bright and smooth,
As any looking-glass; and indeed is call'd
The Virgin's-Milk for the face, oglio reale;
A ceruse, neither cold nor heat will hurt;
And mix'd with oil of myrrh, and the red gilliflower,
Call'd cataputia, and flowers of rovistico,
Makes the best muta or dye of the whole world.

    Lady T. Dear madam, will you let us be familiar?

    Wit. Your ladyship's servant.

    Meer. How do you like her?

    Fitz. Admirable!
But yet I cannot see the ring.

    Pug. Sir!

    Meer. I must
Deliver it, or mar all: this fool's so jealous!   [*Aside.*
Madam—[*whispers Wit.*] Sir, wear this ring, and pray you take
        knowledge,
'Twas sent you by his wife; and give her thanks.
Do not you dwindle, sir, bear up.   [*Aside to Pug.*

    Pug. I thank you, sir.

    Lady T. But for the manner of Spain. Sweet madam, let us

Be bold, now we are in: are all the ladies
There in the fashion?
    Wit. None but grandees, madam,
Of the clasp'd train, which may be worn at length too,
Or thus, upon my arm.
    Lady T. And do they wear
Cioppinos all?
    Wit. If they be drest in punto, madam.
    Lady T. Gilt as those are, madam?
    Wit. Of goldsmith's work, madam,
And set with diamonds; and their Spanish pumps,
Of perfumed leather.
    Lady T. I should think it hard
To go in them, madam.
    Wit. At the first it is, madam.
    Lady T. Do you never fall in them?
    Wit. Never.
    Lady E. I swear I should,
Six times an hour.
    Lady T. But you have men at hand still,
To help you, if you fall?
    Wit. Only one, madam,
The guarda-duennas, such a little old man
As this.   *[Points to Trains.*
    Lady E. Alas, he can do nothing, this!
    Wit. I'll tell you, madam, I saw in the court of Spain once,
A lady fall in the king's sight, along;
And there she lay, flat spread, as an umbrella,
Her hoop here crack'd; no man durst reach a hand
To help her, till the guarda-duennas came,
Who is the person only allow'd to touch
A lady there, and he but by this finger.
    Lady E. Have they no servants, madam, there, nor friends?
    Wit. An escudero, or so, madam, that waits
Upon them in another coach, at distance;
And when they walk or dance, holds by a handkerchief,
Never presumes to touch them.
    Lady E. This is scurvy,
And a forced gravity! I do not like it:
I like our own much better.
    Lady T. 'Tis more French,
And courtly, ours.
    Lady E. And tastes more liberty.
We may have our dozen of visitors at once
Make love to us.
    Lady T. And before our husbands.
    Lady E. Husband!
As I am honest, Tailbush, I do think,
If nobody should love me but my poor husband,

I should e'en hang myself.

Lady T. Fortune forbid, wench,

So fair a neck should have so foul a necklace!

Lady E. 'Tis true, as I am handsome.

Wit. I received, lady,

A token from you, which I would not be

Rude to refuse, being your first remembrance.

Fitz. O, I am satisfied now!   [*Aside to Meer.*

Meer. Do you see it, sir?

Wit. But since you come to know me nearer, lady,

I'll beg the honour you will wear it for me,

It must be so.   [*Gives the ring to Mrs. Fitzdottrel.*

Mrs. Fitz. Sure I have heard this tongue.   [*Aside.*

Meer. What do you mean, sir?   [*Aside to Wit.*

Wit. Would you have me mercenary?

We'll recompense it anon in somewhat else.

[*Exeunt Meer. and Trains.*

Fitz. I do not love to be gull'd, though in a toy;

Wife, do you hear? [*takes Mrs. Fitz. aside.*] you are come into
          the school, wife,

Where you may learn, I do perceive it, any thing.

How to be fine, or fair, or great, or proud,

Or what you will, indeed, wife; here 'tis taught:

And I am glad on't, that you may not say,

Another day, when honours come upon you,

You wanted means.   I have done my parts; been,

To-day, at fifty pound charge; first, for a ring,

To get you enter'd; then left my new play,

To wait upon you here, to see't confirm'd,

That I may say, both to mine eyes and ears,

Senses, you are my witness, she hath enjoy'd

All helps that could be had for love, or money—

Mrs. Fitz. To make a fool of her.

Fitz. Wife, that's your malice,

The wickedness of your nature, to interpret

Your husband's kindness thus: but I'll not leave

Still to do good, for your depraved affections;

Intend it; bend this stubborn will; be great.

Lady T. Good madam, whom do they use in messages?

Wit. They commonly use their slaves, madam.

Lady T. And does your ladyship

Think that so good, madam?

Wit. No indeed, madam; I

Therein prefer the fashion of England far,

Of your young delicate page, or discreet usher.

Fitz. And I go with your ladyship in opinion,

Directly for your gentleman usher:

There's not a finer officer goes on ground.

Wit. If he be made and broken to his place once.

Fitz. Nay, so I presuppose him.

Wit. And they are fitter
Managers too, sir; but I would have them call'd
Our escuderos.

Fitz. Good.

Wit. Say I should send
To your ladyship, who, I presume, has gather'd
All the dear secrets, to know how to make
Pastillos of the dutchess of Braganza,
Coquettas, almoiavanas, mantecadas,
Alcoreas, mustaccioli; or say it were
The peladore of Isabella, or balls
Against the itch, or aqua nanfa, or oil
Of jessamine for gloves, of the marquesse Muja;
Or for the head and hair; why, these are offices—

Fitz. Fit for a gentleman, not a slave.

Wit. They only
Might ask for your piveti, Spanish coal,
To burn, and sweeten a room: but the arcana
Of ladies' cabinets—

Fitz. Should be elsewhere trusted.
You are much about the truth.—Sweet honour'd ladies,
Let me fall in with you: I have my female wit,
As well as my male; and I do know what suits
A lady of spirit, or a woman of fashion.

Wit. And you would have your wife such?

Fitz. Yes, madam, airy,
Light; not to plain dishonesty, I mean:
But somewhat o' this side.

Wit. I take you, sir:—
He has reason, ladies. I'll not give this rush
For any lady that cannot be honest
Within a thread.

Lady T. Yes, madam, and yet venture
As far for the other, in her fame—

Wit. As can be:
Coach it to Pimlico, dance the saraband,
Hear and talk bawdy, laugh as loud as a larum,
Squeak, spring, do any thing.

Lady E. In young company, madam.

Lady T. Or afore gallants. If they be brave, or lords,
A woman is engaged.

Fitz. I say so, ladies.
It is civility to deny us nothing.

Pug. You talk of a university! why, hell is
A grammar-school to this! [*Aside.*

Lady E. But then
She must not lose a look on stuffs or cloth, madam.

Lady T. Nor no coarse fellow.

Wit. She must be guided, madam,
By the clothes he wears, and company he is in,
Whom to salute, how far—
    Fitz. I have told her this;
And how that bawdry too, upon the point,
Is in itself as civil a discourse—
    Wit. As any other affair of flesh whatever.
    Fitz. But she will ne'er be capable, she is not
So much as coming, madam; I know not how
She loses all her opportunities,
With hoping to be forced. I have entertain'd
A gentleman, a younger brother, here,
Whom I would fain breed up her escudero,
Against some expectations that I have,
And she'll not countenance him.
    Wit. What's his name?
    Fitz. Devil of Derbyshire.
    Lady E. Bless us from him!
    Lady T. Devil!
Call him De-vile, sweet madam.
    Mrs. Fitz. What you please, ladies.
    Lady T. De-vile's a prettier name.
    Lady E. And sounds, methinks,
As it came in with the conqueror—
    Man. Over smocks!
What things they are! that nature should be at leisure
Ever to make them! My wooing is at an end.
                 [*Aside, and exit with indignation.*
    Wit. What can he do?
    Lady E. Let's hear him.
    Lady T. Can he manage?
    Fitz. Please you to try him, ladies.—Stand forth, Devil.
    Pug. Was all this but the preface to my torment? [*Aside.*
    Fitz. Come, let their ladyships see your honours.
    Lady E. O,
He makes a wicked leg.
    Lady T. As ever I saw.
    Wit. Fit for a devil.
    Lady T. Good madam, call him De-vile.
    Wit. De-vile, what property is there most required,
In your conceit now, in the escudero?
    Fitz. Why do you not speak?
    Pug. A settled discreet pace, madam.
    Wit. I think, a barren head, sir, mountain-like,
To be exposed to the cruelty of weathers—
    Fitz. Ay, for his valley is beneath the waist, madam,
And to be fruitful there, it is sufficient.
Dullness upon you! could not you hit this?   [*Strikes him.*
    Pug. Good sir—

Wit. He then had had no barren head:
You draw him too much in troth, sir.
 Fitz. I must walk
With the French stick, like an old verger, for you.
 Pug. O chief, call me to hell again, and free me!   [*Aside.*
 Fitz. Do you murmur now?
 Pug. Not I, sir.
 Wit. What do you take,
Master De-vile, the height of your employment,
In the true perfect escudero?
 Fitz. When!
What do you answer?
 Pug. To be able, madam,
First to enquire, then report the working
Of any lady's physic, in sweet phrase.
 Wit. Yes, that's an act of elegance and importance:
But what above?
 Fitz. O, that I had a goad for him.
 Pug. To find out a good corn-cutter.
 Lady T. Out on him!
 Lady E. Most barbarous!
 Fitz. Why did you do this now?
Of purpose to discredit me, you damn'd devil!
 Pug. Sure, if I be not yet, I shall be.—All
My days in hell were holidays, to this!   *Aside.*
 Lady T. 'Tis labour lost, madam.
 Lady E. He is a dull fellow,
Of no capacity.
 Lady T. Of no discourse,
O, if my Ambler had been here!
 Lady E. Ay, madam,
You talk of a man; where is there such another?
 Wit. Master De-vile, put case one of my ladies here
Had a fine brach, and would employ you forth
To treat 'bout a convenient match for her;
What would you observe?
 Pug. The colour and the size, madam.
 Wit. And nothing else?
 Fitz. The moon, you calf, the moon!
 Wit. Ay, and the sign.
 Lady T. Yes, and receipts for proneness.
 Wit. Then when the puppies came, what would you do?
 Pug. Get their nativities cast.
 Wit. This is well. What more?
 Pug. Consult the almanac-man which would be least,
Which cleanliest.
 Wit. And which silent'st? This is well, madam.
And while she were with puppy?
 Pug. Walk her out,

And air her every morning.
   Wit. Very good!
And be industrious to kill her fleas?
   Pug. Yes.
   Wit. He will make a pretty proficient.
   Pug. Who,
Coming from hell, could look for such a catechising?
The Devil is an Ass, I do acknowledge it.   *[Aside.*
   Fitz. The top of woman! all her sex in abstract!
I love her, to each syllable falls from her.
                    [Aside, and looking at Wittipol.
   Lady T. Good madam, give me leave to go aside with him,
And try him a little.
   Wit. Do, and I'll withdraw, madam,
With this fair lady, read to her the while.
   Lady T. Come, sir.
   Pug. Dear chief, relieve me, or I perish!   *[Aside.*
   Wit. Lady, we'll follow.—You are not jealous, sir?
   Fitz. O, madam, you shall see.—Stay, wife;—behold,
I give her up here absolutely to you;
She is your own, do with her what you will:
Melt, cast, and form her as you shall think good;
Set any stamp on: I'll receive her from you
As a new thing, by your own standard.   *[Exit.*
   Wit. Well, sir!
   [Exeunt Wittipol with Mrs. Fitz., and Tailbush and Eitherside
     with Pug.

     SCENE II.—*Another Room in the same.*

     Enter MEERCRAFT *and* FITZDOTTREL.

   Meer. But what have you done in your dependence since?
   Fitz. O, it goes on; I met your cousin, the master—
   Meer. You did not acquaint him, sir?
   Fitz. Faith but I did, sir,
And, upon better thought, not without reason.
He being chief officer might have taken it ill else,
As a contempt against his place, and that
In time, sir, have drawn on another dependence:
No, I did find him in good terms, and ready
To do me any service.
   Meer. So he said to you!
But, sir, you do not know him.
   Fitz. Why, I presumed,
Because this bus'ness of my wife's required me,
I could not have done better: and he told
Me, that he would go presently to your counsel,
A knight here in the lane—
   Meer. Yes, justice Eitherside.

Fitz. And get the feoffment drawn, with a letter of attorney,
For livery and seisin.

Meer. That I know's the course.
But, sir, you mean not to make him feoffee?

Fitz. Nay, that I'll pause on.

Enter PITFALL.

Meer. How now, little Pitfall!

Pit. Your cousin, master Everill, would come in—
But he would know if master Manly were here.

Meer. No, tell him; if he were, I have made his peace.—

                   [*Exit Pitfall.*

He's one, sir, has no state, and a man knows not
How such a trust may tempt him.

Fitz. I conceive you.

Enter EVERILL *and* PLUTARCHUS.

Ever. Sir, this same deed is done here.

Meer. Pretty Plutarchus!
Art thou come with it? and has sir Paul view'd it?

Plu. His hand is to the draught.

Meer. Will you step in, sir,
And read it?

Fitz. Yes.

Ever. I pray you, a word with you.   [*Aside to Fitz.*
Sir Paul Eitherside will'd me give you caution
Whom you did make feoffee; for 'tis the trust
Of your whole state; and though my cousin here
Be a worthy gentleman, yet his valour has
At the tall board been question'd; and we hold
Any man so impeach'd of doubtful honesty.
I will not justify this, but give it you
To make your profit of it; if you utter it,
I can forswear it.

Fitz. I believe you, and thank you, sir.   [*Exeunt.*

SCENE III.—*Another Room in the same.*

Enter WITTIPOL *and* Mrs. FITZDOTTREL.

Wit. Be not afraid, sweet lady; you are trusted
To love, not violence, here: I am no ravisher,
But one whom you by your fair trust again
May of a servant make a most true friend.

MANLY *enters behind.*

Mrs. Fitz. And such a one I need, but not this way.
Sir, I confess me to you, the mere manner
Of your attempting me this morning, took me;
And I did hold my invention, and my manners,

Were both engaged to give it a requital,
But not unto your ends: my hope was then,
Though interrupted ere it could be utter'd,
That whom I found the master of such language,
That brain and spirit for such an enterprise,
Could not, but if those succours were demanded
To a right use, employ them virtuously,
And make that profit of his noble parts
Which they would yield.   Sir, you have now the ground
To exercise them in: I am a woman
That cannot speak more wretchedness of myself,
Than you can read; match'd to a mass of folly,
That every day makes haste to his own ruin;
The wealthy portion that I brought him, spent,
And, through my friends' neglect, no jointure made me.
My fortunes standing in this precipice,
'Tis counsel that I want, and honest aids;
And in this name I need you for a friend;
Never in any other; for his ill
Must not make me, sir, worse.
    Manly. [*comes forward.*] O, friend, forsake not
The brave occasion virtue offers you
To keep you innocent: I have fear'd for both,
And watch'd you, to prevent the ill I fear'd.
But since the weaker side hath so assured me,
Let not the stronger fall by his own vice,
Or be the less a friend, 'cause virtue needs him.
    Wit. Virtue shall never ask my succours twice;
Most friend, most man, your counsels are commands.—
Lady, I can love goodness in you, more
Than I did beauty; and do here intitle
Your virtue to the power upon a life
You shall engage in any fruitful service,
Even to forfeit.

Enter Meercraft.

    Meer. Madam;——Do you hear, sir?   [*Aside to Wittipol.*
We have another leg strain'd for this Dottrel.
He has a quarrel to carry, and has caused
A deed of feoffment of his whole estate
To be drawn yonder: he has't within; and you
Only he means to make feoffee.   He is fallen
So desperately enamour'd on you, and talks
Most like a madman: you did never hear
A phrenetic so in love with his own favour!
Now you do know, 'tis of no validity
In your name, as you stand: therefore advise him
To put in me!—

Enter FITZDOTTREL, EVERILL, *and* PLUTARCHUS.

He's come here.   You shall share, sir.

Fitz. Madam, I have a suit to you; and aforehand
I do bespeak you; you must not deny me,
I will be granted.

Wit. Sir, I must know it, though.

Fitz. No, lady, you must not know it: yet you must too,
For the trust of it, and the fame indeed,
Which else were lost me.   I would use your name,
But in a feoffment, make my whole estate
Over unto you: a trifle, a thing of nothing,
Some eighteen hundred.

Wit. Alas! I understand not
Those things, sir; I am a woman, and most loth
To embark myself—

Fitz. You will not slight me, madam?

Wit. Nor you'll not quarrel me?

Fitz. No, sweet madam.   I have
Already a dependence; for which cause
I do this: let me put you in, dear madam,
I may be fairly kill'd.

Wit. You have your friends, sir,
About you here for choice.

Ever. She tells you right, sir.

Fitz. Death, if she do, what do I care for that?
Say, I would have her tell me wrong!

Wit. Why, sir,
If for the trust you'll let me have the honour
To name you one.

Fitz. Nay, you do me the honour, madam.
Who is't?

Wit. This gentleman.   [*Pointing to Manly.*

Fitz. O no, sweet madam.
He's friend to him with whom I have the dependence.

Wit. Who might he be?

Fitz. One Wittipol, do you know him?

Wit. Alas, sir, he! a toy: this gentleman
A friend to him! no more than I am, sir.

Fitz. But will your ladyship undertake that, madam?

Wit. Yes, and what else, for him, you will engage me.

Fitz. What is his name?

Wit. His name is Eustace Manly.

Fitz. Whence does he write himself?

Wit. Of Middlesex, esquire.

Fitz. Say nothing, madam.—Clerk, come hither;
                                        [*To Plutarchus.*
Write Eustace Manly, squire of Middlesex.

Meer. What have you done, sir?   [*Aside to Wit.*

Wit. Named a gentleman,
That I'll be answerable for to you, sir:
Had I named you, it might have been suspected;
This way 'tis safe.
    Fitz. Come, gentlemen, your hands
For witness.
    Man. What is this?
    Ever. You have made election
Of a most worthy gentleman!
    Man. Would one of worth
Had spoke it! but now whence it comes, it is
Rather a shame unto me than a praise.
    Ever. Sir, I will give you any satisfaction.
    Man. Be silent then: Falsehood commends not truth.
    Plu. You do deliver this, sir, as your deed,
To the use of master Manly?
    Fitz. Yes: and sir—   [*To Manly.*
When did you see young Wittipol? I am ready
For process now: sir, this is publication.
He shall hear from me; he would needs be courting
My wife, sir.
    Man. Yes; so witnesseth his cloke there.
    Fitz. Nay, good sir.—Madam, you did undertake—
    Wit. What?
    Fitz. That he was not Wittipol's friend.
    Wit. I hear,
Sir, no confession of it.
    Fitz. O, she knows not;
Now I remember.—Madam, this young Wittipol
Would have debauch'd my wife, and made me cuckold
Thorough a casement; he did fly her home
To mine own window; but, I think, I sous'd him,
And ravish'd her away out of his pounces.
I have sworn to have him by the ears: I fear
The toy will not do me right.
    Wit. No! that were pity!
What right do you ask, sir? here he is will do't you.
                            [*Discovers himself.*

    Fitz. Ha! W.ttipol!
    Wit. Ay, sir; no more lady now,
Nor Spaniard.
    Man. No indeed, 'tis Wittipol.
    Fitz. Am I the thing I fear'd?
    Wit. A cuckold! No, sir;
But you were late in possibility,
I'll tell you so much.
    Man. But your wife's too virtuous.
    Wit. We'll see her, sir, at home, and leave you here,
To be made duke of Shoreditch with a project.

Fitz. Thieves! ravishers!

Wit. Cry but another note, sir,
I'll mar the tune of your pipe.

Fitz. Give me my deed then.

Wit. Neither: that shall be kept for your wife's good,
Who will know better how to use it.

Fitz. Ha!
To feast you with my land?

Wit. Sir, be you quiet,
Or I shall gag you ere I go; consult
Your master of dependences, how to make this
A second business, you have time, sir.

                [Baffles him, and exit with Manly.

Fitz. Oh!
What will the ghost of my wise grandfather,
My learned father, with my worshipful mother,
Think of me now, that left me in this world
In state to be their heir? that am become
A cuckold, and an ass, and my wife's ward;
Likely to lose my land, have my throat cut;
All by her practice!

Meer. Sir, we are all abused.

Fitz. And be so still! who hinders you, I pray you?
Let me alone, I would enjoy myself,
And be the duke of Drown'd-land you have made me.

Meer. Sir, we must play an after-game of this.

Fitz. But I am not in case to be a gamester,
I tell you once again—

Meer. You must be ruled,
And take some counsel.

Fitz. Sir, I do hate counsel,
As I do hate my wife, my wicked wife!

Meer. But we may think how to recover all,
If you will act.

Fitz. I will not think, nor act,
Nor yet recover; do not talk to me:
I'll run out of my wits, rather than hear;
I will be what I am, Fabian Fitzdottrel,
Though all the world say nay to't.   *[Exit.*

Meer. Let us follow him.   *[Exeunt.*

ACT V

SCENE I.—*A Room in* Tailbush's *House.*

Enter Ambler *and* Pitfall.

Amb. But has my lady miss'd me?
Pit. Beyond telling.
Here has been that infinity of strangers!
And then she would have had you, to have sampled you
With one within, that they are now a teaching,
And does pretend to your rank.
 Amb. Good fellow Pitfall,
Tell master Meercraft I entreat a word with him. [*Exit Pitfall.*
This most unlucky accident will go near
To be the loss of my place, I am in doubt.

Enter Meercraft.

Meer. With me!—What say you, master Ambler?
Amb. Sir,
I would beseech your worship, stand between
Me and my lady's displeasure, for my absence.
 Meer. O, is that all! I warrant you.
 Amb. I would tell you, sir,
But how it happen'd.
 Meer. Brief, good master Ambler,
Put yourself to your rack; for I have task
Of more importance.
 Amb. Sir, you'll laugh at me:
But (so is truth) a very friend of mine,
Finding by conference with me, that I lived
Too chaste for my complexion, and indeed.
Too honest for my place, sir, did advise me,
If I did love myself,—as that I do,
I must confess—
 Meer. Spare your parenthesis.
 Amb. To give my body a little evacuation—
 Meer. Well, and you went to a whore?
 Amb. No, sir, I durst not
(For fear it might arrive at somebody's ear
It should not) trust myself to a common house;
      [*Tells this with extraordinary speed.*
But got the gentlewoman to go with me,
And carry her bedding to a conduit-head,
Hard by the place toward Tyburn, which they call
My Lord Mayor's banqueting-house. Now, sir, this morning
Was execution; and I never dreamt on't,
Till I heard the noise of the people, and the horses;

And neither I, nor the poor gentlewoman,
Durst stir, till all was done and past: so that,
In the interim, we fell asleep again.   [*He flags.*

   Meer. Nay, if you fall from your gallop, I am gone, sir.

   Amb. But when I waked, to put on my clothes, a suit
I made new for the action, it was gone,
And all my money, with my purse, my seals,
My hard-wax, and my table-books, my studies,
And a fine new device I had to carry
My pen and ink, my civet, and my tooth-picks,
All under one.   But that which grieved me, was
The gentlewoman's shoes, (with a pair of roses,
And garters, I had given her for the business,)
So as that made us stay till it was dark:
For I was fain to lend her mine, and walk
In a rug, by her, barefoot, to St. Giles's.

   Meer. A kind of Irish penance! Is this all, sir?

   Amb. To satisfy my lady.

   Meer. I will promise you, sir.

   Amb. I have told the true disaster.

   Meer. I cannot stay with you,
Sir, to condole; but gratulate your return.   [*Exit.*

   Amb. An honest gentleman; but he's never at leisure
To be himself, he has such tides of business.   [*Exit.*

SCENE II.—*Another Room in the same.*

Enter PUG.

   Pug. O call me home again, dear chief, and put me
To yoking foxes, milking of he-goats,
Pounding of water in a mortar, laving
The sea dry with a nut-shell, gathering all
The leaves are fallen this autumn, drawing farts
Out of dead bodies, making ropes of sand,
Catching the winds together in a net,
Mustering of ants, and numbering atoms; all
That hell and you thought exquisite torments, rather
Than stay me here a thought more: I would sooner
Keep fleas within a circle, and be accomptant
A thousand year, which of them, and how far,
Out-leap'd the other, than endure a minute
Such as I have within.   There is no hell
To a lady of fashion; all your tortures there
Are pastimes to it! 'Twould be a refreshing
For me, to be in the fire again, from hence—

Enter AMBLER, *and surveys him.*

   Amb. This is my suit, and those the shoes and roses! [*Aside.*

   Pug. They have such impertinent vexations,

A general council of devils could not hit—
Ha! [*sees Ambler.*] this is he I took asleep with his wench,
And borrow'd his clothes.   What might I do to balk him?   [*Aside.*

Amb. Do you hear, sir?
Pug. Answer him, but not to the purpose.   [*Aside.*
Amb. What is your name, I pray you, sir?
Pug. Is't so late, sir?
Amb. I ask not of the time, but of your name, sir.
Pug. I thank you, sir: yes, it does hold, sir, certain.
Amb. Hold, sir! what holds?   I must both hold, and talk to you,
About these clothes.
Pug. A very pretty lace;
But the tailor cozen'd me.
Amb. No, I am cozen'd
By you; robb'd.
Pug. Why, when you please, sir; I am,
For three-penny gleek, your man.
Amb. Pox o' your gleek,
And three-pence! give me an answer.
Pug. Sir,
My master is the best at it.
Amb. Your master!
Who is your master?
Pug. Let it be Friday night.
Amb. What should be then?
Pug. Your best song's *Tom o' Bethlem.*
Amb. I think you are he.—Does he mock me, trow, from purpose,
Or do not I speak to him what I mean?—
Good sir, your name.
Pug. Only a couple of cocks, sir;
If we can get a widgeon, 'tis in season.
Amb. He hopes to make one of these sciptics of me,
(I think I name them right,) and does not fly me;
I wonder at that: 'tis a strange confidence!
I'll prove another way, to draw his answer.   [*Exeunt severally.*

SCENE III.—*A Room in* FITZDOTTREL'S *House.*

Enter MEERCRAFT, FITZDOTTREL, *and* EVERILL.

Meer. It is the easiest thing, sir, to be done,
As plain as fizzling: roll but with your eyes,
And foam at the mouth.   A little castle-soap
Will do't, to rub your lips; and then a nut-shell,
With tow, and touch-wood in it, to spit fire.
Did you ne'er read, sir, little Darrel's tricks
With the boy of Burton, and the seven in Lancashire,
Somers at Nottingham? all these do teach it.
And we'll give out, sir, that your wife has bewitch'd you.
Ever. And practis'd with those two as sorcerers.

Meer. And gave you potions, by which means you were
Not *compos mentis,* when you made your feoffment.
There's no recovery of your state but this;
This, sir, will sting.

Ever. And move in a court of equity.

Meer. For it is more than manifest, that this was
A plot of your wife's, to get your land.

Fitz. I think it.

Ever. Sir, it appears.

Meer. Nay, and my cousin has known
These gallants in these shapes—

Ever. To have done strange things, sir,
One as the lady, the other as the squire,

Meer. How a man's honesty may be fool'd!   I thought him
A very lady.

Fitz. So did I; renounce me else.

Meer. But this way, sir, you'll be revenged at height.

Ever. Upon them all.

Meer. Yes, faith, and since your wife
Has run the way of woman thus, e'en give her—

Fitz. Lost, by this hand, to me; dead to all joys
Of her dear Dottrel; I shall never pity her,
That could [not] pity herself.

Meer. Princely resolv'd, sir,
And like yourself still, *in potentia.*

Enter GILTHEAD, PLUTARCHUS, SLEDGE, *and* Serjeants.

Meer. Gilthead! what news?

Fitz. O, sir, my hundred pieces!
Let me have them yet.

Gilt. Yes, sir.—Officers,
Arrest him.

Fitz. Me!

1 *Serj.* I arrest you.

Sledge. Keep the peace,
I charge you, gentlemen.

Fitz. Arrest me! why?

Gilt. For better security, sir.   My son Plutarchus
Assures me, you are not worth a groat.

Plu. Pardon me, father,
I said his worship had no foot of land left:
And that I'll justify, for I writ the deed.

Fitz. Have you these tricks in the city?

Gilt. Yes, and more:
Arrest this gallant too, here, at my suit.   [*Points to Meercraft.*

Sledge. Ay, and at mine: he owes me for his lodging
Two year and a quarter.

Meer. Why, master Gilthead,—landlord,
Thou art not mad, though thou art constable,
Puft up with the pride of the place.   Do you hear, sirs,

Have I deserv'd this from you two, for all
My pains at court, to get you each a patent?
   Gilt. For what?
   Meer. Upon my project of the forks.
   Sledge. Forks! what be they?
   Meer. The laudable use of forks,
Brought into custom here, as they are in Italy,
To the sparing of napkins: that, that should have made
Your bellows go at the forge, as his at the furnace.
I have procured it, have the signet for it,
Dealt with the linen-drapers on my private,
Because I fear'd they were the likeliest ever
To stir against, to cross it: for 'twill be
A mighty saver of linen through the kingdom,
As that is one o' my grounds, and to spare washing.
Now, on you two had I laid all the profits:
Gilthead to have the making of all those
Of gold and silver, for the better personages;
And you, of those of steel for the common sort:
And both by patent. I had brought you your seals in,
But now you have prevented me, and I thank you.
   Sledge. Sir, I will bail you, at mine own apperil.
   Meer. Nay, choose.
   Plu. Do you so too, good father.
   Gilt. I like the fashion of the project well,
The forks! it may be a lucky one! and is
Not intricate, as one would say, but fit for
Plain heads, as ours, to deal in.—Do you hear,
Officers, we discharge you.   *[Exeunt Serjeants.*
   Meer. Why, this shews
A little good-nature in you, I confess;
But do not tempt your friends thus.—Little Gilthead,
Advise your sire, great Gilthead, from these courses:
And, here, to trouble a great man in reversion,
For a matter of fifty, in a false alarm!
Away, it shews not well. Let him get the pieces
And bring them: you'll hear more else.
   Plu. Father.   *[Exeunt Gilt. and Plu.*

Enter AMBLER, *dragging in* PUG.

   Amb. O, master Sledge, are you here? I have been to seek you.
You are the constable, they say. Here's one
That I do charge with felony, for the suit
He wears, sir.
   Meer. Who? master Fitzdottrel's man!
Ware what you do, master Ambler.

Enter FITZDOTTREL.

   Amb. Sir, these clothes

I'll swear are mine; and the shoes the gentlewoman's
I told you of: and have him afore a justice
I will.

Pug. My master, sir, will pass his word for me.

Amb. O, can you speak to purpose now?

Fitz. Not I,
If you be such a one, sir, I will leave you
To your godfathers in law: let twelve men work.

Pug. Do you hear, sir, pray, in private.   [*Takes him aside.*

Fitz. Well, what say you?
Brief, for I have no time to lose.

Pug. Truth is, sir,
I am the very Devil, and had leave
To take this body I am in to serve you;
Which was a cut-purse's, and hang'd this morning;
And it is likewise true, I stole this suit
To clothe me with; but, sir, let me not go
To prison for it. I have hitherto
Lost time, done nothing; shewn, indeed, no part
Of my devil's nature: now, I will so help
Your malice, 'gainst these parties; so advance
The business that you have in hand, of witchcraft,
And your possession, as myself were in you;
Teach you such tricks to make your belly swell,
And your eyes turn, to foam, to stare, to gnash
Your teeth together, and to beat yourself,
Laugh loud, and feign six voices—

Fitz. Out, you rogue!
You most infernal counterfeit wretch, avaunt!
Do you think to gull me with your Æsop's fables?
Here, take him to you, I have no part in him.

Pug. Sir—

Fitz. Away! I do disclaim, I will not hear you.
                       [*Exit Sledge with Pug.*

Meer. What said he to you, sir?

Fitz. Like a lying rascal,
Told me he was the Devil.

Meer. How! a good jest.

Fitz. And that he would teach me such fine devil's tricks
For our new resolution.

Ever. O, pox on him!
'Twas excellent wisely done, sir, not to trust him.

Meer. Why, if he were the Devil, we shall not need him,
If you'll be ruled. Go throw yourself on a bed, sir,
And feign you ill. We'll not be seen with you
Till after, that you have a fit; and all
Confirm'd within. Keep you with the two ladies,   [*To Everill.*
And persuade them. I will to justice Eitherside,
And possess him with all. Trains shall seek out Engine,

And they two fill the town with't; every cable
Is to be veer'd.   We must employ out all
Our emissaries now.   Sir, I will send you
Bladders and bellows.   Sir, be confident,
'Tis no hard thing t' outdo the Devil in;
A boy of thirteen year old made him an ass,
But t'other day.
 Fitz. Well, I'll begin to practise,
And scape the imputation of being cuckold,
By mine own act.
 Meer. You are right.   *[Exit Fitz.*
 Ever. Come, you have put
Yourself to a simple coil here, and your friends,
By dealing with new agents, in new plots.
 Meer. No more of that, sweet cousin.
 Ever. What had you
To do with this same Wittipol, for a lady?
 Meer. Question not that; 'tis done.
 Ever. You had some strain
Bove *e-la?*
 Meer. I had indeed.
 Ever. And now you crack for't.
 Meer. Do not upbraid me.
 Ever. Come, you must be told on't;
You are so covetous still to embrace
More than you can, that you lose all.
 Meer. 'Tis right:
What would you more than guilty?   Now, your succours. *[Exeunt.*

SCENE IV.—*A Cell in Newgate.*

Enter SHACKLES, *with* PUG *in chains.*

 Shack. Here you are lodged, sir; you must send your garnish,
If you'll be private.
 Pug. There it is, sir: leave me.   *[Exit Shackles.*
To Newgate brought! how is the name of devil
Discredited in me! what a lost fiend
Shall I be on return! my chief will roar
In triumph, now, that I have been on earth
A day, and done no noted thing, but brought
That body back here, was hang'd out this morning.
Well! would it once were midnight, that I knew
My utmost.   I think Time be drunk and sleeps,
He is so still, and moves not!   I do glory
Now in my torment.   Neither can I expect it,
I have it with my fact.
Enter INIQUITY.
 Iniq. Child of hell, be thou merry:
Put a look on as round, boy, and red as a cherry.

Cast care at thy posterns, and firk in thy fetters:
They are ornaments, baby, have graced thy betters:
Look upon me, and hearken. Our chief doth salute thee,
And lest the cold iron should chance to confute thee,
He hath sent thee grant-parole by me, to stay longer
A month here on earth, against cold, child, or hunger.

    Pug. How! longer here a month?
    Iniq. Yes, boy, till the session,
That so thou mayst have a triumphal egression.
    Pug. In a cart to be hang'd!
    Iniq. No, child, in a car,
The chariot of triumph, which most of them are.
And in the mean time, to be greasy, and bouzy,
And nasty, and filthy, and ragged, and lousy,
With damn me! renounce me! and all the fine phrases,
That bring unto Tyburn the plentiful gazes.
    Pug. He is a devil, and may be our chief,
The great superior devil, for his malice!
Arch-devil! I acknowledge him. He knew
What I would suffer, when he tied me up thus
In a rogue's body; and he has, I thank him,
His tyrannous pleasure on me, to confine me
To the unlucky carcase of a cut-purse,
Wherein I could do nothing.

Enter SATAN.

    Sat. Impudent fiend,
Stop thy lewd mouth. Dost thou not shame and tremble
To lay thine own dull, damn'd defects upon
An innocent case there? Why, thou heavy slave!
The spirit that did possess that flesh before,
Put more true life in a finger and a thumb,
Than thou in the whole mass; yet thou rebell'st
And murmur'st! What one proffer hast thou made,
Wicked enough, this day, that might be call'd
Worthy thine own, much less the name that sent thee?
First, thou didst help thyself into a beating,
Promptly, and with't endangered'st too thy tongue:
A devil, and could not keep a body entire
One day! that, for our credit: and to vindicate it,
Hinder'dst, for aught thou know'st, a deed of darkness:
Which was an act of that egregious folly,
As no one, toward the devil, could have thought on.
This for your acting.—But, for suffering!—why
Thou hast been cheated on, with a false beard,
And a turn'd cloke: faith, would your predecessor
The cut-purse, think you, have been so? Out upon thee!
The hurt thou hast done, to let men know their strength,
And that they are able to outdo a devil

Put in a body, will for ever be
A scar upon our name?   Whom hast thou dealt with,
Woman or man, this day, but have outgone thee
Some way, and most have proved the better fiends?
Yet you would be employ'd! yes; hell shall make you
Provincial of the cheaters, or bawd-ledger,
For this side of the town! no doubt, you'll render
A rare account of things!   Bane of your itch,
And scratching for employment!   I'll have brimstone
To allay it sure, and fire to singe your nails off.—
But that I would not such a damn'd dishonour
Stick on our state, as that the devil were hang'd,
And could not save a body, that he took
From Tyburn, but it must come thither again;
You should e'en ride.   But up, away with him—
                    [*Iniquity takes him on his back.*

Iniq. Mount, dearling of darkness, my shoulders are broad:
He that carries the fiend is sure of his load.
The devil was wont to carry away the Evil,
But now the Evil outcarries the devil.   [*Exeunt.*
                    [*A loud explosion, smoke, etc.*

Enter SHACKLES, *and the* Under-keepers, *affrighted.*

Shack. O me!
1 *Keep.* What's this?
2 *Keep.* A piece of Justice-hall
Is broken down.
3 *Keep.* Fough! what a steam of brimstone
Is here!
4 *Keep.* The prisoner's dead, came in but now.
Shack. Ha! where?
4 *Keep.* Look here.
1 *Keep.* 'Slid, I should know his countenance:
It is Gill Cut-purse, was hang'd out this morning.
Shack. 'Tis he!
2 *Keep.* The devil sure has a hand in this!
3 *Keep.* What shall we do?
Shack. Carry the news of it
Unto the sheriffs.
1 *Keep.* And to the justices.
4 *Keep.* This is strange.
3 *Keep.* And savours of the devil strongly.
2 *Keep.* I have the sulphur of hell-coal in my nose.
1 *Keep.* Fough!
Shack. Carry him in.
1 *Keep.* Away.
2 *Keep.* How rank it is!   [*Exeunt with the body.*

SCENE V.—*A Room in* Fitzdottrel's *House.*

Fitzdottrel *discovered in bed;* Lady Eitherside, Tailbush, Ambler, Trains, *and* Pitfall, *standing by him.*

Enter Sir Paul Eitherside, Meercraft, *and* Everill.

Sir P. Eith. This was the notablest conspiracy
That e'er I heard of.

Meer. Sir, they had given him potions,
That did enamour him on the counterfeit lady—

Ever. Just to the time o' delivery of the deed.

Meer. And then the witchcraft 'gan to appear, for straight
He fell into his fit.

Ever. Of rage at first, sir,
Which since has so increased.

Lady T. Good sir Paul, see him,
And punish the impostors.

Sir P. Eith. Therefore I come, madam.

Lady E. Let master Eitherside alone, madam.

Sir P. Eith. Do you hear?
Call in the constable, I will have him by;
He's the king's officer: and some citizens
Of credit; I'll discharge my conscience clearly.

Meer. Yes, sir, and send for his wife.

Ever. And the two sorcerers,
By any means.   [*Exit Ambler.*

Lady T. I thought one a true lady,
I should be sworn: so did you, Eitherside.

Lady E. Yes, by that light, would I might ne'er stir else, Tailbush.

Lady T. And the other, a civil gentleman.

Ever. But, madam,
You know what I told your ladyship.

Lady T. I now see it.
I was providing of a banquet for them,
After I had done instructing of the fellow,
De-vile, the gentleman's man.

Meer. Who is found a thief, madam,
And to have robb'd your usher, master Ambler,
This morning.

Lady T. How!

Meer. I'll tell you more anon.

Fitz. Give me some garlic, garlic, garlic, garlic!
                                    [He begins his fit.

Meer. Hark, the poor gentleman, how he is tormented!

Fitz. My wife is a whore, I'll kiss her no more: and why?
May'st not thou be a cuckold as well as I?
Ha, ha, ha, ha, ha, ha, ha!

Sir P. Eith. That is the devil speaks and laughs in him.

Meer. Do you think so, sir?

Sir P. Eith. I discharge my conscience.
Fitz. And is not the devil good company ? yes, wis.
Ever. How he changes, sir, his voice!
Fitz. And a cuckold is,
Wherever he put his head, with a wannion,
If his horns be forth, the devil's companion.
Look, look, look, else !
Meer. How he foams!
Ever. And swells!
Lady T. O me, what's that there rises in his belly?
Lady E. A strange thing: hold it down.
Tra. Pit. We cannot, madam.
Sir P. Eith. 'Tis too apparent this!
Fitz. Wittipol, Wittipol !

Enter WITTIPOL, MANLY, *and* Mrs. FITZDOTTREL.

Wit. How now! what play have we here?
Man. What fine new matters?
Wit. The cockscomb and the coverlet.
Meer. O strange impudence,
That these should come to face their sin!
Ever. And outface
Justice! they are the parties, sir.
Sir P. Eith. Say, nothing.
Meer. Did you mark, sir, upon their coming in,
How he call'd Wittipol?
Ever. And never saw them.
Sir P. Eith. I warrant you did I: let them play awhile.
Fitz. Buz, buz, buz, buz !
Lady T. 'Las, poor gentleman,
How he is tortured!
Mrs. Fitz. [*goes to him.*] Fie, master Fitzdottrel,
What do you mean to counterfeit thus?
Fitz. O, O !
She comes with a needle, and thrusts it in,
She pulls out that, and she puts in a pin,
And now, and now, I do not know how, nor where,
But she pricks me here, and she pricks me there: Oh, oh !
Sir P. Eith. Woman, forbear.
Wit. What, sir?
Sir P. Eith. A practice foul
For one so fair.
Wit. Hath this, then, credit with you?
Man. Do you believe in't?
Sir P. Eith. Gentlemen, I'll discharge
My conscience: 'tis a clear conspiracy,
A dark and devilish practice! I detest it.
Wit. The justice sure will prove the merrier man.
Man. This is most strange, sir.

Sir P. Eith. Come not to confront
Authority with impudence; I tell you,
I do detest it.—

Re-enter AMBLER, *with* SLEDGE *and* GILTHEAD.

Here comes the king's constable,
And with him a right worshipful commoner,
My good friend, master Gilthead.   I am glad
I can, before such witnesses, profess
My conscience, and my detestation of it.
Horrible! most unnatural! abominable!
    Ever. You do not tumble enough.
    Meer. Wallow, gnash.   [*They whisper him.*
    Lady T. O, how he is vexed!
    Sir P. Eith. 'Tis too manifest.
    Ever. Give him more soap to foam with. [*To Meer.*] Now lie still.
    Meer. And act a little.
    Lady T. What does he now, sir?
    Sir P. Eith. Shew
The taking of tobacco, with which the devil
Is so delighted.
    Fitz. Hum!
    Sir P. Eith. And calls for hum.
You takers of strong waters and tobacco,
Mark this.
    Fitz. Yellow, yellow, yellow, yellow!
    Sir P. Eith. That's starch! the devil's idol of that colour.
He ratifies it with clapping of his hands;
The proofs are pregnant.
    Gilt. How the devil can act!
    Sir P. Eith. He is the master of players, master Gilthead,
And poets too: you heard him talk in rhyme,
I had forgot to observe it to you, erewhile!
    Lady T. See, he spits fire!
    Sir P. Eith. O no, he plays at figgum;
The devil is the author of wicked figgum.
    Man. Why speak you not unto him?
    Wit. If I had
All innocence of man to be endanger'd,
And he could save or ruin it, I'd not breathe
A syllable in request, to such a fool
He makes himself.
    Fitz. O they whisper, whisper, whisper,
We shall have more of devils a score,
To come to dinner, in me the sinner.
    Lady E. Alas, poor gentleman!
    Sir P. Eith. Put them asunder;
Keep them one from the other.
    Man. Are you phrenetic, sir?

Or what grave dotage moves you to take part
With so much villainy? we are not afraid
Either of law or trial; let us be
Examined what our ends were, what the means
To work by, and possibility of those means:
Do not conclude against us ere you hear us.

Sir P. Eith. I will not hear you, yet I will conclude
Out of the circumstances.

Man. Will you so, sir?

Sir P. Eith. Yes, they are palpable.

Man. Not as your folly.

Sir P. Eith. I will discharge my conscience, and do all,
To the meridian of justice.

Gilt. You do well, sir.

*Fitz. Provide me to eat, three or four dishes o' good meat,
I'll feast them and their trains, a justice head and brains
Shall be the first.—*

Sir P. Eith. The devil loves not justice,
There you may see.

*Fitz. A spare rib of my wife,
And a whore's purtenance; a Gilthead whole.*

Sir P. Eith. Be not you troubled, sir, the devil speaks it.

Fitz. Yes, wis, knight, shite, Poul, joul, owl, foul, troul, boul!

Sir P. Eith. Crambo! another of the devil's games.

Meer. Speak, sir, some Greek, if you can. [*Aside to Fitz.*] Is not
the justice
A solemn gamester?

Ever. Peace.

Fitz. Οἱ μοι, κακοδαίμων,
Καὶ τρισκακοδαίμων, καὶ τετράκις, καὶ πεντάκις,
Καὶ δωδεκάκις καὶ μυριάκις.

Sir P. Eith. He curses
In Greek, I think.

Ever. Your Spanish, that I taught you.   [*Aside to Fitz.*

Fitz. Quebremos el ojo de burlas.

Ever. How!—your rest—
Let's break his neck in jest, the devil says.

Fitz. Di gratia, signor mio, se havete denari fatamene parte.

Meer. What! would the devil borrow money?

Fitz. Ouy, ouy, monsieur, un pauvre diable, diabletin.

Sir P. Eith. It is the devil, by his several languages.

Enter SHACKLES, *with the things found on the body of the* Cut-purse.

Shack. Where's sir Paul Eitherside?

Sir P. Eith. Here; what's the matter?

Shack. O, such an accident fallen out at Newgate, sir:
A great piece of the prison is rent down!
The devil has been there, sir, in the body
Of the young cut-purse, was hang'd out this morning,

But in new clothes, sir; every one of us know him.
These things were found in his pocket.
   Amb. Those are mine, sir.
   Shack. I think he was committed on your charge, sir,
For a new felony.
   Amb. Yes.
   Shack. He's gone, sir, now
And left us the dead body; but withal, sir,
Such an infernal stink and steam behind,
You cannot see St. Pulchre's steeple yet:
They smell't as far as Ware, as the wind lies,
By this time, sure.
   Fitz. [*starts up.*] Is this upon your credit, friend?
   Shack. Sir, you may see, and satisfy yourself.
   Fitz. Nay then, 'tis time to leave off counterfeiting.—
Sir, I am not bewitch'd, nor have a devil,
No more than you; I do defy him, I,
And did abuse you: these two gentlemen
Put me upon it.   (I have faith against him.)
They taught me all my tricks.   I will tell truth,
And shame the fiend.   See here, sir, are my bellows,
And my false belly, and my mouse, and all
That should have come forth.
   Man. Sir, are you not ashamed
Now of your solemn, serious vanity?
   Sir P. Eith. I will make honourable amends to truth.
   Fitz. And so will I.   But these are cozeners still,
And have my land, as plotters, with my wife;
Who, though she be not a witch, is worse, a whore.
   Man. Sir, you belie her: she is chaste and virtuous,
And we are honest.   I do know no glory
A man should hope, by venting his own follies;
But you'll still be an ass in spite of providence.
Please you go in, sir, and hear truths, then judge 'em,
And make amends for your late rashness: when
You shall but hear the pains, and care was taken
To save this fool from ruin, his Grace of Drown'd-land—
   Fitz. My land is drown'd indeed—
   Sir P. Eith. Peace.
   Man. And how much
His modest and too worthy wife hath suffer'd
By misconstruction from him, you will blush,
First, for your own belief, more for his actions.
His land is his; and never by my friend,
Or by myself, meant to another use,
But for her succours, who hath equal right
If any other had worse counsels in it,
(I know I speak to those can apprehend me)
Let them repent them, and be not detected.—

It is not manly to take joy or pride
In human errors: we do all ill things;
They do them worst that love them, and dwell there,
Till the plague comes. The few that have the seeds
Of goodness left, will sooner make their way
To a true life, by shame, than punishment.

                     [*He comes forward for the Epilogue.*

Thus the projector here is overthrown;
But I have now a project of mine own,
If it may pass, that no man would invite
The poet from us, to sup forth to-night,
If the play please. If it displeasant be,
We do presume that no man will, nor we.   [Exeunt.

THE STAPLE OF NEWS

DRAMATIS PERSONÆ

PENNYBOY, *the Son, the Heir and Suitor.*
PENNYBOY, *the Father, the Canter.*
PENNYBOY, *Richer, the Uncle, the Usurer.*
CYMBAL, *Master of the Staple, and Prime Jeerer.*
FITTON, *Emissary Court, and Jeerer.*
ALMANAC, *Doctor in Physic, and Jeerer.*
SHUNFIELD, *Sea Captain, and Jeerer.*
MADRIGAL, *Poetaster, and Jeerer.*
PICKLOCK, *Man o' Law, and Emissary Westminster.*
PIEDMANTLE, *Pursuivant at Arms, and Heraldet.*
REGISTER, *of the Staple, or Office.*
NATHANIEL, *First Clerk of the Office.*
THOMAS, *Barber, Second Clerk of the Office.*
BROKER, *Secretary, and Gentleman-Usher to* PECUNIA.

LICKFINGER, *Master - Cook, and Parcel-Poet.*
FASHIONER, *the Tailor of the times.*
LEATHERLEG, *Shoemaker.*

Linener.
Haberdasher.
Spurrier.
Customers, *Male and Female.*
Porter.
Block *and* Lollard, *two Dogs.*
BUZ, AMBLER, *Grooms ;* Fiddlers, Singing-Boy, Attendants, *etc.*
INTERMEAN *or* CHORUS.
Gossips—MIRTH, TATTLE, EXPECTATION, *and* CENSURE.

PECUNIA, *Infanta of the Mines.*
MORTGAGE, *her Nurse.*
STATUTE, *First Woman.*
BAND, *Second Woman.*
WAX (Rose), *Chambermaid.*

SCENE,—LONDON

THE INDUCTION.

THE STAGE.

Enter PROLOGUE.

Pro. For your own sakes, not his—

Enter Gossip MIRTH, *Gossip* TATTLE, *Gossip* EXPECTATION, *and Gossip* CENSURE, *four Gentlewomen, lady-like attired.*

Mirth. *Come, gossip, be not ashamed. The play is* THE STAPLE OF NEWS, *and you are the mistress and lady of Tattle,—let's have your opinion of it.—Do you hear, gentleman ? what are you, gentleman-usher to the play ? Pray you help us to some stools here.*

Pro. *Where ? on the stage, ladies !*

Mirth. *Yes, on the stage; we are persons of quality, I assure you, and women of fashion, and come to see and to be seen. My gossip Tattle here, and gossip Expectation, and my gossip Censure, and I am Mirth, the daughter of Christmas, and spirit of Shrovetide. They say, It's merry when gossips meet; I hope your play will be a merry one.*

347

Pro. Or you will make it such, ladies. Bring a form here. [A bench is brought in.] But what will the noblemen think, or the grave wits here, to see you seated on the bench thus ?

Mirth. Why, what should they think, but that they had mothers as we had; and those mothers had gossips (if their children were christened) as we are; and such as had a longing to see plays, and sit upon them, as we do, and arraign both them and their poets ?

Pro. O, is that your purpose ! Why, mistress Mirth and madam Tattle, enjoy your delights freely.

Tat. Look your News be new and fresh, master Prologue, and untainted; I shall find them else, if they be stale or fly-blown, quickly.

Pro. We ask no favour from you; only we would entreat of madam Expectation—

Expect. What, master Prologue ?

Pro. That your ladyship would expect no more than you understand.

Expect. Sir, I can expect enough.

Pro. I fear, too much, lady; and teach others to do the like.

Expect. I can do that too, if I have cause.

Pro. Cry you mercy, you never did wrong, but with just cause. What's this lady ?

Mirth. Curiosity, my lady Censure.

Pro. O, Curiosity ! you come to see who wears the new suit to-day; whose clothes are best penn'd, whatever the part be; which actor has the best leg and foot; what king plays without cuffs, and his queen without gloves; who rides post in stockings, and dances in boots.

Cen. Yes, and which amorous prince makes love in drink, or does over-act prodigiously in beaten satin, and having got the trick on't, will be monstrous still, in despite of counsel.

Book-holder. [within.] Mend your lights, gentlemen.—Master Prologue, begin.

Enter the Tire-men to mend the lights.

Tat. Ah me !

Expect. Who's that ?

Pro. Nay, start not, ladies; these carry no fireworks to fright you, but a torch in their hands, to give light to the business. The truth is, there are a set of gamesters within, in travail of a thing called a play, and would fain be deliver'd of it: and they have entreated me to be their man midwife, the prologue; for they are like to have a hard labour on't.

Tat. Then the poet has abused himself, like an ass as he is.

Mirth. No, his actors will abuse him enough, or I am deceived. Yonder he is within (I was in the tiring-house awhile to see the actors drest) rolling himself up and down like a tun in the midst of them, and purges, never did vessel of wort or wine work so ! his sweating put me in mind of a good Shroving-dish (and I believe would be taken up for a service of state somewhere, an't were known), a stewed poet ! he doth sit like an unbraced drum, with one of his heads beaten out; for that you must note, a poet hath two heads, as a drum has; one for making,

the other repeating! and his repeating head is all to pieces; they may
gather it up in the tiring-house; for he hath torn the book in a poetical
fury, and put himself to silence in dead sack, which, were there no
other vexation, were sufficient to make him the most miserable emblem
of patience.

Cen. *The Prologue, peace.*

PROLOGUE.

(FOR THE STAGE.)

For your own sakes, not his, he bad me say,
Would you were come to hear, not see a play.
Though we his actors, must provide for those
Who are our guests here, in the way of shows,
The maker hath not so; he'd have you wise,
Much rather by your ears, than by your eyes;
And prays you'll not prejudge his play for ill,
Because you mark it not, and sit not still;
But have a longing to salute, or talk
With such a female, and from her to walk
With your discourse, to what is done, and where,
How, and by whom, in all the town, but here.
Alas! what is it to his scene, to know
How many coaches in Hyde-park did shew
Last spring, what fare to-day at Medley's was,
If Dunstan or the Phœnix best wine has?
They are things—but yet the stage might stand as well,
If it did neither hear these things, nor tell.
Great noble wits, be good unto yourselves,
And make a difference 'twixt poetic elves,
And poets: all that dabble in the ink,
And defile quills, are not those few can think,
Conceive, express, and steer the souls of men,
As with a rudder, round thus, with their pen.
He must be one that can instruct your youth,
And keep your acme in the state of truth,
Must enterprise this work: mark but his ways,
What flight he makes, how new: and then he says
If that not like you, that he sends to-night,
'Tis you have left to judge, not he to write.

PROLOGUE.

(FOR THE COURT.)

A work not smelling of the lamp, to-night,
But fitted for your Majesty's disport,
And writ to the meridian of your court,
We bring; and hope it may produce delight,

The rather being offered as a rite,
To scholars, that can judge, and fair report
The sense they hear, above the vulgar sort
Of nut-crackers, that only come for sight.
Wherein although our title, sir, be News,
We yet adventure here to tell you none,
But shew you common follies, and so known,
That though they are not truths, the innocent Muse,
Hath made so like, as phant'sy could them state,
Or poetry, without scandal, imitate.

ACT I

SCENE I.—*The Lodgings of* PENNYBOY jun.

Enter PENNYBOY jun., *and* LEATHERLEG *with a new pair of boots.*

P. jun. [*Leath. pulls on his boots.*] Gramercy, Leatherleg: get me the spurrier,
And thou hast fitted me.

Leath. I'll do it presently.   [*Exit.*

P. jun. [*walks up and down in his gown, waistcoat, and trowses, expecting his tailor.*] Look to me, wit, and look to my wit, land,
That is, look on me, and with all thine eyes,
Male, female, yea, hermaphroditic eyes,
And those bring all your helps and perspicils,
To see me at best advantage, and augment
My form as I come forth; for I do feel
I will be one worth looking after shortly;
Now, by and by, that's shortly,—[*draws forth his watch, and sets it on the table.*] It strikes one, two,
Three, four, five, six.   Enough, enough, dear watch,
Thy pulse hath beat enough.   Now sleep and rest;
Would thou couldst make the time to do so too:
I'll wind thee up no more.   The hour is come
So long expected! there, there, drop my wardship,
                            [*Throws off his gown.*
My pupillage and vassalage together.—
And, Liberty, come throw thyself about me,
In a rich suit, cloke, hat, and band, for now
I'll sue out no man's livery, but mine own;
I stand on my own feet, so much a year,
Right round and sound, the lord of mine own ground.
And (to rhyme to it) threescore thousand pound!
Not come? not yet?—[*Goes to the door and looks.*]   Tailor, thou art a vermin,
Worse than the same thou prosecut'st, and prick'st
In subtle seam—Go to, I say no more—

Thus to retard my longings, on the day
I do write man, to beat thee! One and twenty
Since the clock struck, complete! and thou wilt feel it,
Thou foolish animal!—I could pity him,
An I were not heartily angry with him now,
For this one piece of folly he bears about him,
To dare to tempt the fury of an heir
T' above two thousand a year, yet hope his custom!
Well, master Fashioner, there's some must break—
A head, for this your breaking.—

Enter FASHIONER.

                           Are you come, sir?
   Fash. God give your worship joy!
   P. jun. What! of your staying,
And leaving me to stalk here in my trowses,
Like a tame her'nsew for you?
   Fash. I but waited
Below, till the clock struck.
   P. jun. Why, if you had come
Before a quarter, would it so have hurt you,
In reputation, to have waited here?
   Fash. No, but your worship might have pleaded nonage,
If you had got them on, ere I could make
Just affidavit of the time.
   P. jun. That jest
Has gain'd thy pardon, thou hadst lived condemn'd
To thine own hell else, never to have wrought
Stitch more for me, or any Pennyboy,
I could have hinder'd thee: but now thou art mine.
For one and twenty years, or for three lives,
Choose which thou wilt, I'll make thee a copyholder,
And thy first bill unquestion'd. Help me on.
   Fash. Presently, sir: [*says his suit.*] I am bound unto your
      worship.
   P. jun. Thou shalt be, when I have seal'd thee a lease of my
      custom.
   Fash. Your worship's barber is without.
   P. jun. Who? Tom!—
Come in, Tom.

Enter THOMAS, *Barber.*

                 Set thy things upon the board,
And spread thy cloths, lay all forth in *procinctu*,
And tell's what news?
   Tho. O sir, a STAPLE OF NEWS!
Or the New Staple, which you please.
   P. jun. What's that?
   Fash. An office, sir, a brave young office set up:

I had forgot to tell your worship.
 P. jun. For what?
 Tho. To enter all the News, sir, of the time.
 Fash. And vent it as occasion serves: a place
Of huge commerce it will be!
 P. jun. Pray thee, peace;
I cannot abide a talking tailor: let Tom
(He is a barber) by his place relate it.
What is't, an office, Tom?
 Tho. Newly erected
Here in the house, almost on the same floor,
Where all the news of all sorts shall be brought,
And there be examined, and then register'd,
And so be issued under the seal of the office,
As Staple News; no other news be current.
 P. jun. 'Fore me, thou speak'st of a brave business, Tom.
 Fash. Nay, if you knew the brain that hatch'd it, sir—
 P. jun. I know thee well enough: give him a loaf, Tom;
Quiet his mouth, that oven will be venting else.
Proceed—
 Tho. He tells you true, sir; master Cymbal
Is master of the office, he projected it,
He lies here, in the house; and the great rooms
He has taken for the office, and set up
His desks and classes, tables and his shelves,
 Fash. He is my customer, and a wit, sir, too.
But he has brave wits under him—
 Tho. Yes, four emissaries.
 P. jun. Emissaries? stay, there's a fine new word, Tom?
Pray God it signify any thing! what are emissaries?
 Tho. Men employ'd outward, that are sent abroad
To fetch in the commodity.
 Fash. From all regions
Where the best news are made.
 Tho. Or vented forth.
 Fash. By way of exchange, or trade.
 P. jun. Nay, thou wilt speak—
 Fash. My share, sir, there's enough for both.
 P. jun. Go on then,
Speak all thou canst: methinks the ordinaries
Should help them much.
 Fash. Sir, they have ordinaries,
And extraordinaries, as many changes,
And variations, as there are points in the compass.
 Tho. But the four cardinal quarters.
 P. jun. Ay those, Tom—
 Tho. The Court, sir, Paul's, Exchange, and Westminster-hall.
 P. jun. Who is the chief? which hath precedency?
 Tho. The governor of the Staple, master Cymbal,

He is the chief; and after him the emissaries:
First emissary Court, one master Fitton,
He is a jeerer too.

    P. jun. What's that?

    Fash. A wit.

    Tho. Or half a wit, some of them are half-wits,
Two to a wit, there are a set of them.
Then master Ambler, emissary Paul's,
A fine-paced gentleman, as you shall see walk
The middle aisle: and then my froy Hans Buz,
A Dutchman; he is emissary Exchange.

    Fash. I had thought master Burst, the merchant, had had it.

    Tho. No,
He has a rupture, he has sprung a leak.
Emissary Westminster's undisposed of yet;
Then the examiner, register, and two clerks,
They manage all at home, and sort, and file,
And seal the news, and issue them.

    P. jun. Tom, dear Tom,
What may my means do for thee? ask and have it,
I'd fain be doing some good: it is my birthday,
And I would do it betimes, I feel a grudging
Of bounty, and I would not long lie fallow.
I pray thee think and speak, or wish for something.

    Tho. I would I had but one of the clerks' places
In this News-office.

    P. jun. Thou shalt have it, Tom,
If silver or gold will fetch it; what's the rate?
At what is it set in the market?

    Tho. Fifty pound, sir.

    P. jun. An 'twere a hundred, Tom, thou shalt not want it.

    Fash. O noble master!   [*Leaps and embraces him.*

    P. jun. How now, Æsop's ass!
Because I play with Tom, must I needs run
Into your rude embraces? stand you still, sir;
Clowns' fawnings are a horse's salutations.—
How dost thou like my suit, Tom?

    Tho. Master Fashioner
Has hit your measures, sir, he has moulded you,
And made you, as they say.

    Fash. No, no, not I,
I am an *ass,* old *Æsop's ass.*

    P. jun. Nay, Fashioner,
I can do thee a good turn too; be not musty,
Though thou hast moulded me, as little Tom says:
—I think thou hast put me in mouldy pockets.
                      [*Draws out his pockets.*

    Fash. As good,
Right Spanish perfume, the lady Estifania's;—

They cost twelve pound a pair.

    P. jun. Thy bill will say so.
I pray thee tell me, Fashioner, what authors
Thou read'st to help thy invention: Italian prints?
Or arras hangings? they are tailors' libraries.

    Fash. I scorn such helps.

    P. jun. O! though thou art a silkworm,
And deal'st in satins and velvets, and rich plushes,
Thou canst not spin all forms out of thyself;
They are quite other things: I think this suit
Has made me wittier than I was.

    Fash. Believe it, sir,
That clothes do much upon the wit, as weather
Does on the brain; and thence [sir] comes your proverb,
The tailor makes the man: I speak by experience
Of my own customers. I have had gallants,
Both court and country, would have fool'd you up
In a new suit, with the best wits in being,
And kept their speed as long as their clothes lasted
Handsome and neat; but then as they grew out
At the elbows again, or had a stain or spot,
They have sunk most wretchedly.

    P. jun. What thou report'st,
Is but the common calamity, and seen daily;
And therefore you've another answering proverb,
A broken sleeve keeps the arm back.

    Fash. 'Tis true, sir.
And thence we say, that such a one plays at *peep-arm.*

    P. jun. Do you so? it is wittily said. I wonder, gentlemen
And men of means will not maintain themselves
Fresher in wit, I mean in clothes, to the highest:
For he that's out of clothes is out of fashion,
And out of fashion is out of countenance,
And out of countenance is out of wit.
Is not rogue haberdasher come?

    Enter Haberdasher, Linener, *and* Hatter *and* Shoemaker.

    Hab. Yes, here, sir,
I have been without this half hour.

    P. jun. Give me my hat.
Put on my girdle, rascal: fits my ruff well?

    Lin. In print.

    P. jun. Slave!

    Lin. See yourself.

    P. jun. Is this same hat
Of the block-passant? Do not answer me,
I cannot stay for an answer. I do feel
The powers of one and twenty, like a tide,
Flow in upon me, and perceive an heir

Can conjure up all spirits in all circles.
Rogue! rascal! slave! give tradesmen their true names,
And they appear to him presently.
    Lin. For profit.
    P. jun. Come, cast my cloke about me, I'll go see
This office, Tom, and be trimm'd afterwards.
I'll put thee in possession, my prime work!

Enter Spurrier.

Ods so, my spurrier! put them on, boy, quickly;
I had like to have lost my spurs with too much speed.

Enter Pennyboy *Canter, in a patched and ragged cloke, singing.*

    P. Can. Good morning to my joy ! my jolly Pennyboy !
      The lord, and the prince of plenty !
    I come to see what riches, thou bearest in thy breeches,
      The first of thy one and twenty.
    What, do thy pockets jingle ? or shall we need to mingle
      Our strength both of foot and of horses !
    These fellows look so eager, as if they would beleaguer
      An heir in the midst of his forces !
    I hope they be no serjeants, that hang upon thy margents—
      This rogue has the joul of a jailor !
    P. jun. [answers in tune.] *O founder, no such matter, my spurrier,*
      and my hatter,
My linen-man, and my tailor.
Thou should'st have been brought in too, shoemaker,
If the time had been longer, and Tom Barber.
How dost thou like my company, old Canter?
Do I not muster a brave troop, all bill-men?
Present your arms before my founder here,
This is my Founder, this same learned Canter!
He brought me the first news of my father's death.
I thank him, and ever since I call him founder.
Worship him, boys; I'll read only the sums,
And pass them straight.
    Tho. Now ale—
    Rest. And strong ale bless him.
    P. jun. Ods so, some ale and sugar for my founder!
Good bills, sufficient bills, these bills may pass.
[*Puts them in his pockets.*
    P. Can. I do not like these paper-squibs, good master.
They may undo your store, I mean, of credit,
And fire your arsenal, if case you do not
In time make good those outer-works, your pockets,
And take a garrison in of some two hundred,
To beat those pioneers off, that carry a mine
Would blow you up, at last. Secure your casamates.
Here, master Picklock, sir, your man of law,

And learn'd attorney, has sent you a bag of munition.

P. jun. [*takes the bag.*] What is't?

P. Can. Three hundred pieces.

P. jun. I'll dispatch them.

P. Can. Do; I would have your strengths lined, and perfumed
With gold, as well as amber.

P. jun. God-a-mercy,
Come, *ad solvendum*, boys! there, there, and there,
I look on nothing but *totalis*. [*Pays all their bills.*

P. Can. See!
The difference 'twixt the covetous and the prodigal!
The covetous man never has money, and
The prodigal will have none shortly! [*Aside.*

P. jun. Ha,
What says my founder? [*They make legs to him.*] I thank you, I
thank you, sirs.

All. God bless your worship, and your worship's Canter!
[*Exeunt Shoemaker, Linener, Haber., and Hatter.*

P. Can. I say 'tis nobly done, to cherish shop-keepers,
And pay their bills, without examining thus.

P. jun. Alas! they have had a pitiful hard time on't,
A long vacation from their cozening.
Poor rascals! I do it out of charity:
I would advance their trade again, and have them
Haste to be rich, swear and forswear wealthily.
What do you stay for, sirrah? [*To the Spurrier.*

Spur. To my box, sir.

P. jun. Your box! why, there's an angel; if my spurs
Be not right Rippon—

Spur. Give me never a penny
If I strike not thorough your bounty with the rowels. [*Exit.*

P. jun. Dost thou want any money, founder?

P. Can. Who, sir, I?
Did I not tell you I was bred in the mines,
Under sir Bevis Bullion?

P. jun. That is true,
I quite forgot, you mine-men want no money,
Your streets are pav'd with't: there the molten silver
Runs out like cream on cakes of gold.

P. Can. And rubies
Do grow like strawberries.

P. jun. 'Twere brave being there!—
Come, Tom, we'll go to the office now.

P. Can. What office?

P. jun. News-office, the New Staple; thou shalt go too;
'Tis here in the house, on the same floor, Tom says:
Come, founder, let us trade in ale and nutmegs. [*Exeunt.*

SCENE II.—*Another part of the same.   An outer Room*
of the Office.

Enter Register *and* NATHANIEL.

Reg. What, are those desks fit now? Set forth the table,
The carpet and the chair; where are the news
That were examined last? have you filed them up?
  Nath. Not yet, I had no time.
  Reg. Are those news registered
That emissary Buz sent in last night,
Of Spinola and his eggs?
  Nath. Yes, sir, and filed.
  Reg. What are you now upon?
  Nath. That our new emissary
Westminster gave us, of the golden heir.
  Reg. Dispatch; that's news indeed, and of importance.—

Enter a Countrywoman.

What would you have, good woman?
  Wom. I would have, sir,
A groatsworth of any news, I care not what,
To carry down this Saturday to our vicar.
  Reg. O! you are a butter-woman; ask Nathaniel,
The clerk there.
  Nath. Sir, I tell her she must stay
Till emissary Exchange, or Paul's send in,
And then I'll fit her.
  Reg. Do, good woman, have patience;
It is not now, as when the captain lived.
  Nath. You'll blast the reputation of the office,
Now in the bud, if you dispatch these groats
So soon: let them attend, in the name of policy.

Enter CYMBAL *and* FITTON, *introducing* PENNYBOY jun.

  P. jun. In troth they are dainty rooms; what place is this?
  Cym. This is the outer room, where my clerks sit,
And keep their sides, the register in the midst;
The examiner, he sits private there, within;
And here I have my several rolls and files
Of news by the alphabet, and all put up
Under their heads.
  P. jun. But those too subdivided?
  Cym. Into authentical, and apocryphal—
  Fit. Or news of doubtful credit, as barbers' news—
  Cym. And tailors' news, porters' and watermen's news.
  Fit. Whereto, besides the Coranti, and Gazetti—
  Cym. I have the news of the season—

Fit. As vacation-news,
Term-news, and Christmas-news.
   Cym. And news of the faction.
   Fit. As the reformed-news; Protestant-news:—
   Cym. And pontificial-news; of all which several,
The day-books, characters, precedents are kept,
Together with the names of special friends—
   Fit. And men of correspondence in the country—
   Cym. Yes, of all ranks, and all religions.—
   Fit. Factors and agents—
   Cym. Liegers, that lie out
Through all the shires of the kingdom.
   P. jun. This is fine,
And bears a brave relation! But what says
Mercurius Britannicus to this?
   Cym. O sir, he gains by't half in half.
   Fit. Nay more,
I'll stand to't. For where he was wont to get
In hungry captains, obscure statesmen—
   Cym. Fellows
To drink with him in a dark room in a tavern,
And eat a sausage—
   Fit. We have seen it.
   Cym. As fain to keep so many politic pens
Going, to feed the press—
   Fit. And dish out news,
Were't true or false—
   Cym. Now all that charge is saved.
The public chronicler—
   Fit. How do you call him there?
   Cym. And gentle reader—
   Fit. He that has the maidenhead
Of all the books.
   Cym. Yes, dedicated to him—
   Fit. Or rather prostituted—
   P. jun. You are right, sir.
   Cym. No more shall be abused; nor country parsons
Of the inquisition, nor busy justices
Trouble the peace, and both torment themselves,
And their poor ignorant neighbours, with enquiries
After the many and most innocent monsters,
That never came in the counties they were charged with.
   P. jun. Why, methinks, sir, if the honest common people
Will be abused, why should not they have their pleasure,
In the believing lies are made for them;
As you in the office, making them yourselves?
   Fit. O, sir! it is the printing we oppose.
   Cym. We not forbid that any news be made,
But that it be printed; for when news is printed,

It leaves, sir, to be news; while 'tis but written—

Fit. Tho' it be ne'er so false, it runs news still.

P. jun. See divers men's opinions! unto some
The very printing of 'em makes them news;
That have not the heart to believe any thing,
But what they see in print.

Fit. Ay, that's an error
Has abused many; but we shall reform it,
As many things beside, (we have a hope,)
Are crept among the popular abuses.

Cym. Nor shall the stationer cheat upon the time,
By buttering o'er again—

Fit. Once in seven years,
As the age doats—

Cym. And grows forgetful of them,
His antiquated pamphlets with new dates:
But all shall come from the mint.

Fit. Fresh and new-stamp'd.

Cym. With the office-seal, staple commodity.

Fit. And if a man will insure his news, he may;
Two-pence a sheet he shall be warranted,
And have a policy for it.

P. jun. Sir, I admire
The method of your place: all things within't
Are so digested, fitted, and composed,
As it shews Wit had married Order.

Fit. Sir.

Cym. The best we could to invite the times.

Fit. It has
Cost sweat and freezing.

Cym. And some broken sleeps,
Before it came to this.

P. jun. I easily think it.

Fit. But now it has the shape—

Cym. And is come forth—

P. jun. A most polite neat thing, with all the limbs,
As sense can taste!

Cym. It is, sir, though I say it,
As well begotten a business, and as fairly
Help'd to the world.

P. jun. You must be a midwife, sir,
Or else the son of a midwife (pray you pardon me)
Have help'd it forth so happily!—What news have you?
News of this morning? I would fain hear some,
Fresh from the forge; as new as day, as they say.

Cym. And such we have, sir.

Reg. Shew him the last roll,
Of emissary Westminster's, *The heir.*

Enter Barber.

P. jun. Come nearer, Tom!

Nath. There is a brave young heir
Is come of age this morning, master Pennyboy.

P. jun. That's I?   [*Aside.*

Nath. His father died on this day seven-night.

P. jun. True!   [*Aside.*

Nath. At six o' the clock in the morning, just a week
Ere he was one and twenty.

P. jun. I am here, Tom!—
Proceed, I pray thee.

Nath. An old canting beggar
Brought him first news, whom he has entertain'd
To follow him since.

P. jun. Why, you shall see him;—Founder!
Come in—

Enter PENNYBOY Canter.

No follower, but companion:
I pray thee put him in, friend; [*to Nath.*] there's an angel—
Thou dost not know, he is a wise old fellow,
Though he seem patch'd thus, and made up of pieces. [*Exit Nath.*
Founder, we are in here, in, i' the News-office!
In this day's roll already!—I do muse
How you came by us, sirs.

Cym. One master Picklock,
A lawyer that hath purchased here a place
This morning of an emissary under me—

Fit. Emissary Westminster.

Cym. Gave it into the office.

Fit. For his essay, his piece.

P. jun. My man of law!
He's my attorney and solicitor too!
A fine pragmatic! what is his place worth?

Cym. A *nemo-scit*, sir.

Fit. 'Tis as news come in.

Cym. And as they are issued.   I have the just moiety
For my part: then the other moiety
Is parted into seven: the four emissaries,
Whereof my cousin Fitton here's for Court,
Ambler for Paul's, and Buz for the Exchange,
Picklock for Westminster, with the examiner,
And register, they have full parts: and then one part
Is under-parted to a couple of clerks.
And there's the just division of the profits.

P. jun. Have you those clerks, sir?

Cym. There is one desk empty,
But it has many suitors.

P. jun. Sir, may I
Present one more, and carry it, if his parts
Or gifts, which you will call them—
　　Cym. Be sufficient, sir.
　　P. jun. What are your present clerk's abilities?
How is he qualified?
　　Cym. A decay'd stationer
He was, but knows news well, can sort and rank them.
　　Fit. And for a need can make them.
　　Cym. True Paul's, bred
In the church-yard.
　　P. jun. And this at the west-door
On the other side; he is my barber, Tom,
A pretty scholar, and a master of arts
Was made, or went out master of arts in a throng
At the university; as before, one Christmas,
He got into a masque at court, by his wit,
And the good means of his cittern, holding up thus
For one of the music: he's a nimble fellow,
And alike skill'd in every liberal science,
As having certain snaps of all; a neat
Quick vein in forging news too: I do love him,
And promised him a good turn, and I would do it.
What is your price? the value?
　　Cym. Fifty pounds, sir.
　　P. jun. Get in, Tom, take possession, I instal thee.
Here, tell your money.　Give thee joy, good Tom!
And let me hear from thee every minute of news,
While the New Staple stands, or the office lasts,
Which I do wish may ne'er be less, for thy sake.

Re-enter NATHANIEL.

　　Nath. The emissaries, sir, would speak with you
And master Fitton; they have brought in news,
Three bale together.
　　Cym. Sir, you are welcome here.
　　Fit. So is your creature.
　　Cym. Business calls us off, sir,
That may concern the office.
　　P. jun. Keep me fair, sir,
Still in your staple; I am here your friend,
On the same floor.
　　Fit. We shall be your servants.
　　　　　　　　　　　[Exeunt all but P. jun. and P. Cant.
　　P. jun. How dost thou like it, founder?
　　P. Can. All is well,
But that your man of law, methinks, appears not
In his due time.　O! here comes master's worship.

Enter PICKLOCK.

Pick. How does the heir, bright master Pennyboy?
Is he awake yet in his one and twenty?—
Why, this is better far, than to wear cypress,
Dull smutting gloves, or melancholy blacks,
And have a pair of twelve-penny broad ribands,
Laid out like labels.

    P. jun. I should have made shift
To have laugh'd as heartily in my mourner's hood,
As in this suit, if it had pleased my father
To have been buried with the trumpeters

    Pick. The heralds of arms, you mean.

    P. jun. I mean,
All noise that is superfluous!

    Pick. All that idle pomp,
And vanity of a tombstone, your wise father
Did by his will prevent. Your worship had—

    P. jun. A loving and obedient father of him,
I know it [I]; a right kind-natured man,
To die so opportunely.

    Pick. And to settle
All things so well! compounded for your wardship
The week afore, and left your state entire,
Without any charge upon't.

    P. jun. I must needs say,
I lost an officer of him, a good bailiff,
And I shall want him: but all peace be with him!
I will not wish him alive again, not I,
For all my fortune. Give your worship joy
Of your new place, your emissaryship
In the News-office!

    Pick. Know you why I bought it, sir?

    P. jun. Not I.

    Pick. To work for you, and carry a mine
Against the master of it, master Cymbal,
Who hath a plot, upon a gentlewoman
Was once design'd for you, sir.

    P. jun. Me?

    Pick. Your father,
Old master Pennyboy, of happy memory,
And wisdom too, as any in the county,
Careful to find out a fit match for you,
In his own life-time, (but he was prevented,)
Left it in writing in a schedule here,
To be annexed to his will, that you,
His only son, upon his charge and blessing,
Should take due notice of a gentlewoman
Sojourning with your uncle, Richer Pennyboy.

P. jun. A Cornish gentlewoman; I do know her,
Mistress Pecunia Do-all.

    Pick. A great lady,
Indeed, she is, and not of mortal race,
Infanta of the mines; her grace's grandfather
Was duke, and cousin to the king of Ophyr,
The Subterranean. Let that pass. Her name is,
Or rather her three names are (for such she is)
Aurelia Clara Pecunia, a great princess,
Of mighty power, though she live in private,
With a contracted family! Her secretary—

    P. Can. Who is her gentleman-usher too.

    Pick. One Broker;
And then two gentlewomen, mistress Statute
And mistress Band, with Wax the chambermaid,
And mother Mortgage the old nurse, two grooms,
Pawn and his fellow: you have not many to bribe, sir.
The work is feasible, and the approaches easy,
By your own kindred. Now, sir, Cymbal thinks,
The master here, and governor of the Staple,
By his fine arts, and pomp of his great place,
To draw her! He concludes, she is a woman,
And that so soon as she hears of the new office,
She'll come to visit it, as they all have longings,
After new sights and motions! But your bounty,
Person, and bravery, must achieve her.

    P. Can. She is
The talk o' the time! the adventure of the age!

    Pick. You cannot put yourself upon an action
Of more importance.

    P. Can. All the world are suitors to her.

    Pick. All sorts of men, and all professions.

    P. Can. You shall have stall-fed doctors, cramm'd divines,
Make love to her, and with those studied
And perfumed flatteries, as no room can stink
More elegant, than where they are.

    Pick. Well chanted,
Old Canter! thou sing'st true.

    P. Can. And, by your leave,
Good master's worship, some of your velvet coat
Make corpulent curt'sies to her, till they crack for't.

    Pick. There's doctor Almanac woos her, one of the jeerers,
A fine physician.

    P. Can. Your sea-captain, Shunfield,
Gives out, he'll go upon the cannon for her.

    Pick. Though his loud mouthing get him little credit.

    P. Can. Young master Piedmantle, the fine herald,
Professes to derive her through all ages,
From all the kings and queens that ever were.

Pick. And master Madrigal, the crowned poet
Of these our times, doth offer at her praises
As fair as any, when it shall please Apollo
That wit and rhyme may meet both in one subject.

P. Can. And you to bear her from all these, it will be—

Pick. A work of fame.

P. Can. Of honour.

Pick. Celebration.

P. Can. Worthy your name.

Pick. The Pennyboys to live in't.

P. Can. It is an action you were built for, sir.

Pick. And none but you can do it.

P. jun. I'll undertake it.

P. Can. And carry it.

P. jun. Fear me not; for since I came
Of mature age, I have had a certain itch
In my right eye, this corner here, do you see?
To do some work, and worthy of a chronicle.　　　[*Exeunt.*

Mirth. *How now, gossip! how does the play please you?*

Cen. *Very scurvily, methinks, and sufficiently naught.*

Expect. *As a body would wish: here's nothing but a young prodigal come of age, who makes much of the barber, buys him a place in a new office, in the air, I know not where; and his man of law to follow him, with a beggar to boot, and they two help him to a wife.*

Mirth. *Ay, she is a proper piece! that such creatures can broke for.*

Tat. *I cannot abide that nasty fellow, the beggar; if he had been a court-beggar in good clothes, a beggar in velvet, as they say, I could have endured him.*

Mirth. *Or a begging scholar in black, or one of these beggarly poets, gossip, that could hang upon a young heir like a horseleech.*

Expect. *Or a threadbare doctor of physic, a poor quacksalver.*

Cen. *Or a sea-captain half starved.*

Mirth. *Ay, these were tolerable beggars, beggars of fashion! you shall see some such anon.*

Tat. *I would fain see the fool, gossip; the fool is the finest man in the company, they say, and has all the wit: he is the very justice o' peace of the play, and can commit whom he will, and what he will, error, absurdity, as the toy takes him, and no man say black is his eye, but laugh at him.*

Mirth. *But they have no fool in this play, I am afraid, gossip.*

Tat. *It is a wise play, then!*

Expect. *They are all fools, the rather, in that.*

Cen. *Like enough.*

Tat. *My husband, Timothy Tattle, God rest his poor soul! was wont to say, there was no play without a fool and a devil in't; he was for the devil still, God bless him! The devil for his money, would he say, I would fain see the devil. And why would you so fain see the devil? would I say. Because he has horns, wife, and may be a cuckold as well as a devil, he would answer. You are e'en such* another! husband, quoth I. *Was the devil ever married? Where do you read, the devil was ever so honourable to commit matrimony? The play will tell us that, says he, we'll go see it to-morrow, The Devil is an Ass. He is an errant learned man that made it, and can write, they say, and I am foully deceived but he can read too.*

Mirth. I remember it, gossip, I went with you: by the same token Mistress Trouble-truth dissuaded us, and told us he was a profane poet, and all his plays had devils in them; that he kept school upon the stage, could conjure there, above the school of Westminster, and doctor Lamb too: not a play he made but had a devil in it; and that he would learn us all to make our husbands cuckolds at plays: by another token, that a young married wife in the company said, she could find in her heart to steal thither, and see a little of the vanity through her mask, and come practise at home.

Tat. O, it was mistress—

Mirth. Nay, gossip, I name nobody: It may be 'twas myself.

Expect. But was the devil a proper man, gossip?

Mirth. As fine a gentleman of his inches as ever I saw trusted to the stage, or any where else; and loved the commonwealth as well as ever a patriot of them all: he would carry away the Vice on his back, quick to hell, in every play where he came, and reform abuses.

Expect. There was the Devil of Edmonton, no such man, I warrant you.

Cen. The conjuror cozened him with a candle's end; he was an ass.

Mirth. But there was one Smug, a smith, would have made a horse laugh, and broke his halter, as they say.

Tat. O, but the poor man had got a shrewd mischance one day.

Expect. How, gossip?

Tat. He had drest a rogue jade in the morning, that had the staggers, and had got such a spice of them himself by noon, as they would not away all the play-time, do what he could for his heart.

Mirth. 'Twas his part, gossip; he was to be drunk by his part.

Tat. Say you so? I understood not so much.

Expect. Would we had such another part, and such a man in this play! I fear 'twill be an excellent dull thing.

Cen. Expect, intend it.

ACT II

SCENE I.—*A Room in* PENNYBOY senior's *House.*

Enter PENNYBOY sen., PECUNIA, MORTGAGE, STATUTE, BAND, *and* BROKER.

P. sen. Your grace is sad, methinks, and melancholy,
You do not look upon me with that face
As you were wont, my goddess, bright Pecunia!
Altho' your grace be fallen off two in the hundred,
In vulgar estimation; yet am I

Your grace's servant still: and teach this body
To bend, and these my aged knees to buckle,
In adoration, and just worship of you.
Indeed, I do confess, I have no shape
To make a minion of, but I am your martyr,
Your grace's martyr.   I can hear the rogues,
As I do walk the streets, whisper and point,
"There goes old Pennyboy, the slave of money,
Rich Pennyboy, lady Pecunia's drudge.
A sordid rascal, one that never made
Good meal in his sleep, but sells the acates are sent him,
Fish, fowl, and venison, and preserves himself,
Like an old hoary rat, with mouldy pie-crust!"
This I do hear, rejoicing I can suffer
This, and much more for your good grace's sake.

   Pec. Why do you so, my guardian? I not bid you:
Cannot my grace be gotten, and held too,
Without your self-tormentings and your watches,
Your macerating of your body thus,
With cares and scantings of your diet and rest?

   P. sen. O no, your services, my princely lady,
Cannot with too much zeal of rites be done,
They are so sacred.

   Pec. But my reputation
May suffer, and the worship of my family,
When by so servile means they both are sought.

   P. sen. You are a noble, young, free, gracious lady,
And would be every body's in your bounty,
But you must not be so.   They are a few
That know your merit, lady, and can value it.
Yourself scarce understands your proper powers,
They are all-mighty, and that we, your servants,
That have the honour here to stand so near you,
Know and can use too.   All this nether world
Is yours, you command it, and do sway it;
The honour of it, and the honesty,
The reputation, ay, and the religion,
(I was about to say, and had not err'd,)
Is queen Pecunia's: for that style is yours,
If mortals knew your grace, or their own good.

   Mor. Please your grace to retire.

   Band. I fear your grace
Hath ta'en too much of the sharp air.

   Pec. O, no!
I could endure to take a great deal more,
(And with my constitution,) were it left
Unto my choice; what think you of it, Statute?

   Sta. A little now and then does well, and keeps
Your grace in your complexion.

Band. And true temper.

Mor. But too much, madam, may increase cold rheums,
Nourish catarrhs, green sicknesses, and agues,
And put you in consumption.

P. sen. Best to take
Advice of your grave women, noble madam,
They know the state of your body, and have studied
Your grace's health.

Band. And honour. Here'll be visitants,
Or suitors by and by; and 'tis not fit
They find you here.

Sta. 'Twill make your grace too cheap
To give them audience presently.

Mor. Leave your secretary
To answer them.

Pec. Wait you here, broker.

Bro. I shall, madam,   [*Exeunt all but Broker.*
And do your grace's trusts with diligence.

Enter PIEDMANTLE.

Pie. What luck is this? I am come an inch too late!
Do you hear, sir? is your worship of the family
Unto the lady Pecunia?

Bro. I serve her grace, sir,
Aurelia Clara Pecunia, the Infanta.

Pie. Has she all those titles, and her grace besides!
I must correct that ignorance and oversight,
Before I do present. Sir, I have drawn
A pedigree for her grace, though yet a novice
In that so noble study.

Bro. A herald at arms?

Pie. No, sir, a pursuivant, my name is Piedmantle.

Bro. Good master Piedmantle.

Pie. I have deduced her—

Bro. From all the Spanish mines in the West Indies,
I hope; for she comes that way by her mother,
But by her grandmother she is duchess of mines.

Pie. From man's creation I have brought her.

Bro. No farther!
Before, sir, long before, you have done nothing else;
Your mines were before Adam, search your office,
Roll five and twenty, you will find it so.
I see you are but a novice, master Piedmantle,
If you had not told me so.

Pie. Sir, an apprentice
In armory. I have read the Elements,
And Accidence, and all the leading books;
And I have now upon me a great ambition
How to be brought to her grace, to kiss her hands.

Bro. Why, if you have acquaintance with mistress Statute,
Or mistress Band, my lady's gentlewomen,
They can induce you.   One is a judge's daughter,
But somewhat stately; the other mistress Band,
Her father's but a scrivener, but she can
Almost as much with my lady as the other,
Especially if Rose Wax the chambermaid
Be willing.   Do you not know her, sir, neither?
Pie. No, in troth, sir.
Bro. She's a good pliant wench,
And easy to be wrought, sir; but the nurse,
Old mother Mortgage, if you have a tenement,
Or such a morsel, though she have no teeth,
She loves a sweetmeat, any thing that melts
In her warm gums, she could command it for you
On such a trifle, a toy.   Sir, you may see
How for your love, and this so pure complexion,
(A perfect sanguine) I have ventur'd thus,
The straining of a ward, opening a door
Into the secrets of our family.
Pie. I pray you let me know, sir, unto whom
I am so much beholden; but your name.
Bro. My name is Broker; I am secretary
And usher to her grace.
Pie. Good master Broker!
Bro. Good master Piedmantle!
Pie. Why, you could do me,
If you would, now, this favour of yourself.
Bro. Truly I think I could; but if I would,
I hardly should, without, or mistress Band,
Or mistress Statute, please to appear in it;
Or the good nurse I told you of, mistress Mortgage,
We mingle not
One in another's sphere, but all move orderly
In our own orbs; yet we are all concentrics.
Pie. Well, sir, I'll wait a better season.
Bro. Do,   [*Makes a mouth at him.*
And study the right means; get mistress Band
To urge on your behalf, or little Wax.
Pie. I have a hope, sir, that I may, by chance,
Light on her grace, as she is taking the air.
Bro. That air of hope has blasted many an aiery
Of castrils like yourself, good master Piedmantle.
                                              [*Exit Piedmantle.*
P. sen. [*springs forward.*] Well said, master secretary, I
        stood behind
And heard thee all.   I honour thy dispatches.
If they be rude, untrained in our method,
And have not studied the rule, dismiss them quickly.

Where's Lickfinger, my cook, that unctuous rascal?
He'll never keep his hour, that vessel of kitchen-stuff!

Enter LICKFINGER.

Bro. Here he is come, sir.
P. sen. Pox upon him, kidney,
Always too late!
Lick. To wish them you, I confess,
That have them already.
P. sen. What?
Lick. The pox!
P. sen. The piles,
The plague, and all diseases light on him
Knows not to keep his word! I'd keep my word sure;
I hate that man that will not keep his word.
When did I break my word?
Lick. Or I, till now?
And 'tis but half an hour.
P. sen. Half a year,
To me, that stand upon a minute of time:
I am a just man, I love still to be just.
Lick. Why, you think I can run like light-foot Ralph,
Or keep a wheel-barrow with a sail in town here,
To whirl me to you. I have lost two stone
Of suet in the service, posting hither:
You might have followed me like a watering-pot,
And seen the knots I made along the street:
My face dropt like the skimmer in a fritter-pan,
And my whole body is yet, to say the truth,
A roasted pound of butter, with grated bread in't!
P. sen. Believe you he that list; you staid of purpose
To have my venison stink, and my fowl mortified,
That you might have them—
Lick. A shilling or two cheaper!
That is your jealousy.
P. sen. Perhaps it is.
Will you go in, and view, and value all?
Yonder is venison sent me, fowl, and fish,
In such abundance, I am sick to see it;
I wonder what they mean! I have told them of it!
To burden a weak stomach, and provoke
A dying appetite! thrust a sin upon me
I ne'er was guilty of! nothing but gluttony,
Gross gluttony, that will undo this land!
Lick. And bating two in the hundred.
P. sen. Ay, that same's
A crying sin, a fearful damn'd device,
Eats up the poor, devours them—
Lick. Sir, take heed

What you give out.

    P. sen. Against your grave great Solons,
Numæ Pompilii, they that made that law,
To take away the poor's inheritance!
It was their portion, I will stand to it;
And they have robb'd them of it, plainly robb'd them.
I still am a just man, I tell the truth.
When moneys went at ten in the hundred, I,
And such as I, the servants of Pecunia,
Could spare the poor two out of ten, and did it:
How say you, Broker?

    Lick. Ask your echo!

    Bro. You did it.

    P. sen. I am for justice; when did I leave justice?
We knew 'twas theirs, they had right and title to't:
Now—

    Lick. You can spare them nothing.

    P. sen. Very little.

    Lick. As good as nothing.

    P. sen. They have bound our hands
With their wise solemn act, shorten'd our arms.

    Lick. Beware those worshipful ears, sir, be not shorten'd,
And you play Crop in the Fleet, if you use this license.

    P. sen. What license, knave, informer?

    Lick. I am Lickfinger,
Your cook.

    P. sen. A saucy Jack you are, that's once.
What said I, Broker?

    Bro. Nothing that I heard, sir.

    Lick. I know his gift, he can be deaf when he list.

    P. sen. Have you provided me my bushel of eggs
I did bespeak? I do not care how stale
Or stinking that they be; let 'em be rotten:
For ammunition here to pelt the boys
That break my windows.

    Lick. Yes, sir, I have spared them
Out of the custard-politic for you, the mayor's.

    P. sen. 'Tis well; go in, take hence all that excess,
Make what you can of it, your best; and when
I have friends that I invite at home, provide me
Such, such, and such a dish, as I bespeak;
One at a time, no superfluity.
Or if you have it not, return me money:
You know my ways.

    Lick. They are a little crooked.

    P. sen. How, knave?

    Lick. Because you do indent.

    P. sen. 'Tis true, sir,
I do indent you shall return me money.

Lick. Rather than meat, I know it; you are just still.

P. sen. I love it still; and therefore if you spend
The red-deer pies in your house, or sell them forth, sir,
Cast so, that I may have their coffins all
Return'd here, and piled up: I would be thought
To keep some kind of house.

Lick. By the mouldy signs!

P. sen. And then remember meat for my two dogs;
Fat flaps of mutton, kidneys, rumps of veal,
Good plenteous scraps; my maid shall eat the relics.

Lick. When you and your dogs have dined! a sweet reversion.

P. sen. Who's here? my courtier, and my little doctor?
My muster-master? And what plover's that
They have brought to pull?

Bro. I know not, some green plover.
I'll find him out.

Enter FITTON, ALMANAC, SHUNFIELD, *and* MADRIGAL.

P. sen. Do, for I know the rest:
They are the jeerers, mocking, flouting Jacks.

Fit. How now, old Moneybawd! We are come—

P. sen. To jeer me,
As you were wont; I know you.

Alm. No, to give thee
Some good security, and see Pecunia.

P. sen. What is't?

Fit. Ourselves.

Alm. We'll be one bound for another.

Fit. This noble doctor here.

Alm. This worthy courtier.

Fit. This man of war, he was our muster-master.

Alm. But a sea-captain now, brave captain Shunfield.
                                [P. sen. holds up his nose.

Shun. You snuff the air now, has the scent displeased you?

Fit. Thou need'st not fear him, man, his credit is sound.

Alm. And season'd too, since he took salt at sea.

P. sen. I do not love pickled security;
Would I had one good fresh man in for all;
For truth is, you three stink.

Shun. You are a rogue.

P. sen. I think I am; but I will lend no money
On that security, captain.

Alm. Here's a gentleman,
A fresh-man in the world, one master Madrigal.

Fit. Of an untainted credit; what say you to him?
                                [Exit Madrigal with Broker.

Shun. He's gone, methinks; where is he?—Madrigal!

P. sen. He has an odd singing name; is he an heir?

Fit. An heir to a fair fortune.

'ull hopes:

..iolar, and a pretty poet!

... You have said enough. I have no money, gentlemen,
. go to't in rhyme once, not a penny.   [*He snuffs again.*

Shun. Why, he's of years, though he have little beard.

P. sen. His beard has time to grow: I have no money.
Let him still dabble in poetry.   No Pecunia
Is to be seen.

Alm. Come, thou lov'st to be costive
Still in thy courtesy; but I have a pill,
A golden pill, to purge away this melancholy.

Shun. 'Tis nothing but his keeping of the house here
With his two drowsy dogs.

Fit. A drench of sack
At a good tavern, and a fine fresh pullet,
Would cure him.

Lick. Nothing but a young heir in white-broth;
I know his diet better than the doctor.

Shun. What, Lickfinger, mine old host of Ram-alley!
You have some market here.

Alm. Some dosser of fish
Or fowl, to fetch off.

Fit. An odd bargain of venison
To drive.

P. sen. Will you go in, knave?

Lick. I must needs,
You see who drives me, gentlemen.   [*P. sen. thrusts him in.*

Alm. Not the devil.

Fit. He may in time, he is his agent now.

P. sen. You are all cogging Jacks, a covey of wits,
The jeerers, that still call together at meals,
Or rather an aiery; for you are birds of prey,
And fly at all; nothing's too big or high for you;
And are so truly fear'd, but not beloved
One of another, as no one dares break
Company from the rest, lest they should fall
Upon him absent.

Alm. O, the only oracle
That ever peep'd or spake out of a doublet!

Shun. How the rogue stinks! worse than a fishmonger's sleeves.

Fit. Or currier's hands.

Shun. And such a parboil'd visage!

Fit. His face looks like a dyer's apron, just

Alm. A sodden head, and his whole brain a posset-curd.

P. sen. Ay, now you jeer, jeer on; I have no money.

Alm. I wonder what religion he is of.

Fit. No certain species sure: a kind of mule,
That's half an ethnic, half a Christian!

P. sen. I have no money, gentlemen.

Shun. This stock,
He has no sense of any virtue, honour,
Gentry, or merit.

P. sen. You say very right,
My meritorious captain, as I take it,
Merit will keep no house, nor pay no house-rent.
Will mistress Merit go to market, think you,
Set on the pot, or feed the family?
Will gentry clear with the butcher, or the baker,
Fetch in a pheasant, or a brace of partridges,
From good-wife poulter, for my lady's supper?

Fit. See this pure rogue!

P. sen. This rogue has money though;
My worshipful brave courtier has no money;
No, nor my valiant captain.

Shun. Hang you, rascal.

P. sen. Nor you, my learned doctor. I loved you
While you did hold your practice, and kill tripe-wives,
And kept you to your urinal; but since your thumbs
Have greased the Ephemerides, casting figures,
And turning over for your candle-rents,
And your twelve houses in the zodiac,
With your almutens, alma-cantaras,
Troth you shall cant alone for Pennyboy.

Shun. I told you what we should find him, a mere bawd.

Fit. A rogue, a cheater.

P. sen. What you please, gentlemen:
I am of that humble nature and condition,
Never to mind your worships, or take notice
Of what you throw away thus. I keep house here,
Like a lame cobler, never out of doors,
With my two dogs, my friends: and, as you say,
Drive a quick pretty trade, still. I get money:
And as for titles, be they rogue or rascal,
Or what your worships fancy, let them pass,
As transitory things; they are mine to-day,
And yours to-morrow.

Alm. Hang thee, dog!

Shun. Thou cur!

P. sen. You see how I do blush, and am ashamed
Of these large attributes! yet you have no money.

Alm. Well, wolf, hyena, you old pocky rascal,
You will have the hernia fall down again
Into your scrotum, and I shall be sent for:
I will remember then, that, and your fistula
In ano, I cured you of.

P. sen. Thank your dog-leech craft!
They were wholesome piles afore you meddled with them.

Alm. What an ungrateful wretch is this!

Shun. He minds
A courtesy no more than London-bridge
What arch was mended last.

Fit. He never thinks,
More than a log, of any grace at court
A man may do him; or that such a lord
Reach'd him his hand.

P. sen. O yes! if grace would strike
The brewer's tally, or my good lord's hand
Would quit the scores: but, sir, they will not do it;
Here is a piece, my good lord Piece doth all;
Goes to the butcher's, fetches in a mutton;
Then to the baker's, brings in bread, makes fires,
Gets wine, and does more real courtesies
Than all my lords I know: my sweet lord Piece!

                    [Holds up a piece of gold.
You are my lord, the rest are cogging Jacks,
Under the rose.

Shun. Rogue, I could beat you now.

P. sen. True, captain, if you durst beat any other,
I should believe you; but indeed you are hungry;
You are not angry, captain, if I know you
Aright, good captain. No Pecunia
Is to be seen, though mistress Band would speak,
Or little blushet Wax be ne'er so easy;
I'll stop mine ears with her, against the Syrens,
Court, and philosophy. God be wi' you, gentlemen!
Provide you better names, Pecunia is for you.   *[Exit.*

Fit. What a damn'd harpy it is! Where's Madrigal?
Is he sneak'd hence?

Shun. Here he comes with Broker,
Pecunia's secretary.

Re-enter MADRIGAL *and* BROKER.

Alm. He may do some good
With him perhaps.—Where have you been, Madrigal?

Mad. Above, with my lady's women, reading verses.

Fit. That was a favour.—Good morrow, master Secretary!

Shun. Good morrow, master Usher!

Alm. Sir, by both
Your worshipful titles, and your name, mas Broker,
Good morrow!

Mad. I did ask him if he were
Amphibion Broker.

Shun. Why?

Mad. A creature of two natures,
Because he has two offices.

Bro. You may jeer,
You have the wits, young gentlemen: but your hope

Of Helicon will never carry it here,
With our fat family; we have the dullest,
Most unbored ears for verse amongst our females!
I grieved you read so long, sir; old nurse Mortgage
She snored in the chair, and Statute, if you mark'd her,
Fell fast asleep, and mistress Band she nodded,
But not with any consent to what you read.
They must have somewhat else to chink than rhymes.
If you could make an epitaph on your land,
(Imagine it on departure,) such a poem
Would wake them and bring Wax to her true temper.

   Mad. I'faith, sir, and I'll try.

   Bro. It is but earth,
Fit to make bricks and tiles of.

   Shun. Pox upon't,
'Tis but for pots, or pipkins at the best.
If it would keep us in good tobacco-pipes—

   Bro. It were worth keeping.

   Fit. Or in porcelain dishes,
There were some hope.

   Alm. But this is a hungry soil,
And must be help'd.

   Fit. Who would hold any land,
To have the trouble to marle it?

   Shun. Not a gentleman.

   Bro. Let clowns and hinds affect it, that love ploughs,
And carts and harrows, and are busy still
In vexing the dull element.

   Alm. Our sweet songster
Shall rarify't into air.

   Fit. And you, mas Broker,
Shall have a feeling.

   Bro. So it supple, sir,
The nerves.

   Mad. O, it shall be palpable,
Make thee run thorough a hoop, or a thumb-ring,
The nose of a tobacco-pipe, and draw
Thy ductile bones out like a knitting-needle,
To serve my subtile turns.

   Bro. I shall obey, sir,
And run a thread, like an hour-glass.

            Re-enter PENNYBOY sen.

   P. sen. Where is Broker?
Are not these flies gone yet? Pray quit my house,
I'll smoke you out else.

   Fit. O the prodigal!
Will you be at so much charge with us, and loss?

   Mad. I've heard you have offer'd, sir, to lock up smoke,

And calk your windows, spar up all your doors,
Thinking to keep it a close prisoner with you,
And wept when it went out, sir, at your chimney.

    Fit. And yet his eyes were drier than a pumice.

    Shun. A wretched rascal, that will bind about
The nose of his bellows, lest the wind get out
When he's abroad.

    Alm. Sweeps down no cobwebs here,
But sells them for cut fingers; and the spiders,
As creatures rear'd of dust, and cost him nothing,
To fat old ladies' monkeys.

    Fit. He has offer'd
To gather up spilt water, and preserve
Each hair falls from him, to stop balls withal.

    Shun. A slave, and an idolater to Pecunia!

    P. sen. You all have happy memories, gentlemen,
In rocking my poor cradle. I remember too,
When you had lands and credit, worship, friends,
Ay, and could give security: now you have none,
Or will have none right shortly. This can time,
And the vicissitude of things! I have
All these, and money too, and do possess them,
And am right heartily glad of all our memories,
And both the changes.

    Fit. Let us leave the viper.   [*Exeunt all but P. sen. and Broker.*

    P. sen. He's glad he is rid of his torture, and so soon.—
Broker, come hither: up, and tell your lady,
She must be ready presently, and Statute,
Band, Mortgage, Wax: my prodigal young kinsman
Will straight be here to see her; top of our house,
The flourishing and flaunting Pennyboy!
We were but three of us in all the world,
My brother Francis, whom they call'd Frank Pennyboy,
Father to this; he's dead: this Pennyboy
Is now the heir! I, Richer Pennyboy,
Not Richard, but old Harry Pennyboy,
And, to make rhyme, close, wary Pennyboy,
I shall have all at last, my hopes do tell me.
Go, see all ready; and where my dogs have faulted,
Remove it with a broom, and sweeten all
With a slice of juniper, not too much, but sparing,
We may be faulty ourselves else, and turn prodigal,
In entertaining of the prodigal.   [*Exit Broker.*
Here he is, and with him—what? a clapper-dudgeon!
That's a good sign, to have the beggar follow him
So near, at his first entry into fortune.

    Enter PENNYBOY jun., PENNYBOY *Canter, and* PICKLOCK.

    P. jun. How now, old uncle! I am come to see thee,

And the brave lady here, the daughter of Ophir,
They say thou keep'st.

P. sen. Sweet nephew, if she were
The daughter of the Sun, she's at your service,
And so am I, and the whole family,
Worshipful nephew.

P. jun. Say'st thou so, dear uncle!
Welcome my friends then: here is dominie Picklock,
My man of law, solicits all my causes,
Follows my business, makes and compounds my quarrels
Between my tenants and me; sows all my strifes,
And reaps them too; troubles the country for me,
And vexes any neighbour that I please.

P. sen. But with commission?

P. jun. Under my hand and seal.

P. sen. A worshipful place!

Pick. I thank his worship for it.

P. sen. But what is this old gentleman?

P. Can. A rogue,
A very canter, I, sir, one that maunds
Upon the pad: we should be brothers though;
For you are near as wretched as myself,
You dare not use your money, and I have none.

P. sen. Not use my money, cogging Jack! who uses it
At better rates, lets it for more in the hundred
Than I do, sirrah?

P. jun. Be not angry, uncle.

P. sen. What! to disgrace me, with my queen, as if
I did not know her value.

P. Can. Sir, I meant,
You durst not to enjoy it.

P. sen. Hold your peace,
You are a Jack.

P. jun. Uncle, he shall be a John,
An you go to that; as good a man as you are:
And I can make him so, a better man;
Perhaps I will too.   Come, let us go.   [*Going.*

P. sen. Nay, kinsman,
My worshipful kinsman, and the top of our house,
Do not your penitent uncle that affront,
For a rash word, to leave his joyful threshold,
Before you see the lady that you long for,
The Venus of the time and state, Pecunia!
I do perceive your bounty loves the man,
For some concealed virtue that he hides
Under those rags.

P. Can. I owe my happiness to him,
The waiting on his worship, since I brought him
The happy news welcome to all young heirs.

P. jun. Thou didst indeed, for which I thank thee yet.
Your fortunate princess, uncle, is long a coming.

P. Can. She is not rigg'd, sir; setting forth some lady
Will cost as much as furnishing a fleet.—
Here she is come at last, and like a galley
Gilt in the prow.

Enter PECUNIA *in state, attended by* BROKER, STATUTE, BAND,
WAX, *and* MORTGAGE.

P. jun. Is this Pecunia?

P. sen. Vouchsafe my toward kinsman, gracious madam,
The favour of your hand.

    Pec. Nay, of my lips, sir,   [*Kisses him.*
To him.

    P. jun. She kisses like a mortal creature.   [*Aside.*
Almighty madam, I have long'd to see you.

Pec. And I have my desire, sir, to behold
That youth and shape, which in my dreams and wakes
I have so oft contemplated, and felt
Warm in my veins, and native as my blood.
When I was told of your arrival here,
I felt my heart beat, as it would leap out
In speech; and all my face it was a flame:
But how it came to pass, I do not know.

P. jun. O, beauty loves to be more proud than nature,
That made you blush. I cannot satisfy
My curious eyes, by which alone I am happy,
In my beholding you.   [*Kisses her.*

P. Can. They pass the compliment
Prettily well.

Pick. Ay, he does kiss her, I like him.

P. jun. My passion was clear contrary, and doubtful,
I shook for fear, and yet I danced for joy,
I had such motions as the sun-beams make
Against a wall, or playing on a water,
Or trembling vapour of a boiling pot—

P. sen. That's not so good; it should have been a crucible
With molten metal, she had understood it.

    P. jun. I cannot talk, but I can love you, madam:
Are these your gentlewomen? I love them too.   [*Kisses them.*
And which is mistress Statute? mistress Band?
They all kiss close, the last stuck to my lips.

Bro. It was my lady's chambermaid, soft Wax.

P. jun. Soft lips she has, I am sure on't. Mother Mortgage
I'll owe a kiss, till she be younger. Statute,
Sweet mistress Band, and honey little Wax,
We must be better acquainted.   [*Kisses them again.*

Sta. We are but servants, sir.

Band. But whom her grace is so content to grace,

We shall observe.

Wax. And with all fit respect.

Mor. In our poor places.

Wax. Being her grace's shadows.

P. jun. A fine, well-spoken family!—What's thy name?

Bro. Broker.

P. jun. Methinks my uncle should not need thee,
Who is a crafty knave enough, believe it.   [*Aside to Broker.*
Art thou her grace's steward?

Bro. No, her usher, sir.

P. jun. What, of the hall? thou hast a sweeping face,
Thy beard is like a broom.

Bro. No barren chin, sir.
I am no eunuch, though a gentleman-usher.

P. jun. Thou shalt go with us.—Uncle, I must have
My princess forth to-day.

P. sen. Whither you please, sir;
You shall command her.

Pec. I will do all grace
To my new servant.

P. sen. Thanks unto your bounty;
He is my nephew and my chief, the point,
Tip, top, and tuft of all our family!—
But, sir, condition'd always you return
Statute and Band home, with my sweet soft Wax,
And my good nurse, here, Mortgage.

P. jun. O, what else?

P. sen. By Broker.

P. jun. Do not fear.

P. sen. She shall go with you,
Whither you please, sir, any where.

P. Can. I see
A money-bawd is lightly a flesh-bawd too.

Pick. Are you advised? Now, on my faith, this Canter
Would make a good grave burgess in some barn.

P. jun. Come, thou shalt go with us, uncle.

P. sen. By no means, sir.

P. jun. We'll have both sack and fidlers.

P. sen. I'll not draw
That charge upon your worship.

P. Can. He speaks modestly,
And like an uncle.

P. sen. But mas Broker here,
He shall attend you, nephew; her grace's usher.
And what you fancy to bestow on him,
Be not too lavish, use a temperate bounty,
I'll take it to myself.

P. jun. I will be princely,
While I possess my princess, my Pecunia.

P. sen. Where is't you eat?

P. jun. Hard by, at Picklock's lodging,
Old Lickfinger's the cook, here in Ram-alley.

P. sen. He has good cheer; perhaps I'll come and see you.

P. Can. O fie! an alley, and a cook's shop, gross!
'Twill savour, sir, most rankly of them both:
Let your meat rather follow you to a tavern.   [*To P. jun.*

Pick. A tavern's as unfit too for a princess.

P. Can. No, I have known a princess, and a great one,
Come forth of a tavern.

Pick. Not go in, sir, though.

P. Can. She must go in, if she came forth: the blessed
Pokahontas, as the historian calls her,
And great king's daughter of Virginia,
Hath been in womb of tavern;—and besides,
Your nasty uncle will spoil all your mirth,
And be as noisome.—

Pick. That is true.

P. Can. No 'faith,
Dine in Apollo with Pecunia,
At brave duke Wadloe's, have your friends about you,
And make a day on't.

P. jun. Content, i'faith;
Our meat shall be brought thither: Simon the king
Will bid us welcome.

Pick. Patron, I have a suit.

P. jun. What's that?

Pick. That you will carry the Infanta
To see the Staple; her grace will be a grace
To all the members of it.

P. jun. I will do it,
And have her arms set up there, with her titles,
Aurelia Clara Pecunia, the Infanta,
And in Apollo! Come, sweet princess, go.

P. sen. Broker, be careful of your charge.

Bro. I warrant you.   [*Exeunt.*

*Cen. Why this is duller and duller! intolerable, scurvy, neither
devil nor fool in this play! pray God some on us be not a witch, gossip,
to forespeak the matter thus.*

*Mirth. I fear we are all such, an we were old enough: but we are
not all old enough to make one witch. How like you the Vice in the
play?*

Expect. Which is he?

*Mirth. Three or four: Old Covetousness, the sordid Pennyboy, the
Money-bawd, who is a flesh-bawd too, they say.*

*Tat. But here is never a fiend to carry him away. Besides, he has
never a wooden dagger! I would not give a rush for a Vice, that has
not a wooden dagger to snap at every body he meets.*

Mirth. That was the old way, gossip, when Iniquity came in like Hokos Pokos, in a juggler's jerkin, with false skirts, like the knave of clubs; but now they are attired like men and women of the time, the vices male and female. Prodigality, like a young heir, and his mistress Money, (whose favours he scatters like counters,) pranked up like a prime lady, the Infanta of the mines.

Cent. Ay, therein they abuse an honourable princess, it is thought.

Mirth. By whom is it so thought? or where lies the abuse?

Cen. Plain in the styling her Infanta, and giving her three names.

Mirth. Take heed it lie not in the vice of your interpretation; what have Aurelia, Clara, Pecunia, to do with any person? do they any more but express the property of Money, which is the daughter of Earth, and drawn out of the mines? Is there nothing to be call'd Infanta, but what is subject to exception? why not the infanta of the beggars, or infanta of the gypsies, as well as king of beggars, and king of gypsies?

Cen. Well, an there were no wiser than I, I would sew him in a sack, and send him by sea to his princess.

Mirth. Faith, an he heard you, Censure, he would go near to stick the ass's ears to your high dressing, and perhaps to all ours for hearkening to you.

Tat. By'r Lady, but he should not to mine; I would hearken, and hearken, and censure, if I saw cause, for the other princess' sake Pokahontas, surnamed the Blessed, whom he has abused indeed, and I do censure him, and will censure him:—To say she came forth of a tavern, was said like a paltry poet.

Mirth. That's but one gossip's opinion, and my gossip Tattle's too! but what says Expectation here? She sits sullen and silent.

Expect. Troth, I expect their office, their great office, the Staple, what it will be! they have talk'd on't, but we see it not open yet.—Would Butter would come in, and spread itself a little to us!

Mirth. Or the butter-box, Buz, the emissary.

Tat. When it is churn'd and dish'd we shall hear of it.

Expect. If it be fresh and sweet butter; but say it be sour and wheyish?

Mirth. Then it is worth nothing, mere pot butter, fit to be spent in suppositories, or greasing coach-wheels, stale, stinking butter, and such, I fear, it is, by the being barrelled up so long.

Expect. Or rank Irish butter.

Cen. Have patience, gossip; say that, contrary to our expectation, it prove right, seasonable, salt butter?

Mirth. Or to the time of year, in Lent, delicate almond butter! I have a sweet tooth yet, and I will hope the best, and sit down as quiet and calm as butter, look smooth and soft as butter, be merry and melt like butter, laugh and be fat like butter: so butter answer my expectation, and be not mad butter;

—————————————"if it be,
It shall both July and December see!"

I say no more, but——Dixi.

ACT III

SCENE I.—*The Office of the Staple.*

Enter FITTON, CYMBAL, Register, Clerk, *and* THOMAS, *Barber.*

Fit. You hunt upon a wrong scent still, and think
The air of things will carry them; but it must
Be reason and proportion, not fine sounds,
My cousin Cymbal, must get you this lady.
You have entertain'd a pettyfogger here,
Picklock, with trust of an emissary's place,
And he is all for the young prodigal;
You see he has left us.
 Cym. Come, you do not know him,
That thus speak of him: he will have a trick
To open us a gap by a trap-door,
When they least dream on't. Here he comes.

Enter PICKLOCK.

What news?
 Pick. Where is my brother Buz, my brother Ambler?
The register, examiner, and the clerks?
Appear, and let us muster all in pomp,
For here will be the rich Infanta presently,
To make her visit. Pennyboy the heir,
My patron, has got leave for her to play
With all her train, of the old churl her guardian.
Now is your time to make all court unto her,
That she may first but know, then love the place,
And shew it by her frequent visits here:
And afterwards get her to sojourn with you.
She will be weary of the prodigal quickly.
 Cym. Excellent news!
 Fit. And counsel of an oracle!
 Cym. How say you, cousin Fitton?
 Fit. Brother Picklock,
I shall adore thee for this parcel of tidings,
It will cry up the credit of our office
Eternally, and make our Staple immortal!
 Pick. Look your addresses then be fair and fit,
And entertain her and her creatures too,
With all the migniardise, and quaint caresses
You can put on them.
 Fit. Thou seem'st by thy language,
No less a courtier than a man of law.
I must embrace thee.
 Pick. Tut, I am Vertumnus,

On every change, or chance, upon occasion,
A true camelion, I can colour for it.
I move upon my axle like a turnpike,
Fit my face to the parties, and become
Straight one of them.

Enter NATHANIEL, THOMAS, *Barber, and* Register.

Cym. Sirs, up into your desks
And spread the rolls upon the table,—so!
Is the examiner set?
Reg. Yes, sir.
Cym. Ambler and Buz
Are both abroad now.
Pick. We'll sustain their parts.
No matter, let them ply the affairs without,
Let us alone within, I like that well.
On with the cloke, and you with the Staple gown,
     [*Fit. puts on the office cloke, and Cym. the gown.*
And keep your state, stoop only to the Infanta;
We'll have a flight at Mortgage, Statute, Band,
And hard but we'll bring Wax to the retrieve:
Each know his several province, and discharge it.
       [*They take their seats.*

Fit. I do admire this nimble engine, Picklock.
Cym. Coz, what did I say?
Fit. You have rectified my error.

Enter PENNYBOY jun., P. Canter, PECUNIA, STATUTE, BAND,
   MORTGAGE, WAX, *and* BROKER.

P. jun. By your leave, gentlemen, what news? good, good still,
In your new office? Princess, here's the Staple!
This is the governor, kiss him, noble princess,
For my sake.—Tom, how is it, honest Tom?
How does thy place, and thou?—my creature, princess,
This is my creature, give him your hand to kiss,
He was my barber, now he writes clericus!
I bought this place for him, and gave it him.
P. Can. He should have spoke of that, sir, and not you:
Two do not do one office well.
P. jun. 'Tis true,
But I am loth to lose my courtesies.
P. Can. So are all they that do them to vain ends;
And yet you do lose when you pay yourselves.
P. jun. No more of your sentences, Canter, they are stale;
We come for news, remember where you are.
I pray thee let my princess hear some news,
Good master Cymbal.
Cym. What news would she hear?
Or of what kind, sir?

P. jun. Any, any kind,
So it be news, the newest that thou hast,
Some news of state for a princess.

   Cym. Read from Rome there.

   Tho. *They write, the king of Spain is chosen pope.*

   P. jun. How!

   Tho. *And emperor too, the thirtieth of February.*

   P. jun. Is the emperor dead?

   Cym. No, but he has resign'd,
And trails a pike now under Tilly.

   Fit. For penance.

   P. jun. These will beget strange turns in Christendom!

   Tho. *And Spinola is made general of the Jesuits.*

   P. jun. Stranger!

   Fit. Sir, all are alike true and certain.

   Cym. All the pretence to the fifth monarchy
Was held but vain, until the ecclesiastic
And secular powers were united thus,
Both in one person.

   Fit. It has been long the aim
Of the house of Austria.

   Cym. See but Maximilian
His letters to the baron of Bouttersheim,
Or Scheiter-huyssen.

   Fit. No, of Leichtenstein,
Lord Paul, I think.

   P. jun. I have heard of some such thing.
Don Spinola made general of the Jesuits!
A priest!

   Cym. O, no, he is dispens'd withal—
And the whole society, who do now appear
The only enginers of Christendom.

   P. jun. They have been thought so long, and rightly too.

   Fit. Witness the engine that they have presented him,
To wind himself with up into the moon,
And thence make all his discoveries!

   Cym. Read on.

   Tho. *And Vitellesco, he that was last general,*
Being now turn'd cook to the society,
Has drest his excellence such a dish of eggs—

   P. jun. What, potch'd?

   Tho. No, powder'd.

   Cym. All the yolk is wild-fire,
As he shall need beleaguer no more towns,
But throw his egg in.

   Fit. It shall clear consume
Palace and place: demolish and bear down
All strengths before it!

   Cym. Never be extinguish'd,

Till all become one ruin!

    Fit. And from Florence.

    Tho. They write was found in Galilœo's study,
A burning glass, which they have sent him too,
To fire any fleet that's out at sea.—

    Cym. By moonshine, is't not so?

    Tho. Yes, sir, in the water.

    P. jun. His strengths will be unresistible, if this hold.
Have you no news against him on the contrary?

    Nath. Yes, sir. *They write here, one Cornelius-Son,*
Hath made the Hollanders an invisible eel
To swim the haven at Dunkirk, and sink all
The shipping there.

    P. jun. Why have not you this, Tom?

    Cym. Because he keeps the pontificial side.

    P. jun. How! Change sides, Tom, 'twas never in my thought
To put thee up against ourselves. Come down,
Quickly.

    Cym. Why, sir?

    P. jun. I ventured not my money
Upon those terms: if he may change, why so!
I'll have him keep his own side, sure.

    Fit. Why, let him,
It is but writing so much over again.

    P. jun. For that I'll bear the charges: there's two pieces.

    Fit. Come, do not stick with the gentleman.

    Cym. I'll take none, sir,
And yet he shall have the place.

    P. jun. They shall be ten then.
Up, Tom, and the office shall take them. Keep your side, Tom.
                    [*Tho. changes his side.*
Know your own side, do not forsake your side, Tom.

    Cym. Read.

    Tho. They write here, one Cornelius-Son,
Hath made the Hollanders an invisible eel
To swim the haven at Dunkirk, and sink all
The shipping there.

    P. jun. But how is't done?

    Cym. I'll shew you, sir.
It is an automa, runs under water,
With a snug nose, and has a nimble tail
Made like an auger, with which tail she wriggles
Betwixt the costs of a ship, and sinks it straight.

    P. jun. Whence have you this news?

    Fit. From a right hand, I assure you,
The eel boats here, that lie before Queen-hythe,
Came out of Holland.

    P. jun. A most brave device,
To murder their flat bottoms.

Fit. I do grant you:
But what if Spinola have a new project,
To bring an army over in cork-shoes,
And land them here at Harwich? all his horse
Are shod with cork, and fourscore pieces of ordnance,
Mounted upon cork carriages, with bladders
Instead of wheels, to run the passage over
At a spring tide.

P. jun. Is't true?

Fit. As true as the rest.

P. jun. He'll never leave his engines: I would hear now
Some curious news.

Cym. As what?

P. jun. Magic or alchemy,
Or flying in the air, I care not what.

Nath. They write from Libtzig (reverence to your ears)
The art of drawing farts out of dead bodies,
Is by the brotherhood of the Rosie Cross
Produced unto perfection, in so sweet
And rich a tincture—

Fit. As there is no princess
But may perfume her chamber with the extraction.

P. jun. There's for you, princess!

P. Can. What, a fart for her?

P. jun. I mean the spirit.

P. Can. Beware how she resents it.

P. jun. And what hast thou, Tom?

Tho. The perpetual motion,
Is here found out by an ale-wife in Saint-Katherine's,
At the sign of the Dancing Bears.

P. jun. What, from her tap?
I'll go see that, or else I'll send old Canter:
He can make that discovery.

P. Can. Yes, in ale.   [*Noise without.*

P. jun. Let me have all this news made up and seal'd.

Reg. The people press upon us. Please you, sir,
Withdraw with your fair princess: there's a room
Within, sir, to retire to.

P. jun. No, good register,
We'll stand it out here, and observe your office;
What news it issues.

Reg. 'Tis the House of Fame, sir,
Where both the curious and the negligent,
The scrupulous and careless, wild and stay'd,
The idle and laborious, all do meet,
To taste the cornu-copiæ of her rumours,
Which she, the mother of sport, pleaseth to scatter
Among the vulgar: baits, sir, for the people;
And they will bite like fishes.

Enter a crowd of Customers.

P. jun. Let us see it.

1 Cust. Have you in your profane shop any news
Of the saints at Amsterdam?

Reg. Yes; how much would you?

2 Cust. Six penny-worth.

Reg. Lay your money down.—Read, Thomas.

Tho. The saints do write, they expect a prophet shortly,
The prophet Baal, to be sent over to them,
To calculate a time, and half a time,
And the whole time, according to Naometry.

P. jun. What's that?

Tho. The measuring of the temple; a cabal
Found out but lately, and set out by Archie,
Or some such head, of whose long coat they have heard,
And, being black, desire it.

1 Cust. Peace be with them!

Reg. So there had need, for they are still by the ears
One with another.

1 Cust. It is their zeal.

Reg. Most likely.

1 Cust. Have you no other of that species?

Reg. Yes,
But dearer; it will cost you a shilling.

1 Cust. Verily,
There is a nine-pence, I will shed no more.

Reg. Not to the good of the saints?

1 Cust. I am not sure
That man is good.

Reg. Read from Constantinople
Nine penn'orth.

Tho. They give out here, the grand signior
Is certainly turn'd Christian; and to clear
The controversy 'twixt the pope and him,
Which is the Antichrist, he means to visit
The church at Amsterdam this very summer
And quit all marks of the beast.

1 Cust. Now joyful tidings!
Who brought in this! which emissary?

Reg. Buz,
Your countryman.

1 Cust. Now, blessed be the man,
And his whole family, with the nation!

Reg. Yes, for Amboyna, and the justice there!
This is a Dopper, a she Anabaptist!
Seal and deliver her her news, dispatch.

2 Cust. Have you any news from the Indies? any miracle
Done in Japan by the Jesuits, or in China?

Nath. No, but *we hear of a colony of cooks*
To be set ashore on the coast of America,
For the conversion of the cannibals,
And making them good eating Christians.
Here comes the colonel that undertakes it.

Enter LICKFINGER.

3 Cust. Who, captain Lickfinger?
Lick. News, news, my boys,
I am to furnish a great feast to-day,
And I would have what news the office affords.
   Nath. We were venting some of you, of your new project.
   Reg. Afore 'twas paid for! you were somewhat too hasty.
   P. jun. What, Lickfinger! wilt thou convert the cannibals
With spit and pan divinity?
   Lick. Sir, for that
I will not urge, but for the fire and zeal
To the true cause; thus I have undertaken
With two lay brethren, to myself, no more,
One of the broach, the other of the boiler,
In one six months, and by plain cookery,
No magic to it, but old Japhet's physic,
The father of the European arts,
To make such sauces for the savages,
And cook their meats with those enticing steams,
As it would make our cannibal-christians
Forbear the mutual eating one another,
Which they do do more cunningly than the wild
Anthropophagi, that snatch only strangers,
Like my old patron's dogs there.
   P. jun. O, my uncle's!
Is dinner ready, Lickfinger?
   Lick. When you please, sir,
I was bespeaking but a parcel of news,
To strew out the long meal withal, but it seems
You are furnished here already.
   P. jun. O, not half.
   Lick. What court news is there? any proclamations
Or edicts to come forth?
   Tho. Yes, there is one,
That the king's barber has got, for aid of our trade,
Whereof there is a manifest decay.
A precept for the wearing of long hair,
To run to seed, to sow bald pates withal,
And the preserving fruitful heads and chins
To help a mystery almost antiquated.
Such as are bald and barren beyond hope,
Are to be separated and set by
For ushers to old countesses: and coachmen

To mount their boxes reverently, and drive
Like lapwings, with a shell upon their heads
Thorough the streets.

    Lick. Have you no news of the stage?
They'll ask me about new plays at dinner-time,
And I should be as dumb as a fish.

    Tho. O, yes.
There is a legacy left to the king's players,
Both for their various shifting of their scene,
And dextrous change of their persons to all shapes
And all disguises, by the right reverend
Archbishop of Spalato.

    Lick. He is dead
That play'd him!

    Tho. Then he has lost his share of the legacy.

    Lick. What news of Gondomar?

    Tho. *A second fistula,*
Or an excoriation, at the least,
For putting the poor English play, was writ of him,
To such a sordid use, as, is said, he did,
Of cleansing his posteriors.

    Lick. Justice! justice!

    Tho. *Since when, he lives condemn'd to his share at Bruxels,*
And there sits filing certain politic hinges,
To hang the states on he has heaved off the hooks.

    Lick. What must you have for these?

    P. jun. Thou shalt pay nothing,
But reckon them in the bill.　[*Exit Lick.*]　There's twenty pieces,
Her grace bestows upon the office, Tom:
Write thou that down for news.

    Reg. We may well do't,
We have not many such.

    P. jun. There's twenty more,
If you say so; my princess is a princess!
And put that too under the office seal.

    Cym. [*takes Pecunia aside, while Fitton courts the Waiting-women.*]
If it will please your grace to sojourn here,
And take my roof for covert, you shall know
The rites belonging to your blood and birth,
Which few can apprehend: these sordid servants,
Which rather are your keepers, than attendants,
Should not come near your presence. I would have
You waited on by ladies, and your train
Born up by persons of quality and honour;
Your meat should be served in with curious dances,
And set upon the board with virgin hands,
Tuned to their voices; not a dish removed,
But to the music, nor a drop of wine
Mixt with his water, without harmony.

Pec. You are a courtier, sir, or somewhat more,
That have this tempting language.

    Cym. I am your servant,
Excellent princess, and would have you appear
That which you are: come forth the state and wonder
Of these our times, dazzle the vulgar eyes,
And strike the people blind with admiration.

    P. Can. Why that's the end of wealth! thrust riches outward,
And remain beggars within; contemplate nothing
But the vile sordid things of time, place, money,
And let the noble and the precious go:
Virtue and honesty; hang them, poor thin membranes
Of honour! who respects them? O, the fates,
How hath all just true reputation fallen,
Since money, this base money 'gan to have any!   [*Aside.*

    Band. Pity the gentleman is not immortal.

    Wax. As he gives out the place is by description.

    Fit. A very paradise, if you saw all, lady.

    Wax. I am the chamber-maid, sir, you mistake,
My lady may see all.

    Fit. Sweet mistress Statute, gentle mistress Band,
And mother Mortgage, do but get her grace
To sojourn here.

    Pick. I thank you, gentle Wax.

    Mor. If it were a chattel, I would try my credit.

    Pick. So it is, for term of life, we count it so.

    Sta. She means inheritance to him and his heirs:
Or that he could assure a state of years;
I'll be his Statute staple, Statute-merchant,
Or what he please.

    Pick. He can expect no more.

    Band. His cousin, alderman Security,
That he did talk of so, e'en now—

    Sta. Who is
The very brooch of the bench, gem of the city.

    Band. He and his deputy, but assure his life
For one seven years—

    Sta. And see what we'll do for him,
Upon his scarlet motion.

    Band. And old chain,
That draws the city ears.

    Wax. When he says nothing,
But twirls it thus.

    Sta. A moving oratory!

    Band. *Dumb rhetoric, and silent eloquence !*
As the fine poet says.

    Fit. Come, they all scorn us:
Do you not see't? the family of scorn!

    Bro. Do not believe him: gentle master Picklock,

They understood you not; the gentlewomen,
They thought you would have my lady sojourn with you,
And you desire but now and then a visit.

   Pick. Yes, if she pleased, sir, it would much advance
Unto the office, her continual residence:
I speak but as a member.

   Bro. 'Tis enough.
I apprehend you: and it shall go hard,
But I'll so work, as somebody shall work her.

   Pick. Pray you change with our master but a word about it.

   P. jun. Well, Lickfinger, see that our meat be ready.
Thou hast news enough.

   Lick. Something of Bethlem Gabor,
And then I am gone.

   Tho. We hear he has devised
A drum, to fill all Christendom with the sound:
But that he cannot draw his forces near it,
To march yet, for the violence of the noise.
And therefore he is fain, by a design,
To carry them in the air, and at some distance,
'Till he be married, then they shall appear.

   Lick. Or never! well, God be wi' you! stay, who's there?
A little of the Duke of Bavier, and then—

   Nath. *He has taken a grey habit, and is turn'd*
The church's miller, grinds the catholic grist
With every wind; and Tilly takes the toll.

   4 *Cust.* Have you any news of the pageants to send down
Into the several counties? All the country
Expected from the city most brave speeches,
Now, at the coronation.

   Lick. It expected
More than it understood; for they stand mute,
Poor innocent dumb things: they are but wood,
As is the bench, and blocks they were wrought on: yet
If May-day come, and the sun shine, perhaps,
They'll sing like Memnon's statue, and be vocal.

   5 *Cust.* Have you any forest news?

   Tho. None very wild, sir,
Some tame there is, out of the forest of fools.
A new park is a making there, to sever
Cuckolds of antler, from the rascals. Such
Whose wives are dead, and have since cast their heads,
Shall remain cuckolds pollard.

   Lick. I'll have that news.

   1 *Cust.* And I.

   2 *Cust.* And I.

   3 *Cust.* And I.

   4 *Cust.* And I.

   5 *Cust.* And I.

Cym. Sir, I desire to be excused; [*to P. jun.*] and, madam,
I cannot leave my office the first day.
My cousin Fitton here shall wait upon you,
And emissary Picklock.

    P. jun. And Tom Clericus?

    Cym. I cannot spare him yet, but he shall follow you,
When they have order'd the rolls. Shut up the office,
When you have done, till two o'clock.

                            [*Exeunt all but Thomas and Nath.*

Enter SHUNFIELD, ALMANAC, *and* MADRIGAL.

    Shun. By your leave, clerks,
Where shall we dine to-day? do you know?

    Nath. The jeerers.

    Alm. Where is my fellow Fitton?

    Tho. New gone forth.

    Shun. Cannot your office tell us, what brave fellows
Do eat together to-day, in town, and where?

    Tho. Yes, there's a gentleman, the brave heir, young Pennyboy,
Dines in Apollo.

    Mad. Come, let's thither then,
I have supt in Apollo.

    Alm. With the Muses?

    Mad. No,
But with two gentlewomen, call'd the Graces.

    Alm. They were ever three in *poetry*.

    Mad. This was *truth*, sir.

    Tho. Sir, master Fitton's there too.

    Shun. All the better.

    Alm. We may have a jeer, perhaps.

    Shun. Yes, you'll drink, doctor,
If there be any good meat, as much good wine now,
As would lay up a Dutch Ambassador.

    Tho. If he dine there, he's sure to have good meat,
For Lickfinger provides the dinner.

    Alm. Who!
The glory of the kitchen! that holds cookery
A trade from Adam, quotes his broths and sallads,
And swears he is not dead yet, but translated
In some immortal crust, the paste of almonds!

    Mad. The same. He holds no man can be a poet,
That is not a good cook, to know the palates,
And several tastes of the time. He draws all arts
Out of the kitchen, but the art of poetry,
Which he concludes the same with cookery.

    Shun. Tut, he maintains more heresies than that.
He'll draw the magisterium from a minced-pie,
And prefer jellies to your julaps, doctor.

    Alm. I was at an olla podrida of his making,

Was a brave piece of cookery: at a funeral!
But opening the pot-lid, he made us laugh,
Who had wept all day, and sent us such a tickling
Into our nostrils, as the funeral feast
Had been a wedding-dinner!
    Shun. Give him allowance,
And that but a moderate, he will make a syren
Sing in the kettle, send in an Arion,
In a brave broth, and of a watery-green,
Just the sea-colour, mounted on the back
Of a grown conger, but in such a posture,
As all the world would take him for a dolphin.
    Mad. He's a rare fellow, without question! but
He holds some paradoxes.
    Alm. Ay, and pseudodoxes.
Marry for most, he's orthodox in the kitchen.
    Mad. And knows the clergy's taste!
    Alm. Ay, and the laity's!
    Shun. You think not of your time; we shall come too late,
If we go not presently.
    Mad. Away then.
    Shun. Sirs,
You must get of this news, to store your office,
Who dines and sups in the town; where, and with whom;
It will be beneficial: when you are stored,
And as we like our fare, we shall reward you.
    Nath. A hungry trade, 'twill be.
    Tho. Much like duke Humphry's,
But, now and then, as the wholesome proverb says,
'Twill *obsonare famem ambulando.*
    Nath. Shut up the office, gentle brother Thomas.
    Tho. Brother Nathaniel, I have the wine for you.
I hope to see us, one day, emissaries.
    Nath. Why not? 'Slid, I despair not to be master!   [*Exeunt.*

SCENE II.—*A Room in* PENNYBOY senior's *House.*

Enter PENNYBOY sen. *and* BROKER, *at different doors.*

    P. sen. How now! I think I was born under Hercules' star,
Nothing but trouble and tumult to oppress me!
Why come you back? where is your charge?
    Bro. I have brought
A gentleman to speak with you.
    P. sen. To speak with me!
You know 'tis death for me to speak with any man.
What is he? set me a chair.
    Bro. He is the master
Of the great office.
    P. sen. What?

Bro. The Staple of News,
A mighty thing, they talk six thousand a-year.
  P. sen. Well, bring your six in. Where have you left Pecunia?
  Bro. Sir, in Apollo, they are scarce set.
  P. sen. Bring six.   *[Exit Broker, and returns with Cymbal.*
  Bro. Here is the gentleman.
  P. sen. He must pardon me,
I cannot rise, a diseased man,
  Cym. By no means, sir;
Respect your health and ease.
  P. sen. It is no pride in me,
But pain, pain: What's your errand, sir, to me?
Broker, return to your charge, be Argus-eyed,
Awake to the affair you have in hand,
Serve in Apollo, but take heed of Bacchus.   *[Exit Broker.*
Go on, sir.
  Cym. I am come to speak with you.
  P. sen. 'Tis pain for me to speak, a very death;
But I will hear you.
  Cym. Sir, you have a lady,
That sojourns with you.
  P. sen. Ha! I am somewhat short
In my sense too—
  Cym. Pecunia.
  P. sen. O' that side
Very imperfect; on—
  Cym. Whom I would draw
Oftener to a poor office, I am master of—
  P. sen. My hearing is very dead, you must speak quicker.
  Cym. Or, if it please you, sir, to let her sojourn,
In part with me; I have a moiety
We will divide, half of the profits.
  P. sen. Ha!
I hear you better now. How come they in?
Is it a certain business, or a casual?
For I am loth to seek out doubtful courses,
Run any hazardous paths; I love straight ways,
A just and upright man! now all trade totters;
The trade of money is fall'n two in the hundred:
That was a certain trade, while the age was thrifty,
And men good husbands, look'd unto their stocks,
Had their minds bounded; now the public riot
Prostitutes all, scatters away in coaches,
In footmen's coats, and waiting women's gowns,
They must have velvet haunches, with a pox!
Now taken up, and yet not pay the use!
Bate of the use! I am mad with this time's manners.
                    [Vehemently and loud.
  Cym. You said e'en now, it was death for you to speak.

P. sen. Ay, but an anger, a just anger, as this is,
Puts life in man.   Who can endure to see   [*Starts from his chair.*
The fury of men's gullets, and their groins?
What fires, what cooks, what kitchens might be spared?
What stews, ponds, parks, coops, garners, magazines?
What velvets, tissues, scarfs, embroideries,
And laces they might lack?   They covet things
Superfluous still; when it were much more honour
They could want necessary: what need hath nature
Of silver dishes, or gold chamber-pots?
Of perfumed napkins, or a numerous family
To see her eat? poor, and wise, she requires
Meat only; hunger is not ambitious:
Say, that you were the emperor of pleasures,
The great dictator of fashions, for all Europe,
And had the pomp of all the courts, and kingdoms,
Laid forth unto the shew, to make yourself
Gazed and admired at; you must go to bed,
And take your natural rest: then all this vanisheth.
Your bravery was but shewn; 'twas not possest:
While it did boast itself, it was then perishing.
    Cym. This man has healthful lungs.   [*Aside.*
    P. sen. All that excess
Appear'd as little yours, as the spectators':
It scarce fills up the expectation
Of a few hours, that entertains men's lives.
    Cym. He has the monopoly of sole-speaking.   [*Aside.*
Why, good sir, you talk all.
    P. sen. [*angrily.*] Why should I not?
Is it not under mine own roof, my ceiling?
    Cym. But I came here to talk with you.
    P. sen. Why, an I will not
Talk with you, sir! you are answer'd; who sent for you?
    Cym. No body sent for me—
    P. sen. But you came; why then
Go as you came, here's no man holds you; there,
There lies your way, you see the door.
    Cym. This is strange!
    P. sen. 'Tis my civility, when I do not relish
The party, or his business.   Pray you be gone, sir,
I'll have no venture in your shop, the office,
Your bark of six, if 'twere sixteen, good sir.
    Cym. You are a rogue.
    P. sen. I think I am, sir, truly.
    Cym. A rascal, and a money-bawd.
    P. sen. My surnames.
    Cym. A wretched rascal—
    P. sen. You will overflow
And spill all.

Cym. Caterpillar, moth,
Horse-leech, and dung-worm—
P. sen. Still you lose your labour.
I am a broken vessel, all runs out:
A shrunk old dryfat.   Fare you well, good six!   [*Exeunt.*

Cen. A notable tough rascal, this old Pennyboy! right city-bred!

Mirth. In Silver-street, the region of money, a good seat for an usurer.

Tat. He has rich ingredients in him, I warrant you, if they were extracted; a true receipt to make an alderman, an he were well wrought upon, according to art.

Expect. I would fain see an alderman in chimia, *that is, a treatise of aldermanity truly written!*

Cen. To shew how much it differs from urbanity.

Mirth. Ay, or humanity. Either would appear in this Pennyboy, an he were rightly distill'd. But how like you the news? you are gone from that.

Cen. O, they are monstrous! scurvy, and stale, and too exotic! ill cook'd and ill dish'd!

Expect. They were as good, yet, as butter could make them!

Tat. In a word, they were beastly buttered: he shall never come on my bread more, nor in my mouth, if I can help it. I have better news from the bake-house, by ten thousand parts, in a morning; or the conduits in Westminster: all the news of Tuttle-street, and both the Alm'ries, the two Sanctuaries, long and round Wool-staple, with King's-street, and Canon-row to boot.

Mirth. Ay, my gossip Tattle knew what fine slips grew in Gardener's-lane; who kist the butcher's wife with the cow's breath; what matches were made in the Bowling-alley, and what bets were won and lost; how much grist went to the mill, and what besides: who conjured in Tuttle-fields, and how many, when they never came there; and which boy rode upon doctor Lamb in the likeness of a roaring lion, that run away with him in his teeth, and has not devour'd him yet.

Tat. Why, I had it from my maid Joan Hearsay; and she had it from a limb o' the school, she says, a little limb of nine year old; who told her, the master left out his conjuring book one day, and he found it, and so the fable came about. But whether it were true or no, we gossips are bound to believe it, an't be once out, and a-foot: how should we entertain the time else, or find ourselves in fashionable discourse, for all companies, if we do not credit all, and make more of it in the reporting?

Cen. For my part, I believe it: an there were no wiser than I, I would have ne'er a cunning schoolmaster in England. I mean, a cunning man a schoolmaster; that is, a conjurer, or a poet, or that had any acquaintance with a poet. They make all their scholars play-boys! Is't not a fine sight, to see all our children made interluders? Do we pay our money for this? we send them to learn their grammar and their Terence, and they learn their play-books! Well, they talk we

shall have no more parliaments, God bless us ! but an we have, I hope,
Zeal-of-the-land Busy and my gossip Rabbi Troubletruth will start up,
and see we shall have painful good ministers to keep school, and
catechise our youth, and not teach them to speak plays, and act fables
of false news, in this manner, to the super-vexation of town and country,
with a wannion.

ACT IV

SCENE I.—*The* DEVIL TAVERN. *The Apollo.*

PENNYBOY jun., FITTON, SHUNFIELD, ALMANAC, MADRIGAL,
PENNYBOY Canter, *and* PICKLOCK, *discovered at table.*

P. jun. Come, gentlemen, let's breathe from healths awhile.
This Lickfinger has made us a good dinner,
For our Pecunia: what shall's do with ourselves,
While the women water, and the fidlers eat?
Fit. Let's jeer a little.
P. jun. Jeer! what's that?
Shun. Expect, sir.
Alm. We first begin with ourselves, and then at you.
Shun. A game we use.
Mad. We jeer all kind of persons
We meet withal, of any rank or quality,
And if we cannot jeer them, we jeer ourselves.
P. Can. A pretty sweet society, and a grateful!
Pick. Pray let's see some.
Shun. Have at you then, lawyer.
They say there was one of your coat in Bethlem lately.
Alm. I wonder all his clients were not there.
Mad. They were the madder sort.
Pick. Except, sir, one
Like you, and he made verses.
Fit. Madrigal,
A jeer!
Mad. I know.
Shun. But what did you do, lawyer,
When you made love to Mistress Band, at dinner?
Mad. Why, of an advocate, he grew the client.
P. jun. Well play'd, my poet.
Mad. And shew'd the law of nature
Was there above the common-law.
Shun. Quit, quit!
P. jun. Call you this jeering! I can play at this,
'Tis like a ball at tennis.
Fit. Very like;
But we were not well in.
Alm. It is indeed, sir,

When we do speak at volley, all the ill
We can one of another.
  Shun. As this morning,
(I would you had heard us,) of the rogue your uncle.
  Alm. That money-bawd.
  Mad. We call'd him a coat-card,
Of the last order.
  P. jun. What is that, a knave?
  Mad. Some readings have it so, my manuscript
Doth speak it varlet.
  P. Can. And yourself a fool
Of the first rank, and one shall have the leading
Of the right-hand-file, under this brave commander.
  P. jun. What say'st thou, Canter?
  P. Can. Sir, I say this is
A very wholesome exercise, and comely,
Like lepers shewing one another their scabs,
Or flies feeding on ulcers.
  P. jun. What news, gentlemen,
Have you any news for after dinner? methinks
We should not spend our time unprofitably.
  P. Can. They never lie, sir, between meals; 'gainst supper
You may have a bale or two brought in.
  Fit. This Canter
Is an old envious knave!
  Alm. A very rascal!
  Fit. I have mark'd him all this meal, he has done nothing
But mock, with scurvy faces, all we said.
  Alm. A supercilious rogue! he looks as if
He were the patrico—
  Mad. Or arch-priest of Canters.
  Shun. He is some primate metropolitan rascal,
Our shot-clog makes so much of him.
  Alm. The law,
And he does govern him.
  P. jun. What say you, gentlemen?
  Fit. We say, we wonder not, your man of law
Should be so gracious with you; but how it comes,
This rogue, this Canter—
  P. jun. O, good words.
  Fit. A fellow
That speaks no language—
  Alm. But what jingling gypsies,
And pedlars trade in—
  Fit. And no honest Christian
Can understand—
  P. Can. Why, by that argument
You are all Canters, you, and you, and you:
All the whole world are Canters, I will prove it

In your professions.
    P. jun. I would fain hear this:
But stay, my princess comes; provide the while,
I'll call for it anon.

    Enter LICKFINGER, PECUNIA, STATUTE, BAND, WAX, *and*
        MORTGAGE.

        How fares your grace?
    Lick. I hope the fare was good.
    Pec. Yes, Lickfinger,
And we shall thank you for it, and reward you.
    Mad. Nay, I'll not lose my argument, Lickfinger;
Before these gentlewomen, I affirm,
The perfect and true strain of poetry
Is rather to be given the quick cellar,
Than the fat kitchen. [*P. jun. takes Pecunia aside and courts her.*
    Lick. Heretic, I see
Thou art for the vain Oracle of the Bottle.
The hogshead, Trismegistus, is thy Pegasus.
Thence flows thy muse's spring, from that hard hoof.
Seduced poet, I do say to thee,
A boiler, range, and dresser were the fountains
Of all the knowledge in the universe.
And they're the kitchens, where the master-cook—
Thou dost not know the man, nor canst thou know him,
Till thou hast serv'd some years in that deep school,
That's both the nurse and mother of the arts,
And hear'st him read, interpret and demonstrate—
A master-cook! why, he's the man of men,
For a professor! he designs, he draws,
He paints, he carves, he builds, he fortifies,
Makes citadels of curious fowl and fish,
Some he dry-dishes, some motes round with broths;
Mounts marrow bones, cuts fifty-angled custards,
Rears bulwark pies, and for his outer works,
He raiseth ramparts of immortal crust;
And teacheth all the tactics, at one dinner:
What ranks, what files, to put his dishes in;
The whole art military. Then he knows
The influence of the stars upon his meats,
And all their seasons, tempers, qualities,
And so to fit his relishes and sauces.
He has nature in a pot, 'bove all the chymists,
Or airy brethren of the Rosie-cross.
He is an architect, an engineer,
A soldier, a physician, a philosopher,
A general mathematician.
    Mad. It is granted.
    Lick. And that you may not doubt him for a poet—

Alm. This fury shews, if there were nothing else,
And 'tis divine! I shall for ever hereafter
Admire the wisdom of a cook.

Band. And we, sir.

P. jun. O, how my princess draws me with her looks,
And hales me in, as eddies draw in boats,
Or strong Charybdis ships, that sail too near
The shelves of love! The tides of your two eyes,
Wind of your breath, are such as suck in all
That do approach you.

Pec. Who hath changed my servant?

P. jun. Yourself, who drink my blood up with your beams,
As doth the sun the sea! Pecunia shines
More in the world than he; and makes it spring
Where'er she favours! please her but to shew
Her melting wrists, or bare her ivory hands,
She catches still! her smiles they are love's fetters!
Her breasts his apples! her teats strawberries!
Where Cupid, were he present now, would cry,
Farewell my mother's milk, here's sweeter nectar!
Help me to praise Pecunia, gentlemen;
She is your princess, lend your wits.

Fit. A lady
The Graces taught to move!

Alm. The Hours did nurse!

Fit. Whose lips are the instructions of all lovers.

Alm. Her eyes their lights, and rivals to the stars!

Fit. A voice, as if that harmony still spake!

Alm. And polish'd skin, whiter than Venus' foot!

Fit. Young Hebe's neck, or Juno's arms!

Alm. A hair,
Large as the morning's, and her breath as sweet
As meadows after rain, and but new mown!

Fit. Leda might yield unto her for a face!

Alm. Hermione for breasts!

Fit. Flora for cheeks!

Alm. And Helen for a mouth!

P. jun. Kiss, kiss 'em, princess.　　　　　[*Pecunia kisses them.*

Fit. The pearl doth strive in whiteness with her neck—

Alm. But loseth by it: here the snow thaws snow;
One frost resolves another.

Fit. O, she has
A front too slippery to be look'd upon!

Alm. And glances that beguile the seer's eyes!

P. jun. Kiss, kiss again. [*Pecunia kisses Alm. and Fit.*] What
　　　says my man of war?

Shun. I say she's more than fame can promise of her,
A theme that's overcome with her own matter!
Praise is struck blind and deaf and dumb with her:

She doth astonish commendation!

P. jun. Well pump'd, i'faith, old sailor: kiss him too,
Though he be a slug. [*She kisses him.*] What says my poet-sucker?
He's chewing his muse's cud, I do see by him.

Mad. I have almost done. I want but e'en to finish.

Fit. That's the ill luck of all his works still.

P. jun. What?

Fit. To begin many works but finish none.

P. jun. How does he do his mistress' work?

Fit. Imperfect.

Alm. I cannot think he finished that.

P. jun. Let's hear.

Mad. It is a madrigal; I affect that kind
Of poem much.

P. jun. And thence you have the name.

Fit. It is his rose, he can make nothing else.

Mad. I made it to the tune the fiddlers play'd,
That we all liked so well.

P. jun. Good! read it, read it.

Mad. The sun is father of all metals, you know,
Silver and Gold.

P. jun. Ay, leave your prologues, say.

Mad. *As bright as is the sun her sire,*
  Or earth, her mother, in her best attire,
  Or Mint, the midwife, with her fire,
   Comes forth her grace!

P. jun. That Mint, the midwife, does well.
  The splendour of the wealthiest mines,
  The stamp and strength of all imperial lines,
  Both majesty and beauty shines,
   In her sweet face!

Fit. That's fairly said of money.
  Look how a torch of taper light,
  Or of that torch's flame, a beacon bright;

P. jun. Good!

Mad. Now there, I want a line to finish, sir.

P. jun. *Or of that beacon's fire, moonlight.*

Mad. *So takes she place!*

Fit. 'Tis good.

Mad. And then I have a saraband—
  She makes good cheer, she keeps full boards,
  She holds a fair of knights and lords,
  A market of all offices,
  And shops of honours more or less.
  According to Pecunia's grace,
  The bride hath beauty, blood, and place;
  The bridegroom virtue, valour, wit,
  And wisdom as he stands for it.

P. jun. Call in the fiddlers.

Enter the Fiddlers *and* NICHOLAS.

                              Nick the boy shall sing it.
Sweet princess, kiss him, kiss them all, dear madam,
                              [*Pecunia kisses them.*
And at the close vouchsafe to call them cousins.
   Pec. Sweet cousin Madrigal, and cousin Fitton,
My cousin Shunfield, and my learned cousin—
   Pick. Al-manach, though they call him Almanac.
   P. Can. Why, here's the prodigal prostitutes his mistress! [*Aside.*
   P. jun. And Picklock, he must be a kinsman too.
My man of law will teach us all to win,
And keep our own.—Old founder!
   P. Can. Nothing, I, sir.
I am a wretch, a beggar: She the fortunate,
Can want no kindred; we the poor know none.
   Fit. Nor none shall know by my consent.
   Alm. Nor mine.
   P. jun. Sing, boy, stand here.
   Nich. [sings.] *As bright, etc.*   [*Music.*
   P. Can. Look, look, how all their eyes
Dance in their heads, observe, scatter'd with lust,
At sight of their brave idol! how they are tickled
With a light air, the bawdy saraband!
They are a kind of dancing engines all,
And set by nature, thus to run alone
To every sound! all things within, without them,
Move, but their brain, and that stands still! mere monsters,
Here in a chamber, of most subtile feet,
And make their legs in tune, passing the streets!
These are the gallant spirits of the age,
The miracles of the time! that can cry up
And down men's wits, and set what rate on things
Their half-brain'd fancies please! now, pox upon them!
See how solicitously he learns the jig,
As if it were a mystery of his faith.
   Shun. A dainty ditty!
   Fit. O, he's a dainty poet,
When he sets to it!
   P. jun. And a dainty scholar!
   Alm. No, no great scholar; he writes like a gentleman.
   Shun. Pox o' your scholar!
   P. Can. Pox o' your distinction!
As if a scholar were no gentleman.
With these, to write like a gentleman, will in time
Become all one, as to write like an ass.
These gentlemen! these rascals; I am sick
Of indignation at them.   [*Aside.*
   P. jun. How do you like't, sir?

Fit. 'Tis excellent!
Alm. 'Twas excellently sung!
Fit. A dainty air!
P. jun. What says my Lickfinger?
Lick. I am telling mistress Band and mistress Statute,
What a brave gentleman you are, and Wax, here!
How much 'twere better, that my lady's grace
Would here take up, sir, and keep house with you.
P. jun. What say they?
Sta. We could consent, sir, willingly.
Band. Ay, if we knew her grace had the least liking.
Wax. We must obey her grace's will and pleasure.
P. jun. I thank you, gentlewomen.—Ply them, Lickfinger.
Give mother Mortgage, there—
Lick. Her dose of sack.
I have it for her, and her distance of hum.
Pec. Indeed therein, I must confess, dear cousin,
I am a most unfortunate princess.
Alm. And
You still will be so, when your grace may help it!
                    [*The gallants gather all about Pecunia.*
Mad. Who'd lie in a room with a close-stool, and garlic,
And kennel with his dogs that had a prince,
Like this young Pennyboy, to sojourn with!
Shun. He'll let you have your liberty—
Alm. Go forth,
Whither you please, and to what company—
Mad. Scatter yourself amongst us—
P. jun. Hope of Parnassus!
Thy ivy shall not wither, nor thy bays;
Thou shalt be had into her grace's cellar,
And there know sack and claret, all December:
Thy vein is rich, and we must cherish it.
Poets and bees swarm now-a-days; but yet
There are not those good taverns, for the one sort,
As there are flowery fields to feed the other.
Though bees be pleased with dew, ask little wax,
That brings the honey to her lady's hive:
The poet must have wine; and he shall have it.

Enter Pennyboy sen. *hastily.*

P. sen. Broker! what, Broker!
P. jun. Who's that, my uncle?
P. sen. I am abused; where is my knave, my Broker?
Lick. Your Broker is laid out upon a bench, yonder;
Sack hath seized on him, in the shape of sleep.
Pick. He hath been dead to us almost this hour.
P. sen. This hour!
P. Can. Why sigh you, sir? 'cause he's at rest?

P. sen. It breeds my unrest.

Lick. Will you take a cup,
And try if you can sleep?

P. sen. No, cogging Jack,
Thou and thy cups too, perish. [*Strikes the cup out of his hand.*

Shun. O, the sack!

Mad. The sack, the sack!

P. Can. A madrigal on sack!

Pick. Or rather an elegy, for the sack is gone.

Pec. Why do you this, sir? spill the wine, and rave,
For Broker's sleeping?

P. sen. What through sleep and sack,
My trust is wrong'd: but I am still awake,
To wait upon your grace, please you to quit
This strange lewd company, they are not for you.

Pec. No, guardian, I do like them very well.

P. sen. Your grace's pleasure be observ'd; but you,
Statute, and Band, and Wax will go with me?

Sta. Truly, we will not.

Band. We will stay, and wait here
Upon her grace, and this your noble kinsman.

P. sen. Noble! how noble! who hath made him noble?

P. jun. Why, my most noble Money hath, or shall,
My princess here; she that, had you but kept
And treated kindly, would have made you noble,
And wise too: nay, perhaps have done that for you,
An act of parliament could not, made you honest.
The truth is, uncle, that her grace dislikes
Her entertainment, 'specially her lodging.

Pec. Nay, say her jail! never unfortunate princess
Was used so by a jailor. Ask my women:
Band, you can tell, and Statute, how he has used me,
Kept me close prisoner, under twenty bolts—

Sta. And forty padlocks—

Band. All malicious engines
A wicked smith could forge out of his iron;
As locks and keys, shackles and manacles,
To torture a great lady.

Sta. He has abused
Your grace's body.

Pec. No, he would have done;
That lay not in his power: he had the use
Of our bodies, Band and Wax, and sometimes Statute's:
But once he would have smothered me in a chest,
And strangled me in leather, but that you
Came to my rescue then, and gave me air.

Sta. For which he cramm'd us up in a close box,
All three together, where we saw no sun
In one six months.

Wax. A cruel man he is!

Band. He has left my fellow Wax out in the cold—

Sta. Till she was stiff as any frost, and crumbled

Away to dust, and almost lost her form.

Wax. Much ado to recover me.

P. sen. Women jeerers!

Have you learn'd too the subtle faculty?

Come, I will shew you the way home, if drink

Or too full diet have disguised you.

Band. Troth,

We have not any mind, sir, of return—

Sta. To be bound back to back—

Band. And have our legs

Turn'd in, or writh'd about—

Wax. Or else display'd—

Sta. Be lodged with dust and fleas, as we were wont—

Band. And dieted with dog's-dung.

P. sen. Why, you whores,

My bawds, my instruments, what should I call you,

Man may think base enough for you?

P. jun. Hear you, uncle:

I must not hear this of my princess' servants,

And in Apollo, in Pecunia's room.

Go, get you down the stairs; home, to your kennel,

As swiftly as you can. Consult your dogs,

The Lares of your family; or believe it,

The fury of a footman and a drawer

Hangs over you.

Shun. Cudgel and pot do threaten

A kind of vengeance.

Mad. Barbers are at hand.

Alm. Washing and shaving will ensue.

Fit. The pump

Is not far off; if 'twere, the sink is near,

Or a good jordan.

Mad. You have now no money.

Shun. But are a rascal.

P. sen. I am cheated, robb'd,

Jeer'd by confederacy.

Fit. No, you are kick'd,

And used kindly, as you should be.

Shun. Spurn'd

From all commerce of men, who are a cur.   [*They kick him.*

Alm. A stinking dog in a doublet, with foul linen.

Mad. A snarling rascal, hence!

Shun. Out!

P. sen. Well, remember,

I am cozen'd by my cousin, and his whore.

Bane o' these meetings in Apollo!

Lick. Go, sir.
You will be tost like Block in a blanket, else.
    P. jun. Down with him, Lickfinger.
    P. sen. Saucy Jack, away:
Pecunia is a whore.
    P. jun. Play him down, fiddlers,
And drown his noise.   [*Exeunt P. sen. and Lickfinger.*]—Who's this?

Enter PIEDMANTLE *with* PECUNIA'S *pedigree.*

    Fit. O, master Piedmantle!
    Pie. By your leave, gentlemen.
    Fit. Her grace's herald?
    Alm. No herald yet, a heraldet.
    P. jun. What's that?
    P. Can. A canter.
    P. jun. O, thou saidst thou'dst prove us all so!
    P. Can. Sir, here is one will prove himself so, straight;
So shall the rest, in time.
    Pec. My pedigree?
I tell you, friend, he must be a good scholar
Can my descent: I am of princely race;
And as good blood as any is in the mines
Runs through my veins.   I am, every limb, a princess!
Dutchess of mines was my great-grandmother;
And by the father's side, I come from Sol:
My grandfather was duke of Or, and match'd
In the blood-royal of Ophir.
    Pie. Here is his coat.
    Pec. I know it, if I hear the blazon.
    Pie. He bears
In a field azure, a sun proper, beamy,
Twelve of the second.
    P. Can. How far is this from canting?
    P. jun. Her grace doth understand it.
    P. Can. She can cant, sir.
    Pec. What be these, bezants?
    Pie. Yes, an't please your grace.
    Pec. That is our coat too, as we come from Or.
What line is this?
    Pie. The rich mines of Potosi,
The Spanish mines in the West Indies.
    Pec. This?
    Pie. The mines of Hungary, this of Barbary.
    Pec. But this, this little branch?
    Pie. The Welsh mine that.
    Pec. I have Welsh blood in me too; blaze, sir, that coat.
    Pie. She bears, an't please you, argent, three leeks vert,
In canton or, and tassell'd of the first.
    P. Can. Is not this canting? do you understand him?

P. jun. Not I; but it sounds well, and the whole thing
Is rarely painted: I will have such a scroll,
Whate'er it cost me.

Pec. Well, at better leisure
We'll take a view of it, and so reward you.

P. jun. Kiss him, sweet princess, and style him a cousin.

Pec. I will, if you will have it.—Cousin Piedmantle.

[*She kisses him.*

P. jun. I love all men of virtue, from my princess
Unto my beggar here, old Canter. On,
On to thy proof; whom prove you the next canter?

P. Can. The doctor here; I will proceed with the learned.
When he discourseth of dissection,
Or any point of anatomy; that he tells you
Of vena cava, and of vena porta,
The meseraics, and the mesenterium:
What does he else but cant? or if he run
To his judicial astrology,
And trowl the Trine, the Quartile, and the Sextile,
Platic aspect, and Partile, with his Hyleg,
Or Alchochoden, Cuspes, and Horoscope;
Does not he cant? who here does understand him?

Alm. This is no canter, though!

P. Can. Or when my muster-master
Talks of his tactics, and his ranks and files,
His bringers up, his leaders-on, and cries
Faces about to the right hand, the left,
Now, *as you were;* then tells you of redoubts,
Of cats, and cortines; doth not he cant?

P. jun. Yes, faith.

P. Can. My egg-chin'd laureat here, when he comes forth
With dimeters, and trimeters, tetrameters,
Pentameters, hexameters, catalectics,
His hyper and his brachy-catalectics,
His pyrrhics, epitrites, and choriambics:
What is all this, but canting?

Mad. A rare fellow!

Shun. Some begging scholar!

Fit. A decay'd doctor, at least!

P. jun. Nay, I do cherish virtue, though in rags.

P. Can. And you, mas courtier—   [*To Fitton.*

P. jun. Now he treats of you,
Stand forth to him fair.

P. Can. With all your fly-blown projects,
And looks-out of the politics, your shut faces,
And reserv'd questions and answers, that you game with; as,
Is't a clear business? will it manage well?
My name must not be used else   Here 'twill dash—
Your business has receiv'd a taint,—give off,

I may not prostitute myself. Tut, tut,
That little dust I can blow off at pleasure.—
Here's no such mountain, yet, in the whole work,
But a light purse may level.—I will tide
This affair for you; give it freight, and passage:—
And such mint phrase, as 'tis the worst of canting,
By how much it affects the sense it has not.

  Fit. This is some other than he seems!
  P. jun. How like you him?
  Fit. This cannot be a canter!
  P. jun. But he is, sir,
And shall be still, and so shall you be too:
We'll all be canters. Now I think of it,
A noble whimsy's come into my brain:
I'll build a college, I and my Pecunia,
And call it Canters' College: sounds it well?
  Alm. Excellent!
  P. jun. And here stands my father rector,
And you professors; you shall all profess
Something, and live there, with her grace and me,
Your founders: I'll endow it with lands and means,
And Lickfinger shall be my master-cook.
What, is he gone?
  P. Can. And a professor?
  P. jun. Yes.
  P. Can. And read Apicius *de re culinaria*
To your brave doxy and you!
  P. jun. You, cousin Fitton,
Shall, as a courtier, read the politics;
Doctor Almanac he shall read Astrology;
Shunfield shall read the military arts.
  P. Can. As carving and assaulting the cold custard.
  P. jun. And Horace here, the art of poetry,
His lyrics and his madrigals; fine songs,
Which we will have at dinner, steep'd in claret,
And against supper, soused in sack.
  Mad. In troth,
A divine whimsy!
  Shun. And a worthy work,
Fit for a chronicle!
  P. jun. Is it not?
  Shun. To all ages.
  P. jun. And Piedmantle shall give us all our arms:
But Picklock, what wouldst thou be? thou canst cant too.
  Pick. In all the languages in Westminster-hall,
Pleas, Bench, or Chancery. Fee-farm, fee-tail,
Tenant in dower, at will, for term of life,
By copy of court-roll, knight's service, homage,
Fealty, escuage, soccage, or frank almoigne,

Grand serjeantry, or burgage.

    P. jun. Thou appear'st,
Κατ᾽ ἐξοχὴν, a canter. Thou shalt read
All Littleton's Tenures to me, and indeed,
All my conveyances.

    Pick. And make them too, sir:
Keep all your courts, be steward of your lands,
Let all your leases, keep your evidences.
But first, I must procure and pass your mortmain,
You must have license from above, sir.

    P. jun. Fear not,
Pecunia's friends shall do it.

    P. Can. But I shall stop it.
        [*Throws off his patched cloke, etc., and discovers himself.*
Your worship's *loving and obedient father,*
Your *painful steward,* and *lost officer !*
Who have done this, to try how you would use
Pecunia when you had her; which since I see,
I will take home the lady to my charge,
And these her servants, and leave you my cloke,
To travel in to Beggar's-bush! A seat
Is built already, furnish'd too, worth twenty
Of your imagined structures, Canters' College.

    Fit. It is his father!

    Mad. He's alive, methinks.

    Alm. I knew he was no rogue.

    P. Can. Thou prodigal,
Was I so careful for thee, to procure
And plot with my learn'd counsel, master Picklock,
This noble match for thee, and dost thou prostitute,
Scatter thy mistress' favours, throw away
Her bounties, as they were red-burning coals.
Too hot for thee to handle, on such rascals,
Who are the scum and excrements of men!
If thou hadst sought out good and virtuous persons
Of these professions, I had loved thee and them:
For these shall never have that plea against me,
Or colour of advantage, that I hate
Their callings, but their manners and their vices.
A worthy courtier is the ornament
Of a king's palace, his great master's honour;
This is a moth, a rascal, a court-rat,   [*Points to Fitton.*
That gnaws the commonwealth with broking suits,
And eating grievances! so, a true soldier,
He is his country's strength, his sovereign's safety.
And to secure his peace, he makes himself
The heir of danger, nay the subject of it,
And runs those virtuous hazards that this scarecrow
Cannot endure to hear of.

Shun. You are pleasant, sir.

P. Can. With you I dare be! here is Piedmantle;
'Cause he's an ass, do not I love a herald,
Who is the pure preserver of descents,
The keeper fair of all nobility,
Without which all would run into confusion?
Were he a learned herald, I would tell him
He can give arms and marks, he cannot honour;
No more than money can make noble: it may
Give place, and rank, but it can give no virtue:
And he would thank me for this truth. This dog-leach,
You style him doctor, 'cause he can compile
An almanack, perhaps erect a scheme
For my great madam's monkey, when't has ta'en
A glyster, and bewray'd the Ephemerides.
Do I despise a learn'd physician,
In calling him a quacksalver? or blast
The ever-living garland, always green,
Of a good poet, when I say his wreath
Is pieced and patch'd of dirty wither'd flowers?—
Away! I am impatient of these ulcers,
That I not call you worse. There is no sore
Or plague but you to infect the times: I abhor
Your very scent.—Come, lady, since my prodigal
Knew not to entertain you to your worth,
I'll see if I have learn'd how to receive you,
With more respect to you, and your fair train here.
Farewell, my beggar in velvet, for to-day;
To-morrow you may put on that grave robe,

                          [Points to his patch'd cloke.
And enter your great work of *Canters' College,*
Your work, and worthy of a chronicle!   *[Exeunt.*

Tat. *Why, this was the worst of all, the catastrophe!*

Cen. *The matter began to be good but now; and he has spoil'd it all with his beggar there!*

Mirth. *A beggarly Jack it is, I warrant him, and akin to the poet.*

Tat. *Like enough, for he had the chiefest part in his play, if you mark it.*

Expect. *Absurdity on him, for a huge overgrown play-maker! why should he make him live again, when they and we all thought him dead? if he had left him to his rags, there had been an end of him.*

Tat. *Ay, but set a beggar on horseback, he'll never lin till he be a gallop.*

Cen. *The young heir grew a fine gentleman in this last act.*

Expect. *So he did, gossip, and kept the best company.*

Cen. *And feasted them and his mistress.*

Tat. *And shew'd her to them all: was not jealous!*

Mirth. *But very communicative and liberal, and began to be magnificent, if the churl his father would have let him alone.*

Cen. It was spitefully done of the poet, to make the chuff take him off in his height, when he was going to do all his brave deeds.

Expect. To found an academy.

Tat. Erect a college.

Expect. Plant his professors, and water his lectures.

Mirth. With wine, gossips, as he meant to do;—and then to defraud his purposes.

Expect. Kill the hopes of so many towardly young spirits.—

Tat. As the doctor's—

Cen. And the courtier's! I protest I was in love with master Fitton: he did wear all he had, from the hatband to the shoe-tie, so politically, and would stoop, and leer!

Mirth. And lie so in wait for a piece of wit, like a mouse-trap!

Expect. Indeed, gossip, so would the little doctor; all his behaviour was mere glyster. O' my conscience, he would make any party's physic in the world work with his discourse.

Mirth. I wonder they would suffer it; a foolish old fornicating father to ravish away his son's mistress.

Cen. And all her women at once, as he did.

Tat. I would have flown in his gypsy's face, i'faith.

Mirth. It was a plain piece of political incest, and worthy to be brought afore the high commission of wit. Suppose we were to censure him; you are the youngest voice, gossip Tattle, begin.

Tat. Marry, I would have the old coney-catcher cozen'd of all he has, in the young heir's defence, by his learned counsel, master Picklock!

Cen. I would rather the courtier had found out some trick to beg him for his estate!

Expect. Or the captain had courage enough to beat him!

Cen. Or the fine Madrigal-man in rhyme, to have run him out of the country, like an Irish rat.

Tat. No, I would have master Piedmantle, her grace's herald, to pluck down his hatchments, reverse his coat armour, and nullify him for no gentleman.

Expect. Nay, then, let master doctor dissect him, have him opened, and his tripes translated to Lickfinger, to make a probation-dish of.

Cen. Tat. Agreed, agreed!

Mirth. Faith, I would have him flat disinherited by a decree of court, bound to make restitution of the lady Pecunia, and the use of her body, to his son.

Expect. And her train to the gentlemen.

Cen. And both the poet, and himself, to ask them all forgiveness!

Tat. And us too.

Cen. In two large sheets of paper—

Expect. Or to stand in a skin of parchment, which the court please.

Cen. And those fill'd with news!

Mirth. And dedicated to the sustaining of the Staple!

Expect. Which their poet hath let fall most abruptly.

Mirth. Bankruptly indeed.

Cen. You say wittily, gossip; and therefore let a protest go out against him.

Mirth. *A mournival of protests, or a gleek, at least.*

Expect. *In all our names.*

Cen. *For a decay'd wit—*

Expect. *Broken—*

Tat. *Non-solvent—*

Cen. *And for ever forfeit—*

Mirth. *To scorn of Mirth!*

Cen. *Censure!*

Expect. *Expectation!*

Tat. *Subsign'd, Tattle. Stay, they come again.*

ACT V

SCENE I.—PENNYBOY'S *Lodgings.*

Enter PENNYBOY jun. in the patched and ragged cloke his father left him.

P. jun. Nay, they are fit, as they had been made for me,
And I am now a thing worth looking at,
The same I said I would be in the morning!
No rogue, at a comitia of the canters,
Did ever there become his parent's robes
Better than I do these.   Great fool and beggar!
Why do not all that are of those societies
Come forth, and gratulate me one of theirs?
Methinks I should be on every side saluted,
Dauphin of beggars, prince of prodigals!
That have so fallen under the ears, and eyes,
And tongues of all, the fable of the time,
Matter of scorn, and mark of reprehension!
I now begin to see my vanity
Shine in this glass, reflected by the foil!—
Where is my fashioner, my feather man,
My linener, perfumer, barber, all
That tail of riot follow'd me this morning?
Not one! but a dark solitude about me,
Worthy my cloke and patches; as I had
The epidemical disease upon me;
And I'll sit down with it.   [*Seats himself on the floor.*

Enter THOMAS, Barber.

Tho. My master, maker!
How do you? why do you sit thus on the ground, sir?
Hear you the news?

P. jun. No, nor I care to bear none.
Would I could here sit still, and slip away
The other one and twenty, to have this

Forgotten, and the day razed out, expunged
In every ephemerides, or almanac!
Or if it must be in, that time and nature
Have decreed; still let it be a day
Of tickling prodigals about the gills,
Deluding gaping heirs, losing their loves,
And their discretions, falling from the favours
Of their best friends and parents, their own hopes,
And entering the society of canters.
 Tho. A doleful day it is, and dismal times
Are come upon us! I am clear undone.
 P. jun. How, Tom?
 Tho. Why, broke, broke; wretchedly broke.
 P. jun. Ha!
 Tho. Our Staple is all to pieces, quite dissolv'd.
 P. jun. Ha!
 Tho. Shiver'd, as in an earthquake! heard you not
The crack and ruins? we are all blown up!
Soon as they heard the Infanta was got from them,
Whom they had so devoured in their hopes,
To be their patroness, and sojourn with them,
Our emissaries, register, examiner,
Flew into vapour: our grave governor
Into a subtler air, and is return'd,
As we do hear, grand captain of the jeerers.
I and my fellow melted into butter,
And spoil'd our ink, and so the office vanish'd.
The last hum that it made, was, that your father
And Picklock are fall'n out, the man of law.
 P. jun. [*starting up.*] How! this awakes me from my lethargy.
 Tho. And a great suit is like to be between them:
Picklock denies the feoffment, and the trust,
Your father says he made of the whole estate
Unto him, as respecting his mortality,
When he first laid his late device, to try you.
 P. jun. Has Picklock then a trust?
 Tho. I cannot tell.
Here comes the worshipful—
  [*P. jun. makes a sign to Tho., who retires behind the hangings.*

Enter PICKLOCK.

 Pick. What, my velvet heir
Turn'd beggar in mind, as robes!
 P. jun. You see what case
Your, and my father's plots have brought me to.
 Pick. Your father's, you may say, indeed, not mine.
He's a hard-hearted gentleman; I am sorry
To see his rigid resolution!

That any man should so put off affection,
And human nature, to destroy his own,
And triumph in a victory so cruel!
He's fallen out with me, for being yours,
And calls me knave, and traitor to his trust;
Says he will have me thrown over the bar—
　　P. jun. Have you deserv'd it?
　　Pick. O, good Heaven knows
My conscience, and the silly latitude of it;
A narrow-minded man! my thoughts do dwell
All in a lane, or line indeed; no turning,
Nor scarce obliquity in them.　I still look
Right forward, to the intent and scope of that
Which he would go from now.
　　P. jun. Had you a trust then?
　　Pick. Sir, I had somewhat will keep you still lord
Of all the estate, if I be honest, as
I hope I shall.　My tender scrupulous breast
Will not permit me see the heir defrauded,
And like an alien thrust out of the blood.
The laws forbid that I should give consent
To such a civil slaughter of a son!
　　P. jun. Where is the deed? hast thou it with thee?
　　Pick. No.
It is a thing of greater consequence,
Than to be borne about in a black box,
Like a Low-Country vorloffe, or Welsh brief.
It is at Lickfinger's, under lock and key.
　　P. jun. O, fetch it hither.
　　Pick. I have bid him bring it,
That you might see it.
　　P. jun. Knows he what he brings?
　　Pick. No more than a gardener's ass, what roots he carries.
　　P. jun. I was a sending my father, like an ass,
A penitent epistle; but I am glad
I did not now.
　　Pick. Hang him, an austere grape,
That has no juice, but what is verjuice in him!
　　P. jun. I'll shew you my letter.　　　　　　　　　[*Exit.*
　　Pick. Shew me a defiance!
If I can now commit father and son,
And make my profits out of both; commence
A suit with the old man for his whole state,
And go to law with the son's credit, undo
Both, both with their own money, it were a piece
Worthy my night-cap, and the gown I wear,
A Picklock's name in law.—Where are you, sir?
What do you do so long?

Re-enter PENNYBOY jun.

P. jun. I cannot find
Where I have laid it; but I have laid it safe.

Pick. No matter, sir; trust you unto my Trust,
'Tis that that shall secure you, an absolute deed!
And I confess it was in trust for you,
Lest any thing might have happen'd mortal to him:
But there must be a gratitude thought on,
And aid, sir, for the charges of the suit,
Which will be great, 'gainst such a mighty man
As is your father, and a man possest
Of so much land, Pecunia and her friends.
I am not able to wage law with him,
Yet must maintain the thing, as my own right,
Still for your good, and therefore must be bold
To use your credit for moneys.

P. jun. What thou wilt,
So we be safe, and the trust bear it.

Pick. Fear not,
'Tis he must pay arrearages in the end.
We'll milk him and Pecunia, draw their cream down,
Before he get the deed into his hands.
My name is Picklock, but he'll find me a padlock.

Enter PENNYBOY Canter.

P. Can. How now! conferring with your learned counsel
Upon the cheat! Are you of the plot to cozen me?

P. jun. What plot?

P. Can. Your counsel knows there, master Picklock,
Will you restore the trust yet?

Pick. Sir, take patience
And memory unto you, and bethink you,
What trust? where does't appear? I have your deed;
Doth your deed specify any trust? Is it not
A perfect act, and absolute in law,
Seal'd and deliver'd before witnesses,
The day and date emergent?

P. Can. But what conference,
What oaths and vows preceded?

Pick. I will tell you, sir,
Since I am urged of those; as I remember,
You told me you had got a grown estate,
By griping means, sinisterly—

P. Can. How!

Pick. And were
Even weary of it; if the parties lived
From whom you had wrested it—

P. Can. Ha!

Pick. You could be glad
To part with all, for satisfaction:
But since they had yielded to humanity,
And that just Heaven had sent you for a punishment,
You did acknowledge it, this riotous heir,
That would bring all to beggary in the end,
And daily sow'd consumption where he went—

    P. Can. You would cozen both then? your confederate too?

    Pick. After a long mature deliberation,
You could not think where better how to place it—

    P. Can. Than on you, rascal?

    Pick. What you please, in your passion;
But with your reason, you will come about,
And think a faithful and a frugal friend
To be preferr'd.

    P. Can. Before a son?

    Pick. A prodigal,
A tub without a bottom, as you term'd him!
For which I might return you a vow or two,
And seal it with an oath of thankfulness,
I not repent it, neither have I cause; yet—

    P. Can. Forehead of steel, and mouth of brass, hath impudence
Polish'd so gross a lie, and dar'st thou vent it?
Engine, composed of all mixt metals! hence,
I will not change a syllable with thee more,
Till I may meet thee at a bar in court,
Before thy judges.

    Pick. Thither it must come,
Before I part with it to you, or you, sir.

    P. Can. I will not hear thee.

    P. jun. Sir, your ear to me though—
Not that I see through his perplexed plots,
And hidden ends; nor that my parts depend
Upon the unwinding this so knotted skean,
Do I beseech your patience. Unto me,
He hath confest the trust.

    Pick. How! I confess it?

    P. jun. Ay, thou false man.

    P. Can. Stand up to him, and confront him.

    Pick. Where, when, to whom?

    P. jun. To me, even now, and here:
Canst thou deny it?

    Pick. Can I eat or drink,
Sleep, wake, or dream, arise, sit, go, or stand,
Do any thing that's natural?

    P. jun. Yes, lie
It seems thou canst, and perjure; that is natural.

    Pick. O me, what times are these of frontless carriage!
An egg of the same nest! the father's bird!

It runs in a blood, I see.
    P. jun. I'll stop your mouth.
    Pick. With what?
    P. jun. With truth.
    Pick. With noise; I must have witness:
Where is your witness? you can produce witness?
    P. jun. As if my testimony were not twenty,
Balanced with thine!
    Pick. So say all prodigals,
Sick of self-love; but that's not law, young Scattergood:
I live by law.
    P. jun. Why, if thou hast a conscience,
That is a thousand witnesses.
    Pick. No court
Grants out a writ of summons for the conscience,
That I know, nor subpœna, nor attachment.
I must have witness, and of your producing,
Ere this can come to hearing, and it must
Be heard on oath and witness.
    P. jun. Come forth, Tom!

Re-enter THOMAS, *Barber.*

Speak what thou heard'st, the truth, and the whole truth,
And nothing but the truth. What said this varlet?
    Pick. A rat behind the hangings?
    Tho. Sir, he said,
It was a trust! an act, the which your father
Had will to alter; but *his tender breast*
Would not permit to see the heir defrauded,
And, like an alien, thrust out of the blood.
The laws forbid that he should give consent
To such a civil slaughter of a son—
    P. jun. And talk'd of a gratuity to be given,
And aid unto the charges of the suit;
Which he was to maintain in his own name,
But for my use, he said.
    P. Can. It is enough.
    Tho. And he *would milk Pecunia, and draw down*
Her cream, before you got the trust again.
    P. Can. Your ears are in my pocket, knave, go shake 'em
The little while you have them.
    Pick. You do trust
To your great purse.
    P. Can. I have you in a purse-net,
Good master Picklock, with your worming brain,
And wriggling engine-head of maintenance,
Which I shall see you hole with very shortly!
A fine round head, when those two lugs are off,
To trundle through a pillory! You are sure

You heard him speak this?

P. jun. Ay, and more.

Tho. Much more.

Pick. I'll prove yours maintenance and combination,
And sue you all.

P. Can. Do, do, my gowned vulture,
Crop in reversion! I shall see you quoited
Over the bar, as bargemen do their billets.

Pick. This 'tis, when men repent of their good deeds,
And would have 'em in again—They are almost mad:
But I forgive their *lucida intervalla.*

Enter LICKFINGER.

O, Lickfinger! come hither.

[*Comes forward with Lickfinger; while P. jun. discovers the plot,
aside, to his father, and that he is in possession of the deed.*

Where's my writing?

Lick. I sent it you, together with your keys.

Pick. How?

Lick. By the porter that came for it from you,
And by the token, you had given me the keys,
And bade me bring it.

Pick. And why did you not?

Lick. Why did you send a countermand?

Pick. Who, I?

Lick. You, or some other you, you put in trust.

Pick. In trust!

Lick. Your trust's another self, you know;
And without trust, and your trust, how should he
Take notice of your keys, or of my charge?

Pick. Know you the man?

Lick. I know he was a porter,
And a seal'd porter; for he bore the badge
On his breast, I am sure.

Pick. I am lost: a plot! I scent it.

Lick. Why, and I sent it by the man you sent,
Whom else I had not trusted.

Pick. Plague on your trust!
I am truss'd up among you—

P. jun. Or you may be.

Pick. In mine own halter; I have made the noose.   [*Exit.*

P. jun. What was it, Lickfinger?

Lick. A writing, sir,
He sent for't by a token; I was bringing it,
But that he sent a porter, and he seem'd
A man of decent carriage.

P. Can. 'Twas good fortune!
To cheat the cheater, was no cheat, but justice.
Put off your rags, and be yourself again:

This act of piety and good affection
Hath partly reconciled me to you.
 P. jun. Sir—
 P. Can. No vows, no promises; too much protestation
Makes that suspected oft, we could persuade.
 Lick. Hear you the news?
 P. jun. The office is down, how should we?
 Lick. But of your uncle?
 P. jun. No.
 Lick. He is run mad, sir.
 P. Can. How, Lickfinger?
 Lick. Stark staring mad, your brother,
He has almost kill'd his maid—
 P. Can. Now heaven forbid!
 Lick. But that she is cat-lived and squirrel-limb'd,
With throwing bed-staves at her: he has set wide
His outer doors, and now keeps open house
For all the passers-by to see his justice.
First, he has apprehended his two dogs,
As being of the plot to cozen him;
And there he sits like an old worm of the peace,
Wrapp'd up in furs, at a square table, screwing,
Examining, and committing the poor curs
To two old cases of close-stools, as prisons:
The one of which he calls his Lollard's tower,
T'other his Block-house, 'cause his two dogs' names
Are Block and Lollard.
 P. jun. This would be brave matter
Unto the jeerers.
 P. Can. Ay, if so the subject
Were not so wretched.
 Lick. Sure I met them all,
I think, upon that quest.
 P. Can. 'Faith, like enough:
The vicious still are swift to shew their natures.
I'll thither too, but with another aim,
If all succeed well, and my simples take.   [*Exeunt.*

SCENE II.—*A Room in* PENNYBOY senior's *House.*

PENNYBOY sen. *discovered sitting at table with papers, etc., before*
 him; Porter, *and* Block *and* Lollard (*two dogs*).

 P. sen. Where are the prisoners?
 Por. They are forth-coming, sir,
Or coming forth, at least.
 P. sen. The rogue is drunk,
Since I committed them to his charge.—Come hither,
Near me, yet nearer; breathe upon me. [*He smells him.*] Wine!
Wine o' my worship! sack, Canary sack!

Could not your badge have been drunk with fulsom ale,
Or beer, the porter's element? but sack!

Por. I am not drunk; we had, sir, but one pint,
An honest carrier and myself.

P. sen. Who paid for't?

Por. Sir, I did give it him.

P. sen. What, and spend sixpence!
A frock spend sixpence! sixpence!

Por. Once in a year, sir.

P. sen. In seven years, varlet! know'st thou what thou hast done,
What a consumption thou hast made of a state?
It might please heav'n (a lusty knave and young)
To let thee live some seventy years longer,
Till thou art fourscore and ten, perhaps a hundred.
Say seventy years; how many times seven in seventy?
Why seven times ten, is ten times seven, mark me,
I will demonstrate to thee on my fingers.
Sixpence in seven year, use upon use,
Grows in that first seven year to be a twelve-pence;
That, in the next, two shillings; the third, four shillings;
The fourth seven year, eight shillings; the fifth, sixteen;
The sixth, two and thirty; the seventh, three pound four;
The eighth, six pound and eight; the ninth, twelve pound sixteen;
And the tenth seven, five and twenty pound
Twelve shillings. This thou art fall'n from by thy riot,
Should'st thou live seventy years, by spending sixpence
Once in the seven: but in a day to waste it!
There is a sum that number cannot reach!
Out of my house, thou pest of prodigality,
Seed of consumption, hence! a wicked keeper
Is oft worse than the prisoners. There's thy penny,
Four tokens for thee. Out, away! [*Exit Por.*] My dogs
May yet be innocent and honest: if not,
I have an entrapping question or two more,
To put unto them, a cross intergatory,
And I shall catch them. Lollard! Peace: [*He calls forth Lollard.*
What whispering was that you had with Mortgage,
When you last lick'd her feet? the truth now. Ha!
Did you smell she was going? Put down that. *And not,
Not to return?* You are silent: good! And when
Leap'd you on Statute? *As she went forth?* Consent!
There was consent, as she was going forth.
'Twould have been fitter at her coming home,
But you knew *that she would not?* To your tower:
You are cunning, are you? I will meet your craft.

                      [*Commits him again.*
Block, shew your face; leave your caresses: tell me,

                      [*Calls forth Block.*
And tell me truly, what affronts do you know

Were done Pecunia, that she left my house?
None, say you so? *not that you know?* or *will know?*
I fear me, I shall find you an obstinate cur.
Why did your fellow Lollard cry this morning?
'Cause Broker kick'd him? Why did Broker kick him?
Because he pist against my lady's gown?
Why, that was no affront, no, no distaste.
You knew of none? you are a dissembling tyke,
To your hole again, your Block-house. [*Commits him.*] Lollard, arise.
Where did you lift your leg up last, 'gainst what?
Are you struck dummerer now, and whine for mercy?
Whose kirtle was't you gnaw'd too, mistress Band's?
And Wax's stockings? Who? *Did Block bescumber
Statute's white suit, with the parchment lace there;
And Broker's satin doublet?* All will out,
They had offence, offence enough to quit me.
Appear, Block, foh! 'tis manifest; he shews it,
Should he forswear't, make all the affidavits
Against it, that he could afore the bench
And twenty juries, he would be convinced.
He bears an air about him doth confess it.

       Enter CYMBAL, FITTON, SHUNFIELD, ALMANAC, *and*
               MADRIGAL *behind.*

To prison again, close prison. Not you, Lollard;
You may enjoy the liberty of the house:
And yet there is a quirk come in my head,
For which I must commit you too, and close.
Do not repine, it will be better for you—
   Cym. This is enough to make the dogs mad too:
Let's in upon him.   [*They come forward.*
   P. sen. How now, what's the matter?
Come you to force the prisoners? make a rescue?
   Fit. We come to bail your dogs.
   P. sen. They are not bailable,
They stand committed without bail or mainprise,
Your bail cannot be taken.
   Shun. Then the truth is,
We come to vex you.
   Alm. Jeer you.
   Mad. Bait you, rather.
   Cym. A baited usurer will be good flesh.
   Fit. And tender, we are told.
   P. sen. Who is the butcher,
Amongst you, that is come to cut my throat?
   Shun. You would die a calf's death fain; but 'tis an ox's
Is meant you.
   Fit. To be fairly knock'd o' the head.
   Shun. With a good jeer or two.

P. sen. And from your jaw-bone,
Don Assinigo?

Cym. Shunfield, a jeer; you have it.

Shun. I do confess, a swashing blow; but, Snarl,
You that might play the third dog, for your teeth,
You have no money now?

Fit. No, nor no Mortgage.

Alm. Nor Band.

Mad. Nor Statute.

Cym. No, nor blushet Wax.

P. sen. Nor you no office, as I take it.

Shun. Cymbal,
A mighty jeer!

Fit. Pox o' these true jests, I say!

Mad. He'll turn the better jeerer.

Alm. Let's upon him,
And if we cannot jeer him down in wit—

Mad. Let's do't in noise.

Shun. Content.

Mad. Charge, man of war.

Alm. Lay him aboard.

Shun. We'll give him a broadside first.

Fit. Where is your venison now?

Cym. Your red-deer pies?

Shun. With your baked turkeys?

Alm. And your partridges?

Mad. Your pheasants and fat swans!

P. sen. Like you, turn'd geese.

Mad. But such as will not keep your Capitol.

Shun. You were wont to have your breams—

Alm. And trouts sent in.

Cym. Fat carps and salmons.

Fit. Ay, and now and then,
An emblem of yourself, an o'ergrown pike.

P. sen. You are a jack, sir.

Fit. You have made a shift
To swallow twenty such poor jacks ere now.

Alm. If he should come to feed upon poor John—

Mad. Or turn pure Jack-a-lent after all this?

Fit. Tut, he will live like a grasshopper—

Mad. On dew.

Shun. Or like a bear, with licking his own claws.

Cym. Ay, if his dogs were away.

Alm. He'll eat them first,
While they are fat.

Fit. Faith, and when they are gone,
Here's nothing to be seen beyond.

Cym. Except
His kindred spiders, natives of the soil.

Alm. Dust he will have enough here, to breed fleas.

Mad. But by that time he'll have no blood to rear them.

Shun. He will be as thin as a lanthorn, we shall see through him.

Alm. And his gut colon tell his *intestina.*

P. sen. Rogues! rascals!   [*The dogs bark.*   (Bow, wow!)

Fit. He calls his dogs to his aid.

Alm. O, they but rise at mention of his tripes.

Cym. Let them alone, they do it not for him.

Mad. They bark *se defendendo.*

Shun. Or for custom,
As commonly curs do, one for another.

Enter LICKFINGER.

Lick. Arm, arm you, gentlemen jeerers! the old Canter
Is coming in upon you with his forces,
The gentleman that was the Canter.

Shun. Hence!

Fit. Away!

Cym. What is he?

Alm. Stay not to ask questions.

Fit. He is a flame.

Shun. A furnace.

Alm. A consumption,
Kills where he goes.   [*Cym., Fit., Mad., Alm., and Shun. run off.*

Lick. See! the whole covey is scatter'd;
'Ware, 'ware the hawks! I love to see them fly.

Enter PENNYBOY Canter, PENNYBOY jun., PECUNIA, STATUTE,
BAND, WAX, *and* MORTGAGE.

P. Can. You see by this amazement and distraction,
What your companions were, a poor, affrighted,
And guilty race of men, that dare to stand
No breath of truth; but conscious to themselves
Of their no-wit, or honesty, ran routed
At every panic terror themselves bred.
Where else, as confident as sounding brass,
Their tinkling captain, Cymbal, and the rest,
Dare put on any visor, to deride
The wretched, or with buffoon license jest
At whatsoe'er is serious, if not sacred.

P. sen. Who's this? my brother! and restored to life!

P. Can. Yes, and sent hither to restore your wits;
If your short madness be not more than anger
Conceived for your loss! which I return you.
See here, your Mortgage, Statute, Band, and Wax,
Without your Broker, come to abide with you,
And vindicate the prodigal from stealing
Away the lady. Nay, Pecunia herself
Is come to free him fairly, and discharge

All ties, but those of love unto her person,
To use her like a friend, not like a slave,
Or like an idol. Superstition
Doth violate the deity it worships,
No less than scorn doth; and believe it, brother,
The use of things is all, and not the store:
Surfeit and fulness have kill'd more than famine.
The sparrow with his little plumage flies,
While the proud peacock, overcharg'd with pens,
Is fain to sweep the ground with his grown train,
And load of feathers.

   P. sen. Wise and honour'd brother!
None but a brother, and sent from the dead,
As you are to me, could have alter'd me:
I thank my destiny, that is so gracious.
Are there no pains, no penalties decreed
From whence you come, to us that smother money
In chests, and strangle her in bags?

   P. Can. O, mighty,
Intolerable fines, and mulcts imposed,
Of which I come to warn you: forfeitures
Of whole estates, if they be known and taken.

   P. sen. I thank you, brother, for the light you have given me;
I will prevent them all.   First, free my dogs,
Lest what I have done to them, and against law,
Be a præmunire; for by Magna Charta
They could not be committed as close prisoners.
My learned counsel tells me here, my cook:
And yet he shew'd me the way first.

   Lick. Who did? I!
I trench the liberty of the subjects!

   P. Can. Peace,
Picklock, your guest, that Stentor, hath infected you,
Whom I have safe enough in a wooden collar.

   P. sen. Next, I restore these servants to their lady,
With freedom, heart of cheer, and countenance;
It is their year and day of jubilee.

   Omnes. We thank you, sir.

   P. sen. And lastly, to my nephew
I give my house, goods, lands, all but my vices,
And those I go to cleanse; kissing this lady,
Whom I do give him too, and join their hands.

   P. Can. If the spectators will join theirs, we thank 'em.

   P. jun. And wish they may, as I, enjoy Pecunia.

   Pec. And so Pecunia herself doth wish,
That she may still be aid unto their uses,
Not slave unto their pleasures, or a tyrant
Over their fair desires; but teach them all
The golden mean; the prodigal how to live;

The sordid and the covetous how to die:
That, with sound mind; this, safe frugality.   [*Exeunt.*

THE EPILOGUE.

Thus have you seen the maker's double scope,
To profit and delight; wherein our hope
Is, though the clout we do not always hit,
It will not be imputed to his wit:—
A tree so tried, and bent, as 'twill not start:
Nor doth he often crack a string of art;
Though there may other accidents as strange
Happen, the weather of your looks may change,
Or some high wind of misconceit arise,
To cause an alteration in our skies:
If so, we are sorry, that have so misspent
Our time and tackle; yet he's confident,
And vows, the next fair day he'll have us shoot
The same match o'er for him, if you'll come to't.

THE NEW INN; OR, THE LIGHT HEART

TO THE READER

If thou be such, I make thee my patron, and dedicate the piece to thee: if not so much, would I had been at the charge of thy better literature. Howsoever, if thou canst but spell, and join my sense, there is more hope of thee, than of a hundred fastidious impertinents, who were there present the first day, yet never made piece of their prospect the right way. What did they come for, then? thou wilt ask me. I will as punctually answer: To see, and to be seen: to make a general muster of themselves in their clothes of credit; and possess the stage against the play: to dislike all, but mark nothing. And by their confidence of rising between the acts, in oblique lines, make affidavit to the whole house, of their not understanding one scene. Armed with this prejudice, as the stage furniture, or arras-clothes, they were there, as spectators, away: for the faces in the hangings, and they, beheld alike. So I wish they may do ever; and do trust myself and my book, rather to thy rustic candour, than all the pomp of their pride, and solemn ignorance to boot. Fare thee well, and fall to. Read.

BEN JONSON.

But first,

THE ARGUMENT

THE Lord Frampul, a noble gentleman, well educated, and bred a scholar in Oxford, was married young, to a virtuous gentlewoman, Sylly's daughter of the South, whose worth, though he truly enjoyed, he never could rightly value; but, as many green husbands, (given over to their extravagant delights, and some peccant humours of their own,) occasioned in his over-loving wife so deep a melancholy, by his leaving her in the time of her lying-in of her second daughter, she having brought him only two daughters, Frances and Lætitia: and (out of her hurt fancy) interpreting that to be a cause of her husband's coldness in affection, her not being blest with a son, took a resolution with herself, after her month's time, and thanks-giving rightly in the church, to quit her home, with a vow never to return, till by reducing her lord, she could bring a wished happiness to the family.

He in the mean time returning, and hearing of this departure of his lady, began, though over-late, to resent the injury he had done her: and out of his cock-brain'd resolution, entered into as solemn a quest of her. Since when, neither of them had been heard of. But the eldest daughter, Frances, by the title of Lady Frampul, enjoyed the estate, her sister being lost young, and is the sole relict of the family. Here begins our Comedy.

ACT I.

This lady, being a brave, bountiful lady, and enjoying this free and plentiful estate, hath an ambitious disposition to be esteemed the mistress of many servants, but loves none. And hearing of a famous New-Inn, that is kept by a merry host, call'd Goodstock, in Barnet, invites some lords and gentlemen to wait on her thither, as well to see the fashions of the place, as to make themselves merry, with the accidents on the by. It happens there is a melancholy gentleman, one Master Lovel, hath been lodged there some days before in the inn, who (unwilling to be seen) is surprised by the lady, and invited by Prudence, the lady's chambermaid, who is elected governess of the sports in the inn for that day, and install'd their sovereign. Lovel is persuaded by the host, and yields to the lady's invitation, which concludes the first act. Having revealed his quality before to the host.

ACT II.

In this, Prudence and her lady express their anger conceiv'd at the tailor, who had promised to make Prudence a new suit, and bring it home, as on the eve, against this day. But he failing of his word, the lady had commanded a standard of her own best apparel to be brought down; and Prudence is so fitted. The lady being put in mind, that she is there alone without other company of women, borrows, by the advice of Prue, the host's son of the house, whom they dress, with the host's consent, like a lady, and send out the coachman with the empty coach, as for a kinswoman of her ladyship's, Mistress Lætitia Sylly, to bear her company: who attended with his nurse, an old charewoman in the inn, drest odly by the host's counsel, is believed to be a lady of quality, and so receiv'd, entertain'd, and love made to her by the young Lord Beaufort, etc. In the mean time the Fly of the Inn is discover'd to Colonel Glorious, with the Militia of the house, below the stairs, in the Drawer, Tapster, Chamberlain, and Hostler, inferior Officers; with the Coachman, Trundle, Ferret, etc. And the preparation is made to the lady's design upon Lovel, his upon her, and the sovereign's upon both.

ACT III.

Here begins the Epitasis, or business of the Play.

Lovel, by the dexterity and wit of the sovereign of the sports, Prudence, having two hours assign'd him of free colloquy, and love-making to his mistress, one after dinner, the other after supper, the court being set, is demanded by the Lady Frampul, what love is: as doubting if there were any such power, or no. To whom he, first by definition, and after by argument, answers; proving and describing the effects of love so vively, as she who had derided the name of love before, hearing his discourse, is now so taken both with the man and his matter, as she confesseth herself enamour'd of him, and, but for the ambition she hath to enjoy the other hour, had presently declared herself: which gives both him and the spectators occasion to think she yet dissembles, notwithstanding the payment of her kiss, which he celebrates. And the court dissolves, upon news brought of a new lady, a newer coach, and a new coachman call'd Barnaby.

ACT IV.

The house being put into a noise, with the rumour of this new lady, and there being drinking below in the court, the colonel, Sir Glorious, with Bat Burst, a broken citizen, and Hodge Huffle, his champion; she falls into their hands, and being attended but with one footman, is uncivilly entreated by them, and a quarrel commenced, but is rescued by the valour of Lovel; which beheld by the Lady Frampul, from the window, she is invited up for safety, where coming, and conducted by the host, her gown is first discovered to be the same with the whole suit, which was bespoken for Prue, and she herself, upon examination, found to be Pinnacia Stuff, the tailor's wife, who was wont to be pre-occupied in all his customers' best clothes, by the footman her husband. They are both condemned and censured, she stript like a doxy, and sent home a-foot. In the interim, the second hour goes on, and the question, at suit of the Lady Frampul, is changed from love to valour; which ended, he receives his second kiss, and, by the rigour of the sovereign, falls into a fit of melancholy, worse, or more desperate than the first.

ACT V.

Is the catastrophe, or knitting up of all, where Fly brings word to the host of the Lord Beaufort's being married privately in the New Stable, to the supposed lady, his son; which the host receives as an omen of mirth; but complains that Lovel is gone to bed melancholic, when Prudence appears drest in the new suit, applauded by her lady, and employed to retrieve Lovel. The host encounters them, with this relation of Lord Beaufort's marriage, which is seconded by the Lord Latimer, and all the servants of the house. In this while, Lord Beaufort comes in, and professes it, calls for his bed and bride-bowl to be made ready; the host forbids both, shews whom he hath married, and discovers him to be his son, a boy. The lord bridegroom confounded, the nurse enters like a frantic bedlamite, cries out on Fly, says she is undone in her daughter, who is confessed to be the Lord Frampul's child, sister to the other lady, the host to be their father, she his wife. He finding his children, bestows them one on Lovel, the other on the Lord Beaufort, the Inn upon Fly, who had been a gypsy with him; offers a portion with Prudence, for her wit, which is refused; and she taken by the Lord Latimer, to wife; for the crown of her virtue and goodness. And all are contented.

DRAMATIS PERSONÆ

WITH SOME SHORT CHARACTERISM OF THE CHIEF ACTORS

GOODSTOCK, the Host, (play'd well,) alias the Lord FRAMPUL. He pretends to be a gentleman and a scholar, neglected by the times, turns host, and keeps an Inn, the sign of the Light-Heart, in Barnet : is supposed to have one only son, but is found to have none, but two daughters, FRANCES, and LÆTITIA, who was lost young, etc.

LOVEL, a complete Gentleman, a soldier and a scholar, is a melancholy guest in the Inn : first quarrell'd, after much honoured and beloved by the host. He is known to have been Page to the old Lord BEAUFORT, follow'd him in the French wars, after a companion of his studies, and left guardian to his son. He is assisted in his love to the Lady FRAMPUL, by the host and the chambermaid PRUDENCE. He was one that acted well too.

FERRET, who is called STOTE and VERMIN, is LOVEL'S Servant, a fellow of a quick, nimble wit, knows the manners and affections of people, and can make profitable and timely discoveries of them.

FRANK, supposed a boy, and the host's son, borrowed to be drest for a lady, and set up as a stale by PRUDENCE, to catch BEAUFORT or LATIMER, proves to be LÆTITIA, sister to FRANCES, and Lord FRAMPUL'S younger daughter, stolen by a beggar woman, shorn, put into boy's apparel, sold to the host, and brought up by him as his son.

NURSE, a poor Chare-Woman in the Inn, with one eye, that tends the boy, is thought the Irish beggar that sold him, but is truly the Lady FRAMPUL, who left her home melancholic, and jealous that her lord loved her not, because she brought him none but daughters ; and lives unknown to her husband, as he to her.

FRANCES, *supposed the* Lady FRAMPUL, *being reputed his sole daughter and heir, the barony descending upon her, is a lady of great fortune, and beauty, but phantastical ; thinks nothing a felicity, but to have a multitude of servants, and be call'd mistress by them, comes to the Inn to be merry, with a chambermaid only, and her servants her guests, etc.*

PRUDENCE, *the Chambermaid, is elected sovereign of the sports in the Inn, governs all, commands, and so orders, as the* Lord LATIMER *is exceedingly taken with her, and takes her to his wife, in conclusion.*

LORD LATIMER, *and* LORD BEAUFORT, *are a pair of young lords, servants and guests to the Lady* FRAMPUL; *but as* LATIMER *falls enamour'd of* PRUDENCE, *so doth* BEAUFORT *on the boy, the host's son, set up for* LÆTITIA, *the younger sister, which she proves to be indeed.*

SIR GLORIOUS TIPTO, *a Knight, and Colonel, hath the luck to think well of himself, without a rival, talks gloriously of any thing, but very seldom is in the right. He is the* lady's guest, and her servant too ; but this day utterly neglects his service, or that him. For he is so enamour'd on the Fly of the Inn, and the Militia below stairs, with HODGE HUFFLE and BAT BURST, guests that come in, and TRUNDLE, BARNABY, etc., as no other society relisheth with him.

FLY, *is the Parasite of the Inn, visitor-general of the house, one that had been a strolling gypsy, but now is reclaim'd, to be inflamer of the reckonings.*

PIERCE, *the Drawer, knighted by the* Colonel, *styled Sir* PIERCE, *and* Young ANON, *one of the chief of the infantry.*

JORDAN, *the Chamberlain, another of the Militia, and an Officer, commands the tertia of the beds.*

JUG, *the Tapster, a thoroughfare of news.*

PECK, *the Hostler.*

BAT BURST, *a broken Citizen, an in-and-in man.*

HODGE HUFFLE, *a Cheater, his Champion.*

NICK STUFF, *the Ladies' Tailor.*

PINNACIA STUFF, *his Wife.*

TRUNDLE, *a Coachman.*

BARNABY, *a hired Coachman.*

STAGGERS, *the Smith,* ⎫ *only talked*
TREE, *the Sadler,* ⎭ *on.*

SCENE,—BARNET

THE PROLOGUE.

You are welcome, welcome all to the New Inn:
Though the old house, we hope our cheer will win
Your acceptation: we have the same cook
Still, and the fat, who says, you shall not look
Long for your bill of fare, but every dish
Be serv'd in i' the time, and to your wish:
If any thing be set to a wrong taste,
'Tis not the meat there, but the mouth's displaced,
Remove but that sick palate, all is well.
For this the secure dresser bade me tell,
Nothing more hurts just meetings, than a crowd;
Or, when the expectation's grown too loud:
That the nice stomach would have this or that,
And being ask'd, or urged, it knows not what,
When sharp or sweet, have been too much a feast,
And both outlived the palate of the guest.

Beware to bring such appetites to the stage,
They do confess a weak, sick, queasy age;
And a shrewd grudging too of ignorance,
When clothes and faces 'bove the men advance:
Hear for your health, then, but at any hand,
Before you judge, vouchsafe to understand,
Concoct, digest: if then, it do not hit,
Some are in a consumption of wit,
Deep he dares say, he will not think, that all—
For hectics are not epidemical.

ACT I

SCENE I.—*A Room in the Inn.*

Enter Host, *followed by* Ferret.

Host. I am not pleased, indeed, you are in the right;
Nor is my house pleased, if my sign could speak,
The sign of the Light Heart. There you may read it;
So may your master too, if he look on it.
A heart weigh'd with a feather, and outweigh'd too:
A brain-child of my own, and I am proud on't!
And if his worship think, here, to be melancholy,
In spite of me or my wit, he is deceived;
I will maintain the rebus against all humours,
And all complexions in the body of man,
That is my word, or in the isle of Britain!
    Fer. You have reason, good mine host.
    Host. Sir, I have rhyme too.
Whether it be by chance or art,
A heavy purse makes a light heart.
There 'tis exprest: first, by a purse of gold,
A heavy purse, and then two turtles, makes,
A heart with a light stuck in it, a Light Heart.
Old abbot Islip could not invent better,
Or prior Bolton with his bolt and ton.
I am an inn-keeper, and know my grounds,
And study them; brain o' man! I study them.
I must have jovial guests to drive my ploughs,
And whistling boys to bring my harvest home,
Or I shall hear no flails thwack. Here, your master
And you have been this fortnight, drawing fleas
Out of my mats, and pounding them in cages
Cut out of cards, and those roped round with pack-thread
Drawn through birdlime, a fine subtility!
Or poring through a multiplying-glass,
Upon a captived crab-louse, or a cheese-mite,
To be dissected, as the sports of nature,

With a neat Spanish needle! speculations
That do become the age, I do confess!
As measuring an ant's eggs with the silk-worm's,
By a phantastic instrument of thread,
Shall give you their just difference to a hair!
Or else recovering of dead flies with crumbs,
Another quaint conclusion in the physics,
Which I have seen you busy at, through the key-hole—
But never had the fate to see a fly

Enter Lovel.

Alive in your cups, or once heard, *Drink, mine host!*
Or such a cheerful chirping charm come from you.
    Lov. What's that, what's that?
    Fer. A buzzing of mine host
About a fly; a murmur that he has.
    Host. Sir, I am telling your Stote here, monsieur Ferret,
For that I hear's his name, and dare tell you, sir,
If you have a mind to be melancholy, and musty,
There's Footman's inn at the town's end, the stocks,
Or Carrier's place, at sign of the Broken Wain,
Mansions of state! take up your harbour there,
There are both flies and fleas, and all variety
Of vermin, for inspection or dissection.
    Lov. We have set our rest up here, sir, in your Heart.
    Host. Sir, set your heart at rest, you shall not do it,
Unless you can be jovial. Brain of man!
Be jovial first, and drink, and dance, and drink.
Your lodging here, and with your daily dumps,
Is a mere libel 'gain my house and me;
And, then, your scandalous commons—
    Lov. How, mine host!
    Host. Sir, they do scandal me upon the road here,
A poor quotidian rack of mutton, roasted
Dry to be grated! and that driven down
With beer and butter-milk, mingled together.
Or clarified whey instead of claret!
It is against my freehold, my inheritance,
My Magna Charta, *cor lætificat*,
To drink such balderdash, or bonny-clabber!
Give me good wine, or catholic, or christian,
Wine is the word that glads the heart of man:
And mine's the house of wine: Sack, says my bush,
Be merry, and *drink sherry;* that's my posie!
For I shall never joy in my light heart,
So long as I conceive a sullen guest,
Or any thing that's earthy.
    Lov. Humorous host!
    Host. I care not if I be.

Lov. But airy also!
Not to defraud you of your rights, or trench
Upon your privileges, or great charter,
For those are every hostler's language now,
Say, you were born beneath those smiling stars,
Have made you lord and owner of the Heart,
Of the Light Heart in Barnet: suffer us,
Who are more saturnine, to enjoy the shade
Of your round roof yet.
    Host. Sir, I keep no shades
Nor shelters, I, for either owls or rere-mice.

               Enter FRANK.

    Fer. He'll make you a bird of night, sir.
    Host. Bless you, child!—   [*Aside to Frank.*
You'll make yourselves such.
    Lov. That your son, mine host?
    Host. He's all the sons I have, sir.
    Lov. Pretty boy!
Goes he to school?
    Fer. O lord, sir, he prates Latin,
An it were a parrot, or a play-boy.
    Lov. Thou
Commend'st him fitly!
    Fer. To the pitch he flies, sir.
He'll tell you what is Latin for a looking-glass,
A beard-brush, rubber, or quick warming pan.
    Lov. What's that?
    Fer. A wench, in the inn-phrase, is all these;
    A looking-glass in her eye,
    A beard-brush with her lips,
    A rubber with her hand,
    And a warming-pan with her hips.
    Host. This, in your scurril dialect: but my inn
Knows no such language.
    Fer. That's because, mine host,
You do profess the teaching him yourself.
    Host. Sir, I do teach him somewhat: by degrees,
And with a funnel, I make shift to fill
The narrow vessel; he is but yet a bottle.
    Lov. O let him lose no time though.
    Host. Sir, he does not.
    Lov. And less his manners.
    Host. I provide for those too.—
Come hither, Frank, speak to the gentleman
In Latin; he is melancholy: say,
I long to see him merry, and so would treat him.
    *Fra. Subtristis visu' es esse aliquantulum patri, qui te laute
excipere, etiam ac tractare gestit.*

The New Inn

Lov. *Pulchre.*

Host. Tell him, I fear it bodes us some ill luck,
His too reservedness.

Fra. *Veretur pater, ne quid nobis mali ominis apportet iste nimis præclusus vultus.*

Lov. *Belle.* A fine child!
You will not part with him, mine host?

Host. Who told you
I would not?

Lov. I but ask you.

Host. And I answer
To whom? for what?

Lov. To me, to be my page.

Host. I know no mischief yet the child hath done,
To deserve such a destiny.

Lov. Why?

Host. Go down, boy,
And get your breakfast. [*Exeunt Frank and Ferret.*]—Trust me,
        I had rather
Take a fair halter, wash my hands, and hang him
Myself, make a clean riddance of him, than—

Lov. What?

Host. Than damn him to that desperate course of life.

Lov. Call you that desperate, which by a line
Of institution, from our ancestors,
Hath been derived down to us, and received
In a succession, for the noblest way
Of breeding up our youth, in letters, arms,
Fair mein, discourses, civil exercise,
And all the blazon of a gentleman?
Where can he learn to vault, to ride, to fence,
To move his body gracefuller, to speak
His language purer, or to tune his mind,
Or manners, more to the harmony of nature,
Than in these nurseries of nobility?

Host. Ay, that was when the nursery's self was noble,
And only virtue made it, not the market,
That titles were not vented at the drum,
Or common outcry; goodness gave the greatness,
And greatness worship: every house became
An academy of honour, and those parts—
We see departed, in the practice now
Quite from the institution.

Lov. Why do you say so,
Or think so enviously? do they not still
Learn there the Centaur's skill, the art of Thrace,
To ride? or Pollux' mystery, to fence?
The Pyrrhic gestures, both to dance and spring
In armour, to be active for the wars?

To study figures, numbers, and proportions,
May yield them great in counsels, and the arts
Grave Nestor and the wise Ulysses practised,
To make their English sweet upon their tongue,
As reverend Chaucer says?

    Host. Sir, you mistake;
To play sir Pandarus, my copy hath it,
And carry messages to madam Cressid,
Instead of backing the brave steed, o' mornings,
To mount the chambermaid; and for a leap
Of the vaulting-horse, to ply the vaulting-house;
For exercise of arms, a bale of dice,
Or two or three packs of cards to shew the cheat,
And nimbleness of hand; mistake a cloak
From my lord's back, and pawn it; ease his pockets
Of a superfluous watch, or geld a jewel
Of an odd stone or so; twinge three or four buttons
From off my lady's gown: these are the arts,
Or seven liberal deadly sciences
Of pagery, or rather paganism,
As the tides run! to which, if he apply him,
He may, perhaps, take a degree at Tyburn,
A year the earlier; come, to read a lecture
Upon Aquinas at St. Thomas à Waterings,
And so go forth a laureat in hemp circle!

    Lov. You are tart, mine host, and talk above your seasoning,
O'er what you seem: it should not come, methinks,
Under your cap, this vein of salt and sharpness,
These strikings upon learning, now and then.
How long have you, if your dull guest may ask it,
Drove this quick trade, of keeping the Light Heart,
Your mansion, palace, here, or hostelry?

    Host. Troth, I was born to somewhat, sir, above it.

    Lov. I easily suspect that: mine host, your name?

    Host. They call me Goodstock.

    Lov. Sir, and you confess it,
Both in your language, treaty, and your bearing.

    Host. Yet all, sir, are not sons of the white hen:
Nor can we, as the songster says, come all
To be wrapt soft and warm in fortune's smock.
When she is pleas'd to trick or tromp mankind,
Some may be coats, as in the cards; but, then,
Some must be knaves, some varlets, bawds, and ostlers.
As aces, duces, cards of ten, to face it
Out in the game, which all the world is.—

    Lov. But,
It being in your free-will (as 'twas) to choose
What parts you would sustain, methinks a man
Of your sagacity, and clear nostril, should

Have made another choice, than of a place
So sordid, as the keeping of an inn:
Where every jovial tinker, for his chink,
May cry, Mine host, to crambe! *Give us drink;*
And do not slink, but skink, or else you stink.
Rogue, bawd, and cheater, call you by the surnames,
And known synonyma of your profession.

Host. But if I be no such, who then's the rogue,
In understanding, sir, I mean? who errs,
Who tinkles then, or personates Tom Tinker?
Your weazel here may tell you I talk bawdy,
And teach my boy it; and you may believe him;
But, sir, at your own peril, if I do not;
And at his too, if he do lie, and affirm it,
No slander strikes, less hurts, the innocent.
If I be honest, and that all the cheat
Be of myself, in keeping this Light Heart,
Where, I imagine all the world's a play:
The state, and men's affairs, all passages
Of life, to spring new scenes; come in, go out,
And shift, and vanish; and if I have got
A seat to sit at ease here, in mine inn,
To see the comedy; and laugh, and chuck
At the variety and throng of humours
And dispositions, that come justling in
And out still, as they one drove hence another;
Why will you envy me my happiness?
Because you are sad and lumpish; carry a load-stone
In your pocket, to hang knives on; or jet rings,
To entice young straws to leap at them; are not taken
With the alacrities of an host! 'Tis more,
And justlier, sir, my wonder, why you took
My house up, Fidler's-hall, the seat of noise,
And mirth, an inn here, to be drowsy in,
And lodge your lethargy in the Light Heart:
As if some cloud from court had been your harbinger,
Or Cheapside debt-books, or some mistress' charge,
Seeing your love grow corpulent, gave it a diet,
By absence, some such mouldy passion!

    Lov. 'Tis guess'd unhappily.   [*Aside.*

Re-enter FERRET.

    Fer. Mine host, you're call'd.
    Host. I come, boys.   [*Exit.*
    Lov. Ferret, have not you been ploughing
With this mad ox, mine host, nor he with you?
    Fer. For what, sir?
    Lov. Why, to find my riddle out.
    Fer. I hope you do believe, sir, I can find

Other discourse to be at, than my master,
With hosts and hostlers,
   Lov. If you can, 'tis well:
Go down, and see, who they are come in, what guests;
And bring me word.   *[Exit Ferret.*
   Lov. O love, what passion art thou!
So tyrannous and treacherous! first to enslave,
And then betray all that in truth do serve thee!
That not the wisest, nor the wariest creature,
Can more dissemble thee, than he can bear
Hot burning coals, in his bare palm, or bosom:
And less conceal, or hide thee, than a flash
Of enflamed powder, whose whole light doth lay it
Open to all discovery, even of those
Who have but half an eye, and less of nose.
An host, to find me! who is, commonly,
The log, a little of this side the sign-post;
Or at the best some round-grown thing, a jug
Faced with a beard, that fills out to the guests,
And takes in from the fragments of their jests!
But I may wrong this out of sullenness,
Or by mistaking humour: pray thee, phant'sy,
Be laid again: and, gentle melancholy,
Do not oppress me; I will be as silent
As the tame lover should be, and as foolish.

Re-enter HOST.

   Host. My guest, my guest, be jovial, I beseech thee.
I have fresh golden guests, guests of the game,
Three coachful! lords! and ladies! new come in;
And I will cry them to thee, and thee to them,
So I can spring a smile but in this brow,
That, like the rugged Roman alderman,
Old master Gross, surnam'd Ἀγέλαστος,
Was never seen to laugh, but at an ass.

Re-enter FERRET.

   Fer. Sir, here's the lady Frampul.
   Lov. How!
   Fer. And her train,
Lord Beaufort, and lord Latimer, the colonel
Tipto, with mistress Prue, the chambermaid,
Trundle, the coachman—
   Lov. Stop—discharge the house,
And get my horses ready; bid the groom
Bring them to the back gate.   *[Exit Ferret.*
   Host. What mean you, sir?
   Lov. To take fair leave, mine host.
   Host. I hope, my guest,

Though I have talk'd somewhat above my share,
At large, and been in the altitudes, the extravagants,
Neither my self nor any of mine have given you
The cause to quit my house thus on the sudden.

Lov. No, I affirm it on my faith. Excuse me
From such a rudeness; I was now beginning
To taste and love you: and am heartily sorry,
Any occasion should be so compelling,
To urge my abrupt departure thus. But—
Necessity's a tyrant, and commands it.

Host. She shall command me first to fire my bush;
Then break up house: or, if that will not serve,
To break with all the world; turn country bankrupt
In mine own town, upon the market-day,
And be protested for my butter and eggs,
To the last bodge of oats, and bottle of hay.
Ere you shall leave me I will break my Heart;
Coach and coach-horses, lords and ladies pack:
All my fresh guests shall stink. I'll pull my sign down,
Convert mine inn to an alms-house, or a spittle
For lazars, or switch-sellers; turn it to
An academy of rogues; or give it away
For a free-school to breed up beggars in,
And send them to the canting universities,
Before you leave me!

Lov. Troth, and I confess
I am loth, mine host, to leave you: your expressions
Both take and hold me. But, in case I stay,
I must enjoin you and your whole family
To privacy, and to conceal me; for
The secret is, I would not willingly
See, or be seen, to any of this ging,
Especially the lady.

Host. Brain o' man!
What monster is she, or cockatrice in velvet,
That kills thus?

Lov. O good words, mine host. She is
A noble lady, great in blood and fortune,
Fair, and a wit! but of so bent a phant'sy,
As she thinks nought a happiness, but to have
A multitude of servants; and to get them,
Though she be very honest, yet she ventures
Upon these precipices, that would make her
Not seem so, to some prying narrow natures.
We call her, sir, the lady Frances Frampul,
Daughter and heir to the lord Frampul.

Host. Who!
He that did live in Oxford, first a student,
And after, married with the daughter of—

Lov. Sylly.

Host. Right.

Of whom the tale went, to turn puppet-master.

   Lov. And travel with young Goose, the motion-man.

   Host. And lie and live with the gipsies half a year
Together, from his wife.

   Lov. The very same:
The mad lord Frampul! and this same is his daughter,
But as cock-brain'd as e'er the father was!
There were two of them, Frances and Lætitia,
But Lætitia was lost young; and, as the rumour
Flew then, the mother upon it lost herself;
A fond weak woman, went away in a melancholy.
Because she brought him none but girls, she thought
Her husband loved her not: and he as foolish,
Too late resenting the cause given, went after,
In quest of her, and was not heard of since.

   Host. A strange division of a family!

   Lov. And scattered as in the great confusion!

   Host. But yet the lady, the heir, enjoys the land?

   Lov. And takes all lordly ways how to consume it
As nobly as she can: if clothes, and feasting,
And the authorised means of riot will do it.

   Host. She shews her extract, and I honour her for it.

Re-enter FERRET.

   Fer. Your horses, sir, are ready; and the house
Dis—

   Lov. —Pleased, thou think'st?

   Fer. I cannot tell; discharged
I am sure it is.

   Lov. Charge it again, good Ferret,
And make unready the horses; thou know'st how.
Chalk, and renew the rondels, I am now
Resolved to stay.

   Fer. I easily thought so,
When you should hear what's purposed.

   Lov. What?

   Fer. To throw
The house out of the window.

   Host. Brain o' man,
I shall have the worst of that! will they not throw
My household stuff out first, cushions and carpet,
Chairs, stools, and bedding? is not their sport my ruin

   Lov. Fear not, mine host, I am not of the fellowship.

   Fer. I cannot see, sir, how you will avoid it;
They know already, all, you are in the house.

   Lov. Who know?

   Fer. The lords: they have seen me, and enquired it.

Lov. Why were you seen?

Fer. Because indeed I had
No medicine, sir, to go invisible:
No fern seed in my pocket; nor an opal
Wrapt in bay-leaf, in my left fist, to charm
Their eyes with.

Host. He does give you reasons, [sir,]
As round as Gyges' ring; which, say the ancients,
Was a hoop ring; and that is, round as a hoop.

Lov. You will have your rebus still, mine host.

Host. I must.

Fer. My lady too look'd out of the window, and call'd me.
And see where secretary Prue comes from her,
Employ'd upon some embassy unto you.

Host. I'll meet her if she come upon employment:—

Enter PRUDENCE.

Fair lady, welcome, as your host can make you!

Pru. Forbear, sir; I am first to have mine audience,
Before the compliment. This gentleman
Is my address to.

Host. And it is in state.

Pru. My lady, sir, is glad of the encounter
To find a servant here, and such a servant,
Whom she so values; with her best respects,
Desires to be remember'd; and invites
Your nobleness to be a part, to-day,
Of the society, and mirth intended
By her, and the young lords, your fellow-servants,
Who are alike ambitious of enjoying
The fair request; and to that end have sent
Me, their imperfect orator, to obtain it.
Which if I may, they have elected me,
And crown'd me, with the title of a sovereign
Of the day's sports devised in the inn,
So you be pleased to add your suffrage to it.

Lov. So I be pleased, my gentle mistress Prudence!
You cannot think me of that coarse disposition,
To envy you any thing.

Host. That's nobly said,
And like my guest!

Lov. I gratulate your honour,
And should, with cheer, lay hold on any handle
That could advance it: but for me to think,
I can be any rag or particle
Of your lady's care, more than to fill her list,
She being the lady, that professeth still
To love no soul or body, but for ends,
Which are her sports; and is not nice to speak this,

But doth proclaim it, in all companies—
Her ladyship must pardon my weak counsels,
And weaker will, if I decline to obey her.
   Pru. O, master Lovel, you must not give credit
To all that ladies publicly profess,
Or talk o' the volée, unto their servants.
Their tongues and thoughts ofttimes lie far asunder.
Yet when they please, they have their cabinet-counsels,
And reserv'd thoughts, and can retire themselves
As well as others.
   Host. Ay, the subtlest of us.
All that is born within a lady's lips—
   Pru. Is not the issue of their hearts, mine host.
   Host. Or kiss, or drink afore me.
   Pru. Stay, excuse me;
Mine errand is not done. Yet, if her ladyship's
Slighting, or disesteem, sir, of your service,
Hath formerly begot any distaste,
Which I not know of; here I vow unto you,
Upon a chambermaid's simplicity,
Reserving still the honour of my lady,
I will be bold to hold the glass up to her,
To shew her ladyship where she hath err'd,
And how to tender satisfaction;
So you vouchsafe to prove but the day's venture.
   Host. What say you, sir? where are you, are you within?
                      [*Strikes Lovel on the breast.*
   Lov. Yes, I will wait upon her and the company.
   Host. It is enough, queen Prudence; I will bring him:
And on this kiss.—[*Kisses her. Exit Prudence.*] I long'd to kiss a
    queen.
   Lov. There is no life on earth, but being in love!
There are no studies, no delights, no business,
No intercourse, or trade of sense, or soul,
But what is love! I was the laziest creature,
The most unprofitable sign of nothing,
The veriest drone, and slept away my life
Beyond the dormouse, till I was in love!
And now, I can outwake the nightingale,
Outwatch an usurer, and outwalk him too;
Stalk like a ghost, that haunted 'bout a treasure,
And all that phant'sied treasure, it is love.
   Host. But is your name Love-ill, sir, or Love-well?
I would know that.
   Lov. I do not know't myself,
Whether it is; but it is love hath been
The hereditary passion of our house,
My gentle host, and, as I guess, my friend:
The truth is, I have loved this lady long,

And impotently, with desire enough,
But no success: for I have still forborne
To express it, in my person, to her.
    Host. How then?
    Lov. I have sent her toys, verses, and anagrams,
Trials of wit, mere trifles she has commended,
But knew not whence they came, nor could she guess.
    Host. This was a pretty riddling way of wooing!
    Lov. I oft have been too in her company;
And look'd upon her a whole day; admired her;
Loved her, and did not tell her so; loved still,
Look'd still, and loved; and loved, and look'd, and sigh'd:
But, as a man neglected, I came off,
And unregarded—
    Host. Could you blame her, sir,
When you were silent, and not said a word?
    Lov. O but I loved the more; and she might read it
Best in my silence, had she been—
    Host. As melancholic.
As you are! Pray you, why would you stand mute, sir?
    Lov. O, thereon hangs a history, mine host.
Did you e'er know, or hear of the lord Beaufort,
Who serv'd so bravely in France? I was his page,
And ere he died, his friend: I follow'd him,
First, in the wars, and, in the times of peace,
I waited on his studies; which were right.
He had no Arthurs, nor no Rosicleers,
No knights o' the sun, nor Amadis de Gauls,
Primalions, Pantagruels, public nothings;
Abortives of the fabulous dark cloyster,
Sent out to poison courts and infest manners;
But great Achilles, Agamemnon's acts,
Sage Nestor's counsels, and Ulysses' slights,
Tydides' fortitude, as Homer wrought them
In his immortal phant'sy, for examples
Of the heroic virtue. Or, as Virgil,
That master of the epic poem, limn'd
Pious Æneas, his religious prince,
Bearing his aged parent on his shoulders,
Rapt from the flames of Troy, with his young son:
And these he brought to practice, and to use.
He gave me first my breeding, I acknowledge,
Then shower'd his bounties on me, like the Hours,
That open-handed sit upon the clouds,
And press the liberality of heaven
Down to the laps of thankful men! But then
The trust committed to me at his death,
Was above all, and left so strong a tie
On all my powers, as time shall not dissolve,

Till it dissolve itself, and bury all!
The care of his brave heir, and only son:
Who being a virtuous, sweet, young, hopeful lord,
Hath cast his first affections on this lady.
And though I know, and may presume her such,
As, out of humour, will return no love;
And therefore might indifferently be made
The courting-stock, for all to practise on,
As she doth practise on all us, to scorn:
Yet, out of a religion to my charge,
And debt profess'd, I have made a self-decree,
Ne'er to express my person, though my passion
Burn me to cinders.

    Host. Then you are not so subtle
Or half so read in love-craft as I took you;
Come, come, you are no phœnix; an you were,
I should expect no miracle from your ashes.
Take some advice. Be still that rag of love,
You are: burn on till you turn tinder.
This chambermaid may hap to prove the steel,
To strike a sparkle out of the flint, your mistress,
May beget bonfires yet; you do not know,
What light may be forced out, and from what darkness.

    Lov. Nay, I am so resolv'd, as still I'll love,
Though not confess it.

    Host. That's, sir, as it chances;
We'll throw the dice for it: cheer up.

    Lov. I do.   *[Exeunt.*

ACT II

SCENE I.—*A Room in the Inn.*

Enter Lady Frampul, *and* Prudence *pinning on her lady's gown.*

    Lady F. Come, wench, this suit will serve;—dispatch, make
      ready;
It was a great deal with the biggest for me,
Which made me leave it off after once wearing.
How does it fit? will it come together?

    Pru. Hardly.

    Lady F. Thou must make shift with it; pride feels no pain.
Girt thee hard, Prue. Pox o' this errant tailor,
He angers me beyond all mark of patience!
These base mechanics never keep their word,
In any thing they promise.

    Pru. 'Tis their trade, madam,
To swear and break; they all grow rich by breaking
More than their words; their honesties and credits,

Are still the first commodity they put off.

    Lady F. And worst, it seems; which makes them do it so often.
If he had but broke with me, I had not cared,
But with the company! the body politic!—

    Pru. Frustrate our whole design, having that time,
And the materials in, so long before!

    Lady F. And he to fail in all, and disappoint us!
The rogue deserves a torture—

    Pru. To be cropp'd
With his own scissors.

    Lady F. Let's devise him one.

    Pru. And have the stumps sear'd up with his own searing candle.

    Lady F. Close to his head, to trundle on his pillow.—
I'll have the lease of his house cut out in measures.

    Pru. And he be strangled with them.

    Lady F. No, no life
I would have touch'd, but stretch'd on his own yard
He should be a little, have the strappado—

    Pru. Or an ell of taffata
Drawn through his guts, by way of glyster, and fired
With aqua vitæ.

    Lady F. Burning in the hand
With the pressing-iron, cannot save him.

    Pru. Yes,
Now I have got this on; I do forgive him,
What robes he should have brought.

    Lady F. Thou art not cruel,
Although strait-laced, I see, Prue.

    Pru. This is well.

    Lady F. 'Tis rich enough, but 'tis not what I meant thee.
I would have had thee braver than myself,
And brighter far. 'Twill fit the players yet,
When thou hast done with it, and yield thee somewhat.

    Pru. That were illiberal, madam, and mere sordid
In me, to let a suit of yours come there.

    Lady F. Tut, all are players, and but serve the scene, Prue:
Dispatch; I fear thou dost not like the province,
Thou art so long a fitting thyself for it.
Here is a scarf to make thee a knot finer.

    Pru. You send me a-feasting, madam.

    Lady F. Wear it, wench.

    Pru. Yes; but with leave of your ladyship, I would tell you,
This can but bear the face of an odd journey.

    Lady F. Why, Prue?

    Pru. A lady of your rank and quality,
To come to a public inn, so many men,
Young lords and others, in your company,
And not a woman but myself, a chamber-maid!

    Lady F. Thou doubt'st to be o'erlaid, Prue, fear it not,

I'll bear my part, and share with thee in the venture.
　　Pru. O but the censure, madam, is the main.
What will they say of you, or judge of me,
To be translated thus, above all the bound
Of fitness or decorum?
　　Lady F. How now, Prue!
Turn'd fool upon the sudden, and talk idly
In thy best clothes! shoot bolts and sentences
To affright babies with! as if I lived
To any other scale than what's my own,
Or sought myself, without myself, from home!
　　Pru. Your ladyship will pardon me my fault;
If I have over-shot, I'll shoot no more.
　　Lady F. Yes, shoot again, good Prue; I'll have thee shoot,
And aim, and hit; I know 'tis love in thee,
And so I do interpret it.
　　Pru. Then, madam,
I'd crave a farther leave.
　　Lady F. Be it to license,
It shall not want an ear, Prue. Say, what is it?
　　Pru. A toy I have, to raise a little mirth
To the design in hand.
　　Lady F. Out with it, Prue,
If it but chime of mirth.
　　Pru. Mine host has, madam,
A pretty boy in the house, a dainty child,
His son, and is of your ladyship's name, too, Francis,
Whom if your ladyship would borrow of him,
And give me leave to dress him as I would,
Should make the finest lady and kinswoman,
To keep you company, and deceive my lords,
Upon the matter, with a fountain of sport.
　　Lady F. I apprehend thee, and the source of mirth
That it may breed; but is he bold enough,
The child, and well assured?
　　Pru. As I am, madam:
Have him in no suspicion, more than me.
Here comes mine host; will you but please to ask him,
Or let me make the motion?
　　Lady F. Which thou wilt, Prue.

Enter Host.

　　Host. Your ladyship, and all your train are welcome.
　　Lady F. I thank my hearty host.
　　Host. So is your sovereignty,
Madam, I wish you joy of your new gown.
　　Lady F. It should have been, my host; but Stuff, our tailor,
Has broke with us; you shall be of the counsel.
　　Pru. He will deserve it, madam. My lady has heard

You have a pretty son, mine host, she'll see him.

Lady F. Ay, very fair; I pray thee let me see him, host.

Host. Your ladyship shall presently.—   *[Goes to the door.*
Bid Frank come hither anon, unto my lady.—
It is a bashful child, homely brought up,
In a rude hostelry: but the Light Heart
Is now his father's, and it may be his.
Here he comes.—

Enter FRANK.

    Frank, salute my lady.

Frank. I do
What, madam, I am design'd to do, by my birthright,
As heir of the Light Heart, bid you most welcome.

Lady F. And I believe your *most*, my pretty boy,
Being so emphased by you.

Frank. Your ladyship, madam,
If you believe it such, are sure to make it.

Lady F. Prettily answered! Is your name Francis?

Frank. Yes, madam.

Lady F. I love mine own the better.

Frank. If I knew yours,
I should make haste to do so too, good madam.

Lady F. It is the same with yours.

Frank. Mine then acknowledges
The lustre it receives, by being named after.

Lady F. You will win upon me in compliment.

Frank. By silence.

Lady F. A modest and a fair well-spoken child.

Host. Her ladyship shall have him, sovereign Prue,
Or what I have beside; divide my Heart
Between you and your lady: make your use of it:
My house is yours, my son is yours. Behold,
I tender him to your service; Frank, become
What these brave ladies would have you. Only this,
There is a chare-woman in the house, his nurse,
An Irish woman, I took in a beggar,
That waits upon him, a poor, silly fool,
But an impertinent and sedulous one
As ever was; will vex you on all occasions,
Never be off, or from you, but in her sleep;
Or drink which makes it: she doth love him so,
Or rather doat on him. Now, for her, a shape,
And we may dress her, and I'll help to fit her,
With a tuft-taffata cloke, an old French hood,
And other pieces, heterogene enough.

Pru. We have brought a standard of apparel down,
Because this tailor fail'd us in the main.

Host. She shall advance the game.

Pru. About it then,
And send but Trundle hither, the coachman, to me.

 Host. I shall: but, Prue, let Lovel have fair quarter.   [*Aside.*
 Pru. The best.   [*Exit Host.*
 Lady F. Our host, methinks, is very gamesome.
 Pru. How like you the boy?
 Lady F. A miracle!
 Pru. Good madam,
But take him in, and sort a suit for him.
I'll give our Trundle his instructions;
And wait upon your ladyship in the instant.
 Lady F. But, Prue, what shall we call him, when we have drest
  him?
 Pru. My lady Nobody, any thing, what you will.
 Lady F. Call him Lætitia, by my sister's name,
And so 'twill mend our mirth too we have in hand.   [*Exit.*

Enter TRUNDLE.

 Pru. Good Trundle, you must straight make ready the coach,
And lead the horses out but half a mile,
Into the fields, whither you will, and then
Drive in again, with the coach-leaves put down,
At the back gate, and so to the back stairs,
As if you brought in somebody to my lady,
A kinswoman that she sent for. Make that answer,
If you be ask'd; and give it out in the house so.
 Trun. What trick is this, good mistress secretary,
You'd put upon us?
 Pru. Us! do you speak plural?
 Trun. Me and my mares are us.
 Pru. If you so join them,
Elegant Trundle, you may use your figures:
I can but urge, it is my lady's service.
 Trun. Good mistress Prudence, you can urge enough;
I know you are secretary to my lady,
And mistress steward.
 Pru. You will still be trundling,
And have your wages stopt now at the audit.
 Trun. 'Tis true, you are gentlewoman o' the horse too;
Or what you will beside, Prue. I do think it
My best t' obey you.
 Pru. And I think so too, Trundle.   [*Exeunt.*

SCENE II.—*Another Room in the same.*

Enter Lord BEAUFORT *and* Lord LATIMER.

 Lord B. Why, here's return enough of both our ventures,
If we do make no more discovery.
 Lord L. What?

The New Inn

Than of this parasite?
   Lord B. O he's a dainty one!
The parasite of the house.
   Lord L. Here comes mine host.

Enter Host.

   Host. My lords, you both are welcome to the Heart.
   Lord B. To the Light Heart, we hope.
   Lord L. And merry, I swear.
We never yet felt such a fit of laughter,
As your glad Heart hath offered us since we enter'd.
   Lord B. How came you by this property?
   Host. Who, my Fly?
   Lord B. Your Fly, if you call him so.
   Host. Nay, he is that,
And will be still.
   Lord B. In every dish and pot?
   Host. In every cup and company, my lords,
A creature of all liquors, all complexions,
Be the drink what it will, he'll have his sip.
   Lord L. He's fitted with a name.
   Host. And he joys in it.
I had him when I came to take the Inn here,
Assigned me over in the inventory,
As an old implement, a piece of household stuff,
And so he doth remain.
   Lord B. Just such a thing
We thought him.
   Lord L. Is he a scholar?
   Host. Nothing less;
But colours for it as you see; wears black,
And speaks a little tainted, fly-blown Latin,
After the school.
   Lord B. Of Stratford o' the Bow:
For Lillie's Latin is to him unknown.
   Lord L. What calling has he?
   Host. Only to call in still,
Enflame the reckoning, bold to charge a bill,
Bring up the shot in the rear, as his own word is.
   Lord B. And does it in the discipline of the house,
As corporal of the field, maestro del campo?
   Host. And visiter general of all the rooms:
He has form'd a fine militia for the Inn too.
   Lord B. And means to publish it?
   Host. With all his titles;
Some call him deacon Fly, some doctor Fly;
Some captain, some lieutenant: but my folks
Do call him quarter-master Fly, which he is.

Enter Colonel TIPTO *and* FLY.

Tip. Come, quarter-master Fly.

Host. Here's one already
Hath got his titles.

Tip. Doctor.

Fly. Noble colonel,
No doctor, yet a poor professor of ceremony,
Here in the Inn, retainer to the host,
I discipline the house.

Tip. Thou read'st a lecture
Unto the family here: when is the day?

Fly. This is the day.

Tip. I'll hear thee, and I'll have thee a doctor,
Thou shalt be one, thou hast a doctor's look,
A face disputative, of Salamanca.

Host. Who's this?

Lord L. The glorious colonel Tipto, host.

Lord B. One talks upon his tiptoes, if you'll hear him.

Tip. Thou hast good learning in thee; *macte*, Fly.

Fly. And I say *macte* to my colonel.

Host. Well *macted* of them both.

Lord B. They are match'd, i'faith.

Tip. But, Fly, why *macte?*

Fly. *Quasi magis aucte,*
My honourable colonel.

Tip. What a critic!

Host. There is another accession, critic Fly.

Lord L. I fear a taint here in the mathematics.
They say, lines parallel do never meet;
He has met his parallel in wit and school-craft.

Lord B. They side, not meet, man; mend your metaphor,
And save the credit of your mathematics.

Tip. But, Fly, how cam'st thou to be here, committed
Unto this Inn?

Fly. Upon suspicion of drink, sir.
I was taken late one night here with the tapster,
And the under officers, and so deposited.

Tip. I will redeem thee, Fly, and place thee better,
With a fair lady.

Fly. A lady, sweet sir Glorious!

Tip. A sovereign lady. Thou shalt be the bird
To sovereign Prue, queen of our sports, her Fly,
The Fly in household and in ordinary;
Bird of her ear, and she shall wear thee there,
A Fly of gold, enamell'd, and a school-fly.

Host. The school then, are my stables, or the cellar,
Where he doth study deeply, at his hours,
Cases of cups, I do not know how spiced

With conscience, for the tapster and the hostler; as
Whose horses may be cosen'd, or what jugs
Fill'd up with froth? that is his way of learning.
   Tip. What antiquated feather's that that talks?
   Fly. The worshipful host, my patron, master Goodstock,
A merry Greek, and cants in Latin comely,
Spins like the parish top.
   Tip. I'll set him up then.—
Art thou the Dominus?
   Host. Fac-totum here, sir.
   Tip. Host real of the house, and cap of maintenance?
   Host. The lord of the Light Heart, sir, cap-a-pie;
Whereof the feather is the emblem, colonel,
Put up with the ace of hearts.
   Tip. But why in cuerpo?
I hate to see an host, and old, in cuerpo.
   Host. Cuerpo! what's that?
   Tip. Light-skipping hose and doublet,
The horse-boy's garb! poor blank and half blank cuerpo,
They relish not the gravity of an host,
Who should be king at arms, and ceremonies,
In his own house; know all, to the gold weights.
   Lord B. Why, that his Fly doth for him here, your bird.
   Tip. But I would do it myself were I my host,
I would not speak unto a cook of quality,
Your lordship's footman, or my lady's Trundle,
In cuerpo: if a dog but stay'd below,
That were a dog of fashion, and well nosed,
And could present himself; I would put on
The Savoy chain about my neck, the ruff
And cuffs of Flanders, then the Naples hat,
With the Rome hatband, and the Florentine agat,
The Milan sword, the cloke of Genoa, set
With Brabant buttons; all my given pieces,
Except my gloves, the natives of Madrid,
To entertain him in; and compliment
With a tame coney, as with a prince that sent it.
   Host. The same deeds, though, become not every man;
That fits a colonel will not fit an host.
   Tip. Your Spanish host is never seen in cuerpo,
Without his paramentos, cloke and sword.
   Fly. Sir,
He has the father of swords within, a long sword;
Blade Cornish styled of sir Rud Hughdebras.
   Tip. And why a long sword, bully bird? thy sense?
   Fly. To note him a tall man, and a master of fence.
   Tip. But doth he teach the Spanish way of don Lewis?
   Fly. No, the Greek master he.
   Tip. What call you him?

Fly. Euclid.

Tip. Fart upon Euclid, he is stale and antic!
Give me the moderns.

Fly. Sir, he minds no moderns,
Go by, Hieronimo!

Tip. What was he?

Fly. The Italian,
That play'd with abbot Antony in the Friars,
And Blinkinsops the bold.

Tip. Ay, marry, those
Had fencing names; What is become of them?

Host. They had their times, and we can say, they were.
So had Caranza his; so had don Lewis.

Tip. Don Lewis of Madrid is the sole master
Now of the world.

Host. But this of the other world,
Euclid demonstrates. He! he is for all:
The only fencer of name, now in Elysium.

Fly. He does it all by lines and angles, colonel;
By parallels and sections, has his diagrams.

Lord B. Wilt thou be flying, Fly?

Lord L. At all, why not?
The air's as free for a fly as for an eagle.

Lord B. A buzzard! he is in his contemplation.

Tip. Euclid a fencer, and in the Elysium!

Host. He play'd a prize last week with Archimedes,
And beat him, I assure you.

Tip. Do you assure me?
For what?

Host. For four i' the hundred. Give me five,
And I assure you again.

Tip. Host peremptory,
You may be ta'en. But where, whence had you this?

Host. Upon the road. A post that came from thence,
Three days ago, here, left it with the tapster.

Fly. Who is indeed a thoroughfare of news,
Jack Jug with the broken belly, a witty fellow!

Host. Your bird here heard him.

Tip. Did you hear him, bird?

Host. Speak in the faith of a Fly.   [*Exit.*

Fly. Yes, and he told us
Of one that was the prince of Orange' fencer.

Tip. Stevinus?

Fly. Sir, the same had challenged Euclid
At thirty weapons more than Archimedes
E'er saw, and engines; most of his own invention.

Tip. This may have credit, and chimes reason, this!
If any man endanger Euclid, bird,
Observe, that had the honour to quit Europe

This forty year, 'tis he.   He put down Scaliger.
    Fly. And he was a great master.
    Lord B. Not of fence, Fly.
    Tip. Excuse him, lord, he went on the same grounds.
    Lord B. On the same earth, I think, with other mortals.
    Tip. I mean, sweet lord, the mathematics.   Basta!
When thou know'st more, thou wilt take less green honour.
He had his circles, semicircles, quadrants—
    Fly. He writ a book of the quadrature of the circle—
    Tip. Cyclometria, I read—
    Lord B. The title only.
    Lord L. And indice.
    Lord B. If it had one; of that, quære?—
What insolent, half-witted things these are!
    Lord L. So are all smatterers, insolent and impudent.
    Lord B. They lightly go together.
    Lord L. 'Tis my wonder
Two animals should hawk at all discourse thus,
Fly every subject to the mark, or retrieve—
    Lord B. And never have the luck to be in the right!
    Lord L. 'Tis some folks' fortune.
    Lord B. Fortune is a bawd,
And a blind beggar; 'tis their vanity,
And shews most vilely.
    Tip. I could take the heart now
To write unto don Lewis into Spain,
To make a progress to the Elysian fields
Next summer—
    Lord B. And persuade him die for fame,
Of fencing with a shadow!   Where's mine host?
I would he had heard this bubble break, i'faith.

Re-enter Host, *with* PRUDENCE *richly dressed,* FRANK *as a lady,*
    Nurse, *and* Lady FRAMPUL.

    Host. Make place, stand by, for the queen-regent, gentlemen!
    Tip. This is thy queen that shall be, bird, our sovereign.
    Lord B. Translated Prudence!
    Pru. Sweet my lord, hand off:
It is not now, as when plain Prudence lived,
And reach'd her ladyship—
    Host. The chamber-pot.
    Pru. The looking-glass, mine host: lose your house metaphor!
You have a negligent memory indeed.
Speak the host's language.   Here is a young lord
Will make't a precedent else.
    Lord L. Well acted, Prue.
    Host. First minute of her reign!   What will she do
Forty years hence, God bless her!
    Pru. If you'll kiss,

Or compliment, my lord, behold a lady,
A stranger, and my lady's kinswoman.
 Lord B. I do confess my rudeness, that had need
To have mine eye directed to this beauty.
 Frank. It was so little, as it ask'd a perspicil.
 Lord B. Lady, your name?
 Frank. My lord, it is Lætitia.
 Lord B. Lætitia! a fair omen, and I take it:
Let me have still such Lettice for my lips.
But that of your family, lady?
 Frank. Sylly, sir.
 Lord B. My lady's kinswoman?
 Frank. I am so honour'd.
 Host. Already it takes.   [*Aside to Lady F.*
 Lady F. An excellent fine boy.
 Nurse. He is descended of a right good stock, sir.
 Lord B. What's this, an antiquary?
 Host. An antiquity,
By the dress, you'd swear! an old Welsh herald's widow:
She's a wild Irish born, sir, and a hybride,
That lives with this young lady a mile off here,
And studies Vincent against York.
 Lord B. She'll conquer
If she read Vincent. Let me study her.
 Host. She's perfect in most pedigrees, most descents.
 Lord B. A bawd, I hope, and knows to blaze a coat. [*Aside.*
 Host. And judgeth all things with a single eye.
Fly, come you hither! no discovery
Of what you see, to your colonel Toe, or Tip, here,
But keep all close; though you stand in the way o' preferment,
Seek it off from the road; no flattery for't,
No lick-foot, pain of losing your proboscis,
My liquorish fly.   [*Aside to Fly.*
 Tip. What says old velvet-head?
 Fly. He will present me himself, sir, if you will not.
 Tip. Who, he present! what? whom? an host, a groom,
Divide the thanks with me? share in my glories?
Lay up: I say no more.
 Host. Then silence, sir,
And hear the sovereign.
 Tip. Hostlers to usurp
Upon my Sparta or province, as they say!
No broom but mine!
 Host. Still, colonel, you mutter.
 Tip. I dare speak out, as cuerpo.
 Fly. Noble colonel—
 Tip. And carry what I ask—
 Host. Ask what you can, sir,
So it be in the house.

Tip. I ask my rights and privileges;
And though for form I please to call't a suit,
I have not been accustomed to repulse.
   Pru. No, sweet sir Glorious, you may still command—
   Host. And go without.
   Pru. But yet, sir, being the first,
And call'd a suit, you'll look it shall be such
As we may grant.
   Lady F. It else denies itself.
   Pru. You hear the opinion of the court.
   Tip. I mind no court opinions.
   Pru. 'Tis my lady's, though.
   Tip. My lady is a spinster at the law,
And my petition is of right.
   Pru. What is it?
   Tip. It is for this poor learned bird.
   Host. The fly.
   Tip. Professor in the Inn, here, of small matters.
   Lord L. How he commends him!
   Host. As to save himself in him.
   Lady F. So do all politics in their commendations.
   Host. This is a state-bird, and the verier fly.
   Tip. Hear him problematise.
   Pru. Bless us, what's that?
   Tip. Or syllogise, elenchise.
   Lady F. Sure, petards
To blow us up.
   Lord L. Some enginous strong words.
   Host. He means to erect a castle in the air,
And make his fly an elephant to carry it.
   Tip. Bird of the arts he is, and Fly by name.
   Pru. Buz!
   Host. Blow him off. good Prue, they'll mar all else.
   Tip. The sovereign's honour is to cherish learning.
   Pru. What in a fly?
   Tip. In any thing industrious.
   Pru. But flies are busy.
   Lady F. Nothing more troublesome,
Or importune.
   Tip. There's nothing more domestic,
Tame or familiar, than your fly in cuerpo.
   Host. That is when his wings are cut, he is tame indeed, else
Nothing more impudent and greedy; licking—
   Lady F. Or saucy, good sir Glorious.
   Pru. Leave your advocateship,
Except that we shall call you orator Fly,
And send you down to the dresser and the dishes.
   Host. A good flap that!
   Pru. Commit you to the steam.

Lady F. Or else condemn you to the bottles.
Pru. And pots.
There is his quarry.
 Host. He will chirp far better,
Your bird, below.
 Lady F. And make you finer music.
 Pru. His buz will there become him.
 Tip. Come away,
Buz, in their faces: give them all the buz,
Dor in their ears and eyes, hum, dor, and buz!
I will statuminate and under-prop thee.
If they scorn us, let us scorn them—We'll find
The thoroughfare below, and quære him;
Leave these relicts, buz: they shall see that I,
Spite of their jeers, dare drink, and with a fly.
        [Exeunt Tipto and Fly.
 Lord L. A fair remove at once of two impertinents!
Excellent Prue, I love thee for thy wit,
No less than state.
 Pru. One must preserve the other.

      Enter LOVEL.

 Lady F. Who's here?
 Pru. O Lovel, madam, your sad servant.
 Lady F. Sad! he is sullen still, and wears a cloud
About his brows; I know not how to approach him.
 Pru. I will instruct you, madam, if that be all;
Go to him, and kiss him.
 Lady F. How, Prue!
 Pru. Go, and kiss him,
I do command it.
 Lady F. Thou art not wild, wench.
 Pru. No,
Tame, and exceeding tame, but still your sovereign.
 Lady F. Hath too much bravery made thee mad?
 Pru. Nor proud.
Do what I do enjoin you. No disputing
Of my prerogative, with a front, or frown;
Do not detract; you know the authority
Is mine, and I will exercise it swiftly,
If you provoke me.
 Lady F. I have woven a net
To snare myself in!—*[To Lovel.]* Sir, I am enjoin'd
To tender you a kiss: but do not know
Why, or wherefore, only the pleasure royal
Will have it so, and urges——Do not you
Triumph on my obedience, seeing it forced thus.
There 'tis.   *[Kisses him.*
 Lov. And welcome.—Was there ever kiss

That relish'd thus! or had a sting like this,
Of so much nectar, but with aloes mixt! [*Aside.*
   Pru. No murmuring nor repining, I am fixt.
   Lov. It had, methinks, a quintessence of either,
But that which was the better, drown'd the bitter.
How soon it pass'd away, how unrecover'd!
The distillation of another soul
Was not so sweet; and till I meet again
That kiss, those lips, like relish, and this taste,
Let me turn all consumption, and here waste. [*Aside.*
   Pru. The royal assent is past and cannot alter.
   Lady F. You'll turn a tyrant.
   Pru. Be not you a rebel.
It is a name is alike odious.
   Lady F. You'll hear me?
   Pru. No, not on this argument.
Would you make laws, and be the first that break them?
The example is pernicious in a subject,
And of your quality, most.
   Lord L. Excellent princess!
   Host. Just queen!
   Lord L. Brave sovereign!
   Host. A she Trajan, this!
   Lord B. What is't? proceed, incomparable Prue:
I am glad I am scarce at leisure to applaud thee.
   Lord L. It's well for you, you have so happy expressions.
   Lady F. Yes, cry her up with acclamations, do,
And cry me down; run all with sovereignty:
Prince Power will never want her parasites—
   Pru. Nor murmur her pretences: master Lovel,
For so your libel here, or bill of complaint,
Exhibited, in our high court of sovereignty,
At this first hour of our reign, declares
Against this noble lady, a disrespect
You have conceived, if not received, from her.
   Host. Received; so the charge lies in our bill.
   Pru. We see it, his learned counsel, leave your planing.
We that do love our justice above all
Our other attributes, and have the nearness,
To know your extraordinary merit,
As also to discern this lady's goodness,
And find how loth she'd be to lose the honour
And reputation she hath had, in having
So worthy a servant, tho' but for few minutes;
Do here enjoin—
   Host. Good!
   Pru. Charge, will, and command
Her ladyship, pain of our high displeasure,
And the committing an extreme contempt

Unto the court, our crown, and dignity—
    Host. Excellent sovereign, and egregious Prue!
    Pru. To entertain you for a pair of hours,
Choose, when you please, this day, with all respects,
And valuation of a principal servant,
To give you all the titles, all the privileges,
The freedoms, favours, rights, she can bestow—
    Host. Large ample words, of a brave latitude!
    Pru. Or can be expected, from a lady of honour
Or quality, in discourse, access, address—
    Host. Good!
    Pru. Not to give ear, or admit conference
With any person but yourself: nor there,
Of any other argument but LOVE,
And the companion of it, gentle courtship.
For which your two hours' service, you shall take
Two kisses.
    Host. Noble!
    Pru. For each hour a kiss,
To be ta'en freely, fully, and legally,
Before us; in the court here, and our presence.
    Host. Rare!
    Pru. But those hours past, and the two kisses paid,
The binding caution is, never to hope
Renewing of the time, or of the suit,
On any circumstance.
    Host. A hard condition!
    Lord L. Had it been easier, I should have suspected
The sovereign's justice.
    Host. O you are [a] servant,
My lord, unto the lady, and a rival:
In point of law, my lord, you may be challenged.
    Lord L. I am not jealous.
    Host. Of so short a time
Your lordship needs not, and being done *in foro.*
    Pru. What is the answer?
    Host. He craves respite, madam,
To advise with his learned council.
    Pru. Be you he,
And go together quickly.   [*Lovel and Host walk aside.*
    Lady F. You are no tyrant!
    Pru. If I be, madam, you were best appeal me.
    Lord L. Beaufort—
    Lord B. I am busy, prithee let me alone;
I have a cause in hearing too.
    Lord L. At what bar?
    Lord B. Love's court of Requests.
    Lord L. Bring it into the sovereignty,
It is the nobler court, afore judge Prue;

The only learned mother of the law,
And lady of conscience, too!
    Lord B. 'Tis well enough
Before this mistress of requests, where it is.
    Host. Let them not scorn you: bear up, master Lovel,
And take your hours and kisses, they are a fortune.
    Lov. Which I cannot approve, and less make use of.
    Host. Still in this cloud! why cannot you make use of?
    Lov. Who would be rich to be so soon undone?
The beggar's best is wealth he doth not know;
And, but to shew it him, inflames his want.
    Host. Two hours at height!
    Lov. That joy is too, too narrow,
Would bound a love so infinite as mine;
And being past, leaves an eternal loss.
Who so prodigiously affects a feast,
To forfeit health and appetite, to see it?
Or but to taste a spoonful, would forego
All gust of delicacy ever after?
    Host. These, yet, are hours of hope.
    Lov. But all hours following
Years of despair, ages of misery!
Nor can so short a happiness, but spring
A world of fear, with thought of losing it;
Better be never happy, than to feel
A little of it, and then lose it ever.
    Host. I do confess, it is a strict injunction:
But then the hope is, it may not be kept.
A thousand things may intervene; we see
The wind shift often, thrice a day sometimes:
Decrees may alter upon better motion,
And riper hearing. The best bow may start,
And the hand vary. Prue may be a sage
In law, and yet not sour; sweet Prue, smooth Prue,
Soft, debonaire, and amiable Prue,
May do as well as rough and rigid Prue;
And yet maintain her, venerable Prue,
Majestic Prue, and serenissimous Prue.
Try but one hour first, and as you like
The loose of that, draw home and prove the other.
    Lov. If one hour could the other happy make,
I should attempt it.
    Host. Put it on; and do.
    Lov. Or in the blest attempt that I might die!
    Host. Ay, marry, there were happiness indeed!
Transcendent to the melancholy, meant.
It were a fate above a monument,
And all inscription, to die so! A death
For emperors to enjoy, and the kings

Of the rich East to pawn their regions for;
To sow their treasure, open all their mines,
Spend all their spices to embalm their corps,
And wrap the inches up in sheets of gold,
That fell by such a noble destiny!
And for the wrong to your friend, that fear's away,
He rather wrongs himself, following fresh light,
New eyes to swear by. If lord Beaufort change,
It is no crime in you to remain constant,
And upon these conditions, at a game
So urg'd upon you.

Pru. Sir, your resolution?

Host. How is the lady affected?

Pru. Sovereigns use not
To ask their subjects' suffrage where 'tis due,
But where conditional.

Host. A royal sovereign!

Lord L. And a rare stateswoman! I admire her bearing
In her new regiment.

Host. Come, choose your hours,
Better be happy for a part of time,
Than not the whole; and a short part, than never.
Shall I appoint them, pronounce for you?

Lov. Your pleasure.

Host. Then he designs his first hour after dinner;
His second after supper. Say ye, content?

Pru. Content.

Lady F. I am content.

Host. Content.

Frank. Content.

Lord B. What's that? I am content too.

Lord L. You have reason,
You had it on the bye, and we observed it.

Nur. Trot' I am not content: in fait' I am not.

Host. Why art not thou content, good Sheleenien

Nurse. He tauk so desperate, and so debausht,
So baudy like a courtier and a lord,
God bless him, one that tak'th tobacco.

Host. Very well mixt!
What did he say?

Nurse. Nay, nothing to the purposh,
Or very little, nothing at all to purposh.

Host. Let him alone, Nurse.

Nurse. I did tell him of Serly
Was a great family come out of Ireland,
Descended of O Neal, Mac Con, Mac Dermot,
Mac Murrogh, but he mark'd not.

Host. Nor do I;
Good queen of heralds, ply the bottle, and sleep.   [*Exeunt.*

ACT III

SCENE I.—*A Lower Room in the Inn.*

Enter Col. TIPTO, FLY, *and* JUG.

Tip. I like the plot of your militia well.
It is a fine militia, and well order'd,
And the division's neat! 'twill be desired
Only, the expressions were a little more Spanish;
For there's the best militia of the world.
To call them tertias—tertia of the kitchen,
Tertia of the cellar, tertia of the chamber,
And tertia of the stables.

Fly. That I can, sir;
And find out very able, fit commanders
In every tertia.

Tip. Now you are in the right.
As in the tertia of the kitchen, yourself,
Being a person elegant in sauces,
There to command, as prime maestro del campo,
Chief master of the palate, for that tertia,
Or the cook under you; 'cause you are the marshal,
And the next officer in the field, to the host.
Then for the cellar, you have young Anon,
Is a rare fellow—what's his other name?

Fly. Pierce, sir.

Tip. Sir Pierce, I'll have him a cavalier.
Sir Pierce Anon will pierce us a new hogshead.
And then your thoroughfare, Jug here, his alfarez:
An able officer, give me thy beard, round Jug,
I take thee by this handle, and do love
One of thy inches.   In the chambers, Jordan here;
He is the don del campo of the beds.
And for the stables, what's his name?

Fly. Old Peck.

Tip. Maestro del campo, Peck! his name is curt,
A monosyllable, but commands the horse well.

Fly. O, in an inn, sir, we have other horse,
Let those troops rest a while.   Wine is the horse,
That we must charge with here.

Tip. Bring up the troops,
Or call, sweet Fly; 'tis an exact militia,
And thou an exact professor; Lipsius Fly
Thou shalt be call'd, and Jouse:—

Enter FERRET *and* TRUNDLE.

Jack Ferret, welcome.
Old trench-master, and colonel of the pioneers,

What canst thou bolt us now; a coney or two
Out of Tom Trundle's burrow, here, the coach?
This is the master of the carriages.
How is thy driving, Tom, good, as it was?
 Trun. It serves my lady, and our officer Prue.
Twelve miles an hour! Tom has the old trundle still.
 Tip. I am taken with the family here, fine fellows!
Viewing the muster-roll.
 Trun. They are brave men.
 Fer. And of the Fly-blown discipline all, the quarter-master.
 Tip. The Fly is a rare bird in his profession.
Let's sip a private pint with him: I would have him
Quit this light sign of the Light Heart, my bird,
And lighter house. It is not for his tall
And growing gravity, so cedar-like,
To be the second to an host in cuerpo,
That knows no elegances: use his own
Dictamen, and his genius: I would have him
Fly high, and strike at all.—

Enter PIERCE.

       Here's young Anon too.
 Pierce. What wine is't, gentlemen, white or claret?
 Tip. White,
My brisk Anon.
 Pierce. I'll draw you Juno's milk
That dyed the lilies, colonel.   [*Exit.*
 Tip. Do so, Pierce.

Enter PECK.

 Peck. A plague of all jades, what a clap he has gi'en me!
 Fly. Why, how now, cousin?
 Tip. Who's that?
 Fer. The hostler.
 Fly. What ail'st thou, cousin Peck?   [*Takes him aside.*
 Peck. O me, my hanches!
As sure as you live, sir, he knew perfectly
I meant to cozen him. He did leer so on me,
And then he sneer'd, as who would say, take heed, sirrah;
And when he saw our half-peck, which you know
Was but an old court-dish, lord, how he stamp'd,
I thought 't had been for joy: when suddenly
He cuts me a back-caper with his heels,
And takes me just o' the crupper. Down come I
And my whole ounce of oats! Then he neigh'd out,
As if he had a mare by the tail.
 Fly. Troth, cousin,
You are to blame to use the poor dumb Christians
So cruelly, defraud 'em of their *dimensum.*

Yonder's the colonel's horse (there I look'd in)
Keeping our Lady's eve! the devil a bit
He has got, since he came in yet! there he stands
And looks and looks, but 'tis your pleasure, coz,
He should look lean enough.

Peck. He has hay before him.

Fly. Yes, but as gross as hemp, and as soon will choke him,
Unless he eat it butter'd. He had four shoes,
And good ones, when he came in: it is a wonder,
With standing still, he should cast three.

Peck. Troth, quarter-master,
This trade is a kind of mystery, that corrupts
Our standing manners quickly: once a week,
I meet with such a brush to mollify me,
Sometimes a brace, to awake my conscience,
Yet still I sleep securely.

Fly. Cousin Peck,
You must use better dealing, faith, you must.

Peck. Troth, to give good example to my successors,
I could be well content to steal but two girths,
And now and then a saddle-cloth, change a bridle,
For exercise; and stay there.

Fly. If you could,
There were some hope on you, coz: but the fate is,
You are drunk so early, you mistake whole saddles;
Sometimes a horse.

Peck. Ay, there's—

Re-enter PIERCE *with wine.*

Fly. The wine! come, coz,
I'll talk with you anon.   [*They come forward.*

Peck. Do, lose no time,
Good quarter-master.

Tip. There are the horse, come, Fly.

Fly. Charge, in, boys, in—

Enter JORDAN.

Lieutenant of the ordnance,
Tobacco and pipes.

Tip. Who's that? Old Jordan! good.
A comely vessel, and a necessary.
New scour'd he is: Here's to thee, marshal Fly;
In milk, my young Anon says.   [*Drinks.*

Pierce. Cream of the grape,
That dropt from Juno's breasts and sprung the lily!
I can recite your fables, Fly. Here is, too,
The blood of Venus, mother of the rose!   [*Music within.*

Jor. The dinner is gone up.

Jug. I hear the whistle.

Jor. Ay, and the fidlers: We must all go wait.

Pierce. Pox o' this waiting, quarter-master Fly.

Fly. When chambermaids are sovereigns, wait their ladies;
Fly scorns to breathe.—

Peck. Or blow upon them, he.

Pierce. Old parcel Peck, art thou there? how now, lame!

Peck. Yes faith: it is ill halting afore cripples;
I have got a dash of a jade here, will stick by me.

Pierce. O you have had some phant'sy, fellow Peck,
Some revelation—

Peck. What?

Pierce. To steal the hay
Out of the racks again.

Fly. I told him so,
When the guests' backs were turn'd.

Pierce. Or bring his peck,
The bottom upwards, heap'd with oats; and cry,
Here's the best measure upon all the road! when,
You know, the guest put in his hand to feel,
And smell to the oats, that grated all his fingers
Upon the wood—

Peck. Mum!

Pierce. And found out your cheat.

Peck. I have been in the cellar, Pierce.

Pierce. You were then there,
Upon your knees, I do remember it,
To have the fact conceal'd. I could tell more,
Soaping of saddles, cutting of horse-tails,
And cropping—pranks of ale, and hostelry—

Fly. Which he cannot forget, he says, young knight,
No more than you can other deeds of darkness,
Done in the cellar.

Tip. Well said, bold professor.

Fer. We shall have some truth explain'd.

Pierce. We are all mortal,
And have our visions.

Peck. Truly, it seems to me,
That every horse has his whole peck, and tumbles
Up to the ears in litter.

Fly. When, indeed,
There's no such matter, not a smell of provender.

Fer. Not so much straw as would tie up a horse-tail.

Fly. Nor any thing in the rack but two old cobwebs,
And so much rotten hay as had been a hen's nest.

Trun. And yet he's ever apt to sweep the mangers!

Fer. But puts in nothing.

Pierce. These are fits and fancies,
Which you must leave, good Peck.

Fly. And you must pray

It may be reveal'd to you at some times,
Whose horse you ought to cozen; with what conscience;
The how, and when: a parson's horse may suffer—
Pierce. Whose master's double beneficed; put in that.
Fly. A little greasing in the teeth; 'tis wholesome;
And keeps him in a sober shuffle.
Pierce. His saddle too
May want a stirrup.
Fly. And, it may be sworn,
His learning lay o' one side, and so broke it.
Peck. They have ever oats in their cloke-bags, to affront us.
Fly. And therefore 'tis an office meritorious,
To tithe such soundly.
Pierce. And a grazier's may—
Fer. O, they are pinching puckfists!
Trun. And suspicious.
Pierce. Suffer before the master's face, sometimes.
Fly. He shall think he sees his horse eat half a bushel—
Pierce. When the slight is, rubbing his gums with salt
Till all the skin come off, he shall but mumble,
Like an old woman that were chewing brawn,
And drop them out again.
Tip. Well argued, cavalier.
Fly. It may do well; and go for an example.
But, coz, have a care of understanding horses,
Horses with angry heels, nobility horses,
Horses that know the world; let them have meat
Till their teeth ake, and rubbing till their ribs
Shine like a wench's forehead: they are devils else
Will look into your dealings.
Peck. For mine own part,
The next I cozen of the pamper'd breed,
I wish he may be foundred.
Fly. Foun-der-ed.
Prolate it right.
Peck. And of all four, I wish it,
I love no crupper-compliments.
Pierce. Whose horse was it?
Peck. Why, master Burst's.
Pierce. Is Bat Burst come?
Peck. An hour
He has been here.
Tip. What Burst?
Pierce. Mas Bartolmew Burst.
One that hath been a citizen, since a courtier,
And now a gamester: hath had all his whirls,
And bouts of fortune, as a man would say,
Once a bat and ever a bat! a rere-mouse,
And bird of twilight, he has broken thrice.

Tip. Your better man, the Genoway proverb says:
Men are not made of steel.

Pierce.   Nor are they bound
Always to hold.

Fly.   Thrice honourable colonel,
Hinges will crack.

Tip.   Though they be Spanish iron.

Pierce. He is a merchant still, adventurer,
At in-and-in; and is our thoroughfare's friend.

Tip. Who, Jug's?

Pierce. The same; and a fine gentleman
Was with him.

Peck.   Master Huffle.

Pierce.   Who, Hodge Huffle!

Tip. What's he?

Pierce. A cheater, and another fine gentleman,
A friend o' the chamberlain's, Jordan's.   Master Huffle,
He's Burst's protection.

Fly.   Fights and vapours for him.

Pierce. He will be drunk so civilly—

Fly.   So discreetly—

Pierce. And punctually! just at this hour.

Fly.   And then
Call for his Jordan with that hum and state,
As if he piss'd the politics.

Pierce.   And sup
With his tuft-taffata night gear, here, so silently!

Fly. Nothing but music.

Pierce.   A dozen of bawdy songs.

Tip. And knows the general this?

Fly.   O no, sir; *dormit,*
Dormit patronus still, the master sleeps,
They'll steal to bed.

Pierce.   In private, sir, and pay
The fidlers with that modesty, next morning.

Fly. Take a *dejeune* of muskadel and eggs.

Pierce. And pack away in their trundling cheats, like gipsies.

Trun. Mysteries, mysteries, Ferret.

Fer.   Ay, we see, Trundle,
What the great officers in an inn may do; ·
I do not say the officers of the Crown,
But the Light Heart.

Tip. I'll see the Bat and Huffle.

Fer. I have some business, sir, I crave your pardon—

Tip. What?

Fer. To be sober.   [*Exit.*

Tip. Pox, go get you gone then.
Trundle shall stay.

Trun. No, I beseech you, colonel.

The New Inn

Your lordship has a mind to be drunk private,
With these brave gallants; I will step aside
Into the stables, and salute my mares.   [*Exit.*
    Pierce. Yes, do, and sleep with them.—Let him go, base whip-
stock;
He is as drunk as a fish now, almost as dead.
    Tip. Come, I will see the flicker-mouse, my Fly.   [*Exeunt.*

SCENE II.—*Another Room in the same, furnished as a
Tribunal, etc.*

Music. Enter the Host, *ushering* Prudence, *who takes her seat of
judicature, assisted by Lord* Beaufort, *and Lord* Latimer; *the*
Nurse, Frank, Jug, Jordan, Trundle, *and* Ferret.

    Pru. Here set the hour; but first produce the parties;
And clear the court: the time is now of price.
    Host. Jug, get you down, and, Trundle, get you up,
You shall be crier; Ferret here, the clerk.
Jordan, smell you without, till the ladies call you;
Take down the fidlers too, silence that noise,
Deep in the cellar, safe.   [*Exeunt Jug, Jordan, and Musicians.*
    Pru. Who keeps the watch?
    Host. Old Sheelinin, here, is the madam Tell-clock.
    Nurse. No fait' and trot', sweet maister, I shall sleep;
I'fait', I shall.
    Lord B. I prithee do then, screech-owl.
She brings to mind the fable of the dragon,
That kept the Hesperian fruit.   Would I could charm her!
    Host. Trundle will do it with his hum.   Come, Trundle:
Precede him, Ferret, in the form.
    Fer. Oyez, oyez, oyez.
    Trun. Oyez, oyez, oyez.
    Fer. Whereas there hath been awarded,—
    Trun. Whereas there hath, etc.
        [*As Ferret proclaims, Trundle repeats after him, at the breaks
        here, and through the rest of this scene.*
    Fer. By the queen regent of love,—
In this high court of sovereignty,—
Two special hours of address,—
To Herbert Lovel, appellant,—
Against the lady Frampul, defendant.—
Herbert Lovel, come into the court,—
Make challenge to thy first hour,—
And save thee and thy bail,—
    Trun. And save thee, etc.

Enter Lovel, *and ranges himself on the one side.*

    Host. Lo, louting, where he comes into the court!
Clerk of the sovereignty, take his appearance,

And how accoutred, how design'd he comes!

Fer. 'Tis done.   Now, crier, call the lady Frampul
And by the name of
              Frances, lady Frampul, defendant,—

Trun. Frances, lady Frampul, etc.

Fer. Come into the court.—
Make answer to the award,—
And save thee and thy bail,—

Trun. And save thee, etc.

Enter Lady FRAMPUL, *and takes her place on the other side.*

Host. She makes a noble and a just appearance.
Set it down likewise, and how arm'd she comes.

Pru. Usher of Love's court, give them [both] their oath,
According to the form, upon Love's missal.

Host. Arise, and lay your hands upon the book.

Herbert Lovel, appellant, and lady Frances Frampul, defendant, you
shall swear upon the liturgy of Love, *Ovid de arte amandi,* that you neither
have, ne will have, nor in any wise bear about you, thing or things, pointed,
or blunt, within these lists, other than what are natural and allow'd by
the court: no inchanted arms, or weapons, stones of virtue, herb of grace,
charm, character, spell, philtre, or other power than Love's only, and the
justness of your cause.   So help you Love, his mother, and the contents
of this book: kiss it.   [*Lov. kisses the book.*

Return unto your seats.—Crier, bid silence.

Trun. Oyez, oyez, oyez, oyez.

Fer. In the name of the sovereign of Love,—

Trun. In the name of the, etc.

Fer. Notice is given by the court,—
To the appellant, and defendant,—
That the first hour of address proceeds,—
And Love save the sovereign,—

Trun. And Love save, etc.

Every man or woman keep silence, pain of imprisonment.

Pru. Do your endeavours in the name of Love.

Lov. To make my first approaches, then, in love.

Lady F. Tell us what love is, that we may be sure
There's such a thing, and that it is in nature.

Lov. Excellent lady, I did not expect
To meet an infidel, much less an atheist,
Here in Love's list! of so much unbelief
To raise a question of his being!

Host. Well charged!

Lov. I rather thought, and with religion think,
Had all the characters of love been lost,
His lines, dimensions, and whole signature
Razed and defaced, with dull humanity,
That both his nature, and his essence, might
Have found their mighty instauration here;
Here, where the confluence of fair and good

Meets to make up all beauty. For what else
Is love, but the most noble, pure affection
Of what is truly beautiful and fair,
Desire of union with the thing beloved?

Lord B. Have the assistants of the court their votes,
And writ of privilege, to speak them freely?

Pru. Yes, to assist, but not to interrupt.

Lord B. Then I have read somewhere, that man and woman
Were, in the first creation, both one piece,
And being cleft asunder, ever since
— Love was an appetite to be rejoin'd.
As for example—   *[Kisses Frank.*

Nurse. Cramo-cree! what mean'sh tou?

Lord B. Only to kiss and part.

Host. So much is lawful.

Lord L. And stands with the prerogative of Love's court.

Lov. It is a fable of Plato's, in his banquet,
And utter'd there by Aristophanes.

Host. 'Tis well remember'd here, and to good use.
But on with your description, what love is:
Desire of union with the thing beloved.

Lov. I meant a definition. For I make
The efficient cause, what's beautiful and fair;
The formal cause, the appetite of union:
The final cause, the union itself.
But larger if you'll have it; by description,
It is a flame and ardour of the mind,
Dead, in the proper corps, quick in another's;
Transfers the lover into the be-loved.
The he or she that loves, engraves or stamps
The idea of what they love, first in themselves:
Or like to glasses, so their minds take in
The forms of their beloved, and then reflect.
It is the likeness of affections,
Is both the parent and the nurse of love.
Love is a spiritual coupling of two souls,
So much more excellent, as it least relates
Unto the body; circular, eternal,
Not feign'd, or made, but born; and then so precious,
As nought can value it but itself; so free,
As nothing can command it but itself;
And in itself so round and liberal,
As where it favours it bestows itself.

Lord B. And that do I; here my whole self I tender,
According to the practice of the court.   *[To Frank.*

Nurse. Ay, 'tish a naughty practish, a lewd practish,
Be quiet, man, dou shalt not leip her here.

Lord B. Leap her! I lip her, foolish queen at arms,
Thy blazon's false: wilt thou blaspheme thine office?

    Lov. But we must take and understand this love,
Along still, as a name of dignity;
Not pleasure.
    Host. Mark you that, my light young lord?   *[To Lord B.*
    Lov. True love hath no unworthy thought, no light,
Loose, unbecoming appetite, or strain,
But fixed, constant, pure, immutable.
    Lord B. I relish not these philosophical feasts;
Give me a banquet of sense, like that of Ovid:
A form to take the eye; a voice mine ear;
Pure aromatic to my scent: a soft,
Smooth, dainty hand to touch; and for my taste,
Ambrosiac kisses to melt down the palate.
    Lov. They are the earthly, lower form of lovers,
Are only taken with what strikes the senses;
And love by that loose scale. Although I grant,
We like what's fair and graceful in an object,
And, true, would use it, in the all we tend to,
Both of our civil and domestic deeds;
In ordering of an army, in our style,
Apparel, gesture, building, or what not:
All arts and actions do affect their beauty.
But put the case, in travel I may meet
Some gorgeous structure, a brave frontispiece,
Shall I stay captive in the outer court,
Surprised with that, and not advance to know
Who dwells there, and inhabiteth the house?
There is my friendship to be made, within,
With what can love me again: not with the walls,
Doors, windows, architraves, the frieze, and cornice.
My end is lost in loving of a face,
An eye, lip, nose, hand, foot, or other part,
Whose all is but a statue, if the mind
Move not, which only can make the return.
The end of love, is to have two made one
In will, and in affection, that the minds
Be first inoculated, not the bodies.
    Lord B. Give me the body, if it be a good one. *[Kisses Frank.*
    Frank. Nay, sweet my lord, I must appeal the sovereign
For better quarter, if you hold your practice.
    Trun. Silence, pain of imprisonment! hear the court.
    Lov. The body's love is frail, subject to change,
And alters still with it; the mind's is firm,
One and the same, proceedeth first from weighing,
And well examining what is fair and good;
Then what is like in reason, fit in manners;
That breeds good-will: good-will desire of union.
So knowledge first begets benevolence,
Benevolence breeds friendship, friendship love:

And where it starts or steps aside from this,
— It is a mere degenerous appetite,
A lost, oblique, depraved affection,
And bears no mark or character of love.

    Lady F. How am I changed! by what alchemy
Of love, or language, am I thus translated!
His tongue is tipt with the philosopher's stone,
And that hath touched me through every vein!
I feel that transmutation of my blood,
As I were quite become another creature,
And all he speaks it is projection.

    Pru. Well feign'd, my lady: now her parts begin.

    Lord L. And she will act them subtily.

    Pru. She fails me else.

    Lov. Nor do they trespass within bounds of pardon,
That giving way, and license to their love,
Divest him of his noblest ornaments,
Which are his modesty and shamefacedness:
And so they do, that have unfit designs
Upon the parties they pretend to love.
For what's more monstrous, more a prodigy,
Than to hear me protest truth of affection
Unto a person that I would dishonour?
And what's a more dishonour, than defacing
Another's good with forfeiting mine own;
And drawing on a fellowship of sin?
From note of which, though for a while, we may
Be both kept safe by caution, yet the conscience
Cannot be cleans'd: for what was hitherto
Call'd by the name of love, becomes destroy'd
Then, with the fact; the innocency lost,
The bateing of affection soon will follow;
And love is never true that is not lasting:
No more than any can be pure or perfect,
That entertains more than one object. *Dixi.*

    Lady F. O speak, and speak for ever! let mine ear
Be feasted still, and filled with this banquet!
No sense can ever surfeit on such truth,
It is the marrow of all lovers' tenets!
Who hath read Plato, Heliodore, or Tatius,
Sidney, D'Urfé, or all Love's fathers, like him?
He's there the Master of the Sentences,
Their school, their commentary, text, and gloss,
And breathes the true divinity of love!

    Pru. Excellent actor, how she hits this passion!

    Lady F. Where have I lived, in heresy, so long
Out of the congregation of Love,
And stood irregular, by all his canons?

    Lord L. But do you think she plays?

Pru. Upon my sovereignty;
Mark her anon.

Lord L. I shake, and am half jealous.

Lady F. What penance shall I do to be received,
And reconciled to the church of Love?
Go on procession, barefoot, to his image,
And say some hundred penitential verses,
There, out of Chaucer's Troilus and Cressid?
Or to his mother's shrine, vow a wax-candle
As large as the town May-pole is, and pay it?
Enjoin me any thing this court thinks fit,
For I have trespass'd, and blasphemed Love:
I have, indeed, despised his deity,
Whom (till this miracle wrought on me) I knew not.
Now I adore Love, and would kiss the rushes
That bear this reverend gentleman, his priest,
If that would expiate—but I fear it will not.
For, though he be somewhat struck in years, and old
Enough to be my father, he is wise,
And only wise men love, the other covet.
I could begin to be in love with him,
But will not tell him yet, because I hope
To enjoy the other hour with more delight,
And prove him farther.

Pru. Most Socratic lady,
Or, if you will ironic! give you joy
Of your Platonic love here, master Lovel!
But pay him his first kiss yet, in the court,
Which is a debt, and due: for the hour's run.

Lady F. How swift is time, and slily steals away
From them would hug it, value it, embrace it!
I should have thought it scarce had run ten minutes,
When the whole hour is fled. Here, take your kiss, sir,
Which I most willingly tender you in court.   [*Kisses Lov.*

Lord B. And we do imitate.   [*Kisses Frank.*

Lady F. And I could wish,
It had been twenty—so the sovereign's
Poor narrow nature had decreed it so—
But that is past, irrevocable, now:
She did her kind, according to her latitude—

Pru. Beware you do not conjure up a spirit
You cannot lay.

Lady F. I dare you, do your worst:
Shew me but such an injustice; I would thank you
To alter your award.

Lord L. Sure she is serious!
I shall have another fit of jealousy,
I feel a grudging.

Host. Cheer up, noble guest,

—We cannot guess what this may come to yet;
The brain of man or woman is uncertain.
   Lov. Tut, she dissembles; all is personated,
And counterfeit comes from her! if it were not,
The Spanish monarchy, with both the Indies,
Could not buy off the treasure of this kiss,
Or half give balance for my happiness.
   Host. Why, as it is yet, it glads my Light Heart
To see you rouzed thus from a sleepy humour
Of drowsy, accidental melancholy;
—And all those brave parts of your soul awake,
That did before seem drown'd, and buried in you.
That you express yourself as you had back'd
The Muses' horse, or got Bellerophon's arms—

Enter FLY.

What news with Fly?
   Fly. News of a newer lady,
A finer, fresher, braver, bonnier beauty,
A very bona-roba, and a bouncer,
In yellow, glistering, golden satin.
   Lady F. Prue,
Adjourn the court.
   Pru. Cry, Trundle.
   Trun. Oyez,
Any man, or woman, that hath any personal attendance
To give unto the court; keep the second hour,
And Love save the sovereign!   [*Exeunt.*

ACT IV

SCENE I.—*A Room in the Inn.*

Enter JUG, BARNABY, *and* JORDAN.

   Jug. O Barnaby!
   Jor. Welcome, Barnaby! where hast thou been?
   Bar. In the foul weather.
   Jug. Which has wet thee, Barnaby.
   Bar. As dry as a chip. Good Jug, a cast of thy name,
As well as thy office: two jugs.
   Jug. By and by.   [*Exit.*
   Jor. What lady's this thou hast brought here?
   Bar. A great lady!
I know no more; one that will try you, Jordan;
She'll find your gage, your circle, your capacity.
How does old Staggers the smith, and Tree the sadler?
Keep they their penny club still?
   Jor. And the old catch too,
Of *Whoop-Barnaby!*

Bar. Do they sing at me?

Jor. They are reeling at it in the parlour now.

Re-enter Jug *with wine.*

Bar. I'll to them: give me a drink first.   [*Drinks.*

Jor. Where's thy hat?

Bar. I lost it by the way—Give me another.

Jug. A hat!

Bar. A drink.   [*Drinks.*

Jug. Take heed of taking cold, Bar—

Bar. The wind blew't off at Highgate, and my lady
Would not endure me light to take it up;
But made me drive bareheaded in the rain.

Jor. That she might be mistaken for a countess?

Bar. Troth, like enough: she might be an o'ergrown dutchess,
For aught I know.

Jug. What, with one man!

Bar. At a time,
They carry no more, the best of them.

Jor. Nor the bravest.

Bar. And she is very brave.

Jor. A stately gown
And petticoat, she has on!

Bar. Have you spied that, Jordan?
You are a notable peerer, an old rabbi,
At a smock's hem, boy.

Jug. As he is chamberlain,
He may do that by his place.

Jor. What is her squire?

Bar. A toy, that she allows eight-pence a-day,
A slight mannet, to port her up and down:
Come, shew me to my play-fellows, old Staggers,
And father Tree.

Jor. Here, this way, Barnaby.   [*Exeunt.*

SCENE II.—*The Court of the Inn.*

Enter Tipto, Burst, Huffle, *and* Fly.

Tip. Come, let us take in fresco, here, one quart.

Burst. Two quarts, my man of war, let's not be stinted.

Huf. Advance three Jordans, varlet of the house.

Tip. I do not like your Burst, bird; he is saucy:
Some shop-keeper he was?

Fly. Yes, sir.

Tip. I knew it,
A broke-wing'd shop-keeper? I nose them straight.
He had no father, I warrant him, that durst own him;
Some foundling in a stall, or the church-porch;
Brought up in the hospital; and so bound prentice;

Then master of a shop; then one o' the inquest;
Then breaks out bankrupt, or starts alderman:
The original of both is a church-porch—
    Fly. Of some, my colonel.
    Tip. Good faith, of most
Of your shop citizens: they are rude animals!
And let them get but ten mile out of town,
They out-swagger all the wapentake.
    Fly. What's that?
    Tip. A Saxon word to signify the hundred.
    Burst. Come, let us drink, sir Glorious, some brave health
Upon our tip-toes.
    Tip. To the health of the Bursts.
    Burst. Why Bursts?
    Tip. Why Tiptos?
    Burst. O, I cry you mercy!
    Tip. It is sufficient.
    Huf. What is so sufficient?
    Tip. To drink to you is sufficient.
    Huf. On what terms?
    Tip. That you shall give security to pledge me.
    Huf. So you will name no Spaniard, I will pledge you.
    Tip. I rather choose to thirst, and will thirst ever,
Than leave that cream of nations uncried up.
Perish all wine, and gust of wine!   *[Throws the wine at him.*
    Huf. How! spill it?
Spill it at me?
    Tip. I reck not; but I spilt it.
    Fly. Nay, pray you be quiet, noble bloods.
    Burst. No Spaniards,
I cry, with my cousin Huffle.
    Huf. Spaniards! pilchers.
    Tip. Do not provoke my patient blade; it sleeps,
And would not hear thee: Huffle, thou art rude,
And dost not know the Spanish composition.
    Burst. What is the recipe? name the ingredients.
    Tip. Valour.
    Burst. Two ounces!
    Tip. Prudence.
    Burst. Half a dram!
    Tip. Justice.
    Burst. A pennyweight!
    Tip. Religion.
    Burst. Three scruples!
    Tip. And of gravidàd.
    Burst. A face-full.
    Tip. He carries such a dose of it in his looks,
Actions and gestures, as it breeds respect
To him from savages, and reputation

With all the sons of men.

Burst. Will it give him credit
With gamesters, courtiers, citizens, or tradesmen?

Tip. He'll borrow money on the stroke of his beard,
Or turn of his mustaccio! his mere cuello,
Or ruff about his neck, is a bill of exchange
In any bank in Europe: not a merchant
That sees his gait, but straight will furnish him
Upon his pace.

Huf. I have heard the Spanish name
Is terrible to children in some countries;
And used to make them eat their bread and butter
Or take their worm-seed.

Tip. Huffle, you do shuffle.

Enter STUFF, *and* PINNACIA *his wife richly habited.*

Burst. 'Slid, here's a lady!

Huf. *And a lady gay!*

Tip. A well-trimm'd lady!

Huf. Let us lay her aboard.

Burst. Let's hail her first.

Tip. By your sweet favour, lady.

Stuff. Good gentlemen, be civil, we are strangers.

Burst. An you were Flemings, sir—

Huf. Or Spaniards—

Tip. They are here, have been at Sevil in their days,
And at Madrid too.

Pin. He is a foolish fellow,
I pray you mind him not, he is my Protection.

Tip. In your protection he is safe, sweet lady.
So shall you be in mine.

Huf. A share, good colonel.

Tip. Of what?

Huf. Of your fine lady: I am Hodge,
My name is Huffle.

Tip. Huffling Hodge, be quiet.

Burst. And I pray you, be you so, glorious colonel!
Hodge Huffle shall be quiet.

Huf. [singing.] *A lady gay, gay:*
For she is a lady gay, gay, gay.　For she is a lady gay.

Tip. Bird of the vespers, vespertilio Burst,
You are a gentleman of the first head;
But that head may be broke, as all the body is—
Burst, if you tie not up your Huffle quickly.

Huf. Tie dogs, not men.

Burst. Nay, pray thee, Hodge, be still.

Tip. This steel here rides not on this thigh in vain.

Huf. Shew'st thou thy steel and thigh, thou glorious dirt!
Then Hodge sings Samson, and no ties shall hold. [*They fight.*

Enter PIERCE, JUG, *and* JORDAN.

Pierce. Keep the peace, gentlemen: what do you mean?
Tip. I will not discompose myself for Huffle.

[*Exeunt all* (*but Stuff and Pin.*) *fighting.*

Pin. You see what your entreaty and pressure still
Of gentlemen, to be civil, doth bring on:
A quarrel, and perhaps man-slaughter. You
Will carry your goose about you still, your planing-iron!
Your tongue to smooth all! is not here fine stuff!
Stuff. Why, wife?
Pin. Your wife! have not I forbidden you that?
Do you think I'll call you husband in this gown,
Or any thing, in that jacket, but protection?
Here, tie my shoe, and shew my velvet petticoat,
And my silk stocking. Why do you make me a lady,
If I may not do like a lady in fine clothes?
Stuff. Sweet heart, you may do what you will with me.
Pin. Ay, I knew that at home; what to do with you;
But why was I brought hither? to see fashions?
Stuff. And wear them too, sweet heart; but this wild company—
Pin. Why do you bring me in wild company?
You'd have me tame and civil in wild company!
I hope I know wild company are fine company,
And in fine company, where I am fine myself,
A lady may do any thing, deny nothing
To a fine party, I have heard you say it.

Re-enter PIERCE.

Pierce. There are a company of ladies above
Desire your ladyship's company, and to take
The surety of their lodgings from the affront
Of these half beasts were here e'en now, the Centaurs.
Pin. Are they fine ladies?
Pierce. Some very fine ladies.
Pin. As fine as I?
Pierce. I dare use no comparisons,
Being a servant, sent—
Pin. Spoke like a fine fellow!
I would thou wert one; I'd not then deny thee: —
But, thank thy lady.

[*Exit Pierce.*

Enter Host.

Host. Madam, I must crave you
To afford a lady a visit, would excuse
Some harshness of the house, you have received
From the brute guests.
Pin. This is a fine old man!
I'd go with him an he were a little finer.

Stuff. You may, sweet heart, it is mine host.
Pin. Mine host!
Host. Yes, madam, I must bid you welcome.
Pin. Do, then.
Stuff. But do not stay.
Pin. I'll be advised by you! yes.   [*Exeunt.*

SCENE III.—*A Room in the same.*

Enter Lord LATIMER, Lord BEAUFORT, Lady FRAMPUL,
PRUDENCE, FRANK, *and* Nurse.

Lord L. What more than Thracian barbarism was this?
Lord B. The battle of the Centaurs with the Lapithes!
Lady F. There is no taming of the monster, drink.
Lord L. But what a glorious beast our Tipto shew'd!
He would not discompose himself, the don!
Your Spaniard ne'er doth discompose himself.
Lord B. Yet, how he talk'd, and roar'd in the beginning!
Pru. And ran as fast as a knock'd marrow-bone.
Lord B. So they did at last, when Lovel went down,
And chased them 'bout the court.
Lord L. For all's don Lewis,
Or fencing after Euclid.
Lady F. I ne'er saw
A lightning shoot so, as my servant did,
His rapier was a meteor, and he waved it
Over them, like a comet, as they fled him.
I mark'd his manhood! every stoop he made
Was like an eagle's at a flight of cranes:
As I have read somewhere.
Lord B. Bravely exprest.
Lord L. And like a lover.
Lady F. Of his valour, I am.
He seem'd a body rarified to air;
Or that his sword, and arm were of a piece,
They went together so!—Here comes the lady.

Enter Host, *with* PINNACIA.

Lord B. A bouncing bona-roba! as the Fly said.
Frank. She is some giantess: I will stand off,
For fear she swallow me.
Lady F. Is not this our gown, Prue,
That I bespoke of Stuff?
Pru. It is the fashion.
Lady F. Ay, and the silk; feel: sure it is the same!
Pru. And the same petticoat, lace and all!
Lady F. I'll swear it.
How came it hither? make a bill of enquiry.
Pru. You have a fine suit on, madam, and a rich one.

Lady F. And of a curious making.

Pru. And a new.

Pin. As new as day.

Lord L. She answers like a fish-wife.

Pin. I put it on since noon, I do assure you.

Pru. Who is your tailor?

Lady F. Pray you, your fashioner's name?

Pin. My fashioner is a certain man of mine own;
He is in the house: no matter for his name.

Host. O, but to satisfy this bevy of ladies,
Of which a brace, here, long'd to bid you welcome.

Pin. He is one, in truth, I title my Protection:
Bid him come up.

Host. [*calls.*] Our new lady's Protection!
What is your ladyship's style?

Pin. Countess Pinnacia.

Host. Countess Pinnacia's man, come to your lady!

Enter STUFF.

Pru. Your ladyship's tailor! master Stuff!

Lady F. How, Stuff!
He the Protection!

Host. Stuff looks like a remnant.

Stuff. I am undone, discover'd.   [*Falls on his knees.*

Pru. 'Tis the suit, madam,
Now, without scruple: and this some device
To bring it home with.

Pin. Why upon your knees?
Is this your lady godmother?

Stuff. Mum, Pinnacia.
It is the lady Frampul; my best customer.

Lady F. What shew is this that you present us with?

Stuff. I do beseech your ladyship, forgive me;
She did but say the suit on.

Lady F. Who? which she?

Stuff. My wife, forsooth.

Lady F. How! mistress Stuff, your wife!
Is that the riddle?

Pru. We all look'd for a lady,
A dutchess, or a countess at the least.

Stuff. She's my own lawfully begotten wife,
In wedlock: we have been coupled now seven years.

Lady F. And why thus mask'd? you like a footman, ha!
And she your countess!

Pin. To make a fool of himself,
And of me too.

Stuff. I pray thee, Pinnace, peace.

Pin. Nay, it shall out, since you have call'd me wife,
And openly dis-ladied me: Though I am discountess'd

I am not yet dis-countenanced. These shall see.

Host. Silence!

Pin. It is a foolish trick, madam, he has;
For though he be your tailor, he is my beast:
I may be bold with him, and tell his story.
When he makes any fine garment will fit me,
Or any rich thing that he thinks of price,
Then must I put it on, and be his countess,
Before he carry it home unto the owners.
A coach is hired, and four horse; he runs
In his velvet jacket thus, to Rumford, Croydon,
Hounslow, or Barnet, the next bawdy road:
And takes me out, carries me up, and throws me
Upon a bed—

Lady F. Peace, thou immodest woman!—
She glories in the bravery of the vice.

Lord L. It is a quaint one.

Lord B. A fine species
Of fornicating with a man's own wife,
Found out by—what's his name?

Lord L. Master Nic. Stuff.

Host. The very figure of pre-occupation
In all his customers' best clothes.

Lord L. He lies
With his own succuba, in all your names.

Lord B. And all your credits.

Host. Ay, and at all their costs.

Lord L. This gown was then bespoken for the sovereign.

Lord B. Ay, marry was it.

Lord L. And a main offence
Committed 'gainst the sovereignty; being not brought
Home in the time: beside, the profanation
Which may call on the censure of the court.

Host. Let him be blanketted. Call up the quarter-master.
Deliver him o'er to Fly.

Enter FLY.

Stuff. O good my lord.

Host. Pillage the Pinnace.

Lady F. Let his wife be stript.

Lord B. Blow off her upper deck.

Lord L. Tear all her tackle.

Lady F. Pluck the polluted robes over her ears;
Or cut them all to pieces, make a fire of them.

Pru. To rags and cinders burn th' idolatrous vestures.

Host. Fly, and your fellows, see that the whole censure
Be thoroughly executed.

Fly. We'll toss him bravely,
Till the stuff stink again.

Host. And send her home,
Divested to her flannel, in a cart.
Lord L. And let her footman beat the bason afore her.
Fly. The court shall be obey'd.
Host. Fly, and his officers,
Will do it fiercely.
Stuff. Merciful queen Prue!
Pru. I cannot help you.   [*Exit Fly, with Stuff and Pinnacia.*
Lord B. Go thy ways, Nic. Stuff,
Thou hast nickt it for a fashioner of venery.
Lord L. For his own hell! though he run ten mile for it.
Pru. O, here comes Lovel, for his second hour.
Lord B. And after him the type of Spanish valour.

Enter LOVEL *with a Paper, followed by* TIPTO.

Lady F. Servant, what have you there?
Lov. A meditation,
Or rather a vision, madam, and of beauty,
Our former subject.
Lady F. Pray you let us hear it.

Lov.   *It was a beauty that I saw,*
        So pure, so perfect, as the frame
        Of all the universe was lame,
        To that one figure, could I draw,
        Or give least line of it a law!

        A skein of silk without a knot,
        A fair march made without a halt,
        A curious form without a fault,
        A printed book without a blot,
        All beauty, and without a spot!

Lady F. They are gentle words, and would deserve a note,
Set to them, as gentle.
Lov. I have tried my skill,
To close the second hour, if you will hear them;
My boy by that time will have got it perfect.
Lady F. Yes, gentle servant.   In what calm he speaks,
After this noise and tumult, so unmoved,
With that serenity of countenance,
As if his thoughts did acquiesce in that
Which is the object of the second hour,
And nothing else.
Pru. Well then, summon the court.
Lady F. I have a suit to the sovereign of Love,
If it may stand with the honour of the court,
To change the question but from love to valour,
To hear it said, but what true valour is,
Which oft begets true love. —
Lord L. It is a question

Fit for the court to take true knowledge of,
And hath my just assent.

    Pru. Content.

    Lord B. Content.

    Frank. Content. I am content, give him his oath.

    Host. Herbert Lovel, Thou shalt swear upon the Testament of Love, to make answer to this question propounded to thee by the court, What true valour is? and therein to tell the truth, the whole truth, and nothing but the truth. So help thee Love, and thy bright sword at need.

    Lov. So help me, Love, and my good sword at need.
It is the greatest virtue, and the safety
Of all mankind, the object of it is danger.
A certain mean 'twixt fear and confidence:
No inconsiderate rashness or vain appetite
Of false encountering formidable things;
But a true science of distinguishing
What's good or evil. It springs out of reason,
And tends to perfect honesty, the scope
Is always honour, and the public good:
It is no valour for a private cause. —

    Lord B. No! not for reputation?

    Lov. That's man's idol,
Set up 'gainst God, the maker of all laws,
Who hath commanded us we should not kill;
And yet we say, we must for reputation.
What honest man can either fear his own,
Or else will hurt another's reputation?
Fear to do base unworthy things is valour;
If they be done to us, to suffer them,
Is valour too. The office of a man
That's truly valiant, is considerable,
Three ways: the first is in respect of matter,
Which still is danger; in respect of form,
Wherein he must preserve his dignity;
And in the end, which must be ever lawful.

    Lord L. But men, when they are heated, and in passion,
Cannot consider.

    Lov. Then it is not valour.
I never thought an angry person valiant:
Virtue is never aided by a vice.
What need is there of anger and of tumult;
When reason can do the same things, or more?

    Lord B. O yes, 'tis profitable, and of use;
It makes us fierce, and fit to undertake.

    Lov. Why, so will drink make us both bold and rash,
Or Phrensy if you will: do these make valiant?
They are poor helps, and virtue needs them not.
No man is valianter by being angry,

But he that could not valiant be without:
So that it comes not in the aid of virtue,
But in the stead of it.

    Lord L. He holds the right.

    Lov. And 'tis an odious kind of remedy,
To owe our health to a disease.

    Tip. If man
Should follow the *dictamen* of his passion,
He could not 'scape—

    Lord B. To discompose himself.

    Lord L. According to don Lewis!

    Host. Or Caranza!

    Lov. Good colonel Glorious, whilst we treat of valour,
Dismiss yourself.

    Lord L. You are not concern'd.

    Lov. Go drink,
And congregate the hostlers and the tapsters,
The under-officers of your regiment;
Compose with them, and be not angry valiant.   *[Exit Tipto.*

    Lord B. How does that differ from true valour?

    Lov. Thus.
In the efficient, or that which makes it:
For it proceeds from passion, not from judgment:
Then brute beasts have it, wicked persons; there
It differs in the subject; in the form,
'Tis carried rashly, and with violence:
Then in the end, where it respects not truth,
Or public honesty, but mere revenge.
Now confident, and undertaking valour,
Sways from the true, two other ways, as being
A trust in our own faculties, skill, or strength,
And not the right, or conscience of the cause,
That works it: then in the end, which is the victory,
And not the honour.

    Lord B. But the ignorant valour.
That knows not why it undertakes, but doth it
To escape the infamy merely—

    Lov. Is worst of all:
That valour lies in the eyes o' the lookers on;
And is called valour with a witness.

    Lord B. Right.

    Lov. The things true valour's exercised about,
Are poverty, restraint, captivity,
Banishment, loss of children, long disease:
The least is death. Here valour is beheld,
Properly seen; about these it is present:
Not trivial things, which but require our confidence.
And yet to those we must object ourselves,
Only for honesty; if any other

Respects be mixt, we quite put out her light.
And as all knowledge, when it is removed,
Or separate from justice, is call'd craft,
Rather than wisdom; so a mind affecting,
Or undertaking dangers, for ambition,
Or any self-pretext not for the public,
Deserves the name of daring, not of valour.
And over-daring is as great a vice,
As over-fearing.
　　Lord L. Yes, and often greater.
　　Lov. But as it is not the mere punishment,
But cause that makes a martyr, so it is not
Fighting or dying, but the manner of it,
Renders a man himself.　A valiant man
Ought not to undergo, or tempt a danger,
But worthily, and by selected ways:
He undertakes with reason, not by chance.
His valour is the salt to his other virtues,
They are all unseasoned without it.　The waiting maids,
Or the concomitants of it, are his patience,
His magnanimity, his confidence,
His constancy, security, and quiet;
He can assure himself against all rumour,
Despairs of nothing, laughs at contumelies,
As knowing himself advanced in a height
Where injury cannot reach him, nor aspersion
Touch him with soil!
　　Lady F. Most manly utter'd all!
As if Achilles had the chair in valour,
And Hercules were but a lecturer.
Who would not hang upon those lips for ever,
That strike such music!　I could run on them;
But modesty is such a school-mistress
To keep our sex in awe—
　　Pru. Or you can feign;
My subtle and dissembling lady mistress.
　　Lord L. I fear she means it, Prue, in too good earnest.
　　Lov. The purpose of an injury 'tis to vex
And trouble me; now nothing can do that
To him that's valiant.　He that is affected
With the least injury, is less than it.
It is but reasonable to conclude
That should be stronger still which hurts, than that
Which is hurt.　Now no wickedness is stronger
Than what opposeth it: not Fortune's self,
When she encounters virtue, but comes off
Both lame and less!　why should a wise man then
Confess himself the weaker, by the feeling
Of a fool's wrong?　There may an injury

Be meant me. I may choose, if I will take it.
But we are now come to that delicacy,
And tenderness of sense, we think an insolence
Worse than an injury, bear words worse than deeds;
We are not so much troubled with the wrong,
As with the opinion of the wrong; like children,
We are made afraid with visors: such poor sounds
As is the lie or common words of spite,
Wise laws thought never worthy a revenge;
And 'tis the narrowness of human nature,
Our poverty, and beggary of spirit,
To take exception at these things. He laugh'd at me!
He broke a jest! a third took place of me!
How most ridiculous quarrels are all these?
Notes of a queasy and sick stomach, labouring
With want of a true injury: the main part
Of the wrong, is our vice of taking it.
    Lord L. Or our interpreting it to be such.
    Lov. You take it rightly. If a woman, or child
Give me the lie, would I be angry? no,
Not if I were in my wits, sure, I should think it
No spice of a disgrace. No more is theirs,
If I will think it, who are to be held
In as contemptible a rank, or worse.
I am kept out a masque, sometime thrust out,
Made wait a day, two, three, for a great word,
Which, when it comes forth, is all frown and forehead:
What laughter should this breed, rather than anger!
Out of the tumult of so many errors,
To feel with contemplation, mine own quiet!
If a great person do me an affront,
A giant of the time, sure I will bear it
Or out of patience, or necessity:
Shall I do more for fear, than for my judgment?
For me now to be angry with Hodge Huffle,
Or Burst, his broken charge, if he be saucy,
Or our own type of Spanish valour, Tipto,
Who were he now necessited to beg,
Would ask an alms, like Conde Olivares,
Were just to make myself such a vain animal
As one of them. If light wrongs touch me not,
No more shall great; if not a few, not many.
There's nought so sacred with us but may find
A sacrilegious person, yet the thing is
No less divine, 'cause the profane can reach it.
He is shot free, in battle, is not hurt,
Not he that is not hit: so he is valiant,
That yields not unto wrongs; not he that 'scapes them.
They that do pull down churches, and deface

The holiest altars, cannot hurt the Godhead.
A calm wise man may shew as much true valour, —
Amidst these popular provocations,
As can an able captain shew security
By his brave conduct, through an enemy's country.
A wise man never goes the people's way:
But as the planets still move contrary
To the world's motion; so doth he, to opinion.
He will examine, if those accidents
Which common fame calls injuries, happen to him
Deservedly or no? Come they deservedly,
They are no wrongs then, but his punishments:
If undeservedly, and he not guilty,
The doer of them, first, should blush, not he.

    Lord L. Excellent!
    Lord B. Truth, and right!
    Frank. An oracle
Could not have spoken more!
    Lady F. Been more believed!
    Pru. The whole court runs into your sentence, sir:
And see your second hour is almost ended.
    Lady F. It cannot be! O clip the wings of time,
Good Prue, or make him stand still with a charm.
Distil the gout into it, cramps, all diseases
To arrest him in the foot, and fix him here:
O, for an engine, to keep back all clocks,
Or make the sun forget his motion!—
If I but knew what drink the time now loved,
To set my Trundle at him, mine own Barnaby!
    Pru. Why, I'll consult our Shelee-nien Thomas.   *[Shakes her.*
    Nurse. *Er grae Chreest.*
    Lord B. Wake her not.
    Nurse. *Tower een cuppaw*
D'usque-bagh, doone.
    Pru. Usquebaugh's her drink,
But 'twill not make the time drunk.
    Host. As it hath her.
Away with her, my lord, but marry her first.
                        [Exit Lord B. with Frank.

    Pru. Ay,
That will be sport anon too for my lady,
But she hath other game to fly at yet.—
The hour is come, your kiss.
    Lady F. My servant's song, first.
    Pru. I say the kiss, first; and I so enjoin'd it:
At your own peril, do, make the contempt.
    Lady F. Well, sir, you must be pay'd, and legally. *[Kisses Lovel.*
    Pru. Nay, nothing, sir, beyond.
    Lov. One more—I except.

This was but half a kiss, and I would change it.

Pru. The court's dissolv'd, removed, and the play ended,
No sound, or air of love more, I decree it.

Lov. From what a happiness hath that one word
Thrown me into the gulph of misery!
To what a bottomless despair! how like
A court removing, or an ended play,
Shews my abrupt precipitate estate,
By how much more my vain hopes were increased
By these false hours of conversation!
Did not I prophesy this of myself,
And gave the true prognostics? O my brain,
How art thou turned! and my blood congeal'd,
My sinews slacken'd, and my marrow melted,
That I remember not where I have been,
Or what I am! only my tongue's on fire;
And burning downward, hurls forth coals and cinders,
To tell, this temple of love will soon be ashes!
Come, indignation, now, and be my mistress.
No more of Love's ungrateful tyranny;
His wheel of torture, and his pits of birdlime,
His nets of nooses, whirlpools of vexation,
His mills to grind his servants into powder—
I will go catch the wind first in a sieve,
Weigh smoak, and measure shadows: plough the water,
And sow my hopes there, ere I stay in love.

Lord L. My jealousy is off, I am now secure. [*Aside and exit.*

Lov. Farewell the craft of crocodiles, women's piety,
And practice of it, in this art of flattering,
And fooling men! I have not lost my reason,
Though I have lent myself out for two hours,
Thus to be baffled by a chambermaid,
And the good actor, her lady, afore mine host
Of the Light Heart, here, that hath laugh'd at all—

Host. Who, I?

Lov. Laugh on, sir, I'll to bed and sleep,
And dream away the vapour of love, if the house
And your leer drunkards let me.

[*Exeunt all but Lady F., Prudence, and Nurse.*

Lady F. Prue!

Pru. Sweet madam.

Lady F. Why would you let him go thus?

Pru. In whose power
Was it to stay him, properer than my lady's?

Lady F. Why in your lady's? are not you the sovereign?

Pru. Would you in conscience, madam, have me vex
His patience more?

Lady F. Not, but apply the cure,
Now it is vext.

Pru. That's but one body's work;
Two cannot do the same thing handsomely.
    Lady F. But had not you the authority absolute?
    Pru. And were not you in rebellion, lady Frampul,
From the beginning?
    Lady F. I was somewhat froward,
I must confess, but frowardness, sometime
Becomes a beauty, being but a visor
Put on.   You'll let a lady wear her mask, Prue!
    Prue. But how do I know, when her ladyship is pleased
To leave it off, except she tell me so?
    Lady F. You might have known that by my looks, and language,
Had you been or regardant, or observant.
One woman reads another's character
Without the tedious trouble of deciphering,
If she but give her mind to't; you knew well,
It could not sort with any reputation
Of mine, to come in first, having stood out
So long, without conditions for mine honour.
    Pru. I thought you did expect none, you so jeer'd him,
And put him off with scorn.
    Lady F. Who, I, with scorn?
I did express my love to idolatry rather,
And so am justly plagued, not understood.
    Pru. I swear I thought you had dissembled, madam,
And doubt you do so yet.
    Lady F. Dull, stupid wench!
Stay in thy state of ignorance still, be damn'd,
An idiot chambermaid!   Hath all my care,
My breeding thee in fashion, thy rich clothes,
Honour, and titles wrought no brighter effects
On thy dark soul, than thus?   Well! go thy ways;
Were not the tailor's wife to be demolish'd,
Ruin'd, uncased, thou should'st be she, I vow.
    Pru. Why, take your spangled properties, your gown
And scarfs.   [*Tearing off her gown.*
    Lady F. Prue, Prue, what dost thou mean?
    Pru. I will not buy this play-boy's bravery
At such a price, to be upbraided for it,
Thus, every minute.
    Lady F. Take it not to heart so.
    Pru. The tailor's wife! there was a word of scorn!
    Lady F. It was a word fell from me, Prue, by chance.
    Pru. Good madam, please to undeceive yourself,
I know when words do slip, and when they are darted
With all their bitterness: *uncased, demolish'd!*
An *idiot chambermaid, stupid* and *dull!*
Be *damn'd for ignorance!*   I will be so;
And think I do deserve it, that, and more,

Much more I do.

Lady F. Here comes mine host: no crying,
Good Prue!—

Re-enter Host.

Where is my servant Lovel, host?

Host. You have sent him up to bed, would you would follow him,
And make my house amends!

Lady F. Would you advise it?

Host. I would I could command it!   My light heart
Should leap till midnight.

Lady F. Pray thee be not sullen,
I yet must have thy counsel.   Thou shalt wear, Prue,
The new gown yet.

Pru. After the tailor's wife!

Lady F. Come, be not angry or grieved: I have a project.
[*Exeunt Lady F. and Pru.*

Host. Wake, Shelee-nien Thomas!   Is this your heraldry,
And keeping of records to lose the main?
Where is your charge?

Nurse. Grae Chreest!

Host. Go ask the oracle
Of the bottle, at your girdle, there you lost it:
You are a sober setter of the watch!

[*Exeunt.*

ACT V

SCENE I.—*A Room in the Inn.*

Enter Host *and* FLY.

Host. Come, Fly and Legacy, the bird o' the Heart:
Prime insect of the Inn, professor, quarter-master,
As ever thou deserved'st thy daily drink,
Padling in sack, and licking in the same,
Now shew thyself an implement of price,
And help to raise a nap to us out of nothing.—
Thou saw'st them married?

Fly. I do think I did,
And heard the words, *I Philip, take thee Lætice.*
I gave her too, was then the father Fly,
And heard the priest do his part, far as five nobles
Would lead him in the lines of matrimony.

Host. Where were they married?

Fly. In the new stable.

Host. Ominous!
I have known many a church been made a stable,
But not a stable made a church till now:
I wish them joy.   Fly, was he a full priest?

Fly. He belly'd for it, had his velvet sleeves,
And his branch'd cassock, a side sweeping gown,
All his formalities, a good cramm'd divine!
I went not far to fetch him, the next inn,
Where he was lodged, for the action.

Host. Had they a license?

Fly. License of love; I saw no other; and purse
To pay the duties both of church and house:
The angels flew about.

Host. Those birds send luck;
And mirth will follow. I had thought to have sacrificed
To merriment to-night in my Light Heart, Fly,
And like a noble poet, to have had
My last act best; but all fails in the plot.
Lovel is gone to bed; the lady Frampul
And sovereign Prue fall'n out: Tipto and his regiment
Of mine-men, all drunk dumb, from his whoop Barnaby,
To his hoop Trundle: they are his two tropics.
No project to rear laughter on, but this,
The marriage of lord Beaufort with Lætitia.
Stay, what is here? the satin gown redeem'd,
And Prue restored in't to her lady's grace!

Fly. She is set forth in't, rigg'd for some employment!

Host. An embassy at least.

Fly. Some treaty of state.

Host. 'Tis a fine tack about; and worth the observing.

[They stand aside.

Enter Lady FRAMPUL, *and* PRUDENCE *magnificently dressed.*

Lady F. Sweet Prue, ay, now thou art a queen indeed!
These robes do royally, and thou becom'st them!
So they do thee! rich garments only fit
The parties they are made for; they shame others.
How did they shew on goody tailor's back?
Like a caparison for a sow, God save us!
Thy putting 'em on hath purged and hallow'd them
From all pollution meant by the mechanics.

Pru. Hang him, poor snip, a secular shop-wit!
He hath nought but his sheers to claim by, and his measures:
His prentice may as well put in for his needle,
And plead a stitch.

Lady F. They have no taint in them
Now of the tailor.

Pru. Yes, of his wife's hanches,
Thus thick of fat; I smell them, of the say.

Lady F. It is restorative, Prue: with thy but chafing it.
A barren hind's grease may work miracles.—
Find but his chamber-door, and he will rise
To thee; or if thou pleasest, feign to be
The wretched party herself, and com'st unto him

In forma pauperis, to crave the aid
Of his knight-errant valour, to the rescue
Of thy distressed robes: name but thy gown,
And he will rise to that.
 Pru. I'll fire the charm first,
I had rather die in a ditch with mistress Shore,
Without a smock, as the pitiful matter has it,
Than owe my wit to clothes, or have it beholden.
 Host. Still spirit of Prue!
 Fly. And smelling of the sovereign!
 Pru. No, I will tell him, as it is indeed;
I come from the fine, froward, frampul lady,
One was run mad with pride, wild with self-love,
But late encountering a wise man who scorn'd her,
And knew the way to his own bed, without
Borrowing her warming-pan, she hath recover'd
Part of her wits; so much as to consider
How far she hath trespass'd, upon whom, and how,
And now sits penitent and solitary,
Like the forsaken turtle, in the volary
Of the Light Heart, the cage, she hath abused,
Mourning her folly, weeping at the height
She measures with her eyes, from whence she is fall'n,
Since she did branch it on the top o' the wood.
 Lady F. I prithee, Prue, abuse me enough, that's use me
As thou think'st fit, any coarse way, to humble me,
Or bring me home again, or Lovel on:
Thou dost not know my sufferings, what I feel,
My fires and fears are met; I burn and freeze,
My liver's one great coal, my heart shrunk up
With all the fibres, and the mass of blood
Within me, is a standing lake of fire,
Curl'd with the cold wind of my gelid sighs,
That drive a drift of sleet through all my body,
And shoot a February through my veins.
Until I see him, I am drunk with thirst,
And surfeited with hunger of his presence.
I know not whêr I am, or no; or speak,
Or whether thou dost hear me.
 Pru. Spare expressions.
I'll once more venture for your ladyship,
So you will use your fortunes reverently.
 Lady F. Religiously, dear Prue: Love and his mother,
I'll build them several churches, shrines, and altars,
And over head, I'll have, in the glass windows,
The story of this day be painted, round,
For the poor laity of love to read:
I'll make myself their book, nay, their example,
To bid them take occasion by the forelock,

And play no after-games of love hereafter.
 Host. [*coming forward with Fly.*] And here your host and's Fly
  witness your vows,
And like two lucky birds, bring the presage
Of a loud jest; Lord Beaufort's married.
 Lady F. Ha!
 Fly. All to-be-married.
 Pru. To whom, not your son?
 Host. The same, Prue. If her ladyship could take truce
A little with her passion, and give way
To their mirth now running—
 Lady F. Runs it mirth! let it come,
It shall be well received, and much made of it.
 Pru. We must of this, it was our own conception.

Enter Lord LATIMER.

 Lord L. Room for green rushes, raise the fidlers, chamberlain,
Call up the house in arms!
 Host. This will rouse Lovel.
 Fly. And bring him on too.
 Lord L. Sheelee-nien Thomas
Runs like a heifer bitten with the brize,
About the court, crying on Fly, and cursing.
 Fly. For what, my lord?
 Lord L. You were best hear that from her,
It is no office, Fly, fits my relation.
Here come the happy couple!—

Enter Lord BEAUFORT, FRANK, FERRET, JORDAN, *and* JUG,
Fidlers, Servants, etc.

Joy, lord Beaufort!

 Fly. And my young lady too.
 Host. Much joy, my lord!
 Lord B. I thank you all; I thank thee, father Fly.
Madam, my cousin, you look discomposed,
I have been bold with a sallad after supper,
Of your own lettice here.
 Lady F. You have, my lord:
But laws of hospitality, and fair rites,
Would have made me acquainted.
 Lord B. In your own house,
I do acknowledge; else I much had trespass'd.
But in an inn, and public, where there is license
Of all community; a pardon of course
May be sued out.
 Lord L. It will, my lord, and carry it.
I do not see, how any storm or tempest
Can help it now.
 Pru. The thing being done and past,

You bear it wisely, and like a lady of judgment.

Lord B. She is that, secretary Prue.

Pru. Why secretary,
My wise lord? is your brain [too] lately married!

Lord B. Your reign is ended, Prue, no sovereign now:
Your date is out, and dignity expired.

Pru. I am annull'd; how can I treat with Lovel,
Without a new commission?

Lady F. Thy gown's commission.

Host. Have patience, Prue, expect, bid the lord joy.

Pru. And this brave lady too. I wish them joy!

Pierce. Joy!

Jor. Joy!

Jug. All joy!

Host. Ay, the house full of joy.

Fly. Play the bells, fidlers, crack your strings with joy.   [*Music.*

Pru. But, lady Lætice, you shew'd a neglect
Un-to-be-pardon'd, to'ards my lady, your kinswoman,
Not to advise with her.

Lord B. Good politic Prue,
Urge not your state-advice, your after-wit;
'Tis near upbraiding. Get our bed ready, chamberlain,
And host, a bride-cup; you have rare conceits,
And good ingredients; ever an old host,
Upon the road, has his provocative drinks.

Lord L. He is either a good bawd, or a physician.

Lord B. 'Twas well he heard you not, his back was turn'd.
A bed, the genial bed! a brace of boys,
To-night, I play for.

Pru. Give us points, my lord.

Lord B. Here take them, Prue, my cod-piece point, and all.
I have clasps, my Lætice' arms; here take them, boys.
                                   [*Throws off his doublet, etc.*
What, is the chamber ready? Speak, why stare you
On one another?

Jor. No, sir.

Lord B. And why no?

Jor. My master has forbid it: he yet doubts,
That you are married.

Lord B. Ask his vicar-general,
His Fly, here.

Fly. I must make that good; they are married.

Host. But I must make it bad, my hot young lord.—
Give him his doublet again, the air is piercing;
You may take cold, my lord. See whom you have married,
Your host's son, and a boy!   [*Pulls off Frank's head-dress.*

Fly. You are abused.

Lady F. Much joy, my lord!

Pru. If this be your Lætitia,

She'll prove a counterfeit mirth, and a clipp'd lady.

Ser. A boy, a boy, my lord has married a boy!

Lord L. Raise all the house in shout and laughter, a boy!

Host. Stay, what is here! peace, rascals, stop your throats.—

Enter Nurse, *hastily.*

Nurse. That maggot, worm, that insect! O my child,
My daughter! where's that Fly? I'll fly in his face,
The vermin, let me come to him.

Fly. Why, nurse Sheelee?

Nurse. Hang thee, thou parasite, thou son of crumbs
And orts, thou hast undone me, and my child,
My daughter, my dear daughter!

Host. What means this?

Nurse. O, sir, my daughter, my dear child is ruin'd,
By this your Fly, here, married in a stable,
And sold unto a husband.

Host. Stint thy cry,
Harlot, if that be all; didst thou not sell him
To me for a boy, and brought'st him in boy's rags
Here to my door, to beg an alms of me?

Nurse. I did, good master, and I crave your pardon:
But 'tis my daughter, and a girl.

Host. Why saidst thou
It was a boy, and sold'st him then to me
With such entreaty, for ten shillings, carlin?

Nurse. Because you were a charitable man,
I heard, good master, and would breed him well;
I would have given him you for nothing gladly.
Forgive the lie of my mouth, it was to save
The fruit of my womb. A parent's needs are urgent,
And few do know that tyrant o'er good natures:
But you relieved her, and me too, the mother,
And took me into your house to be the nurse,
For which heaven heap all blessings on your head,
Whilst there can one be added.

Host. Sure thou speak'st
Quite like another creature than thou hast lived
Here, in the house, a Sheelee-nien Thomas,
An Irish beggar.

Nurse. So I am, God help me.

Host. What art thou? tell: the match is a good match,
For aught I see; ring the bells once again.　　　　*[Music.*

Lord B. Stint, I say, fidlers.

Lady F. No going off, my lord.

Lord B. Nor coming on, sweet lady, things thus standing.

Fly. But what's the heinousness of my offence,
Or the degrees of wrong you suffer'd by it?
In having your daughter match'd thus happily,

Into a noble house, a brave young blood,
And a prime peer of the realm?
   Lord B. Was that your plot, Fly?
Give me a cloke, take her again among you.
I'll none of your Light Heart fosterlings, no inmates,
Supposititious fruits of an host's brain,
And his Fly's hatching, to be put upon me.
There is a royal court of the Star-chamber,
Will scatter all these mists, disperse these vapours,
And clear the truth: Let beggars match with beggars—
That shall decide it; I will try it there.
   Nurse. Nay then, my lord, it's not enough, I see,
You are licentious, but you will be wicked.
You are not alone content to take my daughter,
Against the law; but having taken her,
You would repudiate and cast her off,
Now at your pleasure, like a beast of power,
Without all cause, or colour of a cause,
That, or a noble, or an honest man,
Should dare to except against, her poverty;
Is poverty a vice?
   Lord B. The age counts it so.
   Nurse. God help your lordship, and your peers that think so,
If any be; if not, God bless them all,
And help the number of the virtuous,
If poverty be a crime! You may object
Our beggary to us, as an accident,
But never deeper, no inherent baseness.
And I must tell you now, young lord of dirt,
As an incensed mother, she hath more,
And better blood, running in those small veins,
Than all the race of Beauforts have in mass,
Though they distil their drops from the left rib
Of John o' Gaunt.
   Host. Old mother of records,
Thou know'st her pedigree then: whose daughter is she?
   Nurse. The daughter and co-heir to the lord Frampul,
This lady's sister.
   Lady F. Mine! what is her name?
   Nurse. Lætitia.
   Lady F. That was lost!
   Nurse. The true Lætitia.
   Lady F. Sister, O gladness! Then you are our mother?
   Nurse. I am, dear daughter.
   Lady F. On my knees I bless
The light I see you by.
   Nurse. And to the author
Of that blest light, I ope my other eye,
Which hath almost, now, seven years been shut,

Dark as my vow was, never to see light,
Till such a light restored it, as my children,
Or your dear father, who, I hear, is not.

   Lord B. Give me my wife, I own her now, and will have her.

   Host. But you must ask my leave first, my young lord.
Leave is but light.—Ferret, go bolt your master,
Here's gear will startle him.   [*Exit Ferret.*]—I cannot keep
The passion in me, I am e'en turn'd child,
And I must weep.—Fly, take away mine host,
                              [*Pulls off his disguise.*
My beard and cap here from me, and fetch my lord.—   [*Exit Fly.*
I am her father, sir, and you shall now
Ask my consent, before you have her.—Wife!
My dear and loving wife! my honour'd wife!
Who here hath gain'd but I? I am lord Frampul,
The cause of all this trouble; I am he
Have measured all the shires of England over,
Wales, and her mountains, seen those wilder nations
Of people in the Peak, and Lancashire;
Their pipers, fidlers, rushers, puppet-masters,
Jugglers, and gipsies, all the sorts of canters,
And colonies of beggars, tumblers, ape-carriers;
For to these savages I was addicted,
To search their natures, and make odd discoveries:
And here my wife, like a she-Mandevile,
Ventured in disquisition after me.

Re-enter FLY, with Lord FRAMPUL's robes.

   Nurse. I may look up, admire, I cannot speak
Yet to my lord.

   Host. Take heart, and breathe, recover,
Thou hast recover'd me, who here had coffin'd
Myself alive, in a poor hostelry,
In penance of my wrongs done unto thee,
Whom I long since gave lost.

   Nurse. So did I you,
Till stealing mine own daughter from her sister,
I lighted on this error hath cured all.

   Lord B. And in that cure, include my trespass, mother,
And father, for my wife—

   Host. No, the *Star-chamber.*

   Lord B. Away with that, you sour the sweetest lettice
Was ever tasted.

   Host. Give you joy, my son;
Cast her not off again.—

Enter LOVEL.

        O call me father,
Lovel, and this your mother, if you like.

conclusion too coincidental.
— but a period piece.

But take your mistress, first, my child; I have power
To give her now, with her consent; her sister
Is given already to your brother Beaufort.

Lov. Is this a dream now, after my first sleep,
Or are these phant'sies made in the Light Heart,
And sold in the New Inn?

Host. Best go to bed,
And dream it over all.   Let's all go sleep,
Each with his turtle.   Fly, provide us lodgings,
Get beds prepared; you are master now of the inn,
The lord of the Light Heart, I give it you.
Fly was my fellow-gipsy.   All my family,
Indeed, were gipsies, tapsters, ostlers, chamberlains,
Reduced vessels of civility.—
But here stands Prue, neglected, best deserving
Of all that are in the house, or in my Heart,
Whom though I cannot help to a fit husband,
I'll help to that will bring one, a just portion:
I have two thousand pound in bank for Prue,
Call for it when she will.

Lord B. And I as much.

Host. There's somewhat yet, four thousand pound! that's better
Than sounds the proverb, *four bare legs in a bed.*

Lov. Me and her mistress, she hath power to coin
Up into what she will.

Lady F. Indefinite Prue!

Lord L. But I must do the crowning act of bounty.

Host. What's that, my lord?

Lord L. Give her myself, which here
By all the holy vows of love I do.
Spare all your promised portions; she's a dowry
So all-sufficient in her virtue and manners,
That fortune cannot add to her.

Pru. My lord,
Your praises are instructions to mine ears,
Whence you have made your wife to live your servant.

Host. Lights! get us several lights!

Lov. Stay, let my mistress
But hear my vision sung, my dream of beauty,
Which I have brought, prepared, to bid us joy,
And light us all to bed, 'twill be instead
Of airing of the sheets with a sweet odour.

Host. 'Twill be an incense to our sacrifice
Of love to-night, where I will woo afresh,
And like Mæcenas, having but one wife,
I'll marry her every hour of life hereafter.   [*Exeunt with a song.*

EPILOGUE.

Plays in themselves have neither hopes nor fears;
Their fate is only in their hearers' ears:
If you expect more than you had to-night,
The maker is sick, and sad.   But do him right:
He meant to please you: for he sent things fit,
In all the numbers both of sense and wit;
If they have not miscarried ! if they have,
All that his faint and faltering tongue doth crave,
Is, that you not impute it to his brain,
That's yet unhurt, although, set round with pain,
It cannot long hold out.   All strength must yield;
Yet judgment would the last be in the field,
With a true poet.   He could have haled in
The drunkards, and the noises of the Inn,
In his last act; if he had thought it fit
To vent you vapours in the place of wit:
But better 'twas that they should sleep, or spue,
Than in the scene to offend or him or you.
This he did think; and this do you forgive:
Whene'er the carcass dies, this art will live.
And had he lived the care of king and queen,
His art in something more yet had been seen;
But mayors and shrieves may yearly fill the stage:
A king's, or poet's birth doth ask an age.

ANOTHER EPILOGUE THERE WAS, MADE FOR THE PLAY, IN THE
POET'S DEFENCE, BUT THE PLAY LIVED NOT, IN OPINION,
TO HAVE IT SPOKEN.

A jovial host, and lord of the New Inn,
'Clept the Light Heart, with all that past therein,
Hath been the subject of our play to-night,
To give the king, and queen, and court delight.
But then we mean the court above the stairs,
And past the guard; men that have more of ears,
Than eyes to judge us: such as will not hiss,
Because the chambermaid was named Cis.
We think it would have served our scene as true,
If, as it is, at first we had call'd her Prue,
For any mystery we there have found,
Or magic in the letters, or the sound.
She only meant was for a girl of wit,
To whom her lady did a province fit:
Which she would have discharg'd, and done as well,
Had she been christen'd Joyce, Grace, Doll, or Nell.

ODE

(TO HIMSELF).

COME leave the loathed stage,
    And the more loathsome age;
Where pride and impudence, in faction knit,
      Usurp the chair of wit!
Indicting and arraigning every day,
      Something they call a play.
    Let their fastidious, vain
    Commission of the brain
Run on and rage, sweat, censure and condemn;
They were not made for thee, less thou for them

    Say that thou pour'st them wheat,
    And they will acorns eat;
'Twere simple fury still thyself to waste
      On such as have no taste!
To offer them a surfeit of pure bread,
      Whose appetites are dead!
    No, give them grains their fill,
    Husks, draff to drink and swill:
If they love lees, and leave the lusty wine,
Envy them not, their palate's with the swine.

    No doubt some mouldy tale,
    Like Pericles, and stale
As the shrieve's crusts, and nasty as his fish—
      Scraps, out of every dish
Thrown forth, and raked into the common tub,
      May keep up the Play-club:
    There, sweepings do as well
    As the best-order'd meal;
For who the relish of these guests will fit,
Needs set them but the alms-basket of wit.

    And much good do't you then:
    Brave plush and velvet-men,
Can feed on orts; and, safe in your stage-clothes,
      Dare quit, upon your oaths,
The stagers and the stage-wrights too, your peers,
      Of larding your large ears
    With their foul comic socks,
    Wrought upon twenty blocks;
Which if they are torn, and turn'd, and patch'd enough,
The gamesters share your gilt, and you their stuff.—

Leave things so prostitute,
　　And take the Alcaic lute;
Or thine own Horace, or Anacreon's lyre;
　　　Warm thee by Pindar's fire:
And though thy nerves be shrunk, and blood be cold
　　　Ere years have made thee old,
　　Strike that disdainful heat
　　Throughout, to their defeat,
As curious fools, and envious of thy strain,
May, blushing, swear no palsy's in thy brain.

　　But when they hear thee sing
　　The glories of thy king,
His zeal to God, and his just awe o'er men:
　　　They may, blood-shaken then,
Feel such a flesh-quake to possess their powers
　　　As they shall cry " Like ours,
　　In sound of peace or wars,
　　No harp e'er hit the stars,
In tuning forth the acts of his sweet reign;
And raising Charles his chariot 'bove his Wain."

AN ANSWER TO THE ODE,

" *Come leave the loathed Stage,*" *etc.*

(BY OWEN FELTHAM.)

Come leave this saucy way
　　Of baiting those that pay
Dear for the sight of your declining wit:
　　　'Tis known it is not fit,
That a sale poet, just contempt once thrown,
　　　Should cry up thus his own.
　　I wonder by what dower,
　　Or patent, you had power
From all to rape a judgment.　Let 't suffice,
Had you been modest, you'd been granted wise.

　　'Tis known you can do well,
　　And that you do excell,
As a Translator:　But when things require
　　　A genius, and fire,
Not kindled heretofore by others' pains;
　　　As oft you've wanted brains
　　And art to strike the white,
　　As you have levell'd right:
Yet if men vouch not things apocryphal,
You bellow, rave, and spatter round your gall.

Jug, Pierce, Peck, Fly, and all
    Your jests so nominal,
Are things so far beneath an able brain,
    As they do throw a stain
Through all th' unlikely plot, and do displease
    As deep as Pericles,
    Where, yet, there is not laid
    Before a chambermaid
Discourse so weigh'd as might have serv'd of old
For schools, when they of love and valour told.

    Why rage then! when the show
    Should judgment be and know-
ledge, there are in plush who scorn to drudge
    For stages, yet can judge
Not only poets' looser lines, but wits,
    And all their perquisits.
    A gift as rich, as high
    Is noble poesie:
Yet though in sport it be for kings a play,
'Tis next mechanics, when it works for pay.

    Alcæus' lute had none,
    Nor loose Anacreon
Ere taught so bold assuming of the bays,
    When they deserv'd no praise.
To rail men into approbation,
    Is new to yours alone;
    And prospers not: for know,
    Fame is as coy, as you
Can be disdainful; and who dares to prove
A rape on her, shall gather scorn, not love.

    Leave then this humour vain,
    And this more humorous strain,
Where self-conceit, and choler of the blood
    Eclipse what else is good:
Then if you please those raptures high to touch,
    Whereof you boast so much;
    And but forbear your crown,
    Till the world puts it on:
No doubt from all you may amazement draw,
Since braver theme no Phœbus ever saw.

AN ANSWER TO BEN JONSON'S ODE,

TO PERSUADE HIM NOT TO LEAVE THE STAGE.

(BY T. RANDOLPH.)

BEN, do not leave the stage,
   'Cause 'tis a loathsome age:
For pride and impudence will grow too bold,
     When they shall hear it told
They frighted thee; stand high as is thy cause,
     Their hiss is thy applause:
     More just were thy disdain,
     Had they approved thy vein:
So thou for them, and they for thee were born,
They to incense, and thou as much to scorn.

Will't thou engross thy store
   Of wheat, and pour no more,
Because their bacon-brains have such a taste,
     As more delight in mast:
No! set them forth a board of dainties, full
     As thy best Muse can cull;
     Whilst they the while do pine
     And thirst, midst all their wine.
What greater plague can hell itself devise,
Than to be willing thus to tantalise?

Thou canst not find them stuff,
   That will be bad enough
To please their palates: let 'em them refuse,
     For some Pye-Corner Muse;
She is too fair an hostess, 'twere a sin
     For them to like thine *Inn:*
     'Twas made to entertain
     Guests of a nobler strain;
Yet if they will have any of thy store,
Give them some scraps, and send them from thy door.

And let those things in plush,
   Till they be taught to blush,
Like what they will, and more contented be
     With what Brome swept from thee.
I know thy worth, and that thy lofty strains
     Write not to clothes, but brains;
     But thy great spleen doth rise,
     'Cause moles will have no eyes:
This only in my Ben I faulty find,
He's angry, they'll not see him that are blind.

Why should the scene be mute,
  'Cause thou canst touch thy lute,
And string thy Horace? let each Muse of nine
  Claim thee, and say, Thou'rt mine.
'Twere fond to let all other flames expire,
    To sit by Pindar's fire:
    For by so strange neglect,
    I should myself suspect,
The palsy were as well thy brain's disease,
If they could shake thy Muse which way they please.

    And though thou well canst sing
    The glories of thy King;
And on the wings of verse his chariot bear,
    To heaven, and fix it there;
Yet let thy Muse as well some raptures raise,
    To please him, as to praise.
    I would not have thee choose
    Only a treble Muse;
But have this envious, ignorant age to know,
Thou that canst sing so high, canst reach as low.

TO BEN JONSON,

UPON OCCASION OF HIS ODE OF DEFIANCE ANNEXED TO HIS
PLAY OF THE NEW INN.

(BY T. CAREW.)

'TIS true, dear Ben, thy just chastising hand
Hath fix'd upon the sotted age a brand
To their swoln pride, and empty scribbling due;
It can nor judge, nor write: and yet 'tis true,
Thy comic Muse from the exalted line
Touch'd by the Alchemist, doth since decline
From that her zenith, and foretells a red
And blushing evening, when she goes to bed;
Yet such, as shall outshine the glimmering light,
With which all stars shall gild the following night.
Nor think it much (since all thy eaglets may
Endure the sunny trial) if we say
This hath the stronger wing, or that doth shine,
Trick'd up in fairer plumes, since all are thine:
Who hath his flock of cackling geese compared
With thy tuned quire of swans? or else who dared
To call thy births deform'd? but if thou bind,
By city custom, or by gavel-kind,
In equal shares thy love on all thy race,
We may distinguish of their sex, and place;

Though one hand form them, and though one brain strike
Souls into all, they are not all alike.
Why should the follies then of this dull age
Draw from thy pen such an immodest rage,
As seems to blast thy else-immortal bays,
When thine own tongue proclaims thy itch of praise?
Such thirst will argue drought. No, let be hurl'd
Upon thy works, by the detracting world,
What malice can suggest: let the rout say,
" The running sands, that, ere thou make a play,
Count the slow minutes, might a Godwin frame,
To swallow, when thou hast done, thy shipwreck'd name."
Let them the dear expense of oil upbraid,
Suck'd by thy watchful lamp, " that hath betray'd
To theft the blood of martyr'd authors, spilt
Into thy ink, whilst thou grow'st pale with guilt."
Repine not at the taper's thrifty waste,
That sleeks thy terser poems; nor is haste
Praise, but excuse; and if thou overcome
A knotty writer, bring the booty home:
Nor think it theft if the rich spoils, so torn
From conquer'd authors, be as trophies worn.
Let others glut on the extorted praise
Of vulgar breath, trust thou to after days:
Thy labour'd works shall live, when Time devours
The abortive offspring of their hasty hours.
Thou art not of their rank; the quarrel lies
Within thine own verge: then let this suffice,
The wiser world doth greater thee confess
Than all men else, than thyself only less.

ODE TO BEN JONSON,

UPON HIS ODE TO HIMSELF.

(BY J. CLEVELAND.)

PROCEED in thy brave rage,
    Which hath rais'd up our stage
Unto that height, as Rome in all her state,
    Or Greece might emulate;
Whose greatest senators did silent sit,
      Hear and applaud the wit,
    Which those more temperate times,
    Used when it tax'd their crimes:
Socrates stood, and heard with true delight,
All that the sharp Athenian Muse could write

The New Inn

Against his supposed fault;
And did digest the salt
That from that full vein did so freely flow:
And though that we do know
The Graces jointly strove to make that breast
A temple for their rest,
We must not make thee less
Than Aristophanes:
He got the start of thee in time and place,
But thou hast gain'd the goal in art and grace.

But if thou make thy feasts
For the high-relish'd guests,
And that a cloud of shadows shall break in,
It were almost a sin
To think that thou shouldst equally delight
Each several appetite;
Though Art and Nature strive
Thy banquets to contrive:
Thou art our whole Menander, and dost look
Like the old Greek; think, then, but on his Cook.

If thou thy full cups bring
Out of the Muses' spring,
And there are some foul mouths had rather drink
Out of the common sink;
There let them seek to quench th' hydropic thirst,
Till the swoln humour burst.
Let him who daily steals
From thy most precious meals,
Since thy strange plenty finds no loss by it,
Feed himself with the fragments of thy wit.

And let those silken men
That know not how, or when
To spend their money, or their time, maintain
With their consumed no-brain,
Their barbarous feeding on such gross base stuff
As only serves to puff
Up the weak empty mind,
Like bubbles, full with wind,
And strive t' engage the scene with their damn'd oaths,
As they do with the privilege of their clothes.

Whilst thou tak'st that high spirit,
Well purchas'd by thy merit:
Great Prince of Poets, though thy head be grey,
Crown it with Delphic bay,

And from the chief [pin] in Apollo's quire,
 Take down thy best-tuned lyre,
 Whose sound shall pierce so far
 It shall strike out the star,
Which fabulous Greece durst fix in heaven, whilst thine
With all due glory, here on earth shall shine.

 Sing, English Horace, sing
 The wonders of thy King;
Whilst his triumphant chariot runs his whole
 Bright course about each pole:
Sing down the Roman harper; he shall rain
 His bounties on thy vein;
 And with his golden rays,
 So gild thy glorious bays,
That Fame shall bear on her unwearied wing,
What the best Poet sung of the best King.

THE MAGNETIC LADY; OR,
HUMOURS RECONCILED

DRAMATIS PERSONÆ

COMPASS, *a Scholar Mathematic.*
CAPTAIN IRONSIDE, *his Brother, a Soldier.*
PARSON PALATE, *Prelate of the Parish.*
RUT, *Physician to* Lady LOADSTONE.
TIM. ITEM, *his Apothecary.*
SIR DIAPHANOUS SILKWORM, *a Courtier.*
PRACTICE, *a Lawyer.*
SIR MOTH INTEREST, *an Usurer, or Money-Bawd.*
BIAS, *a Vi-Politic, or Sub-Secretary.*
NEEDLE, *the* Lady's *Steward and Tailor.*

LADY LOADSTONE, *the* MAGNETIC LADY.
POLISH, *her Gossip and She-Parasite.*
PLACENTIA, *her Niece.*
PLEASANCE, *her Waiting-Woman.*
KEEP, *the Niece's Nurse.*
CHAIR, *the Midwife.*

Servant *to* Sir MOTH, Serjeants, etc.

The Chorus (PROBEE, DAMPLAY, *and* Boy *of the house*) *by way of* Induction.

SCENE,—LONDON

INDUCTION, OR CHORUS.

THE STAGE.

Enter Master PROBEE and Master DAMPLAY, met by a Boy of the house.

Boy. *What do you lack, gentlemen, what is't you lack? any fine fancies, figures, humours, characters, ideas, definitions of lords and ladies? Waiting-women, parasites, knights, captains, courtiers, lawyers? what do you lack?*

Pro. *A pretty prompt boy for the poetic shop!*

Dam. *And a bold! Where's one of your masters, sirrah, the poet?*

Boy. *Which of them, sir? we have divers that drive that trade, now; poets, poetaccios, poetasters, poetitos—*

Dam. *And all haberdashers of small wit, I presume; we would speak with the poet of the day, boy.*

Boy. *Sir, he is not here. But I have the dominion of the shop, for this time, under him, and can shew you all the variety the stage will afford for the present.*

Pro. *Therein you will express your own good parts, boy.*

Dam. *And tie us two to you for the gentle office.*

Pro. *We are a pair of public persons (this gentleman and myself) that are sent thus coupled unto you, upon state-business.*

Boy. It concerns but the state of the stage, I hope.

Dam. O, you shall know that by degrees, boy. No man leaps into a business of state, without fording first the state of the business.

Pro. We are sent unto you, indeed, from the people.

Boy. The people ! which side of the people ?

Dam. The venison side, if you know it, boy.

Boy. That's the left side. I had rather they had been the right.

Pro. So they are. Not the fæces, or grounds of your people, that sit in the oblique caves and wedges of your house, your sinful sixpenny mechanics—

Dam. But the better and braver sort of your people, plush and velvet outsides ! that stick your house round like so many eminences—

Boy. Of clothes, not understandings ! they are at pawn. Well, I take these as a part of your people though; what bring you to me from these people ?

Dam. You have heard, boy, the ancient poets had it in their purpose, still to please this people.

Pro. Ay, their chief aim was—

Dam. Populo ut placerent: if he understands so much.—

Boy. Quas fecissent fabulas.—I understand that since I learn'd Terence, in the third form at Westminster: go on, sir.

Pro. Now, these people have employed us to you, in all their names, to entreat an excellent play from you.

Dam. For they have had very mean ones from this shop of late, the stage as you call it.

Boy. Troth, gentlemen, I have no wares which I dare thrust upon the people with praise. But this, such as it is, I will venture with your people, your gay gallant people: so as you, again, will undertake for them, that they shall know a good play when they hear it; and will have the conscience and ingenuity beside to confess it.

Pro. We'll pass our words for that; you shall have a brace of us to engage ourselves.

Boy. You'll tender your names, gentlemen, to our book then ?

Dam. Yes; here's master Probee, a man of most powerful speech, and parts to persuade.

Pro. And master Damplay will make good all he undertakes.

Boy. Good master Probee, and master Damplay ! I like your securities: whence do you write yourselves ?

Pro. Of London, gentlemen; but knights' brothers, and knights' friends, I assure you.

Dam. And knights' fellows too: every poet writes squire now.

Boy. You are good names ! very good men, both of you; I accept you.

Dam. And what is the title of your play here, The Magnetic Lady ?

Boy. Yes, sir, an attractive title the author has given it.

Pro. A magnete, I warrant you.

Dam. O no, from magnus, magna, magnum.

Boy. This gentleman hath found the true magnitude—

Dam. Of his portal or entry to the work, according to Vitruvius.

Boy. Sir, all our work is done without a portal, or Vitruvius. In *foro, as a true comedy should be. And what is conceal'd within, is brought out, and made present by report.*

Dam. We *see not that always observed by your authors of these times; or scarce any other.*

Boy. Where *it is not at all known, how should it be observed ? The most of those your people call authors, never dreamt of any decorum, or what was proper in the scene; but grope at it in the dark, and feel or fumble for it: I speak it, both with their leave, and the leave of your people.*

Dam. But, why Humours Reconciled, *I would fain know ?*

Boy. I can satisfy you there too, if you will. But perhaps you desire not to be satisfied.

Dam. No ! why should you conceive so, boy ?

Boy. My conceit is not ripe yet ; I'll tell you that anon. The author beginning his studies of this kind, with Every Man in his Humour; *and after* Every Man *out of his Humour; and since, continuing in all his plays, especially those of the comic thread, whereof the* New Inn *was the last, some recent humours still, or manners of men, that went along with the times; finding himself now near the close, or shutting up of his circle, hath fancied to himself, in idea, this Magnetic Mistress: a lady, a brave bountiful housekeeper, and a virtuous widow; who having a young niece, ripe for a man, and marriageable, he makes that his centre attractive, to draw thither a diversity of guests, all persons of different humours to make up his perimeter. And this he hath called* Humours Reconciled.

Pro. A bold undertaking, and far greater than the reconciliation of both churches; the quarrel between humours having been much the ancienter; and, in my poor opinion, the root of all schism and faction both in church and commonwealth.

Boy. Such is the opinion of many wise men, that meet at this shop still; but how he will speed in it, we cannot tell, and he himself, it seems, less cares: for he will not be entreated by us, to give it a prologue. He has lost too much that way already, he says. He will not woo the gentle ignorance so much. But careless of all vulgar censure, as not depending on common approbation, he is confident it shall super-please judicious spectators, and to them he leaves it to work with the rest, by example or otherwise.

Dam. He may be deceived in that, boy: few follow examples now, especially if they be good.

Boy. The play is ready to begin, gentlemen; I tell you, lest you might defraud the expectation of the people, for whom you are delegates: please you take a couple of seats, and plant yourselves, here, as near my standing as you can: fly every thing you see to the mark, and censure it freely; so you interrupt not the series or thread of the argument, to break or pucker it, with unnecessary questions. For, I must tell you, (not out of mine own dictamen, but the author's,) a good play is like a skein of silk; which if you take by the right end, you may wind off at pleasure, on the bottom or card of your discourse, in a tale or so; how you will: but if you light on the wrong end, you will pull all into a knot or elf-lock; which nothing but the sheers, or a candle, will undo or separate.

Dam. *Stay, who be these, I pray you?*

Boy. *Because it is your first question, and these be the prime persons, it would in civility require an answer: but I have heard the poet affirm, that to be the most unlucky scene in a play, which needs an interpreter; especially, when the auditory are awake: and such are you he presumes; ergo—*

ACT I

SCENE I.—*The Street before* Lady LOADSTONE'S *House.*

Enter COMPASS, *and* Captain IRONSIDE, *meeting.*

Com. Welcome, good captain Ironside, and brother;
You shall along with me. I am lodged hard by,
Here, at a noble lady's house in the street,
The lady Loadstone's, one will bid us welcome;
Where there are gentlewomen and male guests,
Of several humours, carriage, constitution,
Profession too; but so diametral
One to another, and so much opposed,
As if I can but hold them altogether,
And draw them to a sufferance of themselves,
But till the dissolution of the dinner,
I shall have just occasion to believe
My wit is magisterial; and ourselves
Take infinite delight in the success.

Iron. Troth, brother Compass, you shall pardon me;
I love not so to multiply acquaintance
At a meal's cost; 'twill take off o' my freedom
So much; or bind me to the least observance.

Com. Why, Ironside, you know I am a scholar,
And part a soldier; I have been employ'd
By some the greatest statesmen of the kingdom,
These many years; and in my time convers'd
With sundry humours, suiting so myself
To company, as honest men and knaves,
Good-fellows, hypocrites, all sorts of people,
Though never so divided in themselves,
Have studied to agree still in the usage
And handling of me, which hath been fair too.

Iron. Sir, I confess you to be one well read
In men and manners; and that usually,
The most ungovern'd persons, you being present,
Rather subject themselves unto your censure,
Than give you least occasion of distaste,
By making you the subject of their mirth.
But, to deal plainly with you, as a brother,

The Magnetic Lady

Whenever I distrust in my own valour,
I'll never bear me on another's wit,
Or offer to bring off, or save myself,
On the opinion of your judgment, gravity,
Discretion, or what else.   But, being away,
You are sure to have less wit-work, gentle brother,
My humour being as stubborn as the rest,
And as unmanageable.
   Com. You do mistake
My caract of your friendship all this while,
Or at what rate I reckon your assistance;
Knowing by long experience, to such animals,
Half-hearted creatures, as these are, your fox there,
Unkennell'd with a choleric, ghastly aspect,
On two or three comminatory terms,
Would run their fears to any hole of shelter,
Worth a day's laughter!   I am for the sport;
For nothing else.
   Iron. But, brother, I have seen
A coward meeting with a man as valiant
As our St. George, not knowing him to be such,
Or having least opinion that he was so,
Set to him roundly, ay, and swinge him soundly;
And in the virtue of that error, having
Once overcome, resolv'd for ever after
To err; and think no person, nor no creature
More valiant than himself.
   Com. I think that too:
But, brother, could I over-entreat you,
I have some little plot upon the rest,
If you would be contented to endure
A sliding reprehension at my hands,
To hear yourself or your profession glanced at
In a few slighting terms; it would beget
Me such a main authority, on the bye,
And do yourself no disrepute at all.
   Iron. Compass, I know that universal causes
In nature produce nothing, but as meeting
Particular causes to determine those,
And specify their acts.   This is a piece
Of Oxford science, stays with me e'er since
I left that place; and I have often found
The truth thereof, in my [own] private passions:
For I do never feel myself perturb'd
With any general words 'gainst my profession,
Unless by some smart stroke upon myself
They do awake, and stir me: else, to wise
And well-experienced men, words do not signify;
They have no power, save with dull grammarians.

Whose souls are nought but a syntaxis of them.
   Com. Here comes our parson, parson Palate here,
A venerable youth, (I must salute him,)
And a great clerk! he's going to the ladies;
And though you see him thus, without his cope,
I do assure you he's our parish pope.—

Enter PALATE.

God save my reverend clergy, parson Palate!
   Pal. The witty master Compass! how is't with you?
   Com. My lady stays for you, and for your counsel,
Touching her niece, mistress Placentia Steel,
Who strikes the fire of full fourteen to-day,
Ripe for a husband!
   Pal. Ay, she chimes, she chimes.
Saw you the doctor Rut, the house physician?
He's sent for too.
   Com. To council! time you were there:
Make haste, and give it a round quick dispatch,
That we may go to dinner betimes, parson;
And drink a health or two more to the business.   [*Exit Palate.*
   Iron. This is a strange put off; *a reverend youth!*
You use him most surreverently methinks.
What call you him? Palate Please, or Parson Palate?
   Com. All's one, but shorter. I can give you his character.

> *He is the prelate of the parish here,*
> *And governs all the dames, appoints the cheer,*
> *Writes down the bills of fare, pricks all the guests,*
> *Makes all the matches and the marriage feasts*
> *Within the ward; draws all the parish wills,*
> *Designs the legacies, and strokes the gills*
> *Of the chief mourners; and, whoever lacks,*
> *Of all the kindred, he hath first his blacks.*
> *Thus holds his weddings up, and burials,*
> *As his main tithing; with the gossips' stalls,*
> *Their pews; he's top still, at the public mess:*
> *Comforts the widow, and the fatherless,*
> *In funeral sack; sits 'bove the alderman;*
> *For of the wardmote quest, he better can*
> *The mystery, than the Levitic law:*
> *That piece of clerkship doth his vestry awe.*
> *He is as he conceives himself, a fine*
> *Well-furnish'd, and apparelled divine.*

   Iron. Who made this epigram, you?
   Com. No, a great clerk
As any is of his bulk, Ben Jonson, made it.
   Iron. But what's the other character, doctor Rut?

Com. The same man made them both; but his is shorter,
And not in rhyme, but blanks: I'll tell you that, too.

> *Rut is a young physician to the family:*
> *That, letting God alone, ascribes to nature*
> *More than her share; licentious in discourse,*
> *And in his life a profest voluptuary;*
> *The slave of money, a buffoon in manners;*
> *Obscene in language, which he vents for wit;*
> *Is saucy in his logics, and disputing,*
> *Is anything but civil, or a man—*

Re-enter PALATE *with* RUT *and* Lady LOADSTONE, *in discourse.*

See here they are! and walking with my lady,
In consultation, afore the door;
We will slip in, as if we saw them not.

                 [Iron. and Com. go into the house.

Lady L. Ay, 'tis his fault she's not bestow'd,
My brother Interest's.

Pal. Who, old sir Moth?

Lady L. He keeps off all her suitors, keeps the portion
Still in his hands; and will not part withal,
On any terms.

Pal. Hinc illæ lachrymæ:
Thence flows the cause of the main grievance.

Rut. That!—

It is a main one; how much is the portion?

Lady L. No petty sum.

Pal. But sixteen thousand pound.

Rut. He should be forced, madam, to lay it down:
When is it payable?

Lady L. When she is married.

Pal. Marry her, marry her, madam.

Rut. Get her married.

Lose not a day, an hour—

Pal. Not a minute.

Pursue your project real, master Compass
Advised you to: he is the perfect instrument
Your ladyship should sail by.

Rut. Master Compass

Is a fine witty man: I saw him go in, now.

Lady L. Is he gone in?

Pal. Yes, and a feather with him;
He seems a soldier.

Rut. Some new suitor, madam.

Lady L. I am beholding to him; he brings ever
Variety of good persons to my table,
And I must thank him, though my brother Interest
Dislike of it a little.

Pal. He likes nothing
That runs your way.
  Rut. Troth, and the other cares not.
He'll go his own way, if he think it right.
  Lady L. He's a true friend: and there is master Practice,
The fine young man of law, comes to the house:
My brother brooks him not, because he thinks
He is by me assigned for my niece:
He will not hear of it.
  Rut. Not of that ear;
But yet your ladyship doth wisely in it.
  Pal. 'Twill make him to lay down the portion sooner,
If he but dream you'll match her with a lawyer.
  Lady L. So master Compass says. It is between
The lawyer, and the courtier, which shall have her.
  Pal. Who, sir Diaphanous Silkworm?
  Rut. A fine gentleman,
Old master Silkworm's heir.
  Pal. And a neat courtier,
Of a most elegant thread.
  Lady L. And so my gossip
Polish assures me. Here she comes.—

     Enter Mistress POLISH.

          Good Polish,
Welcome in troth! how dost thou, gentle Polish?
  Rut. Who's this?   [*Aside to Palate.*
  Pal. Dame Polish, her she-parasite,
Her talking, soothing, sometime governing gossip.
  Pol. Your ladyship is still the lady Loadstone,
That draws, and draws unto you, guests of all sorts;
The courtiers, and the soldiers, and the scholars,
The travellers, physicians, and divines,
As doctor Ridley wrote, and doctor Barlow:
They both have writ of you and master Compass.
  Lady L. We mean they shall write more ere it be long.
  Pol. Alas, they are both dead, an't please you! but
Your ladyship means well, and shall mean well,
So long as I live. How does your fine niece,
My charge, mistress Placentia Steel?
  Lady L. She is not well.
  Pol. Not well?
  Lady L. Her doctor says so.
  Rut. Not very well; she cannot shoot at butts,
Or manage a great horse; but she can cranch
A sack of small-coal, eat you lime, and hair,
Soap-ashes, loam, and has a dainty spice
Of the green sickness—
  Pol. 'Od shield!

Rut. Or the dropsy:
A toy, a thing of nothing. But my lady, here,
Her noble aunt—
    Pol. She is a noble aunt;
And a right worshipful lady, and a virtuous;
I know it well!
    Rut. Well, if you know it, peace.
    Pal. Good sister Polish, hear your betters speak.
    Pol. Sir, I will speak, with my good lady's leave,
And speak, and speak again; I did bring up
My lady's niece, mistress Placentia Steel,
With my own daughter, who's Placentia too,
And waits upon my lady, is her woman:—
Her ladyship well knows, mistress Placentia
Steel, as I said, her curious niece, was left
A legacy to me, by father and mother,
With the nurse Keep that tended her: her mother
She died in child-bed of her, and her father
Lived not long after; for he loved her mother!
They were a godly couple; yet both died,
As we must all.—No creature is immortal,
I have heard our pastor say; no, not the faithful!
And they did die, as I said, both in one month—
    Rut. Sure, she is not long-lived if she spend breath thus.
    Pol. And did bequeath her to my care and hand,
To polish and bring up. I moulded her,
And fashion'd her, and form'd her; she had the sweat
Both of my brows and brains, my lady knows it,
Since she could write a quarter old.
    Lady L. I know not
That she could write so early, my good gossip:
But I do know she was so long your care,
Till she was twelve year old; that I call'd for her,
And took her home; for which I thank you, Polish,
And am beholden to you.
    Rut. I sure thought
She had a lease of talking for nine lives—
    Pal. It may be she has.
    Pol. Sir, sixteen thousand pound
Was then her portion, for she was, indeed,
Their only child: and this was to be paid
Upon her marriage, so she married still
With my good lady's liking here, her aunt:
I heard the will read. Master Steel, her father,
The world condemn'd him to be very rich,
And very hard; and he did stand condemn'd
With that vain world, till, as 'twas proved after,
He left almost as much more to good uses
In sir Moth Interest's hands, my lady's brother,

Whose sister he had married: he holds all
In his close gripe.　But master Steel was liberal,
And a fine man;　and she a dainty dame,
And a religious, and a bountiful—

Enter COMPASS, *and* IRONSIDE *from the house.*

You knew her, master Compass—
　Com. Spare the torture,
I do confess without it.
　Pol. And her husband,
What a fine couple they were, and how they lived—
　Com. Yes.
　Pol. And loved together like a pair of turtles—
　Com. Yes.
　Pol. And feasted all the neighbours?
　Com. Take her off,
Somebody that hath mercy—
　Rut. O he knows her,
It seems.
　Com. Or any measure of compassion:
Doctors, if you be Christians, undertake
One for the soul, the other for the body.
　Pol. She would dispute with the doctors of divinity,
At her own table;　and the Spittle preachers:
And find out the Armenians.
　Rut. The Arminians.
　Pol. I say, the Armenians.
　Com. Nay, I say so too.
　Pol. So master Polish call'd them, the Armenians.
　Com. And Medes and Persians, did he not?
　Pol. Yes, he knew them,
And so did mistress Steel; she was his pupil.
The Armenians, he would say, were worse than papists:
And then the Persians were our Puritans,
Had the fine piercing wits.
　Com. And who, the Medes?
　Pol. The middle men, the luke-warm protestants.
　Rut. Out, out!
　Pol. Sir, she would find them by their branching:
Their branching sleeves, branch'd cassocks, and branch'd doctrine,
Beside their texts.
　Rut. Stint, carline; I'll not hear.
Confute her, parson.
　Pol. I respect no parsons,
Chaplains, or doctors, I will speak.
　Lady L. Yes, so it be reason,
Let her.
　Rut. Death, she cannot speak reason.
　Com. Nor sense, if we be master of our senses.

Iron. What mad woman have they got here to bait?

Pol. Sir, I am mad in truth, and to the purpose;
And cannot but be mad, to hear my lady's
Dead sister slighted, witty mistress Steel.

Iron. If she had a wit, death has gone near to spoil it,
Assure yourself.

Pol. She was both witty and zealous,
And lighted all the tinder of the truth
(As one said) of religion, in our parish;
She was too learned to live long with us!
She could the Bible in the holy tongue,
And read it without pricks; had all her Masoreth,
Knew Burton and his Bull, and scribe Prynne gent.
Præsto-be-gone, and all the Pharisees.

Lady L. Dear gossip,
Be you gone, at this time, too, and vouchsafe
To see your charge, my niece.

Pol. I shall obey
If your wise ladyship think fit: I know
To yield to my superiors.   *[Exit.*

Lady L. A good woman!
But when she is impertinent, grows earnest,
A little troublesome, and out of season:
Her love and zeal transport her.

Com. I am glad
That any thing could port her hence: we now
Have hope of dinner, after her long grace.
I have brought your ladyship an hungry guest here,
A soldier, and my brother, captain Ironside;
Who being by custom grown a sanguinary,
The solemn and adopted son of slaughter,
Is more delighted in the chase of an enemy,
An execution of three days and nights,
Than all the hope of numerous succession,
Or happiness of issue could bring to him.

Rut. He is no suitor then!   *[Aside to Pal.*

Pal. So it should seem.

Com. And if he can get pardon at heaven's hand
For all his murthers, is in as good case
As a new christen'd infant: his employments
Continued to him, without interruption,
And not allowing him or time or place
To commit any other sin, but those.—
Please you to make him welcome for a meal, madam?

Lady L. The nobleness of his profession makes
His welcome perfect; though your coarse description
Would seem to sully it.

Iron. Never, where a beam
Of so much favour doth illustrate it,

Right knowing lady.
Pal. She hath cured all well.
Rut. And he hath fitted well the compliment.

Enter Sir DIAPHANOUS SILKWORM *and* PRACTICE.

Com. No, here they come; the prime magnetic guests
Our lady Loadstone so respects: the Arctic,
And the Antarctic! sir Diaphanous Silkworm,
A courtier extraordinary; who by diet
Of meats and drinks, his temperate exercise,
Choice music, frequent baths, his hoary shifts
Of shirts and waistcoats, means to immortalise
Mortality itself, and makes the essence
Of his whole happiness the trim of court.
Sir Dia. I thank you, master Compass, for your short
Encomiastic.
Rut. It is much in little, sir.
Pal. Concise and quick; the true style of an orator.
Com. But master Practice here, my lady's lawyer,
Or man of law, (for that is the true writing,)
A man so dedicate to his profession,
And the preferments go along with it,
As scarce the thundering bruit of an invasion,
Another eighty-eight, threatening his country
With ruin, would no more work upon him,
Than Syracusa's sack on Archimede;
So much he loves that night-cap! the bench-gown,
With the broad gard on the back! these shew a man
Betroth'd unto the study of our laws.
Prac. Which you but think the crafty impositions
Of subtile clerks, feats of fine understanding,
To abuse clots and clowns with, master Compass;
Having no ground in nature to sustain it,
Or light, from those clear causes, to the inquiry
And search of which, your mathematical head
Hath so devow'd itself.
Com. Tut, all men are
Philosophers, to their inches.   There's within
Sir Interest, as able a philosopher,
In buying and selling! has reduced his thrift
To certain principles, and in that method,
As he will tell you instantly, by logarithms,
The utmost profit of a stock employed;
Be the commodity what it will: the place,
Or time, but causing very very little,
Or, I may say, no parallax at all,
In his pecuniary observations!
He has brought your niece's portion with him, madam;
At least, the man that must receive it: here

They come negociating the affair;
You may perceive the contract in their faces,
And read the indenture. If you'll sign them, so!

Enter Sir Moth Interest *and* Bias.

Pal. What is he, master Compass!
Com. A vi-politic,
Or a sub-aiding instrument of state:
A kind of a laborious secretary
To a great man, and likely to come on;
Full of attendance, and of such a stride
In business politic or economic,
As well his lord may stoop to advise with him,
And be prescribed by him in affairs
Of highest consequence, when he is dull'd,
Or wearied with the less.
Sir Dia. 'Tis master Bias,
Lord Whach'um's politic.
Com. You know the man.
Sir Dia. I have seen him wait at court, there, with his maniples
Of papers and petitions.
Prac. He is one
That over-rules though, by his authority
Of living there; and cares for no man else:
Neglects the sacred letter of the law;
And holds it all to be but a dead heap
Of civil institutions: the rest only
Of common men, and their causes, a farrago,
Or a made dish in court; a thing of nothing.
Com. And that's your quarrel at him! a just plea.
Sir Moth. I tell you, sister Loadstone—
Com. Hang your ears
This way, and hear his praises: now Moth opens.   [*Aside.*
Sir Moth. I have brought you here the very man, the jewel
Of all the court, close master Bias, sister!
Apply him to your side: or you may wear him
Here on your breast, or hang him in your ear,
He's a fit pendant for a lady's tip!
A chrysolite, a gem, the very agate
Of state and policy, cut from the quar
Of Machiavel; a true Cornelian
As Tacitus himself, and to be made
The brooch to any true state-cap in Europe!
Lady L. You praise him, brother, as you had hope to sell him.
Com. No, madam, as he had hope to sell your niece
Unto him.
Lady L. 'Ware your true jests, master Compass;
They will not relish.
Sir Moth. I will tell you, sister,

I cannot cry his caract up enough;
He is unvaluable: all the lords
Have him in that esteem for his relations,
Corants, avisos, correspondences
With this ambassador, and that agent! he
Will screw you out a secret from a statist—
   Com. So easy, as some cobler worms a dog.
   Sir Moth. And lock it in the cabinet of his memory—
   Com. Till it turn a politic insect or a fly,
Thus long!
   Sir Moth. You may be merry, master Compass;
But though you have the reversion of an office,
You are not in it, sir.
   Bias. Remember that.
   Com. Why should that fright me, master Bi—, from telling
Whose—ass you are?
   Sir Moth. Sir, he is one can do
His turns there, and deliver too his letters
As punctually, and in as good a fashion,
As e'er a secretary can in court.
   Iron. Why, is it any matter in what fashion
A man deliver his letters, so he not open them?
   Bias. Yes, we have certain precedents in court,
From which we never swerve once in an age:
And (whatsoever he thinks) I know the arts
And sciences do not directlier make
A graduate in our universities,
Than an habitual gravity prefers
A man in court.
   Com. Which, by the truer style,
Some call a formal flat servility.
   Bias. Sir, you may call it what you please; but we
That tread the path of public businesses,
Know what a tacit shrug is, or a shrink;
The wearing the callot, the politic hood,
And twenty other parerga, on the bye,
You seculars understand not: I shall trick him,
If his reversion come in my lord's way.
   Sir Dia. What is that, master Practice? you sure know;
Master Compasses reversion?
   Prac. A fine place,
Surveyor of the projects general;
I would I had it.
   Pal. What is't worth?
   Prac. O sir,
A *nemo scit.*
   Lady L. We'll think on't afore dinner.   *[Exeunt.*

   Boy. Now, gentlemen, what censure you of our protasis, or first act?

Pro. Well, boy, it is a fair presentment of your actors; and a handsome promise of somewhat to come hereafter.

Dam. But there is nothing done in it, or concluded: therefore I say, no act.

Boy. A fine piece of logic! do you look, master Damplay, for conclusions in a protasis? I thought the law of comedy had reserved [them] to the catastrophe; and that the epitasis, as we are taught, and the catastasis, had been intervening parts, to have been expected. But you would have all come together, it seems: the clock should strike five at once, with the acts.

Dam. Why, if it could do so, it were well, boy.

Boy. Yes, if the nature of a clock were to speak, not strike. So, if a child could be born in a play, and grow up to a man, in the first scene, before he went off the stage: and then after to come forth a squire, and be made a knight: and that knight to travel between the acts, and do wonders in the Holy Land or elsewhere; kill Paynims, wild boars, dun cows, and other monsters; beget him a reputation and marry an emperor's daughter for his mistress: convert her father's country; and at last come home lame, and all-to-be laden with miracles.

Dam. These miracles would please, I assure you, and take the people: for there be of the people, that will expect miracles, and more than miracles from this pen.

Boy. Do they think this pen can juggle? I would we had Hokospokos for 'em then, your people; or Travitanto Tudesco.

Dam. Who's that, boy?

Boy. Another juggler, with a long name. Or that your expecters would be gone hence now, at the first act; or expect no more hereafter than they understand.

Dam. Why so, my peremptory Jack?

Boy. My name is John, indeed——Because, who expect what is impossible or beyond nature, defraud themselves.

Pro. Nay, there the boy said well; they do defraud themselves, indeed.

Boy. And therefore, master Damplay, unless, like a solemn justice of wit, you will damn our play unheard or unexamined, I shall entreat your mistress, madam Expectation, if she be among these ladies, to have patience but a pissing while: give our springs leave to open a little, by degrees; a source of ridiculous matter may break forth anon, that shall steep their temples, and bathe their brains in laughter, to the fomenting of stupidity itself, and the awaking any velvet lethargy in the house.

Pro. Why do you maintain your poet's quarrel so with velvet and good clothes, boy? we have seen him in indifferent good clothes ere now.

Boy. And may do in better, if it please the king his master to say Amen to it, and allow it, to whom he acknowledgeth all. But his clothes shall never be the best thing about him, though; he will have somewhat beside, either of human letters, or severe honesty, shall speak him a man, though he went naked.

Pro. He is beholden to you, if you can make this good, boy.

Boy. Himself hath done that already, against envy.

Dam. What is your name, sir, or your country ?

Boy. John Try-gust my name; a Cornish youth, and the poet's servant.

Dam. West country breed I thought, you were so bold.

Boy. Or rather saucy; to find out your palate, master Damplay. 'Faith we do call a spade a spade, in Cornwall. If you dare damn our play in the wrong place, we shall take heart to tell you so !

Pro. Good boy.

ACT II

SCENE I.—*A Room in* Lady LOADSTONE'S *House.*

Enter Nurse KEEP, PLACENTIA, *and* PLEASANCE.

Keep. Sweet mistress, pray you be merry; you are sure
To have a husband now.

Pla. Ay, if the store
Hurt not the choice.

Plea. Store is no sore, young mistress,
My mother is wont to say.

Keep. And she'll say wisely
As any mouth in the parish.   Fix on one,
Fix upon one, good mistress.

Pla. At this call too.
Here's master Practice who is call'd to the bench
Of purpose.

Keep. Yes, and by my lady's means.

Plea. 'Tis thought to be the man.

Keep. A lawyer's wife.

Plea. And a fine lawyer's wife.

Keep. Is a brave calling.

Plea. Sweet mistress Practice!

Keep. Gentle mistress Practice!

Plea. Fair, open mistress Practice!

Keep. Ay, and close,
And cunning mistress Practice!

Pla. I not like that;
The courtier's is the neater calling.

Plea. Yes,
My lady Silkworm.

Keep. And to shine in plush.

Plea. Like a young night-crow, a Diaphanous Silkworm.

Keep. Lady Diaphanous sounds most delicate.

Plea. Which would you choose now, mistress?

Pla. 'Cannot tell.
The copy does confound one.

Plea. Here's my mother.

Enter POLISH.

Pol. How now, my dainty charge, and diligent nurse?
What were you chanting on?   [*Pleasance kneels.*]   God bless you,
     maiden.
    Keep. We are inchanting all; wishing a husband
For my young mistress here: a man to please her.
    Pol. She shall have a man, good nurse, and must have a man,
A man and a half, if we can choose him out;
We are all in council within, and sit about it:
The doctors and the scholars, and my lady,
Who's wiser than all us.—Where's master Needle?
Her ladyship so lacks him to prick out
The man!   [*Exit Pleasance.*]   How does my sweet young mistress?
You look not well, methinks; how do you, dear charge?
You must have a husband, and you shall have a husband,
There's two put out to making for you; a third
Your uncle promises: but you must still
Be ruled by your aunt, according to the will
Of your dead father and mother, who are in heaven.
Your lady-aunt has choice in the house for you:
We do not trust your uncle: he would keep you
A batchelor still, by keeping of your portion;
And keep you not alone without a husband,
But in a sickness; ay, and the green sickness,
The maiden's malady; which is a sickness:
A kind of a disease, I can assure you,
And like the fish our mariners call *remora*—
    Keep. A remora, mistress!
    Pol. How now, goody nurse,
Dame Keep of Katerns? what! have you an oar
In the cock-boat, 'cause you are a sailor's wife,
And come from Shadwell?

Enter NEEDLE.

           I say a remora,
For it will stay a ship that's under sail;
And stays are long and tedious things to maids!
And maidens are young ships that would be sailing
When they be rigg'd; wherefore is all their trim else?
    Nee. True; and for them to be staid—
    Pol. The stay is dangerous:
You know it, master Needle.
    Nee. I know somewhat;
And can assure you from the doctor's mouth,
She has a dropsy, and must change the air,
Before she can recover.
    Pol. Say you so, sir?
    Nee. The doctor says so.

Pol. Says his worship so?
I warrant them he says true then; they sometimes
Are soothsayers, and always cunning men.
Which doctor was it?
 Nee. E'en my lady's doctor,
The neat house doctor; but a true stone doctor.
 Pol. Why, hear you, nurse? how comes this geer to pass?
This is your fault in truth; it shall be your fault,
And must be your fault: why is your mistress sick?
She had her health the while she was with me.
 Keep. Alas, good mistress Polish, I am no saint,
Much less my lady, to be urged give health,
Or sickness, at my will: but to await
The stars' good pleasure, and to do my duty.
 Pol. You must do more than your duty, foolish nurse:
You must do all you can, and more than you can,
More than is possible; when folks are sick,
Especially a mistress, a young mistress.
 Keep. Here's master doctor himself cannot do that. [*Exit.*

Enter Lady LOADSTONE *and* RUT.

Pol. Doctor Do-all can do it; thence he's call'd so.
 Rut. Whence? what is he call'd?
 Pol. Doctor, do all you can,
I pray you, and beseech you, for my charge here.
 Lady L. She is my tendering gossip, loves my niece.
 Pol. I know you can do all things, that you please, sir,
For a young damsel, my young lady's niece, here;
You can do what you list.
 Rut. Peace, Tiffany.
 Pol. Especially in this new case of the dropsy.
The gentlewoman, I do fear, is leaven'd.
 Rut. Leaven'd! what's that?
 Pol. Puft, blown, an't please your worship.
 Rut. What! dark by darker? what is blown, puft? speak
English—
 Pol. Tainted, an't please you, some do call it.
She swells, and so swells with it—
 Rut. Give her vent,
If she do swell. A gimlet must be had;
It is a tympanites she is troubled with.
There are three kinds: the first is anasarca,
Under the flesh a tumour; that's not her's.
The second is ascites, or aquosus,
A watery humour; that is not her's neither.
But tympanites, which we call the drum,
A wind-bombs in her belly, must be unbraced,
And with a faucet or a peg, let out,
And she'll do well: get her a husband.

Pol. Yes,
I say so, master doctor, and betimes too.

Lady L. As soon as we can: let her bear up to-day,
Laugh and keep company at gleek or crimp.

Pol. Your ladyship says right, crimp sure will cure her.

Rut. Yes, and gleek too; peace, gossip Tittle-tattle.
She must to-morrow down into the country,
Some twenty miles; a coach and six brave horses:
Take the fresh air a month there, or five weeks;
And then return a bride up to the town,
For any husband in the hemisphere
To chuck at, when she has dropt her tympany.

Pol. Must she then drop it?

Rut. Thence 'tis call'd a dropsy.
The tympanites is one spice of it:
A toy, a thing of nothing, a mere vapour;
I'll blow't away.

Lady L. Needle, get you the coach
Ready, against to-morrow morning.

Nee. Yes, madam.   [*Exit.*

Lady L. I'll down with her myself, and thank the doctor.

Pol. We all shall thank him: but, dear madam, think,
Resolve upon a man this day.

Lady L. I have done it.
To tell you true, sweet gossip—here is none
But master doctor, he shall be of the council.—
The man I have design'd her to, indeed,
Is master Practice; he's a neat young man,
Forward, and growing up in a profession:
Like to be somebody, if the Hall stand,
And pleading hold! A prime young lawyer's wife,
Is a right happy fortune.

Rut. And she bringing
So plentiful a portion, they may live
Like king and queen at common law together:
Sway judges, guide the courts, command the clerks,
And fright the evidence; rule at their pleasures,
Like petty sovereigns in all cases.

Pol. O, that
Will be a work of time; she may be old
Before her husband rise to a chief judge,
And all her flower be gone. No, no, a lady
Of the first head I would have her, and in court,
The lady Silkworm, a Diaphanous lady:
And be a vicountess, to carry all
Before her, as we say, her gentleman-usher,
And cast off pages, bare, to bid her aunt
Welcome unto her honour, at her lodgings.

Rut. You say well, lady's gossip; if my lady

Could admit that, to have her niece precede her.

Lady L. For that, I must consult mine own ambition,
My zealous gossip.

Pol. O, you shall precede her:
You shall be a countess, sir Diaphanous
Shall get you made a countess! here he comes
Has my voice, certain.

Enter behind Sir Diaphanous Silkworm *and* Palate *in
discourse.*

           O fine courtier!
O blessed man! the bravery pick'd out,
To make my dainty charge a vicountess,
And my good lady, her aunt, countess at large!

Sir Dia. I tell thee, parson, if I get her, reckon
Thou hast a friend in court; and shalt command
A thousand pound, to go on any errand,
For any church-preferment thou hast a mind to.

Pal. I thank your worship; I will so work for you,
As you shall study all the ways to thank me:
I'll work my lady, and my lady's friends;
Her gossip, and this doctor, and squire Needle,
And master Compass, who is all in all;
The very fly she moves by: he is one
That went to sea with her husband, sir John Loadstone,
And brought home the rich prizes; all that wealth
Is left her; for which service she respects him:
A dainty scholar in the mathematics;
And one she wholly employs. Now dominus Practice
Is yet the man, appointed by her ladyship;
But there's a trick to set his cap awry,
If I know any thing: he hath confest
To me in private that he loves another,
My lady's woman, mistress Pleasance; therefore
Secure you of rivalship.

Sir Dia. I thank thee,
My noble parson; there's five hundred pound
Waits on thee more for that.

Pal. Accost the niece,
Yonder she walks alone; I'll move the aunt:
But here's the gossip; she expects a morsel.
Have you ne'er a ring or toy to throw away?

Sir Dia. Yes, here's a diamond of some threescore pound,
I pray you give her that.

Pal. If she will take it.

Sir Dia. And there's an emerald for the doctor too:
Thou parson, thou shalt coin me; I am thine.

Pal. Here master Compass comes.

Enter COMPASS.

                      Do you see my lady,
And all the rest, how they do flutter about him?
He is the oracle of the house and family.
Now is your time; go nick it with the niece: [*Exit Sir Dia.*
I will walk by, and hearken how the chimes go. [*Walks aside.*

   Com. Nay, parson, stand not off: you may approach;
This is no such hid point of state we handle,
But you may hear it; for we are all of counsel.
The gentle master Practice hath dealt clearly,
And nobly with you, madam.

   Lady L. Have you talk'd with him,
And made the overture?

   Com. Yes, first I moved
The business trusted to me by your ladyship,
In your own words, almost your very syllables,
Save where my memory trespass'd 'gainst their elegance,
For which I hope your pardon.   Then I enlarged,
In my own homely style, the special goodness
And greatness of your bounty in your choice,
And free conferring of a benefit
So without ends, conditions, any tie
But his mere virtue, and the value of it,
To call him to your kindred, to your veins,
Insert him in your family, and to make him
A nephew by the offer of a niece,
With such a portion; which when he had heard,
And most maturely acknowledg'd (as his calling
Tends all unto maturity) he return'd
A thanks as ample as the courtesy,
In my opinion: said it was a grace
Too great to be rejected or accepted
By him: but as the terms stood with his fortune,
He was not to prevaricate with your ladyship,
But rather to require ingenuous leave,
He might with the same love that it was offer'd
Refuse it, since he could not with his honesty,
(Being he was engaged before,) receive it.

   Pal. The same he said to me.

   Com. And named the party?

   Pal. He did and he did not.

   Com. Come, leave your schemes,
And fine amphibolies, parson.

   Pal. You'll hear more.

   Pol. Why, now your ladyship is free to choose
The courtier sir Diaphanous: he shall do it,
I'll move it to him myself.

   Lady L. What will you move to him?

Pol. The making you a countess.

Lady L. Stint, fond woman.
Know you the party master Practice means?

Com. No, but your parson says he knows, madam.

Lady L. I fear he fables; parson, do you know
Where master Practice is engaged?

Pal. I'll tell you,
But under seal; her mother must not know:
'Tis with your Ladyship's woman, mistress Pleasance.

Com. How!

Lady L. He is not mad?

Pal. O hide the hideous secret
From her; she'll trouble all else.　You do hold
A cricket by the wing.

Com. Did he name Pleasance?
Are you sure, parson?

Lady L. O 'tis true, your mistress!
I find where your shoe wrings you, master Compass:
But you'll look to him there.

Com. Yes; here's sir Moth,
Your brother, with his Bias, and the party
Deep in discourse; 'twill be a bargain and sale,
I see, by their close working of their heads,
And running them together so in counsel.

Enter at a distance, in discourse, Sir MOTH INTEREST, PRACTICE,
and BIAS.

Lady L. Will master Practice be of counsel against us?

Com. He is a lawyer, and must speak for his fee,
Against his father and mother, all his kindred,
His brothers or his sisters; no exception
Lies at the common law.　He must not alter
Nature for form, but go on in his path;
It may be, he'll be for us.　Do not you
Offer to meddle, let them take their course.
Dispatch, and marry her off to any husband;
Be not you scrupulous; let who can have her:
So he lay down the portion, though he geld it,
It will maintain the suit against him, somewhat;
Something in hand is better than no birds;
He shall at last accompt for the utmost farthing,
If you can keep your hand from a discharge.　　　*[Exit Lady L.*

Pol. [*to Diaphanous.*] Sir, do but make her worshipful aunt a
　　　　countess,
And she is yours, her aunt has worlds to leave you:
The wealth of six East-Indian fleets at least.
Her husband, sir John Loadstone, was the governor
Of the company seven years.

Sir Dia. And came there home

Six fleets in seven years?
   Pol. I cannot tell,
I must attend my gossip her good ladyship.   [*Exit.*
   Pla. And will you make me a vicountess too, sir?
How do they make a countess; in a chair,
Or on a bed?
   Sir Dia. Both ways, sweet bird; I'll shew you.
                [*Exeunt Sir Diaphanous and Placentia.*
   Sir Moth. [*coming forward.*] The truth is, master Practice,
                now we are sure
That you are off, we dare come on the bolder;
The portion left was sixteen thousand pound,
I do confess it, as a just man should.
And call here master Compass, with these gentlemen,
To the relation; I will still be just.
Now for the profits every way arising,
It was the donor's wisdom, those should pay
Me for my watch, and breaking of my sleeps;
It is no petty charge, you know, that sum,
To keep a man awake for fourteen year.
   Prac. But, as you knew to use it in that time,
It would reward your waking.
   Sir Moth. That's my industry,
As it might be your reading, study, and counsel,
And now your pleading; who denies it you?
I have my calling too. Well, sir, the contract
Is with this gentleman; ten thousand pound.
An ample portion for a younger brother,
With a soft, tender, delicate rib of man's flesh,
That he may work like wax, and print upon.—
He expects no more than that sum to be tender'd,
And he receive it; these are the conditions.
   Prac. A direct bargain, and sale in open market.
   Sir Moth. And what I have furnish'd him withal o' the by,
To appear or so; a matter of four hundred,
To be deduced upon the payment—
   Bia. Right:
You deal like a just man still.
   Sir Moth. Draw up this,
Good master Practice, for us, and be speedy.
   Prac. But here's a mighty gain, sir, you have made
Of this one stock: the principal first doubled,
In the first seven year; and that redoubled
In the next seven! beside six thousand pound,
There's threescore thousand got in fourteen year,
After the usual rate of ten in the hundred,
And the ten thousand paid.
   Sir Moth. I think it be.
   Prac. How will you 'scape the clamour and the envy?

Sir Moth. Let them exclaim and envy, what care I?
Their murmurs raise no blisters in my flesh.
My monies are my blood, my parents, kindred;
And he that loves not these, he is unnatural.
I am persuaded that the love of money
Is not a virtue only in a subject,
But might befit a prince: and were there need,
I find me able to make good the assertion,
To any reasonable man's understanding,
And make him to confess it.
    Com. Gentlemen,
Doctors, and scholars, you'll hear this, and look for
As much true secular wit, and deep lay-sense,
As can be shewn on such a common place.
    Sir Moth. First, we all know the soul of man is infinite
In what it covets.   Who desireth knowledge,
Desires it infinitely; who covets honour,
Covets it infinitely: It will be then
No hard thing for a coveting man to prove,
Or to confess, he aims at infinite wealth.
    Com. His soul lying that way.
    Sir Moth. Next, every man
Is in the hope or possibility
Of a whole world; this present world being nothing,
But the dispersed issue of [the] first one.
And therefore I not see, but a just man
May, with just reason, and in office ought
Propound unto himself—
    Com. An infinite wealth!
I'll bear the burden; go you on, sir Moth.
    Sir Moth. Thirdly, if we consider man a member
But of the body politic, we know
By just experience, that the prince hath need
More of one wealthy, than ten fighting men.
    Com. There you went out of the road, a little from us.
    Sir Moth. And therefore, if the prince's aims be infinite,
It must be in that which makes all.
    Com. Infinite wealth!
    Sir Moth. Fourthly, 'tis natural to all good subjects,
To set a price on money, more than fools
Ought on their mistress' picture; every piece,
From the penny to the twelve-pence, being the hieroglyphic,
And sacred sculpture of the sovereign.
    Com. A manifest conclusion, and a safe one!
    Sir Moth. Fifthly, wealth gives a man the leading voice
At all conventions; and displaceth worth,
With general allowance to all parties:
It makes a trade to take the wall of virtue,
And the mere issue of a shop right honourable.

Sixthly, it doth enable him that hath it,
To the performance of all real actions,
Referring him to himself still, and not binding
His will to any circumstance, without him.
It gives him precise knowledge of himself;
For, be he rich, he straight with evidence knows
Whether he have any compassion,
Or inclination unto virtue, or no;
Where the poor knave erroneously believes,
If he were rich, he would build churches, or
Do such mad things.   Seventhly, your wise poor men
Have ever been contented to observe
Rich fools, and so to serve their turns upon them;
Subjecting all their wit to the others' wealth,
And become gentlemen parasites, squire bawds,
To feed their patron's honourable humours.
Eighthly, 'tis certain that a man may leave
His wealth, or to his children, or his friends;
His wit he cannot so dispose by legacy,
As they shall be a Harrington the better for't.

Enter Captain IRONSIDE.

Com. He may entail a jest upon his house,
Or leave a tale to his posterity,
To be told after him.
    Iron. As you have done here?
To invite your friend and brother to a feast,
Where all the guests are so mere heterogene,
And strangers, no man knows another, or cares
If they be Christians, or Mahometans,
That here are met.
    Com. Is't any thing to you, brother,
To know religions more than those you fight for?
    Iron. Yes, and with whom I eat.   I may dispute,
And how shall I hold argument with such,
I neither know their humours, nor their heresies,
Which are religions now, and so received?
Here's no man among these that keeps a servant,
To enquire his master of; yet in the house
I hear it buzz'd there are a brace of doctors,
A fool, and a physician; with a courtier,
That feeds on mulberry leaves, like a true silkworm:
A lawyer, and a mighty money-bawd,
Sir Moth, has brought his politic Bias with him,
A man of a most animadverting humour;
Who, to endear himself unto his lord,
Will tell him, you and I, or any of us,
That here are met, are all pernicious spirits,
And men of pestilent purpose, meanly affected

Unto the state we live in; and beget
Himself a thanks with the great men of the time,
By breeding jealousies in them of us,
Shall cross our fortunes, frustrate our endeavours,
Twice seven years after: and this trick be call'd
Cutting of throats with a whispering, or a pen-knife.
I must cut his throat now: I am bound in honour,
And by the law of arms, to see it done;
I dare to do it, and I dare profess
The doing of it; being to such a rascal,
Who is the common offence grown of mankind,
And worthy to be torn up from society.

   Com. You shall not do it here, sir.

   Iron. Why, will you
Entreat yourself into a beating for him,
My courteous brother? If you will, have at you.
No man deserves it better, now I think on't,
Than you, that will keep consort with such fidlers,
Pragmatic flies, fools, publicans, and moths,
And leave your honest and adopted brother.

   Sir Moth. Best raise the house upon him to secure us;
He'll kill us all!   [*Exit.*

   Pal. I love no blades in belts.   [*Exit.*

   Rut. Nor I.   [*Exit.*

   Bia. Would I were at my shop again,
In court, safe stow'd up with my politic bundles.   [*Exit.*

   Com. How they are scattered!

   Iron. Run away like *cimici*,
Into the crannies of a rotten bed-stead.

   Com. I told you, such a passage would disperse them,
Although the house were their fee-simple in law,
And they possest of all the blessings in it.

   Iron. Pray heaven they be not frighted from their stomachs,
That so my lady's table be disfurnish'd
Of the provisions!

   Com. No, the parson's calling,
By this time, all the covey again together.
Here comes good tidings—

Enter PLEASANCE.

                      Dinner's on the board.—   [*Exit Ironside.*
Stay, mistress Pleasance, I must ask you a question:
Have you any suits in law?

   Plea. I, master Compass!

   Com. Answer me briefly, it is dinner-time.
They say you have retain'd brisk master Practice,
Here, of your counsel; and are to be join'd
A patentee with him.

   Plea. In what? who says so?

You are disposed to jest.

   Com. No, I am in earnest.
'Tis given out in the house so, I assure you;
But keep your right to yourself, and not acquaint
A common lawyer with your case: if he
Once find the gap, a thousand will leap after.
I'll tell you more anon.   *[Exit.*

   Plea. This riddle shews
A little like a love trick, o' one face,
If I could understand it.   I will study it.   *[Exit.*

   *Dam. But whom doth your poet mean now by this master Bias?
what lord's secretary doth he purpose to personate or perstringe?*

   *Boy. You might as well ask me, what alderman, or alderman's mate,
he meant by sir Moth Interest, or what eminent lawyer, by the ridiculous
master Practice? who hath rather his name invented for laughter, than
any offence or injury it can stick on the reverend professors of the law:
and so the wise ones will think.*

   *Pro. It is an insidious question, brother Damplay: iniquity itself
would not have urged it. It is picking the lock of the scene, not opening
it the fair way with a key. A play, though it apparel and present vices
in general, flies from all particularities in persons. Would you ask
of Plautus, and Terence, if they both lived now, who were Davus or
Pseudolus in the scene, who Pyrgopolinices or Thraso? who Euclio or
Menedemus?*

   *Boy. Yes, he would: and enquire of Martial, or any other epigram-
matist, whom he meant by Titius or Seius, (the common John a Noke,
or John a Stile,) under whom they note all vices and errors taxable to
the times? as if there could not be a name for a folly fitted to the stage,
but there must be a person in nature found out to own it.*

   Dam. Why, I can fancy a person to myself, boy, who shall hinder me?

   *Boy. And in not publishing him, you do no man an injury. But if
you will utter your own ill meaning on that person, under the author's
words, you make a libel of his comedy.*

   Dam. O, he told us that in a prologue, long since.

   *Boy. If you do the same reprehensible ill things, still the same
reprehension will serve you, though you heard it afore: they are his
own words, I can invent no better, nor he.*

   *Pro. It is the solemn vice of interpretation that deforms the figure of
many a fair scene, by drawing it awry; and, indeed, is the civil murder
of most good plays: if I see a thing vively presented on the stage, that
the glass of custom, which is comedy, is so held up to me by the poet,
as I can therein view the daily examples of men's lives, and images of
truth, in their manners, so drawn for my delight or profit, as I may,
either way, use them: and will I, rather than make that true use, hunt
out the persons to defame by my malice of misapplying, and imperil
the innocence and candour of the author by this calumny! It is an
unjust way of hearing and beholding plays, this, and most unbecoming
a gentleman to appear malignantly witty in another's work.*

*Boy. They are no other but narrow and shrunk natures, shrivell'd
up, poor things, that cannot think well of themselves, who dare to
detract others. That signature is upon them, and it will last. A
half-witted barbarism, which no barber's art, or his balls will ever
expunge or take out!*

*Dam. Why, boy, this were a strange empire, or rather a tyranny,
you would entitle your poet to, over gentlemen, that they should come to
hear and see plays, and say nothing for their money.*

Boy. O, yes, say what you will; so it be to purpose, and in place.

*Dam. Can any thing be out of purpose at a play? I see no reason,
if I come here, and give my eighteen-pence or two shillings for my seat,
but I should take it out in censure on the stage.*

*Boy. Your two shilling worth is allow'd you: but you will take
your ten shilling worth, your twenty shilling worth, and more; and
teach others about you to do the like, that follow your leading face; as
if you were to cry up and down every scene by confederacy, be it right
or wrong.*

Dam. Who should teach us the right or wrong at a play?

*Boy. If your own science cannot do it, or the love of modesty and
truth; all other entreaties or attempts are vain. You are fitter spectators for the bears, than us, or the puppets. This is a popular ignorance
indeed, somewhat better apparelled in you, than the people; but a hard-
handed and stiff ignorance worthy a trowel or a hammerman; and
not only fit to be scorned, but to be triumphed over.*

Dam. By whom, boy?

*Boy. No particular, but the general neglect and silence. Good master
Damplay, be yourself still, without a second: few here are of your
opinion to-day, I hope; to-morrow, I am sure there will be none, when
they have ruminated this.*

*Pro. Let us mind what you come for, the play, which will draw on
to the epitasis now.*

ACT III

SCENE I.—*A Room in Lady* LOADSTONE'S *House.*

Enter TIMOTHY ITEM, NEEDLE, *and Nurse* KEEP.

Item. Where's master doctor?

Nee. O, master Timothy Item,
His learned pothecary, you are welcome!
He is within at dinner.

Item. Dinner! death,
That he will eat now, having such a business,
That so concerns him!

Nee. Why, can any business
Concern a man like his meat?

Item. O, twenty millions,
To a physician that's in practice: I

Do bring him news from all the points o' the compass,
That's all the parts of the sublunary globe,
Of times and double times.

Nee. In, in, sweet Item,
And furnish forth the table with your news:
Deserve your dinner, sow out your whole bagfull;
The guests will hear it.

Item. I heard they were out.

Nee. But they are pieced, and put together again;
You may go in, you'll find them at high eating:
The parson has an edifying stomach,
And a persuading palate, like his name;
He hath begun three draughts of sack in doctrines,
And four in uses.

Item. And they follow him?

Nee. No, sir Diaphanous is a recusant
In sack; he only takes it in French wine,
With an allay of water. In, in, Item,
And leave your peeping.   [*Exit Item.*

Keep. I have a month's mind
To peep a little too. Sweet master Needle,
How are they set?

Nee. At the board's end, my lady—

Keep. And my young mistress by her?

Nee. Yes, the parson
On the right hand (as he'll not lose his place
For thrusting) and against him mistress Polish;
Next, sir Diaphanous against sir Moth;
Knights, one again another: then the soldier,
The man of war; and man of peace, the lawyer;
Then the pert doctor, and the politic Bias,
And master Compass circumscribeth all.   [*A noise within.*

Plea. [*within.*] Nurse Keep, nurse Keep!

Nee. What noise is that within?

Plea. [*within.*] Come to my mistress, all their weapons are out.

Nee. Mischief of men, what day, what hour is this!

Keep. Run for the cellar of strong waters, quickly.   [*Exeunt.*

SCENE II.—*Another Room in the Same.*

Enter IRONSIDE, *followed by* COMPASS.

Com. Were you a madman, to do this at table,
And trouble all the guests, to affright the ladies,
And gentlewomen?

Iron. Pox upon your women.
And your half-man there, court sir Ambergris,
A perfumed braggart! he must drink his wine
With three parts water; and have amber in that too!

Com. And you must therefore break his face with a glass,

And wash his nose in wine?
   Iron. Cannot he drink
In orthodox, but he must have his gums,
And paynim drugs?
   Com. You should have used the glass
Rather as balance, than the sword of Justice:
But you have cut his face with it, he bleeds.
Come, you shall take your sanctuary with me;
The whole house will be up in arms against you else,
Within this half hour: this way to my lodging.   [*Exeunt.*

SCENE III.—*Another Room in the same.*

Enter RUT, *Lady* LOADSTONE, POLISH, *and* KEEP *carrying*
    PLACENTIA: PLEASANCE *and* ITEM *following.*

   Rut. A most rude action! carry her to her bed;
And use the fricace to her, with those oils.
Keep your news, Item, now, and tend this business.
   Lady L. Good gossip, look to her.
   Pol. How do you, sweet charge?
   Keep. She's in a sweat.
   Pol. Ay, and a faint sweat, marry.
   Rut. Let her alone to Tim; he has directions:
I'll hear your news, Tim Item, when you have done.
    [*Exeunt Item, Polish, Keep, and Pleasance, with Placentia.*
   Lady L. Was ever such a guest brought to my table?
   Rut. These boisterous soldiers have no better breeding.
Here master Compass comes:

Enter COMPASS.

                             Where is your captain,
Rudhudibrass de Ironside?
   Com. Gone out of doors.
   Lady L. Would he had ne'er come in them, I may wish!
He has discredited my house and board,
With his rude swaggering manners, and endanger'd
My niece's health, by drawing of his weapon,
God knows how far; for master doctor does not.
   Com. The doctor is an ass then, if he say so,
And cannot with his conjuring names, Hippocrates,
Galen or Rasis, Avicen, Averroes,
Cure a poor wench's falling in a swoon;
Which a poor farthing changed in rosa solis,
Or cinnamon water would.

Re-enter KEEP *and* POLISH.

   Lady L. How now! how does she?
   Keep. She's somewhat better: master Item has brought her
A little about.
   Pol. But there's sir Moth, your brother,

Is fallen into a fit o' the happyplex;—
It were a happy place for him and us,
If he could steal to heaven thus! all the house
Are calling master doctor, master doctor.   *[Exit Rut.*
The parson he has given him gone, this half hour;
He's pale in the mouth already for the fear
Of the fierce captain.

 Lady L. Help me to my chamber,
Nurse Keep: would I could see the day no more,
But night hung over me, like some dark cloud;
That, buried with this loss of my good name,
I and my house might perish thus forgotten!
     [Exeunt Lady L., Keep, and Polish.
 Com. Her taking it to heart thus more afflicts me
Than all these accidents, for they'll blow over.

   Enter PRACTICE *and* Sir DIAPHANOUS SILKWORM.

 Prac. It was a barbarous injury, I confess:
But if you will be counsell'd, sir, by me,
The reverend law lies open to repair
Your reputation. That will give you damages:
Five thousand pound for a finger, I have known
Given in court; and let me pack your jury.
 Sir Dia. There's nothing vexes me, but that he has stain'd
My new white satin doublet, and bespatter'd
My spick and span silk stockings on the day
They were drawn on; and here's a spot in my hose too!
 Com. Shrewd maims! your clothes are wounded desperately;
And that, I think, troubles a courtier more,
An exact courtier, than a gash in his flesh.
 Sir Dia. My flesh! I swear had he given me twice so much,
I never should have reckon'd it: but my clothes
To be defaced and stigmatised so foully!
I take it as a contumely done me,
Above the wisdom of our laws to right.
 Com. Why, then you'll challenge him?
 Sir Dia. I will advise;
Though master Practice here doth urge the law,
And reparation it will make me of credit,
Beside great damages—let him pack my jury.
 Com. He speaks like master Practice, one that is
The child of a profession he is vow'd to,
And servant to the study he hath taken,
A pure apprentice at law! but you must have
The counsel of the sword, and square your action
Unto their canons, and that brotherhood,
If you do right.
 Prac. I tell you, master Compass,
You speak not like a friend unto the laws,

Nor scarce a subject, to persuade him thus
Unto the breach of the peace: sir, you forget
There is a court above, of the Star-chamber,
To punish routs and riots.
   Com. No, young master,
Although your name be Practice there in term-time,
I do remember it. But you'll not hear
What I was bound to say; but like a wild
Young haggard justice, fly at breach of the peace,
Before you know whether the amorous knight
Dares break the peace of conscience in a duel.
   Sir Dia. Troth, master Compass, I take you my friend;
You shall appoint of me in any matter
That's reasonable, so we may meet fair,
On even terms.
   Com. I shall persuade no other;
And take your learned counsel to advise you,
I'll run along with him. You say you'll meet him
On even terms. I do not see indeed
How that can be 'twixt Ironside and you,
Now I consider it: he is my brother,
I do confess we have call'd so twenty year:
But you are, sir, a knight in court, allied there,
And so befriended, you may easily answer
The worst success: he a known, noted, bold
Boy of the sword, hath all men's eyes upon him;
And there's no London jury, but are led
In evidence, as far by common fame,
As they are by present deposition.
Then you have many brethren, and near kinsmen.
If he kill you, it will be a lasting quarrel
'Twixt them and him: whereas Rud Ironside,
Although he have got his head into a beaver,
With a huge feather, is but a currier's son,
And has not two old cordovan skins to leave
In leather caps to mourn him in, if he die.
Again; you are generally beloved, he hated
So much, that all the hearts and votes of men
Go with you, in the wishing all prosperity
Unto your purpose: he is a fat, corpulent,
Unwieldy fellow; you, a dieted spark,
Fit for the combat. He has kill'd so many,
As it is ten to one his turn is next:
You never fought with any, less, slew any;
And therefore have the [better] hopes before you.
I hope these things, thus specified unto you,
Are fair advantages; you cannot encounter
Him upon equal terms. Beside, sir Silkworm,
He hath done you wrong in a most high degree;

And sense of such an injury received
Should so exacuate, and whet your choler,
As you should count yourself an host of men,
Compared to him: and therefore you, brave sir,
Have no more reason to provoke, or challenge
Him than the huge great porter has to try
His strength upon an infant.

Sir Dia. Master Compass,
You rather spur me on, than any way
Abate my courage to the enterprise.

Com. All counsel's as 'tis taken: if you stand
On point of honour, not to have any odds,
I have rather then dissuaded you, than otherwise:
If upon terms of humour and revenge,
I have encouraged you.   So that I think,
I have done the part of a friend on either side;
In furnishing your fear with matter first,
If you have any; or, if you dare fight,
To heighten and confirm your resolution.

Prac. I now do crave your pardon, master Compass:
I did not apprehend your way before,
The true perimeter of it: you have circles,
And such fine draughts about!

Sir Dia. Sir, I do thank you,
I thank you, master Compass, heartily.
I must confess, I never fought before,
And I'd be glad to do things orderly,
In the right place; I pray you instruct me, sir:
Is't best I fight ambitiously, or maliciously?

Com. Sir, if you never fought before, be wary,
Trust not yourself too much.

Sir Dia. Why? I assure you,
I am very angry.

Com. Do not suffer, though,
The flatuous, windy choler of your heart,
To move the clapper of your understanding,
Which is the guiding faculty, your reason:
You know not, if you'll fight, or no, being brought
Upon the place.

Sir Dia. O yes, I have imagined
Him treble arm'd, provoked too, and as furious
As Homer makes Achilles; and I find
Myself not frighted with his fame one jot.

Com. Well, yet take heed.   These fights imaginary,
Are less than skirmishes; the fight of shadows:
For shadows have their figure, motion,
And their umbratil action, from the real
Posture and motion of the body's act:
Whereas imaginarily, many times,

Those men may fight dare scarce eye one another,
And much less meet. But if there be no help,
Faith I would wish you send him a fair challenge.
    Sir Dia. I will go pen it presently.
    Com. But word it
In the most generous terms.
    Sir Dia. Let me alone.
    Prac. And silken phrase; the courtliest kind of quarrel.
    Com. He'll make it a petition for his peace.
    Prac. O, yes, of right, and he may do't by law.   [*Exeunt.*

SCENE IV.—*Another Room in the Same.*

Enter RUT, PALATE, *and* BIAS, *bringing out* Sir MOTH INTEREST
in a chair: ITEM *and* POLISH *following.*

    Rut. Come, bring him out into the air a little:
There, set him down. Bow him, yet bow him more,
Dash that same glass of water in his face;
Now tweak him by the nose—hard, harder yet:
If it but call the blood up from the heart,
I ask no more. See, what a fear can do!
Pinch him in the nape of the neck now; nip him, nip him.
    Item. He feels; there's life in him.
    Pal. He groans, and stirs.
    Rut. Tell him the captain's gone.
    Sir Moth. Ha!
    Pal. He's gone, sir.
    Rut. Give him a box, hard, hard, on his left ear.
    Sir Moth. O!
    Rut. How do you feel yourself?
    Sir Moth. Sore, sore.
    Rut. But where?
    Sir Moth. In my neck.
    Rut. I nipt him there.
    Sir Moth. And in my head.
    Rut. I box'd him twice or thrice, to move those sinews.
    Bias. I swear you did.
    Pol. What a brave man's a doctor,
To beat one into health! I thought his blows
Would e'en have kill'd him; he did feel no more
Than a great horse.
    Sir Moth. Is the wild captain gone,
That man of murder?
    Bias. All is calm and quiet.
    Sir Moth. Say you so, cousin Bias, then all's well.
    Pal. How quickly a man is lost!
    Bias. And soon recover'd!
    Pol. Where there are means, and doctors learned men,
And there apothecaries, who are not now,

As Chaucer says, their friendship to begin.
Well, could they teach each other how to win
In their swath bands—
   Rut. Leave your poetry, good gossip,
Your Chaucer's clouts, and wash your dishes with them;
We must rub up the roots of his disease,
And crave your peace a while, or else your absence.
   Pol. Nay, I know when to hold my peace.
   Rut. Then do it.—
Give me your hand, sir Moth.   Let's feel your pulse;
It is a pursiness, a kind of stoppage,
Or tumour of the purse, for want of exercise,
That you are troubled with: some ligatures
In the neck of your *vesica*, or *marsupium*,
Are so close knit, that you cannot evaporate;
And therefore you must use relaxatives.
Beside, they say, you are so restive grown,
You cannot but with trouble put your hand
Into your pocket to discharge a reckoning,
And this we sons of physic do call *chiragra*,
A kind of cramp, or hand-gout.   You shall purge for't.
   Item. Indeed your worship should do well to advise him
To cleanse his body, all the three high-ways;
That is, by sweat, purge, and phlebotomy.
   Rut. You say well, learned Tim; I'll first prescribe him
To give his purse a purge, once, twice a-week
At dice, or cards; and when the weather is open,
Sweat at a bowling-alley; or be let blood
In the lending vein, and bleed a matter of fifty
Or threescore ounces at a time; then put your thumbs
Under your girdle, and have somebody else
Pull out your purse for you, till with more ease,
And a good habit, you can do it yourself,
And then be sure always to keep good diet,
And have your table furnish'd from one end
Unto the t'other; it is good for the eyes:
But feed you on one dish still, have your diet-drink
Ever in bottles ready, which must come
From the King's-head: I will prescribe you nothing,
But what I'll take before you mine own self;
That is my course with all my patients.
   Pal. Very methodical, *secundùm artem.*
   Bias. And very safe *pro captu recipientis.*
   Pol. All errant learned men, how they 'spute Latin!
   Rut. I had it of a Jew, and a great rabbi,
Who every morning cast his cup of white-wine
With sugar, and by the residence in the bottom,
Would make report of any chronic malady,
Such as sir Moth's is, being an oppilation

In that you call the neck of the money-bladder,
Most anatomical, and by dissection—

Enter Nurse KEEP, *hastily.*

Keep. O, master doctor, and his 'pothecary,
Good master Item, and my mistress Polish,
We need you all above! she's fallen again
In a worse fit than ever.

Pol. Who?

Keep. Your charge.

Pol. Come away, gentlemen.

Sir Moth. This fit with the doctor
Hath mended me past expectation.   [*Exeunt all but Bias.*

Enter COMPASS, Sir DIAPHANOUS SILKWORM, *and* PRACTICE.

Com. O sir Diaphanous! have you done?

Sir Dia. I have brought it.

Prac. That's well.

Com. But who shall carry it now?

Sir Dia. A friend:
I'll find a friend to carry it; master Bias here
Will not deny me that.

Bias. What is't?

Sir Dia. To carry
A challenge I have writ unto the captain.

Bias. Faith, but I will, sir; you shall pardon me
For a twi-reason of state: I'll bear no challenges;
I will not hazard my lord's favour so;
Or forfeit mine own judgment with his honour,
To turn a ruffian: I have to commend me
Nought but his lordship's good opinion;
And to it my kalligraphy, a fair hand,
Fit for a secretary: now you know, a man's hand
Being his executing part in fight,
Is more obnoxious to the common peril.

Sir Dia. You shall not fight, sir, you shall only search
My antagonist; commit us fairly there
Upon the ground on equal terms.

Bias. O, sir,
But if my lord should hear I stood at end
Of any quarrel, 'twere an end of me
In a state-course! I have read the politics;
And heard the opinions of our best divines.

Com. The gentleman has reason. Where was first
The birth of your acquaintance, or the cradle
Of your strict friendship made?

Sir Dia. We met in France, sir.

Com. In France! that garden of humanity,
The very seed-plot of all courtesies:
I wonder that your friendship suck'd that aliment,

The milk of France; and see this sour effect
It doth produce, 'gainst all the sweets of travel.
There, every gentleman professing arms,
Thinks he is bound in honour to embrace
The bearing of a challenge for another,
Without or questioning the cause, or asking
Least colour of a reason. There's no cowardice,
No poltronery, like urging why? wherefore?
But carry a challenge, do the thing, and die.
    Bias. Why, hear you, master Compass, I but crave
Your ear in private: [*takes him aside.*] I would carry his challenge,
If I but hoped your captain angry enough
To kill him; for, to tell you truth, this knight
Is an impertinent in court, we think him,
And troubles my lord's lodgings, and his table
With frequent, and unnecessary visits,
Which we, the better sort of servants, like not:
Being his fellows in all other places,
But at our master's board; and we disdain
To do those servile offices, oft-times,
His foolish pride and empire will exact,
Against the heart, or humour of a gentleman.
    Com. Truth, master Bias, I would not have you think
I speak to flatter you; but you are one
Of the deepest politics I ever met,
And the most subtly rational. I admire you.
But do not you conceive in such a case,
That you are accessary to his death,
From whom you carry a challenge with such purpose?
    Bias. Sir, the corruption of one thing in nature,
Is held the generation of another;
And therefore, I had as lief be accessary
Unto his death, as to his life.
    Com. A new
Moral philosophy too! you'll carry it then?
    Bias. If I were sure 'twould not incense his choler
To beat the messenger.
    Com. O, I'll secure you;
You shall deliver it in my lodging, safely,
And do your friend a service worthy thanks.

Enter IRONSIDE.

    Bias. I'll venture it upon so good induction,
To rid the court of an impediment,
This baggage knight.
    Iron. Peace to you all, gentlemen,
Save to this mushroom, who I hear is menacing
Me with a challenge; which I come to anticipate,

And save the law a labour.—Will you fight, sir?
    Sir Dia. Yes, in my shirt.   [*Throws off his doublet.*
    Iron. O, that's to save your doublet;
I know it a court-trick; you had rather have
An ulcer in your body, than a pink
More in your clothes.
    Sir Dia. Captain, you are a coward,
If you'll not fight in your shirt.
    Iron. Sir, I do not mean
To put it off for that, nor yet my doublet:
You have cause to call me coward, that more fear
The stroke of the common and life-giving air,
Than all your fury, and the panoply—
    Prac. Which is at best, but a thin linen armour.
I think a cup of generous wine were better,
Than fighting in your shirts.
    Sir Dia. Sir, sir, my valour,
It is a valour of another nature,
Than to be mended by a cup of wine.
    Com. I should be glad to hear of any valours,
Differing in kind; who have known hitherto,
Only one virtue they call fortitude,
Worthy the name of valour.
    Iron. Which who hath not,
Is justly thought a coward; and he is such.
    Sir Dia. O, you have read the play there, the *New Inn,*
Of Jonson's, that decries all other valour,
But what is for the public.
    Iron. I do that too,
But did not learn it there; I think no valour
Lies for a private cause.
    Sir Dia. Sir, I'll redargue you
By disputation.
    Com. O, let's hear this:
I long to hear a man dispute in his shirt
Of valour, and his sword drawn in his hand!
    Prac. His valour will take cold, put on your doublet.
    Com. His valour will keep cold, you are deceived;
And relish much the sweeter in our ears;
It may be too, in the ordinance of nature,
Their valours are not yet so combatant,
Or truly antagonistic, as to fight,
But may admit to hear of some divisions
Of fortitude, may put them off their quarrel.
    Sir Dia. I would have no man think me so ungovern'd,
Or subject to my passion but I can
Read him a lecture 'twixt my undertakings
And executions: I do know all kinds
Of doing the business, which the town calls valour.

Com. Yes, he has read the town, Town-top's his author!
Your first?

Sir Dia. Is a rash headlong unexperience.

Com. Which is in children, fools, or your street-gallants
Of the first head.

Prac. A pretty kind of valour!

Com. Commend him, he will spin it out in's shirt,
Fine as that thread.

Sir Dia. The next, an indiscreet
Presumption, grounded upon often scapes.

Com. Or the insufficiency of adversaries,
And this is in your common fighting brothers,
Your old Perdue's, who, after time, do think,
The one, that they are shot-free, the other sword-free.
Your third?

Sir Dia. Is nought but an excess of choler,
That reigns in testy old men—

Com. Noblemen's porters,
And self-conceited poets.

Sir Dia. And is rather
A pevishness, than any part of valour.

Prac. He but rehearses, he concludes no valour.

Com. A history of distempers as they are practised,
His harangue undertaketh, and no more.
Your next?

Sir Dia. Is a dull desperate resolving.

Com. In case of some necessitous misery, or
Incumbent mischief.

Prac. Narrowness of mind,
Or ignorance being the root of it.

Sir Dia. Which you shall find in gamesters quite blown up.

Com. In bankrupt merchants, and discovered traitors.

Prac. Or your exemplified malefactors,
That have survived their infamy and punishment.

Com. One that hath lost his ears by a just sentence
Of the Star-chamber, a right valiant knave—
And is a histrionical contempt
Of what a man fears most; it being a mischief
In his own apprehension unavoidable.

Prac. Which is in cowards wounded mortally,
Or thieves adjudged to die.

Com. This is a valour
I should desire much to see encouraged;
As being a special entertainment
For our rogue people, and make oft good sport
Unto them, from the gallows to the ground.

Sir Dia. But mine is a judicial resolving,
Or liberal undertaking of a danger—

Com. That might be avoided.

Sir Dia. Ay, and with assurance,
That it is found in noblemen and gentlemen
Of the best sheaf.

Com. Who having lives to lose,
Like private men, have yet a world of honour
And public reputation to defend.

Sir Dia. Which in the brave historified Greeks,
And Romans, you shall read of.

Com. And no doubt,
May in our aldermen meet it, and their deputies,
The soldiers of the city, valiant blades,
Who, rather than their houses should be ransack'd,
Would fight it out, like so many wild beasts;
Not for the fury they are commonly arm'd with,
But the close manner of their fight and custom
Of joining head to head, and foot to foot.

Iron. And which of these so well-prest resolutions
Am I to encounter now? for commonly,
Men that have so much choice before them, have
Some trouble to resolve of any one.

Bias. There are three valours yet, which sir Diaphanous
Hath, with his leave, not touch'd.

Sir Dia. Yea! which are those?

Prac. He perks at that.

Com. Nay, he does more, he chatters.

Bias. A philosophical contempt of death
Is one; then an infused kind of valour,
Wrought in us by our genii, or good spirits;
Of which the gallant ethnics had deep sense,
Who generally held that no great statesman,
Scholar, or soldier, e'er did any thing
Sine divino aliquo afflatu.

Prac. But there's a Christian valour 'bove these two.

Bias. Which is a quiet patient toleration
Of whatsoever the malicious world
With injury doth unto you; and consists
In passion more than action, sir Diaphanous.

Sir Dia. Sure, I do take mine to be Christian valour.

Com. You may mistake though. Can you justify,
On any cause, this seeking to deface
The divine image in a man?

Bias. O, sir,
Let them alone: is not Diaphanous
As much a divine image, as is Ironside?
Let images fight, if they will fight, a God's name.

Enter Nurse KEEP, *hastily.*

Keep. Where's master Needle? saw you master Needle?
We are undone.

Com. What ails the frantic nurse?

Keep. My mistress is undone! she's crying out!
Where is this man trow, master Needle?

Enter NEEDLE.

Nee. Here. [*Takes her aside.*

Keep. Run for the party, mistress Chair, the midwife.
Nay, look how the man stands as he were gowk'd!
She's lost if you not haste away the party.

Nee. Where is the doctor?

Keep. Where a scoffing man is,
And his apothecary little better;
They laugh and jeer at all: will you dispatch,
And fetch the party quickly to our mistress?
We are all undone! the tympany will out else.

[*Exeunt Needle and Keep.*

Enter Sir MOTH INTEREST.

Sir Moth. News, news, good news, better than butter'd news!
My niece is found with child, the doctor tells me,
And fallen in labour.

Com. How! [*Exit.*

Sir Moth. The portion's paid,
The portion——O the captain! is he here? [*Exit.*

Prac. He has spied your swords out: put them up, put up,
You have driven him hence, and yet your quarrel's ended.

Iron. In a most strange discovery.

Prac. Of light gold.

Sir Dia. And cracked within the ring. I take the omen
As a good omen.

Prac. Then put up your sword,
And on your doublet. Give the captain thanks.

Sir Dia. I have been slurr'd else. Thank you, noble captain!
Your quarrelling caused all this.

Iron. Where's Compass?

Prac. Gone,
Shrunk hence, contracted to his centre, I fear.

Iron. The slip is his then.

Sir Dia. I had like t' have been
Abused in the business, had the slip slurr'd on me,
A counterfeit.

Bias. Sir, we are all abused,
As many as were brought on to be suitors;
And we will join in thanks all to the captain,
And to his fortune that so brought us off. [*Exeunt.*

Dam. This was a pitiful poor shift of your poet, boy, to make his prime woman with child, and fall in labour, just to compose a quarrel,
Boy. *With whose borrowed ears have you heard, sir, all this while.*

that you can mistake the current of our scene so? The stream of the argument threatened her being with child from the very beginning; for it presented her in the first of the second act with some apparent note of infirmity or defect, from knowledge of which the auditory were rightly to be suspended by the author, till the quarrel, which was but the accidental cause, hastened on the discovery of it, in occasioning her affright, which made her fall into her throes presently, and within that compass of time allowed to the comedy: wherein the poet exprest his prime artifice, rather than any error, that the detection of her being with child should determine the quarrel, which had produced it.

Pro. The boy is too hard for you, brother Damplay; best mark the play, and let him alone.

Dam. I care not for marking the play; I'll damn it, talk, and do that I come for. I will not have gentlemen lose their privilege, nor I myself my prerogative, for never an overgrown or superannuated poet of them all. He shall not give me the law: I will censure and be witty, and take my tobacco, and enjoy my *Magna Charta* of reprehension, as my predecessors have done before me.

Boy. Even to license and absurdity.

Pro. Not now, because the gentlewoman is in travail, and the midwife may come on the sooner, to put her and us out of our pain.

Dam. Well, look to your business afterward, boy, that all things be clear, and come properly forth, suited and set together; for I will search what follows severely, and to the nail.

Boy. Let your nail run smooth then, and not scratch, lest the author be bold to pare it to the quick, and make it smart: you'll find him as severe as yourself.

Dam. A shrewd boy, and has me every where! The midwife is come, she has made haste.

ACT IV

SCENE I.—*A Room in* Lady LOADSTONE's *House.*

Enter Mother CHAIR *and* NEEDLE.

Chair. Stay, master Needle, you do prick too fast
Upon the business, I must take some breath;
Lend me my stool; you have drawn a stitch upon me,
In faith, son Needle, with your haste.

Nee. Good mother,
Piece up this breach; I'll give you a new gown,
A new silk grogoran gown: I'll do it, mother.

Enter Nurse KEEP.

Keep. What will you do! you have done too much already,
With your prick-seam, and through-stitch, master Needle.
I pray you sit not fabling here old tales,
Good mother Chair, the midwife, but come up.
[*Exeunt Chair and Needle.*

Enter COMPASS *and* PRACTICE.

Com. How now, Nurse! where's my lady?
Keep. In her chamber,
Lock'd up, I think: she'll speak with nobody.
   Com. Knows she of this accident?
   Keep. Alas, sir, no:
Would she might never know it!   [*Exit.*
   Prac. I think her ladyship
Too virtuous, and too nobly innocent,
To have a hand in so ill-form'd a business.
   Com. Your thought, sir, is a brave thought, and a safe one:
The child now to be born is not more free
From the aspersion of all spot than she.
She have her hand in a plot 'gainst master Practice,
If there were nothing else, whom she so loves,
Cries up, and values! knows to be a man
Mark'd out for a chief justice in his cradle,
Or a lord paramount, the head of the hall,
The top, or the top-gallant of our law!
Assure yourself she could not so deprave
The rectitude of her judgment, to wish you
Unto a wife might prove your infamy,
Whom she esteem'd that part of the commonwealth,
And had [raised] up for honour to her blood.
   Prac. I must confess a great beholdingness
Unto her ladyship's offer, and good wishes:
But the truth is, I never had affection,
Or any liking to this niece of hers.
   Com. You foresaw somewhat then?
   Prac. I had my notes,
And my prognostics.
   Com. You read almanacs,
And study them to some purpose, I believe.
   Prac. I do confess I do believe, and pray too,
According to the planets, at some times.
   Com. And do observe the sign in making love?
   Prac. As in phlebotomy.
   Com. And choose your mistress
By the good days, and leave her by the bad?
   Prac. I do and I do not.
   Com. A little more
Would fetch all his astronomy from Allestree.
   Prac. I tell you, master Compass, as my friend,
And under seal, I cast my eyes long since
Upon the other wench, my lady's woman,
Another manner of piece for handsomeness,
Than is the niece: but that is *sub sigillo*,
And as I give it you, in hope of your aid

And counsel in the business.

   Com. You need counsel!
The only famous counsel of the kingdom,
And in all courts! That is a jeer in faith,
Worthy your name, and your profession too,
Sharp master Practice.

   Prac. No, upon my law,
As I am a bencher, and now double reader,
I meant in mere simplicity of request.

   Com. If you meant so, the affairs are now perplex'd,
And full of trouble; give them breath and settling,
I'll do my best. But in mean time do you
Prepare the parson.—I am glad to know
This; for myself liked the young maid before,
And loved her too. [*Aside.*]—Have you a license?

   Prac. No;
But I can fetch one straight.

   Com. Do, do, and mind
The parson's pint, to engage him [in] the business;
A knitting cup there must be.

   Prac. I shall do it.   [*Exit.*

Enter BIAS *and* SIR MOTH INTEREST.

   Bias. 'Tis an affront from you, sir; you here brought me
Unto my lady's, and to woo a wife,
Which since is proved a crack'd commodity:
She hath broke bulk too soon.

   Sir Moth. No fault of mine,
If she be crack'd in pieces, or broke round:
It was my sister's fault that owns the house
Where she hath got her clap, makes all this noise.
I keep her portion safe, that is not scatter'd;
The monies rattle not, nor are they thrown,
To make a muss yet, 'mong the gamesome suitors.

   Com. Can you endure that flout, close master Bias,
And have been so bred in the politics?
The injury is done you, and by him only:
He lent you imprest money, and upbraids it;
Furnish'd you for the wooing, and now waves you.

   Bias. That makes me to expostulate the wrong
So with him, and resent it as I do.

   Com. But do it home then.

   Bias. Sir, my lord shall know it.

   Com. And all the lords of the court too.

   Bias. What a Moth
You are, sir Interest!

   Sir Moth. Wherein, I entreat you,
Sweet master Bias?

   Com. To draw in young statesmen,

And heirs of policy into the noose
Of an infamous matrimony.

 Bias. Yes,
Infamous, *quasi in communem famam:*
And matrimony, *quasi* matter of money.

 Com. Learnedly urged, my cunning master Bias.

 Bias. With his lewd known and prostituted niece.

 Sir Moth. My *known* and *prostitute !* how you mistake,
And run upon a false ground, master Bias!
Your lords will do me right. Now she is prostitute,
And that I know it, please you understand me,
I mean to keep the portion in my hands,
And pay no monies.

 Com. Mark you that, don Bias?
And you shall still remain in bonds to him,
For wooing furniture, and imprest charges.

 Sir Moth. Good master Compass, for the sums he has had
Of me, I do acquit him; they are his own:
Here, before you, I do release him.

 Com. Good!

 Bias. O sir—

 Com. 'Slid, take it; I do witness it:
He cannot hurl away his money better.

 Sir Moth. He shall get so much, sir, by my acquaintance,
To be my friend; and now report to his lords
As I deserve, no otherwise.

 Com. But well;
And I will witness it, and to the value:
Four hundred is the price, if I mistake not,
Of your true friend in court. Take hands, you have bought him,
And bought him cheap.

 Bias. I am his worship's servant.

 Com. And you his slave, sir Moth, seal'd and deliver'd.
Have you not studied the court-compliment?—

[Exeunt Sir Moth and Bias.

Here are a pair of HUMOURS RECONCILED now,
That money held at distance, or their thoughts,
Baser than money.

Enter POLISH, driving in Nurse KEEP.

 Pol. Out, thou caitiff witch,
Bawd, beggar, gipsey; any thing, indeed,
But honest woman!

 Keep. What you please, dame Polish,
My lady's stroker.

 Com. What is here to do!
The gossips out!

 Pol. Thou art a traitor to me,   [*Aside.*
An Eve, the apple, and the serpent too:

A viper, that hast eat a passage through me,
Through mine own bowels, by thy recklessness.

Com. What frantic fit is this? I'll step aside,
And hearken to it.   [*Retires.*

Pol. Did I trust thee, wretch,
With such a secret, of that consequence,
Did so concern me, and my child, our livelihood,
And reputation! and hast thou undone us,
By thy connivance, nodding in a corner,
And suffering her be got with child so basely?
Sleepy, unlucky hag!—thou bird of night,
And all mischance to me!

Keep. Good lady empress,
Had I the keeping of your daughter's clicket
In charge, was that committed to my trust?

Com. Her daughter!   [*Aside.*

Pol. Softly, devil, not so loud:
You'd have the house hear and be witness, would you?

Keep. Let all the world be witness: afore I'll
Endure the tyranny of such a tongue,
And such a pride—

Pol. What will you do?

Keep. Tell truth,
And shame the she-man-devil in puff'd sleeves;
Run any hazard, by revealing all
Unto my lady; how you changed the cradles,
And changed the children in them.

Pol. Not so high!

Keep. Calling your daughter Pleasance there Placentia,
And my true mistress by the name of Pleasance.

Com. A horrid secret this; worth the discovery.

Pol. And must you be thus loud?

Keep. I will be louder,
And cry it through the house, through every room,
And every office of the laundry-maids,
Till it be borne hot to my lady's ears:
Ere I will live in such a slavery,
I'll do away myself.

Pol. Didst thou not swear
To keep it secret! And upon what book?—
I do remember now, *The Practice of Piety.*

Keep. It was a practice of impiety,
Out of your wicked forge, I know it now,
My conscience tells me: first, against the infants,
To rob them of their names and their true parents;
To abuse the neighbourhood, keep them in error;
But most my lady; she has the main wrong,
And I will let her know it instantly.
Repentance, if it be true, ne'er comes too late.   [*Exit.*

Pol. What have I done? conjured a spirit up,
I shall not lay again! drawn on a danger
And ruin on myself thus, by provoking
A peevish fool, whom nothing will pray off
Or satisfy, I fear! her patience stirr'd,
Is turn'd to fury. I have run my bark
On a sweet rock, by mine own arts and trust;
And must get off again, or dash in pieces.   [*Exit.*

Com. [*coming forward.*] This was a business worth the listening
    after.

Enter PLEASANCE.

Plea. O master Compass, did you see my mother?
Mistress Placentia, my lady's niece,
Is newly brought to bed of the bravest boy!
Will you go see it?
    Com. First, I'll know the father,
Ere I approach these hazards.
    Plea. Mistress midwife
Has promised to find out a father for it,
If there be need.
    Com. She may the safelier do it,
By virtue of her place.—But, pretty Pleasance,
I have a news for you I think will please you.
    Plea. What is it, master Compass?
    Com. Stay, you must
Deserve it ere you know it. Where's my lady?
    Plea. Retired unto her chamber, and shut up.
    Com. She hears of none of this yet? Well, do you
Command the coach, and fit yourself to travel
A little way with me.
    Plea. Whither, for God's sake?
    Com. Where I'll entreat you not to your loss, believe it,
If you dare trust yourself.
    Plea. With you the world o'er.
    Com. The news will well requite the pains, I assure you,
And in this tumult you will not be miss'd.
Command the coach, it is an instant business,
Will not be done without you.   [*Exit Pleasance.*

Enter PALATE.

                    Parson Palate!
Most opportunely met; step to my chamber;
I'll come to you presently: there is a friend
Or two will entertain you.   [*Exit Palate.*

Enter PRACTICE.

                    Master Practice,
Have you the license?
    Prac. Here it is.

Com. Let's see it:
Your name's not in it.
   Prac. I'll fill that presently.
It has the seal, which is the main, and register'd;
The clerk knows me, and trusts me.
   Com. Have you the parson?
   Prac. They say he's here, he 'pointed to come hither.
   Com. I would not have him seen here for a world,
To breed suspicion.   Do you intercept him,
And prevent that.   But take your license with you,
And fill the blank; or leave it here with me,
I'll do it for you: stay you for us at his church,
Behind the Old Exchange, we'll come in the coach,
And meet you there within this quarter at least.
   Prac. I am much bound unto you, master Compass;
You have all the law and parts of squire Practice
For ever at your use.   I'll tell you news too:
Sir, your reversion's fallen; Thinwit's dead,
Surveyor of the projects general.
   Com. When died he?
   Prac. Even this morning; I received it
From a right hand.
   Com. Conceal it, master Practice,
And mind the main affair you are in hand with.   [*Exit Practice.*

Re-enter PLEASANCE.

Plea. The coach is ready, sir.
   Com. 'Tis well, fair Pleasance,
Though now we shall not use it; bid the coachman
Drive to the parish church, and stay about there,
Till master Practice come to him, and employ him.
                         [*Exit Pleasance.*
I have a license now, which must have entry
Before my lawyer's.—

Re-enter PALATE.

Noble parson Palate,
Thou shalt be a mark advanced; here is a piece, [*Gives him money.*
And do a feat for me.
   Pal. What, master Compass?
   Com. But run the words of matrimony over
My head and mistress Pleasance's in my chamber;
There's captain Ironside to be a witness,
And here's a license to secure thee.—Parson,
What do you stick at?
   Pal. It is afternoon, sir;
Directly against the canon of the church:
You know it, master Compass: and beside,
I am engaged unto your worshipful friend,

The learned master Practice, in that business.
Com. Come on, engage yourself: who shall be able
To say you married us but in the morning,
The most canonical minute of the day,
If you affirm it? That's a spiced excuse,
And shews you have set the canon law before
Any profession else, of love or friendship.

Re-enter PLEASANCE.

Come, mistress Pleasance, we cannot prevail
With the rigid Parson here; but, sir, I'll keep you
Lock'd in my lodging, till't be done elsewhere,
And under fear of Ironside.
Pal. Do you hear, sir?
Com. No, no, it matters not.
Pal. Can you think, sir,
I would deny you any thing, not to loss
Of both my livings? I will do it for you;
Have you a wedding ring?
Com. Ay, and a posie:
Annulus hic nobis, quod sic uterque, dabit.
Pal. Good!
This ring will give you what you both desire.
I'll make the whole house chant it, and the parish.
Com. Why, well said, parson. Now, to you my news,
That comprehend my reasons, mistress Pleasance.   [*Exeunt.*

SCENE II.—*Another Room in the same.*

Enter Mother CHAIR *with a child,* POLISH, KEEP, *and* NEEDLE.

Chair. Go, get a nurse, procure her at what rate
You can; and out of the house with it, son Needle;
It is a bad commodity.
Nee. Good mother,
I know it, but the best would now be made on't.
                    [*Exit with the child.*
Chair. And shall. You should not fret so, mistress Polish,
Nor you, dame Keep; my daughter shall do well,
When she has ta'en my caudle. I have known
Twenty such breaches pieced up and made whole,
Without a bum of noise. You two fall out,
And tear up one another!
Pol. Blessed woman!
Blest be the peace-maker!
Keep. The pease-dresser!
I'll hear no peace from her. I have been wrong'd,
So has my lady, my good lady's worship,
And I will right her, hoping she'll right me.
Pol. Good gentle Keep, I pray thee, mistress nurse,

Pardon my passion, I was misadvised;
Be thou yet better, by this grave sage woman,
Who is the mother of matrons and great persons,
And knows the world.

   Keep. I do confess, she knows
Something—and I know something—

   Pol. Put your somethings
Together then.

   Chair. Ay, here's a chance fallen out
You cannot help; less can this gentlewoman;
I can, and will, for both. First, I have sent
By-chop away; the cause gone, the fame ceaseth.
Then by my caudle and my cullice, I set
My daughter on her feet, about the house here;
She's young, and must stir somewhat for necessity,
Her youth will bear it out. She shall pretend
To have had a fit o' the mother; there is all.
If you have but a secretary laundress,
To blanch the linen—Take the former counsels
Into you; keep them safe in your own breasts,
And make your market of them at the highest.
Will you go peach, and cry yourself a fool
At grannam's cross! be laugh'd at and despised!
Betray a purpose, which the deputy
Of a double ward, or scarce his alderman,
With twelve of the wisest questmen could find out,
Employed by the authority of the city!
Come, come, be friends; and keep these women-matters,
Smock-secrets to ourselves, in our own verge:
We shall mar all, if once we ope the mysteries
Of the tiring-house, and tell what's done within.
No theatres are more cheated with appearances,
Or these shop-lights, than the ages, and folk in them,
That seem most curious.

   Pol. Breath of an oracle!
You shall be my dear mother; wisest woman
That ever tipp'd her tongue with point of reasons,
To turn her hearers! Mistress Keep, relent,
I did abuse thee; I confess to penance,
And on my knees ask thee forgiveness.   [*Kneels.*

   Chair. Rise,
She doth begin to melt, I see it.

   Keep. Nothing
Grieved me so much as when you call'd me bawd:
Witch did not trouble me, nor gipsey; no,
Nor beggar: but a bawd was such a name!

   Chair. No more rehearsals; repetitions
Make things the worse: the more we stir—you know
The proverb, and it signifies—a stink.

What's done and dead, let it be buried:
New hours will fit fresh handles to new thoughts.   [*Exeunt.*

SCENE III.—*Another Room in the same.*

Enter Sir MOTH INTEREST *and* Servant.

Sir Moth. Run to the church, sirrah; get all the drunkards
To ring the bells, and jangle them for joy:
My niece has brought an heir unto the house,
A lusty boy! [*Exit Servant.*]   Where is my sister Loadstone?—

Enter Lady LOADSTONE.

Asleep at afternoons! it is not wholesome;
Against all rules of physic, lady sister.
The little doctor will not like it.   Our niece
Is new deliver'd of a chopping child,
Can call the father by the name already,
If it but ope the mouth round.   Master Compass,
He is the man, they say, fame gives it out,
Hath done that act of honour to our house,
And friendship, to pump out a son and heir
That shall inherit nothing, surely nothing
From me, at least.

Enter COMPASS.

                    I come to invite your ladyship
To be a witness; I will be your partner,
And give it a horn spoon, and a treen-dish,
Bastard, and beggar's badges, with a blanket
For dame the doxy to march round the circuit,
With bag and baggage.
    Com. Thou malicious knight,
Envious sir Moth, that eats on that which feeds thee,
And frets her goodness that sustains thy being!
What company of mankind would own thy brotherhood,
But as thou hast a title to her blood,
Whom thy ill-nature hath chose out t' insult on,
And vex thus, for an accident in her house,
As if it were her crime, good innocent lady!
Thou shew'st thyself a true corroding vermin,
Such as thou art.
    Sir Moth. Why, gentle master Compass?
Because I wish you joy of your young son,
And heir to the house, you have sent us?
    Com. I have sent you!
I know not what I shall do.   Come in, friends:

Enter IRONSIDE, Sir DIAPHANOUS SILKWORM, PALATE, *and*
PLEASANCE.

Madam, I pray you be pleased to trust yourself
Unto our company.
    Lady L. I did that too late;
Which brought on this calamity upon me,
With all the infamy I hear; your soldier,
That swaggering guest.
    Com. Who is return'd here to you,
Your vowed friend and servant; comes to sup with you,
(So we do all,) and will prove he hath deserv'd
That special respect and favour from you,
As not your fortunes, with yourself to boot,
Cast on a feather-bed, and spread on the sheets
Under a brace of your best Persian carpets,
Were scarce a price to thank his happy merit.
    Sir Moth. What impudence is this! can you endure
To hear it, sister?
    Com. Yes, and you shall hear it,
Who will endure it worse. What deserves he,
In your opinion, madam, or weigh'd judgment,
That, things thus hanging as they do in doubt,
Suspended and suspected, all involv'd,
And wrapt in error, can resolve the knot?
Redintegrate the fame first of your house,
Restore your ladyship's quiet, render then
Your niece a virgin and unvitiated,
And make all plain and perfect as it was,
A practice to betray you, and your name?
    Sir Moth. He speaks impossibilities.
    Com. Here he stands,
Whose fortune hath done this, and you must thank him.
To what you call his swaggering, we owe all this:
And that it may have credit with you, madam,
Here is your niece, whom I have married, witness
These gentlemen, the knight, captain, and parson,
And this grave politic tell-troth of the court.
    Lady L. What's she that I call niece then?
    Com. Polish's daughter:
Her mother, goody Polish, has confess'd it
To grannam Keep, the nurse, how they did change
The children in their cradles.
    Lady L. To what purpose?
    Com. To get the portion, or some part of it,
Which you must now disburse entire to me, sir,
If I but gain her ladyship's consent.
    Lady L. I bid God give you joy, if this be true.
    Com. *As true it is lady, lady,* in the song.

The Magnetic Lady

The portion's mine, with interest, sir Moth;
I will not bate you a single Harrington,
Of interest upon interest: In mean time,
I do commit you to the guard of Ironside,
My brother here, captain Rudhudibrass;
From whom I will expect you or your ransom.

Sir Moth. Sir, you must prove it, and the possibility,
Ere I believe it.

Com. For the possibility,
I leave to trial.

Enter PRACTICE.

Truth shall speak itself.
O, master Practice, did you meet the coach?

Prac. Yes, sir, but empty.

Com. Why, I sent it for you.
The business is dispatch'd here ere you come:
Come in, I'll tell you how; you are a man
Will look for satisfaction, and must have it.

All. So we do all, and long to hear the right. [*Exeunt.*

Dam. Troth, I am one of those that labour with the same longing, for it is almost pucker'd, and pulled into that knot by your poet, which I cannot easily, with all the strength of my imagination, untie.

Boy. Like enough, nor is it in your office to be troubled or perplexed with it, but to sit still, and expect. The more your imagination busies itself the more it is intangled, especially if (as I told in the beginning) you happen on the wrong end.

Pro. He hath said sufficient, brother Damplay: our parts that are the spectators, or should hear a comedy, are to wait the process and events of things, as the poet presents them, not as we would corruptly fashion them. We come here to behold plays, and censure them, as they are made, and fitted for us; not to beslave our own thoughts, with censorious spittle tempering the poet's clay, as we were to mould every scene anew: that were a mere plastic or potter's ambition, most unbecoming the name of a gentleman. No, let us mark, and not lose the business on foot, by talking. Follow the right thread, or find it.

Dam. Why, here his play might have ended, if he would have let it; and have spared us the vexation of a fifth act yet to come, which every one here knows the issue of already, or may in part conjecture.

Boy. That conjecture is a kind of figure-flinging, or throwing the dice, for a meaning was never in the poet's purpose perhaps. Stay, and see his last act, his catastrophe, how he will perplex that, or spring some fresh cheat, to entertain the spectators, with a convenient delight, till some unexpected and new encounter break out to rectify all, and make good the conclusion.

Pro. Which ending here, would have shown dull, flat, and unpointed: without any shape or sharpness, brother Damplay.

Dam. Well, let us expect then: and wit be with us, on the poet's part.

ACT V

SCENE I.—*A Room in* Lady LOADSTONE's *House.*

Enter NEEDLE *and* ITEM.

Nee. Troth, master Item, here's a house divided,
And quarter'd into parts, by your doctor's ingine.
He has cast out such aspersions on my lady's
Niece here, of having had a child; as hardly
Will be wiped off, I doubt.
  Item. Why, is't not true?
  Nee. True! did you think it?
  Item. Was she not in labour,
The midwife sent for?
  Nee. There's your error now!
You have drunk of the same water.
  Item. I believed it,
And gave it out too.
  Nee. More you wrong'd the party;
She had no such thing about her, innocent creature!
  Item. What had she then?
  Nee. Only a fit of the mother:
They burnt old shoes, goose-feathers, assafœtida,
A few horn-shavings, with a bone or two,
And she is well again, about the house.
  Item. Is't possible?
  Nee. See it, and then report it.
  Item. Our doctor's urinal judgment is half-crack'd then.
  Nee. Crack'd in the case most hugely with my lady,
And sad sir Moth, her brother; who is now
Under a cloud a little.
  Item. Of what? disgrace?
  Nee. He is committed to Rudhudibrass,
The captain Ironside, upon displeasure,
From master Compass; but it will blow off.
  Item. The doctor shall reverse this instantly,
And set all right again; if you'll assist
But in a toy, squire Needle, comes in my noddle now.
  Nee. Good! Needle and noddle! what may't be? I long for't.
  Item. Why, but to go to bed, feign a distemper,
Of walking in your sleep, or talking in't
A little idly, but so much, as on it
The doctor may have ground to raise a cure
For his reputation.
  Nee. Any thing, to serve
The worship of the man I love and honour.   [*Exeunt.*

SCENE II.—*Another Room in the same.*

Enter POLISH *and* PLEASANCE.

Pol. O! give you joy, mademoiselle Compass,
You are his whirlpool now: all-to-be-married,
Against your mother's leave, and without counsel!
He has fish'd fair, and caught a frog, I fear it.
What fortune have you to bring him in dower?
You can tell stories now; you know a world
Of secrets to discover.
 Plea. I know nothing
But what is told me, nor can I discover
Any thing.
 Pol. No, you shall not, I'll take order.
Go, get you in there: [*Exit Pleasance.*] It is Ember-week,
I'll keep you fasting from his flesh awhile.

Enter CHAIR *and* KEEP *with* PLACENTIA.

 Chair. See who is here! she has been with my lady,
Who kist her, all-to-be-kist her, twice or thrice.
 Keep. And call'd her niece again, and view'd her linen.
 Pol. You have done a miracle, mother Chair.
 Chair. Not I,
My caudle has done it: thank my caudle heartily.
 Pol. It shall be thank'd, and you too, wisest mother;
You shall have a new, brave, four-pound beaver hat,
Set with enamell'd studs, as mine is here;
And a right pair of crystal spectacles,
Crystal o' the rock, thou mighty mother of dames!
Hung in an ivory case, at a gold belt;
And silver bells to gingle, as you pace
Before your fifty daughters in procession
To church, or from the church.
 Chair. Thanks, mistress Polish.
 Keep. She does deserve as many pensions
As there be pieces in a—maiden-head,
Were I a prince to give them.
 Pol. Come, sweet charge,
You shall present yourself about the house;
Be confident, and bear up; you shall be seen.   [*Exeunt.*

SCENE III.—*Another Room in the same.*

Enter COMPASS, IRONSIDE, *and* PRACTICE.

 Com. What! I can make you amends, my learned counsel,
And satisfy a greater injury
To chafed master Practice. Who would think
That you could be thus testy?
 Iron. A grave head,

Given over to the study of our laws.

    Com. And the prime honours of the commonwealth.

    Iron. And you to mind a wife!

    Com. What should you do
With such a toy as a wife, that might distract you,
Or hinder you in your course?

    Iron. He shall not think on't.

    Com. I will make over to you my possession
Of that same place is fall'n, you know, to satisfy;
Surveyor of the projects general.

    Iron. And that's an office you know how to stir in.

    Com. And make your profits of.

    Iron. Which are indeed
The ends of a gown'd man: shew your activity,
And how you are built for business.

    Prac. I accept it
As a possession, be it but a reversion.

    Com. You first told me 'twas a possession.

    Prac. Ay,
I told you that I heard so.

    Iron. All is one,
He'll make a reversion a possession quickly.

    Com. But I must have a general release from you.

    Prac. Do one, I'll do the other.

    Com. It's a match,
Before my brother Ironside.

    Prac. 'Tis done.

    Com. We two are RECONCILED then.

    Iron. To a lawyer,
That can make use of a place, any half title
Is better than a wife.

    Com. And will save charges
Of coaches, vellute gowns, and cut-work smocks.

    Iron. He is to occupy an office wholly.

    Com. True; I must talk with you nearer, master Practice,
About recovery of my wife's portion,
What way I were best to take.

    Prac. The plainest way.

    Com. What's that, for plainness?

    Prac. Sue him at common law:
Arrest him on an action of choke-bail,
Five hundred thousand pound; it will affright him,
And all his sureties. You can prove your marriage?

    Com. Yes.
We'll talk of it within, and hear my lady.   *[Exeunt.*

SCENE IV.—*Another Room in the same.*

Enter Sir MOTH INTEREST, *and* Lady LOADSTONE.

Sir Moth. I am sure the vogue of the house went all that way;
She was with child, and master Compass got it.

Lady L. Why, that, you see, is manifestly false;
He has married the other, our true niece, he says,
He would not woo them both: he is not such
A stallion, to leap all.   Again, no child
Appears, that I can find with all my search,
And strictest way of inquiry, I have made
Through all my family.   A fit of the mother,
The women say she had, which the midwife cured,
With burning bones and feathers.

Enter RUT.

Here's the doctor.
Sir Moth. O, noble doctor, did not you and your Item
Tell me our niece was in labour?

Rut. If I did,
What follows?

Sir Moth. And that mother Midnight
Was sent for?

Rut. So she was, and is in the house still.

Sir Moth. But here has a noise been since, she was deliver'd
Of a brave boy, and master Compass's getting.

Rut. I know no rattle of gossips, nor their noises:
I hope you take not me for a pimp-errant,
To deal in smock affairs.   Where is the patient,
The infirm man I was sent for, squire Needle?

Lady L. Is Needle sick?

Rut. My pothecary tells me
He is in danger—

Enter ITEM.

How is it, Tim? where is he?
Item. I cannot hold him down.   He is up and walks,
And talks, in his perfect sleep, with his eyes shut,
As sensibly as he were broad awake.
See, here he comes; he's fast asleep, observe him.

Enter NEEDLE, *followed by* POLISH, CHAIR, KEEP, *and* PLACENTIA.

Rut. He'll tell us wonders.   What do these women here,
Hunting a man half naked? you are fine beagles,
You'd have his doucets!

Nee. I have linen breeks on.

Rut. He hears, but he sees nothing.

Nee. Yes, I see
Who hides the treasure yonder.

Sir Moth. Ha! what treasure?

Rut. If you ask questions, he wakes presently,
And then you'll hear no more till his next fit.

Nee. And whom she hides it for.

Rut. Do you mark, sir, list.

Nee. A fine she spirit it is, an Indian magpye.
She was an alderman's widow, and fell in love
With our sir Moth, my lady's brother.

Rut. Hear you?

Nee. And she has hid an alderman's estate,
Dropt through her bill, in little holes, in the garden,
And scrapes earth over them; where none can spy
But I, who see all by the glow-worm's light,
That creeps before.   [*Exeunt Needle, Chair, Keep, and Placentia.*

Pol. I knew the gentlewoman,
Alderman Parrot's widow, a fine speaker,
As any was in the clothing, or the bevy;
She did become her scarlet and black velvet,
Her green and purple—

Rut. Save thy colours, rainbow!
Or she will run thee o'er, and all thy lights.

Pol. She dwelt in Do-little-lane, a top o' the hill there,
In the round cage was after sir Chime Squirrel's:
She would eat nought but almonds, I assure you.

Rut. Would thou hadst a dose of pills, a double dose,
Of the best purge to make thee turn tail t'other way!

Pol. You are a foul-mouth'd, purging, absurd doctor;
I tell you true, and I did long to tell it you.
You have spread a scandal in my lady's house here,
On her sweet niece, you never can take off
With all your purges, or your plaister of oaths;
Though you distil your damn-me, drop by drop,
In your defence.   That she hath had a child,
Here she doth spit upon thee, and defy thee,
Or I do't for her!

Rut. Madam, pray you bind her
To her behaviour: tie your gossip up,
Or send her unto Bethlem.

Pol. Go thou thither,
That better hast deserv'd it, shame of doctors!
Where could she be deliver'd? by what charm,
Restored to her strength so soon? who is the father,
Or where the infant? ask your oracle,
That walks and talks in his sleep.

Rut. Where is he gone?
You have lost a fortune, listening to her tabor.

[*Aside to Sir Moth.*

Good madam, lock her up.

Lady L. You must give losers

Their leave to speak, good doctor.

Rut. Follow his footing
Before he get to his bed; this rest is lost else.

          [Exeunt Rut and Sir Moth.

Enter COMPASS, PRACTICE, *and* IRONSIDE.

Com. Where is my wife? what have you done with my wife,
Gossip of the counsels?

Pol. I, sweet master Compass!
I honour you and your wife.

Com. Well, do so still?
I will not call you mother though, but Polish.
Good gossip Polish, where have you hid my wife?

Pol. I hide your wife!

Com. Or she is run away.

Lady L. That would make all suspected, sir, afresh:
Come, we will find her if she be in the house.

Pol. Why should I hide your wife, good master Compass?

Com. I know no cause, but that you are goody Polish,
That's good at malice, good at mischief, all
That can perplex or trouble a business thoroughly.

Pol. You may say what you will; you are master Compass,
And carry a large sweep, sir, in your circle.

Lady L. I'll sweep all corners, gossip, to spring this,
If't be above ground. I will have her cried
By the common-crier, thorough all the ward,
But I will find her.

Iron. It will be an act
Worthy your justice, madam.

Prac. And become
The integrity and worship of her name.   *[Exeunt.*

SCENE V.—*Another Room in the same.*

Enter RUT *and* Sir MOTH INTEREST.

Rut. 'Tis such a fly, this gossip, with her buz,
She blows on every thing, in every place!

Sir Moth. A busy woman is a fearful grievance!
Will he not sleep again?

Rut. Yes, instantly,
As soon as he is warm. It is the nature
Of the disease, and all these cold dry fumes
That are melancholic, to work at first,
Slow and insensibly in their ascent;
Till being got up, and then distilling down
Upon the brain, they have a pricking quality
That breeds this restless rest, which we, the sons
Of physic, call a walking in the sleep,
And telling mysteries, that must be heard

Softly, with art, as we were sewing pillows
Under the patient's elbows; else they'd fly
Into a phrensy, run into the woods,
Where there are noises, huntings, shoutings, hallowings,
Amidst the brakes and furzes, over bridges
Fall into waters, scratch their flesh, sometimes
Drop down a precipice, and there be lost.

Enter ITEM.

How now! what does he?
  Item. He is up again,
And 'gins to talk.
  Sir Moth. Of the former matter, Item?
  Item. The treasure and the lady, that's his argument.
  Sir Moth. O me, [most] happy man! he cannot off it:
I shall know all then.
  Rut. With what appetite
Our own desires delude us! [*Aside.*]—Hear you, Tim,
Let no man interrupt us.
  Item. Sir Diaphanous
And master Bias, his court-friends, desire
To kiss his niece's hands, and gratulate
The firm recovery of her good fame
And honour.
  Sir Moth. Good! Say to them, master Item,
My niece is on my lady's side; they'll find her there.
I pray to be but spared for half an hour:
I'll see them presently.
  Rut. Do, put them off, Tim,
And tell them the importance of the business.
Here, he is come! sooth; and have all out of him.

Enter NEEDLE, *talking as in his sleep.*

  Nee. How do you, lady-bird? so hard at work, still!
What's that you say? do you bid me walk, sweet bird,
And tell your knight? I will, How! *walk, knave, walk!*
I think you're angry with me, Pol. Fine Pol!
Pol is a fine bird! O find lady Pol!
Almond for Parrot. Parrot's a brave bird.
Three hundred thousand pieces have you stuck
Edge-long into the ground, within the garden?
O bounteous bird!
  Sir Moth. And me most happy creature!
  Rut. Smother your joy.
  Nee. How! and dropp'd twice so many—
  Sir Moth. Ha! where?
  Rut. Contain yourself.
  Nee. In the old well?
  Sir Moth. I cannot, I am a man of flesh and blood:

Who can contain himself, to hear the ghost
Of a dead lady do such works as these,
And a city lady too of the strait waist?

    Nee. I will go try the truth of it.   [*Exit.*

    Rut. He's gone.

Follow him, Tim; see what he does.   [*Exit Item.*]   If he bring you

A say of it now!—

    Sir Moth. I'll say he's a rare fellow,

And has a rare disease.

    Rut. And I will work

As rare a cure upon him.

    Sir Moth. How, good doctor?

    Rut. When he hath utter'd all that you would know of him,

I'll cleanse him with a pill as small as a pease,

And stop his mouth: for there his issue lies,

Between the muscles of the tongue.

Re-enter ITEM.

    Sir Moth. He's come.

    Rut. What did he, Item?

    Item. The first step he stept

Into the garden, he pull'd these five pieces

Up, in a finger's breadth one of another:

The dirt sticks on them still.

    Sir Moth. I know enough.

Doctor, proceed with your cure, I'll make thee famous,

Famous among the sons of the physicians,

Machaon, Podalirius, Esculapius.

Thou shalt have a golden beard, as well as he had;

And thy Tim Item here, have one of silver;

A livery beard! and all thy pothecaries

Belong to thee.—Where is squire Needle? gone?

    Item. He is prick'd away, now he has done the work.

    Rut. Prepare his pill, and give it him afore supper. [*Exit Item.*

    Sir Moth. I'll send for a dozen of labourers to-morrow,

To turn the surface of the garden up.

    Rut. In mold! bruise every clod.

    Sir Moth. And have all sifted,

For I'll not lose a piece of the bird's bounty;

And take an inventory of all.

    Rut. And then,

I would go down into the well—

    Sir Moth. Myself;

No trusting other hands: six hundred thousand,

To the first three; nine hundred thousand pound—

    Rut. 'Twill purchase the whole bench of aldermanity,

Stript to their shirts.

    Sir Moth. There never did accrue

So great a gift to man, and from a lady

I never saw but once: now I remember,
We met at Merchant-tailors'-hall, at dinner,
In Threadneedle-street.

Rut. Which was a sign squire Needle
Should have the threading of this thread.

Sir Moth. 'Tis true;
I shall love parrots better while I know him.

Rut. I'd have her statue cut now in white marble.

Sir Moth. And have it painted in most orient colours.

Rut. That's right! all city statues must be painted,
Else they be worth nought in their subtle judgments.

Enter BIAS.

Sir Moth. My truest friend in court, dear master Bias!
You hear of the recovery of our niece
In fame and credit?

Bias. Yes, I have been with her,
And gratulated to her; but I am sorry
To find the author of the foul aspersion
Here in your company, this insolent doctor.

Sir Moth. You do mistake him; he is clear got off on't:
A gossip's jealousy first gave the hint.
He drives another way now as I would have him;
He's a rare man, the doctor, in his way.
He has done the noblest cure here in the house,
On a poor squire, my sister's tailor, Needle,
That talk'd in's sleep; would walk to St. John's-wood,
And Waltham-forest, scape by all the ponds
And pits in the way; run over two-inch bridges,
With his eyes fast, and in the dead of night!—
I'll have you better acquainted with him. Doctor,
Here is my dear, dear, dearest friend in court,
Wise, powerful master Bias; pray you salute
Each other, not as strangers, but true friends.

Rut. This is the gentleman you brought to-day,
A suitor to your niece.

Sir Moth. Yes.

Rut. You were
Agreed, I heard; the writings drawn between you.

Sir Moth. And seal'd.

Rut. What broke you off?

Sir Moth. This rumour of her:
Was it not, master Bias?

Bias. Which I find
Now false, and therefore come to make amends
In the first place. I stand to the old conditions.

Rut. Faith, give them him, sir Moth, whate'er they were.
You have a brave occasion now to cross
The flanting master Compass, who pretends

Right to the portion, by the other intail.
  Sir Moth. And claims it. You do hear he's married?
  Bias. We hear his wife is run away from him,
Within: she is not to be found in the house,
With all the hue and cry is made for her
Through every room; the larders have been search'd,
The bake-houses and boulting tub, the ovens,
Wash-house and brew-house, nay the very furnace,
And yet she is not heard of.
  Sir Moth. Be she ne'er heard of,
The safety of Great Britain lies not on't.
You are content with the ten thousand pound,
Defalking the four hundred garnish-money?
That's the condition here, afore the doctor,
And your demand, friend Bias?
  Bias. It is, sir Moth.

Enter PALATE.

  Rut. Here comes the parson then, shall make all sure.
  Sir Moth. Go you with my friend Bias, parson Palate,
Unto my niece; assure them we are agreed.
  Pal. And mistress Compass too is found within.
  Sir Moth. Where was she hid?
  Pal. In an old bottle-house,
Where they scraped trenchers ; there her mother had thrust her.
  Rut. You shall have time, sir, to triumph on him,
When this fine feat is done, and his Rud-Ironside.   [*Exeunt.*

SCENE VI.—Another Room in the same.

Enter COMPASS, Lady LOADSTONE, PRACTICE, POLISH, CHAIR,
and KEEP.

  Com. Was ever any gentlewoman used
So barbarously by a malicious gossip,
Pretending to be mother to her too?
  Pol. Pretending! sir, I am her mother, and challenge
A right and power for what I have done.
  Com. Out, hag!
Thou that hast put all nature off, and woman,
For sordid gain, betray'd the trust committed
Unto thee by the dead, as from the living;
Changed the poor innocent infants in their cradles;
Defrauded them of their parents, changed their names,
Calling Placentia, Pleasance: Pleasance, Placentia.
  Pol. How knows he this?   [*Aside.*
  Com. Abused the neighbourhood;
But most this lady: didst enforce an oath
To this poor woman, on a pious book,
To keep close thy impiety.

Pol. Have you told this?   [*Aside to the Nurse.*
Keep. I told it! no, he knows it, and much more,
As he's a cunning man.
Pol. A cunning fool,
If that be all.
Com. But now to your true daughter,
That had the child, and is the proper Pleasance,
We must have an account of that too, gossip.
Pol. This is like all the rest of master Compass.

Enter RUT, *running.*

Rut. Help, help, for charity! sir Moth Interest
Is fallen into the well.
Lady L. Where, where?
Rut. In the garden.
A rope to save his life!
Com. How came he here?
Rut. He thought to take possession of a fortune
There newly dropt him, and the old chain broke,
And down fell he in the bucket.
Com. Is it deep?
Rut. We cannot tell.   A rope, help with a rope!

Enter Sir DIAPHANOUS SILKWORM, IRONSIDE, ITEM, *and* NEEDLE, *leading in* Sir MOTH INTEREST.

Sir Dia. He is got out again.   The knight is saved.
Iron. A little soused in the water; Needle saved him.
Item. The water saved him, 'twas a fair escape.
Nee. Have you no hurt?
Sir Moth. A little wet.
Nee. That's nothing.
Rut. I wish'd you stay, sir, till to-morrow; and told you
It was no lucky hour: since six o'clock
All stars were retrograde.
Lady L. In the name
Of fate or folly, how came you in the bucket?
Sir Moth. That is a *quære* of another time, sister;
The doctor will resolve you—who hath done
The admirablest cure upon your Needle!
Give me thy hand, good Needle; thou cam'st timely.
Take off my hood and coat; and let me shake
Myself a little.   I have a world of business.
Where is my nephew Bias? and his wife?

Enter BIAS *and* PLACENTIA.

Who bids God give them joy? here they both stand,
As sure affianced as the parson, or words,
Can tie them.
Rut. We all wish them joy and happiness.

Sir Dia. I saw the contract, and can witness it.

Sir Moth. He shall receive ten thousand pounds to-morrow.
You look'd for't, Compass, or a greater sum,
But 'tis disposed of, this, another way:
I have but one niece, verily, [master] Compass.

Enter a Serjeant.

Com. I'll find another.—Varlet, do your office.

Serj. I do arrest your body, sir Moth Interest,
In the king's name; at suit of master Compass,
And dame Placentia his wife. The action's enter'd,
Five hundred thousand pound.

Sir Moth. Hear you this, sister?
And hath your house the ears to hear it too,
And to resound the affront?

Lady L. I cannot stop
The laws, or hinder justice: I can be
Your bail, if it may be taken.

Com. With the captain's,
I ask no better.

Rut. Here are better men,
Will give their bail.

Com. But yours will not be taken,
Worshipful doctor; you are good security
For a suit of clothes to the tailor that dares trust you:
But not for such a sum as is this action.—
Varlet, you know my mind.

Serj. You must to prison, sir,
Unless you can find bail the creditor likes.

Sir Moth. I would fain find it, if you'd shew me where.

Sir Dia. It is a terrible action; more indeed
Than many a man is worth; and is call'd Fright-bail.

Iron. Faith, I will bail him at mine own apperil.
Varlet, begone: I'll once have the reputation,
To be security for such a sum.
Bear up, sir Moth.

Rut. He is not worth the buckles
About his belt, and yet this Ironside clashes!

Sir Moth. Peace, lest he hear you, doctor; we'll make use of him.
What doth your brother Compass, captain Ironside,
Demand of us, by way of challenge, thus?

Iron. Your niece's portion; in the right of his wife.

Sir Moth. I have assured one portion to one niece,
And have no more to account for, that I know of:
What I may do in charity—if my sister
Will bid an offering for her maid and him,
As a benevolence to them, after supper,
I'll spit into the bason, and entreat
My friends to do the like.

Com. Spit out thy gall,
And heart, thou viper! I will now no mercy,
No pity of thee, thy false niece, and Needle;

Enter PLEASANCE.

Bring forth your child, or I appeal you of murder,
You, and this gossip here, and mother Chair.
    Chair. The gentleman's fallen mad!
    Plea. No, mistress midwife.
I saw the child, and you did give it me,
And put it in my arms; by this ill token,
You wish'd me such another; and it cried.
    Prac. The law is plain; if it were heard to cry,
And you produce it not, he may indict
All that conceal it, of felony and murder.
    Com. And I will take the boldness, sir, to do it,
Beginning with sir Moth here, and his doctor.
    Sir Dia. Good faith, this same is like to turn a business.
    Pal. And a shrewd business, marry; they all start at it.
    Com. I have the right thread now, and I will keep it.
You, goody Keep, confess the truth to my lady,
The truth, the whole truth, nothing but the truth.
    Pol. I scorn to be prevented of my glories.
I plotted the deceit, and I will own it.
Love to my child, and lucre of the portion
Provoked me; wherein, though the event hath fail'd
In part, I will make use of the best side.
This is my daughter, [*points to Placentia.*] and she hath had a child
This day, unto her shame, I now profess it,
By this mere false stick, squire Needle; but
Since this wise knight hath thought it good to change
The foolish father of it, by assuring
Her to his dear friend, master Bias; and him
Again to her, by clapping of him on
With his free promise of ten thousand pound,
Afore so many witnesses—
    Sir Dia. Whereof I
Am one.
    Pal. And I another.
    Pol. I should be unnatural
To my own flesh and blood, would I not thank him.—
I thank you, sir; and I have reason for it.
For here your true niece stands, fine mistress Compass,
(I'll tell you truth, you have deserv'd it from me,)
To whom you are by bond engaged to pay
The sixteen thousand pound, which is her portion,
Due to her husband, on her marriage-day.
I speak the truth, and nothing but the truth.
    Iron. You'll pay it now, sir Moth, with interest:

You see the truth breaks out on every side of you.

Sir Moth. Into what nets of cozenage am I cast
On every side! each thread is grown a noose,
A very mesh: I have run myself into
A double brake, of paying twice the money.

Bias. You shall be released of paying me a penny,
With these conditions.

Pol. Will you leave her then?

Bias. Yes, and the sum twice told, ere take a wife,
To pick out monsieur Needle's basting-threads.

Com. Gossip, you are paid: though he be a fit nature,
Worthy to have a whore justly put on him;
He is not bad enough to take your daughter,
On such a cheat.   Will you yet pay the portion?

Sir Moth. What will you bate?

Com. No penny the law gives.

Sir Moth. Yes, Bias's money.

Com. What, your friend in court!
I will not rob you of him, nor the purchase,
Nor your dear doctor here; stand all together,
Birds of a nature all, and of a feather.

Lady L. Well, we are all now reconciled to truth.
There rests yet a gratuity from me,
To be conferr'd upon this gentleman;
Who, as my nephew Compass says, was cause
First of the offence, but since of all the amends.
The quarrel caused the affright, that fright brought on
The travail, which made peace; the peace drew on
This new discovery, which endeth all
In RECONCILEMENT.

Com. When the portion
Is tender'd, and received.

Sir Moth. Well, you must have it;
As good at first as last.

Lady L. 'Tis well said, brother.
And I, if this good captain will accept me,
Give him myself, endow him with my estate,
And make him lord of me, and all my fortunes:
He that hath saved my honour, though by chance,
I'll really study his, and how to thank him.

Iron. And I embrace you, lady, and your goodness,
And vow to quit all thought of war hereafter;
Save what is fought under your colours, madam.

Pal. More work then for the parson; I shall cap
The Loadstone with an Ironside, I see.

Iron. And take in these, the forlorn couple, with us,
Needle and his Thread, whose portion I will think on;
As being a business waiting on my bounty:
Thus I do take possession of you, madam,
My true MAGNETIC mistress, and my LADY.   [*Exeunt.*

CHORUS

CHANGED INTO AN EPILOGUE TO THE KING.

Well, gentlemen, I now must, under seal,
And the author's charge, wave you, and make my appeal
To the supremest power, my lord the king;
Who best can judge of what we humbly bring.
He knows our weakness, and the poet's faults;
Where he doth stand upright, go firm, or halts;
And he will doom him.   To which voice he stands,
And prefers that, 'fore all the people's hands.

A TALE OF A TUB

DRAMATIS PERSONÆ

CHANON (Canon) HUGH, *Vicar of Pancras, and* CAPTAIN THUMS.

SQUIRE TUB, *or* TRIPOLY, *of Totten-Court.*

BASKET - HILTS, *his Man and Governor.*

JUSTICE PREAMBLE, *alias* BRAMBLE, *of Maribone.*

MILES METAPHOR, *his Clerk.*

POL MARTIN, *Huisher to* LADY TUB.

TOBIE TURFE, *High Constable of Kentish-Town.*

JOHN CLAY, *of Kilborn, Tilemaker, the Bridegroom.*

IN-AND-IN MEDLAY, *of Islington, Cooper and Headborough.*

RASI' CLENCH, *of Hamstead, Farrier and Petty Constable.*

TO-PAN, *Tinker, or Metal-Man of Belsise, Thirdborough.*

DIOGENES SCRIBEN, *of Chalcot, the great Writer.*

HANNIBAL (Ball) PUPPY, *the High Constable's Man.*

FATHER ROSIN, *the Minstrel, and his two Boys.*

BLACK JACK, *Lady* TUB'S *Butler.*

LADY TUB, *of Totten, the Squire's Mother.*

DIDO WISPE, *her Woman.*

SIBIL TURFE, *Wife to the High Constable.*

AWDREY TURFE, *her Daughter, the Bride.*

JOAN, JOYCE, MADGE, PARNEL, GRISEL, *and* KATE, *Maids of the Bridal.*

Servants.

SCENE.—FINSBURY HUNDRED

PROLOGUE.

No state-affairs, nor any politic club,
Pretend we in our Tale, here, of a Tub:
But acts of clowns and constables, to-day
Stuff out the scenes of our ridiculous play.
A cooper's wit, or some such busy spark,
Illumining the high constable, and his clerk,
And all the neighbourhood, from old records,
Of antique proverbs, drawn from Whitson-lords
And their authorities, at Wakes and Ales,
With country precedents, and old wives' tales,
We bring you now, to shew what different things
The cotes of clowns are from the courts of kings

ACT I

SCENE I.—*Totten-Court.*—*Before* Lady TUB's *House.*

Enter Canon HUGH.

Hugh. Now on my faith, old bishop Valentine,
You have brought us nipping weather.—*Februere*
Doth cut and shear—your day and diocese
Are very cold. All your parishioners,
As well your laics as your quiristers,
Had need to keep to their warm feather beds,
If they be sped of loves: this is no season,
To seek new makes in; though sir Hugh of Pancras
Be hither come to Totten, on intelligence,
To the young lord of the manor, 'squire Tripoly.
On such an errand as a mistress is.
What, 'squire! I say.—[*Calls.*] Tub I should call him too:
Sir Peter Tub was his father, a saltpetre-man;
Who left his mother, lady Tub of Totten-
Court, here, to revel, and keep open house in;
With the young 'squire her son, and's governor Basket-
Hilts, both by sword and dagger: [*Calls again.*] *Domine*
Armiger Tub, 'squire Tripoly! *Expergiscere!*
I dare not call aloud lest she should hear me,
And think I conjured up the spirit, her son,
In priest's lack-Latin: O she is jealous
Of all mankind for him.

   Tub. [*appears at the window.*] Canon, is't you?
   Hugh. The vicar of Pancras, 'squire Tub! wa'hoh!
   Tub. I come, I stoop unto the call, sir Hugh!
   Hugh. He knows my lure is from his love, fair Awdrey,
The high constable's daughter of Kentish-town here, master
Tobias Turfe.

Enter TUB *in his night-gown.*

   Tub. What news of him?
   Hugh. He has waked me
An hour before I would, sir; and my duty
To the young worship of Totten-Court, 'squire Tripoly!
Who hath my heart, as I have his: Your mistress
Is to be made away from you this morning,
St. Valentine's day: there are a knot of clowns,
The council of Finsbury, so they are styled,
Met at her father's; all the wise of the hundred;
Old Rasi' Clench of Hamstead, petty constable,
In-and-In Medlay, cooper of Islington,
And headborough; with loud To-Pan, the tinker
Or metal-man of Belsise, the thirdborough;

And D'ogenes Scriben, the great writer of Chalcot.

Tub. And why all these?

Hugh. Sir, to conclude in council,
A husband or a make for mistress Awdrey;
Whom they have named and pricked down, Clay of Kilborn,
A tough young fellow, and a tilemaker.

Tub. And what must he do?

Hugh. Cover her, they say;
And keep her warm, sir: mistress Awdrey Turfe,
Last night did draw him for her Valentine;
Which chance, it hath so taken her father and mother,
(Because themselves drew so on Valentine's eve
Was thirty year,) as they will have her married
To-day by any means; they have sent a messenger
To Kilborn, post, for Clay; which when I knew,
I posted with the like to worshipful Tripoly,
The 'squire of Totten: and my advice to cross it.

Tub. What is't, sir Hugh?

Hugh. Where is your governor Hilts?
Basket must do it.

Tub. Basket shall be call'd.—
Hilts! can you see to rise?   [*Aloud.*

Hilts. [*appears at the window.*] Cham not blind, sir,
With too much light.

Tub. Open your t'other eye,
And view if it be day.

Hilts. Che can spy that
At's little a hole as another, through a milstone.   [*Exit above.*

Tub. He will have the last word, though he talk bilk for't.

Hugh. Bilk! what's that?

Tub. Why, nothing: a word signifying
Nothing; and borrowed here to express nothing.

Hugh. A fine device!

Tub. Yes, till we hear a finer.
What's your device now, canon Hugh?

Hugh. In private,
Lend it your ear; I will not trust the air with it,
Or scarce my shirt; my cassock shall not know it;
If I thought it did I'd burn it.

Tub. That's the way,
You have thought to get a new one, Hugh: is't worth it?
Let's hear it first.

Hugh. Then hearken, and receive it.   [*Whispers him.*
This 'tis, sir. Do you relish it?

      Enter HILTS, *and walks by, making himself ready.*

Tub. If Hilts
Be close enough to carry it; there's all.

Hilts. It is no sand, nor butter-milk: if it be,
Ich'am no zive, or watering-pot, to draw

Knots i' your 'casions. If you trust me, zo;
If not, praform it your zelves. Cham no man's wife,
But resolute Hilts: you'll vind me in the buttry.   *[Exit.*

   Tub. A testy, but a tender clown as wool,
And melting as the weather in a thaw!
He'll weep you like all April; but he'll roar you
Like middle March afore: he will be as mellow,
And tipsy too, as October; and as grave
And bound up like a frost (with the new year)
In January; as rigid as he is rustic.

   Hugh. You know his nature, and describe it well;
I'll leave him to your fashioning.

   Tub. Stay, sir Hugh;
Take a good angel with you for your guide;
                [Gives him a piece of money.
And let this guard you homeward, as the blessing
To our device.   *[Exit.*

   Hugh. I thank you, 'squire's worship,
Most humbly—for the next: for this I am sure of.
O for a quire of these voices, now,
To chime in a man's pocket, and cry chink!
One doth not chirp, it makes no harmony.
Grave justice Bramble next must contribute;
His charity must offer at this wedding:
I'll bid more to the bason and the bride-ale,
Although but one can bear away the bride.
I smile to think how like a lottery
These weddings are. Clay hath her in possession,
The 'squire he hopes to circumvent the Tile-kin;
And now, if justice Bramble do come off,
'Tis two to one but Tub may lose his bottom.   *[Exit.*

   SCENE II.—*Kentish-Town.*—*A Room in* TURFE'S *House.*

   Enter CLENCH, MEDLAY, D'OGE SCRIBEN, BALL, PUPPY,
         and PAN.

   Clench. Why, it is thirty year, e'en as this day now,
Zin Valentine's day, of all days kursin'd, look you;
And the zame day o' the month as this Zin Valentine,
Or I am vowly deceived—

   Med. That our high constable,
Master Tobias Turfe, and his dame were married:
I think you are right. But what was that Zin Valentine?
Did you ever know 'un, goodman Clench?

   Clench. Zin Valentine!
He was a deadly zin, and dwelt at Highgate,
As I have heard; but 'twas avore my time:
He was a cooper too, as you are, Medlay,
An In-and-In: a woundy brag young vellow,

As the 'port went o' hun then, and in those days.

Scri. Did he not write his name Sim Valentine?
Vor I have met no Sin in Finsbury books;
And yet I have writ them six or seven times over.

Pan. O you mun look for the nine deadly Sins,
In the church-books, D'oge: not [in] the high constable's;
Nor in the county's: zure, that same zin Valentine,
He was a stately zin, an' he were a zin,
And kept brave house.

Clench. At the Cock-and-Hen in Highgate.
You have fresh'd my memory well in't, neighbour Pan:
He had a place in last king Harry's time,
Of sorting all the young couples; joining them,
And putting them together; which is yet
Praform'd, as on his day—zin Valentine:
As being the zin of the shire, or the whole county:
I am old Rivet still, and bear a brain,
The Clench, the varrier, and true leach of Hamstead.

Pan. You are a shrew antiquity, neighbour Clench,
And a great guide to all the parishes!
The very bell-weather of the hundred, here,
As I may zay. Master Tobias Turfe,
High constable, would not miss you, for a score on us,
When he do 'scourse of the great charty to us.

Pup. What's that, a horse? can 'scourse nought but a horse,
And that in Smithveld. Charty! I ne'er read o' hun,
In the old Fabian's chronicles; nor I think
In any new: he may be a giant there,
For aught I know.

Scri. You should do well to study
Records, fellow Ball, both law and poetry.

Pup. Why, all's but writing and reading, is it, Scriben?
An it be any more, it is mere cheating zure,
Vlat cheating; all your law and poets too.

Pan. Master high constable comes.

Enter TURFE.

Pup. I'll zay't afore hun.

Turfe. What's that makes you all so merry and loud, sirs, ha?
I could have heard you to my privy walk.

Clench. A contrevarsie 'twixt two learned men here:
Hannibal Puppy says that law and poetry
Are both flat cheating; all's but writing and reading,
He says, be't verse or prose.

Turfe. I think in conzience,
He do zay true: who is't do thwart 'un, ha?

Med. Why, my friend Scriben, an it please your worship.

Turfe. Who, D'oge, my D'ogenes? a great writer, marry!
He'll vace me down [sirs,] me myself sometimes,

That verse goes upon veet, as you and I do:
But I can gi' 'un the hearing; zit me down,
And laugh at 'un; and to myself conclude,
The greatest clerks are not the wisest men
Ever.   Here they are both! what, sirs, disputing,
And holding arguments of verse and prose,
And no green thing afore the door, that shews,
Or speaks a wedding!
   Scri. Those were verses now,
Your worship spake, and run upon vive veet.
   Turfe. Feet, vrom my mouth, D'oge! leave your 'zurd upinions,
And get me in some boughs.
   Scri. Let them have leaves first.
There's nothing green but bays and rosemary.
   Pup. And they are too good for strewings, your maids say.
   Turfe. You take up 'dority still to vouch against me.
All the twelve smocks in the house, zure, are your authors.
Get some fresh hay then, to lay under foot;
Some holly and ivy to make vine the posts:
Is't not zon Valentine's day, and mistress Awdrey,
Your young dame, to be married?   [*Exit Puppy.*]   I wonder Clay
Should be so tedious? he's to play son Valentine:
And the clown sluggard is not come fro' Kilborn yet!
   Med. Do you call your son-in-law clown, an't please your worship?
   Turfe. Yes and vor worship too, my neighbour Medlay,
A Middlesex clown, and one of Finsbury.
They were the first colons of the kingdom here,
The primitory colons, my Diogenes says,
Where's D'ogenes, my writer, now?   What were those
You told me, D'ogenes, were the first colons
Of the country, that the Romans brought in here?
   Scri. The *coloni,* sir; *colonus* is an inhabitant,
A clown original: as you'd say, a farmer,
A tiller of the earth, e'er since the Romans
Planted their colony first; which was in Middlesex.
   Turfe. Why so!   I thank you heartily, good Diogenes,
You ha' zertified me.   I had rather be
An ancient colon, (as they say,) a clown of Middlesex,
A good rich farmer, or high constable.
I'd play hun 'gain a knight, or a good 'squire,
Or gentleman of any other county
In the kingdom.
   Pan. Outcept Kent, for there they landed
All gentlemen, and came in with the conqueror,
Mad Julius Cæsar, who built Dover-castle:
My ancestor To-Pan, beat the first kettle-drum
Avore 'hun, here vrom Dover on the march.
Which piece of monumental copper hangs
Up, scour'd, at Hammersmith yet; for there they came

Over the Thames, at a low water-mark;
Vore either London, ay, or Kingston-bridge,
I doubt, were kursin'd.

Re-enter PUPPY *with* JOHN CLAY.

Turfe. Zee, who is here: John Clay!
Zon Valentine, and bridegroom! have you zeen
Your Valentine-bride yet, sin' you came, John Clay?
  Clay. No, wusse. Che lighted I but now in the yard,
Puppy has scarce unswaddled my legs yet.
  Turfe. What, wisps on your wedding-day, zon! this is right
Originous Clay, and Clay o' Kilborn too!
I would ha' had boots on this day, zure, zon John.
  Clay. I did it to save charges: we mun dance,
On this day, zure; and who can dance in boots?
No, I got on my best straw-colour'd stockings,
And swaddled them over to zave charges, I.
  Turfe. And his new chamois doublet too with points!
I like that yet: and his long sausage-hose,
Like the commander of four smoking tile-kilns,
Which he is captain of, captain of Kilborn;
Clay with his hat turn'd up o' the leer side too,
As if he would leap my daughter yet ere night,
And spring a new Turfe to the old house!—

Enter JOYCE, JOAN, *and the other* Maids, *with ribands, rosemary,
and bay for the bride-men.*

Look! an the wenches ha' not found 'un out,
And do prazent 'un with a van of rosemary,
And bays, to vill a bow-pot, trim the head
Of my best vore-horse! we shall all ha' bride-laces,
Or points, I zee; my daughter will be valiant,
And prove a very Mary Ambry in the business.
  Clench. They zaid your worship had 'sured her to 'squire Tub
Of Totten-Court here; all the hundred rings on't.
  Turfe. A TALE OF A TUB, sir, a mere Tale of a Tub.
Lend it no ear, I pray you: the 'squire Tub
Is a fine man, but he is too fine a man,
And has a lady Tub too to his mother;
I'll deal with none of these fine silken Tubs:
John Clay and cloth-breech for my money and daughter.
Here comes another old boy too vor his colours,

Enter ROSIN, *and his two* Boys.

Will stroak down my wive's udder of purses, empty
Of all her milk-money this winter quarter:
Old father Rosin, the chief minstrel here,
Chief minstrel too of Highgate, she has hired him
And all his two boys for a day and a half;

And now they come for ribanding and rosemary:
Give them enough, girls, give them enough, and take it
Out in his tunes anon.

   Clench. I'll have *Tom Tiler*,
For our John Clay's sake, and the tile-kilns, zure.

   Med. And I the *Jolly Joiner* for mine own sake.

   Pan. I'll have the *Jovial Tinker* for To-Pan's sake.

   Turfe. We'll all be jovy this day vor son Valentine,
My sweet son John's sake.

   Scri. There's another reading now:
My master reads it Son and not Sin Valentine.

   Pup. Nor Zim: and he's in the right; he is high constable,
And who should read above 'un, or avore hun?

   Turfe. Son John shall bid us welcome all, this day;
We'll zerve under his colours: lead the troop, John,
And Puppy, see the bells ring. Press all noises
Of Finsbury, in our name: Diogenes Scriben
Shall draw a score of warrants vor the business.
Does any wight perzent hir majesty's person
This hundred, 'bove the high constable?

   All. No, no.

   Turfe. Use our authority then to the utmost on't. [*Exeunt.*

SCENE III.—*Maribone.*—*A Room in* Justice PREAMBLE'S
House.

Enter Canon HUGH *and* Justice PREAMBLE.

   Hugh. So you are sure, sir, to prevent them all,
And throw a block in the bridegroom's way, John Clay,
That he will hardly leap o'er.

   Pre. I conceive you,
Sir Hugh; as if your rhetoric would say,
Whereas the father of her is a Turfe,
A very superficies of the earth;
He aims no higher than to match in clay,
And there hath pitch'd his rest.

   Hugh. Right, justice Bramble;
You have the winding wit, compassing all.

   Pre. Subtle sir Hugh, you now are in the wrong,
And err with the whole neighbourhood, I must tell you,
For you mistake my name. Justice Preamble
I write myself; which, with the ignorant clowns here,
Because of my profession of the law,
And place of the peace, is taken to be Bramble:
But all my warrants, sir, do run Preamble,
Richard Preamble.

   Hugh. Sir, I thank you for it,
That your good worship would not let me run
Longer in error, but would take me up thus.

Pre. You are my learned and canonic neighbour,
I would not have you stray; but the incorrigible
Nott-headed beast, the clowns, or constables,
Still let them graze, eat sallads, chew the cud:
All the town music will not move a log.
    Hugh. The beetle and wedges will where you will have them.
    Pre. True, true, sir Hugh.—

Enter METAPHOR.

                            Here comes Miles Metaphor,
My clerk; he is the man shall carry it, canon,
By my instructions.
    Hugh. He will do it *ad unguem*,
Miles Metaphor! he is a pretty fellow.
    Pre. I love not to keep shadows, or half-wits,
To foil a business.—Metaphor, you have seen
A king ride forth in state.
    Met. Sir, that I have:
King Edward our late liege, and sovereign lord;
And have set down the pomp.
    Pre. Therefore I ask'd you.
Have you observ'd the messengers of the chamber,
What habits they were in?
    Met. Yes, minor coats,
Unto the guard, a dragon and a greyhound,
For the supporters of the arms.
    Pre. Well mark'd!
You know not any of them?
    Met. Here's one dwells
In Maribone.
    Pre. Have you acquaintance with him,
To borrow his coat an hour?
    Hugh. Or but his badge,
'Twill serve; a little thing he wears on his breast.
    Pre. His coat, I say, is of more authority:
Borrow his coat for an hour.   I do love
To do all things completely, canon Hugh;
Borrow his coat, Miles Metaphor, or nothing.
    Met. The taberd of his office I will call it,
Or the coat-armour of his place; and so
Insinuate with him by that trope.
    Pre. I know
Your powers of rhetoric, Metaphor.   Fetch him off
In a fine figure for his coat, I say.   [*Exit Metaphor.*
    Hugh. I'll take my leave, sir, of your worship too,
Because I may expect the issue anon.
    Pre. Stay, my diviner counsel, take your fee:
We that take fees, allow them to our counsel;
And our prime learned counsel, double fees.

There are a brace of angels to support you
In your foot-walk this frost, for fear of falling,
Or spraying of a point of matrimony,
When you come at it—
   Hugh. In your worship's service:
That the exploit is done, and you possess
Of mistress Awdrey Turfe.—
   Pre. I like your project.   [*Exit.*
   Hugh. And I, of this effect of two to one;
It worketh in my pocket, 'gainst the 'squire,
And his half bottom here, of half a piece,
Which was not worth the stepping o'er the stile for:
His mother has quite marr'd him, lady Tub,
She's such a vessel of fæces: all dried earth,
Terra damnata! not a drop of salt,
Or petre in her! all her nitre is gone.   [*Exit.*

SCENE IV.—*Totten-Court.*—*Before* Lady Tub's *House.*

Enter Lady Tub *and* Pol Martin.

   Lady T. Is the nag ready, Martin? call the 'squire,
This frosty morning we will take the air,
About the fields; for I do mean to be
Somebody's Valentine, in my velvet gown,
This morning, though it be but a beggar-man.
Why stand you still, and do not call my son?
   Pol. Madam, if he had couched with the lamb,
He had no doubt been stirring with the lark:
But he sat up at play, and watch'd the cock,
Till his first warning chid him off to rest.
Late watchers are no early wakers, madam:
But if your ladyship will have him call'd—
   Lady T. Will have him call'd! wherefore did I, sir, bid him
Be call'd, you weazel, vermin of an huisher?
You will return your wit to your first stile
Of Martin Polecat, by these stinking tricks,
If you do use them; I shall no more call you
Pol Martin, by the title of a gentleman,
If you go on thus.
   Pol. I am gone.   [*Exit.*
   Lady T. Be quick then,
In your come off; and make amends, you stote!
Was ever such a fulmart for an huisher,
To a great worshipful lady, as myself!
Who, when I heard his name first, Martin Polecat,
A stinking name, and not to be pronounced
In any lady's presence without a reverence;
My very heart e'en yearn'd, seeing the fellow
Young, pretty, and handsome; being then, I say,

A basket-carrier, and a man condemn'd
To the salt-petre works; made it my suit
To master Peter Tub, that I might change it;
And call him as I do now, by Pol Martin,
To have it sound like a gentleman in an office,
And made him mine own foreman, daily waiter.
And he to serve me thus! ingratitude,
Beyond the coarseness yet of any clownage,
Shewn to a lady!—

Re-enter POL MARTIN.

                    What now, is he stirring?
Pol. Stirring betimes out of his bed, and ready.
Lady T. And comes he then?
Pol. No, madam, he is gone.
Lady T. Gone! whither?   Ask the porter where is he gone.
  Pol. I met the porter, and have ask'd him for him;
He says, he let him forth an hour ago.
  Lady T. An hour ago! what business could he have
So early; where is his man, grave Basket-hilts,
His guide and governor?
  Pol. Gone with his master.
  Lady T. Is he gone too!   O that same surly knave
Is his right-hand; and leads my son amiss.
He has carried him to some drinking match or other.
Pol Martin,—I will call you so again,
I am friends with you now—go, get your horse and ride
To all the towns about here, where his haunts are,
And cross the fields to meet, and bring me word;
He cannot be gone far, being a-foot.
Be curious to inquire him: and bid Wispe,
My woman, come, and wait on me.   [*Exit Pol.*]   The love
We mothers bear our sons we have brought with pain,
Makes us oft view them with too careful eyes,
And overlook them with a jealous fear,
Out-fitting mothers.

Enter DIDO WISPE.

  Lady T. How now, Wispe! have you
A Valentine yet?   I am taking the air to choose one.
  Wispe. Fate send your ladyship a fit one then.
  Lady T. What kind of one is that?
  Wispe. A proper man
To please your ladyship.
  Lady T. Out of that vanity
That takes the foolish eye! any poor creature,
Whose want may need my alms or courtesy,
I rather wish; so bishop Valentine
Left us example to do deeds of charity;

To feed the hungry, clothe the naked, visit
The weak and sick; to entertain the poor,
And give the dead a Christian funeral;
These were the works of piety he did practise,
And bade us imitate; not look for lovers,
Or handsome images to please our senses.—
I pray thee, Wispe, deal freely with me now,
We are alone, and may be merry a little:
Thou art none of the court glories, nor the wonders
For wit or beauty in the city; tell me,
What man would satisfy thy present fancy,
Had thy ambition leave to choose a Valentine,
Within the queen's dominion, so a subject?
   Wispe. You have given me a large scope, madam, I confess,
And I will deal with your ladyship sincerely;
I'll utter my whole heart to you.   I would have him
The bravest, richest, and the properest, man
A tailor could make up; or all the poets,
With the perfumers: I would have him such,
As not another woman but should spite me;
Three city ladies should run mad for him,
And country madams infinite.
   Lady T. You would spare me,
And let me hold my wits?
   Wispe. I should with you,
For the young 'squire, my master's sake, dispense
A little, but it should be very little.
Then all the court-wives I'd have jealous of me,
As all their husbands jealous too of them;
And not a lawyer's puss of any quality,
But lick her lips for a snatch in the term-time.
   Lady T. Come,
Let's walk; we'll hear the rest as we go on:
You are this morning in a good vein, Dido;
Would I could be as merry!   My son's absence
Troubles me not a little, though I seek
These ways to put it off; which will not help:
Care that is entered once into the breast,
Will have the whole possession ere it rest.
                                         [Exeunt.

ACT II

SCENE I.—*The Fields near* PANCRAS.

Enter, in procession, with ribands, rosemary and bay, TURFE, CLAY,
MEDLAY, CLENCH, TO-PAN, SCRIBEN, *and* PUPPY *with the bride-
cake, as going to church.*

Turfe. Zon Clay, cheer up, the better leg avore,
This is a veat is once done, and no more.
   Clench. And then 'tis done vor ever, as they say.
   Med. Right! vor a man has his hour, and a dog his day.
   Turfe. True, neighbour Medlay, you are still In-and-In.
   Med. I would be, master constable, if che could win.
   Pan. I zay, John Clay keep still on his old gate:
Wedding and hanging both go at a rate.
   Turfe. Well said, To-Pan; you have still the hap to hit
The nail o' the head at a close: I think there never
Marriage was managed with a more avisement,
Than was this marriage, though I say it that should not;
Especially 'gain mine own flesh and blood,
My wedded wife.   Indeed my wife would ha' had
All the young batchelors, and maids forsooth,
Of the zix parishes hereabouts; but I
Cried *none, sweet Sybil; none of that gear, I:*
It would lick zalt, I told her, by her leave.
No, three or vour our wise, choice, honest neighbours,
Ubstantial persons, men that have born office,
And mine own family would be enough
To eat our dinner.   What! dear meat's a thief;
I know it by the butchers and the market-volk.
Hum drum, I cry.   No half ox in a pye:
A man that's bid to a bride-ale, if he have cake
And drink enough, he need not vear his stake.
   Clench. 'Tis right; he has spoke as true as a gun, believe it.

Enter Dame TURFE *and* AWDREY, *followed by* JOAN, JOYCE, MADGE,
PARNEL, GRISEL, *and* KATE, *dressed for the wedding.*

Turfe. Come, Sybil, come; did not I tell you o' this,
This pride and muster of women would mar all?
Six women to one daughter, and a mother!
The queen (God save her) ha' no more herself.
   Dame T. Why, if you keep so many, master Turfe,
Why should not all present our service to her?
   Turfe. Your service! good! I think you'll write to her shortly,
Your very loving and obedient mother.
Come, send your maids off, I will have them sent
Home again, wife; I love no trains of Kent,
Or Christendom, as they say.

Joyce. We will not back,
And leave our dame.

Madge. Why should her worship lack
Her tail of maids, more than you do of men?

Turfe. What, mutining, Madge?

Joan. Zend back your clowns agen,
And we will vollow.

All. Else we'll guard our dame.

Turfe. I ha' zet the nest of wasps all on a flame.

Dame T. Come, you are such another, master Turfe,
A clod you should be call'd, of a high constable:
To let no music go afore your child
To church, to chear her heart up this cold morning!

Turfe. You are for father Rosin and his consort
Of Fiddling boys, the great Feates and the less;
Because you have entertain'd them all from Highgate.
To shew your pomp, you'd have your daughters and maids
Dance o'er the fields like faies to church, this frost.
I'll have no rondels, I, in the queen's paths;
Let 'em scrape the gut at home, where they have fill'd it,
At afternoon.

Dame T. I'll have them play at dinner.

Clench. She is in the right, sir; vor your wedding-dinner
Is starv'd without the music.

Med. If the pies
Come not in piping hot, you have lost that proverb.

Turfe. I yield to truth: wife, are you sussified?

Pan. A right good man! when he knows right, he loves it.

Scri. And he will know't and shew't too by his place
Of being high constable, if no where else.

Enter HILTS, *with a false beard, booted and spurred.*

Hilts. Well overtaken, gentlemen! I pray you
Which is the queen's high constable among you?

Pup. The tallest man; who should be else, do you think?

Hilts. It is no matter what I think, young clown;
Your answer savours of the cart.

Pup. How! *cart*
And *clown!* do you know whose team you speak to?

Hilts. No, nor I care not: Whose jade may you be?

Pup. Jade! cart! and *clown!* O for a lash of whip-cord,
Three-knotted cord!

Hilts. Do you mutter! sir, snorle this way,
That I may hear, and answer what you say,
With my school-dagger 'bout your costard, sir.
Look to't, young growse: I'll lay it on, and sure;
Take't off who wull.   [*Draws his sword.*

Clench. Nay, 'pray you, gentleman—

Hilts. Go to, I will not bate him an ace on't.
What rowly-powly, maple face! all fellows!

Pup. Do you hear, friend? I would wish you, for your good,
Tie up your brended bitch there, your dun, rusty,
Pannier-hilt poniard; and not vex the youth
With shewing the teeth of it. We now are going
To church in way of matrimony, some on us;
They ha' rung all in a' ready. If it had not,
All the horn-beasts are grazing in this close
Should not have pull'd me hence, till this ash-plant
Had rung noon on your pate, master Broombeard.

Hilts. That I would fain zee, quoth the blind George
Of Holloway: come, sir.

Awd. O their naked weapons!

Pan. For the passion of man, hold gentleman and Puppy.

Clay. Murder, O murder!

Awd. O my father and mother!

Dame T. Husband, what do you mean? son Clay, for God's
sake—

Turfe. I charge you in the queen's name, keep the peace.

Hilts. Tell me o' no queen or keysar; I must have
A leg or a hanch of him ere I go.

Med. But, zir,
You must obey the queen's high officers.

Hilts. Why must I, goodman Must?

Med. You must an' you wull.

Turfe. Gentlemen, I am here for fault, high constable—

Hilts. Are you zo! what then?

Turfe. I pray you, sir, put up
Your weapons; do, at my request: for him,
On my authority, he shall lie by the heels,
Verbatim continente, an I live.

Dame T. Out on him for a knave, what a dead fright
He has put me into! come, Awdrey, do not shake.

Awd. But is not Puppy hurt, nor the t'other man?

Clay. No bun? but had not I cried murder, I wuss—

Pup. Sweet goodman Clench, I pray you revise my master,
I may not zit in the stocks till the wedding be past,
Dame, mistress Awdrey: I shall break the bride-cake else.

Clench. Zomething must be to save authority, Puppy.

Dame T. Husband—

Clench. And gossip—

Awd. Father—

Turfe. 'Treat me not,
It is in vain. If he lie not by the heels,
I'll lie there for 'un; I will teach the hind
To carry a tongue in his head to his superiors.

Hilts. This's a wise constable! where keeps he school?

Clench. In Kentish-town; a very servere man.

Hilts. But, as servere as he is, let me, sir, tell him
He shall not lay his man by the heels for this.

This was my quarrel; and by his office' leave,
If it carry 'un for this, it shall carry double;
Vor he shall carry me too.

 Turfe. Breath of man!
He is my chattel, mine own hired goods:
An if you do abet 'un in this matter,
I'll clap you both by the heels, ankle to ankle.

 Hilts. You'll clap a dog of wax as soon, old Blurt.
Come, spare not me, sir, I am no man's wife;
I care not, I, sir, not three skips of a louse for you,
An you were ten tall constables, not I.

 Turfe. Nay, pray you, sir, be not angry, but content;
My man shall make you what amends you'll ask 'un.

 Hilts. Let 'un mend his manners then, and know his betters;
It's all I ask 'un; and 'twill be his own,
And's master's too another day; che vore 'un.

 Med. As right as a club still! Zure this angry man
Speaks very near the mark when he is pleased.

 Pup. I thank you, sir, an' I meet you at Kentish-town,
I ha' the courtesy o' the hundred for you.

 Hilts. Gramercy, good high constable's hind! But hear you?
Mass constable, I have other manner of matter
To bring you about than this. And so it is,
I do belong to one of the queen's captains,
A gentleman o' the field, one captain Thums,
I know not whether you know 'un or no: it may be
You do, and it may be you do not again.

 Turfe. No, I assure you on my constableship,
I do not know 'un.

 Hilts. Nor I neither, i'faith.—
It skills not much; my captain and myself
Having occasion to come riding by here
This morning, at the corner of St. John's-wood,
Some mile [west] o' this town, were set upon
By a sort of country-fellows, that not only
Beat us, but robb'd us most sufficiently,
And bound us to our behaviour hand and foot;
And so they left us. Now, don constable,
I am to charge you in her majesty's name,
As you will answer it at your apperil,
That forthwith you raise hue and cry in the hundred,
For all such persons as you can despect,
By the length and breadth of your office: for I tell you,
The loss is of some value; therefore look to't.

 Turfe. As fortune mend me now, or any office
Of a thousand pound, if I know what to zay.
Would I were dead, or vaire hang'd up at Tyburn,
If I do know what course to take, or how
To turn myself just at this time too, now

My daughter is to be married! I'll but go
To Pancridge-church hard by, and return instantly,
And all my neighbourhood shall go about it.

   Hilts. Tut, Pancridge me no Pancridge! if you let it
Slip, you will answer it, an your cap be of wool;
Therefore take heed, you'll feel the smart else, constable. [*Going.*

   Turfe. Nay, good sir, stay.—Neighbours, what think you of this?

   Dame T. Faith, man—

   Turfe. Odds precious, woman, hold your tongue,
And mind your pigs on the spit at home; you must
Have [an] oar in every thing.—Pray you, sir, what kind
Of fellows were they?

   Hilts. Thieves-kind, I have told you.

   Turfe. I mean, what kind of men?

   Hilts. Men of our make.

   Turfe. Nay, but with patience, sir: We that are officers
Must 'quire the special marks, and all the tokens
Of the despected parties; or perhaps else
Be ne'er the near of our purpose in 'prehending them.
Can you tell what 'parrel any of them wore?

   Hilts. Troth, no; there were so many o' 'em all like
So one another; now I remember me,
There was one busy fellow was their leader,
A blunt squat swad, but lower than yourself;
He had on a leather-doublet with long points,
And a pair of pinn'd-up breeches, like pudding-bags
With yellow stockings, and his hat turn'd up
With a silver clasp on his leer side.

   Dame T. By these
Marks it should be John Clay, now bless the man!

   Turfe. Peace, and be nought! I think the woman be phrensic.

   Hilts. John Clay! what's he, good mistress?

   Awd. He that shall be
My husband.

   Hilts. How! your husband, pretty one?

   Awd. Yes, I shall anon be married; that is he.

   Turfe. Passion o' me, undone!

   Pup. Bless master's son!

   Hilts. O, you are well 'prehended: know you me, sir?

   Clay. No's my record; I never zaw you avore.

   Hilts. You did not! where were your eyes then, out at washing?

   Turfe. What should a man zay, who should he trust
In these days? Hark you, John Clay, if you have
Done any such thing, tell troth and shame the devil.

   Clench. Vaith, do; my gossip Turfe zays well to you, John.

   Med. Speak, man; but do not convess, nor be avraid.

   Pan. A man is a man, and a beast's a beast, look to't.

   Dame T. In the name of men or beasts, what do you do?
Hare the poor fellow out on his five wits,

And seven senses! do not weep, John Clay.
I swear the poor wretch is as guilty from it
As the child was, was born this very morning.

 Clay. No, as I am a kyrsin soul, would I were hang'd
If ever I——alas, I would I were out
Of my life; so I would I were, and in again——

 Pup. Nay, mistress Awdrey will say nay to that;
No, in-and-out: an you were out of your life,
How should she do for a husband? who should fall
Aboard of her then?—Ball? he's a puppy!
No, Hannibal has no breeding! well, I say little;
But hitherto all goes well, pray it prove no better. [*Aside.*

 Awd. Come, father; I would we were married! I am a-cold.

 Hilts. Well, master constable, this your fine groom here,
Bridegroom, or what groom else soe'er he be,
I charge him with the felony, and charge you
To carry him back forthwith to Paddington
Unto my captain, who stays my return there:
I am to go to the next justice of peace,
To get a warrant to raise hue and cry,
And bring him and his fellows all afore 'un.
Fare you well, sir, and look to 'un, I charge you
As you will answer it. Take heed; the business
If you defer, may prejudicial you
More than you think for; zay I told you so. [*Exit.*

 Turfe. Here's a bride-ale indeed! ah, zon John, zon Clay!
I little thought you would have proved a piece
Of such false metal.

 Clay. Father, will you believe me?
Would I might never stir in my new shoes,
If ever I would do so voul a fact.

 Turfe. Well, neighbours, I do charge you to assist me
With 'un to Paddington. Be he a true man, so!
The better for 'un. I will do mine office,
An he were my own begotten a thousand times.

 Dame T. Why, do you hear, man? husband, master Turfe?
What shall my daughter do? Puppy, stay here.
     [*Exeunt all but Awdrey and Puppy.*

 Awd. Mother, I'll go with you and with my father.

 Pup. Nay, stay, sweet mistress Awdrey: here are none
But one friend, as they zay, desires to speak
A word or two, cold with you: how do you veel
Yourself this frosty morning?

 Awd. What have you
To do to ask, I pray you? I am a-cold.

 Pup. It seems you are hot, good mistress Awdrey.

 Awd. You lie; I am as cold as ice is, feel else.

 Pup. Nay, you have cool'd my courage; I am past it,
I ha' done feeling with you.

Awd. Done with me!
I do defy you, so I do, to say
You ha' done with me: you are a saucy Puppy.
 Pup. O you mistake! I meant not as you mean.
 Awd. Meant you not knavery, Puppy?
 Pup. No, not I.
Clay meant you all the knavery, it seems,
Who rather than he would be married to you,
Chose to be wedded to the gallows first.
 Awd. I thought he was a dissembler; he would prove
A slippery merchant in the frost. He might
Have married one first, and have been hang'd after,
If he had had a mind to't. But you men—
Fie on you!
 Pup. Mistress Awdrey, can you vind
In your heart to fancy Puppy? me poor Ball?
 Awd. You are disposed to jeer one, master Hannibal.—

Re-enter HILTS.

Pity o' me, the angry man with the beard!
 Hilts. Put on thy hat, I look for no despect.
Where is thy master?
 Pup. Marry, he is gone
With the picture of despair to Paddington.
 Hilts. Prithee run after 'un, and tell 'un he shall
Find out my captain lodged at the Red-Lion,
In Paddington; that's the inn. Let 'un ask
Vor captain Thums; and take that for thy pains:
He may seek long enough else. Hie thee again.
 Pup. Yes, sir; you'll look to mistress bride the while?
 Hilts. That I will: prithee haste.   *[Exit Puppy.*
 Awd. What, Puppy! Puppy!
 Hilts. Sweet mistress bride, he'll come again presently.—
Here was no subtle device to get a wench!
This Canon has a brave pate of his own,
A shaven pate, and a right monger y' vaith;
This was his plot. I follow captain Thums!
We robb'd in St. John's-wood! In my t'other hose!—
I laugh to think what a fine fool's finger they have
O' this wise constable, in pricking out
This captain Thums to his neighbours: you shall see
The tile-man too set fire on his own kiln,
And leap into it to save himself from hanging.
You talk of a bride-ale, here was a bride-ale broke
In the nick! Well, I must yet dispatch this bride
To mine own master, the young 'squire, and then
My task is done.—[*Aside.*]—Gentlewoman, I have in sort
Done you some wrong, but now I'll do you what right
I can: it's true, you are a proper woman;

But to be cast away on such a clown-pipe
As Clay! methinks your friends are not so wise
As nature might have made 'em; well, go to:
There's better fortune coming towards you,
An you do not deject it. Take a vool's
Counsel, and do not stand in your own light;
It may prove better than you think for, look you.
  Awd. Alas, sir, what is't you would have me do?
I'd fain do all for the best, if I knew how.
  Hilts. Forsake not a good turn when it is offer'd you,
Fair mistress Awdrey—that's your name, I take it.
  Awd. No mistress, sir, my name is Awdrey.
  Hilts. Well; so it is, there is a bold young 'squire,
The blood of Totten, Tub, and Tripoly—
  Awd. 'Squire Tub, you mean: I know him, he knows me too.
  Hilts. He is in love with you; and more, he's mad for you.
  Awd. Ay, so he told me in his wits, I think.
But he's too fine for me; and has a lady
Tub to his mother.

Enter TUB.

              Here he comes himself!
  Tub. O you are a trusty governor!
  Hilts. What ails you?
You do not know when you are well, I think.
You'd ha' the calf with the white face, sir, would you?
I have her for you here; what would you more?
  Tub. Quietness, Hilts, and hear no more of it.
  Hilts. No more of it, quoth you! I do not care
If some on us had not heard so much of it.
I tell you true; a man must carry and vetch
Like Bungy's dog for you.
  Tub. What's he?
  Hilts. A spaniel—
And scarce be spit in the mouth for't. A good dog
Deserves, sir, a good bone, of a free master;
But, an your turns be serv'd, the devil a bit
You care for a man after, e'er a laird of you.
Like will to like, y-faith, quoth the scabb'd 'squire
To the mangy knight, when both met in a dish
Of butter'd vish. One bad, there's ne'er a good;
And not a barrel the better herring among you.
  Tub. Nay, Hilts, I pray thee grow not frampull now.
Turn not the bad cow after thy good soap.
Our plot hath hitherto ta'en good effect,
And should it now be troubled or stopp'd up,
'Twould prove the utter ruin of my hopes.
I pray thee haste to Pancridge, to the Canon,
And give him notice of our good success.

Will him that all things be in readiness:
Fair Awdrey and myself will cross the fields
The nearest path.   Good Hilts, make thou some haste,
And meet us on the way.—Come, gentle Awdrey.

Hilts. Vaith, would I had a few more geances on't!
An you say the word, send me to Jericho.
Outcept a man were a post-horse, I have not known
The like on it;   yet, an he had [had] kind words,
'Twould never irke 'un: but a man may break
His heart out in these days, and get a flap
With a fox-tail, when he has done—and there is all!

Tub. Nay, say not so, Hilts: hold thee, there are crowns
My love bestows on thee for thy reward;
If gold will please thee, all my land shall drop
In bounty thus, to recompense thy merit.

Hilts. Tut, keep your land, and your gold too, sir, I
Seek neither—neither of 'un.   Learn to get
More;   you will know to spend that zum you have
Early enough;   you are assured of me:
I love you too too well to live o' the spoil—
For your own sake, would there were no worse than I!
All is not gold that glisters.   I'll to Pancridge.   [*Exit crying.*

Tub. See how his love does melt him into tears!
An honest faithful servant is a jewel.—
Now the advent'rous 'squire hath time and leisure
To ask his Awdrey how she does, and hear
A grateful answer from her.   She not speaks.—
Hath the proud tyrant Frost usurp'd the seat
Of former beauty, in my love's fair cheek;
Staining the roseate tincture of her blood
With the dull dye of blue congealing cold?
No, sure the weather dares not so presume
To hurt an object of her brightness.   Yet,
The more I view her, she but looks so, so.
Ha! give me leave to search this mystery—
O now I have it: Bride, I know your grief;
The last night's cold hath bred in you such horror
Of the assigned bridegroom's constitution,
The Kilborn clay-pit;   that frost-bitten marl,
That lump in courage, melting cake of ice:
That the conceit thereof hath almost kill'd thee:
But I must do thee good, wench, and refresh thee.

Awd. You are a merry man, 'squire Tub of Totten!
I have heard much o' your words, but not o' your deeds.

Tub. Thou sayst true, sweet;   I have been too slack in deeds.

Awd. Yet I was never so strait-laced to you, 'squire.

Tub. Why, did you ever love me, gentle Awdrey?

Awd. Love you!   I cannot tell: I must hate no body,
My father says.

Tub. Yes, Clay and Kilborn, Awdrey,
You must hate them.

Awd. It shall be for your sake then.

Tub. And for my sake shall yield you that gratuity.

[Offers to kiss her.

Awd. Soft and fair, 'squire, there go two words to a bargain.

[Puts him back.

Tub. What are those, Awdrey?

Awd. Nay, I cannot tell.
My mother said, zure, if you married me,
You'd make me a lady the first week; and put me
In—I know not what, the very day.

Tub. What was it?
Speak, gentle Awdrey, thou shalt have it yet.

Awd. A velvet dressing for my head, it is,
They say, will make one brave; I will not know
Bess Moale, nor Margery Turn-up: I will look
Another way upon them, and be proud.

Tub. Troth, I could wish my wench a better wit;
But what she wanteth there, her face supplies.
There is a pointed lustre in her eye
Hath shot quite through me, and hath hit my hearts:
And thence it is I first received the wound,
That rankles now, which only she can cure.
Fain would I work myself from this conceit;
But, being flesh, I cannot. I must love her,
The naked truth is; and I will go on,
Were it for nothing but to cross my rivals. *[Aside.*
Come, Awdrey, I am now resolv'd to have thee.

Enter Justice PREAMBLE, *and* METAPHOR *disguised as a pursuivant.*

Pre. Nay, do it quickly, Miles; why shak'st thou, man?
Speak but his name, I'll second thee myself.

Met. What is his name?

Pre. 'Squire Tripoly, or Tub;
Any thing—

Met. 'Squire Tub, I do arrest you
In the queen's majesty's name, and all the council's.

Tub. Arrest me, varlet!

Pre. Keep the peace, I charge you.

Tub. Are you there, justice Bramble! where's your warrant?

Pre. The warrant is directed here to me,
From the whole table; wherefore I would pray you,
Be patient, 'squire, and make good the peace.

Tub. Well, at your pleasure, justice. I am wrong'd:
Sirrah, what are you have arrested me?

Pre. He is a pursuivant at arms, 'squire Tub.

Met. I am a pursuivant; see by my coat else.

Tub. Well, pursuivant, go with me: I'll give you bail.

Pre. Sir, he may take no bail: it is a warrant
In special from the council, and commands
Your personal appearance. Sir, your weapon
I must require; and then deliver you
A prisoner to this officer, 'squire Tub.
I pray you to conceive of me no other,
Than as your friend and neighbour: let my person
Be sever'd from my office in the fact,
And I am clear. Here, pursuivant, receive him
Into your hands, and use him like a gentleman.

Tub. I thank you, sir: but whither must I go now?

Pre. Nay, that must not be told you till you come
Unto the place assign'd by his instructions:
I'll be the maiden's convoy to her father,
For this time, 'squire.

Tub. I thank you, master Bramble.
I doubt or fear you will make her the balance
To weigh your justice in. Pray ye do me right,
And lead not her, at least, out of the way:
Justice is blind, and having a blind guide,
She may be apt to slip aside.

Pre. I'll see to her.   [*Exit Pre. with Awd.*

Tub. I see my wooing will not thrive. Arrested,
As I had set my rest up for a wife!
And being so fair for it as I was!—Well, fortune,
Thou art a blind bawd and a beggar too,
To cross me thus; and let my only rival
To get her from me! that's the spight of spights.
But most I muse at, is, that I, being none
O' the court, am sent for thither by the council:
My heart is not so light as it was in the morning.

Re-enter HILTS.

Hilts. You mean to make a hoiden or a hare
Of me, to hunt counter thus, and make these doubles:
And you mean no such thing as you send about.
Where is your sweet heart now, I marle?

Tub. Oh Hilts!

Hilts. I know you of old! ne'er halt afore a cripple.
Will you have a caudle? where's your grief, sir? speak.

Met. Do you hear, friend, do you serve this gentleman?

Hilts. How then, sir? what if I do? peradventure yea,
Peradventure nay; what's that to you, sir? say.

Met. Nay, pray you, sir, I meant no harm in truth;
But this good gentleman is arrested.

Hilts. How!
Say me that again.

Tub. Nay, Basket, never storm;

I am arrested here, upon command
From the queen's council; and I must obey.

Met. You say, sir, very true, you must obey.
An honest gentleman, in faith.

Hilts. He must!

Tub. But that which most tormenteth me is this,
That justice Bramble hath got hence my Awdrey.

Hilts. How! how! stand by a little, sirrah, you
With the badge on your breast. [*Draws his sword.*] Let's know, sir,
    what you are.

Met. I am, sir,—pray you do not look so terribly—
A pursuivant.

Hilts. A pursuivant! your name, sir?

Met. My name, sir—

Hilts. What is't? speak.

Met. Miles Metaphor;
And justice Preamble's clerk.

Tub. What says he?

Hilts. Pray you,
Let us alone. You are a pursuivant?

Met. No, faith, sir, would I might never stir from you,
I is made a pursuivant against my will.

Hilts. Ha! and who made you one? tell true, or my will
Shall make you nothing instantly.

Met. [*kneels.*] Put up
Your frightful blade, and your dead-doing look,
And I shall tell you all.

Hilts. Speak then the truth,
And the whole truth, and nothing but the truth.

Met. My master, justice Bramble, hearing your master,
The 'squire Tub, was coming on this way,
With mistress Awdrey, the high constable's daughter,
Made me a pursuivant, and gave me warrant
To arrest him; so that he might get the lady,
With whom he is gone to Pancridge, to the vicar,
Not to her father's. This was the device,
Which I beseech you do not tell my master.

Tub. O wonderful! well, Basket, let him rise;
And for my free escape forge some excuse.
I'll post to Paddington to acquaint old Turfe
With the whole business, and so stop the marriage.   [*Exit.*

Hilts. Well, bless thee: I do wish thee grace to keep
Thy master's secrets better, or be hang'd.

Met. [*rises.*] I thank you for your gentle admonition.
Pray you, let me call you god-father hereafter:
And as your godson Metaphor, I promise
To keep my master's privities seal'd up
In the vallies of my trust, lock'd close for ever,
Or let me be truss'd up at Tyburn shortly.

Hilts. Thine own wish save or choke thee! come away. [*Exeunt.*

ACT III

SCENE I.—KENTISH-TOWN.

Enter TURFE, CLENCH, MEDLAY, TO-PAN, SCRIBEN, *and* CLAY.

   Turfe. Passion of me, was ever a man thus cross'd!
All things run arsie versie, up-side down.
High constable! now by our lady of Walsingham,
I had rather be mark'd out Tom Scavinger,
And with a shovel make clean the highways,
Than have this office of a constable,
And a high constable! the higher charge,
It brings more trouble, more vexation with it.
Neighbours, good neighbours, 'vize me what to do;
How we shall bear us in this hue and cry.
We cannot find the captain, no such man
Lodged at the Lion, nor came thither hurt,
The morning we have spent in privy search;
And by that means the bride-ale is deferr'd:
The bride, she's left alone in Puppy's charge;
The bridegroom goes under a pair of sureties,
And held of all as a respected person.
How should we bustle forward? give some counsel
How to bestir our stumps in these cross ways.
   Clench. Faith, gossip Turfe, you have, you say, remission
To comprehend all such as are despected:
Now would I make another privy search
Thorough this town, and then you have search'd two towns.
   Med. Masters, take heed, let us not vind too many:
One is enough to stay the hangman's stomach.
There is John Clay, who is yvound already,
A proper man, a tile-man by his trade,
A man, as one would zay, moulded in clay;
As spruce as any neighbour's child among you:
And he (you zee) is taken on conspition,
And two or three, they zay, what call you 'em?
Zuch as the justices of *coram nobis*
Grant—I forget their names, you have many on 'em,
Master high constable, they come to you.—
I have it at my tongue's ends—coney-boroughs,
To bring him strait avore the zessions-house.
   Turfe. O you mean warrens, neighbour, do you not?
   Med. Ay, ay, thik same! you know 'em well enough.
   Turfe. Too well, too well; would I had never known them!
We good vreeholders cannot live in quiet,
But every hour new purcepts, hues and cries,
Put us to requisitions night and day —

What shud a man say? shud we leave the zearch,
I am in danger to reburse as much
As he was robb'd on; ay, and pay his hurts.
If I should vollow it, all the good cheer
That was provided for the wedding-dinner
Is spoil'd and lost.   O, there are two vat pigs
A zindging by the vire: now by St. Tony,
Too good to eat, but on a wedding-day;
And then a goose will bid you all, come cut me.
Zon Clay, zon Clay, for I must call thee so,
Be of good comfort: take my muckinder,
And dry thine eyes.   If thou be'st true and honest,
And if thou find'st thy conscience clear vrom it,
Pluck up a good heart, we'll do well enough:
If not, confess a-truth's name.   But in faith,
I durst be sworn upon all holy books,
John Clay would ne'er commit a robbery
On his own head.
   Clay.   No, truth is my rightful judge;
I have kept my hands herehence from evil-speaking,
Lying, and slandering; and my tongue from stealing.
He do not live this day can say, John Clay,
I have zeen thee, but in the way of honesty.
   Pan.   Faith, neighbour Medlay, I durst be his burrough,
He would not look a true man in the vace.
   Clay.   I take the town to concord, where I dwell,
All Kilborn be my witness, if I were not
Begot in bashfulness, brought up in shamefacedness.
Let 'un bring a dog but to my vace that can
Zay I have beat 'un, and without a vault;
Or but a cat will swear upon a book,
I have as much as zet a vire her tail,
And I'll give him or her a crown for 'mends.
But to give out and zay I have robb'd a captain!
Receive me at the latter day, if I
E'er thought of any such matter, or could mind it.
   Med.   No, John, you are come of too good personage:
I think my gossip Clench and master Turfe
Both think you would ratempt no such voul matter.
   Turfe.   But how unhappily it comes to pass
Just on the wedding-day!   I cry me mercy,
I had almost forgot the hue and cry:
Good neighbour Pan, you are the thirdborough,
And D'ogenes Scriben, you my learned writer,
Make out a new purcept—Lord for thy goodness,
I had forgot my daughter all this while!
The idle knave hath brought no news from her.
Here comes the sneaking puppy.—

Enter Puppy *and* Dame Turfe, *on different sides.*

What's the news?
My heart! my heart! I fear all is not well,
Something's mishapp'd; that he is come without her.

   Pup. O, where's my master, my master, my master?

   Dame T. Thy master! what would'st have with thy master, man?
There is thy master.

   Turfe. What's the matter, Puppy?

   Pup. O master, oh dame! oh dame! oh master!

   Dame T. What say'st thou to thy master or thy dame?

   Pup. Oh John Clay, John Clay, John Clay!

   Turfe. What of John Clay?

   Med. Luck grant he bring not news he shall be hang'd

   Clench. The world forfend! I hope it is not so well.

   Clay. O Lord! oh me! what shall I do? poor John!

   Pup. Oh John Clay, John Clay, John Clay!

   Clay. Alas,
That ever I was born! I will not stay by't,
For all the tiles in Kilborn.   *[Runs off.*

   Dame T. What of Clay?
Speak, Puppy; what of him?

   Pup. He hath lost, he hath lost—

   Turfe. For luck sake speak, Puppy, what hath he lost!

   Pup. Oh Awdrey, Awdrey, Awdrey!

   Dame T. What of my daughter Awdrey?

   Pup. I tell you, Awdrey—do you understand me?
Awdrey, sweet master, Awdrey, my dear dame—

   Turfe. Where is she? what's become of her, I pray thee?

   Pup. Oh, the serving-man, the serving-man, the serving-man!

   Turfe. What talk'st thou of the serving-man! where's Awdrey?

   Pup. Gone with the serving-man, gone with the serving-man.

   Dame T. Good Puppy, whither is she gone with him?

   Pup. I cannot tell: he bade me bring you word
The captain lay at the Lion, and before
I came again, Awdrey was gone with the serving-man;
I tell you, Awdrey's run away with the serving-man.

   Turfe. 'Od'socks, my woman, what shall we do now?

   Dame T. Now, so you help not, man, I know not, I.

   Turfe. This was your pomp of maids! I told you on't.
Six maids to vollow you, and not leave one
To wait upon your daughter! I zaid pride
Would be paid one day her old vi'pence, wife.

   Med. What of John Clay, Ball Puppy?

   Pup. He hath lost—

   Med. His life for velony?

   Pup. No, his wife by villainy.

   Turfe. Now villains both! oh that same hue and cry!
Oh neighbours! oh that cursed serving-man!

O maids! O wife! but John Clay, where is he?—
How! fled for fear, zay ye? will he slip us now?
We that are sureties must require 'un out.
How shall we do to find the serving-man?
Cock's bodikins, we must not lose John Clay;
Awdrey, my daughter Awdrey too! let us zend
To all the towns and zeek her;—but, alas,
The hue and cry, that must be look'd unto.

Enter TUB.

Tub. What, in a passion, Turfe?
Turfe. Ay, good 'squire Tub.
Were never honest varmers thus perplext.
Tub. Turfe, I am privy to thy deep unrest:
The ground of which springs from an idle plot,
Cast by a suitor to your daughter Awdrey—
And thus much, Turfe, let me advertise you;
Your daughter Awdrey met I on the way,
With justice Bramble in her company;
Who means to marry her at Pancras-church.
And there is canon Hugh to meet them ready:
Which to prevent, you must not trust delay;
But winged speed must cross their sly intent:
Then hie thee, Turfe, haste to forbid the banes.
Turfe. Hath justice Bramble got my daughter Awdrey?
A little while shall he enjoy her, zure.
But O, the hue and cry! that hinders me;
I must pursue that, or neglect my journey:
I'll e'en leave all, and with the patient ass,
The over-laden ass, throw off my burden,
And cast mine office: pluck in my large ears
Betimes, lest some disjudge 'em to be horns:
I'll leave to beat it on the broken hoof,
And ease my pasterns; I'll no more high constables.
Tub. I cannot choose but smile to see thee troubled
With such a bald, half-hatched circumstance.
The captain was not robb'd, as is reported;
That trick the justice craftily devised,
To break the marriage with the tileman Clay.
The hue and cry was merely counterfeit:
The rather may you judge it to be such,
Because the bridegroom was described to be
One of the thieves first in the felony;
Which, how far 'tis from him, yourselves may guess.
'Twas justice Bramble's fetch to get the wench.
Turfe. And is this true, 'squire Tub?
Tub. Believe me, Turfe,
As I am a 'squire; or less, a gentleman.
Turfe. I take my office back, and my authority,

Upon your worship's words:—Neighbours, I am
High constable again. Where's my zon Clay?
He shall be zon yet; wife, your meat by leisure:
Draw back the spits.

   Dame T. That's done already, man.

   Turfe. I'll break this marriage off; and afterward,
She shall be given to her first betroth'd.
Look to the meat, wife, look well to the roast.

                   [Exit, followed by his neighbours.

   Tub. I'll follow him aloof to see the event.   *[Exit.*

   Pup. Dame, mistress, though I do not turn the spit,
I hope yet the pig's head.

   Dame T. Come up, Jack sauce;
It shall be serv'd into you.

   Pup. No, no service,
But a reward for service.

   Dame T. I still took you
For an unmannerly Puppy: will you come,
And vetch more wood to the vire, master Ball?   *[Exit.*

   Pup. I, wood to the vire! I shall piss it out first:
You think to make me e'en your ox or ass,
Or any thing: though I cannot right myself
On you, I'll sure revenge me on your meat.   *[Exit.*

   SCENE II.—*The same.—Before* TURFE's *House.*

   Enter Lady TUB, POL MARTIN, *and* WISPE.

   Pol. Madam, to Kentish-town we are got at length;
But by the way we cannot meet the 'squire,
Nor by inquiry can we hear of him.
Here is Turfe's house, the father of the maid.

   Lady T. Pol Martin, see! the streets are strew'd with herbs;
And here hath been a wedding, Wispe, it seems.
Pray heaven this bride-ale be not for my son!
Good Martin, knock, knock quickly; ask for Turfe.
My thoughts misgive me, I am in such a doubt—

   Pol. [*knocking.*] Who keeps the house here?

   Pup. [*within.*] Why the door and walls
Do keep the house.

   Pol. I ask then, who's within?

   Pup. [*within.*] Not you that are without.

   Pol. Look forth, and speak
Into the street here. Come before my lady.

   Pup. [*within.*] Before my lady! Lord have mercy upon me:
If I do come before her, she will see
The handsomest man in all the town, pardee!

   Enter PUPPY *from the house.*

Now stand I vore her, what zaith velvet she?

   Lady T. Sirrah, whose man are you?

Pup. Madam, my master's.

Lady T. And who's thy master?

Pup. What you tread on, madam.

Lady T. I tread on an old Turfe.

Pup. That Turfe's my master.

Lady T. A merry fellow! what's thy name?

Pup. Ball Puppy

They call me at home: abroad Hannibal Puppy.

Lady T. Come hither, I must kiss thee, valentine Puppy.

Wispe, have you got a valentine?

Wispe. None, madam:

He's the first stranger that I saw.

Lady T. To me

He is so, and as such, let's share him equally.

> [*They struggle to kiss him.*

Pup. Help, help, good dame! A rescue, and in time.

Instead of bills, with colstaves come; instead of spears, with spits;

Your slices serve for slicing swords, to save me and my wits:

A lady and her woman here, their huisher eke by side,

(But he stands mute,) have plotted how your Puppy to divide.

Enter Dame TURFE, JOAN, JOYCE, MADGE, *etc.*

Dame T. How now, what noise is this with you, Ball Puppy?

Pup. Oh dame, and fellows of the kitchen! arm,

Arm, for my safety; if you love your Ball:

Here is a strange thing call'd a lady, a mad-dame,

And a device of hers, yclept her woman,

Have plotted on me in the king's highway,

To steal me from myself, and cut me in halfs,

To make one valentine to serve them both;

This for my right-side, that for my left-hand love.

Dame T. So saucy, Puppy! to use no more reverence

Unto my lady and her velvet gown?

Lady T. Turfe's wife, rebuke him not; your man doth please me

With his conceit: hold, there are ten old nobles,

To make thee merrier yet, half-valentine.

Pup. I thank you, right-side; could my left as much,

'Twould make me a man of mark, young Hannibal!

Lady T. Dido shall make that good, or I will for her.

Here, Dido Wispe, there's for your Hannibal;

He is your countryman as well as valentine.

Wispe. Here, master Hannibal, my lady's bounty

For her poor woman, Wispe.

Pup. Brave Carthage queen!

And such was Dido: I will ever be

Champion to her, who Juno is to thee.

Dame T. Your ladyship is very welcome here.

Please you, good madam, to go near the house.

Lady T. Turfe's wife, I come thus far to seek your husband.

Having some business to impart unto him;
Is he at home?

Dame T. O no, an it shall please you:
He is posted hence to Pancridge, with a witness.
Young justice Bramble has kept level coyl
Here in our quarters, stole away our daughter,
And master Turfe's run after, as he can,
To stop the marriage, if it will be stopp'd.

Pol. Madam, these tidings are not much amiss:
For if the justice have the maid in keep,
You need not fear the marriage of your son.

Lady T. That somewhat easeth my suspicious breast.
Tell me, Turfe's wife, when was my son with Awdrey?
How long is it since you saw him at your house?

Pup. Dame, let me take this rump out of your mouth.

Dame T. What mean you by that, sir?

Pup. Rump and taile's all one,
But I would use a reverence for my lady:
I would not zay, sur-reverence, the tale
Out of your mouth, but rather take the rump.

Dame T. A well-bred youth! and vull of favour you are.

Pup. What might they zay, when I were gone, if I
Not weigh'd my words? This Puppy is a vool,
Great Hannibal's an ass; he hath no breeding:
No, lady gay, you shall not zay
That your Val. Puppy, was so unlucky,
In speech to fail, as to name a tail,
Be as be may be, 'vore a fair lady.

Lady T. Leave jesting; tell us when you saw our son.

Pup. Marry, it is two hours ago.

Lady T. Since you saw him?

Pup. You might have seen him too, if you had look'd up;
For it shined as bright as day.

Lady T. I mean my son.

Pup. Your sun, and our sun, are they not all one?

Lady T. Fool, thou mistak'st; I ask'd thee for my son.

Pup. I had thought there had been no more sons than one.
I know not what you ladies have, or may have.

Pol. Didst thou ne'er hear my lady had a son?

Pup. She may have twenty; but for a son, unless
She mean precisely, 'squire Tub, her zon,
He was here now, and brought my master word
That justice Bramble had got mistress Awdrey:
But whither he be gone, here's none can tell.

Lady T. Martin, I wonder at this strange discourse:
The fool, it seems, tells true; my son the 'squire
Was doubtless here this morning: for the match,
I'll smother what I think, and staying here,
Attend the sequel of this strange beginning.—

Turfe's wife, my people and I will trouble thee
Until we hear some tidings of thy husband;
The rather for my party-valentine.　　　　　　　　[*Exeunt.*

SCENE III.—PANCRAS.

Enter TURFE, AWDREY, CLENCH, MEDLAY, PAN, *and* SCRIBEN.

    Turfe. Well, I have carried it, and will triumph
Over this justice as becomes a constable,
And a high constable: next our St. George,
Who rescued the king's daughter, I will ride;
Above prince Arthur.
    Clench. Or our Shoreditch duke.
    Med. Or Pancridge earl.
    Pan. Or Bevis, or sir Guy,
Who were high constables both.
    Clench. One of Southampton—
    Med. The t'other of Warwick-castle.
    Turfe. You shall work it
Into a story for me, neighbour Medlay,
Over my chimney.
    Scri. I can give you, sir,
A Roman story of a petty-constable,
That had a daughter that was call'd Virginia,
Like mistress Awdrey, and as young as she;
And how her father bare him in the business,
'Gainst justice Appius, a decemvir in Rome,
And justice of assize.
    Turfe. That, that, good D'ogenes!
A learned man is a chronicle.
    Scri. I can tell you
A thousand of great Pompey, Cæsar, Trajan,
All the high constables there.
    Turfe. That was their place!
They were no more.
    Scri. Dictator and high constable
Were both the same.
    Med. High constable was more though:
He laid Dick Tator by the heels.
    Pan. Dick Toter!
He was one o' the waights o' the city, I have read o' 'un;
He was a fellow would be drunk, debauch'd—
And he did zet 'un in the stocks indeed:
His name was Vadian, and a cunning toter.
    Awd. Was ever silly maid thus posted off,
That should have had three husbands in one day;
Yet, by bad fortune, am possest of none!
I went to church to have been wed to Clay,
Then 'squire Tub he seized me on the way,

And thought to have had me, but he mist his aim;
And justice Bramble, nearest of the three,
Was well-nigh married to me; when by chance,
In rush'd my father, and broke off that dance.

Turfe. Ay, girl, there's ne'er a justice on 'em all
Shall teach the constable to guard his own:
Let's back to Kentish-town, and there make merry:
These news will be glad tidings to my wife.
Thou shalt have Clay, my wench: that word shall stand.
He's found by this time, sure, or else he's drown'd;
The wedding-dinner will be spoil'd: make haste.

Awd. Husbands, they say, grow thick, but thin are sown;
I care not who it be, so I have one.

Turfe. Ay, zay you zo! perhaps you shall ha' none for that.

Awd. None, out upon me! what shall I do then?

Med. Sleep, mistress Awdrey, dream on proper men. [*Exeunt.*

SCENE IV.—*Another part of the same.*

Enter Sir HUGH *and* PREAMBLE.

Hugh. O *bone Deus,* have you seen the like!
Here was, Hodge hold thine ear fair, whilst I strike.
Body o' me, how came this geer about?

Pre. I know not, Canon, but it falls out cross.
Nor can I make conjecture by the circumstance
Of these events; it was impossible,
Being so close and politicly carried,
To come so quickly to the ears of Turfe.
O priest! had but thy slow delivery
Been nimble, and thy lazy Latin tongue
But run the forms o'er with that swift dispatch
As had been requisite, all had been well.

Hugh. What should have been, that never loved the friar;
But thus you see the old adage verified,
Multa cadunt inter——you can guess the rest,
Many things fall between the cup and lip;
And though they touch, you are not sure to drink.
You lack'd good fortune, we had done our parts:
Give a man fortune, throw him in the sea,
The properer man, the worse luck: stay a time;
Tempus edax—In time the stately ox,—
Good counsels lightly never come too late.

Pre. You, sir, will run your counsels out of breath.

Hugh. Spur a free horse, he'll run himself to death.
Sancti Evangelistæ ! here comes Miles!

Enter METAPHOR.

Pre. What news, man, with our new-made pursuivant?

Met. A pursuivant! would I were—or more pursie,

And had more store of money; or less pursie,
And had more store of breath: you call me pursuivant,
But I could never vaunt of any purse
I had, sin' you were my godfathers and godmothers,
And gave me that nick-name.

Pre. What's now the matter?

Met. Nay, 'tis no matter, I have been simply beaten.

Hugh. What is become of the 'squire and thy prisoner?

Met. The lines of blood run streaming from my head,
Can speak what rule the 'squire hath kept with me.

Pre. I pray thee, Miles, relate the manner how.

Met. Be't known unto you by these presents then,
That I, Miles Metaphor, your worship's clerk,
Have e'en been beaten to an allegory,
By multitude of hands.   Had they been but
Some five or six, I had whipp'd them all, like tops
In Lent, and hurl'd them into Hobler's hole,
Or the next ditch; I had crack'd all their costards,
As nimbly as a squirrel will crack nuts,
And flourished like to Hercules the porter
Among the pages.   But when they came on
Like bees about a hive, crows about carrion,
Flies about sweetmeats; nay, like watermen
About a fare: then was poor Metaphor
Glad to give up the honour of the day,
To quit his charge to them, and run away
To save his life, only to tell this news.

Hugh. How indirectly all things are fallen out!
I cannot choose but wonder what they were
Rescued your rival from the keep of Miles;
But most of all, I cannot well digest
The manner how our purpose came to Turfe.

Pre. Miles, I will see that all thy hurts be drest.
As for the 'squire's escape, it matters not,
We have by this means disappointed him;
And that was all the main I aimed at.
But canon Hugh, now muster up thy wits,
And call thy thoughts into the consistory,
Search all the secret corners of thy cap,
To find another quaint devised drift,
To disappoint her marriage with this Clay:
Do that, and I'll reward thee jovially.

Hugh. Well said, magister justice.   If I fit you not
With such a new and well-laid stratagem,
As never yet your ears did hear a finer,
Call me with Lilly, *Bos, Fur, Sus atque Sacerdos.*

Pre. I hear there's comfort in thy words yet, Canon.
I'll trust thy regulars, and say no more. [*Exeunt Hugh and Pre.*

Met. I'll follow too.   And if the dapper priest

Be but as cunning, point in his device,
As I was in my lie, my master Bramble
Will stalk, as led by the nose with these new promises,
And fatted with supposes of fine hopes.   [*Exit.*

SCENE V.—*Kentish-Town.*—*Before* TURFE's *House.*

Enter TURFE, Dame TURFE, Lady TUB, POL MARTIN, AWDREY, *and* PUPPY.

Turfe. Well, madam, I may thank the 'squire your son;
For, but for him, I had been over-reach'd.
Dame T. Now heaven's blessing light upon his heart!
We are beholden to him, indeed, madam.
Lady T. But can you not resolve me where he is,
Nor about what his purposes were bent?
Turfe. Madam, they no whit were concerning me,
And therefore was I less inquisitive.
Lady T. Fair maid, in faith, speak truth, and not dissemble;
Does he not often come and visit you?
Awd. His worship now and then, please you, takes pains
To see my father and mother; but, for me,
I know myself too mean for his high thoughts
To stoop at, more than asking a light question,
To make him merry, or to pass his time.
Lady T. A sober maid! call for my woman, Martin.
Pol. The maids and her half-valentine have plied her
With courtesy of the bride-cake and the bowl,
As she is laid awhile.
Lady T. O let her rest.
We will cross o'er to Canbury in the interim,
And so make home.—Farewell, good Turfe, and thy wife;
I wish your daughter joy.   [*Exeunt Lady T. and Pol.*
Turfe. Thanks to your ladyship.—
Where is John Clay now, have you seen him yet?
Dame T. No, he has hid himself out of the way,
For fear of the hue and cry.
Turfe. What, walks that shadow
Avore 'un still?—Puppy, go seek 'un out,
Search all the corners that he haunts unto,
And call 'un forth. We'll once more to the church,
And try our vortunes: luck, son Valentine!
Where are the wise men all of Finsbury?
Pup. Where wise men should be; at the ale and bride-cake.
I would this couple had their destiny,
Or to be hang'd, or married out o' the way:

Enter CLENCH, MEDLAY, SCRIBEN, *etc.*

Man cannot get the mount'nance of an egg-shell
To stay his stomach. Vaith, for mine own part,

I have zupp'd up so much broth as would have cover'd
A leg o' beef o'er head and ears in the porridge-pot,
And yet I cannot sussifie wild nature.
Would they were once dispatch'd, we might to dinner.
I am with child of a huge stomach, and long,
Till by some honest midwife piece of beef
I be deliver'd of it: I must go now
And hunt out for this Kilborn calf, John Clay,
Whom where to find, I know not, nor which way.　　　　　　*[Exit.*

　　　　　Enter Sir HUGH, *disguised as a captain.*

　Hugh. Thus as a beggar in a king's disguise,
Or an old cross well sided with a may-pole,
Comes canon Hugh accoutred as you see.
Disguised, soldado-like. Mark his device:
The canon is that captain Thums was robb'd,
These bloody scars upon my face are wounds,
This scarf upon mine arm shews my late hurts,
And thus am I to gull the constable.
Now have I among you for a man at arms!　　　　　　*[Aside.*
Friends, by your leave, which of you is one Turfe?
　Turfe. Sir, I am Turfe, if you would speak with me.
　Hugh. With thee, Turfe, if thou be'st high constable.
　Turfe. I am both Turfe, sir, and high constable.
　Hugh. Then, Turfe or Scurfe, high or low constable,
Know, I was once a captain at St. Quintin's,
And passing cross the ways over the country,
This morning, betwixt this and Hampstead-heath,
Was by a crew of clowns robb'd, bobb'd and hurt.
No sooner had I got my wounds bound up,
But with much pain I went to the next justice,
One master Bramble, here at Maribone:
And here a warrant is, which he hath directed
For you, one Turfe, if your name be Toby Turfe,
Who have let fall, they say, the hue and cry;
And you shall answer it afore the justice.
　Turfe. Heaven and hell, dogs and devils, what is this!
Neighbours, was ever constable thus cross'd?
What shall we do?
　Med. Faith, all go hang ourselves;
I know no other way to escape the law.

　　　　　　　Re-enter PUPPY.

　Pup. News, news, O news—
　Turfe. What, hast thou found out Clay?
　Pup. No, sir, the news is, that I cannot find him.
　Hugh. Why do you dally, you damn'd russet-coat?
You peasant, nay, you clown, you constable!
See that you bring forth the suspected party,

Or by mine honour, which I won in field,
I'll make you pay for it afore the justice.

   Turfe. Fie, fie! O wife, I'm now in a fine pickle.
He that was most suspected is not found;
And which now makes me think he did the deed,
He thus absents him, and dares not be seen.
Captain, my innocence will plead for me.
Wife, I must go, needs, whom the devil drives:
Pray for me, wife and daughter, pray for me.

   Hugh. I'll lead the way—thus is the match put off,—
And if my plot succeed, as I have laid it,
My captainship shall cost him many a crown.

            [*Aside. Exeunt all but Dame T., Awd., and Puppy.*

   Dame T. So, we have brought our eggs to a fair market.
Out on that villain Clay! would he do a robbery?
I'll ne'er trust smooth-faced tileman for his sake.

   Awd. Mother, the still sow eats up all the draff.

                  [*Exeunt Dame T. and Awd.*

   Pup. Thus is my master, Toby Turfe, the pattern
Of all the painful adventures now in print!
I never could hope better of this match,
This bride-ale; for the night before to-day,
(Which is within man's memory, I take it,)
At the report of it an ox did speak,
Who died soon after; a cow lost her calf;
The bell-weather was flay'd for't; a fat hog
Was singed, and wash'd, and shaven all over, to
Look ugly 'gainst this day: the ducks they quack'd,
The hens too cackled; at the noise whereof
A drake was seen to dance a headless round;
The goose was cut in the head to hear it too:
Brave chant-it-clear, his noble heart was done,
His comb was cut; and two or three of his wives
Or fairest concubines, had their necks broke
Ere they would zee this day: to mark the verven
Heart of a beast! the very pig, the pig
This very morning, as he was a roasting,
Cried out his eyes, and made a shew, as he would
Have bit in two the spit; as he would say,
There shall no roast-meat be this dismal day.
And zure, I think, if I had not got his tongue
Between my teeth and eat it, he had spoke it.
Well, I will in and cry too; never leave
Crying until our maids may drive a buck
With my salt tears at the next washing-day.

                                  [*Exit.*

ACT IV

SCENE I.—*Maribone.*—*A Room in* Justice PREAMBLE'S *House.*

Enter Justice PREAMBLE, Sir HUGH, *disguised as before*, TURFE, *and* METAPHOR.

   Pre. Keep out those fellows; I'll have none come in
But the high constable, the man of peace,
And the queen's captain, the brave man of war.
Now, neighbour Turfe, the cause why you are call'd
Before me by my warrant, but unspecified,
Is this; and pray you mark it thoroughly.
Here is a gentleman, and, as it seems,
Both of good birth, fair speech, and peaceable;
Who was this morning robb'd here in the wood:
You, for your part, a man of good report,
Of credit, landed, and of fair demeans,
And by authority, high constable;
Are, notwithstanding, touch'd in this complaint,
Of being careless in the hue and cry.
I cannot choose but grieve a soldier's loss;
And I am sorry too for your neglect,
Being my neighbour: this is all I object.
   Hugh. This is not all; I can allege far more,
And almost urge him for an accessary.
Good master justice, give me leave to speak,
For I am plaintiff: let not neighbourhood
Make him secure, or stand on privilege.
   Pre. Sir, I dare use no partiality;
Object then what you please, so it be truth.
   Hugh. This more, and which is more than he can answer;
Besides his letting fall the hue and cry,
He doth protect the man charged with the felony,
And keeps him hid, I hear, within his house,
Because he is affied unto his daughter.
   Turfe. I do defy 'un, so shall she do too.
I pray your worship's favour let me have hearing.
I do convess, 'twas told me such a velony,
And't not disgrieved me a little, when 'twas told me,
Vor I was going to church to marry Awdrey:
And who should marry her but this very Clay,
Who was charged to be the chief thief o' 'em all.
Now I (the halter stick me if I tell
Your worships any leazins) did fore-think 'un
The truest man, till he waz run away:
I thought I had had 'un as zure as in a zaw-pit,
Or in mine oven; nay, in the town-pound:

I was zo zure o' 'un, I'd have gi'n my life for 'un,
Till he did start: but now I zee 'un guilty,
Az var as I can look at 'un. Would you ha' more?
Hugh. Yes, I will have, sir, what the law will give me.
You gave your word to see him safe forth-coming;
I challenge that: but that is forfeited;
Beside, your carelessness in the pursuit,
Argues your slackness and neglect of duty,
Which ought be punish'd with severity.
Pre. He speaks but reason, Turfe. Bring forth the man
And you are quit; but otherwise, your word
Binds you to make amends for all his loss,
And think yourself befriended, if he take it
Without a farther suit or going to law.
Come to a composition with him, Turfe,
The law is costly, and will draw on charge.
Turfe. Yes, I do know, I vurst mun vee a returney,
And then make legs to my great man o' law,
To be o' my counsel, and take trouble-vees,
And yet zay nothing for me, but devise
All district means, to ransackle me o' my money.
A pest'lence prick the throats o' 'em! I do know 'em,
As well az I waz in their bellies, and brought up there.
What would you ha' me do, what would you ask of me?
Hugh. I ask the restitution of my money,
And will not bate one penny of the sum;
Fourscore and five pound: and I ask, besides,
Amendment for my hurts; my pain and suffering
Are loss enough for me, sir, to sit down with.
I'll put it to your worship; what you award me,
I'll take, and give him a general release.
Pre. And what say you now, neighbour Turfe?
Turfe. I put it
Even to your worship's bitterment, hab, nab.
I shall have a chance o' the dice for't, I hope, let 'em e'en run: and—
Pre. Faith, then I'll pray you, 'cause he is my neighbour,
To take a hundred pound, and give him day.
Hugh. Saint Valentine's day, I will, this very day,
Before sun-set; my bond is forfeit else.
Turfe. Where will you have it paid?
Hugh. Faith, I am a stranger
Here in the country; know you canon Hugh,
The vicar of Pancras?
Turfe. Yes, who [knows] not him?
Hugh. I'll make him my attorney to receive it,
And give you a discharge.
Turfe. Whom shall I send for't?
Pre. Why, if you please, send Metaphor my clerk:
And, Turfe, I much commend thy willingness;

It's argument of thy integrity.

Turfe. But my integrity shall be my zelf still:
Good master Metaphor, give my wife this key,
And do but whisper it into her hand;
She knows it well enough; bid her, by that,
Deliver you the two zeal'd bags of silver,
That lie in the corner of the cupboard, stands
At my bed-side, they are vifty pound a piece;
And bring them to your master.

Met. If I prove not
As just a carrier as my friend Tom Long was,
Then call me his curtal; change my name of Miles,
To Guiles, Wiles, Piles, Biles, or the foulest name
You can devise, to crambo with for ale.

Hugh. [*takes Met. aside.*] Come hither, Miles; bring by that token
    too
Fair Awdrey; say, her father sent for her.
Say, Clay is found, and waits at Pancras-church,
Where I attend to marry them in haste:
For, by this means, Miles, I may say't to thee,
Thy master must to Awdrey married be.
But not a word but mum: go, get thee gone,
Be wary of thy charge, and keep it close.

Met. O super-dainty canon, vicar incony!
Make no delay, Miles, but away;
And bring the wench and money.   *[Exit.*

Hugh. Now, sir, I see you meant but honestly:
And, but that business calls me hence away,
I would not leave you till the sun were lower.—
But, master justice, one word, sir, with you.   *[Aside to Pre.*
By the same token, is your mistress sent for
By Metaphor, your clerk, as from her father;
Who, when she comes, I'll marry her to you,
Unwitting to this Turfe, who shall attend
Me at the parsonage: this was my plot,
Which I must now make good, turn canon again,
In my square cap. I humbly take my leave.   *[Exit.*

Pre. Adieu, good captain.—Trust me, neighbour Turfe,
He seems to be a sober gentleman:
But this distress hath somewhat stirr'd his patience.
And men, you know, in such extremities,
Apt not themselves to points of courtesy;
I'm glad you have made this end.

Turfe. You stood my friend,
I thank your justice-worship; pray you be
Prezent anon at tendering of the money,
And zee me have a discharge; vor I have no craft
In your law quiblins.

Pre. I'll secure you, neighbour.   *[Exeunt.*

SCENE II.—*The Country near* MARIBONE.

Enter MEDLAY, CLENCH, PAN, *and* SCRIBEN.

Med. Indeed there is a woundy luck in names, sirs,
And a vain mystery, an a man knew where
To vind it. My godsire's name, I'll tell you,
Was In-and-In Shittle, and a weaver he was,
And it did fit his craft: for so his shittle
Went in and in still; this way, and then that way.
And he named me In-and-In Medlay; which serves
A joiner's craft, because that we do lay
Things in and in, in our work. But I am truly
Architectonicus professor, rather;
That is, as one would zay, an architect.

   Clench. As I am a várrier and a visicary;
Horse-smith of Hamstead, and the whole town leach.

   Med. Yes, you have done woundy cures, gossip Clench.

   Clench. An I can zee the stale once through a urine-hole,
I'll give a shrewd guess, be it man or beast.
I cured an ale-wife once that had the staggers
Worse than five horses, without rowelling.
My god-phere was a Rabian or a Jew,
(You can tell, D'oge,) they call'd 'un doctor Rasi.

   Scri. One Rasis was a great Arabic doctor.

   Clench. He was king Harry's doctor, and my god-phere.

   Pan. Mine was a merry Greek, To-Pan of Twiford,
A jovial tinker, and a stopper of holes;
Who left me metal-man of Belsise, his heir.

   Med. But what was yours, D'oge?

   Scri. Vaith, I cannot tell,
If mine were kyrsin'd or no: but zure he had
A kyrsin name, that he left me, Diogenes.
A mighty learned man, but pestilence poor;
Vor he had no house, save an old tub, to dwell in,
(I vind that in records,) and still he turn'd it
In the wind's teeth, as't blew on his backside,
And there they would lie routing one at other,
A week sometimes.

   Med. Thence came, *A Tale of a Tub*,
And the virst *Tale of a Tub*, old D'ogenes' Tub.

   Scri. That was avore sir Peter Tub or his lady.

   Pan. Ay, or the 'squire their son, Tripoly Tub.

   Clench. The 'squire is a fine gentleman.

   Med. He is more,
A gentleman and a half; almost a knight,
Within zix inches; that is his true measure.

   Clench. Zure you can gage 'un.

   Med. To a streak, or less;

I know his d'ameters and circumference:
A knight is six diameters, and a 'squire
Is vive, and zomewhat more; I know't by compass
And scale of man. I have upon my rule here
The just perportions of a knight, a 'squire;
With a tame justice, or an officer rampant,
Upon the bench, from the high constable
Down to the headborough, or tithing-man,
Or meanest minister of the peace, God save 'un!

    Pan. Why you can tell us by the 'squire, neighbour,
Whence he is call'd a constable, and whaffore.

    Med. No, that's a book-case: Scriben can do that.
That's writing and reading, and records.

    Scri. Two words,
Cyning and staple, make a constable;
As we would say, a hold or stay for the king.

    Clench. All constables are truly Johns for the king,
Whate'er their names are, be they Tony or Roger.

    Med. And all are sworn as vingars o' the one hand,
To hold together 'gainst the breach o' the peace;
The high constable is the thumb, as one would zay,
The hold-fast o' the rest.

    Pan. Pray luck he speed
Well in the business between captain Thums
And him!

    Med. I'll warrant 'un for a groat;
I have his measures here in rithmetique,
How he should hear 'un self in all the lines
Of's place and office: let us zeek 'un out.   *[Exeunt.*

SCENE III.—*The Country near* KENTISH-TOWN.
Enter TUB *and* HILTS.

    Tub. Hilts, how dost thou like of this our good day's work?

    Hilts. As good e'en ne'er a whit, as ne'er the better.

    Tub. Shall we to Pancridge or to Kentish-town, Hilts?

    Hilts. Let Kentish-town or Pancridge come to us,
If either will: I will go home again.

    Tub. Faith, Basket, our success hath been but bad,
And nothing prospers that we undertake;
For we can neither meet with Clay nor Awdrey,
The canon Hugh, nor Turfe the constable:
We are like men that wander in strange woods,
And lose ourselves in search of them we seek.

    Hilts. This was because we rose on the wrong side;
But as I am now here, just in the mid-way,
I'll zet my sword on the pummel, and that line
The point valls to, we'll take, whether it be
To Kentish-town, the church, or home again.

    Tub. Stay, stay thy hand: here's justice Bramble's clerk,

Enter METAPHOR.

The unlucky hare hath crossed us all this day.
I'll stand aside whilst thou pump'st out of him
His business, Hilts; and how he's now employed.   [*Walks aside.*
  Hilts. Let me alone, I'll use him in this kind.
  Met. Oh for a pad-horse, pack-horse, or a post-horse,
To bear me on his neck, his back, or his croup!
I am as weary with running as a mill-horse
That hath led the mill once, twice, thrice about,
After the breath hath been out of his body.
I could get up upon a pannier, a pannel,
Or, to say truth, a very pack-saddle,
Till all my honey were turn'd into gall,
And I could sit in the seat no longer:—
Oh [for] the legs of a lackey now, or a footman,
Who is the surbater of a clerk currant,
And the confounder of his trestles dormant!
But who have we here, just in the nick?
  Hilts. I am neither nick, nor in the nick; therefore
You lie, sir Metaphor.
  Met. Lie! how?
  Hilts. Lie so, sir.   [*Strikes up his heels.*
  Met. I lie not yet in my throat.
  Hilts. Thou liest on the ground.
Dost thou know me?
  Met. Yes, I did know you too late.
  Hilts. What is my name, then?
  Met. Basket.
  Hilts. Basket what?
  Met. Basket the great—
  Hilts. The great what?
  Met. Lubber—
I should say, lover, of the 'squire his master.
  Hilts. Great is my patience, to forbear thee thus,
Thou scrape-hill scoundrel, and thou scum of man;
Uncivil, orange-tawney-coated clerk!
Thou cam'st but half a thing into the world,
And wast made up of patches, parings, shreds:
Thou, that when last thou wert put out of service,
Travell'dst to Hamstead-heath on an Ash-We'nesday,
Where thou didst stand six weeks the Jack of Lent,
For boys to hurl, three throws a penny, at thee,
To make thee a purse: seest thou this bold bright blade?
This sword shall shred thee as small unto the grave,
As minced meat for a pye.   I'll set thee in earth
All, save thy head and thy right arm at liberty,
To keep thy hat off while I question thee
What, why, and whither thou wert going now,

With a face ready to break out with business?
And tell me truly, lest I dash't in pieces.

    Met. Then, Basket, put thy smiter up, and hear;
I dare not tell the truth to a drawn sword.

    Hilts. 'Tis sheath'd; stand up, speak without fear or wit.

    Met. [*rises.*] I know not what they mean; but constable Turfe
Sends here his key for monies in his cupboard,
Which he must pay the captain that was robb'd
This morning. Smell you nothing?

    Hilts. No, not I;
Thy breeches yet are honest.

    Met. As my mouth.
Do you not smell a rat? I tell you truth,
I think all's knavery; for the canon whisper'd
Me in the ear, when Turfe had gi'n me his key,
By the same token to bring mistress Awdrey,
As sent for thither; and to say, John Clay
Is found, which is indeed to get the wench
Forth for my master, who is to be married
When she comes there: the canon has his rules
Ready, and all there, to dispatch the matter.

    Tub. [*comes forward.*] Now, on my life, this is the canon's plot.—
Miles, I have heard all thy discourse to Basket.
Wilt thou be true, and I'll reward thee well,
To make me happy in my mistress Awdrey?

    Met. Your worship shall dispose of Metaphor,
Through all his parts, e'en from the sole of the head
To the crown of the foot, to manage of your service.

    Tub. Then do thy message to the mistress Turfe,
Tell her thy token, bring the money hither,
And likewise take young Awdrey to thy charge;
Which done, here, Metaphor, we will attend,
And intercept thee: and for thy reward
You two shall share the money, I the maid;
If any take offence, I'll make all good.

    Met. But shall I have half the money, sir, in faith?

    Tub. Ay, on my 'squireship shalt thou, and my land.

    Met. Then, if I make not, sir, the cleanliest 'scuse
To get her hither, and be then as careful
To keep her for you, as 'twere for myself,
Down on your knees, and pray that honest Miles
May break his neck ere he get o'er two stiles.

    Tub. Make haste, then; we will wait here thy return. [*Exit Met.*
This luck unlook'd for hath reviv'd my hopes,
Which were opprest with a dark melancholy:
In happy time we linger'd on the way,
To meet these summons of a better sound,
Which are the essence of my soul's content.

    Hilts. This heartless fellow, shame to serving-men,

Stain of all liveries, what fear makes him do!
How sordid, wretched and unworthy things!
Betray his master's secrets, ope the closet
Of his devices, force the foolish justice
Make way for your love, plotting of his own;
Like him that digs a trap to catch another,
And falls into't himself!

 Tub. So would I have it,
And hope 'twill prove a jest to twit the justice with.

 Hilts. But that this poor white-liver'd rogue should do it,
And merely out of fear!

 Tub. And hope of money, Hilts:
A valiant man will nibble at that bait.

 Hilts. Who, but a fool, will refuse money proffer'd?

 Tub. And sent by so good chance? Pray heaven he speed.

 Hilts. If he come empty-handed, let him count
To go back empty-headed; I'll not leave him
So much of brain in's pate, with pepper and vinegar,
To be serv'd in for sauce to a calf's head.

 Tub. Thou [wilt] serve him rightly, Hilts.

 Hilts. I'll seal [to] as much
With my hand, as I dare say now with my tongue.
But if you get the lass from Dargison,
What will you do with her?

 Tub. We'll think of that
When once we have her in possession, governor.   [*Exeunt.*

SCENE IV.—*Another Part of the same.*

Enter PUPPY, *and* METAPHOR *with* AUDREY.

 Pup. You see we trust you, master Metaphor,
With mistress Awdrey; pray you use her well,
As a gentlewoman should be used. For my part,
I do incline a little to the serving-man;
We have been of a coat—I had one like yours;
Till it did play me such a sleeveless errand,
As I had nothing where to put mine arms in,
And then I threw it off. Pray you go before her,
Serving-man-like, and see that your nose drop not.
As for example, you shall see me: mark,
How I go afore her! so do you, sweet Miles.
She for her own part is a woman cares not
What man can do unto her in the way
Of honesty and good manners: so farewell,
Fair mistress Awdrey; farewell, master Miles.
I have brought you thus far onward o' your way:
I must go back now to make clean the rooms,
Where my good lady has been. Pray you commend me
To bridegroom Clay, and bid him bear up stiff.

Met. Thank you, good Hannibal Puppy; I shall fit
The leg of your commands with the strait buskins
Of dispatch presently.

Pup. Farewell, fine Metaphor.   [*Exit.*

Met. Come, gentle mistress, will you please to walk?

Awd. I love not to be led; I would go alone.

Met. Let not the mouse of my good meaning, lady,
Be snapp'd up in the trap of your suspicion,
To lose the tail there, either of her truth,
Or swallow'd by the cat of misconstruction.

Awd. You are too finical for me; speak plain, sir.

Enter Tub *and* Hilts.

Tub. Welcome again, my Awdrey, welcome, love!
You shall with me; in faith deny me not:
I cannot brook the second hazard, mistress.

Awd. Forbear, 'squire Tub, as mine own mother says,
I am not for your mowing: you'll be flown
Ere I be fledge.

Hilts. Hast thou the money, Miles?

Met. Here are two bags, there's fifty pound in each.

Tub. Nay, Awdrey, I possess you for this time—
Sirs, take that coin between you, and divide it.
My pretty sweeting, give me now the leave
To challenge love and marriage at your hands.

Awd. Now, out upon you, are you not asham'd!
What will my lady say? In faith, I think
She was at our house, and I think she ask'd for you;
And I think she hit me in the teeth with you,
I thank her ladyship: and I think she means
Not to go hence till she has found you.

Tub. How say you!
Was then my lady mother at your house?
Let's have a word aside.

Awd. Yes, twenty words.   [*They walk aside.*

Enter Lady Tub *and* Pol Martin.

Lady T. 'Tis strange, a motion, but I know not what,
Comes in my mind, to leave the way to Totten,
And turn to Kentish-town again my journey—
And see! my son, Pol Martin, with his Awdrey!
Erewhile we left her at her father's house,
And hath he thence removed her in such haste!
What shall I do, shall I speak fair, or chide?

Pol. Madam, your worthy son with duteous care
Can govern his affections; rather then,
Break off their conference some other way,
Pretending ignorance of what you know.

Tub. An this be all, fair Awdrey, I am thine.

Lady T. [*comes forward.*] Mine you were once, though scarcely
    now your own.

Hilts. 'Slid, my lady, my lady!

Met. Is this my lady bright?   [*Exit.*

Tub. Madam, you took me now a little tardy.

Lady T. At prayers I think you were: what, so devout
Of late, that you will shrive you to all confessors
You meet by chance! come, go with me, good 'squire,
And leave your linen: I have now a business,
And of importance, to impart unto you.

Tub. Madam, I pray you spare me but an hour:
Please you to walk before, I follow you.

Lady T. It must be now, my business lies this way.

Tub. Will not an hour hence, madam, excuse me?

Lady T. 'Squire, these excuses argue more your guilt.
You have some new device now to project,
Which the poor tileman scarce will thank you for.
What! will you go?

Tub. I have ta'en a charge upon me,
To see this maid conducted to her father,
Who, with the canon Hugh, stays her at Pancras,
To see her married to the same John Clay.

Lady T. 'Tis very well; but, 'squire, take you no care,
I'll send Pol Martin with her for that office:
You shall along with me; it is decreed.

Tub. I have a little business with a friend, madam.

Lady T. That friend shall stay for you, or you for him.—
Pol Martin, take the maiden to your care;
Commend me to her father.

Tub. I will follow you.

Lady T. Tut, tell not me of following.

Tub. I'll but speak
A word.

Lady T. No whispering; you forget yourself,
And make your love too palpable: a 'squire,
And think so meanly! fall upon a cowshard!
You know my mind. Come, I will to Turfe's house,
And see for Dido and our Valentine.—
Pol Martin, look to your charge, I'll look to mine.
           [*Exeunt Lady T., Tub, and Hilts.*

Pol. I smile to think, after so many proffers
This maid hath had, she now should fall to me,
That I should have her in my custody!
'Twere but a mad trick to make the essay,
And jump a match with her immediately.
She's fair and handsome, and she's rich enough;
Both time and place minister fair occasion:
Have at it then! [*Aside.*]—Fair lady, can you love?

Awd. No, sir; what's that?

Pol. A toy which women use.

Awd. If it be a toy, it's good to play withal.

Pol. We will not stand discoursing of the toy;
The way is short, please you to prove it, mistress.

Awd. If you do mean to stand so long upon it,
I pray you let me give it a short cut, sir.

Pol. It's thus, fair maid: are you disposed to marry?

Awd. You are disposed to ask.

Pol. Are you to grant?

Awd. Nay, now I see you are disposed indeed.

Pol. I see the wench wants but a little wit,
And that defect her wealth may well supply:
In plain terms, tell me, will you have me, Awdrey?

Awd. In as plain terms, I tell you who would have me,
John Clay would have me, but he hath too hard hands,
I like not him; besides, he is a thief.
And justice Bramble, he would fain have catch'd me:
But the young 'squire, he rather than his life,
Would have me yet; and make me a lady, he says,
And be my knight to do me true knight's service,
Before his lady mother. Can you make me
A lady, would I have you?

Pol. I can give you
A silken gown and a rich petticoat,
And a French hood.—All fools love to be brave:
I find her humour, and I will pursue it.   [*Aside. Exeunt.*

SCENE V.—Kentish-Town.

Enter Lady Tub, Dame Turfe, Squire Tub, *and* Hilts.

Lady T. And, as I told thee, she was intercepted
By the 'squire, here, my son, and this bold ruffian,
His man, who safely would have carried her
Unto her father, and the canon Hugh;
But for more care of the security,
My huisher hath her now in his grave charge.

Dame T. Now on my faith and holydom, we are
Beholden to your worship. She's a girl,
A foolish girl, and soon may tempted be;
But if this day pass well once o'er her head,
I'll wish her trust to herself: for I have been
A very mother to her, though I say it.

Tub. Madam, 'tis late, and Pancridge is in your way;
I think your ladyship forgets yourself.

Lady T. Your mind runs much on Pancridge. Well, young
                 'squire,
The black ox never trod yet on your foot;
These idle phant'sies will forsake you one day.
Come, mistress Turfe, will you go take a walk

Over the fields to Pancridge, to your husband?

Dame T. Madam, I had been there an hour ago,
But that I waited on my man, Ball Puppy.—
What, Ball, I say!—I think the idle slouch
Be fallen asleep in the barn, he stays so long.

Enter PUPPY *hastily from the barn.*

Pup. Sattin, in the name of velvet-sattin, dame!
The devil, O the devil is in the barn!
Help, help! a legion [of] spirits, [a] legion,
Is in the barn! in every straw a devil!

Dame T. Why dost thou bawl so, Puppy? speak, what ails thee?

Pup. My name's Ball Puppy, I have seen the devil
Among the straw. O for a cross! a collop
Of friar Bacon, or a conjuring stick
Of doctor Faustus! spirits are in the barn.

Tub. How, spirits in the barn!—Basket, go see.

Hilts. Sir, an you were my master ten times over,
And 'squire to boot; I know, and you shall pardon me:
Send me 'mong devils! I zee you love me not.
Hell be at their game; I will not trouble them.

Tub. Go see; I warrant thee there's no such matter.

Hilts. An they were giants, 'twere another matter,
But devils! no, if I be torn in pieces,
What is your warrant worth? I'll see the fiend
Set fire o' the barn, ere I come there.

Dame T. Now all zaints bless us, and if he be there,
He is an ugly spright, I warrant.

Pup. As ever
Held flesh-hook, dame, or handled fire-fork rather,
They have put me in a sweet pickle, dame;
But that my lady Valentine smells of musk,
I should be ashamed to press into this presence.

Lady T. Basket, I pray thee see what is the miracle.

Tub. Come, go with me; I'll lead. Why stand'st thou, man?

Hilts. Cock's precious, master, you are not mad indeed.
You will not go to hell before your time?

Tub. Why art thou thus afraid?

Hilts. No, not afraid?
But, by your leave, I'll come no nearer the barn.

Dame T. Puppy, wilt thou go with me?

Pup. How, go with you!
Whither, into the barn? to whom, the devil?
Or to do what there? to be torn amongst 'um!
Stay for my master, the high constable,
Or In-and-In the headborough; let them go
Into the barn with warrant, seize the fiend,
And set him in the stocks for his ill rule:
'Tis not for me that am but flesh and blood,

To meddle with 'un; vor I cannot, nor I wu' not.

Lady T. I pray thee, Tripoly, look what is the matter.

Tub. That shall I, madam.   [*Goes into the barn.*

Hilts. Heaven protect my master!
I tremble every joint till he be back.

Pup. Now, now, even now, they are tearing him in pieces;
Now are they tossing of his legs and arms,
Like loggets at a pear-tree; I'll to the hole,
Peep in, and look whether he lives or dies.

Hilts. I would not be in my master's coat for thousands.

Pup. Then pluck it off, and turn thyself away.
O the devil, the devil, the devil!

Hilts. Where, man, where?

Dame T. Alas, that ever we were born! So near too?

Pup. The 'squire hath him in his hand, and leads him
Out by the collar.

Re-enter Tub, *dragging in* Clay.

Dame T. O this is John Clay.

Lady T. John Clay at Pancras, is there to be married.

Tub. This was the spirit revell'd in the barn.

Pup. The devil he was! was this he was crawling
Among the wheat-straw? had it been the barley,
I should have ta'en him for the devil in drink;
The spirit of the bride-ale: but poor John,
Tame John of Clay, that sticks about the bung-hole—

Hilts. If this be all your devil, I would take
In hand to conjure him: but hell take me,
If e'er I come in a right devil's walk,
If I can keep me out on't.

Tub. Well meant, Hilts.   [*Exit.*

Lady T. But how came Clay thus hid here in the straw,
When news was brought to you all he was at Pancridge,
And you believed it?

Dame T. Justice Bramble's man
Told me so, madam; and by that same token,
And other things, he had away my daughter,
And two seal'd bags of money.

Lady T. Where's the 'squire,
Is he gone hence?

Dame T. He was here, madam, but now.

Clay. Is the hue and cry past by?

Pup. Ay, ay, John Clay.

Clay. And am I out of danger to be hang'd?

Pup. Hang'd, John! yes, sure; unless, as with the proverb,
You mean to make the choice of your own gallows.

Clay. Nay, then all's well: hearing your news, Ball Puppy
You brought from Paddington, I e'en stole home here,
And thought to hide me in the barn e'er since.

Pup. O wonderful! and news was brought us here,
You were at Pancridge, ready to be married.

Clay. No, faith, I ne'er was further than the barn.

Dame T. Haste, Puppy, call forth mistress Dido Wispe,
My lady's gentlewoman, to her lady;
And call yourself forth, and a couple of maids,
To wait upon me: we are all undone,
My lady is undone, her fine young son,
The 'squire, is got away.

Lady T. Haste, haste, good Valentine.

Dame T. And you, John Clay, you are undone too! all!
My husband is undone by a true key,
But a false token; and myself's undone,
By parting with my daughter, who'll be married
To somebody that she should not, if we haste not.   [*Exeunt.*

ACT V

SCENE I.—*The Fields near* KENTISH-TOWN.

Enter Squire TUB *and* POL MARTIN.

Tub. I pray thee, good Pol Martin, shew thy diligence,
And faith in both; get her, but so disguised
The canon may not know her, and leave me
To plot the rest: I will expect thee here.   [*Exit.*

Pol. You shall, 'squire. I'll perform it with all care,
If all my lady's wardrobe will disguise her.—
Come, mistress Awdrey.

Enter AWDREY.

Awd. Is the 'squire gone?

Pol. He'll meet us by and by, where he appointed;
You shall be brave anon, as none shall know you.   [*Exeunt.*

SCENE II.—KENTISH-TOWN.

Enter CLENCH, MEDLAY, PAN, *and* SCRIBEN.

Clench. I wonder where the queen's high constable is,
I vear they ha' made 'un away.

Med. No zure; the justice
Dare not conzent to that: he'll zee 'un forth-coming.

Pan. He must, vor we can all take corpulent oath
We zaw 'un go in there.

Scri. Ay, upon record:
The clock dropt twelve at Maribone.

Med. You are right, D'oge,
Zet down to a minute; now 'tis a' most vowre.

Clench. Here comes 'squire Tub.

Scri. And's governor, master Basket—

Enter Tub *and* Hilts.

Hilts; do you know 'un? a valiant wise fellow,
As tall a man on his hands as goes on veet!
Bless you, mass' Basket.

   Hilts. Thank you, good D'oge.

   Tub. Who's that?

   Hilts. D'oge Scriben the great writer, sir, of Chalcot.

   Tub. And who the rest?

   Hilts. The wisest heads o' the hundred.
Medlay the joiner, headborough of Islington,
Pan of Belsise, and Clench the leach of Hamstead,
The high constable's counsel here of Finsbury.

   Tub. Present me to them, Hilts, 'squire Tub of Totten.

   Hilts. Wise men of Finsbury, make place for a 'squire,
I bring to your acquaintance, Tub of Totten.
'Squire Tub, my master, loves all men of virtue,
And longs, as one would zay, till he be one o' you.

   Clench. His worship's welcum to our company:
Would it were wiser for 'un!

   Pan. Here be some on us
Are call'd the witty men over a hundred.

   Scri. And zome a thousand, when the muster-day comes.

   Tub. I long, as my man Hilts said, and my governor,
To be adopt in your society.
Can any man make a masque here in this company?

   Pan. A masque! what's that?

   Scri. A mumming or a show,
With vizards and fine clothes.

   Clench. A disguise, neighbour,
Is the true word: There stands the man can do't, sir;
Medlay the joiner, In-and-In of Islington,
The only man at a disguise in Middlesex.

   Tub. But who shall write it?

   Hilts. Scriben, the great writer.

   Scri. He'll do't alone, sir; he will join with no man,
Though he be a joiner, in design he calls it,
He must be sole inventer. In-and-In
Draws with no other in's project, he will tell you,
It cannot else be feazible, or conduce:
Those are his ruling words; pleaze you to hear 'un?

   Tub. Yes; master In-and-In, I have heard of you.

   Med. I can do nothing, I.

   Clench. He can do all, sir.

   Med. They'll tell you so.

   Tub. I'd have a toy presented,
A Tale of a Tub, a story of myself,
You can express a Tub?

   Med. If it *conduce*

To the design, whate'er is *feasible:*
I can express a wash-house, if need be,
With a whole pedigree of Tubs.

    Tub. No, one
Will be enough to note our name and family;
'Squire Tub of Totten, and to shew my adventures
This very day. I'd have it in Tub's Hall,
At Totten-Court, my lady mother's house;
My house indeed, for I am heir to it.

    Med. If I might see the place, and had survey'd it,
I could say more: for all invention, sir,
Comes by degrees, and on the view of nature;
A world of things concur to the design,
Which makes it *feasible,* if art *conduce.*

    Tub. You say well, witty master In-and-In.
How long have you studied ingine?

    Med. Since I first
Join'd, or did in-lay in wit, some forty year.

    Tub. A pretty time!—Basket, go you and wait
On master In-and-In to Totten-Court,
And all the other wise masters; shew them the hall,
And taste the language of the buttery to them.
Let them see all the tubs about the house,
That can raise matter, till I come—which shall be
Within an hour at least.

    Clench. It will be glorious,
If In-and-In will undertake it, sir:
He has a monstrous Medlay-wit of his own.

    Tub. Spare for no cost, either in boards or hoops,
To architect your tub: have you ne'er a cooper,
At London, call'd Vitruvius? send for him;
Or old John Heywood, call him to you, to help.

    Scri. He scorns the motion, trust to him alone.

                      [Exeunt all but Tub.

Enter Lady TUB, Dame TURFE, CLAY, PUPPY, *and* WISPE.

    Lady T. O, here's the 'squire! you slipp'd us finely, son.
These manners to your mother will commend you;
But in another age, not this: well, Tripoly,
Your father, good sir Peter, rest his bones,
Would not have done this; where's my huisher, Martin,
And your fair mistress Awdrey?

    Tub. I not see them,
No creature but the four wise masters here,
Of Finsbury hundred, came to cry their constable,
Who, they do say, is lost.

    Dame T. My husband lost,
And my fond daughter lost, I fear me too!
Where is your gentleman, madam? poor John Clay,

Thou has lost thy Awdrey.

Clay. I have lost my wits,
My little wits, good mother; I am distracted.

Pup. And I have lost my mistress, Dido Wispe,
Who frowns upon her Puppy, Hannibal.
Loss, loss on every side! a public loss!
Loss of my master! loss of his daughter! loss
Of favour, friends, my mistress! loss of all!

Enter TURFE *and* PREAMBLE.

Pre. What cry is this?

Turfe. My man speaks of some loss.

Pup. My master's found! good luck, an't be thy will,
Light on us all.

Dame T. O husband, are you alive!
They said you were lost.

Turfe. Where's justice Bramble's clerk?
Had he the money that I sent for?

Dame T. Yes,
Two hours ago, two fifty pounds in silver,
And Awdrey too.

Turfe. Why Awdrey? who sent for her?

Dame T. You, master Turfe, the fellow said.

Turfe. He lied.
I am cozen'd, robb'd, undone: your man's a thief,
And run away with my daughter, master Bramble,
And with my money.

Lady T. Neighbour Turfe, have patience;
I can assure you that your daughter's safe,
But for the monies, I know nothing of.

Turfe. My money is my daughter, and my daughter
She is my money, madam.

Pre. I do wonder
Your ladyship comes to know any thing
In these affairs.

Lady T. Yes, justice Preamble,
I met the maiden in the fields by chance,
In the 'squire's company, my son: how he
Lighted upon her, himself best can tell.

Tub. I intercepted her as coming hither,
To her father, who sent for her by Miles Metaphor,
Justice Preamble's clerk. And had your ladyship
Not hinder'd it, I had paid fine master justice
For his young warrant, and new pursuivant,
He serv'd it by this morning.

Pre. Know you that, sir?

Lady T. You told me, 'squire, a quite other tale,
But I believed you not; which made me send
Awdrey another way, by my Pol Martin,

And take my journey back to Kentish-town,
Where we found John Clay hidden in the barn,
To scape the hue and cry; and here he is.
   Turfe. John Clay agen! nay, then—set cock-a-hoop:
I have lost no daughter, nor no money, justice.
John Clay shall pay; I'll look to you now, John.
Vaith, out it must, as good at night as morning.
I am e'en as vull as a piper's bag with joy,
Or a great gun upon carnation-day.
I could weep lions' tears to see you, John:
'Tis but two vifty pounds I have ventured for you,
But now I have you, you shall pay whole hundred.
Run from your burroughs, son! faith, e'en be hang'd.
An you once earth yourself, John, in the barn,
I have no daughter vor you: who did verret 'un?
   Dame T. My lady's son, the 'squire here, vetch'd 'un out.
Puppy had put us all in such a vright,
We thought the devil was in the barn; and nobody
Durst venture on 'un.
   Turfe. I am now resolv'd
Who shall have my daughter.
   Dame T. Who?
   Turfe. He best deserves her.
Here comes the vicar.—

Enter Sir Hugh.

                   Canon Hugh, we have vound
John Clay agen! the matter's all come round.
   Hugh. Is Metaphor return'd yet?   [*Aside to Pre.*
   Pre. All is turn'd
Here to confusion, we have lost our plot;
I fear my man is run away with the money,
And Clay is found, in whom old Turfe is sure
To save his stake.
   Hugh. What shall we do then, justice?
   Pre. The bride was met in the young 'squire's hands.
   Hugh. And what's become of her?
   Pre. None here can tell.
   Tub. Was not my mother's man, Pol Martin, with you,
And a strange gentlewoman in his company,
Of late here, canon?
   Hugh. Yes, and I dispatch'd them.
   Tub. Dispatch'd them! how do you mean?
   Hugh. Why, married them,
As they desired, but now.
   Tub. And do you know
What you have done, sir Hugh?
   Hugh. No harm, I hope.
   Tub. You have ended all the quarrel: Awdrey is married.

Lady T. Married! to whom?

Turfe. My daughter Awdrey married,
And she not know of it!

Dame T. Nor her father or mother!

Lady T. Whom hath she married?

Tub. Your Pol Martin, madam;
A groom was never dreamt of.

Turfe. Is he a man?

Lady T. That he is, Turfe, and a gentleman I have made him.

Dame T. Nay, an he be a gentleman, let her shift.

Hugh. She was so brave, I knew her not, I swear;
And yet I married her by her own name:
But she was so disguised, so lady-like,
I think she did not know herself the while!
I married them as a mere pair of strangers,
And they gave out themselves for such.

Lady T. I wish them
Much joy, as they have given me heart's ease.

Tub. Then, madam, I'll entreat you now remit
Your jealousy of me; and please to take
All this good company home with you to supper:
We'll have a merry night of it, and laugh.

Lady T. A right good motion, 'squire, which I yield to;
And thank them to accept it.—Neighbour Turfe,
I'll have you merry, and your wife; and you,
Sir Hugh, be pardon'd this your happy error,
By justice Preamble, your friend and patron.

Pre. If the young 'squire can pardon it, I do.

[*Exeunt all but Puppy, Wispe, and Hugh.*

Pup. Stay, my dear Dido; and, good vicar Hu⌐
We have a business with you; in short, this:
If you dare knit another pair of strangers,
Dido of Carthage, and her countryman,
Stout Hannibal stands to't. I have ask'd consent,
And she hath granted.

Hugh. But saith Dido so?

Wispe. From what Ball Hanny hath said, I dare not go.

Hugh. Come in then, I'll dispatch you: a good supper
Would not be lost, good company, good discourse;
But above all, where wit hath any source. [*Exeunt.*

SCENE III.—Totten-Court.—*Before the House.*

Enter Pol Martin, Awdrey, Tub, Lady Tub, Preamble,
Turfe, Dame Turfe, *and* Clay.

Pol. After the hoping of your pardon, madam,
For many faults committed, here my wife
And I do stand expecting your mild doom.

Lady T. I wish thee joy, Pol Martin, and thy wife

As much, mistress Pol Martin. Thou hast trick'd her
Up very fine, methinks.

   Pol. For that I made
Bold with your ladyship's wardrobe, but have trespass'd
Within the limits of your leave—I hope.

   Lady T. I give her what she wears; I know all women
Love to be fine: thou hast deserv'd it of me;
I am extremely pleased with thy good fortune.
Welcome, good justice Preamble; and, Turfe,
Look merrily on your daughter: she has married
A gentleman.

   Turfe. So methinks. I dare not touch her,
She is so fine; yet I will say, God bless her!

   Dame T. And I too, my fine daughter! could love her
Now twice as well as if Clay had her.

   Tub. Come, come, my mother is pleased; I pardon all:
Pol Martin, in and wait upon my lady.
Welcome, good guests! see supper be serv'd in,
With all the plenty of the house and worship.
I must confer with master In-and-In
About some alterations in my masque:
Send Hilts out to me; bid him bring the council
Of Finsbury hither. [*Exeunt all but Tub.*] I'll have such a night
Shall make the name of Totten-Court immortal,
And be recorded to posterity.—

Enter MEDLAY, CLENCH, PAN, *and* SCRIBEN.

O master In-and-In! what have you done?

   Med. Survey'd the place, sir, and design'd the ground,
Or stand-still of the work: and this it is.
First, I have fixed in the earth a tub,
And an old tub, like a salt-petre tub,
Preluding by your father's name, sir Peter,
And the antiquity of your house and family,
Original from salt-petre.

   Tub. Good, i'faith,
You have shewn reading and antiquity here, sir.

   Med. I have a little knowledge in design,
Which I can vary, sir, to *infinito*.

   Tub. *Ad infinitum*, sir, you mean.

   Med. I do,
I stand not on my Latin; I'll invent,
But I must be alone then, join'd with no man:
This we do call the stand-still of our work.

   Tub. Who are those We you now join'd to yourself?

   Med. I mean myself still in the plural number.
And out of this we raise Our Tale of a Tub.

   Tub. No, master In-and-In, My Tale of a Tub,
By your leave; I am Tub, the Tale's of me,

And my adventures! I am 'squire Tub,
Subjectum fabulæ.

   Med. But I the author.

   Tub. The workman, sir, the artificer; I grant you.
So Skelton-laureat was of Elinour Rumming,
But she the subject of the rout and tunning.

   Clench. He has put you to it, neighbour In-and-In.

   Pan. Do not dispute with him; he still will win
That pays for all.

   Scri. Are you revised o' that?
A man may have wit, and yet put off his hat.

   Med. Now, sir, this Tub I will have capt with paper,
A fine oil'd lanthorn paper that we use.

   Pan. Yes, every barber, every cutler has it.

   Med. Which in it doth contain the light to the business;
And shall with the very vapour of the candle
Drive all the motions of our matter about,
As we present them. For example, first,
The worshipful lady Tub—

   Tub. Right worshipful,
I pray you, I am worshipful myself.

   Med. Your 'squireship's mother passeth by (her huisher,
Master Pol Martin, bare-headed before her)
In her velvet gown.

   Tub. But how shall the spectators,
As it might be I, or Hilts, know 'tis my mother,
Or that Pol Martin, there, that walks before her?

   Med. O we do nothing, if we clear not that.

   Clench. You have seen none of his works, sir!

   Pan. All the postures
Of the trained bands of the country.

   Scri. All their colours.

   Pan. And all their captains.

   Clench. All the cries of the city,
And all the trades in their habits.

   Scri. He has
His whistle of command, seat of authority,
And virge to interpret, tipt with silver, sir;
You know not him.

   Tub. Well, I will leave all to him.

   Med. Give me the brief of your subject. Leave the whole
State of the thing to me.

Enter HILTS.

   Hilts. Supper is ready, sir,
My lady calls for you.

   Tub. I'll send it you in writing.

   Med. Sir, I will render *feasible* and facile
What you expect.

Tub. Hilts, be it your care,
To see the wise of Finsbury made welcome:
Let them want nothing.   Is old Rosin sent for?
    Hilts. He's come within.   *[Exit Tub.*
    Scri. Lord, what a world of business
The 'squire dispatches!
    Med. He's a learned man:
I think there are but vew o' the inns of court,
Or the inns of chancery like him.
    Clench. Care to fit 'un then.   *[Exeunt.*

SCENE IV.—*The same.—A Room in the House.*

Enter Black JACK *and* HILTS.

Jack. Yonder's another wedding, master Basket,
Brought in by vicar Hugh.
    Hilts. What are they, Jack?
    Jack. The high constable's man, Ball Hanny, and mistress Wispe,
Our lady's woman.
    Hilts. And are the table merry?
    Jack. There's a young tilemaker makes 'em all laugh;
He will not eat his meat, but cries at the board,
He shall be hang'd.
    Hilts. He has lost his wench already:
As good be hang'd.
    Jack. Was she that is Pol Martin,
Our fellow's mistress, wench to that sneak-John?
    Hilts. I'faith, Black Jack, he should have been her bridegroom:
But I must go to wait on my wise masters.
Jack, you shall wait on me, and see the masque anon;
I am half lord chamberlain in my master's absence.
    Jack. Shall we have a masque? who makes it?
    Hilts. In-and-In,
The maker of Islington: come, go with me
To the sage sentences of Finsbury.   *[Exeunt.*

SCENE V.—*Another Room in the same, with a curtain drawn
across it.*

Enter TUB, *followed by two* Grooms, *with chairs, etc., and* ROSIN
and his two Boys.

1 *Groom.* Come, give us in the great chair for my lady,
And set it there; and this for justice Bramble.
    2 *Groom.* This for the 'squire my master, on the right hand.
    1 *Groom.* And this for the high constable.
    2 *Groom.* This his wife.
    1 *Groom.* Then for the bride and bridegroom here, Pol Martin.
    2 *Groom.* And she Pol Martin at my lady's feet.
    1 *Groom.* Right.
    2 *Groom.* And beside them master Hannibal Puppy.

1 Groom. And his She-Puppy, mistress Wispe that was:
Here's all are in the note.

2 Groom. No, master vicar;
The petty canon Hugh.

1 Groom. And cast-by Clay:
There they are all.

Tub. Then cry *a hall! a hall!*
'Tis merry in Tottenham-hall, when beards wag all:
Come, father Rosin, with your fiddle now,
And two tall toters; flourish to the masque.   [*Loud music.*

Enter PREAMBLE, Lady TUB, TURFE, Dame TURFE, POL MARTIN,
AWDREY, PUPPY, WISPE, HUGH, CLAY; *all take their seats.*
HILTS *waits on the by.*

Lady T. Neighbours all, welcome! Now doth Totten-hall
Shew like a court: and hence shall first be call'd so.
Your witty short confession, master vicar,
Within, hath been the prologue, and hath open'd
Much to my son's device, his Tale of a Tub.

Tub. Let my masque shew itself, and In-and-In,
The architect, appear: I hear the whistle.

Hilts. Peace!

MEDLAY *appears above the curtain.*

*Med. Thus rise I first in my light linen breeches,
To run the meaning over in short speeches.
Here is a Tub, a Tub of Totten-Court,
An ancient Tub has call'd you to this sport:
His father was a knight, the rich sir Peter,
Who got his wealth by a Tub, and by salt-petre;
And left all to his lady Tub, the mother
Of this bold 'squire Tub, and to no other.
Now of this Tub and's deeds, not done in ale,
Observe, and you shall see the very Tale.*
[He draws the curtain, and discovers the top of the Tub.

THE FIRST MOTION.

*Med. Here canon Hugh first brings to Totten-hall
The high constable's council, tells the 'squire all;
Which, though discover'd, give the devil his due,
The wise of Finsbury do still pursue.
Then with the justice doth he counterplot,
And his clerk Metaphor, to cut that knot;
Whilst lady Tub, in her sad velvet gown,
Missing her son, doth seek him up and down.*

Tub. With her Pol Martin bare before her.

Med. Yes,
*I have exprest it here in figure, and Mis-
tress Wispe, her woman, holding up her train.*

Tub. In the next page report your second strain.

THE SECOND MOTION.

Med. Here the high constable and sages walk
To church: the dame, the daughter, bride-maids tal
Of wedding-business; till a fellow in comes,
Relates the robbery of one captain Thums:
Chargeth the bridegroom with it, troubles all,
And gets the bride; who in the hands doth fall
Of the bold 'squire; but thence soon is ta'en
By the sly justice and his clerk profane,
In shape of pursuivant; which he not long
Holds, but betrays all with his trembling tongue:
As truth will break out and shew—

    Tub. O thou hast made him kneel there in a corner,
I see now: there's a simple honour for you, Hilts!

    Hilts. Did I not make him to confess all to you?

    Tub. True, In-and-In hath done you right, you see—
Thy third, I pray thee, witty In-and-In.

    Clench. The 'squire commends 'un; he doth like all well.

    Pan. He cannot choose: this is gear made to sell.

THE THIRD MOTION.

    Med. The careful constable here drooping comes
In his deluded search of captain Thums.
Puppy brings word his daughter's run away
With the tall serving-man, he frights groom Clay
Out of his wits: Returneth then the 'squire,
Mocks all their pains, and gives fame out a liar,
For falsely charging Clay, when 'twas the plot
Of subtle Bramble, who had Awdrey got
Into his hand by this winding device.
The father makes a rescue in a trice:
And with his daughter, like St. George on foot,
Comes home triumphing to his dear heart-root,
And tells the lady Tub, whom he meets there,
Of her son's courtesies, the batchelor,
Whose words had made 'em fall the hue and cry.
When captain Thums coming to ask him, why
He had so done; he cannot yield him cause:
But so he runs his neck into the laws.

THE FOURTH MOTION.

    Med. The laws, who have a noose to crack his neck,
As justice Bramble tells him, who doth peck
A hundred pound out of his purse, that comes
Like his teeth from him, unto captain Thums.
Thums is the vicar in a false disguise;
And employs Metaphor to fetch this prize.
Who tells the secret unto Basket-Hilts,
For fear of beating. This the 'squire quilts

Within his cap; and bids him but purloin
The wench for him; they two shall share the coin.
Which the sage lady in her 'foresaid gown,
Breaks off, returning unto Kentish-town,
To seek her Wispe; taking the 'squire along,
Who finds Clay John, as hidden in straw throng.

Hilts. O how am I beholden to the inventor,
That would not, on record, against me enter,
My slackness here to enter in the barn:
Well, In-and-In, I see thou canst discern!

Tub. On with your last, and come to a conclusion.

THE FIFTH MOTION.

Med. The last is known, and needs but small infusion
Into your memories, by leaving in
These figures as you sit.　I, In-and-In,
Present you with the show: first, of a lady
Tub, and her son, of whom this masque here made I.
Then bridegroom Pol, and mistress Pol the bride,
With the sub-couple, who sit them beside.

Tub. That only verse I alter'd for the better.
Ευφονια *gratia.*

Med. Then justice Bramble, with sir Hugh the canon:
And the bride's parents, which I will not stan' on,
Or the lost Clay, with the recovered Miles:
Who thus unto his master him reconciles,
On the 'squire's word, to pay old Turfe his club.
And so doth end our TALE HERE OF A TUB.

[Exeunt.

THE EPILOGUE,

BY 'SQUIRE TUB.

This tale of me, the Tub of Totten-Court,
A poet first invented for your sport.
Wherein the fortune of most empty tubs,
Rolling in love, are shewn; and with what rubs
We are commonly encountered: when the wit
Of the whole hundred so opposeth it,
Our petty canon's forked plot in chief,
Sly justice' arts, with the high constable's brief
And brag commands; my lady mother's care,
And her Pol Martin's fortune; with the rare
Fate of poor John, thus tumbled in the cask;
Got In-and-In to give it you in a masque:
That you be pleased, who come to see a play,
With those that hear, and mark not what we say.
Wherein the poet's fortune is, I fear,
Still to be early up, but ne'er the near.

THE SAD SHEPHERD;

OR, A TALE OF ROBIN HOOD

THE ARGUMENT

ACT I.

ROBIN HOOD, having invited all the shepherds and shepherdesses of the vale of Belvoir to a feast in the forest of Sherwood, and trusting to his mistress, maid Marian, with her woodmen, to kill him venison against the day: having left the like charge with friar Tuck, his chaplain and steward, to command the rest of his merry men to see the bower made ready, and all things in order for the entertainment: meeting with his guests at their entrance into the wood, welcomes and conducts them to his bower. Where, by the way, he receives the relation of the SAD SHEPHERD, Æglamour, who is fallen into a deep melancholy for the loss of his beloved Earine, reported to have been drowned in passing over the Trent, some few days before. They endeavour in what they can to comfort him: but his disease having taken such strong root, all is in vain, and they are forced to leave him. In the mean time, Marian is come from hunting with the huntsmen, where the lovers interchangeably express their loves. Robin Hood inquires if she hunted the deer at force, and what sport he made? how long he stood, and what head he bore? All which is briefly answered, with a relation of breaking him up, and the raven and her bone. The suspect had of that raven to be Maudlin, the witch of Paplewick, whom one of the huntsmen met in the morning at the rousing of the deer, and [which] is confirmed, by her being then in Robin Hood's kitchen, in the chimney-corner, broiling the same bit which was thrown to the raven at the quarry or fall of the deer. Marian being gone in to shew the deer to some of the shepherdesses, returns instantly to the scene, discontented; sends away the venison she had killed, to her they call the witch; quarrels with her love Robin Hood, abuseth him, and his guests the shepherds; and so departs, leaving them all in wonder and perplexity.

ACT II.

The witch Maudlin having taken the shape of Marian to abuse Robin Hood, and perplex his guests, cometh forth with her daughter Douce, reporting in what confusion she had left them; defrauded them of their venison, made them suspicious each of the other, but most of all, Robin Hood so jealous of his Marian, as she hopes no effect of love would ever reconcile them; glorying so far in the extent of her mischief, as she confesseth to have surprised Earine, stripp'd her of her garments, to make her daughter appear fine at this feast in them; and to have shut the maiden up in a tree, as her son's prize, if he could win her; or his prey, if he would force her. Her son, a rude bragging swineherd, comes to the tree to woo her, (his mother and sister stepping aside to overhear him) and first boasts his wealth to her, and his possessions; which move not. Then he presents her gifts, such as himself is taken with, but she utterly shews a scorn and lothing both of him and them. His mother is angry, rates him, instructs him what to do the next time, and persuades her daughter to shew herself about the bower: tells how she shall know her mother, when she is transform'd, by her broidered belt. Mean while the young shepherdess Amie, being kist by Karolin, Earine's brother, falls in love; but knows not what love is: but describes her disease so innocently, that Marian pities her. When Robin Hood and the rest of his guests invited, enter to Marian, upbraiding her with sending away their venison to mother Maudlin by Scathlock, which she denies; Scathlock affirms it; but seeing his mistress weep, and to forswear it, begins to doubt his own understanding, rather than affront her farther; which makes Robin Hood and the rest to examine themselves better. But Maudlin, the witch, entering like herself, comes to thank her for her bounty; at which Marian is more angry, and more denies the deed. Scathlock enters, tells he has brought it again, and delivered it to the cook. The witch is inwardly vext the venison is so recover'd from her by the rude huntsman, and murmurs and curses; bewitches the cook, mocks poor Amie and the rest; discovereth her ill nature, and is a means of reconciling them all. For the sage shepherd suspecteth her mischief, if she be not prevented: and so persuadeth to seize on her. Whereupon Robin Hood dispatcheth out his woodmen to hunt and take her.

ACT III.

Puck-Hairy discovereth himself in the forest, and discourseth his offices, with their necessities, briefly; after which, Douce entering in the habit of Earine, is pursued by Karol; who (mistaking her at first to be his sister) questions her how she came by those garments. She answers, by her mother's gift. The Sad Shepherd coming in the while, she runs away affrighted, and leaves Karol suddenly; Æglamour thinking it to be Earine's ghost he saw, falls into a melancholic expression of his phant'sie to Karol, and questions him sadly about that point, which moves compassion in Karol of his mistake still. When Clarion and Lionel enter to call Karol to Amie, Karol reports to them Æglamour's passion, with much regret. Clarion resolves to seek him. Karol to return with Lionel. By the way, Douce and her mother (in the shape of Marian) meet them, and would divert them, affirming Amie to be recovered, which Lionel wondered at to be so soon. Robin Hood enters, they tell him the relation of the witch, thinking her to be Marian; Robin suspecting her to be Maudlin, lays hold of her girdle suddenly, but she striving to get free, they both run out, and he returns with the belt broken. She following in her own shape, demanding it, but at a distance, as fearing to be seized upon again; and seeing she cannot recover it, falls into a rage, and cursing, resolving to trust to her old arts, which she calls her daughter to assist in. The shepherds, content with this discovery, go home triumphing, make the relation to Marian. Amie is gladded with the sight of Karol, etc. In the mean time, enters Lorel, with purpose to ravish Earine, and calling her forth to that lewd end, he by the hearing of Clarion's footing is staid, and forced to commit her hastily to the tree again; where Clarion coming by, and hearing a voice singing, draws near unto it; but Æglamour hearing it also, and knowing it to be Earine's, falls into a superstitious commendation of it; as being an angel's, and in the air; when Clarion espies a hand put forth from the tree, and makes towards it, leaving Æglamour to his wild phant'sie, who quitteth the place: and Clarion beginning to court the hand, and make love to it, there ariseth a mist suddenly, which darkening all the place, Clarion loseth himself and the tree where Earine is inclosed, lamenting his misfortune, with the unknown nymph's misery. The air clearing, enters the witch, with her son and daughter, tells them how she had caused that late darkness, to free Lorel from surprisal, and his prey from being rescued from him: bids him look to her, and lock her up more carefully, and follow her, to assist a work she hath in hand of recovering her lost girdle; which she laments the loss of with cursings, execrations, wishing confusion to their feast and meeting, sends her son and daughter to gather certain simples for her purpose, and bring them to her dell. This Puck hearing, prevents, and shews her error still. The huntsmen having found her footing, follow the track, and prick after her. She gets to her dell, and takes her form. Enter [the huntsmen,] Alken has spied her sitting with her spindle, threads, and images. They are eager to seize her presently, but Alken persuades them to let her begin her charms, which they do. Her son and daughter come to her; the huntsmen are affrighted as they see her work go forward. And over-hasty to apprehend her, she escapeth them all, by the help and delusions of Puck.

DRAMATIS PERSONÆ

ROBIN HOOD, *the Chief Woodman, Master of the Feast.*
FRIAR TUCK, *his Chaplain and Steward.*
LITTLE JOHN, *Bow-bearer.*
SCARLET, } *two Brothers, Hunts-*
SCATHLOCK, } *men.*
GEORGE-A-GREEN, *Huisher of the Bower.*
MUCH, *Bailiff, or Acater.*

THE GUESTS INVITED.

ÆGLAMOUR, *the* SAD, }
CLARION, *the Rich,* }
LIONEL, *the Courteous,* } *Shepherds.*
ALKEN, *the Sage,* }
KAROLIN, *the Kind,* }

LOREL, *the Rude, a Swineherd, the Witch's Son.*
PUCK-HAIRY, *or* ROBIN GOOD-FELLOW, *their Hind.*
REUBEN, *the Reconciler, a devout Hermit.*

MARIAN, ROBIN HOOD'S *Lady.*
EARINE, *the Beautiful,* }
MELLIFLEUR, *the Sweet,* } *Shepherd-*
AMIE, *the Gentle,* } *esses.*
MAUDLIN, *the Envious, the Witch of Paplewick.*
DOUCE, *the Proud, her Daughter.*

Musicians, Foresters, *etc.*

SCENE,—SHERWOOD

PROLOGUE.

Enter THE PROLOGUE.

He that hath feasted you these forty years,
And fitted fables for your finer ears,
Although at first he scarce could hit the bore;
Yet you, with patience harkening more and more,
At length have grown up to him, and made known
The working of his pen is now your own:
He prays you would vouchsafe, for your own sake,
To hear him this once more, but sit awake.
And though he now present you with such wool
As from mere English flocks his muse can pull,
He hopes when it is made up into cloth,
Not the most curious head here will be loth
To wear a hood of it, it being a fleece,
To match or those of Sicily or Greece.
His scene is Sherwood, and his play a Tale,

Of Robin Hood's inviting from the vale
Of Belvoir, all the shepherds to a feast:
Where, by the casual absence of one guest,
The mirth is troubled much, and in one man
As much of sadness shewn as passion can:
The sad young shepherd, whom we here present,
Like his woes figure, dark and discontent,

[The Sad Shepherd passeth silently over the stage.

For his lost love, who in the Trent is said
To have miscarried; alas ! what knows the head
Of a calm river, whom the feet have drown'd ?—
Hear what his sorrows are; and if they wound
Your gentle breasts, so that the end crown all,
Which in the scope of one day's chance may fall;
Old Trent will send you more such tales as these,
And shall grow young again as one doth please.

[Exit, but instantly re-enters.

But here's an heresy of late let fall,
That mirth by no means fits a pastoral;
Such say so, who can make none, he presumes:
Else there's no scene more properly assumes
The sock.   For whence can sport in kind arise,
But from the rural routs and families ?
Safe on this ground then, we not fear to-day,
To tempt your laughter by our rustic play;
Wherein if we distaste, or be cried down,
We think we therefore shall not leave the town;
Nor that the fore-wits that would draw the rest
Unto their liking, always like the best.
The wise and knowing critic will not say,
This worst, or better is, before he weigh
Wher every piece be perfect in the kind:
And then, though in themselves he difference find,
Yet if the place require it where they stood,
The equal fitting makes them equal good.
You shall have love and hate, and jealousy,
As well as mirth, and rage, and melancholy:
Or whatsoever else may either move,
Or stir affections, and your likings prove.
But that no style for pastoral should go
Current, but what is stamp'd with Ah! and O!
Who judgeth so, may singularly err;
As if all poesie had one character
In which what were not written, were not right;
Or that the man who made such one poor flight,
In his whole life, had with his winged skill
Advanced him upmost on the muses' hill.
When he like poet yet remains, as those
Are painters who can only make a rose.

From such your wits redeem you, or your chance,
Lest to a greater height you do advance
Of folly, to contemn those that are known
Artificers, and trust such as are none!

ACT I

SCENE I.—SHERWOOD FOREST.—*A distant prospect of hills, valleys,*
cottages, a castle, river, pastures, herds, flocks, etc. ROBIN
HOOD'S *bower in the foreground.*

Enter ÆGLAMOUR.

Æg. Here she was wont to go! and here! and here!
Just where those daisies, pinks, and violets grow:
The world may find the spring by following her,
For other print her airy steps ne'er left.
Her treading would not bend a blade of grass,
Or shake the downy blow-ball from his stalk!
But like the soft west wind she shot along,
And where she went, the flowers took thickest root,
As she had sow'd them with her odorous foot.

[*Exit.*

SCENE II.—*Another Part of the same.*

Enter MARIAN, Friar TUCK, JOHN, GEORGE-A-GREEN, MUCH,
Woodmen, *etc.*

Mar. Know you, or can you guess, my merry men,
What 'tis that keeps your master, Robin Hood,
So long, both from his Marian, and the wood?
Tuck. Forsooth, madam, he will be here by noon,
And prays it of your bounty, as a boon,
That you by then have kill'd him venison some,
To feast his jolly friends, who hither come
In threaves to frolic with him, and make cheer:
Here's Little John hath harbour'd you a deer,
I see by his tackling.
John. And a hart of ten,
I trow he be, madam, or blame your men:
For by his slot, his entries, and his port,
His frayings, fewmets, he doth promise sport,
And standing 'fore the dogs; he bears a head
Large and well-beam'd, with all rights summ'd and spread.
Mar. Let's rouze him quickly, and lay on the hounds.
John. Scathlock is ready with them on the grounds;
So is his brother Scarlet: now they have found
His lair, they have him sure within the pound.
Mar. Away then, when my Robin bids a feast,
'Twere sin in Marian to defraud a guest.

[*Exeunt Marian and John with the Woodmen.*

Tuck. And I, the chaplain, here am left to be
Steward to-day, and charge you all in fee,
To d'on your liveries, see the bower drest,
And fit the fine devices for the feast:
You, George, must care to make the baldrick trim,
And garland that must crown, or her, or him,
Whose flock this year hath brought the earliest lamb.

   George. Good father Tuck, at your commands I am
To cut the table out o' the green sword,
Or any other service for my lord;
To carve the guests large seats; and these lain in
With turf, as soft and smooth as the mole's skin:
And hang the bulled nosegays 'bove their heads,

.   .   .   .   .   .

The piper's bank, whereon to sit and play;
And a fair dial to mete out the day.
Our master's feast shall want no just delights,
His entertainments must have all the rites.

   Much. Ay, and all choice that plenty can send in;
Bread, wine, acates, fowl, feather, fish or fin,
For which my father's nets have swept the Trent—

Enter ÆGLAMOUR.

   Æg. And have you found her?
   Much. Whom?
   Æg. My drowned love,
Earine! the sweet Earine,
The bright and beautiful Earine!
Have you not heard of my Earine?
Just by your father's mill—I think I am right—
Are not you Much the Miller's son?
   Much. I am.
   Æg. And bailiff to brave Robin Hood?
   Much. The same.
   Æg. Close by your father's mills, Earine,
Earine was drown'd! O my Earine!
Old Maudlin tells me so, and Douce her daughter—
Have you swept the river, say you, and not found her?
   Much. For fowl and fish, we have.
   Æg. O, not for her!
You are goodly friends! right charitable men!
Nay, keep your way and leave me; make your toys,
Your tales, your posies, that you talk'd of; all
Your entertainments: you not injure me.
Only if I may enjoy my cypress wreath,
And you will let me weep, 'tis all I ask,
Till I be turn'd to water, as was she!
And troth, what less suit can you grant a man?
   Tuck. His phantasie is hurt, let us now leave him;

The wound is yet too fresh to admit searching.   [*Exit.*

  Æg. Searching! where should I search, or on what track?
Can my slow drop of tears, or this dark shade
About my brows, enough describe her loss!
Earine! O my Earine's loss!
No, no, no, no; this heart will break first.

  George. How will this sad disaster strike the ears
Of bounteous Robin Hood, our gentle master!

  Much. How will it mar his mirth, abate his feast;
And strike a horror into every guest!   [*Exeunt George and Much.*

  Æg. If I could knit whole clouds about my brows,
And weep like Swithin, or those watery signs,
The Kids, that rise then, and drown all the flocks
Of those rich shepherds, dwelling in this vale·
Those careless shepherds that did let her drown!
Then I did something: or could make old Trent
Drunk with my sorrow, to start out in breaches,
To drown their herds, their cattle, and their corn;
Break down their mills, their dams, o'erturn their weirs,
And see their houses and whole livelihood
Wrought into water with her, all were good:
I'd kiss the torrent, and those whirls of Trent,
That suck'd her in, my sweet Earine!
When they have cast her body on the shore,
And it comes up as tainted as themselves,
All pale and bloodless, I will love it still,
For all that they can do, and make them mad
To see how I will hug it in mine arms!
And hang upon her looks, dwell on her eyes,
Feed round about her lips, and eat her kisses,
Suck off her drowned flesh!—and where's their malice!
Not all their envious sousing can change that.
But I will still study some revenge past this—
                     [*Music of all sorts is heard.*
I pray you give me leave, for I will study,
Though all the bells, pipes, tabors, timburines ring,
That you can plant about me; I will study.

   Enter ROBIN HOOD, CLARION, MELLIFLEUR, LIONEL, AMIE,
            ALKEN, TUCK, Musicians, *etc.*

  Rob. Welcome, bright Clarion, and sweet Mellifleur,
The courteous Lionel, fair Amie; all
My friends and neighbours, to the jolly bower
Of Robin Hood, and to the green-wood walks!
Now that the shearing of your sheep is done,
And the wash'd flocks are lighted of their wool,
The smoother ewes are ready to receive
The mounting rams again; and both do feed,
As either promised to increase your breed

At eaning-time, and bring you lusty twins:
Why should or you or we so much forget
The season in ourselves, as not to make
Use of our youth and spirits, to awake
The nimble horn-pipe, and the timburine,
And mix our songs and dances in the wood,
And each of us cut down a triumph-bough?—
Such are the rites the youthful June allow.

　Cla. They *were*, gay Robin; but the sourer sort
Of shepherds now disclaim in all such sport:
And say, our flock the while are poorly fed,
When with such vanities the swains are led.

　Tuck. Would they, wise Clarion, were not hurried more
With covetise and rage, when to their store
They add the poor man's yeanling, and dare sell
Both fleece and carcass, not gi'ing him the fell!
When to one goat they reach that prickly weed,
Which maketh all the rest forbear to feed;
Or strew tods' hairs, or with their tails do sweep
The dewy grass, to do'ff the simpler sheep;
Or dig deep pits their neighbour's neat to vex,
To drown the calves, and crack the heifers' necks;
Or with pretence of chasing thence the brock,
Send in a cur to worry the whole flock!

　Lio. O friar, those are faults that are not seen,
Ours open, and of worst example been.
They call ours Pagan pastimes, that infect
Our blood with ease, our youth with all neglect;
Our tongues with wantonness, our thoughts with lust;
And what they censure ill, all others must.

　Rob. I do not know what their sharp sight may see,
Of late, but I should think it still might be
As 'twas, an happy age, when on the plains
The woodmen met the damsels, and the swains
The neat-herds, ploughmen, and the pipers loud,
And each did dance, some to the kit or crowd,
Some to the bag-pipe; some the tabret mov'd,
And all did either love, or were belov'd.

　Lio. The dextrous shepherd then would try his sling,
Then dart his hook at daisies, then would sing;
Sometimes would wrestle.

　Cla. Ay, and with a lass:
And give her a new garment on the grass;
After a course at barley-break, or base.

　Lio. And all these deeds were seen without offence,
Or the least hazard of their innocence.

　Rob. Those charitable times had no mistrust:
Shepherds knew how to love, and not to lust.

　Cla. Each minute that we lose thus, I confess,

Deserves a censure on us, more or less;
But that a sadder chance hath given allay
Both to the mirth and music of this day.
Our fairest shepherdess we had of late,
Here upon Trent, is drown'd; for whom her mate,
Young Æglamour, a swain, who best could tread
Our country dances, and our games did lead,
Lives like the melancholy turtle, drown'd
Deeper in woe, than she in water: crown'd
With yew, and cypress, and will scarce admit
The physic of our presence to his fit.

    Lio. Sometimes he sits, and thinks all day, then walks,
Then thinks again, and sighs, weeps, laughs, and talks;
And 'twixt his pleasing frenzy, and sad grief,
Is so distracted, as no sought relief
By all our studies can procure his peace.

    Cla. The passion finds in him that large increase,
As we doubt hourly we shall lose him too.

    Rob. You should not cross him then, whate'er you do.
For phant'sie stopp'd, will soon take fire, and burn
Into an anger, or to a phrensie turn.

    Cla. Nay, so we are advised by Alken here,
A good sage shepherd, who, although he wear
An old worn hat and cloke, can tell us more
Than all the forward fry, that boast their lore.

    Lio. See, yonder comes the brother of the maid,
Young Karolin: how curious and afraid
He is at once! willing to find him out,
And loth to offend him.

Enter KAROLIN.

    Kar. Sure he's here about.

    Cla. See where he sits.

                [*Points to Æglamour, sitting upon a bank hard by.*

    Æg. It will be rare, rare, rare!
An exquisite revenge! but peace, no words!
Not for the fairest fleece of all the flock:
If it be known afore, 'tis all worth nothing!
I'll carve it on the trees, and in the turf,
On every green sward, and in every path,
Just to the margin of the cruel Trent.
There will I knock the story in the ground,
In smooth great pebble, and moss fill it round,
Till the whole country read how she was drown'd;
And with the plenty of salt tears there shed,
Quite alter the complexion of the spring.
Or I will get some old, old, grandam thither,
Whose rigid foot but dipp'd into the water,
Shall strike that sharp and sudden cold throughout,

As it shall lose all virtue; and those nymphs,
Those treacherous nymphs pull'd in Earine,
Shall stand curl'd up like images of ice,
And never thaw! mark, never! a sharp justice!
Or stay, a better! when the year's at hottest,
And that the dog-star foams, and the stream boils,
And curls, and works, and swells ready to sparkle,
To fling a fellow with a fever in,
To set it all on fire, till it burn
Blue as Scamander, 'fore the walls of Troy,
When Vulcan leap'd into him to consume him.

    Rob. A deep hurt phant'sie!   [*They approach him.*

    Æg. Do you not approve it?

    Rob. Yes, gentle Æglamour, we all approve,
And come to gratulate your just revenge:
Which, since it is so perfect, we now hope
You'll leave all care thereof, and mix with us,
In all the proffer'd solace of the spring.

    Æg. A spring, now she is dead! of what? of thorns,
Briars, and brambles? thistles, burs and docks?
Cold hemlock, yew? the mandrake or the box?
These may grow still; but what can spring beside?
Did not the whole earth sicken when she died?
As if there since did fall one drop of dew,
But what was wept for her! or any stalk
Did bear a flower, or any branch a bloom,
After her wreath was made! In faith, in faith,
You do not fair to put these things upon me,
Which can in no sort be: Earine,
Who had her very being, and her name,
With the first knots or buddings of the spring,
Born with the primrose, or the violet,
Or earliest roses blown; when Cupid smiled;
And Venus led the Graces out to dance,
And all the flowers and sweets in nature's lap
Leap'd out, and made their solemn conjuration,
To last but while she lived! Do not I know
How the vale wither'd the same day? how Dove,
Dean, Eye, and Erwash, Idel, Snite and Soare,
Each broke his urn, and twenty waters more,
That swell'd proud Trent, shrunk themselves dry? that since
No sun or moon, or other cheerful star,
Look'd out of heaven, but all the cope was dark,
As it were hung so for her exequies!
And not a voice or sound to ring her knell;
But of that dismal pair, the screeching-owl,
And buzzing hornet! Hark! hark! hark! the foul
Bird! how she flutters with her wicker wings!
Peace! you shall hear her screech.

Cla. Good Karolin, sing,
Help to divert this phant'sie.
    Kar. All I can.   *[Sings, while Æg. reads the song.*

> Though I am young and cannot tell
> Either what Death or Love is well,
> Yet I have heard they both bear darts,
> And both do aim at human hearts:
> And then again, I have been told,
> Love wounds with heat, as Death with cold;
> So that I fear they do but bring
> Extremes to touch, and mean one thing.
>
> As in a ruin we it call
> One thing to be blown up or fall;
> Or to our end, like way may have
> By flash of lightning, or a wave:
> So Love's inflamed shaft or brand
> May kill as soon as Death's cold hand,
> Except Love's fires the virtue have
> To fright the frost out of the grave.

    Æg. Do you think so? are you in that good heresy,
I mean, opinion? if you be, say nothing:
I'll study it as a new philosophy,
But by myself alone: now you shall leave me.
Some of these nymphs here will reward you; this,
This pretty maid, although but with a kiss.
                [He forces Amie to kiss Karolin.
Lived my Earine, you should have twenty;
For every line here, one; I would allow them
From mine own store, the treasure I had in her:
Now I am poor as you.   *[Exit.*
    Kar. And I a wretch!
    Cla. Yet keep an eye upon him, Karolin.   *[Exit Karolin.*
    Mel. Alas, that ever such a generous spirit
As Æglamour's should sink by such a loss!
    Cla. The truest lovers are least fortunate:
Look all their lives and legends, what they call
The lover's scriptures, Heliodores or Tatii,
Longi, Eustathii, Prodomi, you'll find it!
What think you, father?
    Alken. I have known some few,
And read of more who have had their dose, and deep,
Of these sharp bitter-sweets.
    Lio. But what is this
To jolly Robin, who the story is
Of all beatitude in love?
    Cla. And told
Here every day with wonder on the wold.
    Lio. And with fame's voice.

Alken. Save that some folk delight
To blend all good of others with some spight.

Cla. He and his Marian are the sum and talk
Of all that breathe here in the green-wood walk.

Mel. Or Belvoir vale.

Lio. The turtles of the wood.

Cla. The billing pair.

Alken. And so are understood
For simple loves, and sampled lives beside.

Mel. Faith, so much virtue should not be envied.

Alken. Better be so than pitied, Mellifleur:
For 'gainst all envy virtue is a cure;
But wretched pity ever calls on scorns.—　　　*[Horns within.*
The deer's brought home; I hear it by their horns.

Enter Marian, John, *and* Scarlet.

Rob. My Marian, and my mistress!

Mar. My loved Robin!　　　　　　　　　*[They embrace.*

Mel. The moon's at full, the happy pair are met.

Mar. How hath this morning paid me for my rising!
First, with my sports; but most with meeting you.
I did not half so well reward my hounds,
As she hath me to-day; although I gave them
All the sweet morsels call'd tongue, ears, and dowcets!

Rob. What, and the inch-pin?

Mar. Yes.

Rob. Your sports then pleased you?

Mar. You are a wanton.

Rob. *One,* I do confess,
I *want*-ed till you came; but now I have you,
I'll grow to your embraces, till two souls
Distilled into kisses through our lips,
Do make one spirit of love.　　　　　　　*[Kisses her.*

Mar. O Robin, Robin!

Rob. Breathe, breathe awhile; what says my gentle Marian?

Mar. Could you so long be absent?

Rob. What, a week!
Was that so long?

Mar. How long are lovers' weeks,
Do you think, Robin, when they are asunder?
Are they not prisoners' years?

Rob. To some they seem so;
But being met again, they are schoolboys' hours.

Mar. That have got leave to play, and so we use them.

Rob. Had you good sport in your chase to-day?

John. O prime!

Mar. A lusty stag.

Rob. And hunted ye at force?

Mar. In a full cry.

John. And never hunted change!

Rob. You had stanch hounds then?

Mar. Old and sure; I love
No young rash dogs, no more than changing friends.

Rob. What relays set you?

John. None at all: we laid not
In one fresh dog.

Rob. He stood not long then?

Scar. Yes,
Five hours and more. A great, large dear!

Rob. What head?

John. Forked: a hart of ten.

Mar. He is good venison,
According to the season in the blood,
I'll promise all your friends, for whom he fell.

John. But at his fall there hapt a chance.

Mar. Worth mark.

Rob. Ay, what was that, sweet Marian?   [*Kisses her.*

Mar. You'll not hear?

Rob. I love these interruptions in a story;   [*Kisses her again.*
They make it sweeter.

Mar. You do know as soon
As the assay is taken—   [*Kisses her again.*

Rob. On, my Marian:
I did but take the assay.

Mar. You stop one's mouth,
And yet you bid one speak—when the arbor's made—

Rob. Pull'd down, and paunch turn'd out.

Mar. He that undoes him,
Doth cleave the brisket bone, upon the spoon
Of which a little gristle grows; you call it—

Rob. The raven's bone.

Mar. Now o'er head sat a raven,
On a sere bough, a grown great bird, and hoarse!
Who, all the while the deer was breaking up,
So croak'd and cried for it, as all the huntsmen,
Especially old Scathlock, thought it ominous;
Swore it was mother Maudlin, whom he met
At the day-dawn, just as he roused the deer
Out of his lair: but we made shift to run him
Off his four legs, and sunk him ere we left.

Enter SCATHLOCK.

Is the deer come?

Scath. He lies within on the dresser.

Mar. Will you go see him, Mellifleur?

Mel. I attend you.

Mar. Come, Amie, you'll go with us?

Amie. I am not well.

Lio. She's sick of the young shepherd that bekiss'd her.
Mar. Friend, cheer your friends up, we will eat him merrily.
                                [*Exeunt Mar., Mel., and Amie.*

  Alken. Saw you the raven, friend?
  Scath. Ay, quha suld let me?
I suld be afraid o' you, sir, suld I?
  Clar. Huntsman,
A dram more of civility would not hurt you.
  Rob. Nay, you must give them all their rudenesses;
They are not else themselves without their language.
  Alken. And what do you think of her?
  Scath. As of a witch.
They call her a wise woman, but I think her
An arrant witch.
  Clar. And wherefore think you so?
  Scath. Because I saw her since broiling the bone
Was cast her at the quarry.
  Alken. Where saw you her?
  Scath. In the chimley-nuik, within: she's there now.

Re-enter MARIAN.

  Rob. Marian!
Your hunt holds in his tale still; and tells more.
  Mar. My hunt! what tale?
  Rob. How! cloudy, Marian!
What look is this?
  Mar. A fit one, sir, for you.
Hand off, rude ranger!—Sirrah, get you in,   [*To Scathlock.*
And bear the venison hence: it is too good
For these coarse rustic mouths, that cannot open,
Or spend a thank for't. A starv'd mutton's carcase
Would better fit their palates. See it carried
To mother Maudlin's, whom you call the witch, sir.
Tell her I sent it to make merry with.
She'll turn us thanks at least! why stand'st thou, groom?
  Rob. I wonder he can move, that he's not fix'd,
If that his feeling be the same with mine!
I dare not trust the faith of mine own senses,
I fear mine eyes and ears: this is not Marian!
Nor am I Robin Hood! I pray you ask her,
Ask her, good shepherds, ask her all for me:
Or rather ask yourselves, if she be she;
Or I be I.
  Mar. Yes, and you are the spy;
And the spied spy that watch upon my walks,
To inform what deer I kill or give away!
Where! when! to whom! but spy your worst, good spy,
I will dispose of this where least you like!
Fall to your cheese-cakes, curds, and clouted cream,

Your fools, your flawns; and [swill] of ale a stream
To wash it from your livers: strain ewes' milk
Into your cyder syllabubs, and be drunk
To him whose fleece hath brought the earliest lamb
This year; and wears the baudric at your board!
Where you may all go whistle and record
This in your dance; and foot it lustily.   [*Exit.*

 Rob. I pray you, friends, do you hear and see as I do?
Did the same accents strike your ears? and objects
Your eyes, as mine?

 Alken. We taste the same reproaches.

 Lio. Have seen the changes.

 Rob. Are we not all changed,
Transformed from ourselves?

 Lio. I do not know.
The best is silence.

 Alken. And to wait the issue.

 Rob. The dead or lazy wait for't! I will find it.   [*Exeunt.*

ACT II

SCENE I.—*The Forest as before.*—*The* Witch's *Dimble, cottage,*
     oak, well, etc.

Enter MAUDLIN *in her proper shape, and* DOUCE *in the dress*
     of EARINE.

 Maud. Have I not left them in a brave confusion?
Amazed their expectation, got their venison,
Troubled their mirth and meeting, made them doubtful
And jealous of each other, all distracted,
And, in the close, uncertain of themselves?
This can your mother do, my dainty Douce!
Take any shape upon her, and delude
The senses best acquainted with their owners!—
The jolly Robin, who hath bid this feast,
And made this solemn invitation,
I have possessed so with syke dislikes
Of his own Marian, that allbe he know her,
As doth the vauting hart his venting hind,
He ne'er fra' hence sall neis her in the wind,
To his first liking.

 Douce. Did you so distaste him?

 Maud. As far as her proud scorning him could 'bate,
Or blunt the edge of any lover's temper.

 Douce. But were ye like her, mother?

 Maud. So like, Douce,
As had she seen me her sel', her sel' had doubted
Whether had been the liker of the twa—

This can your mother do, I tell you, daughter!—
I ha' but dight ye yet in the out-dress,
And 'parel of Earine; but this raiment,
These very weeds sall make ye, as but coming
In view or ken of Æglamour, your form
Shall shew too slippery to be look'd upon,
And all the forests swear you to be she!
They shall rin after ye, and wage the odds,
Upon their own deceived sights, ye are her;
Whilst she, poor lass, is stock'd up in a tree:
Your brother Lorel's prize! for so my largess
Hath lotted her to be,—your brother's mistress,
Gif she can be reclaim'd; gif not, his prey!
And here he comes new claithed, like a prince
Of swineherds! syke he seems, dight in the spoils
Of those he feeds, a mighty lord of swine!
He's command now to woo.   Let's step aside,
And hear his love-craft.   [*They stand aside.*

Enter LOREL *gaily dressed, and releases* EARINE *from the oak.*

            See he opes the door,
And takes her by the hand, and helps her forth:
This is true courtship, and becomes his ray.
     Lor. [*leading Earine forward.*] Ye kind to others, but ye
         coy to me,
Deft mistress! whiter than the cheese new prest,
Smoother than cream, and softer than the curds!
Why start ye from me ere ye hear me tell
My wooing errand, and what rents I have?
Large herds and pastures! swine and kie mine own!
And though my nase be camused, my lips thick,
And my chin bristled, Pan, great Pan, was such,
Who was the chief of herdsmen, and our sire!
I am na fay, na incubus, na changlin,
But a good man, that lives o' my awn geer:
This house, these grounds, this stock is all my awn.
     Ear. How better 'twere to me, this were not known!
     Maud. She likes it not; but it is boasted well.
     Lor. An hundred udders for the pail I have,
That give me milk and curds, that make me cheese
To cloy the markets! twenty swarm of bees,
Whilk all the summer hum about the hive,
And bring me wax and honey in bilive.
An aged oak, the king of all the field,
With a broad breech there grows before my dur,
That mickle mast unto the ferm doth yield.
A chesnut, whilk hath larded mony a swine,
Whose skins I wear to fend me fra the cold;
A poplar green, and with a kerved seat,

Under whose shade I solace in the heat;
And thence can see gang out and in my neat,
Twa trilland brooks, each, from his spring, doth meet,
And make a river to refresh my feet;
In which each morning, ere the sun doth rise,
I look myself, and clear my pleasant eyes,
Before I pipe; for therein I have skill
'Bove other swineherds. Bid me, and I will
Straight play to you, and make you melody.
    Ear. By no means. Ah! to me all minstrelsy
Is irksome, as are you.
    Lor. Why scorn you me?
Because I am a herdsman, and feed swine!
I am a lord of other geer:—This fine
Smooth bawson cub, the young grice of a gray,
Twa tiny urchins, and this ferret gay.
    Ear. Out on 'em! what are these?
    Lor. I give 'em ye,
As presents, mistress.
    Ear. O the fiend on thee!
Gae, take them hence; they fewmand all the claithes,
And prick my coats: hence with 'em, limmer lown,
Thy vermin and thyself, thyself art one!
Ay, lock me up—all's well when thou art gone.
                    [*Lorel leads her to the tree and shuts her in.*
                    [*Maudlin and Douce come forward.*
    Lor. Did you hear this? she wish'd me at the fiend,
With all my presents!
    Maud. A tu lucky end
She wishand thee, foul limmer, dritty lown!
Gud faith, it duills me that I am thy mother:
And see, thy sister scorns thee for her brother.
Thou woo thy love, thy mistress, with twa hedgehogs:
A stinkand brock, a polecat? out, thou houlet!
Thou shouldst have given her a madge-owl, and then
Thou'dst made a present o' thy self, owl-spiegle!
    Douce. Why, mother, I have heard ye bid to give;
And often as the cause calls.
    Maud. I know well,
It is a witty part sometimes to give;
But what? to wham? no monsters, nor to maidens.
He suld present them with mare pleasand things,
Things natural, and what all women covet
To see, the common parent of us all,
Which maids will twire at 'tween their fingers thus:
With which his sire gat him, he's get another,
And so beget posterity upon her;
This he should do!—False gelden, gang thy gait,
And do thy turns betimes; or I'se gar take

Thy new breikes fra' thee, and thy dublet tu:—
The tailleur and the sowter sall undu'
All they have made, except thou manlier woo!   [*Exit Lorel.*
    Douce. Gud mother, gif you chide him, he'll do wairs.
    Maud. Hang him! I geif him to the devil's eirs.
But ye, my Douce, I charge ye, shew your sell
Tu all the shepherds bauldly; gaing amang 'em,
Be mickel in their eye, frequent and fugeand:
And gif they ask ye of Earine,
Or of these claithes, say, that I gave 'em ye,
And say no more.   I have that wark in hand,
That web upon the luime, shall gar 'em think
By then, they feeling their own frights and fears,
I'se pu' the world or nature 'bout their ears.—
But, hear ye, Douce, because ye may meet me
In mony shapes to-day, where'er you spy
This browder'd belt with characters, 'tis I.
A Gypsan lady, and a right beldame,
Wrought it by moonshine for me, and star-light,
Upon your grannam's grave, that very night
We earth'd her in the shades; when our dame Hecate
Made it her gaing night over the kirk-yard,
With all the barkand parish-tikes set at her,
While I sat whyrland of my brazen spindle:
At every twisted thrid my rock let fly
Unto the sewster, who did sit me nigh,
Under the town turnpike; which ran each spell
She stitched in the work, and knit it well.
See ye take tent to this, and ken your mother.   [*Exeunt.*

SCENE II.—*Another part of the Forest.*—*The Entrance to*
           ROBIN HOOD'S *Bower.*

AMIE *discovered lying on a bank,* MARIAN *and* MELLIFLEUR
           sitting by her.

    Mar. How do you, sweet Amie, yet?
    Mel. She cannot tell;
If she could sleep, she says, she should do well.
She feels a hurt, but where, she cannot shew
Any least sign, that she is hurt or no:
Her pain's not doubtful to her, but the seat
Of her pain is: her thoughts too work and beat,
Opprest with cares; but why she cannot say:
All matter of her care is quite away.
    Mar. Hath any vermin broke into your fold?
Or any rot seized on your flock, or cold?
Or hath your feighting ram burst his hard horn,
Or any ewe her fleece, or bag hath torn,
My gentle Amie?

Amie. Marian, none of these.

Mar. Have you been stung by wasps, or angry bees,
Or rased with some rude bramble or rough briar?

Amie. No, Marian, my disease is somewhat nigher.
I weep, and boil away myself in tears;
And then my panting heart would dry those fears:
I burn, though all the forest lend a shade;
And freeze, though the whole wood one fire were made.

Mar. Alas!

Amie. I often have been torn with thorn and briar,
Both in the leg and foot, and somewhat higher;
Yet gave not then such fearful shrieks as these.   [*Sighs.*
I often have been stung too with curst bees,
Yet not remember that I then did quit
Either my company or mirth for it.   [*Sighs again.*
And therefore what it is that I feel now,
And know no cause of it, nor where, nor how
It enter'd in me, nor least print can see,
I feel, afflicts me more than briar or bee.   [*Again.*
How often when the sun, heaven's brightest birth,
Hath with his burning fervour cleft the earth,
Under a spreading elm or oak, hard by
A cool clear fountain, could I sleeping lie,
Safe from the heat! but now no shady tree,
Nor purling brook, can my refreshing be.
Oft when the meadows were grown rough with frost,
The rivers ice-bound, and their currents lost,
My thick warm fleece I wore, was my defence;
Or large good fires I made, drave winter thence:
But now my whole flock's fells, nor this thick grove,
Enflam'd to ashes, can my cold remove.
It is a cold and heat that does outgo
All sense of winters, and of summers so.

Enter ROBIN HOOD, CLARION, LIONEL, *and* ALKEN.

Rob. O are you here, my mistress?

Mar. I, my love!   [*Runs to embrace him.*
Where should I be but in my Robin's arms,
The sphere which I delight in so to move?

Rob. [*he puts her back.*] What, *the rude ranger, and spied spy !
hand off;*
You are for no such rustics.

Mar. What means this,
Thrice worthy Clarion, or wise Alken? know ye?

Rob. 'Las, no, not they: *a poor starv'd mutton's carcase
Would better fit their palates than your venison.*

Mar. What riddle's this? unfold yourself, dear Robin.

Rob. You have not sent your venison hence by Scathlock,
To mother Maudlin?

Mar. I, to mother Maudlin!
Will Scathlock say so?
 Rob. Nay, we will all swear so.
For all did hear it when you gave the charge so,
Both Clarion, Alken, Lionel, and myself.
 Mar. Good honest shepherds, masters of your flocks,
Simple and virtuous men, no others' hirelings;
Be not you made to speak against your conscience,
That which may soil the truth. I send the venison
Away by Scathlock, and to mother Maudlin!
I came to shew it here to Mellifleur,
I do confess; but Amie's falling ill
Did put us off it: since, we employ'd ourselves
In comforting of her.

Enter SCATHLOCK.

O, here he is!
Did I, sir, bid you bear away the venison
To mother Maudlin?
 Scath. Ay, gud faith, madam,
Did you, and I ha' done it.
 Mar. What have you done?
 Scath. Obey'd your hests, madam; done your commands.
 Mar. Done my commands, dull groom! fetch it again,
Or kennel with the hounds. Are these the arts, [*Weeps.*
Robin, you read your rude ones of the wood,
To countenance your quarrels and mistakings?
Or are the sports to entertain your friends
Those formed jealousies? ask of Mellifleur,
If I were ever from her, here, or Amie,
Since I came in with them; or saw this Scathlock
Since I related to you his tale of the raven.
 Scath. Ay, say you so!   [*Exit.*
 Mel. She never left my side
Since I came here, nor I hers.
 Cla. This is strange:
Our best of senses were deceived, our eyes, then!
 Lio. And ears too.
 Mar. What you have concluded on,
Make good, I pray you.
 Amie. O my heart, my heart!
 Mar. My heart it is wounded, pretty Amie;
Report not you your griefs: I'll tell for all.
 Mel. Somebody is to blame, there is a fault.
 Mar. Try if you can take rest: a little slumber
Will much refresh you, Amie.   [*Amie sleeps.*
 Alken. What's her grief?
 Mar. She does not know: and therein she is happy.

Enter JOHN *and* MAUDLIN.

John. Here's mother Maudlin come to give you thanks,
Madam, for some late gift she hath received—
Which she's not worthy of, she says, but cracks,
And wonders of it; hops about the house,
Transported with the joy.

    Maud. Send me a stag,
A whole stag, madam, and so fat a deer!
So fairly hunted, and at such a time too,
When all your friends were here!   *[Skips and dances.*

    Rob. Do you mark this, Clarion?
Her own acknowledgment!

    Maud. 'Twas such a bounty
And honour done to your poor beadswoman,
I know not how to owe it, but to thank you;
And that I come to do: I shall go round,
And giddy with the joy of the good turn.

        Look out, look out, gay folk about,
        And see me spin the ring I am in
        Of mirth and glee, with thanks for fee
        The heart puts on, for th' venison
        My lady sent, which shall be spent
        In draughts of wine, to fume up fine
        Into the brain, and down again
        Fall in a swoun, upon the groun.
        [Turns rapidly round as she speaks, till she falls.

    Rob. Look to her, she is mad.

    Maud. [*rising.*] My son hath sent you
A pot of strawberries gather'd in the wood,
His hogs would else have rooted up, or trod;
With a choice dish of wildings here to scald
And mingle with your cream.

    Mar. Thank you, good Maudlin,
And thank your son. Go, bear them in to Much,
The acater, let him thank her. Surely, mother,
You were mistaken, or my woodmen more,
Or most myself, to send you all our store
Of venison, hunted for ourselves this day:
You will not take it, mother, I dare say,
If we entreat you, when you know our guests;
Red deer is head still of the forest feasts.

    Maud. But I knaw ye, a right free-hearted lady,
Can spare it out of superfluity;
I have departit it 'mong my poor neighbours,
To speak your largess.

    Mar. I not gave it, mother;
You have done wrong then: I know how to place

My gifts, and where; and when to find my seasons
To give, not throw away my courtesies.

   Maud. Count you this thrown away?

   Mar. What's ravish'd from me
I count it worse, as stolen; I lose my thanks.
But leave this quest: they fit not you nor me,
Maudlin, contentions of this quality.—

Re-enter SCATHLOCK.

How now!

   Scath. Your stag's return'd upon my shoulders,
He has found his way into the kitchen again
With his two legs; if now your cook can dress him.—
'Slid, I thought the swineherd would have beat me,
He look'd so big! the sturdy karl, lewd Lorel!

   Mar. There, Scathlock, for thy pains; [*gives him money.*]
       thou hast deserv'd it.   [*Exit Scath.*

   Maud. Do you give a thing, and take a thing, madam?

   Mar. No, Maudlin, *you had imparted to your neighbours;*
And much good do it them! I have done no wrong.

   Maud. *The spit stand still, no broches turn*
        Before the fire, but let it burn
        Both sides and hanches, till the whole
        Converted be into one coal!

   Cla. What devil's pater noster mumbles she?

   Alken. Stay, you will hear more of her witchery.

   Maud. *The swilland dropsy enter in*
        The lazy cuke, and swell his skin;
        And the old mortmal on his shin
        Now prick, and itch, withouten blin.

   Cla. Speak out, hag, we may hear your devil's mattins.

   Maud. *The pain we call St. Anton's fire,*
        The gout, or what we can desire,
        To cramp a cuke, in every limb,
        Before they dine, yet, seize on him.

   Alken. A foul ill spirit hath possessed her.

   Amie [*starting.*] O Karol, Karol! call him back again.

   Lio. Her thoughts do work upon her in her slumber,
And may express some part of her disease.

   Rob. Observe, and mark, but trouble not her ease.

   Amie. O, O!

   Mar. How is it, Amie?

   Mel. Wherefore start you?

   Amie. O Karol! he is fair and sweet.

   Maud. What then?
Are there not flowers as sweet and fair as men?
The lily is fair, and rose is sweet.

   Amie. Ay, so!
Let all the roses and the lilies go:

Karol is only fair to me.

Mar. And why?

Amie. Alas, for Karol, Marian, I could die!
Karol, he singeth sweetly too.

Maud. What then?
Are there not birds sing sweeter far than men?

Amie. I grant the linnet, lark, and bull-finch sing,
But best the dear good angel of the spring,
The nightingale.

Maud. Then why, then why, alone,
Should his notes please you?

Amie. I not long agone
Took a delight with wanton kids to play,
And sport with little lambs a summer's-day,
And view their frisks: methought it was a sight
Of joy to see my two brave rams to fight!
Now Karol only all delight doth move,
All that is Karol, Karol I approve!
This very morning but—I did bestow
(It was a little 'gainst my will I know)
A single kiss upon the silly swain,
And now I wish that very kiss again.
His lip is softer, sweeter than the rose,
His mouth, and tongue, with dropping honey flows;
The relish of it was a pleasing thing.

Maud. Yet, like the bees, it had a little sting.

Amie. And sunk, and sticks yet in my marrow deep;
And what doth hurt me, I now wish to keep.

Mar. Alas, how innocent her story is!

Amie. I do remember, Marian, I have oft
With pleasure kist my lambs and puppies soft;
And once a dainty fine roe-fawn I had,
Of whose out-skipping bounds I was as glad
As of my health; and him I oft would kiss;
Yet had his no such sting or pain as this:
They never prick'd or hurt my heart; and, for
They were so blunt and dull, I wish no more.
But this, that hurts and pricks, doth please; this sweet
Mingled with sour, I wish again to meet:
And that delay, methinks, most tedious is,
That keeps or hinders me of Karol's kiss.

Mar. We'll send for him, sweet Amie, to come to you.

Maud. But I will keep him off, if charms will do it.

[*Exit muttering.*

Cla. Do you mark the murmuring hag, how she doth mutter?

Rob. I like her not; and less her manners now.

Alken. She is a shrewd deformed piece, I vow.

Lio. As crooked as her body.

Rob. I believe

She can take any shape, as Scathlock says.

Alken. She may deceive the sense, but really
She cannot change herself.

Rob. Would I could see her
Once more in Marian's form! for I am certain
Now, it was she abused us; as I think
My Marian, and my love, now innocent:
Which faith I seal unto her with this kiss,
And call you all to witness of my pennance.   [*Kisses Marian.*

Alken. It was believed before, but now confirm'd,
That we have seen the monster.

Enter Friar TUCK, JOHN, MUCH, *and* SCARLET.

Tuck. Hear you how
Poor Tom the cook is taken! all his joints
Do crack, as if his limbs were tied with points:
His whole frame slackens; and a kind of rack
Runs down along the spondils of his back;
A gout or cramp now seizeth on his head,
Then falls into his feet; his knees are lead;
And he can stir his either hand no more
Than a dead stump, to his office, as before.

Alken. He is bewitch'd.

Cla. This is an argument
Both of her malice and her power, we see.

Alken. She must by some device restrained be,
Or she'll go far in mischief.

Rob. Advise how,
Sage shepherd; we shall put it straight in practice.

Alken. Send forth your woodmen then into the walks,
Or let them prick her footing hence; a witch
Is sure a creature of melancholy,
And will be found or sitting in her fourm,
Or else, at relief, like a hare.

Cla. You speak,
Alken, as if you knew the sport of witch-hunting,
Or starting of a hag.

Enter GEORGE.

Rob. Go, sirs, about it,
Take George, here, with you, he can help to find her;
Leave Tuck and Much behind to dress the dinner,
In the cook's stead.

Much. We'll care to get that done.

Rob. Come, Marian, let's withdraw into the bower.
            [*Exeunt all but John, Scarlet, Scathlock, and George.*

John. Rare sport, I swear, this hunting of the witch
Will make us.

Scar. Let's advise upon't like huntsmen.

George. An we can spy her once, she is our own.

Scath. First, think which way she fourmeth, on what wind;
Or north, or south.

George. For as the shepherd said,
A witch is a kind of hare.

Scath. And marks the weather,
As the hare does.

John. Where shall we hope to find her?

Re-enter ALKEN.

Alken. I have ask'd leave to assist you, jolly huntsmen,
If an old shepherd may be heard among you;
Not jeer'd or laugh'd at.

John. Father, you will see
Robin Hood's household know more courtesy.

Scath. Who scorns at eld, peels off his own young hairs.

Alken. Ye say right well: know ye the witch's dell?

Scath. No more than I do know the walks of hell.

Alken. Within a gloomy dimble she doth dwell,
Down in a pit, o'ergrown with brakes and briars,
Close by the ruins of a shaken abbey,
Torn with an earthquake down unto the ground,
'Mongst graves and grots, near an old charnel-house,
Where you shall find her sitting in her fourm,
As fearful and melancholic as that
She is about; with caterpillars' kells,
And knotty cob-webs, rounded in with spells.
Thence she steals forth to relief in the fogs,
And rotten mists, upon the fens and bogs,
Down to the drowned lands of Lincolnshire;
To make ewes cast their lambs, swine eat their farrow,
The housewives' tun not work, nor the milk churn!
Writhe children's wrists, and suck their breath in sleep,
Get vials of their blood! and where the sea
Casts up his slimy ooze, search for a weed
To open locks with, and to rivet charms,
Planted about her in the wicked feat
Of all her mischiefs, which are manifold.

John. I wonder such a story could be told
Of her dire deeds.

George. I thought a witch's banks
Had inclosed nothing but the merry pranks
Of some old woman.

Scar. Yes, her malice more.

Scath. As it would quickly appear had we the store
Of his collects.

George. Ay, this gud learned man
Can speak her right.

Scar. He knows her shifts and haunts.

Alken. And all her wiles and turns. The venom'd plants
Wherewith she kills! where the sad mandrake grows,
Whose groans are deathful; the dead-numbing night-shade,
The stupifying hemlock, adder's tongue,
And martagan: the shrieks of luckless owls
We hear, and croaking night-crows in the air!
Green-bellied snakes, blue fire-drakes in the sky,
And giddy flitter-mice with leather wings!
The scaly beetles, with their habergeons,
That make a humming murmur as they fly!
There in the stocks of trees, white faies do dwell,
And span-long elves that dance about a pool,
With each a little changeling in their arms!
The airy spirits play with falling stars,
And mount the sphere of fire to kiss the moon!
While she sits reading by the glow-worm's light,
Or rotten wood, o'er which the worm hath crept,
The baneful schedule of her nocent charms,
And binding characters, through which she wounds
Her puppets, the sigilla of her witchcraft.
All this I know, and I will find her for you;
And shew you her sitting in her fourm; I'll lay
My hand upon her, make her throw her skut
Along her back, when she doth start before us.
But you must give her law: and you shall see her
Make twenty leaps and doubles; cross the paths,
And then squat down beside us.

John. Crafty croan!
I long to be at the sport, and to report it.

Scar. We'll make this hunting of the witch as famous,
As any other blast of venery.

Scath. Hang her, foul hag! she'll be a stinking chase.
I had rather ha' the hunting of her heir.

George. If we should come to see her, cry, *So ho !* once.

Alken. That I do promise, or I am no good hag-finder. [*Exeunt.*

ACT III

SCENE I.—*The Forest.*

Enter PUCK-HAIRY.

Puck. The fiend hath much to do, that keeps a school,
Or is the father of a family;
Or governs but a country academy:
His labours must be great, as are his cares,
To watch all turns, and cast how to prevent them.
This dame of mine here, Maud, grows high in evil,
And thinks she does all, when 'tis I, her devil,

That both delude her, and must yet protect her.
She's confident in mischief, and presumes
The changing of her shape will still secure her;
But that may fail, and divers hazards meet
Of other consequence, which I must look to,
Nor let her be surprised on the first catch.
I must go dance about the forest now,
And firk it like a goblin, till I find her.
Then will my service come worth acceptation.
When not expected of her; when the help
Meets the necessity, and both do kiss,
'Tis call'd the timing of a duty, this.   [*Exit.*

SCENE II.—*Another Part of the same.*

Enter KAROL, *and* DOUCE *in the dress of* EARINE.

Kar. Sure, you are very like her! I conceived
You had been she, seeing you run afore me:
For such a suit she made her 'gainst this feast,
In all resemblance, or the very same;
I saw her in it; had she lived to enjoy it,
She had been there an acceptable guest
To Marian, and the gentle Robin Hood,
Who are the crown and ghirland of the wood.
  Douce. I cannot tell, my mother gave it me,
And bade me wear it.
  Kar. Who, the wise good woman,
Old Maud of Paplewick?

Enter ÆGLAMOUR.

Douce. Yes:—this sullen man
I cannot like him. I must take my leave.   [*Exit,*
  Æg. What said she to you?
  Kar. Who?
  Æg. Earine.
I saw her talking with you, or her ghost;
For she indeed is drown'd in old Trent's bottom.
Did she not tell who would have pull'd her in,
And had her maidenhead upon the place,
The river's brim, the margin of the flood?
No ground is holy enough, (you know my meaning)
Lust is committed in kings' palaces,
And yet their majesties not violated!
No words!   [*Exit.*
  Kar. How sad and wild his thoughts are! gone?

Re-enter ÆGLAMOUR.

Æg. But she, as chaste as was her name, Earine,
Died undeflower'd: and now her sweet soul hovers
Here in the air above us, and doth haste

To get up to the moon and Mercury;
And whisper Venus in her orb; then spring
Up to old Saturn, and come down by Mars,
Consulting Jupiter, and seat herself
Just in the midst with Phœbus, tempering all
The jarring spheres, and giving to the world
Again his first and tuneful planetting.
O what an age will here be of new concords!
Delightful harmony! to rock old sages,
Twice infants, in the cradle of speculation,
And throw a silence upon all the creatures!   [*Exit.*
    Kar. A cogitation of the highest rapture!

Re-enter ÆGLAMOUR.

    Æg. The loudest seas, and most enraged winds,
Shall lose their clangor; tempest shall grow hoarse,
Loud thunder dumb, and every speece of storm,
Laid in the lap of listening nature, hush'd
To hear the changed chime of this eighth sphere.
Take tent, and hearken for it, lose it not.   [*Exit.*

Enter CLARION *and* LIONEL.

    Cla. O here is Karol! was not that the Sad
Shepherd slipp'd from him?
    Lio. Yes, I guess it was.
Who was that left you, Karol?
    Kar. The lost man;
Whom we shall never see himself again,
Or ours, I fear; he starts away from hand so,
And all the touches or soft strokes of reason
You can apply! no colt is so unbroken,
Or hawk yet half so haggard or unmann'd!
He takes all toys that his wild phant'sie proffers,
And flies away with them: he now conceives
That my lost sister, his Earine,
Is lately turn'd a sphere amid the seven;
And reads a music-lecture to the planets!
And with this thought he's run to call 'em hearers.
    Cla. Alas, this is a strain'd but innocent phant'sie!
I'll follow him, and find him if I can:
Mean time, go you with Lionel, sweet Karol:
He will acquaint you with an accident,
Which much desires your presence on the place.
    Kar. What is it, Lionel, wherein I may serve you?
Why do you so survey and circumscribe me,
As if you struck one eye into my breast,
And with the other took my whole dimensions?
    Lio. I wish you had a window in your bosom,
Or in your back, I might look thorough you,

And see your in-parts, Karol, liver, heart;
For there the seat of Love is: whence the boy,
The winged archer, hath shot home a shaft
Into my sister's breast, the innocent Amie,
Who now cries out, upon her bed, on Karol,
Sweet-singing Karol, the delicious Karol,
That kiss'd her like a Cupid! In your eyes,
She says, his stand is, and between your lips
He runs forth his divisions to her ears,
But will not 'bide there, less yourself do bring him.
Go with me, Karol, and bestow a visit
In charity upon the afflicted maid,
Who pineth with the languor of your love.

> [*As they are going out, enter Maudlin (in the shape*
> *of Marian,) and Douce.*

Maud. Whither intend you? Amie is recover'd,
Feels no such grief as she complain'd of lately.
This maiden hath been with her from her mother
Maudlin, the cunning woman, who hath sent her
Herbs for her head, and simples of that nature,
Have wrought upon her a miraculous cure;
Settled her brain to all our wish and wonder.

Lio. So instantly! you know I now but left her,
Possess'd with such a fit almost to a phrensie:
Yourself too fear'd her, Marian, and did urge
My haste to seek out Karol, and to bring him.

Maud. I did so: but the skill of that wise woman,
And her great charity of doing good,
Hath by the ready hand of this deft lass,
Her daughter, wrought effects beyond belief,
And to astonishment; we can but thank,
And praise, and be amazed, while we tell it. [*Exit with Douce.*

Lio. 'Tis strange, that any art should so help nature
In her extremes.

Kar. Then it appears most real,
When the other is deficient.

Enter ROBIN HOOD.

Rob. Wherefore stay you
Discoursing here, and haste not with your succours
To poor afflicted Amie, that so needs them?

Lio. She is recovered well, your Marian told us
But now here:

Re-enter MAUDLIN *as before.*

> See, she is return'd to affirm it.

Rob. My Marian!

Maud. Robin Hood! is he here?   [*Attempts to run out.*

Rob. Stay;

What was't you told my friend?

> [*He seizes Maud. by the girdle, and runs out with her, but returns immediately with the broken girdle in his hand, followed at a distance by the witch, in her own shape.*

Maud. Help, murder, help!
You will not rob me, outlaw? thief, restore
My belt that ye have broken!

Rob. Yes, come near.

Maud. Not in your gripe.

Rob. Was this the charmed circle,
The copy that so cozen'd and deceiv'd us?
I'll carry hence the trophy of your spoils:
My men shall hunt you too upon the start,
And course you soundly.

Maud. I shall make them sport,
And send some home without their legs or arms.
I'll teach them to climb stiles, leap ditches, ponds,
And lie in the waters, if they follow me.

Rob. Out, murmuring hag.　　　　　[*Exeunt all but Maud.*

Maud. I must use all my powers,
Lay all my wits to piecing of this loss.
Things run unluckily: where's my Puck-hairy?
Hath he forsook me?

Enter PUCK-HAIRY.

Puck. At your beck, madam.

Maud. O Puck, my goblin! I have lost my belt,
The strong thief, Robin Outlaw, forced it from me.

Puck. They are other clouds and blacker threat you, dame;
You must be wary, and pull in your sails,
And yield unto the weather of the tempest.
You think your power's infinite as your malice,
And would do all your anger prompts you to;
But you must wait occasions, and obey them:
Sail in an egg-shell, make a straw your mast,
A cobweb all your cloth, and pass unseen,
Till you have 'scaped the rocks that are about you.

Maud. What rocks about me?

Puck. I do love, madam,
To shew you all your dangers,—when you're past them!
Come, follow me, I'll once more be your pilot,
And you shall thank me.　　　　　[*Exit.*

Maud. Lucky, my loved goblin!

　　　　　[*As she is going out, Lorel meets her.*
Where are you gaang now?

Lor. Unto my tree,
To see my maistress.

Maud. Gang thy gait, and try
Thy turns with better luck, or hang thysel.—

THE CASE IS ALTERED

DRAMATIS PERSONÆ

Count Ferneze.
Lord Paulo Ferneze, *his Son.*
Camillo Ferneze, *supposed* Gasper.
Maximilian, *General of the Forces.*
Chamont, *Friend to* Gasper.
Angelo, *Friend to* Paulo.
Francisco Colonnia.
Jaques de Prie, *a Beggar.*
Antonio Balladino, *Pageant Poet.*
Christophero, Count Ferneze's
  Steward.
Sebastian,
Martino,
Vincentio, } *his Servants.*
Balthasar,

Valentine, *Servant to* Colonnia.
Peter Onion, *Groom of the Hall.*
Juniper, *a Cobler.*
Pacue, *Page to* Gasper.
Finio, *Page to* Camillo.
Page *to* Paulo.

Aurelia,   } *Daughters to* Count
Phœnixella, }   Ferneze.
Rachel de Prie.

Sewer, Messenger, Servants, *etc.*

SCENE —Milan.

ACT I

SCENE I.—*After a Flourish.*

Juniper *is discovered, sitting at work in his shop, and singing.*

Jun. You woful wights, give ear a while,
And mark the tenor of my style,
Which shall such trembling hearts unfold,
As seldom hath to-fore been told.
Such chances rare, and doleful news,

Enter Onion, *in haste.*

Oni. Fellow Juniper! peace a God's name.
Jun. As may attempt your wits to muse.
Oni. Od's so, hear, man! a pox on you!
Jun. And cause such trickling tears to pass,
Except your hearts be flint, or brass :
Oni. Juniper! Juniper!
Jun. To hear the news which I shall tell,
That in Castella once befel.—
'Sblood, where didst thou learn to corrupt a man in the midst of a
verse, ha?

Oni. Od'slid, man, service is ready to go up, man; you must slip on your coat, and come in; we lack waiters pitifully.

Jun. A pitiful hearing; for now must I of a merry cobler become [a] mourning creature.

Oni. Well, you'll come?

Jun. Presto. Go to, a word to the wise; away, fly, vanish!

[*Exit Onion.*

Lie there the weeds that I disdain to wear.

Enter ANTONIO BALLADINO.

Ant. God save you, master Juniper!

Jun. What, signior Antonio Balladino! welcome, sweet ingle.

Ant. And how do you, sir?

Jun. Faith you see, put to my shifts here, as poor retainers be oftentimes. Sirrah Antony, there's one of my fellows mightily enamour'd of thee; and i'faith, you slave, now you are come, I'll bring you together: it's Peter Onion, the groom of the hall; do you know him?

Ant. No, not yet, I assure you.

Jun. O, he is one as right of thy humour as may be, a plain simple rascal, a true dunce; marry, he hath been a notable villain in his time: he is in love, sirrah, with a wench, and I have preferred thee, to him; thou shalt make him some pretty paradox or some allegory. How does my coat sit? well?

Ant. Ay, very well.

Re-enter ONION.

Oni. Nay, God's so, fellow Juniper, come away.

Jun. Art thou there, mad slave? I come with a powder! Sirrah, fellow Onion, I must have you peruse this gentleman well, and do him good offices of respect and kindness, as instance shall be given.

[*Exit.*

Ant. Nay, good master Onion, what do you mean? I pray you, sir—you are too respective, in good faith.

Oni. I would not you should think so, sir: for though I have no learning, yet I honour a scholar in any ground of the earth, sir. Shall I request your name, sir?

Ant. My name is Antonio Balladino.

Oni. Balladino! you are not pageant poet to the city of Milan, sir, are you?

Ant. I supply the place, sir, when a worse cannot be had, sir.

Oni. I cry you mercy, sir; I love you the better for that, sir; by Jesu, you must pardon me, I knew you not; but I would pray to be better acquainted with you, sir: I have seen of your works.

Ant. I am at your service, good master Onion: but concerning this maiden that you love, sir, what is she?

Oni. O, did my fellow Juniper tell you? Marry, sir, she is, as one may say, but a poor man's child indeed, and for mine own part, I am no gentleman born, I must confess; but *my mind to me a kingdom is.*

Ant. Truly a very good saying.

Oni. 'Tis somewhat stale; but that's no matter.

Ant. O 'tis the better; such things ever are like bread, which the staler it is, the more wholesome.

Oni. This is but a hungry comparison, in my judgment.

Ant. Why I'll tell you, master Onion, I do use as much stale stuff, though I say it myself, as any man does in that kind, I am sure. Did you see the last pageant I set forth?

Oni. No faith, sir; but there goes a huge report on't.

Ant. Why you shall be one of my Mæcen-asses: I'll give you one of the books; O you'll like it admirably.

Oni. Nay, that's certain; I'll get my fellow Juniper to read it.

Ant. Read it, sir! I'll read it to you.

Oni. Tut, then I shall not choose but like it.

Ant. Why look you, sir, I write so plain, and keep that old decorum, that you must of necessity like it: marry you shall have some now (as for example, in plays) that will have every day new tricks, and write you nothing but humours: indeed this pleases the gentlemen, but the common sort they care not for't; they know not what to make on't; they look for good matter they, and are not edified with such toys.

Oni. You are in the right, I'll not give a halfpenny to see a thousand of them. I was at one the last term; but an ever I see a more roguish thing, I am a piece of cheese, and no Onion; nothing but kings and princes in it; the fool came not out a jot.

Ant. True, sir; they would have me make such plays: but as I tell them, an they'll give me twenty pounds a-play, I'll not raise my vein.

Oni. No, it were a vain thing an you should, sir.

Ant. Tut, give me the penny, give me the penny. I care not for the gentlemen, I; let me have a good ground, no matter for the pen, the plot shall carry it.

Oni. Indeed that's right, you are in print already for the best plotter.

Ant. Ay, I might as well have been put in for a dumb shew too.

Oni. Ay, marry, sir, I marle you were not. Stand aside, sir, a while.— [*Exit Antonio.*

[*An armed Sewer, followed by Juniper, Sebastian, Martino, Balthasar, Vincentio, and other Servants in mourning, with dishes, etc., passes over the stage.*

Enter VALENTINE.

How now, friend, what are you there? be uncovered. Would you speak with any man here?

Val. Ay, or else I must have returned you no answer.

Oni. Friend, you are somewhat too peremptory, let's crave your absence; nay, never scorn it, I am a little your better in this place.

Val. I do acknowledge it.

Oni. Do you acknowledge it? nay, then you shall go forth. I'll

teach you how [you] shall acknowledge it another time; go to, void,
I must have the hall purged; no setting up of a rest here; pack,
begone!

Val. I pray you, sir, is not your name Onion?

Oni. Your friend as you may use him, and master Onion;
say on.

Val. Master Onion, with a murrain! come, come, put off this
lion's hide, your ears have discovered you. Why, Peter! do not I
know you, Peter?

Oni. God's so, Valentine!

Val. O, can you take knowledge of me now, sir?

Oni. Good Lord, sirrah, how thou art altered with thy travel!

Val. Nothing so much as thou art with thine office; but, sirrah
Onion, is the count Ferneze at home?

Oni. Ay, bully, he is above, and the lord Paulo Ferneze, his son,
and madam Aurelia and madam Phœnixella, his daughters; but,
O Valentine!

Val. How now, man! how dost thou?

Oni. Faith, sad, heavy, as a man of my coat ought to be.

Val. Why, man, thou wert merry enough even now.

Oni. True; but thou knowest

> All creatures here sojourning,
> Upon this wretched earth,
> Sometimes have a fit of mourning,
> As well as a fit of mirth.

O Valentine, mine old lady is dead, man.

Val. Dead!

Oni. I'faith.

Val. When died she?

Oni. Marry, to-morrow shall be three months, she was seen going
to heaven, they say, about some five weeks agone—how now?
trickling tears, ha!

Val. Faith, thou hast made me weep with this news.

Oni. Why I have done but the part of an Onion; you must
pardon me.

Re-enter the Sewer, *followed by the* Servants *with dishes, as before;
they all pass over the stage but* JUNIPER.

Jun. What, Valentine! fellow Onion, take my dish, I prithee.
[*Exit Onion with the dish.*] You rogue, sirrah, tell me how thou dost,
sweet ingle.

Val. Faith, Juniper, the better to see thee thus frœlich.

Jun. Nay! slid I am no changeling, I am Juniper still, I keep
the pristinate; ha, you mad hieroglyphic, when shall we swagger?

Val. Hieroglyphic! what meanest thou by that?

Jun. Mean! od'so, is it not a good word, man? what, stand upon
meaning with your friends? Puh! abscond.

Val. Why, but stay, stay; how long has this sprightly humour
haunted thee?

Jun. Foh, humour! a foolish natural gift we have in the Æqui-noxial.

Val. Natural! slid it may be supernatural, this.

Jun. Valentine, I prithee ruminate thyself welcome. What, *fortuna de la guerra!*

Val. O how pitifully are these words forced! as though they were pumpt out on's belly.

Jun. Sirrah ingle, I think thou hast seen all the strange countries in Christendom since thou went'st.

Val. I have seen some, Juniper.

Jun. You have seenConstantinople?

Val. Ay, that I have.

Jun. And Jerusalem, and the Indies, and Goodwin-sands, and the tower of Babylon, and Venice, and all?

Val. Ay, all; no marle an he have a nimble tongue, if he practise to vault thus from one side of the world to another.   [*Aside.*

Jun. O, it's a most heavenly thing to travel, and see countries; especially at sea, an a man had a patent not to be sick.

Val. O, sea-sick jest, and full of the scurvy!

Re-enter SEBASTIAN, MARTINO, VINCENTIO, *and* BALTHASAR.

Seb. Valentine! welcome, i'faith; how dost, sirrah?

Mar. How do you, good Valentine?

Vin. Troth, Valentine, I am glad to see you.

Bal. Welcome, sweet rogue.

Seb. Before God, he never look'd better in his life.

Bal. And how is't, man? what *allo coragio!*

Val. Never better, gentlemen, i'faith.

Jun. 'Swill! here comes the steward.

Enter CHRISTOPHERO.

Chris. Why, how now, fellows! all here, and nobody to wait above, now they are ready to rise? look up, one or two. [*Exeunt. Juniper, Martino, and Vincentio.*] Signior Francisco Colonnia's man, how does our good master?

Val. In health, sir; he will be here anon.

Chris. Is he come home, then?

Val. Ay, sir; he is not past six miles hence; he sent me before to learn if count Ferneze were here, and return him word.

Chris. Yes, my lord is here; and you may tell your master, he shall come very happily to take his leave of lord Paulo Ferneze; who is now instantly to depart, with other noble gentlemen, upon special service.

Val. I will tell him, sir.

Chris. I pray you do; fellows, make him drink.

Val. Sirs, what service is it they are employed in?

Seb. Why, against the French; they mean to have a fling at Milan again, they say.

Val. Who leads our forces, can you tell?

Seb. Marry, that does Signior Maximilian; he is above now.

Val. Who, Maximilian of Vincenza?

Balt. Ay, he; do you know him?

Val. Know him! O yes, he's an excellent brave soldier.

Balt. Ay, so they say; but one of the most vain-glorious men in Europe.

Val. He is, indeed; marry, exceeding valiant.

Seb. And that is rare.

Balt. What?

Seb. Why, to see a vain-glorious man valiant.

Val. Well, he is so, I assure you.

Re-enter JUNIPER.

Jun. What, no further yet! come on, you precious rascal, sir Valentine, I'll give you a health i'faith, for the heavens, you mad Capricio, hold hook and line.   [*Exeunt.*

SCENE II.—*A Room in* Count FERNEZE'S *House.*

Enter Lord PAULO FERNEZE, *followed by his* Page.

Pau. Boy!

Page. My lord.

Pau. Sirrah, go up to signior Angelo,
And pray him, if he can, devise some means
To leave my father, and come speak with me.

Page. I will, my lord.   [*Exit.*

Pau. Well, heaven be auspicious in the event,
For I do this against my Genius!
And yet my thoughts cannot propose a reason
Why I should fear, or faint thus in my hopes,
Of one so much endeared to my love.
Some spark it is, kindled within the soul,
Whose light yet breaks not to the outward sense
That propagates this timorous suspect;
His actions never carried any face
Of change, or weakness; then I injure him
In being thus cold-conceited of his faith.
O, here he comes.

Re-enter Page *with* ANGELO.

Ang. How now, sweet lord, what's the matter?

Pau. Good faith, his presence makes me half ashamed
Of my stray'd thoughts.—Boy, bestow yourself.—   [*Exit Page.*
Where is my father, signior Angelo?

Ang. Marry, in the gallery, where your lordship left him.

Pau. That's well.   Then, Angelo, I will be brief
Since time forbids the use of circumstance.
How well you are received in my affection,
Let it appear by this one instance only,
That now I will deliver to your trust

The dearest secrets, treasured in my bosom.
Dear Angelo, you are not every man,
But one, whom my election hath design'd,
As the true proper object of my soul.
I urge not this to insinuate my desert,
Or supple your tried temper with soft phrases;
True friendship loathes such oily compliment:
But from the abundance of that love that flows
Through all my spirits, is my speech enforced.

Ang. Before your lordship do proceed too far,
Let me be bold to intimate thus much;
That whatsoe'er your wisdom hath to expose,
Be it the weightiest and most rich affair
That ever was included in your breast,
My faith shall poise it, if not—

Pau. O, no more;
Those words have rapt me with their sweet effects,
So freely breath'd, and so responsible
To that which I endeavour'd to extract;
Arguing a happy mixture of our souls.

Ang. Why, were there no such sympathy, sweet lord,
Yet the impressure of those ample favours
I have derived from your unmatched spirit,
Would blind my faith to all observances.

Pau. How! favours, Angelo! O speak not of them,
They are mere paintings, and import no merit.
Looks my love well? thereon my hopes are placed;
Faith, that is bought with favours cannot last.

Re-enter Page.

Page. My lord.
Pau. How now!
Page. You are sought for all about the house within; the count
your father calls for you.
Pau. Lord!
What cross events do meet my purposes!
Now will he violently fret and grieve
That I am absent.—Boy, say I come presently.   [*Exit Boy.*
Sweet Angelo, I cannot now insist
Upon particulars, I must serve the time;
The main of all this is, I am in love.
Ang. Why starts your lordship?
Pau. I thought I heard my father coming hitherward,
List, ah!
Ang. I hear not any thing,
It was but your imagination sure.
Pau. No!
Ang. No, I assure your lordship.
Pau. I would work safely.

Ang. Why,
Has he no knowledge of it then?
    Pau. O no;
No creature yet partakes it but yourself,
In a third person; and believe me, friend,
The world contains not now another spirit,
To whom I would reveal it.   Hark! hark!
    Servants [*within.*] Signior Paulo! lord Ferneze!
    Ang. A pox upon those brazen-throated slaves!
What are they mad, trow?
    Pau. Alas, blame not them,
Their services are, clock-like, to be set
Backward and forward, at their lord's command.
You know my father's wayward, and his humour
Must not receive a check; for then all objects
Feed both his grief and his impatience.
And those affections in him are like powder,
Apt to inflame with every little spark,
And blow up reason; therefore, Angelo, peace.
    Count F. [*within.*] Why, this is rare; is he not in the garden?
    Chris. [*within.*] I know not, my lord.
    Count F. [*within.*] See, call him.
    Pau. He is coming this way, let's withdraw a little.   [*Exeunt.*
    Ser. [*within.*] Signior Paulo! lord Ferneze! lord Paulo!

    Enter Count FERNEZE, MAXIMILIAN, AURELIA, PHŒNIXELLA,
                SEBASTIAN, *and* BALTHASAR.

    Count F. Where should he be, trow? did you look in the armory?
    Seb. No, my lord.
    Count F. No? why there!   O, who would keep such drones!—
                                        [*Exeunt Seb. and Bal.*
                        Enter MARTINO.
How now, have you found him?
    Mart. No, my lord.
    Count F. *No, my lord!*
I shall have shortly all my family speak nought but, *No, my lord.*
Where is Christophero?   Look how he stands! you sleepy knave—
                                        [*Exit Martino.*
                    Enter CHRISTOPHERO.
What, is he not in the garden?
    Chris. No, my good lord.
    Count F. Your *good lord!*   O, how this smells of fennel!
You have been in the garden, it appears: well, well.

            Re-enter SEBASTIAN *and* BALTHASAR.
    Bal. We cannot find him, my lord.
    Seb. He is not in the armory.
    Count F. He is not! he is no where, is he?
    Max. Count Ferneze!

Count F. Signior.

Max. Preserve your patience, honourable count.

Count F. Patience!
A saint would lose his patience, to be crost
As I am, with a sort of motley brains;
See, see, how like a nest of rooks they stand
Gaping on one another!

Enter ONION.

Now, Diligence,
What news bring you?

Oni. An't please your honour—

Count F. Tut, tut, leave pleasing of my honour, Diligence.
You double with me, come.

Oni. How! does he find fault with *please his honour?* 'Swounds,
it has begun a serving-man's speech, ever since I belonged to the
blue order; I know not how it may shew, now I am in black;
but—   [*Aside.*

Count F. What's that you mutter, sir; will you proceed?

Oni. An't like your good lordship—

Count F. Yet more! od's precious!

Oni. What, does not this like him neither?   [*Aside.*

Count F. What say you, sir knave?

Oni. Marry, I say your lordship were best to set me to school
again, to learn how to deliver a message.

Count F. What, do you take exceptions at me then?

Oni. Exceptions! I take no exceptions; but, by god's so, your
humours—

Count F. Go to, you are a rascal; hold your tongue.

Oni. Your lordship's poor servant, I.

Count F. Tempt not my patience.

Oni. Why I hope I am no spirit, am I?

Max. My lord, command your steward to correct the slave.

Oni. Correct him! 'sblood, come you and correct him, an you
have a mind to it. Correct him! that's a good jest, i'faith: the
steward and you both come and correct him.

Count F. Nay, see! away with him, pull his cloth over his ears.

Oni. Cloth! tell me of your cloth! here's your cloth; nay, an I
mourn a minute longer, I am the rottenest Onion that ever spake
with a tongue.   [*They thrust him out.*

Max. What call [you] your hind's [name], count Ferneze?

Count F. His name is Onion, signior.

Max. I thought him some such saucy companion.

Count F. Signior Maximilian.

Max. Sweet lord.

Count F. Let me entreat you, you would not regard
Any contempt flowing from such a spirit;
So rude, so barbarous.

Max. Most noble count,
Under your favour—

Count F. Why, I'll tell you, signior;
He'll bandy with me word for word; nay more,
Put me to silence, strike me perfect dumb;
And so amaze me, that oftentimes I know not
Whether to check or cherish his presumption:
Therefore, good signior—

Max. Sweet lord, satisfy yourself, I am not now to learn how to manage my affections; I have observed, and know the difference between a base wretch and a true man; I can distinguish them: the property of the wretch is, he would hurt, and cannot; of the man, he can hurt, and will not.   [*Aurelia smiles.*

Count F. Go to, my merry daughter; O, these looks
Agree well with your habit, do they not?

Enter Juniper, *in his Cobler's dress.*

Jun. Tut, let me alone. By your favour,—this is the gentleman, I think: sir, you appear to be an honourable gentleman; I understand, and could wish for mine own part, that things were conden't otherwise than they are: but, the world knows, a foolish fellow, somewhat proclive and hasty, he did it in a prejudicate humour; marry now, upon better computation, he wanes, he melts, his poor eyes are in a cold sweat. Right noble signior, you can have but compunction; I love the man; tender your compassion.

Max. Doth any man here understand this fellow?

Jun. O Lord, sir! I may say *frustra* to the comprehension of your intellection.

Max. Before the Lord, he speaks all riddle, I think. I must have a comment ere I can conceive him.

Count F. Why he sues to have his fellow Onion pardon'd; and you must grant it, signior.

Max. O, with all my soul, my lord; is that his motion?

Jun. Ay, sir; and we shall retort these kind favours with all alacrity of spirit we can, sir, as may be most expedient, as well for the quality as the cause; till when, in spite of this compliment, I rest a poor cobler, servant to my honourable lord here, your friend and Juniper.   [*Exit.*

Max. How, Juniper!

Count F. Ay, signior.

Max. He is a sweet youth, his tongue has a happy turn when he sleeps.

Enter Paulo Ferneze, Francisco Colonnia, Angelo,
and Valentine.

Count F. Ay, for then it rests.—O, sir, you're welcome.
Why, God be thanked, you are found at last:
Signior Colonnia, truly you are welcome,
I am glad to see you, sir, so well return'd.

Fran. I gladly thank your honour; yet, indeed,
I am sorry for such cause of heaviness

As hath possest your lordship in my absence.

Count F. O, Francisco, you knew her what she was!

Fran. She was a wise and honourable lady.

Count F. Ay, was she not! well, weep not, she is gone.
Passion's dull'd eye can make two griefs of one.
Whom death marks out, virtue nor blood can save:
Princes, as beggars, all must feed the grave.

Max. Are your horses ready, lord Paulo?

Pau. Ay, signior; they stay for us at the gate.

Max. Well, 'tis good.—Ladies, I will take my leave of you; be
your fortunes, as yourselves, fair!—Come, let us to horse; Count
Ferneze, I bear a spirit full of thanks for all your honourable
courtesies.

Count F. Sir, I could wish the number and value of them more,
in respect of your deservings. But, signior Maximilian, I pray you
a word in private. [*They walk aside.*

Aur. I'faith, brother, you are fitted for a general yonder. Beshrew my heart if I had Fortunatus' hat here, an I would not wish
myself a man, and go with you, only to enjoy his presence.

Pau. Why, do you love him so well, sister?

Aur. No, by my troth; but I have such an odd pretty apprehension of his humour, methinks, that I am e'en tickled with the
conceit of it. O, he is a fine man.

Ang. And methinks another may be as fine as he.

Aur. O, Angelo! do you think I urge any comparison against you?
no, I am not so ill bred, as to be a depraver of your worthiness:
believe me, if I had not some hope of your abiding with us, I should
never desire to go out of black whilst I lived; but learn to speak
in the nose, and tarn puritan presently.

Ang. I thank you, lady; I know you can flout.

Aur. Come, do you take it so? i'faith, you wrong me.

Fran. Ay, but madam,
Thus to disclaim in all the effects of pleasure,
May make your sadness seem too much affected;
And then the proper grace of it is lost.

Phœn. Indeed, sir, if I did put on this sadness
Only abroad, and in society,
And were in private merry, and quick humour'd,
Then might it seem affected, and abhorr'd:
But, as my looks appear, such is my spirit,
Drown'd up with confluence of grief and melancholy;
That, like to rivers, run through all my veins,
Quenching the pride and fervour of my blood.

Max. My honourable lord, no more.
There is the honour of my blood engaged
For your son's safety.

Count F. Signior, blame me not
For tending his security so much;
He is mine only son, and that word *only*

Hath, with his strong and repercussive sound,
Struck my heart cold, and given it a deep wound.

Max. Why, but stay, I beseech you; had your lordship ever any more sons than this?

Count F. Why, have not you known it, Maximilian?

Max. Let my sword fail me then.

Count F. I had one other, younger born than this,
By twice so many hours as would fill
The circle of a year, his name Camillo,
Whom in that black and fearful night I lost,
('Tis now a nineteen years agone at least,
And yet the memory of it sits as fresh
Within my brain as 'twere but yesterday)
It was that night wherein the great Chamont,
The general for France, surprised Vicenza;
Methinks the horror of that clamorous shout
His soldiers gave, when they attain'd the wall,
Yet tingles in mine ears: methinks I see
With what amazed looks, distracted thoughts,
And minds confused, we, that were citizens,
Confronted one another; every street
Was fill'd with bitter self-tormenting cries,
And happy was that foot, that first could press
The flowery champain bordering on Verona.
Here I, employ'd about my dear wife's safety,
Whose soul is now in peace, lost my Camillo;
Who sure was murder'd by the barbarous soldiers,
Or else I should have heard—my heart is great.
" Sorrow is faint, and passion makes me sweat."

Max. Grieve not, sweet count, comfort your spirits; you have a son, a noble gentleman, he stands in the face of honour; for his safety let that be no question; I am master of my fortune, and he shall share with me. Farewell, my honourable lord: ladies, once more adieu. For yourself, madam, you are a most rare creature, I tell you so, be not proud of it: I love you.—Come, lord Paulo, to horse.

Pau. Adieu, good signior Francisco; farewell, sisters.

         [*A tucket sounds. Exeunt severally.*

SCENE III.—*The Street before* JAQUES DE PRIE'S *House.*

Enter PAULO FERNEZE, *and* ANGELO, *followed by* MAXIMILIAN.

Ang. How shall we rid him hence?

Pau. Why well enough.—Sweet signior Maximilian,
I have some small occasion to stay;
If it may please you but take horse afore,
I'll overtake you ere your troops be ranged.

Max. Your motion doth taste well; lord Ferneze, I go.   [*Exit.*

Pau. Now, if my love, fair Rachel, were so happy
But to look forth.—See, fortune doth me grace

Enter RACHEL.

Before I can demand.—How now, love!
Where is your father?

Rach. Gone abroad, my lord.

Pau. That's well.

Rach. Ay, but I fear he'll presently return.
Are you now going, my most honour'd lord?

Pau. Ay, my sweet Rachel.

Ang. Before God, she is a sweet wench.   [*Aside.*

Pau. Rachel, I hope I shall not need to urge
The sacred purity of our affects,
As if it hung in trial or suspense;
Since, in our hearts, and by our mutual vows,
It is confirm'd and seal'd in sight of heaven.
Nay, do not weep; why start you? fear not, love!
Your father cannot be return'd so soon.
I prithee do not look so heavily;
Thou shalt want nothing.

Rach. No! is your presence nothing?
I shall want that, and wanting that, want all;
For that is all to me.

Pau. Content thee, sweet!
I have made choice here of a constant friend,
This gentleman; one, [on] whose zealous love
I do repose more, than on all the world,
Thy beauteous self excepted; and to him
Have I committed my dear care of thee,
As to my genius, or my other soul.
Receive him, gentle love! and what defects
My absence proves, his presence shall supply.
The time is envious of our longer stay.
Farewell, dear Rachel!

Rach. Most dear lord, adieu!
Heaven and honour crown your deeds and you.   [*Exit.*

Pau. Faith, tell me, Angelo, how dost thou like her?

Ang. Troth, well, my lord; but, shall I speak my mind?

Pau. I prithee do.

Ang. She is derived too meanly to be wife
To such a noble person, in my judgment.

Pau. Nay, then thy judgment is too mean, I see;
Didst thou ne'er read, in difference of good,
'Tis more to shine in virtue than in blood?

Ang. Come, you are so sententious, my lord.

Enter JAQUES.

Pau. Here comes her father.—How dost thou, good Jaques?

Ang. God save thee, Jaques!

Jaq. What should this mean?—Rachel! open the door.   [*Exit.*

Ang. S'blood how the poor slave looks [aghast], as though
He had been haunted by the spirit, Lar;
Or seen the ghost of some great Satrapas
In an unsavoury sheet.
    Pau. I muse he spake not;
Belike he was amazed, coming so suddenly,
And unprepared.—Well, let us go.   [*Exeunt.*

ACT II

SCENE I.—*The Court-yard at the back of* JAQUES' *House.*

Enter JAQUES.

So, now enough, my heart, beat now no more;
At least for this affright. What a cold sweat
Flow'd on my brows, and over all my bosom!
Had I not reason? to behold my door
Beset with unthrifts, and myself abroad?
Why, Jaques! was there nothing in the house
Worth a continual eye, a vigilant thought,
Whose head should never nod, nor eyes once wink?
Look on my coat, my thoughts, worn quite threadbare,
That time could never cover with a nap,
And by it learn, never with naps of sleep
To smother your conceits of that you keep.
But yet, I marvel why these gallant youths
Spoke me so fair, and I esteem'd a beggar!
The end of flattery is gain, or lechery:
If they seek gain of me, they think me rich;
But that they do not: for their other object,
'Tis in my handsome daughter, if it be:
And, by your leave, her handsomeness may tell them
My beggary counterfeits, and, that her neatness
Flows from some store of wealth, that breaks my coffers
With this same engine, love to mine own breed;
But this is answer'd: Beggars will keep fine
Their daughters, being fair, though themselves pine.
Well, then, it is for her; ay, 'tis sure for her:
And I make her so brisk for some of them.
That I might live alone once with my gold!
O, 'tis a sweet companion! kind and true;
A man may trust it when his father cheats him.
Brother, or friend, or wife. O, wondrous pelf
That which makes all men false, is true itself.—
But now, this maid is but supposed my daughter;
For I being steward to a lord of France,
Of great estate and wealth, call'd lord Chamont,
He gone into the wars, I stole his treasure;

(But hear not any thing) I stole his treasure.
And this his daughter, being but two years old,
Because it loved me so, that it would leave
The nurse herself, to come into mine arms;
And had I left it, it would sure have died.
Now herein I was kind, and had a conscience:
And since her lady-mother, that did die
In child-bed of her, loved me passing well,
It may be nature fashion'd this affection,
Both in the child and her: but he's ill bred
That ransacks tombs, and doth deface the dead.
I'll therefore say no more; suppose the rest.
Here have I changed my form, my name and hers,
And live obscurely, to enjoy more safe
My dearest treasure: But I must abroad.—
Rachel!

Enter RACHEL.

Rach. What is your pleasure, sir?
Jaq. Rachel, I must abroad.
Lock thyself in, but yet take out the key;
That whosoever peeps in at the key-hole
May yet imagine there is none at home.
Rach. I will, sir.
Jaq. But hark thee, Rachel; say a thief should come,
And miss the key, he would resolve indeed
None were at home, and so break in the rather:
Ope the door, Rachel; set it open, daughter;
But sit in it thyself, and talk aloud,
As if there were some more in th' house with thee:
Put out the fire, kill the chimney's heart,
That it may breathe no more than a dead man;
The more we spare, my child, the more we gain.　　　*[Exeunt.*

SCENE II.—*A Room in* Count FERNEZE'S *House.*

Enter CHRISTOPHERO, JUNIPER, *and* ONION.

Chris. What says my fellow Onion? come on.
Oni. All of a house, sir, but no fellows; you are my lord's steward: but, I pray you, what think you of love, sir?
Chris. Of love, Onion? why, it is a very honourable humour.
Oni. Nay, if it be but worshipful, I care not.
Jun. Go to, it is honourable; check not at the conceit of the gentleman.
Oni. But, in truth, sir, you shall do well to think well of love: for it thinks well of you, in me, I assure you.
Chris. Gramercy, fellow Onion; I do think well, thou art in love; art thou?
Oni. Partly, sir; but I am ashamed to say wholly.

Chris. Well, I will further it in thee, to any honest woman, or maiden, the best I can.

Jun. Why, now you come near him, sir; he doth vail, he doth remunerate, he doth chew the cud, in the kindness of an honest imperfection to your worship.

Chris. But, who is it thou lovest, fellow Onion?

Oni. Marry, a poor man's daughter; but none of the honestest, I hope.

Chris. Why, wouldst thou not have her honest?

Oni. O no, for then I am sure she would not have me. 'Tis Rachel de Prie.

Chris. Why she hath the name of a very virtuous maiden.

Jun. So she is, sir; but the fellow talks in quiddits, he.

Chris. What wouldst thou have me do in the matter?

Oni. Do nothing, sir, I pray you, but speak for me.

Chris. In what manner?

Oni. My fellow Juniper can tell you, sir.

Jun. Why, as thus, sir. Your worship may commend him for a fellow fit for consanguinity, and that he shaketh with desire of procreation, or so.

Chris. That were not so good, methinks.

Jun. No, sir! why so, sir? What if you should say to her, Corroborate thyself, sweet soul, let me distinguish thy paps with my fingers, divine Mumps, pretty Pastorella! lookest thou so sweet and bounteous? comfort my friend here.

Chris. Well, I perceive you wish I should say something may do him grace, and further his desires; and that, be sure, I will.

Oni. I thank you, sir; God save your life, I pray, sir.

Jun. Your worship is too good to live long: you'll contaminate me no service.

Chris. Command, thou wouldst say; no, good Juniper.

Jun. Health and wealth, sir.   [*Exeunt Onion and Juniper.*

Chris. This wench will I solicit for myself,
Making my lord and master privy to it;
And if he second me with his consent,
I will proceed, as having long ere this,
Thought her a worthy choice to make my wife.   [*Exit.*

SCENE III.—*Another Room in the same.*

Enter AURELIA and PHŒNIXELLA.

Aur. Room for a case of matrons, colour'd black,
How motherly my mother's death hath made us!
I would I had some girls now to bring up.
O I could make a wench so virtuous,
She should say grace to every bit of meat,
And gape no wider than a wafer's thickness;
And she should make French court'sies so most low,
That every touch should turn her over backward.

Phœn. Sister, these words become not your attire,
Nor your estate; our virtuous mother's death
Should print more deep effects of sorrow in us,
Than may be worn out in so little time.

Aur. Sister, i'faith, you take too much tobacco,
It makes you black within, as you are without.
What, true-stitch, sister! both your sides alike!
Be of a slighter work; for of my word,
You shall be sold as dear, or rather dearer.
Will you be bound to customs and to rites?
Shed profitable tears, weep for advantage,
Or else do all things as you are inclined:
Eat when your stomach serves, saith the physician,
Not at eleven and six. So if your humour
Be now affected with this heaviness,
Give it the reins, and spare not, as I do
In this my pleasurable appetite.
It is precisianism to alter that
With austere judgment, that is given by nature.
I wept, you saw too, when my mother died;
For then I found it easier to do so,
And fitter with my mood, than not to weep:
But now 'tis otherwise; another time
Perhaps I shall have such deep thoughts of her,
That I shall weep afresh some twelvemonth hence;
And I will weep, if I be so disposed,
And put on black as grimly then as now.
Let the mind go still with the body's stature,
Judgment is fit for judges, give me nature.

Enter Francisco Colonnia *and* Angelo.

Fran. See, signior Angelo, here are the ladies;
Go you and comfort one, I'll to the other.

Ang. Therefore I come, sir; I will to the eldest.
God save you, ladies! these sad moods of yours,
That make you choose these solitary walks,
Are hurtful for your beauties.

Aur. If we had them.

Ang. Come, that condition might be for your hearts,
When you protest faith, since we cannot see them:
But this same heart of beauty, your sweet face,

Aur. O, you cut my heart
With your sharp eye.

Ang. Nay, lady, that's not so,
Your heart's too hard.

Aur. My beauty's heart?

Ang. O no.
I mean that regent of affection, madam,

That tramples on all love with such contempt
In this fair breast.

Aur. No more, your drift is savour'd;
I had rather seem hard-hearted—

Ang. Than hard-favour'd;
Is that your meaning, lady?

Aur. Go to, sir;
Your wits are fresh, I know, they need no spur.

Ang. And therefore you will ride them.

Aur. Say I do,
They will not tire, I hope.

Ang. No, not with you.
Hark you, sweet lady.   *[Walks aside with Aur.*

Fran. 'Tis much pity, madam,
You should have any reason to retain
This sign of grief, much less the thing design'd.

Phœn. Griefs are more fit for ladies than their pleasures.

Fran. That is for such as follow nought but pleasures.
But you that temper them so well with virtues,
Using your griefs so, it would prove them pleasures;
And you would seem, in cause of griefs and pleasures,
Equally pleasant.

Phœn. Sir, so I do now.
It is the excess of either that I strive
So much to shun, in all my proved endeavours,
Although perhaps, unto a general eye,
I may appear most wedded to my griefs;
Yet doth my mind forsake no taste of pleasure,
I mean that happy pleasure of the soul,
Divine and sacred contemplation
Of that eternal and most glorious bliss,
Proposed as the crown unto our souls.

Fran. I will be silent; yet that I may serve
But as a decade in the art of memory,
To put you still in mind of your own virtues,
When your too serious thoughts make you too sad,
Accept me for your servant, honour'd lady.

Phœn. Those ceremonies are too common, signior,
For your uncommon gravity and judgment,
And fit them only that are nought but ceremony.

Ang. Come, I will not sue stalely to be your servant,
But a new term, will you be my refuge?   *[Comes forward with Aur.*

Aur. Your refuge! why, sir?

Ang. That I might fly to you when all else fail me.

Aur. An you be good at flying, be my plover.

Ang. Nay, take away the P.

Aur. Tut, then you cannot fly.

Ang. I'll warrant you: I'll borrow Cupid's wings.

Aur. Mass, then I fear me you will do strange things.

I pray you blame me not, if I suspect you;
Your own confession simply doth detect you.
Nay, an you be so great in Cupid's books,
'Twill make me jealous. You can with your looks,
I warrant you, inflame a woman's heart,
And at your pleasure take Love's golden dart,
And wound the breast of any virtuous maid.
Would I were hence! good faith, I am afraid
You can constrain one, ere they be aware,
To run mad for your love.   •
    Ang. O, this is rare!

Enter Count FERNEZE.

    Count F. Close with my daughters, gentlemen! well done,
'Tis like yourselves: nay, lusty Angelo,
Let not my presence make you baulk your sport:
I will not break a minute of discourse
'Twixt you and one of your fair mistresses.
    Ang. One of my mistresses! why thinks your lordship
I have so many?
    Count F. Many! no, Angelo,
I do not think thou hast many; some fourteen
I hear thou hast, even of our worthiest dames
Of any note, in Milan.
    Ang. Nay, good my lord, fourteen! it is not so.
    Count F. By the mass that is't; here are their names to shew,
Fourteen or fifteen to one. Good Angelo,
You need not be ashamed of any of them,
They are gallants all.
    Ang. 'Sblood! you are such a lord.   [*Exit.*
    Count F. Nay, stay, sweet Angelo, I am disposed
A little to be pleasant past my custom—
He's gone, he's gone! I have disgraced him shrewdly.—
Daughters, take heed of him, he's a wild youth;
Look what he says to you, believe him not,
He will swear love to every one he sees.
Francisco, give them counsel, good Francisco,
I dare trust thee with both, but him with neither.
    Fran. Your lordship yet may trust both them with him.
    Count F. Well, go your ways, away!—
                  [*Exeunt Aur., Phœn., and Francisco.*

Enter CHRISTOPHERO.

How now, Christophero! What news with you?
    Chris. I have an humble suit to your good lordship.
    Count F. A suit, Christophero! what suit, I prithee?
    Chris. I would crave pardon at your lordship's hands,
If it seem vain or simple in your sight.

Count F. I'll pardon all simplicity, Christophero.
What — thy suit?

Chris. Perhaps, being now so old a batchelor,
I shall seem half unwise, to bend myself
In strict affection to a poor young maid.

Count F. What, is it touching love, Christophero?
Art thou disposed to marry! why, 'tis well.

Chris. Ay, but your lordship may imagine now,
That I, being steward of your honour's house,
If I be married once, will more regard
The maintenance of my wife, and of my charge,
Than the due discharge of my place and office.

Count F. No, no, Christophero, I know thee honest.

Chris. Good faith, my lord, your honour may suspect it;
But—

Count F. Then I should wrong thee; thou hast ever been
Honest and true; and wilt be still, I know.

Chris. Ay, but this marriage alters many men,
And you may fear it will do me, my lord:
But ere it do so, I will undergo
Ten thousand several deaths.

Count F. I know it, man.
Who wouldst thou have, I prithee?

Chris. Rachel de Prie,
If your good lordship grant me your consent,

Count F. Rachel de Prie! what, the poor beggar's daughter?
She's a right handsome maid, how poor soever,
And thou hast my consent with all my heart.

Chris. I humbly thank your honour; I'll now ask
Her father.   [*Exit.*

Count F. Do so, Christophero; thou shalt do well.
'Tis strange, she being so poor, he should affect her!
But this is more strange that myself should love her.
I spied her lately at her father's door,
And if I did not see in her sweet face
Gentry and nobleness, ne'er trust me more;
But this persuasion fancy wrought in me,
That fancy being created with her looks;
For where love is, he thinks his basest object
Gentle and noble; I am far in love,
And shall be forced to wrong my honest steward,
For I must sue and seek her for myself.
How much my duty to my late dead wife,
And my own dear renown, soe'er it sways:
I'll to her father straight, love hates delays.   [*Exit.*

SCENE IV.—*A Hall in the Same.*

Enter ONION, JUNIPER, VALENTINE, SEBASTIAN, BALTHASAR, MARTINO.

Oni. Come on, i'faith, let's to some exercise or other, my hearts.— Fetch the hilts.   [*Exit Martino.*
—Fellow Juniper, wilt thou play?

Jun. I cannot resolve you: 'tis as I am fitted with the ingenuity, quantity, or quality of the cudgel.

Val. How dost thou bastinado the poor cudgel with terms!

Jun. O ingle, I have the phrases, man, and the anagrams, and the epitaphs, fitting the mystery of the noble science.

Oni. I'll be hang'd an he were not misbegotten of some fencer.

Seb. Sirrah, Valentine, you can resolve me now, have they their masters of defence in other countries, as we have here in Italy?

Val. O Lord, ay; especially they in Utopia: there they perform their prizes and challenges with as great ceremony as the Italian, or any nation else.

Bal. Indeed! how is the manner of it, for God's love, good Valentine?

Jun. Ingle, I prithee make recourse unto us; we are thy friends and familiars, sweet ingle.

Val. Why thus, sir—

Oni. God a mercy, good Valentine; nay, go on.

Jun. *Silentium, bonus socius Onionus*, good fellow Onion, be not so ingenious and turbulent. So, sir; and how? how, sweet ingle?

Val. Marry, first they are brought to the public theatre.

Jun. What, have they theatres there?

Val. Theatres! ay, and plays too, both tragedy and comedy, and set forth with as much state as can be imagined.

Jun. By god's so, a man is nobody till he has travelled.

Seb. And how are their plays? as ours are, extemporal?

Val. O no; all premeditated things, and some of them very good, i'faith; my master used to visit them often when he was there.

Bal. Why how, are they in a place where any man may see them?

Val. Ay, in the common theatres, I tell you. But the sport is at a new play, to observe the sway and variety of opinion that passeth it. A man shall have such a confused mixture of judgment, poured out in the throng there, as ridiculous as laughter itself. One says he likes not the writing, another likes not the plot, another not the playing: and sometimes a fellow, that comes not there past once in five years, at a parliament time, or so, will be as deep mired in censuring as the best, and swear by god's foot he would never stir his foot to see a hundred such as that is.

Oni. I must travel to see these things, I shall never think well of myself else.

Jun. Fellow Onion, I'll bear thy charges, an thou wilt but pilgrimise it along with me to the land of Utopia.

Seb. Why, but methinks such rooks as these should be ashamed to judge.

Val. Not a whit; the rankest stinkard of them all will take upon him as peremptory, as if he had writ himself *in artibus magister.*

Seb. And do they stand to a popular censure for any thing they present?

Val. Ay, ever, ever; and the people generally are very acceptive, and apt to applaud any meritable work; but there are two sorts of persons that most commonly are infectious to a whole auditory.

Bal. What be they?

Jun. Ay, come, let's know them.

Oni. It were good they were noted.

Val. Marry, one is the rude barbarous crew, a people that have no brains, and yet grounded judgments; these will hiss any thing that mounts above their grounded capacities; but the other are worth the observation, i'faith.

Omnes. What be they, what be they?

Val. Faith, a few capricious gallants.

Jun. Capricious! stay, that word's for me.

Val. And they have taken such a habit of dislike in all things, that they will approve nothing, be it never so conceited or elaborate; but sit dispersed, making faces, and spitting wagging their upright ears, and cry, *filthy! filthy!* simply uttering their own condition, and using their wryed countenances instead of a vice, to turn the good aspects of all that shall sit near them from what they behold.

Re-enter MARTINO *with cudgels.*

Oni. O that's well said; lay them down; come, sirs, who plays? fellow Juniper, Sebastian, Balthasar? somebody take them up, come.

Jun. Ingle Valentine.

Val. Not I, sir, I profess it not.

Jun. Sebastian.

Seb. Balthasar.

Bal. Who, I?

Oni. Come, but one bout; I'll give them thee, i'faith.

Bal. Why, here's Martino.

Oni. Foh, he! alas, he cannot play a whit, man.

Jun. That's all one; no more could you *in statu quo prius.*—Martino, play with him; every man has his beginning and conduction.

Mart. Will you not hurt me, fellow Onion?

Oni. Hurt thee! no; an I do, put me among pot-herbs, and chop me to pieces. Come on.

Jun. By your favour, sweet bullies, give them room, back, so!—Martino, do not look so thin upon the matter.

[*Mart. and Onion play a bout at cudgels.*

Oni. Ha! well play'd, fall over to my leg now: so, to your guard again; excellent! to my head now; make home your blow; spare not me, make it home, good, good again!

[Mart. breaks his head.

Seb. Why how now, Peter!

Val. Odso, Onion has caught a bruise.

Jun. Coragio! be not capricious; what!

Oni. Capricious! not I, I scorn to be capricious for a scratch. Martino, I must have another bout; come.

Jun. No, no, play no more, play no more.

Oni. Foh, 'tis nothing, a fillip, a device; fellow Juniper, prithee get me a plantain; I had rather play with one that had skill by half.

Mart. By my troth, fellow Onion, 'twas against my will.

Oni. Nay, that's not so, 'twas against my head; but come, we'll have one bout more.

Jun. Not a bout, not a stroke.

Omnes. No more, no more. *[Exit Martino.*

Jun. Why, I'll give you demonstration how it came: thou open'dst the dagger to falsify over with the backsword trick, and he interrupted before he could fall to the close.

Oni. No, no, I know best how it was, better than any man here. I felt his play presently; for look you, I gathered upon him thus, thus, do you see, for the double lock, and took it single on the head.

Val. He says very true, he took it single on the head.

Seb. Come, let's go.

Re-enter MARTINO *with a cobweb.*

Mart. Here, fellow Onion, here's a cobweb.

Oni. How, a cobweb, Martino! I will have another bout with you. 'Swounds, do you first break my head, and then give me a plaister in scorn? Come, to it, I will have a bout.

Mart. God's my witness.—

Oni. Tut! your witness cannot serve.

Jun. 'Sblood, why what! thou art not lunatic, art thou? an thou be'st, avoid, Mephostophilus! Say the sign should be in Aries now, as it may be for all us, where were your life? answer me that?

Seb. He says well, Onion.

Val. Indeed does he.

Jun. Come, come, you are a foolish naturalist; go, get a white of an egg, and a little flax, and close the breach of the head, it is the most conducible thing that can be. Martino, do not insinuate upon your good fortune, but play an honest part, and bear away the bucklers. *[Exeunt.*

ACT III

SCENE I.—*The Street before* JAQUES DE PRIE'S *House.*

Enter ANGELO.

Ang. My young and simple friend, Paulo Ferneze,
Bound me with mighty solemn conjurations
To be true to him, in his love to Rachel;
And to solicit his remembrance still
In his enforced absence. Much, i'faith!
True to my friend in cases of affection!
In women's cases! what a jest it is,
How silly he is that imagines it!
He is an ass that will keep promise strictly
In any thing that checks his private pleasure,
Chiefly in love. 'Sblood, am not I a man,
Have I not eyes that are as free to look,
And blood to be inflamed as well as his?
And when it is so, shall I not pursue
Mine own love's longings, but prefer my friends'?
Ay, 'tis a good fool, do so; hang me then.
Because I swore? alas, who does not know
That lovers' perjuries are ridiculous?
Have at thee, Rachel; I'll go court her sure,
For now I know her father is abroad—
'Sblood, see, he's here.

Enter JAQUES.

O what damn'd luck is this!
This labour's lost, I must by no means see him.
Tau, dery, dery.   [*Exit singing.*
    Jaq. Mischief and hell! what is this man? a spirit!
Haunts he, my house's ghost, still at my door?—
He has been at my door, he has been in,
In my dear door; pray God my gold be safe!

Enter CHRISTOPHERO.

Od's pity, here's another!—Rachel! ho, Rachel!
    Chris. God save you, honest father.
    Jaq. Rachel! odslight, come to me; Rachel! Rachel!   [*Exit.*
    Chris. Now in God's name what ails he? this is strange!
He loves his daughter so, I'll lay my life
That he's afraid, having been now abroad,
I come to seek her love unlawfully.

Re-enter JAQUES.

    Jaq. 'Tis safe, 'tis safe, they have not robb'd my treasure. [*Aside.*
    Chris. Let it not seem offensive to you, sir.
    Jaq. Sir! God's my life, *sir! sir!* call me *sir!*   [*Aside.*

Chris. Good father, hear me.

Jaq. You are most welcome, sir;
I meant almost: and would your worship speak,
Would you abase yourself to speak to me?

Chris. 'Tis no abasing, father; my intent
Is to do further honour to you, sir,
Than only speak; which is, to be your son.

Jaq. My gold is in his nostrils, he has smelt it;
Break breast, break heart, fall on the earth, my entrails,
With this same bursting admiration!
He knows my gold, he knows of all my treasure—   [*Aside.*
How do you know, sir? whereby do you guess?

Chris. At what, sir? what is it you mean?

Jaq. I ask,
An't please your gentle worship, how you know—
I mean, how I should make your worship know
That I have nothing—
To give with my poor daughter? I have nothing:
The very air, bounteous to every man,
Is scant to me, sir.

Chris. I do think, good father,
You are but poor.

Jaq. He thinks so; hark! but thinks so.
He thinks not so, he knows of all my treasure.   [*Aside and exit.*

Chris. Poor man, he is so overjoy'd to hear
His daughter may be past his hopes bestow'd,
That betwixt fear and hope, if I mean simply,
He is thus passionate.

Re-enter JAQUES.

Jaq. Yet all is safe within: is none without?
Nobody break my walls?

Chris. What say you, father, shall I have your daughter?

Jaq. I have no dowry to bestow upon her.

Chris. I do expect none, father.

Jaq. That is well.
Then I beseech your worship make no question
Of that you wish; 'tis too much favour to me.

Chris. I'll leave him now to give his passions breath,
Which being settled, I will fetch his daughter;
I shall but move too much, to speak now to him.   [*Exit.*

Jaq. So! he is gone; would all were dead and gone,
That I might live with my dear gold alone!

Enter Count FERNEZE.

Count F. Here is the poor old man.

Jaq. Out o' my soul, another! comes he hither?

Count F. Be not dismay'd, old man, I come to cheer you.

Jaq. To me, by heaven!

Turn ribs to brass, turn voice into a trumpet,
To rattle out the battles of my thoughts;
One comes to hold me talk, while t'other robs me.   [*Aside and exit.*

   Count F. He has forgot me, sure; what should this mean?
He fears authority, and my want of wife
Will take his daughter from him to defame her:
He that has nought on earth but one poor daughter,
May take this extasy of care to keep her.

Re-enter JAQUES.

   Jaq. And yet 'tis safe: they mean not to use force,
But fawning cunning. I shall easily know,
By his next question, if he think me rich.   [*Aside.*
Whom see I? my good lord?

   Count F. Stand up, good father,
I call thee not [good] father for thy age,
But that I gladly wish to be thy son,
In honour'd marriage with thy beauteous daughter.

   Jaq. O, so, so, so, so, so! this is for gold.
Now it is sure this is my daughter's neatness
Makes them believe me rich. [*Aside.*]—No, my good lord,
I'll tell you all, how my poor hapless daughter
Got that attire she wears from top to toe.

   Count F. Why, father, this is nothing.

   Jaq. O yes, good my lord.

   Count F. Indeed it is not.

   Jaq. Nay, sweet lord, pardon me; do not dissemble;
Hear your poor beadsman speak: 'tis requisite
That I, so huge a beggar, make account
Of things that pass my calling. She was born
To enjoy nothing underneath the sun;
But that, if she had more than other beggars,
She should be envied: I will tell you then
How she had all she wears. Her warm shoes, God wot,
A kind maid gave her, seeing her go barefoot
In a cold frosty morning; God requite her!
Her homely stockings—

   Count F. Father, I'll hear no more, thou mov'st too much
With thy too curious answer for thy daughter,
That doth deserve a thousand times as much.
I'll be thy son-in-law, and she shall wear
The attire of countesses.

   Jaq. O, good my lord,
Mock not the poor; remembers not your lordship
That poverty is the precious gift of God,
As well as riches? tread upon me, rather   [*Kneels.*
Than mock my poorness.

   Count F. Rise, I say;
When I mock poorness, then heaven make me poor.   [*Exit Jaques.*

Enter a Messenger.

Mes. See, here's the count Ferneze, I will tell him
The hapless accident of his brave son,
That he may seek the sooner to redeem him.—
God save your lordship!

Count F. You are right welcome, sir.

Mes. I would I brought such news as might deserve it.

Count F. What! bring you me ill news?

Mes. 'Tis ill, my lord,
Yet such as usual chance of war affords,
And for which all men are prepared that use it,
And those that use it not but in their friends,
Or in their children.

Count F. Ill news of my son,
My dear and only son, I'll lay my soul!
Ah me accurs'd! thought of his death doth wound me,
And the report of it will kill me quite.

Mes. 'Tis not so ill, my lord.

Count F. How then?

Mes. He's taken prisoner,
And that is all.

Count F. That is enough, enough;
I set my thoughts on love, on servile love,
Forget my virtuous wife, feel not the dangers,
The bands and wounds of mine own flesh and blood,
And therein am a madman; therein plagued
With the most just affliction under heaven.
Is Maximilian taken prisoner too?

Mes. No, good my lord; he is return'd with prisoners.

Count F. Is't possible! can Maximilian
Return and view my face without my son,
For whom he swore such care as for himself?

Mes. My lord, no care can change the events of war.

Count F. O, in what tempests do my fortunes sail!
Still wrack'd with winds more foul and contrary
Than any northern gust, or southern flaw,
That ever yet inforced the sea to gape,
And swallow the poor merchant's traffic up.
First in Vicenza lost I my first son,
Next here in Milan my most dear-loved lady,
And now my Paulo prisoner to the French;
Which last being printed with my other griefs,
Doth make so huge a volume, that my breast
Cannot contain them. But this is my love!
I must make love to Rachel! heaven hath thrown
This vengeance on me most deservedly,
Were it for nought but wronging of my steward.

Mes. My lord, since only money may redress

The worst of this misfortune, be not grieved;
Prepare his ransom, and your noble son
Shall greet your cheered eyes with the more honour.

   Count F. I will prepare his ransom; gracious heaven
Grant his imprisonment may be his worst,
Honour'd and soldier-like imprisonment,
And that he be not manacled and made
A drudge to his proud foe! And here I vow,
Never to dream of seemless amorous toys,
Nor aim at any other joy on earth,
But the fruition of my only son.   *[Exeunt.*

SCENE II.—*A Court-yard, at the back of* JAQUES' *House.*

   Enter JAQUES *with his gold, and a scuttle full of dung.*

   Jaq. He's gone: I knew it; this is our hot lover.
I will believe them, I! they may come in
Like simple wooers, and be arrant thieves,
And I not know them! 'Tis not to be told
What servile villainies men will do for gold.—
O it began to have a huge strong smell,
With lying so long together in a place;
I'll give it vent, it shall have shift enough;
And if the devil, that envies all goodness,
Have told them of my gold, and where I kept it,
I'll set his burning nose once more a work,
To smell where I removed it. Here it is;
I'll hide, and cover it with this horse dung.
      [Digs a hole in the ground.
Who will suppose that such a precious nest
Is crown'd with such a dunghill excrement?
In, my dear life! sleep sweetly, my dear child!
Scarce lawfully begotten, but yet gotten,
And that's enough. Rot all hands that come near thee,
Except mine own! burn out all eyes that see thee,
Except mine own! all thoughts of thee be poison
To their enamour'd hearts, except mine own!
I'll take no leave, sweet prince, great emperor,
But see thee every minute: king of kings,
I'll not be rude to thee, and turn my back
In going from thee, but go backward out,
With my face toward thee, with humble courtesies.
None is within, none overlooks my wall;
To have gold, and to have it safe, is all.   *[Exit.*

SCENE III.—*A Gallery in* Count FERNEZE'S *House.*

Enter MAXIMILIAN, *with* Soldiers, CHAMONT, CAMILLO, *and*
PACUE.

Max. Lord Chamont, and your valiant friend there, I cannot
say, welcome to Milan; your thoughts and that word are not
musical; but I can say, you are come to Milan.

Pac. Mort dieu!

Cha. Garçon!   [*Takes Pacue aside.*

Max. Gentlemen, (I would call an emperor so,) you are now my
prisoners; I am sorry: marry this, spit in the face of your fortunes,
for your usage shall be honourable.

Cam. We know it, signior Maximilian;
The fame of all your actions sounds nought else
But perfect honour, from her swelling cheeks.

Max. It shall do so still, I assure you, and I will give you reason:
there is in this last action, you know, a noble gentleman of our
party, and a right valiant, semblably prisoner to your general, as
your honour'd selves to me; for whose safety this tongue has given
warrant to his honourable father, the count Ferneze. You conceive
me?

Cam. Ay, signior.

Max. Well, then I must tell you your ransoms be to redeem him.
What think you? your answer.

Cam. Marry, with my lord's leave here, I say, signior,
This free and ample offer you have made
Agrees well with your honour, but not ous ;
For I think not but Chamont is as well born
As is Ferneze; then, if I mistake not,
He scorns to have his worth so underprised,
That it should need an adjunct in exchange
Of any equal fortune. Noble signior,
I am a soldier, and I love Chamont;
Ere I would bruise his estimation
With the least ruin of mine own respect
In this vile kind, these legs should rot with irons,
This body pine in prison, till the flesh
Dropt from my bones in flakes, like wither'd leaves,
In heart of autumn, from a stubborn oak.

Max. Monsieur Gasper, (I take it so is your name,) misprise me
not; I will trample on the heart, on the soul of him that shall say
I will wrong you: what I purpose you cannot now know, but you
shall know, and, doubt not, to your contentment.—Lord Chamont,
I will leave you, whilst I go in and present myself to the honourable
count; till my regression, so please you, your noble feet may
measure this private, pleasant, and most princely walk.—Soldiers,
regard them and respect them.   [*Exit.*

Pac. O ver bon! excellenta gull, he taka my lord Chamont for

monsieur Gaspra, and monsieur Gaspra for my lord Chamont. Oh
dis be brave for make a me laugha, ha, ha, ha! O my heart tickla.
                                                       [*Aside.*

Cam. Ay, but your lordship knows not what hard fate
Might have pursued us, therefore, howsoe'er,
The changing of our names was necessary,
And we must now be careful to maintain
This error strongly, which our own device
Hath thrust into their ignorant conceits;
For should we (on the taste of this good fortune)
Appear ourselves, 'twould both create in them
A kind of jealousy, and perchance invert
Those honourable courses they intend.

Cha. True, my dear Gasper; but this hang-by here
Will, at one time or other, on my soul,
Discover us. A secret in his mouth
Is like a wild bird put into a cage,
Whose door no sooner opens, but 'tis out,—
But, sirrah, if I may but know thou utter'st it—

Pac. Uttera vat, monsieur?

Cha. That he is Gasper, and I true Chamont.

Pac. O pardonnez moy, fore my tongue shall put out de secreta,
shall breed de cankra in my mouth.

Cam. Speak not so loud, Pacue.

Pac. Foh! you shall not hear de fool, for all your long ear.
Regardez, monsieur: you be Chamont, Chamont be Gaspra.

    Re-enter MAXIMILIAN, *with* Count FERNEZE, FRANCISCO,
        AURELIA, PHŒNIXELLA, *and* FINIO.

Cha. Peace, here comes Maximilian.

Cam. O, belike
That is the count Ferneze, that old man.

Cha. Are those his daughters, trow?

Cam. Ay sure, I think they are.

Cha. Fore God, the taller is a gallant lady.

Cam. So are they both, believe me.

Max. True, my honourable lord, that Chamont was the father
of this man.

Count F. O that may be, for when I lost my son,
This was but young, it seems.

Fran. Faith, had Camillo lived,
He had been much about his years, my lord.

Count F. He had indeed! Well, speak no more of him.

Max. Signior, perceive you the error? 'twas no good office in us
to stretch the remembrance of so dear a loss. Count Ferneze, let
summer sit in your eye; look cheerfully, sweet count; will you do
me the honour to confine this noble spirit within the circle of your
arms?

Count F. Honour'd Chamont, reach me your valiant hand;

I could have wish'd some happier accident
Had made the way unto this mutual knowledge,
Which either of us now must take of other;
But since it is the pleasure of our fates,
That we should thus be rack'd on fortune's wheel,
Let us prepare with steeled patience
To tread on torment, and with minds confirm'd,
Welcome the worst of envy.

    Max. Noble lord, 'tis thus. I have here, in mine honour, set
this gentleman free, without ransom: he is now himself, his valour
hath deserved it, in the eye of my judgment.—Monsieur Gasper,
you are dear to me: *fortuna non mutat genus.* But, to the main;—
if it may square with your lordship's liking, and his love, I could
desire that he were now instantly employed to your noble general
in the exchange of Ferneze for yourself! it is a business that requires
the tender hand of a friend.

    Count F. Ay, and it would be with more speed effected,
If he would undertake it.

    Max. True, my lord.—Monsieur Gasper, how stand you affected
to this motion?

    Cha. My duty must attend his lordship's will.

    Max. What says the lord Chamont?

    Cam. My will doth then approve what these have urged.

    Max. Why there is good harmony, good music in this. Monsieur
Gasper, you shall protract no time, only I will give you a bowl of
rich wine to the health of your general, another to the success of
your journey, and a third to the love of my sword. Pass.

                          [Exeunt all but Aur. and Phœn.

    Aur. Why, how now, sister! in a motley muse?
Go to, there's somewhat in the wind, I see.
Faith, this brown study suits not with your black,
Your habit and your thoughts are of two colours.

    Phœn. Good faith, methinks that this young lord Chamont
Favours my mother, sister; does he not?

    Aur. A motherly conceit; O blind excuse,
Blinder than Love himself! Well, sister, well;
Cupid has ta'en his stand in both your eyes,
The case is altered.

    Phœn. And what of that?

    Aur. Nay, nothing:—But, a saint!
Another Bridget! one that for a face
Would put down Vesta, in whose looks doth swim
The very sweetest cream of modesty,
You, to turn tippet! fie, fie! Will you give
A packing penny to virginity!
I thought you'd dwell so long in Cypres isle,
You'd worship madam Venus at the length:
But come, the strongest fall, and why not you?
Nay, do not frown.

Phœn. Go, go, you fool. Adieu!   [*Exit.*

Aur. Well, I may jest, or so; but Cupid knows
My taking is as bad, or worse than hers.
O, monsieur Gasper, if thou be'st a man,
Be not afraid to court me; do but speak,
Challenge thy right, and wear it; for I swear,
Till thou arriv'dst, ne'er came affection here.   [*Exit.*

ACT IV

SCENE I.—*A Room in* Count FERNEZE'S *House.*

Enter PACUE *and* FINIO.

Fin. Come on, my sweet finical Pacue, the very prime of pages, here's an excellent place for us to practise in; nobody sees us here; come, let's to it.

Enter ONION.

Pac. Contenta; Regardez vous le premier.

Oni. Sirrah, Finio.

Pac. Mort dieu, le paisant!

Oni. Didst thou see Valentine?

Fin. Valentine, no.

Oni. No!

Fin. No. Sirrah Onion, whither goest?

Oni. O, I am vext; he that would trust **any** of these lying travellers.—

Fin. I prithee stay, good Onion.

Pac. Monsieur Onion, venez ça, come hidera, je vous prie. By gar, me ha see two, tree, four hundra tousand of your cousan hang. Lend me your hand, shall pray for know you bettra.

Oni. I thank you, good signior Parlez-vous. O that I were in another world, in the Ingies, or somewhere, that I might have room to laugh!

Pac. Ah, oui, fort bien! stand, you dere—now, me come, Bon jour, monsieur.

Fin. Good morrow, good signior.

Pac. By gar, me be much glad for see you.

Fin. I return you most kind thanks, sir.

Oni. How, how! 'sblood this is rare.

Pac. Nay, shall make you say rare, by and by; reguardez: monsieur Finio.

Fin. Signior Pacue.

Pac. Dieu vous garde, monsieur.

Fin. God save you, sweet signior.

Pac. Monsieur Onion, is not fort bien?

Oni. Bean, quoth he! would I were in debt of a pottle of beans, I could do as much!

Fin. Welcome, signior: what's next?

Pac. O here; voyez de grand admiration, as should meet perchance monsieur Finio.

Fin. Monsieur Pacue.

Pac. By gar, who think we shall meete here?

Fin. By this hand, I am not a little proud of it, sir.

Oni. This trick is only for the chamber, it cannot be cleanly done abroad.

Pac. Vell, vat say you for dis den, monsieur?

Fin. Nay, pray, sir.

Pac. Par ma foy, vous voilà bien encountré!

Fin. What do you mean, sir? let your glove alone.

Pac. Comment se porte la santé?

Fin. Faith, exceeding well, sir.

Pac. Trot, be mush joy for hear.

Fin. And how is it with you, sweet signior Pacue?

Pac. Fait, comme vous voyez.

Oni. Young gentlemen, spirits of blood, if ever you'll taste of a sweet piece of mutton, do Onion a good turn now.

Pac. Que, que? parlez, monsieur, vat ist?

Oni. Faith, teach me one of these tricks.

Pac. O me shall do presently; stand you dere, you signior dere, myself is here; so, fort bien! now I parlez to monsieur Onion, Onion pratla to you, you speaka to me, so: and as you parlez, change the bonet.—Monsieur Onion!

Oni. Monsieur Finio!

Fin. Monsieur Pacue!

Pac. Pray be covera.

Oni. Nay, I beseech you, sir.

Fin. What do you mean?

Pac. Pardonnez moi, shall be so.

Oni. O Lord, sir!

Fin. Not I, in good faith, sir.

Pac. By gar, you must.

Oni. It shall be yours.

Fin. Nay, then you wrong me.

Oni. Well, an ever I come to be great—

Pac. You be big enough for de Onion already.

Oni. I mean a great man.

Fin. Then thou'dst be a monster.

Oni. Well, God knows not what fortune may do, command me, use me from the soul to the crown, and the crown to the soul; meaning not only from the crown of the head, and the sole of the foot, but also the foot of the mind and the crowns of the purse. I cannot stay now, young gentlemen; but—*time was, time is, and time shall be.*   [*Exeunt.*

SCENE II.—*Another Room in the Same.*

Enter CHAMONT *and* CAMILLO.

Cha. Sweet Gasper, I am sorry we must part;
But strong necessity enforces it.
Let not the time seem long unto my friend,
Till my return; for, by our love I swear,
(The sacred sphere wherein our souls are knit,)
I will endeavour to effect this business
With all industrious care and happy speed.
Cam. My lord, these circumstances would come well
To one less capable of your desert
Than I; in whom your merit is confirm'd
With such authentical and grounded proofs.
Cha. Well, I will use no more. Gasper, adieu.
Cam. Farewell, my honour'd lord.
Cha. Commend me to the lady, my good Gasper.
Cam. I had remember'd that, had not you urged it.
Cha. Once more adieu, sweet Gasper.
Cam. My good lord.   [*Exit.*
Cha. Thy virtues are more precious than thy name;
Kind gentleman, I would not sell thy love
For all the earthly objects that mine eyes
Have ever tasted. Sure thou art nobly born,
However, fortune hath obscured thy birth;
For native honour sparkles in thine eyes.
How may I bless the time wherein Chamont,
My honour'd father, did surprise Vicenza,
Where this my friend (known by no name) was found,
Being then a child, and scarce of power to speak,
To whom my father gave this name of Gasper,
And as his own respected him to death:
Since when we two have shared our mutual fortunes
With equal spirits, and, but death's rude hand,
No violence shall dissolve this sacred band.   [*Exit.*

SCENE III.—JUNIPER *is discovered in his shop, singing.*

Enter ONION.

Oni. Fellow Juniper, no more of thy songs and sonnets; sweet Juniper, no more of thy hymns and madrigals; thou sing'st, but I sigh.

Jun. What's the matter, Peter, ha? what, in an academy still? still in sable and costly black array, ha?

Oni. Prithee rise, mount, mount, sweet Juniper; for I go down the wind, and yet I puff, for I am vext.

Jun. Ha, bully, vext! what, intoxicate! is thy brain in a quintessence, an idea, a metamorphosis, an apology, ha, rogue? Come, this love feeds upon thee, I see by thy cheeks, and drinks healths of vermilion tears, I see by thine eyes.

Oni. I confess Cupid's carouse, he plays super negulum with my liquor of life.

Jun. Tut, thou art a goose to be Cupid's gull; go to; no more of these contemplations and calculations; mourn not, for Rachel's thine own.

Oni. For that let the higher powers work: but, sweet Juniper, I am not sad for her, and yet for her in a second person, or if not so, yet in a third.

Jun. How, second person! away, away. In thy crotchets already! longitude and latitude! what second, what person, ha?

Oni. Juniper, I'll bewray myself before thee, for thy company is sweet unto me; but I must intreat thy helping hand in the case.

Jun. Tut, no more of this surquedry; I am thine own ad unguem, upsie freeze, pell mell; come, what case, what case?

Oni. For the case, it may be any man's case, as well as mine. Rachel I mean; but I'll meddle with her anon: in the mean time, Valentine is the man hath wronged me.

Jun. How, my ingle wrong thee! is't possible?

Oni. Your ingle! hang him, infidel. Well, and if I be not revenged on him, let Peter Onion (by the infernal gods) be turned to a leek, or a scallion. I spake to him for a ditty for this handkerchief.

Jun. Why, has he not done it?

Oni. Done it? not a verse, by this hand.

Jun. O in diebus illis! O preposterous! well, come, be blithe; the best inditer of them all is sometimes dull. Fellow Onion, pardon mine ingle; he is a man has imperfections and declinations, as other men have; his muse sometimes cannot curvet, nor prognosticate and come off, as it should; no matter, I'll hammer out a paraphrase for thee myself.

Oni. No, sweet Juniper, no; danger doth breed delay: love makes me choleric, I can bear no longer.

Jun. Not bear what, my mad meridian slave? not bear what?

Oni. Cupid's burthen; 'tis too heavy, too tolerable; and as for the handkerchief and the posie, I will not trouble thee; but if thou wilt go with me into her father's back-side, old Jaques' back-side, and speak for me to Rachel, I will not be ingratitude: the old man is abroad and all.

Jun. Art thou sure on't?

Oni. As sure as an obligation.

Jun. Let's away then; come, we spend time in a vain circumference; trade, I cashier thee till to-morrow: fellow Onion, for thy sake I finish this workday.

Oni. God-a-mercy; and for thy sake I'll at any time make a holiday.   [*Exeunt.*

SCENE IV.—*The Court-yard at the back of* JAQUES' *House.*

Enter ANGELO *and* RACHEL.

Ang. Nay, I prithee, Rachel; I come to comfort thee,
Be not so sad.

Rach. O, signior Angelo,
No comfort but his presence can remove
This sadness from my heart.

Ang. Nay, then you are fond,
And want that strength of judgment and election
That should be attendant on your years and form.
Will you, because your lord is taken prisoner,
Blubber and weep, and keep a peevish stir,
As though you would turn turtle with the news?
Come, come, be wise. 'Sblood, say your lord should die,
And you go mar your face as you begin,
What would you do, trow? who would care for you?
But this it is, when nature will bestow
Her gifts on such as know not how to use them;
You shall have some, that had they but one quarter
Of your fair beauty, they would make it shew
A little otherwise than you do this,
Or they would see the painter twice an hour,
And I commend them, I, that can use art
With such judicial practice.

Rach. You talk idly;
If this be your best comfort, keep it still,
My senses cannot feed on such sour cates.

Ang. And why, sweet heart?

Rach. Nay, leave, good signior.

Ang. Come, I have sweeter viands yet in store.

Jun. [*within.*] Ay, in any case.—Mistress Rachel!

Ang. Rachel!

Rach. Od's pity, signior Angelo, I hear my father; away for
God's sake.

Ang. 'Sblood, I am bewitch'd, I think; this is twice now I have
been served thus.   [*Exit.*

Rach. Pray God he meet him not.   [*Exit.*

Enter ONION *and* JUNIPER.

Oni. O brave! she's yonder: O terrible! she's gone.

Jun. Yea, so nimble in your dilemmas, and your hyperboles!
Hey my love! O my love! at the first sight, by the mass.

Oni. O how she scudded! O sweet scud, how she tripped! O
delicate trip and go!

Jun. Come, thou art enamoured with the influence of her pro-
fundity; but, sirrah, hark a little.

Oni. O rare! what, what? passing, i'faith! what is't, what is't?

Jun. What wilt thou say now, if Rachel stand now, and play hity-tity through the key hole, to behold the equipage of thy person?

Oni. O sweet equipage! try, good Juniper, tickle her, talk, talk; O rare!

Jun. Mistress Rachel!—watch then if her father come.—[*Goes to the door.*]—Rachel! Madona! Rachel! No?

Oni. Say I am here; Onion, or Peter, or so.

Jun. No, I'll knock; we'll not stand upon horizons and tricks, but fall roundly to the matter.

Oni. Well said, sweet Juniper. Horizons, hang 'em! knock, knock. [*Juniper knocks.*

Rach. [*within*]. Who's there? father?

Jun. Father! no; and yet a father, if you please to be a mother.

Oni. Well said, Juniper; to her again; a smack or two more of the mother.

Jun. Do you hear, sweet soul, sweet Radamant, sweet Machavel? one word, Melpomene, are you at leisure?

Rach. [*within.*] At leisure! what to do?

Jun. To do what! to do nothing, but to be liable to the extacy of true love's exigent, or so; you smell my meaning.

Oni. Smell! filthy, fellow Juniper, filthy! smell! O most odious!

Jun. How, filthy?

Oni. Filthy, by this finger! Smell! smell a rat, smell a pudding. Away, these tricks are for trulls; a plain wench loves plain dealing; I'll upon her myself. Smell! to a marchpane wench?

Jun. With all my heart: I'll be legitimate and silent as an apple-squire; I'll see nothing, and say nothing.

Oni. Sweet heart! sweet heart!

Jun. And bag pudding, ha, ha, ha!

Jaq. [*within.*] What, Rachel, my girl! what, Rachel!

Oni. Od's lid.

Jaq. [*within.*] What, Rachel!

Rach. [*within.*] Here I am.

Oni. What rakehell calls Rachel? O treason to my love!

Jun. It is her father, on my life; how shall we intrench and edify ourselves from him?

Oni. O coney-catching Cupid! [*Gets up into a tree.*

Enter JAQUES.

Jaq. How, in my back-side! where? what come they for? Where are they? Rachel! thieves! thieves! Stay, villain, slave! [*Seizes Jun. as he is running out.*] Rachel, untie my dog. Nay, thief, thou canst not 'scape.

Jun. I pray you, sir.

Oni. [*above.*] Ah, pitiful Onion, that thou hadst a rope!

Jaq. Why, Rachel, when, I say! let loose my dog, Garlick, my mastiff, let him loose, I say.

Jun. For God's sake hear me speak, keep up your cur.

Oni. [*above.*] I fear not Garlick, he'll not bite Onion, his kinsman; pray God he come out, and then they'll not smell me.

Jaq. Well then deliver; come, deliver, slave.

Jun. What should I deliver?

Jaq. O thou wouldst have me tell thee, wouldst thou? Shew me thy hands, what hast thou in thy hands?

Jun. Here be my hands.

Jaq. Stay, are thy fingers' ends begrimed with dirt? no, thou hast wiped them.

Jun. Wiped them!

Jaq. Ay, thou villain; thou art a subtle knave. Put off thy shoes; come, I will see them; give me a knife here, Rachel, I'll rip the soles.

Oni. [*above.*] No, matter, he's a cobler, he can mend them.

Jun. What, are you mad, are you detestable? would you make an anatomy of me? think you I am not true orthography?

Jaq. Orthography! anatomy!

Jun. For God's sake be not so inviolable, I am no ambuscado. What predicament call you this? why do you intimate so much?

Jaq. I can feel nothing.

Oni. [*above.*] By'r Lady, but Onion feels something.

Jaq. Soft, sir, you are not yet gone; shake your legs, come; and your arms, be brief:—stay, let me see these drums, these kilderkins, these bombard slops, what is it crams them so?

Jun. Nothing but hair.

Jaq. That's true, I had almost forgot this rug, this hedgehog's nest, this hay-mow, this bear's skin, this heath, this furze-bush.

                                       [*Pulls him by the hair.*

Jun. O, let me go! you tear my hair, you revolve my brains and understanding.

Jaq. Heart, thou art somewhat eased; half of my fear
Hath ta'en his leave of me, the other half
Still keeps possession in despight of hope,
Until these amorous eyes court my fair gold.
Dear, I come to thee. [*Aside.*]—Fiend, why art not gone?
Avoid, my soul's vexation! Satan, hence!
Why dost thou stare on me? why dost thou stay,
Why por'st thou on the ground with thievish eyes?
What seest thou there, thou cur, what gap'st thou at?
Hence from my house.—Rachel, send Garlick forth.

    Jun. I am gone, sir, I am gone; for God's sake, stay.   [*Exit.*

    Jaq. Pack; and thank God thou scap'st so well away.

    Oni. [*above.*] If I scape this tree, destinies I defy you.

    Jaq. I cannot see, by any characters
Writ on this earth, that any felon foot
Hath ta'en acquaintance of this hallow'd ground.
None sees me: knees, do homage to your lord.

        [*Kneels down and removes the dung from his treasure.*

'Tis safe! 'tis safe! it lies and sleeps so soundly,

'Twould do one good to look on't.   If this bliss
Be given to any man that hath much gold,
Justly to say *'tis safe*, I say 'tis safe.
O! what a heavenly round these two words dance
Within me and without me! first I think them:
And then I speak them; then I watch their sound,
And drink it greedily with both mine ears:
Then think, then speak, then drink their sound again,
And racket round about this body's court,
These two sweet words, *'tis safe*.   Stay, I will feed
My other senses. [*Takes up some of the gold and smells to it.*] O how
sweet it smells!

    Oni. [*above.*] I marle he smells not Onion, being so near it.

    Jaq. Down to thy grave again, thou beauteous ghost!
Angels, men say, are spirits; spirits be
Invisible; bright angels, are you so?—
Be you invisible to every eye,
Save only these: sleep, I'll not break your rest,
Though you break mine.   Dear saints, adieu, adieu!
My feet part from you, but my soul dwells with you.   [*Rises and exit.*

    Oni. Is he gone? O Fortune my friend, and not *Fortune my foe,*
I come down to embrace thee, and kiss thy great toe.

                       [*Comes down from the tree.*

Re-enter JUNIPER.

    Jun. Fellow Onion! Peter!

    Oni. Fellow Juniper.

    Jun. What's the old Panurgo gone, departed, cosmografied, ha?

    Oni. O, ay! and hark, sirrah.—Shall I tell him? no.

    Jun. Nay, be brief, and declare; stand not upon conundrums
now: thou knowest what contagious speeches I have suffered for
thy sake: an he should come again and invent me here—

    Oni. He says true, it was for my sake: I will tell him.—Sirrah,
Juniper!—and yet I will not.

    Jun. What sayst thou, sweet Onion?

    Oni. An thou hadst smelt the scent of me when I was in the
tree, thou wouldst not have said so; but, sirrah, *the case is altered*
with me, my heart has given love a box of the ear, made him kick
up the heels, i'faith.

    Jun. Sayst thou me so, mad Greek! how haps it, how chances it?

    Oni. I cannot hold it.—Juniper, have an eye, look; have an eye
to the door; the old proverb's true, I see, Gold is but muck.   Nay,
god's so, Juniper, to the door; an eye to the main chance. [*Removes
the dung, and shews him the gold.*] Here, you slave, have an eye!

    Jun. O inexorable! O infallible; O intricate, divine, and super-
ficial fortune!

    Oni. Nay, it will be sufficient anon; here, look here!

    Jun. O insolent good luck! how didst thou produce the intelli-
gence of the gold minerals?

Oni. I'll tell you that anon! here, make shift, convey, cram. I'll teach you how you shall call for Garlick again, i'faith.

Jun. 'Sblood, what shall we do with all this? we shall never bring it to a consumption.

Oni. Consumption! why we'll be most sumptuously attired, man.

Jun. By this gold, I will have three or four most stigmatical suits presently.

Oni. I'll go in my foot-cloth, I'll turn gentleman.

Jun. So will I.

Oni. But what badge shall we give, what cullison?

Jun. As for that, let's use the infidelity and commiseration of some harrot of arms, he shall give us a gudgeon.

Oni. A gudgeon! a scutcheon thou wouldst say, man.

Jun. A scutcheon, or a gudgeon, all is one.

Oni. Well, our arms be good enough, let's look to our legs.

Jun. Content; we'll be jogging.

Oni. Rachel, we retire; Garlick, god b'ye.

Jun. Farewell, sweet Jaques!

Oni. Farewell, sweet Rachel! sweet dog, adieu! [*Exeunt.*

SCENE V.—*A Room in* Count FERNEZE'S *House.*

Enter MAXIMILIAN, Count FERNEZE, AURELIA, PHŒNIXELLA, *and* PACUE.

Max. Nay, but sweet count.

Count F. Away! I'll hear no more;
Never was man so palpably abused:—
My son so basely marted, and myself
Am made the subject of your mirth and scorn.

Max. Count Ferneze, you tread too hard upon my patience; do not persist, I advise your lordship.

Count F. I will persist, and unto thee I speak;
Thou, *Maximilian,* thou hast injured me.

Max. Before the Lord—

Aur. Sweet signior.

Phœn. O my father.

Max. Lady, let your father thank your beauty.

Pac. By gar, me shall be hang for tella dis same; me tella mademoiselle, she tell her fadera.

Count F. The true Chamont set free, and one left here
Of no descent, clad barely in his name!
Sirrah, boy, come hither, and be sure you speak the simple truth.

Pac. O pardonnez moy, monsieur.

Count F. Come, leave your pardons, and directly say,
What villain is the same that hath usurp'd
The honour'd name and person of Chamont.

Pac. O, monsieur, no point villain, brave chevalier, monsieur Gasper.

Count F. Monsieur Gasper!

On what occasion did they change their names,
What was their policy, or their pretext?

Pac. Me canno tell, par ma foy, monsieur.

Max. My honourable lord!

Count F. Tut, tut, be silent.

Max. Silent, count Ferneze! I tell thee, if Amurath, the great
Turk, were here, I would speak, and he should hear me.

Count F. So will not I.

Max. By my father's hand, but thou shalt, count. I say, till
this instant I was never touch'd in my reputation. Hear me, you
shall know that you have wrong'd me, and I will make you acknowledge it; if I cannot, my sword shall.

Count F. By heaven I will not, I will stop mine ears,
My senses loath the savour of thy breath;
'Tis poison to me; I say, I will not hear.
What shall I know? 'tis you have injured me.
What will you make? make me acknowledge it!
Fetch forth that Gasper, that lewd counterfeit;
I'll make him to your face approve your wrongs.

Enter Servants *with* CAMILLO.

Come on, false substance, shadow to Chamont,
Had you none else to work upon but me?
Was I your fittest project? well, confess
What you intended by this secret plot,
And by whose policy it was contrived.
Speak truth, and be intreated courteously;
But double with me, and resolve to prove
The extremest rigour that I can inflict.

Cam. My honour'd lord, hear me with patience;
Nor hope of favour, nor the fear of torment,
Shall sway my tongue from uttering of truth.

Count F. 'Tis well, proceed then.

Cam. The morn before this battle did begin,
Wherein my lord Chamont and I were ta'en,
We vow'd one mutual fortune, good or bad,
That day should be embraced of us both;
And urging that might worse succeed our vow,
We there concluded to exchange our names.

Count F. Then Maximilian took you for Chamont?

Cam. True, noble lord.

Count F. 'Tis false, ignoble wretch;
'Twas but a complot to betray my son.

Max. Count, thou lies in thy bosom, count.

Count F. Lie!

Cam. Nay, I beseech you, honour'd gentlemen,
Let not the untimely ruin of your love
Follow these slight occurrents; be assured
Chamont's return will heal these wounds again,

And break the points of your too piercing thoughts.

Count F. Return! ay, when? when will Chamont return?
He'll come to fetch you, will he? ay, 'tis like!
You'd have me think so, that's your policy.
No, no, young gallant, your device is stale;
You cannot feed me with so vain a hope.

Cam. My lord, I feed you not with a vain hope;
I know assuredly he will return,
And bring your noble son along with him.

Max. Ay, I dare pawn my soul he will return.

Count F. O impudent derision! open scorn!
Intolerable wrong! is't not enough
That you have play'd upon me all this while,
But still to mock me, still to jest at me?
Fellows, away with him; thou ill-bred slave,
That sett'st no difference 'twixt a noble spirit
And thy own slavish humour, do not think
But I'll take worthy vengeance on thee, wretch.

Cam. Alas, these threats are idle, like the wind,
And breed no terror in a guiltless mind.

Count F. Nay, thou shalt want no torture, so resolve;
Bring him away.   [*Exit.*

Cam. Welcome the worst, I suffer for a friend,
Your tortures will, my love shall never, end.
                     [*Exeunt Servants with Camillo and Pacue.*

Phœn. Alas, poor gentleman! my father's rage
Is too extreme, too stern and violent.
O that I knew with all my strongest powers
How to remove it from thy patient breast!
But that I cannot, yet my willing heart
Shall minister, in spite of tyranny,
To thy misfortune; something there is in him
That doth enforce this strange affection
With more than common rapture in my breast:
For being but Gasper, he is still as dear
To me, as when he did Chamont appear.   [*Aside and exit.*

Aur. But in good sadness, signior, do you think Chamont will
return?

Max. Do I see your face, lady?

Aur. Ay sure, if love have not blinded you.

Max. That is a question; but I will assure you no: I can see,
and yet love is in mine eye. Well, the count your father simply
hath dishonoured me, and this steel shall engrave it on his burgonet.

Aur. Nay, sweet signior!

Max. Lady, I do prefer my reputation to my life;—but you shall
rule me. Come, let's march.   [*Exit.*

Aur. I'll follow, signior. O sweet queen of love!
Sovereign of all my thoughts, and thou, fair Fortune,
Who more to honour my affections,

Hast thus translated Gasper to Chamont!
Let both your flames now burn in one bright sphere,
And give true light to my aspiring hopes:
Hasten Chamont's return, let him affect me,
Though father, friends, and all the world reject me.   [*Exit.*

ACT V

SCENE I.—*The Court at the back of* JAQUES' *House.*

Enter ANGELO *and* CHRISTOPHERO.

Ang. Sigh for a woman! Would I fold mine arms,
Rave in my sleep, talk idly being awake,
Pine and look pale, make love-walks in the night,
To steal cold comfort from a day-star's eyes!
Kit, thou'rt a fool; wilt thou be wise? then, lad,
Renounce this boy-god's nice idolatry,
Stand not on compliment, and coying tricks;
Thou lov'st Old Jaques' daughter, dost thou?
    Chris. Love her!
    Ang. Come, come, I know't; be ruled, and she's thine own.
Thou'lt say, her father Jaques, the old beggar,
Hath pawn'd his word to thee, that none but thou
Shalt be his son-in-law.
    Chris. He has.
    Ang. He has!
Wilt thou believe him, and be made a cokes,
To wait on such an antique weathercock?
Why, he is more inconstant than the sea,
His thoughts, camelion-like, change every minute:
No, Kit, work soundly, steal the wench away,
Wed her, and bed her; and when that is done,
Then say to Jaques, Shall I be your son?
But come, to our device, where is this gold?
    Chris. Here, signior Angelo.
    Ang. Bestow it, bid thy hands shed golden drops;
Let these bald French crowns be uncovered,
In open sight to do obeïsance
To Jaques' staring eyes when he steps forth;
The needy beggar will be glad of gold.—
So! now keep thou aloof, and as he treads
This gilded path, stretch out his ambling hopes
With scattering more and more, and as thou goest,
Cry Jaques! Jaques!
    Chris. Tush, let me alone.
    Ang. But first I'll play the ghost, I'll call him out;
Kit, keep aloof.
    Chris. But, signior Angelo,

Where will yourself and Rachel stay for me,
After the jest is ended?
 Ang. Mass, that's true:
At the old priory behind St. Foy's.
 Chris. Agreed, no better place; I'll meet you there.
          [*Retires, dropping the gold.*
 Ang. Do, good fool, do; but I'll not meet you there.
Now to this gear.—Jaques! Jaques! what, Jaques?
 Jaq. [*within.*] Who calls? who's there?
 Ang. Jaques!
 Jaq. [*within.*] Who calls?
 Ang. Steward, he comes, he comes.—Jaques!   [*Retires.*

Enter Jaques.

 Jaq. What voice is this?
No body here! was I not call'd? I was;
And one cried Jaques with a hollow voice.
I was deceived; no, I was not deceived.   [*Sees the gold.*
See, see, it was an angel call'd me forth.
Gold, gold, man-making gold; another star!
Drop they from heaven? no, no, my house, I hope,
Is haunted with a fairy. My dear Lar,
My household god, my fairy, on my knees—
 Chris. [*within.*] Jaques!
 Jaq. My Lar doth call me; O sweet voice,
Musical as the spheres! see, see, more gold!
 Chris. [*within.*] Jaques!
 Jaq. What, Rachel, Rachel!

Enter Rachel.

       Lock my door,
Look to my house.
 Chris. [*within.*] Jaques!
 Jaq. Shut fast my door.
A golden crown! Jaques shall be a king.
   [*Exit, following the sound, and picking up the gold.*
 Ang. [*comes forward.*] To a fool's paradise that path will bring
Thee and thy household Lar.
 Rach. What means my father?
I wonder what strange humour—
 Ang. Come, sweet soul,
Leave wondering, start not, 'twas I laid this plot,
To get thy father forth.
 Rach. O, Angelo!
 Ang. O me no O's, but hear; my lord, your love,
Paulo Ferneze, is return'd from war,
Lingers at Pont Valerio, and from thence,
By post, at midnight last, I was conjured
To man you thither. Stand not on replies,

A horse is saddled for you, will you go?
And I am for you; if you will stay, why so.
 Rach. O Angelo, each minute is a day
Till my Ferneze come; come, we'll away.   [*Exit.*
 Ang. Sweet soul, I guess thy meaning by thy looks.
At Pont Valerio thou thy love shalt see,
But not Ferneze. Steward, fare you well;
You wait for Rachel too: when! can you tell? [*Exit hastily.*

  Re-enter JAQUES, *with his hands full of money.*

 Jaq. O in what golden circle have I danced!
Milan, these odorous and enflower'd fields
Are none of thine; no, here's Elysium;
Here blessed ghosts do walk; this is the court
And glorious palace, where the god of gold
Shines like the sun, of sparkling majesty.
O [my] fair-feather'd, my red-breasted birds,
Come fly with me, I'll bring you to a choir,
Whose consort being sweeten'd with your sound,
The music will be fuller, and each hour
The ears shall banquet with your harmony.
O! O! O!   [*Exit.*
    Re-enter CHRISTOPHERO.

 Chris. At the old priory behind St. Foy's,
That was the place of our appointment, sure;
I hope he will not make me lose my gold,
And mock me too; perhaps they are within;
I'll knock.
 Jaq. [*within.*] O lord! THE CASE IS ALTERED.
 Chris. Rachel! Angelo! signior Angelo!

    Re-enter JAQUES.

 Jaq. Angels! ay, where? mine angels! where's my gold?
Why, Rachel! O thou thievish cannibal!
Thou eat'st my flesh in stealing of my gold.
 Chris. What gold?
 Jaq. What gold? Rachel! call help, come forth!
I'll rip thine entrails, but I'll have my gold.
Rachel! why com'st thou not? I am undone.
Ah me, she speaks not! thou hast slain my child. [*Exit.*
 Chris. What, is the man possest, trow? this is strange!
Rachel, I see, is gone with Angelo.
Well, I will once again unto the priory,
And see if I can meet them.   [*Exit.*

    Re-enter JAQUES.
 Jaq. 'Tis too true,
Thou hast made away my child, thou hast my gold:
O what hyena call'd me out of doors?

The thief is gone, my gold's gone, Rachel's gone,
All's gone! save I that spend my cries in vain;
But I'll hence too, and die, or end this pain.   [*Exit.*

SCENE II.—*The Street before* Count FERNEZE's *House.*

Enter JUNIPER *and* ONION *richly dressed, and drunk, followed
by* FINIO *and* VALENTINE.

Jun. 'Swounds, let me go; hey, catso! catch him alive; I call,
I call, boy; I come, I come, sweetheart.

Oni. Page, hold my rapier, while I hold my friend here.

Val. O here's a sweet metamorphosis, a couple of buzzards turn'd
to a pair of peacocks.

Jun. Signior Onion, lend me thy boy to unhang my rapier.

Oni. Signior Juniper, for once or so; but troth is, you must
inveigle, as I have done, my lord's page here, a poor follower of mine.

Jun. Hey ho! your page then shall not be superintendant upon
me? he shall not be addicted? he shall not be incident, he shall not
be incident, he shall not be incident, shall he?

                                        [*He foins with his rapier.*

Fin. O sweet signior Juniper.

Jun. 'Sblood, stand away, princox! do not aggravate my joy.

Val. Nay, good master Onion.

Oni. Nay, an he have the heart to draw my blood, let him come.

Jun. I'll slice you, Onion; I'll slice you.

Oni. I'll cleave you, Juniper.

Val. Why hold, hold, ho! what do you mean?

Jun. Let him come, ingle; stand by, boy, his alabaster blade
cannot fear me.

Fin. Why hear you, sweet signior, let not there be any contention
between my master and you about me; if you want a page, sir, I
can help you to a proper stripling.

Jun. Canst thou! what parentage, what ancestry, what genealogy
is he?

Fin. A French boy, sir.

Jun. Has he his French linguist? has he?

Fin. Ay, sir.

Jun. Then transport him; here's a crusado for thee.

Oni. You will not embezzle my servant with your benevolence,
will you? hold, boy, there's a portmanteau for thee.

Fin. Lord, sir!

Oni. Do, take it, boy; it's three pounds ten shillings, a portmanteau.

Fin. I thank your lordship.   [*Exit.*

Jun. Sirrah, ningle, thou art a traveller, and I honour thee. I
prithee discourse, cherish thy muse, discourse.

Val. Of what, sir?

Jun. Of what thou wilt; 'sblood, hang sorrow.

Oni. Prithee, Valentine, assoil me one thing.

Val. 'Tis pity to soil you, sir, your new apparel—

Oni. Mass, thou say'st true, apparel makes a man forget himself.

Jun. Begin, find your tongue, ningle.

Val. Now will I gull these ganders rarely. Gentlemen, having in my peregrination through Mesopotamia—

Jun. Speak legibly, this game's gone without the great mercy of— Here's a fine tragedy indeed! there's a keisar royal! 'slid, nor king, nor keisar shall—

Re-enter FINIO *with* PACUE, BALTHASAR, *and* MARTINO.

Bal. Where, where, Finio, where be they?

Jun. Go to, I'll be with you anon.

Oni. O here's the page, signior Juniper.

Jun. What says monsieur Onion, boy?

Fin. What say you, sir?

Jun. Tread out, boy.

Fin. Take up, you mean, sir.

Jun. Tread out, I say; so! I thank you,—is this the boy?

Pac. Oui, monsieur.

Jun. Who gave you that name?

Pac. Give me de name, vat name?

Oni. He thought your name had been *We.* Young gentleman, you must do more than his legs can do for him, bear with him, sir.

Jun. Sirrah, give me instance of your carriage; you'll serve my turn, will you?

Pac. Vat turn? upon the toe!

Fin. O signior, no.

Jun. Page, will you follow me? I'll give you good exhibition.

Pac. By gar, shall not alone follow you, but shall lead you too.

Oni. Plaguy boy! he sooths his humour; these French villains have pocky wits.

Jun. Here, disarm me, take my semitary.

Val. O rare! this would be a rare man, an he had a little travel.— Balthasar, Martino, put off your shoes, and bid him cobble them.

Jun. Friends, friends, but pardon me for fellows, no more in occupation, no more in corporation; 'tis so, pardon me; the case is altered; this is law, but I'll stand to nothing.

Pac. Fait, so me tink.

Jun. Well, then God save the duke's majesty; is this any harm now? speak, is this any harm now?

Oni. No, nor good neither, 'sblood!—

Jun. Do you laugh at me, do you laugh at me, do you laugh at me?

Val. Ay, sir, we do.

Jun. You do indeed?

Val. Ay, indeed, sir.

Jun. 'Tis sufficient; page, carry my purse; dog me.   [*Exit.*

Oni. Gentlemen, leave him not! you see in what case he is; he is not in adversity, his purse is full of money; leave him not.

                                        [*Exeunt.*

SCENE III.—*The open Country.*

Enter ANGELO *with* RACHEL.

Ang. Nay, gentle Rachel.
Rach. Away! forbear, ungentle Angelo!
Touch not my body with those impious hands,
That, like hot irons, sear my trembling heart,
And make it hiss at your disloyalty.

Enter PAULO FERNEZE *and* CHAMONT, *at a distance.*

Was this your drift, to use Ferneze's name?
Was he your fittest stale? O vile dishonour!
   Pau. Stay, noble sir.   [*Holding back Chamont.*
   Ang. 'Sblood, how like a puppet do you talk now!
Dishonour! what dishonour? come, come, fool;
Nay, then I see you are peevish. S'heart, dishonour!
To have you to a priest, and marry you,
And put you in an honourable state.
   Rach. To marry me! O heaven! can it be,
That men should live with such unfeeling souls,
Without or touch or conscience of religion?
Or that their warping appetites should spoil
Those honoured forms, that the true seal of friendship
Had set upon their faces?
   Ang. Do you hear?
What needs all this? say, will you have me, or no?
   Rach. I'll have you gone, and leave me if you would.
   Ang. Leave you! I was accurst to bring you hither,
And make so fair an offer to a fool.
A pox upon you, why should you be coy,
What good thing have you in you to be proud of?
Are you any other than a beggar's daughter?—
Because you have beauty!—O God's light! a blast!
   Pau. Ay, Angelo!
   Ang. You scornful baggage,
I loved thee not so much, but now I hate thee.
   Rach. Upon my knees, you heavenly powers, I thank you,
That thus have tamed his wild affections.
   Ang. This will not do, I must to her again.   [*Aside.*
Rachel!
O that thou saw'st my heart, or didst behold
The place from whence that scalding sigh evented!
Rachel, by Jesu, I love thee as my soul,
Rachel, sweet Rachel!
   Rach. What, again return'd
Unto this violent passion!
   Ang. Do but hear me;
By heaven I love you, Rachel.

Rach. Pray forbear.
O that my lord Ferneze were but here!
    Ang. 'Sblood! an he were, what would he do?
    Pau. [*rushes forward.*] This would he do, base villain.
                                [*Flings him off.*
    Rach. My dear lord!   [*Runs into his arms.*
    Pau. Thou monster, even the soul of treachery!
O what dishonour'd title of reproach
May my tongue spit in thy deserved face!
Methinks my very presence should invert
The steeled organs of those traitorous eyes.
To take into thy heart, and pierce it through.
Turn'st thou them on the ground? wretch, dig a grave
With their sharp points, to hide thy abhorred head.—
Sweet love, thy wrongs have been too violent
Since my departure from thee, I perceive;
But now true comfort shall again appear,
And, like an armed angel, guard thee safe
From all the assaults of cover'd villainy.
Come, monsieur, let us go, and leave this wretch
To his despair.
    Ang. My noble [lord] Ferneze!
    Pau. What, canst thou speak to me, and not thy tongue,
Forced with the torment of thy guilty soul,
Break that infected circle of thy mouth,
Like the rude clapper of a crazed bell!
I, [I] that in thy bosom lodg'd my soul,
With all her train of secrets, thinking them
To be as safe and richly entertain'd
As in a prince's court, or tower of strength;
And thou to prove a traitor to my trust,
And basely to expose it! O this world!
    Ang. My honourable lord.
    Pau. The very owl,
Whom other birds do stare and wonder at,
Shall hoot at thee; and snakes in every bush,
Shall deaf thine ears with their—
    Cha. Nay, good my lord,
Give end unto your passions.
    Ang. You shall see
I will redeem your lost opinion.
    Rach. My lord, believe him.
    Cha. Come, be satisfied:
Sweet lord, you know our haste; let us to horse.
The time for my engaged return is past.
Be friends again, take him along with you.
    Pau. Come, Angelo, hereafter prove more true.   [*Exeunt.*

SCENE IV.—*A Room in* Count FERNEZE'S *House.*

Enter Count FERNEZE, MAXIMILIAN, *and* FRANCISCO.

Count F. Tut, Maximilian, for your honour'd self
I am persuaded; but no words shall turn
The edge of purposed vengeance on that wretch:
Come bring him forth to execution.—

Enter Servants *with* CAMILLO *bound.*

I'll hang him for my son, he shall not 'scape,
Had he a hundred lives.—Tell me, vile slave,
Think'st thou I love my son? is he my flesh?
Is he my blood, my life? and shall all these
Be tortured for thy sake, and not revenged?—
Truss up the villain.

Max. My lord, there is no law to confirm this action: 'tis dishonourable.

Count F. Dishonourable, Maximilian!
It is dishonourable in Chamont:
The day of his prefixed return is past,
And he shall pay for it.

Cam. My lord, my lord,
Use your extremest vengeance; I'll be glad
To suffer ten times more for such a friend.

Count F. O resolute and peremptory wretch!

Fran. My honour'd lord, let us intreat a word!

Count F. I'll hear no more; I say, he shall not live;
Myself will do it. Stay, what form is this
Stands betwixt him and me, and holds my hand?
What miracle is this? 'tis my own fancy
Carves this impression in me; my soft nature,
That ever hath retain'd such foolish pity
Of the most abject creature's misery,
That it abhors it. What a child am I
To have a child? ah me! my son, my son!

[*Weeps, and walks aside.*

Enter CHRISTOPHERO.

Chris. O my dear love, what is become of thee?
What unjust absence layest thou on my breast,
Like weights of lead, when swords are at my back,
That run me thorough with thy unkind flight!
My gentle disposition waxeth wild;
I shall run frantic: O my love, my love!

Enter JAQUES.

Jaq. My gold, my gold, my wife, my soul, my heaven!
What is become of thee? see, I'll impart

My miserable loss to my good lord.—
Let me have search, my lord, my gold is gone.

Count F. My son, Christophero, think'st thou it possible
I ever shall behold his face again?

Chris. O father, where's my love? were you so careless
To let an unthrift steal away your child?

Jaq. I know your lordship may find out my gold.
For God's sake pity me; justice, sweet lord!

Count F. Now they have young Chamont, Christophero,
Surely they never will restore my son.

Chris. Who would have thought you could have been so careless,
To lose your only daughter?

Jaq. Who would think
That looking to my gold with such hare's eyes,
That ever open, ay, even when they sleep,
I thus should lose my gold! my noble lord,
What says your lordship?

Count F. O my son, my son!

Chris. My dearest Rachel!

Jaq. My most honey gold!

Count F. Hear me, Christophero.

Chris. Nay, hear me, Jaques.

Jaq. Hear me, most honour'd lord.

Max. What rule is here?

Count F. O God, that we should let Chamont escape!

Chris. Ay, and that Rachel, such a virtuous maid,
Should be thus stolen away!

Jaq. And that my gold,
Being so hid in earth, should be found out!

Max. O confusion of languages, and yet no tower of Babel!

Enter AURELIA *and* PHŒNIXELLA.

Fran. Ladies, beshrew me, if you come not fit
To make a jangling consort; will you laugh
To see three constant passions?

Max. Stand by, I will urge them.
Sweet count, will you be comforted?

Count F. It cannot be
But he is handled the most cruelly
That ever any noble prisoner was.

Max. Steward, go cheer my lord.

Chris. Well, if Rachel took her flight willingly—

Max. Sirrah, speak you touching your daughter's flight.

Jaq. O that I could so soon forget to know
The thief again that had my gold, my gold!

Max. Is not this pure?

Count F. O thou base wretch, I'll drag three through the streets;
And as a monster make thee wonder'd at.—

Enter BALTHASAR.

How now?   [*Balthasar whispers with him.*
  Phœn. Sweet gentleman, how too unworthily
Art thou thus tortured!—Brave Maximilian,
Pity the poor youth, and appease my father.
  Count F. How! my son return'd! O Maximilian,
Francisco, daughters! bid him enter here.
Dost thou not mock me?—

Enter PAULO FERNEZE, RACHEL, CHAMONT, *and* ANGELO.

                    O, my dear Paulo, welcome.
  Max. My lord Chamont!
  Cha. My Gasper!
  Chris. Rachel!
  Jaq. My gold, Rachel, my gold!
  Count F. Somebody bid the beggar cease his noise.
  Chris. O signior Angelo, would you deceive
Your honest friend, that simply trusted you?—
Well, Rachel, I am glad thou art here again.
  Ang. I'faith, she is not for you, steward.
  Jaq. I beseech you, madam, urge your father.
  Phœn. I will anon; good Jaques, be content.
  Aur. Now God a mercy Fortune, and sweet Venus:
Let Cupid do his part, and all is well.
  Phœn. Methinks my heart's in heaven with this comfort.
  Cha. Is this the true Italian courtesy?
Ferneze, were you tortured thus in France?
By my soul's safety—
  Count F. My most noble lord,   [*Kneels.*
I do beseech your lordship.
  Cha. Honour'd count,   [*Raises him.*
Wrong not your age with flexure of a knee,
I do impute it to those cares and griefs
That did torment you in your absent son.
  Count F. O worthy gentleman, I am ashamed
That my extreme affection to my son
Should give my honour so uncured a maim;
But my first son being in Vicenza lost—
  Cha. How! in Vicenza! lost you a son there?
About what time, my lord?
  Count F. O, the same night
Wherein your noble father took the town.
  Cha. How long's that since, my lord, can you remember?
  Count F. 'Tis now well nigh upon the twentieth year.
  Cha. And how old was he then?
  Count F. I cannot tell;
Between the years of three and four, I take it.
  Cha. Had he no special note in his attire,

Or otherwise, that you call to mind?

   Count F. I cannot well remember his attire;
But I have often heard his mother say,
He had about his neck a tablet,
Given to him by the emperor Sigismund,
His godfather, with this inscription,
Under the figure of a silver globe,
In minimo mundus.

   Cha. How did you call
Your son, my lord?

   Count F. Camillo, lord Chamont.

   Cha. Then, no more my Gasper, but Camillo,
Take notice of your father.—Gentlemen,
Stand not amazed; here is a tablet,
With that inscription, found about his neck,
That night and in Vicenza, by my father,
Who, being ignorant what name he had,
Christen'd him Gasper; nor did I reveal
This secret, till this hour, to any man.

   Count F. O happy revelation!   O blest hour!
O my Camillo!

   Phœn. O strange! my brother!

   Fran. Maximilian,
Behold now the abundance of his joy
Drowns him in tears of gladness.

   Count F. O, my boy,
Forgive thy father's late austerity.

   Max. My lord, I delivered as much before, but your honour
would not be persuaded; I will hereafter give more observance to
my visions; I dreamt of this.

   Jaq. I can be still no longer; my good lord,
Do a poor man some grace 'mongst all your joys.

   Count F. Why, what's the matter, Jaques?

   Jaq. I am robb'd;
I am undone, my lord; robb'd and undone.
A heap of thirty thousand golden crowns
Stolen from me in one minute, and I fear
By her confederacy that calls me father;
But she is none of mine, therefore, sweet lord,
Let her be tortured to confess the truth.

   Max. More wonders yet.

   Count F. How, Jaques! is not Rachel then thy daughter?

   Jaq. No, I disclaim in her; I spit at her;
She is a harlot, and her customers,
Your son, this gallant, and your steward here,
Have all been partners with her in my spoil;
No less than thirty thousand.

   Count F. Jaques, Jaques,
This is impossible; how shouldst thou come

To the possession of so huge a heap,
Being always a known beggar?

   Jaq. Out, alas!
I have betray'd myself with my own tongue;
The case is alter'd.   *[Going.*

   Count F. Some one stay him here.

   Max. What, means he to depart?—Count Ferneze, upon my
soul, this beggar is a counterfeit. Urge him.—Didst thou lose gold?

   Jaq. O no, I lost no gold.

   Max. Said I not true?

   Count F. How! didst thou first lose thirty thousand crowns,
And now no gold? was Rachel first thy child,
And is she now no daughter? sirrah, Jaques,
You know how far our Milan laws extend
For punishment of liars.

   Jaq. Ay, my lord.—
What shall I do? I have no starting-holes.   *[Aside.*
Monsieur Chamont, stand you my honour'd lord.

   Cha. For what, old man?

   Jaq. Ill-gotten goods ne'er thrive;
I play'd the thief, and now am robb'd myself.
I am not what I seem, Jaques de Prie,
Nor was I born a beggar as I am;
But some time steward to your noble father.

   Cha. What, Melun!
That robb'd my father's treasure, stole my sister?

   Jaq. Ay, ay; that treasure's lost, but Isabel,
Your beauteous sister, here survives in Rachel;
And therefore on my knees—

   Max. Stay, Jaques, stay;
The case still alters.

   Count F. Fair Rachel, sister to the lord Chamont!

   Ang. Steward, your cake is dough, as well as mine.

   Pau. I see that honour's flames cannot be hid,
No more than lightning in the blackest cloud.

   Max. Then, sirrah, it is true, you have lost this gold?

   Jaq. Ay, worthy signior, thirty thousand crowns.

   Count F. Mass, who was it told me, that a couple of my men
were become gallants of late?

   Fran. Marry 'twas I, my lord; my man told me.

          Enter ONION *and* JUNIPER, *dressed as before.*

   Max. How now! what pageant is this?

   Jun. Come, signior Onion, let's not be ashamed to appear; keep
state, look not ambiguous now.

   Oni. Not I, while I am in this suit.

   Jun. Lordlings, equivalence to you all.

   Oni. We thought good to be so good as see you, gentlemen.

   Max. What, monsieur Onion!

Oni. How dost thou, good captain?

Count F. What, are my hinds turn'd gentlemen?

Oni. Hinds, sir! 'sblood, an that word will bear an action, it shall cost us a thousand pound a piece, but we'll be revenged.

Jun. Wilt thou sell thy lordship, count?

Count F. What! peasants purchase lordships?

Jun. Is that any novels, sir?

Max. O transmutation of elements! it is certified you had pages.

Jun. Ay, sir; but it is known they proved ridiculous, they did pilfer, they did purloin, they did procrastinate our purses; for the which wasting of our stock, we have put them to the stocks.

Count F. And thither shall you two presently.
These be the villains that stole Jaques' gold;
Away with them, and set them with their men.

Max. Onion, you will now be peel'd.

Fran. The case is alter'd now.

Oni. Good my lord, good my lord!—

Jun. Away, scoundrel! dost thou fear a little elocution? shall we be confiscate now? shall we droop now? shall we be now in helogabolus?

Oni. Peace, peace, leave thy gabling.

Count F. Away, away with them; what's this they prate?

                     [Exeunt Servants with Jun. and Onion.
Keep the knaves sure, strict inquisition
Shall presently be made for Jaques' gold,
To be disposed at pleasure of Chamont.

Cha. She is your own, lord Paulo, if your father
Give his consent.

Ang. How now, Christophero! The case is alter'd.

Chris. With you as well as me; I am content, sir.

Count F. With all my heart; and in exchange of her,
If with your fair acceptance it may stand,
I tender my Aurelia to your love.

Cha. I take her from your lordship with all thanks,
And bless the hour wherein I was made prisoner,
For the fruition of this present fortune,
So full of happy and unlook'd-for joys.—
Melun, I pardon thee; and for the treasure,
Recover it, and hold it as thine own:
It is enough for me to see my sister
Live in the circle of Ferneze's arms,
My friend, the son of such a noble father;
And my unworthy self rapt above all,
By being the lord to so divine a dame.

Max. Well, I will now swear the CASE IS ALTERED.—Lady, fare you well; I will subdue my affections.—Madam, as for you, you are a profest virgin, and I will be silent.—My honourable lord Ferneze, it shall become you at this time not be frugal, but boun-teous, and open-handed; your fortune hath been so to you.—Lord

Chamont, you are now no stranger; you must be welcome; you
have a fair, amiable, and splendid lady:—but, signior Paulo, signior
Camillo, I know you valiant, be loving.—Lady, I must be better
known to you.—Signiors, for you, I pass you not, though I let you
pass; for in truth I pass not of you.—Lovers to your nuptials,
lordings to your dances. March fair all, for a *fair March is worth
a king's ransom !*   *[Exeunt.*

GLOSSARY

ABATE, cast down, subdue

ABHORRING, repugnant (to), at variance

ABJECT, base, degraded thing, outcast

ABRASE, smooth, blank

ABSOLUTE(LY), faultless(ly)

ABSTRACTED, abstract, abstruse

ABUSE, deceive, insult, dishonour, make ill use of

ACATER, caterer

ACATES, cates

ACCEPTIVE, willing, ready to accept, receive

ACCOMMODATE, fit, befitting. (The word was a fashionable one and used on all occasions. *See* "Henry IV.," pt. 2, iii. 4)

ACCOST, draw near, approach

ACKNOWN, confessedly acquainted with

ACME, full maturity

ADALANTADO, lord deputy or governor of a Spanish province

ADJECTION, addition

ADMIRATION, astonishment

ADMIRE, wonder, wonder at

ADROP, philosopher's stone, or substance from which obtained

ADSCRIBE, subscribe

ADULTERATE, spurious, counterfeit

ADVANCE, lift

ADVERTISE, inform, give intelligence

ADVERTISED, "be —," be it known to you

ADVERTISEMENT, intelligence

ADVISE, consider, bethink oneself, deliberate

ADVISED, informed, aware; "are you —?" have you found that out?

AFFECT, love, like; aim at; move

AFFECTED, disposed; beloved

AFFECTIONATE, obstinate; prejudiced

AFFECTS, affections

AFFRONT, "give the —," face

AFFY, have confidence in; betroth

AFTER, after the manner of

AGAIN, AGAINST, in anticipation of

AGGRAVATE, increase, magnify, enlarge upon

AGNOMINATION. *See* Paranomasie

AIERY, nest, brood

AIM, guess

ALL HID, children's cry at hide-and-seek

ALL-TO, completely, entirely (" all-to-be-laden ")

ALLOWANCE, approbation, recognition

ALMA-CANTARAS (astron.), parallels of altitude

ALMAIN, name of a dance

ALMUTEN, planet of chief influence in the horoscope

ALONE, unequalled, without peer

ALUDELS, subliming pots

AMAZED, confused, perplexed

AMBER, AMBRE, ambergris

AMBREE, MARY, a woman noted for her valour at the siege of Ghent, 1458

AMES-ACE, lowest throw at dice

AMPHIBOLIES, ambiguities

AMUSED, bewildered, amazed

AN, if

ANATOMY, skeleton, or dissected body

ANDIRONS, fire-dogs

ANGEL, gold coin worth 10s., stamped with the figure of the archangel Michael

ANNESH CLEARE, spring known as Agnes le Clare

ANSWER, return hit in fencing

ANTIC, ANTIQUE, clown, buffoon

ANTIC, like a buffoon

ANTIPERISTASIS, an opposition which enhances the quality it opposes

APOZEM, decoction

APPERIL, peril

APPLE-JOHN, APPLE-SQUIRE, pimp, pander

APPLY, attach

APPREHEND, take into custody

APPREHENSIVE, quick of perception; able to perceive and appreciate

APPROVE, prove, confirm

APT, suit, adapt; train, prepare; dispose, incline

APT(LY), suitable(y), opportune(ly)

APTITUDE, suitableness

ARBOR, "make the —," cut up the game (Gifford)

ARCHES, Court of Arches

ARCHIE, Archibald Armstrong, jester to James I. and Charles I.

ARGAILE, argol, crust or sediment in wine casks

ARGENT-VIVE, quicksilver

ARGUMENT, plot of a drama; theme, subject; matter in question; token, proof

ARRIDE, please

ARSEDINE, mixture of copper and zinc, used as an imitation of gold-leaf

ARTHUR, PRINCE, reference to an archery show by a society who assumed arms, etc., of Arthur's knights

ARTICLE, item

ARTIFICIALLY, artfully

ASCENSION, evaporation, distillation

ASPIRE, try to reach, obtain, long for

ASSALTO (Ital.), assault

ASSAY, draw a knife along the belly of the deer, a ceremony of the hunting-field

ASSOIL, solve

ASSURE, secure possession or reversion of

ATHANOR, a digesting furnace, calculated to keep up a constant heat

ATONE, reconcile

ATTACH, attack, seize

AUDACIOUS, having spirit and confidence

AUTHENTIC(AL), of authority, authorised, trustworthy, genuine

AVISEMENT, reflection, consideration

AVOID, begone! get rid of

AWAY WITH, endure

AZOCH, Mercurius Philosophorum

BABION, baboon

BABY, doll

BACK-SIDE, back premises

BAFFLE, treat with contempt

BAGATINE, Italian coin, worth about the third of a farthing

BAIARD, horse of magic powers known to old romance

BALDRICK, belt worn across the breast to support bugle, etc.

BALE (of dice), pair

BALK, overlook, pass by, avoid

BALLACE, ballast

BALLOO, game at ball

BALNEUM (BAIN MARIE), a vessel for holding hot water in which other vessels are stood for heating

BANBURY, "brother of —," Puritan

BANDOG, dog tied or chained up

BANE, woe, ruin

BANQUET, a light repast; dessert

BARB, to clip gold

BARBEL, fresh-water fish

BARE, meer; bareheaded; it was "a particular mark of state and grandeur for the coachman to be uncovered" (Gifford)

BARLEY-BREAK, game somewhat similar to base

BASE, game of prisoner's base

BASES, richly embroidered skirt reaching to the knees, or lower

BASILISK, fabulous reptile, believed to slay with its eye

BASKET, used for the broken provision collected for prisoners

BASON, basons, etc., were beaten by the attendant mob when bad characters were "carted"

BATE, be reduced; abate, reduce

BATOON, baton, stick

BATTEN, feed, grow fat

BAWSON, badger

BEADSMAN, prayer-man, one engaged to pray for another

BEAGLE, small hound; fig. spy

BEAR IN HAND, keep in suspense, deceive with false hopes

BEARWARD, bear leader

BEDPHERE. See Phere

BEDSTAFF, (?) wooden pin in the side of the bedstead for supporting the bedclothes (Johnson); one of the sticks or "laths"; a stick used in making a bed

BEETLE, heavy mallet

BEG, "I'd — him," the custody of minors and idiots was begged for; likewise property fallen forfeit to the Crown ("your house had been begged")

BELL-MAN, night watchman

BENJAMIN, an aromatic gum

BERLINA, pillory

BESCUMBER, defile

BESLAVE, beslabber

BESOGNO, beggar

BESPAWLE, bespatter

BETHLEM GABOR, Transylvanian hero, proclaimed King of Hungary

BEVER, drinking

BEVIS, SIR, knight of romance whose horse was equally celebrated

BEWRAY, reveal, make known

BEZANT, heraldic term: small gold circle

BEZOAR'S STONE, a remedy known by this name was a supposed antidote to poison

BID-STAND, highwayman

BIGGIN, cap, similar to that worn by the Beguines; nightcap

BILIVE (belive), with haste

BILK, nothing, empty talk

BILL, kind of pike

BILLET, wood cut for fuel, stick

BIRDING, thieving

BLACK SANCTUS, burlesque hymn, any unholy riot

BLANK, originally a small French coin

BLANK, white

BLANKET, toss in a blanket

BLAZE, outburst of violence

BLAZE, (her.) blazon; publish abroad

BLAZON, armorial bearings; fig. all that pertains to good birth and breeding

BLIN, "withouten —," without ceasing

BLOW, puff up

BLUE, colour of servants' livery, hence "— order," "— waiters"

BLUSHET, blushing one

BOB, jest, taunt

BOB, beat, thump

BODGE, measure

BODKIN, dagger, or other short, pointed weapon; long pin with which the women fastened up their hair

BOLT, roll (of material)

BOLT, dislodge, rout out; sift (boulting-tub)

BOLT'S-HEAD, long, straight-necked vessel for distillation

BOMBARD SLOPS, padded, puffed-out breeches

BONA ROBA, "good, wholesome, plum-cheeked wench" (Johnson)—not always used in compliment

BONNY-CLABBER, sour butter-milk

BOOKHOLDER, prompter

BOOT, "to —," into the bargain; "no —," of no avail

BORACHIO, bottle made of skin

BORDELLO, brothel

BORNE IT, conducted, carried it through

BOTTLE (of hay), bundle, truss

BOTTOM, skein or ball of thread; vessel

BOURD, jest

BOVOLI, snails or cockles dressed in the Italian manner (Gifford)

BOW-POT, flower vase or pot

BOYS, "terrible —," "angry —," roystering young bucks. (See Nares)

BRABBLES (BRABBLESH), brawls

BRACH, bitch

BRADAMANTE, a heroine in Orlando Furioso

BRADLEY, ARTHUR OF, a lively character commemorated in ballads

BRAKE, frame for confining a horse's feet

while being shod, or strong curb or bridle; trap

BRANCHED, with "detached sleeve ornaments, projecting from the shoulders of the gown" (Gifford)

BRANDISH, flourish of weapon

BRASH, brace

BRAVE, bravado, braggart speech

BRAVE (adv.), gaily, finely (apparelled)

BRAVERIES, gallants

BRAVERY, extravagant gaiety of apparel

BRAVO, bravado, swaggerer

BRAZEN-HEAD, speaking head made by Roger Bacon

BREATHE, pause for relaxation; exercise

BREATHE UPON, speak dispraisingly of

BREND, burn

BRIDE-ALE, wedding feast

BRIEF, abstract; (mus.) breve

BRISK, smartly dressed

BRIZE, breeze, gadfly

BROAD-SEAL, state seal

BROCK, badger (term of contempt)

BROKE, transact business as a broker

BROOK, endure, put up with

BROUGHTON, HUGH, an English divine and Hebrew scholar

BRUIT, rumour

BUCK, wash

BUCKLE, bend

BUFF, leather made of buffalo skin, used for military and serjeants' coats, etc.

BUFO, black tincture

BUGLE, long-shaped bead

BULLED, (?) bolled, swelled

BULLIONS, trunk hose

BULLY, term of familiar endearment

BUNGY, Friar Bungay, who had a familiar in the shape of a dog

BURDEN, refrain, chorus

BURGONET, closely-fitting helmet with visor

BURGULLION, braggadocio

BURN, mark wooden measures ("—ing of cans")

BURROUGH, pledge, security

BUSKIN, half-boot, foot gear reaching high up the leg

BUTT-SHAFT, barbless arrow for shooting at butts

BUTTER, NATHANIEL ("Staple of News"), a compiler of general news. (See Cunningham)

BUTTERY-HATCH, half-door shutting off the buttery, where provisions and liquors were stored

BUY, "he bought me," formerly the guardianship of wards could be bought

BUZ, exclamation to enjoin silence

BUZZARD, simpleton

BY AND BY, at once

BY(E), "on the —," incidentally, as of minor or secondary importance; at the side

BY-CHOP, by-blow, bastard

CADUCEUS, Mercury's wand

CALIVER, light kind of musket

CALLET, woman of ill repute

CALLOT, coif worn on the wigs of our judges or serjeants-at-law (Gifford)

CALVERED, crimped, or sliced and pickled. (See Nares)

CAMOUCCIO, wretch, knave

CAMUSED, flat

CAN, knows

CANDLE-RENT, rent from house property

CANDLE-WASTER, one who studies late

CANTER, sturdy beggar

CAP OF MAINTENCE, an insignia of dignity, a cap of state borne before kings at their coronation; also an heraldic term

CAPABLE, able to comprehend, fit to receive instruction, impression

CAPANEUS, one of the "Seven against Thebes"

CARACT, carat, unit of weight for precious stones, etc.; value, worth

CARANZA, Spanish author of a book on duelling

CARCANET, jewelled ornament for the neck

CARE, take care; object

CAROCH, coach, carriage

CARPET, table-cover

CARRIAGE, bearing, behaviour

CARWHITCHET, quip, pun

CASAMATE, casemate, fortress

CASE, a pair

CASE, "in —," in condition

CASSOCK, soldier's loose overcoat

CAST, flight of hawks, couple

CAST, throw dice; vomit; forecast, calculate

CAST, cashiered

CASTING-GLASS, bottle for sprinkling perfume

CASTRIL, kestrel, falcon

CAT, structure used in sieges

CATAMITE, old form of "ganymede"

CATASTROPHE, conclusion

CATCHPOLE, sheriff's officer

CATES, dainties, provisions

CATSO, rogue, cheat

CAUTELOUS, crafty, artful

CENSURE, criticism; sentence

CENSURE, criticise; pass sentence, doom

CERUSE, cosmetic containing white lead

CESS, assess

CHANGE, "hunt —," follow a fresh scent

CHAPMAN, retail dealer

CHARACTER, handwriting

CHARGE, expense

CHARM, subdue with magic, lay a spell on, silence

CHARMING, exercising magic power

CHARTEL, challenge

CHEAP, bargain, market

CHEAR, CHEER, comfort, encouragement; food, entertainment

CHECK AT, aim reproof at

CHEQUIN, gold Italian coin

CHEVRIL, from kidskin, which is elastic and pliable

CHIAUS, Turkish envoy; used for a cheat, swindler

CHILDERMASS DAY, Innocents' Day

CHOKE-BAIL, action which does not allow of bail

CHRYSOPŒIA, alchemy

CHRYSOSPERM, ways of producing gold

CIBATION, adding fresh substances to supply the waste of evaporation

CIMICI, bugs

CINOPER, cinnabar

CIOPPINI, chopine, lady's high shoe

CIRCLING BOY, "a species of roarer; one who in some way drew a man into a snare, to cheat or rob him" (Nares)

CIRCUMSTANCE, circumlocution, beating about the bush; ceremony, everything pertaining to a certain condition; detail, particular

CITRONISE, turn citron colour

CITTERN, kind of guitar

CITY-WIRES, woman of fashion, who made use of wires for hair and dress

CIVIL, legal

CLAP, clack, chatter

CLAPPER-DUDGEON, downright beggar

CLAPS HIS DISH, a clap, or clack, dish (dish with a movable lid) was carried by beggars and lepers to show that the vessel was empty, and to give sound of their approach

CLARIDIANA, heroine of an old romance

CLARISSIMO, Venetian noble

CLEM, starve

CLICKET, latch

CLIM O' THE CLOUGHS, etc., wordy heroes of romance

CLIMATE, country

CLOSE, secret, private; secretive

CLOSENESS, secrecy

CLOTH, arras, hangings

CLOUT, mark shot at, bull's-eye

CLOWN, countryman, clodhopper

COACH-LEAVES, folding blinds

COALS, "bear no —," submit to no affront

COAT-ARMOUR, coat of arms

COAT-CARD, court-card

COB-HERRING, HERRING-COB, a young herring

COB-SWAN, male swan

COCK-A-HOOP, denoting unstinted jollity; thought to be derived from turning on the tap that all might drink to the full of the flowing liquor

COCKATRICE, reptile supposed to be produced from a cock's egg and to kill by its eye—used as a term of reproach for a woman

COCK-BRAINED, giddy, wild

COCKER, pamper

COCKSCOMB, fool's cap

COCKSTONE, stone said to be found in a cock's gizzard, and to possess particular virtues

CODLING, softening by boiling

COFFIN, raised crust of a pie

COG, cheat, wheedle

COIL, turmoil, confusion, ado

COKELY, master of a puppet-show (Whalley)

COKES, fool, gull

COLD-CONCEITED, having cold opinion of, coldly affected towards

COLE-HARBOUR, a retreat for people of all sorts

COLLECTION, composure; deduction

COLLOP, small slice, piece of flesh

COLLY, blacken

COLOUR, pretext

COLOURS, "fear no —," no enemy (quibble)

COLSTAFF, cowlstaff, pole for carrying a cowl=tub

COME ABOUT, charge, turn round

COMFORTABLE BREAD, spiced gingerbread

COMING, forward, ready to respond, com plaisant

COMMENT, commentary; "sometime it is taken for a lie or fayned tale" (Bullokar, 1616)

COMMODITY, "current for —," allusion to practice of money-lenders, who forced the borrower to take part of the loan in the shape of worthless goods on which the latter had to make money if he could

COMMUNICATE, share

COMPASS, "in —," within the range, sphere

COMPLEMENT, completion, completement; anything required for the perfecting or carrying out of a person or affair; accomplishment

COMPLEXION, natural disposition, constitution

COMPLIMENT. See Complement

COMPLIMENTARIES, masters of accomplishments

COMPOSITION, constitution; agreement, contract

COMPOSURE, composition

COMPTER, COUNTER, debtors' prison

CONCEALMENT, a certain amount of church property had been retained at the dissolution of the monasteries; Elizabeth sent commissioners to search it out, and the courtiers begged for it

CONCEIT, idea, fancy, witty invention, conception, opinion

CONCEIT, apprehend

CONCEITED, fancifully, ingeniously devised or conceived; possessed of intelligence, witty, ingenious (hence well conceited, etc.); disposed to joke; of opinion, possessed of an idea

CONCEIVE, understand

CONCENT, harmony, agreement

CONCLUDE, infer, prove

CONCOCT, assimilate, digest

CONDEN'T, probably conducted

CONDUCT, escort, conductor

CONEY-CATCH, cheat

CONFECT, sweetmeat

CONFER, compare

CONGIES, bows

CONNIVE, give a look, wink, of secret intelligence

CONSORT, company, concert

CONSTANCY, fidelity, ardour, persistence

CONSTANT, confirmed, persistent, faithful.

CONSTANTLY, firmly, persistently

CONTEND, strive

CONTINENT, holding together

CONTROL (the point), bear or beat down

CONVENT, assembly, meeting

CONVERT, turn (oneself)

CONVEY, transmit from one to another

CONVINCE, evince, prove; overcome, over-power; convict

Cop, head, top; tuft on head of birds; "a cop" may have reference to one or other meaning; Gifford and others interpret as "conical, terminating in a point"

Cope-man, chapman

Copesmate, companion

Copy (Lat. *copia*), abundance, copiousness

Corn ("powder —"), grain

Corollary, finishing part or touch

Corsive, corrosive

Cortine, curtain, (arch.) wall between two towers, etc.

Coryat, famous for his travels, published as *Coryat's Crudities*

Cosset, pet lamb, pet

Costard, head

Costard - monger, apple - seller, coster-monger

Costs, ribs

Cote, hut

Cothurnal, from "cothurnus," a particular boot worn by actors in Greek tragedy

Cotquean, hussy

Counsel, secret

Countenance, means necessary for support; credit, standing

Counter. *See* Compter

Counter, pieces of metal or ivory for calculating at play

Counter, "hunt —," follow scent in reverse direction

Counterfeit, false coin

Counterpane, one part or counterpart of a deed or indenture

Counterpoint, opposite, contrary point

Court-dish, a kind of drinking-cup (Halliwell); N.E.D. quotes from Bp. Goodman's *Court of James I.*: "The king . . . caused his carver to cut him out a court-dish, that is, something of every dish, which he sent him as part of his reversion," but this does not sound like short allowance or small receptacle

Court-dor, fool

Courteau, curtal, small horse with docked tail

Courtship, courtliness

Covetise, avarice

Cowshard, cow dung

Coxcomb, fool's cap, fool

Coy, shrink; disdain

Coystrel, low varlet

Cozen, cheat

Crack, lively young rogue, wag

Crack, crack up, boast; come to grief

Crambe, game of crambo, in which the players find rhymes for a given word

Cranch, craunch

Cranion, spider-like; also fairy appellation for a fly (Gifford, who refers to lines in Drayton's "Nimphidia")

Crimp, game at cards

Crincle, draw back, turn aside

Crisped, with curled or waved hair

Crop, gather, reap

Cropshire, a kind of herring. (*See* N.E.D.)

Cross, any piece of money, many coins being stamped with a cross

Cross and pile, heads and tails

Crosslet, crucible

Crowd, fiddle

Crudities, undigested matter

Crump, curl up

Crusado, Portuguese gold coin, marked with a cross

Cry ("he that cried Italian"), "speak in a musical cadence," intone, or declaim (?); cry up

Cucking-stool, used for the ducking of scolds, etc.

Cucurbite, a gourd-shaped vessel used for distillation

Cuerpo, "in —," in undress

Cullice, broth

Cullion, base fellow, coward

Cullisen, badge worn on their arm by servants

Culverin, kind of cannon

Cunning, skill

Cunning, skilful

Cunning-man, fortune-teller

Cure, care for

Curious(ly), scrupulous, particular; elaborate, elegant(ly), dainty(ly) (hence "incurious")

Curst, shrewish, mischievous

Curtal, dog with docked tail, of inferior sort

Custard, "quaking —," "— politic," reference to a large custard which formed part of a city feast and afforded huge entertainment, for the fool jumped into it, and other like tricks were played. (*See* "All's Well, etc." ii. 5, 40)

Cutwork, embroidery, open-work

Cypres (Cyprus) (quibble), cypress (or cyprus) being a transparent material, and when black used for mourning

Dagger ("— frumety "), name of tavern

Dargison, apparently some person known in ballad or tale

Dauphin my boy, refrain of old comic song

Daw, daunt

Dead lift, desperate emergency

Dear, applied to that which in any way touches us nearly

Decline, turn off from; turn away, aside

Defalk, deduct, abate

Defend, forbid

Degenerous, degenerate

Degrees, steps

Delate, accuse

Demi-culverin, cannon carrying a ball of about ten pounds

Denier, the smallest possible coin, being the twelfth part of a sou

Depart, part with

Dependance, ground of quarrel in duello language

Desert, reward

Designment, design

Desperate, rash, reckless

Detect, allow to be detected, betray, inform against

Determine, terminate

Detract, draw back, refuse

DEVICE, masque, show; a thing moved by wires, etc., puppet
DEVISE, exact in every particular
DEVISED, invented
DIAPASM, powdered aromatic herbs, made into balls of perfumed paste. (*See* Pomander)
DIBBLE, (?) moustache (N.E.D.); (?) dagger (Cunningham)
DIFFUSED, disordered, scattered, irregular
DIGHT, dressed
DILDO, refrain of popular songs; vague term of low meaning
DIMBLE, dingle, ravine
DIMENSUM, stated allowance
DISBASE, debase
DISCERN, distinguish, show a difference between
DISCHARGE, settle for
DISCIPLINE, reformation; ecclesiastical system
DISCLAIM, renounce all part in
DISCOURSE, process of reasoning, reasoning faculty
DISCOURTSHIP, discourtesy
DISCOVER, betray, reveal; display
DISFAVOUR, disfigure
DISPARAGEMENT, legal term applied to the unfitness in any way of a marriage arranged for in the case of wards
DISPENSE WITH, grant dispensation for
DISPLAY, extend
DIS'PLE, discipline, teach by the whip
DISPOSED, inclined to merriment
DISPOSURE, disposal
DISPRISE, depreciate
DISPUNCT, not punctilious
DISQUISITION, search
DISSOLVED, enervated by grief
DISTANCE, (?) proper measure
DISTASTE, offence, cause of offence
DISTASTE, render distasteful
DISTEMPERED, upset, out of humour
DIVISION (mus.), variation, modulation
DOG-BOLT, term of contempt
DOLE, given in dole, charity
DOLE OF FACES, distribution of grimaces
DOOM, verdict, sentence
DOP, dip, low bow
DOR, beetle, buzzing insect, drone, idler
DOR, (?) buzz; "give the —," make a fool of
DOSSER, pannier, basket
DOTES, endowments, qualities
DOTTEREL, plover; gull, fool
DOUBLE, behave deceitfully
DOXY, wench, mistress
DRACHM, Greek silver coin
DRESS, groom, curry
DRESSING, coiffure
DRIFT, intention
DRYFOOT, track by mere scent of foot
DUCKING, punishment for minor offences
DUILL, grieve
DUMPS, melancholy, originally a mournful melody
DURINDANA, Orlando's sword
DWINDLE, shrink away, be overawed

EAN, yean, bring forth young

EASINESS, readiness
EBOLITION, ebullition
EDGE, sword
EECH, eke
EGREGIOUS, eminently excellent
EKE, also, moreover
E-LA, highest note in the scale
EGGS ON THE SPIT, important business on hand
ELF-LOCK, tangled hair, supposed to be the work of elves
EMMET, ant
ENGAGE, involve
ENGHLE. *See* Ingle
ENGHLE, cajole; fondle
ENGIN(E), device, contrivance; agent; ingenuity, wit
ENGINER, engineer, deviser, plotter
ENGINOUS, crafty, full of devices; witty, ingenious
ENGROSS, monopolise
ENS, an existing thing, a substance
ENSIGNS, tokens, wounds
ENSURE, assure
ENTERTAIN, take into service
ENTREAT, plead
ENTREATY, entertainment
ENTRY, place where a deer has lately passed
ENVOY, dénouement, conclusion
ENVY, spite, calumny, dislike, odium
EPHEMERIDES, calendars
EQUAL, just, impartial
ERECTION, elevation in esteem
ERINGO, candied root of the sea-holly, formerly used as a sweetmeat and aphrodisiac
ERRANT, arrant
ESSENTIATE, become assimilated
ESTIMATION, esteem
ESTRICH, ostrich
ETHNIC, heathen
EURIPUS, flux and reflux
EVEN, just, equable
EVENT, fate, issue
EVENT(ED), issue(d)
EVERT, overturn
EXACUATE, sharpen
EXAMPLESS, without example or parallel
EXCALIBUR, King Arthur's sword
EXEMPLIFY, make an example of
EXEMPT, separate, exclude
EXEQUIES, obsequies
EXHALE, drag out
EXHIBITION, allowance for keep, pocket-money
EXORBITANT, exceeding limits of propriety or law, inordinate
EXORNATION, ornament
EXPECT, wait
EXPIATE, terminate
EXPLICATE, explain, unfold
EXTEMPORAL, extempore, unpremeditated
EXTRACTION, essence
EXTRAORDINARY, employed for a special or temporary purpose
EXTRUDE, expel
EYE, "in —," in view
EYEBRIGHT, (?) a malt liquor in which the

herb of this name was infused, or a person who sold the same (Gifford)

EYE-TINGE, least shade or gleam

FACE, appearance

FACES ABOUT, military word of command

FACINOROUS, extremely wicked

FACKINGS, faith

FACT, deed, act, crime

FACTIOUS, seditious, belonging to a party, given to party feeling

FAECES, dregs

FAGIOLI, French beans

FAIN, forced, necessitated

FAITHFUL, believing

FALL, ruff or band turned back on the shoulders; or, veil

FALSIFY, feign (fencing term)

FAME, report

FAMILIAR, attendant spirit

FANTASTICAL, capricious, whimsical

FARCE, stuff

FAR-FET. See Fet

FARTHINGAL, hooped petticoat

FAUCET, tapster

FAULT, lack; loss, break in line of scent; "for —," in default of

FAUTOR, partisan

FAYLES, old table game similar to back-gammon

FEAR(ED), affright(ed)

FEAT, activity, operation; deed, action

FEAT, elegant, trim

FEE, "in — " by feudal obligation

FEIZE, beat, belabour

FELLOW, term of contempt

FENNEL, emblem of flattery

FERE, companion, fellow

FERN-SEED, supposed to have power of rendering invisible

FET, fetched

FETCH, trick

FEUTERER (Fr. vautrier), dog-keeper

FEWMETS, dung

FICO, fig

FIGGUM, (?) jugglery

FIGMENT, fiction, invention

FIRK, frisk, move suddenly, or in jerks; "— up," stir up, rouse; "firks mad," suddenly behaves like a madman

FIT, pay one out, punish

FITNESS, readiness

FITTON (FITTEN), lie, invention

FIVE-AND-FIFTY, "highest number to stand on at primero" (Gifford)

FLAG, to fly low and waveringly

FLAGON CHAIN, for hanging a smelling-bottle (Fr. flacon) round the neck (?). (See N.E.D.)

FLAP-DRAGON, game similar to snap-dragon

FLASKET, some kind of basket

FLAW, sudden gust or squall of wind

FLAWN, custard

FLEA, catch fleas

FLEER, sneer, laugh derisively

FLESH, feed a hawk or dog with flesh to incite it to the chase; initiate in blood-shed; satiate

FLICKER-MOUSE, bat

FLIGHT, light arrow

FLITTER-MOUSE, bat

FLOUT, mock, speak and act contemptuously

FLOWERS, pulverised substance

FLY, familiar spirit

FOIL, weapon used in fencing; that which sets anything off to advantage

FOIST, cut-purse, sharper

FOND(LY), foolish(ly)

FOOT-CLOTH, housings of ornamental cloth which hung down on either side a horse to the ground

FOOTING, foothold; footstep; dancing

FOPPERY, foolery

FOR, "— failing," for fear of failing

FORBEAR, bear with; abstain from

FORCE, "hunt at —," run the game down with dogs

FOREHEAD, modesty; face, assurance, effrontery

FORESLOW, delay

FORESPEAK, bewitch; foretell

FORETOP, front lock of hair which fashion required to be worn upright

FORGED, fabricated

FORM, state formally

FORMAL, shapely; normal; conventional

FORTHCOMING, produced when required

FOUNDER, disable with over-riding

FOURM, form, lair

FOX, sword

FRAIL, rush basket in which figs or raisins were packed

FRAMPULL, peevish, sour-tempered

FRAPLER, blusterer, wrangler

FRAYING, "a stag is said to fray his head when he rubs it against a tree to . . . cause the outward coat of the new horns to fall off " (Gifford)

FREIGHT (of the gazetti), burden (of the newspapers)

FREQUENT, full

FRICACE, rubbing

FRICATRICE, woman of low character

FRIPPERY, old clothes shop

FROCK, smock-frock

FROLICS, (?) humorous verses circulated at a feast (N.E.D.); couplets wrapped round sweetmeats (Cunningham)

FRONTLESS, shameless

FROTED, rubbed

FRUMETY, hulled wheat boiled in milk and spiced

FRUMP, flout, sneer

FUCUS, dye

FUGEAND, (?) figent: fidgety, restless (N.E.D.)

FULLAM, false dice

FULMART, polecat

FULSOME, foul, offensive

FURIBUND, raging, furious

GALLEY-FOIST, city-barge, used on Lord Mayor's Day, when he was sworn into his office at Westminster (Whalley)

GALLIARD, lively dance in triple time

GAPE, be eager after

GARAGANTUA, Rabelais' giant

GARB, sheaf (Fr. *gerbe*); manner, fashion, behaviour

GARD, guard, trimming, gold or silver lace, or other ornament

GARDED, faced or trimmed

GARNISH, fee

GAVEL-KIND, name of a land-tenure existing chiefly in Kent; from 16th century often used to denote custom of dividing a deceased man's property equally among his sons (N.E.D.)

GAZETTE, small Venetian coin worth about three-farthings

GEANCE, jaunt, errand

GEAR (GEER), stuff, matter, affair

GELID, frozen

GEMONIES, steps from which the bodies of criminals were thrown into the river

GENERAL, free, affable

GENIUS, attendant spirit

GENTRY, gentlemen; manners characteristic of gentry, good breeding

GIB-CAT, tom-cat

GIGANTOMACHIZE, start a giants' war

GIGLOT, wanton

GIMBLET, gimlet

GING, gang

GLASS ("taking in of shadows, etc."), crystal or beryl

GLEEK, card game played by three; party of three, trio; side glance

GLICK (GLEEK), jest, gibe

GLIDDER, glaze

GLORIOUSLY, of vain glory

GODWIT, bird of the snipe family

GOLD-END-MAN, a buyer of broken gold and silver

GOLL, hand

GONFALIONIER, standard-bearer, chief magistrate, etc.

GOOD, sound in credit

GOOD-YEAR, good luck

GOOSE-TURD, colour of. (*See* Turd)

GORCROW, carrion crow

GORGET, neck armour

GOSSIP, godfather

GOWKED, from "gowk," to stand staring and gaping like a fool

GRANNAM, grandam

GRASS, (?) grease, fat

GRATEFUL, agreeable, welcome

GRATIFY, give thanks to

GRATITUDE, gratuity

GRATULATE, welcome, congratulate

GRAVITY, dignity

GRAY, badger

GRICE, cub

GRIEF, grievance

GRIPE, vulture, griffin

GRIPE'S EGG, vessel in shape of

GROAT, fourpence

GROGRAN, coarse stuff made of silk and mohair, or of coarse silk

GROOM-PORTER, officer in the royal household

GROPE, handle, probe

GROUND, pit (hence "grounded judgments")

GUARD, caution, heed

GUARDANT, heraldic term: turning the head only

GUILDER, Dutch coin worth about 4*d*.

GULES, gullet, throat; heraldic term for red

GULL, simpleton, dupe

GUST, taste

HAB NAB, by, on, chance

HABERGEON, coat of mail

HAGGARD, wild female hawk; hence coy, wild

HALBERD, combination of lance and battle-axe

HALL, "a —!" a cry to clear the room for the dancers

HANDSEL, first money taken

HANGER, loop or strap on a sword-belt from which the sword was suspended

HAP, fortune, luck

HAPPILY, haply

HAPPINESS, appropriateness, fitness

HAPPY, rich

HARBOUR, track, trace (an animal) to its shelter

HARD-FAVOURED, harsh-featured

HARPOCRATES, Horus the child, son of Osiris, figured with a finger pointing to his mouth, indicative of silence

HARRINGTON, a patent was granted to Lord H. for the coinage of tokens (*q.v.*)

HARROT, herald

HARRY NICHOLAS, founder of a community called the "Family of Love"

HAY, net for catching rabbits, etc.

HAY! (Ital. *hai!*), you have it (a fencing term)

HAY IN HIS HORN, ill-tempered person

HAZARD, game at dice; that which is staked

HEAD, "first —," young deer with antlers first sprouting; fig. a newly-ennobled man

HEADBOROUGH, constable

HEARKEN AFTER, inquire; "hearken out," find, search out

HEARTEN, encourage

HEAVEN AND HELL ("Alchemist"), names of taverns

HECTIC, fever

HEDGE IN, include

HELM, upper part of a retort

HER'NSEW, hernshaw, heron

HIERONIMO (JERONIMO), hero of Kyd's "Spanish Tragedy"

HOBBY, nag

HOBBY-HORSE, imitation horse of some light material, fastened round the waist of the morrice-dancer, who imitated the movements of a skittish horse

HODDY-DODDY, fool

HOIDEN, hoyden, formerly applied to both sexes (ancient term for leveret? Gifford)

HOLLAND, name of two famous chemists

HONE AND HONERO, wailing expressions of lament or discontent

HOOD-WINK'D, blindfolded

HORARY, hourly

HORN-MAD, stark mad (quibble)

HORN-THUMB, cut-purses were in the habit of wearing a horn shield on the thumb

HORSE-BREAD-EATING, horses were often fed on coarse bread

HORSE-COURSER, horse-dealer

HOSPITAL, Christ's Hospital

HOWLEGLAS, Eulenspiegel, the hero of a popular German tale which relates his buffooneries and knavish tricks

HUFF, hectoring, arrogance

HUFF IT, swagger

HUISHER (Fr. *huissier*), usher

HUM, beer and spirits mixed together

HUMANITIAN, humanist, scholar

HUMOROUS, capricious, moody, out of humour; moist

HUMOUR, a word used in and out of season in the time of Shakespeare and Ben Jonson, and ridiculed by both

HUMOURS, manners

HUMPHREY, DUKE, those who were dinnerless spent the dinner-hour in a part of St. Paul's where stood a monument, said to be that of the duke's; hence "dine with Duke Humphrey," to go hungry

HURTLESS, harmless

IDLE, useless, unprofitable

ILL-AFFECTED, ill-disposed

ILL-HABITED, unhealthy

ILLUSTRATE, illuminate

IMBIBITION, saturation, steeping

IMBROCATA, fencing term: a thrust in tierce

IMPAIR, impairment

IMPART, give money

IMPARTER, any one ready to be cheated and to part with his money

IMPEACH, damage

IMPERTINENCIES, irrelevancies

IMPERTINENT(LY), irrelevant(ly), without reason or purpose

IMPOSITION, duty imposed by

IMPOTENTLY, beyond power of control

IMPRESS, money in advance

IMPULSION, incitement

IN AND IN, a game played by two or three persons with four dice

INCENSE, incite, stir up

INCERATION, act of covering with wax; or reducing a substance to softness of wax

INCH, "to their —es," according to their stature, capabilities

INCH-PIN, sweet-bread

INCONVENIENCE, inconsistency, absurdity

INCONY, delicate, rare (used as a term of affection)

INCUBEE, incubus

INCUBUS, evil spirit that oppresses us in sleep, nightmare

INCURIOUS, unfastidious, uncritical

INDENT, enter into engagement

INDIFFERENT, tolerable, passable

INDIGESTED, shapeless, chaotic

INDUCE, introduce

INDUE, supply

INEXORABLE, relentless

INFANTED, born, produced

INFLAME, augment charge

INGENIOUS, used indiscriminately for ingenuous; intelligent, talented

INGENUITY, ingenuousness

INGENUOUS, generous

INGINE. *See* Engin

INGINER, engineer. (*See* Enginer)

INGLE, OR ENGHLE, bosom friend, intimate, minion

INHABITABLE, uninhabitable

INJURY, insult, affront

IN-MATE, resident, indwelling

INNATE, natural

INNOCENT, simpleton

INQUEST, jury, or other official body of inquiry

INQUISITION, inquiry

INSTANT, immediate

INSTRUMENT, legal document

INSURE, assure

INTEGRATE, complete, perfect

INTELLIGENCE, secret information, news

INTEND, note carefully, attend, give ear to, be occupied with

INTENDMENT, intention

INTENT, intention, wish

INTENTION, concentration of attention or gaze

INTENTIVE, attentive

INTERESSED, implicated

INTRUDE, bring in forcibly or without leave

INVINCIBLY, invisibly

INWARD, intimate

IRPE (uncertain), "a fantastic grimace, or contortion of the body" (Gifford)

JACK, Jack o' the clock, automaton figure that strikes the hour; Jack-a-lent, puppet thrown at in Lent

JACK, key of a virginal

JACOB'S STAFF, an instrument for taking altitudes and distances

JADE, befool

JEALOUSY, JEALOUS, suspicion, suspicious

JERKING, lashing

JEW'S TRUMP, Jew's harp

JIG, merry ballad or tune; a fanciful dialogue or light comic act introduced at the end or during an interlude of a play

JOINED (JOINT)-STOOL, folding stool

JOLL, jowl

JOLTHEAD, blockhead

JUMP, agree, tally

JUST YEAR, no one was capable of the consulship until he was forty-three

KELL, cocoon

KELLY, an alchemist

KEMB, comb

KEMIA, vessel for distillation

KIBE, chap, sore

KILDERKIN, small barrel

KILL, kiln

KIND, nature; species; "do one's —," act according to one's nature

KIRTLE, woman's gown of jacket and petticoat

KISS OR DRINK AFORE ME, "this is a familiar expression, employed when what the speaker is just about to say is anticipated by another" (Gifford)

KIT, fiddle

KNACK, snap, click

KNIPPER-DOLING, a well-known Anabaptist

KNITTING CUP, marriage cup

KNOCKING, striking, weighty

KNOT, company, band; a sandpiper, or robin snipe (*Tringa canutus*); flower-bed laid out in fanciful design

KURSINED, KYRSIN, christened

LABOURED, wrought with labour and care

LADE, load(ed)

LADING, load

LAID, plotted

LANCE-KNIGHT (*Lanzknecht*), a German mercenary foot-soldier

LAP, fold

LAR, household god

LARD, garnish

LARGE, abundant

LARUM, alarum, call to arms

LATTICE, tavern windows were furnished with lattices of various colours

LAUNDER, to wash gold in *aqua regia*, so as imperceptibly to extract some of it

LAVE, ladle, bale

LAW, " give —," give a start (term of chase)

LAXATIVE, loose

LAY ABOARD, run alongside generally with intent to board

LEAGUER, siege, or camp of besieging army

LEASING, lying

LEAVE, leave off, desist

LEER, leering, or " empty, hence, perhaps, leer horse, a horse without a rider; leer is an adjective meaning uncontrolled, hence ' leer drunkards ' " (Halliwell); according to Nares, a leer (empty) horse meant also a led horse; leeward, left

LEESE, lose

LEGS, " make —," do obeisance

LEIGER, resident representative

LEIGERITY, legerdemain

LEMMA, subject proposed, or title of the epigram

LENTER, slower

LET, hinder

LET, hindrance

LEVEL COIL, a rough game . . . in which one hunted another from his seat. Hence used for any noisy riot (Halliwell)

LEWD, ignorant

LEYSTALLS, receptacles of filth

LIBERAL, ample

LIEGER, ledger, register

LIFT(ING), steal(ing); theft

LIGHT, alight

LIGHTLY, commonly, usually, often

LIKE, please

LIKELY, agreeable, pleasing

LIME-HOUND, leash-, blood-hound

LIMMER, vile, worthless

LIN, leave off

LINE, " by —," by rule

LINSTOCK, staff to stick in the ground, with forked head to hold a lighted match for firing cannon

LIQUID, clear

LIST, listen, hark; like, please

LIVERY, legal term, delivery of the possession, etc.

LOGGET, small log, stick

LOOSE, solution; upshot, issue; release of an arrow

LOSE, give over, desist from; waste

LOUTING, bowing, cringing

LUCULENT, bright of beauty

LUDGATHIANS, dealers on Ludgate Hill

LURCH, rob, cheat

LUTE, to close a vessel with some kind of cement

MACK, unmeaning expletive

MADGE-HOWLET or OWL, barn-owl

MAIM, hurt, injury

MAIN, chief concern (used as a quibble on heraldic term for " hand ")

MAINPRISE, becoming surety for a prisoner so as to procure his release

MAINTENANCE, giving aid, or abetting

MAKE, mate

MAKE, MADE, acquaint with business, prepare(d), instruct(ed)

MALLANDERS, disease of horses

MALT HORSE, dray horse

MAMMET, puppet

MAMMOTHREPT, spoiled child

MANAGE, control (term used for breaking in horses); handling, administration

MANGO, slave-dealer

MANGONISE, polish up for sale

MANIPLES, bundles, handfuls

MANKIND, masculine, like a virago

MANKIND, humanity

MAPLE FACE, spotted face (N.E.D.)

MARCHPANE, a confection of almonds, sugar, etc.

MARK, " fly to the —," " generally said of a goshawk when, having ' put in ' a covey of partridges, she takes stand, marking the spot where they disappeared from view until the falconer arrives to put them out to her " (Harting, Bibl. Accip, Gloss. 226)

MARLE, marvel

MARROW-BONE MAN, one often on his knees for prayer

MARRY! exclamation derived from the Virgin's name

MARRY GIP, " probably originated from By Mary Gipcy = St. Mary of Egypt " (N.E.D.)

MARTAGAN, Turk's cap lily

MARYHINCHCO, stringhalt

MASORETH, Masora, correct form of the scriptural text according to Hebrew tradition

MASS, abb. for master

MAUND, beg

MAUTHER, girl, maid

MEAN, moderation

MEASURE, dance, more especially a stately one

MEAT, " carry — in one's mouth," be a source of money or entertainment

MEATH, metheglin

MECHANICAL, belonging to mechanics; mean, vulgar

MEDITERRANEO, middle aisle of St. Paul's, a general resort for business and amusement

MEET WITH, even with

MELICOTTON, a late kind of peach

MENSTRUE, solvent

MERCAT, market

MERD, excrement

MERE, undiluted; absolute, unmitigated

MESS, party of four

METHEGLIN, fermented liquor, of which one ingredient was honey

METOPOSCOPY, study of physiognomy

MIDDLING GOSSIP, go-between

MIGNIARD, dainty, delicate

MILE-END, training-ground of the city

MINE-MEN, sappers

MINION, form of cannon

MINSITIVE, (?) mincing, affected (N.E.D.)

MISCELLANY MADAM, "a female trader in miscellaneous articles; a dealer in trinkets or ornaments of various kinds, such as kept shops in the New Exchange" (Nares)

MISCELLINE, mixed grain; medley

MISCONCEIT, misconception

MISPRISE, MISPRISION, mistake, misunderstanding

MISTAKE AWAY, carry away as if by mistake

MITHRIDATE, an antidote against poison

MOCCINIGO, small Venetian coin, worth about ninepence

MODERN, in the mode; ordinary, commonplace

MOMENT, force or influence of value

MONTANTO, upward stroke

MONTH'S MIND, violent desire

MOORISH, like a moor or waste

MORGLAY, sword of Bevis of Southampton

MORRICE-DANCE, dances on May Day, etc., in which certain personages were represented

MORTALITY, death

MORT-MAL, old sore, gangrene

MOSCADINO, confection flavoured with musk

MOTHER, *Hysterica passio*

MOTION, proposal, request; puppet, puppet-show; "one of the small figures on the face of a large clock which was moved by the vibration of the pendulum" (Whalley)

MOTION, suggest, propose

MOTLEY, parti-coloured dress of a fool; hence used to signify pertaining to, or like, a fool

MOTTE, motto

MOURNIVAL, set of four aces or court cards in a hand; a quartette

Mow, setord hay or sheaves of grain

MUCH! expressive of irony and incredulity

MUCKINDER, handkerchief

MULE, "born to ride on —," judges or serjeants-at-law formerly rode on mules when going in state to Westminster (Whalley)

MULLETS, small pincers

MUM-CHANCE, game of chance, played in silence

MUN, must

MUREY, dark crimson red

MUSCOVY-GLASS, mica

MUSE, wonder

MUSICAL, in harmony

MUSS, mouse; scramble

MYROBOLANE, foreign conserve, "a dried plum, brought from the Indies"

MYSTERY, art, trade, profession

NAIL, "to the —" (*ad unguem*), to perfection, to the very utmost

NATIVE, natural

NEAT, cattle

NEAT, smartly apparelled; unmixed; dainty

NEATLY, neatly finished

NEATNESS, elegance

NEIS, nose, scent

NEUF (NEAF, NEIF), fist

NEUFT, newt

NIAISE, foolish, inexperienced person

NICE, fastidious, trivial, finical, scrupulous

NICENESS, fastidiousness

NICK, exact amount; right moment; "set in the —," meaning uncertain

NICK, suit, fit; hit, seize the right moment, etc., exactly hit on, hit off

NOBLE, gold coin worth 6s. 8d.

NOCENT, harmful

NIL, not will

NOISE, company of musicians

NOMENTACK, an Indian chief from Virginia

NONES, nonce

NOTABLE, egregious

NOTE, sign, token

NOUGHT, "be —," go to the devil, be hanged, etc.

NOWT-HEAD, blockhead

NUMBER, rhythm

NUPSON, oaf, simpleton

OADE, woad

OBARNI, preparation of mead

OBJECT, oppose; expose; interpose

OBLATRANT, barking, railing

OBNOXIOUS, liable, exposed; offensive

OBSERVANCE, homage, devoted service

OBSERVANT, attentive, obsequious

OBSERVE, show deference, respect

OBSERVER, one who shows deference, or waits upon another

OBSTANCY, legal phrase, "juridical opposition"

OBSTREPEROUS, clamorous, vociferous

OBSTUPEFACT, stupefied

ODLING, (?) "must have some relation to tricking and cheating" (Nares)

OMINOUS, deadly, fatal

ONCE, at once; for good and all; used also for additional emphasis

ONLY, pre-eminent, special

OPEN, make public; expound

OPPILATION, obstruction

OPPONE, oppose

OPPOSITE, antagonist

OPPRESS, suppress

ORIGINOUS, native

ORT, remnant, scrap

OUT, "to be —," to have forgotten one's part; not at one with each other

OUTCRY, sale by auction

OUTRECUIDANCE, arrogance, presumption

OUTSPEAK, speak more than

OVERPARTED, given too difficult a part to play

OWLSPIEGEL. *See* Howleglass

OYEZ! (O YES!), hear ye! call of the public crier when about to make a proclamation

PACKING PENNY, "give a —," dismiss, send packing

PAD, highway

PAD-HORSE, road-horse

PAINED (PANED) SLOPS, full breeches made of strips of different colour and material

PAINFUL, diligent, painstaking

PAINT, blush

PALINODE, ode of recantation

PALL, weaken, dim, make stale

PALM, triumph

PAN, skirt of dress or coat

PANNEL, pad, or rough kind of saddle

PANNIER-ALLY, inhabited by tripe-sellers

PANNIER-MAN, hawker; a man employed about the inns of court to bring in provisions, set the table, etc.

PANTOFLE, indoor shoe, slipper

PARAMENTOS, fine trappings

PARANOMASIE, a play upon words

PARANTORY, (?) peremptory

PARCEL, particle, fragment (used contemptuously); article

PARCEL, part, partly

PARCEL-POET, poetaster

PARERGA, subordinate matters

PARGET, to paint or plaster the face

PARLE, parley

PARLOUS, clever, shrewd

PART, apportion

PARTAKE, participate in

PARTED, endowed, talented

PARTICULAR, individual person

PARTIZAN, kind of halberd

PARTRICH, partridge

PARTS, qualities, endowments

PASH, dash, smash

PASS, care, trouble oneself

PASSADO, fencing term: a thrust

PASSAGE, game at dice

PASSINGLY, exceedingly

PASSION, effect caused by external agency

PASSION, "in —," in so melancholy a tone, so pathetically

PATOUN, (?) Fr. *pâton*, pellet of dough; perhaps the "moulding of the tobacco . . . for the pipe " (Gifford); (?) variant of Petun, South American name of tobacco

PATRICO, the recorder, priest, orator of strolling beggars or gipsies

PATTEN, shoe with wooden sole; "go —," keep step with, accompany

PAUCA VERBA, few words

PAVIN, a stately dance

PEACE, "with my master's —," by leave, favour

PECULIAR, individual, single

PEDANT, teacher of the languages

PEEL, baker's shovel

PEEP, speak in a small or shrill voice

PEEVISH(LY), foolish(ly), capricious(ly); childish(ly)

PELICAN, a retort fitted with tube or tubes, for continuous distillation

PENCIL, small tuft of hair

PERDUE, soldier accustomed to hazardous service

PEREMPTORY, resolute, bold; imperious; thorough, utter, absolute(ly)

PERIMETER, circumference of a figure

PERIOD, limit, end

PERK, perk up

PERPETUANA, "this seems to be that glossy kind of stuff now called *everlasting*, and anciently worn by serjeants and other city officers " (Gifford)

PERSPECTIVE, a view, scene or scenery; an optical device which gave a distortion to the picture unless seen from a particular point; a relief, modelled to produce an optical illusion

PERSPICIL, optic glass

PERSTRINGE, criticise, censure

PERSUADE, inculcate, commend

PERSWAY, mitigate

PERTINACY, pertinacity

PESTLING, pounding, pulverising, like a pestle

PETASUS, broad-brimmed hat or winged cap worn by Mercury

PETITIONARY, supplicatory

PETRONEL, a kind of carbine or light gun carried by horsemen

PETULANT, pert, insolent

PHERE. *See* Fere

PHLEGMA, watery distilled liquor (old chem. " water ")

PHRENETIC, madman

PICARDIL, stiff upright collar fastened on to the coat (Whalley)

PICKT-HATCH, disreputable quarter of London

PIECE, person, used for woman or girl; a gold coin worth in Jonson's time 20s. or 22s.

PIECES OF EIGHT, Spanish coin: piastre equal to eight reals

PIED, variegated

PIE-POUDRES (Fr. *pied-poudreux*, dusty-foot), court held at fairs to administer justice to itinerant vendors and buyers

PILCHER, term of contempt; one who wore a buff or leather jerkin, as did the serjeants of the counter; a pilferer

PILED, pilled, peeled, bald

PILL'D, polled, fleeced

PIMLICO, " sometimes spoken of as a person —perhaps master of a house famous for a particular ale " (Gifford)

PINE, afflict, distress

PINK, stab with a weapon; pierce or cut in scallops for ornament

PINNACE, a go-between in infamous sense

PISMIRE, ant

PISTOLET, gold coin, worth about 6s.

PITCH, height of a bird of prey's flight

PLAGUE, punishment, torment

Glossary

PLAIN, lament

PLAIN SONG, simple melody

PLAISE, plaice

PLANET, "struck with a —," planets were supposed to have powers of blasting or exercising secret influences

PLAUSIBLE, pleasing

PLAUSIBLY, approvingly

PLOT, plan

PLY, apply oneself to

POESIE, posy, motto inside a ring

POINT IN HIS DEVICE, exact in every particular

POINTS, tagged laces or cords for fastening the breeches to the doublet

POINT-TRUSSER, one who trussed (tied) his master's points (q.v.)

POISE, weigh, balance

POKING-STICK, stick used for setting the plaits of ruffs

POLITIC, politician

POLITIC, judicious, prudent, political

POLITICIAN, plotter, intriguer

POLL, strip, plunder, gain by extortion

POMANDER, ball of perfume, worn or hung about the person to prevent infection, or for foppery

POMMADO, vaulting on a horse without the aid of stirrups

PONTIC, sour

POPULAR, vulgar, of the populace

POPULOUS, numerous

PORT, gate; print of a deer's foot

PORT, transport

PORTAGUE, Portuguese gold coin, worth over £3 or £4

PORTCULLIS, "— of coin," some old coins have a portcullis stamped on their reverse (Whalley)

PORTENT, marvel, prodigy; sinister omen

PORTENTOUS, prophesying evil, threatening

PORTER, references appear "to allude to Parsons, the king's porter, who was . . . near seven feet high" (Whalley)

POSSESS, inform, acquaint

POST AND PAIR, a game at cards

POSY, motto. (See Poesie)

POTCH, poach

POULT-FOOT, club-foot

POUNCE, claw, talon

PRACTICE, intrigue, concerted plot

PRACTISE, plot, conspire

PRAGMATIC, an expert, agent

PRAGMATIC, officious, conceited, meddling

PRECEDENT, record of proceedings

PRECEPT, warrant, summons

PRECISIAN(ISM), Puritan(ism), preciseness

PREFER, recommend

PRESENCE, presence chamber

PRESENT(LY), immediate(ly), without delay; at the present time; actually

PRESS, force into service

PREST, ready

PRETEND, assert, allege

PREVENT, anticipate

PRICE, worth, excellence

PRICK, point, dot used in the writing of Hebrew and other languages

PRICK, prick out, mark off, select; trace, track; "— away," make off with speed

PRIMERO, game of cards

PRINCOX, pert boy

PRINT, "in —," to the letter, exactly

PRISTINATE, former

PRIVATE, private interests

PRIVATE, privy, intimate

PROCLIVE, prone to

PRODIGIOUS, monstrous, unnatural

PRODIGY, monster

PRODUCED, prolonged

PROFESS, pretend

PROJECTION, the throwing of the "powder of projection" into the crucible to turn the melted metal into gold or silver

PROLATE, pronounce drawlingly

PROPER, of good appearance, handsome; own, particular

PROPERTIES, stage necessaries

PROPERTY, duty; tool

PRORUMPED, burst out

PROTEST, vow, proclaim (an affected word of that time); formally declare non-payment, etc., of bill of exchange; fig. failure of personal credit, etc.

PROVANT, soldier's allowance — hence, of common make

PROVIDE, foresee

PROVIDENCE, foresight, prudence

PUBLICATION, making a thing public or common property (N.E.D.)

PUCKFIST, puff-ball; insipid, insignificant, boasting fellow

PUFF-WING, shoulder puff

PUISNE, judge of inferior rank, a junior

PULCHRITUDE, beauty

PUMP, shoe

PUNGENT, piercing

PUNTO, point, hit

PURCEPT, precept, warrant

PURE, fine, capital, excellent

PURELY, perfectly, utterly

PURL, pleat or fold of a ruff

PURSE-NET, net of which the mouth is drawn together with a string

PURSUIVANT, state messenger who summoned the persecuted seminaries; warrant officer

PURSY, PURSINESS, shortwinded(ness)

PUT, make a push, exert yourself (N.E.D.)

PUT OFF, excuse, shift

PUT ON, incite, encourage; proceed with, take in hand, try

QUACKSALVER, quack

QUAINT, elegant, elaborated, ingenious, clever

QUAR, quarry

QUARRIED, seized, or fed upon, as prey

QUEAN, hussy, jade

QUEASY, hazardous, delicate

QUELL, kill, destroy

QUEST, request; inquiry

QUESTION, decision by force of arms

QUESTMAN, one appointed to make official inquiry

QUIB, QUIBLIN, quibble, quip

QUICK, the living

QUIDDIT, quiddity, legal subtlety

QUIRK, clever turn or trick

QUIT, requite, repay; acquit, absolve; rid; forsake, leave

QUITTER-BONE, disease of horses

QUODLING, codling

QUOIT, throw like a quoit, chuck

QUOTE, take note, observe, write down

RACK, neck of mutton or pork (Halliwell)

RAKE UP, cover over

RAMP, rear, as a lion, etc.

RAPT, carry away

RAPT, enraptured

RASCAL, young or inferior deer

RASH, strike with a glancing oblique blow, as a boar with its tusk

RATSEY, GOMALIEL, a famous highwayman

RAVEN, devour

REACH, understand

REAL, regal

REBATU, ruff, turned-down collar

RECTOR, RECTRESS, director, governor

REDARGUE, confute

REDUCE, bring back

REED, rede, counsel, advice

REEL, run riot

REFEL, refute

REFORMADOES, disgraced or disbanded soldiers

REGIMENT, government

REGRESSION, return

REGULAR (" Tale of a Tub "), regular noun (quibble) (N.E.D.)

RELIGION, " make — of," make a point of, scruple of

RELISH, savour

REMNANT, scrap of quotation

REMORA, species of fish

RENDER, depict, exhibit, show

REPAIR, reinstate

REPETITION, recital, narration

REREMOUSE, bat

RESIANT, resident

RESIDENCE, sediment

RESOLUTION, judgment, decision

RESOLVE, inform; assure; prepare, make up one's mind; dissolve; come to a decision, be convinced; relax, set at ease

RESPECTIVE, worthy of respect; regardful, discriminative

RESPECTIVELY, with reverence

RESPECTLESS, regardless

RESPIRE, exhale; inhale

RESPONSIBLE, correspondent

REST, musket-rest

REST, " set up one's —," venture one's all, one's last stake (from game of primero)

REST, arrest

RESTIVE, RESTY, dull, inactive

RETCHLESS(NESS), reckless(ness)

RETIRE, cause to retire

RETRICATO, fencing term

RETRIEVE, rediscovery of game once sprung

RETURNS, ventures sent abroad, for the safe return of which so much money is received

REVERBERATE, dissolve or blend by reflected heat

REVERSE, REVERSO, back-handed thrust, etc., in fencing

REVISE, reconsider a sentence

RHEUM, spleen, caprice

RIBIBE, abusive term for an old woman

RID, destroy, do away with

RIFLING, raffling, dicing

RING, " cracked within the —," coins so cracked were unfit for currency

RISSE, risen, rose

RIVELLED, wrinkled

ROARER, swaggerer

ROCHET, fish of the gurnet kind

ROCK, distaff

RODOMONTADO, braggadocio

ROGUE, vagrant, vagabond

RONDEL, " a round mark in the score of a public-house " (Nares); roundel

ROOK, sharper; fool, dupe

ROSAKER, similar to ratsbane

ROSA-SOLIS, a spiced spirituous liquor

ROSES, rosettes

ROUND, " gentlemen of the —," officers of inferior rank

ROUND TRUNKS, trunk hose, short loose breeches reaching almost or quite to the knees

ROUSE, carouse, bumper

ROVER, arrow used for shooting at a random mark at uncertain distance

ROWLY-POWLY, roly-poly

RUDE, RUDENESS, unpolished, rough(ness), coarse(ness)

RUFFLE, flaunt, swagger

RUG, coarse frieze

RUG-GOWNS, gown made of rug

RUSH, reference to rushes with which the floors were then strewn

RUSHER, one who strewed the floor with rushes

RUSSET, homespun cloth of neutral or reddish-brown colour

SACK, loose, flowing gown

SADLY, seriously, with gravity

SAD(NESS), sober, serious(ness)

SAFFI, bailiffs

ST. THOMAS à WATERINGS, place in Surrey where criminals were executed

SAKER, small piece of ordnance

SALT, leap

SALT, lascivious

SAMPSUCHINE, sweet marjoram

SARABAND, a slow dance

SATURNALS, began December 17

SAUCINESS, presumption, insolence

SAUCY, bold, impudent, wanton

SAUNA (Lat.), a gesture of contempt

SAVOUR, perceive; gratify, please; to partake of the nature

SAY, sample

SAY, assay, try

SCALD, word of contempt, implying dirt and disease

SCALLION, shalot, small onion

SCANDERBAG, " name which the Turks (in allusion to Alexander the Great) gave to the brave Castriot, chief of Albania, with whom they had continual wars. His romantic life had just been translated " (Gifford)

SCAPE, escape

SCARAB, beetle

SCARTOCCIO, fold of paper, cover, cartouch, cartridge

SCONCE, head

SCOPE, aim

SCOT AND LOT, tax, contribution (formerly a parish assessment)

SCOTOMY, dizziness in the head

SCOUR, purge

SCOURSE, deal, swap

SCRATCHES, disease of horses

SCROYLE, mean, rascally fellow

SCRUPLE, doubt

SEAL, put hand to the giving up of property or rights

SEALED, stamped as genuine

SEAM-RENT, ragged

SEAMING LACES, insertion or edging

SEAR UP, close by searing, burning

SEARCED, sifted

SECRETARY, able to keep a secret

SECULAR, worldly, ordinary, commonplace

SECURE, confident

SEELIE, happy, blest

SEISIN, legal term: possession

SELLARY, lewd person

SEMBLABLY, similarly

SEMINARY, a Romish priest educated in a foreign seminary

SENSELESS, insensible, without sense or feeling

SENSIBLY, perceptibly

SENSIVE, sensitive

SENSUAL, pertaining to the physical or material

SERENE, harmful dew of evening

SERICON, red tincture

SERVANT, lover

SERVICES, doughty deeds of arms

SESTERCE, Roman copper coin

SET, stake, wager

SET UP, drill

SETS, deep plaits of the ruff

SEWER, officer who served up the feast, and brought water for the hands of the guests

SHAPE, a suit by way of disguise

SHIFT, fraud, dodge

SHIFTER, cheat

SHITTLE, shuttle; "shittle-cock," shuttlecock

SHOT, tavern reckoning

SHOT-CLOG, one only tolerated because he paid the shot (reckoning) for the rest

SHOT-FREE, scot-free, not having to pay

SHOVE-GROAT, low kind of gambling amusement, perhaps somewhat of the nature of pitch and toss

SHOT-SHARKS, drawers

SHREWD, mischievous, malicious, curst

SHREWDLY, keenly, in a high degree

SHRIVE, sheriff; posts were set up before his door for proclamations, or to indicate his residence

SHROVING, Shrovetide, season of merriment

SIGILLA, seal, mark

SILENCED BRETHREN, MINISTERS, those of the Church or Nonconformists who had been silenced, deprived, etc.

SILLY, simple, harmless

SIMPLE, silly, witless; plain, true

SIMPLES, herbs

SINGLE, term of chase, signifying when the hunted stag is separated from the herd, or forced to break covert

SINGLE, weak, silly

SINGLE-MONEY, small change

SINGULAR, unique, supreme

SI-QUIS, bill, advertisement

SKELDRING, getting money under false pretences; swindling

SKILL, "it —s not," matters not

SKINK(ER), pour, draw(er), tapster

SKIRT, tail

SLEEK, smooth

SLICE, fire shovel or pan (dial.)

SLICK, sleek, smooth

'SLID, 'SLIGHT, 'SPRECIOUS, irreverent oaths

SLIGHT, sleight, cunning, cleverness; trick

SLIP, counterfeit coin, bastard

SLIPPERY, polished and shining

SLOPS, large loose breeches

SLOT, print of a stag's foot

SLUR, put a slur on; cheat (by sliding a die in some way)

SMELT, gull, simpleton

SNORLE, "perhaps snarl, as Puppy is addressed" (Cunningham)

SNOTTERIE, filth

SNUFF, anger, resentment; "take in —," take offence at

SNUFFERS, small open silver dishes for holding snuff, or receptacle for placing snuffers in (Halliwell)

SOCK, shoe worn by comic actors

SOD, seethe

SOGGY, soaked, sodden

SOIL, "take —," said of a hunted stag when he takes to the water for safety

SOL, sou

SOLDADOES, soldiers

SOLICIT, rouse, excite to action

SOOTH, flattery, cajolery

SOOTHE, flatter, humour

SOPHISTICATE, adulterate

SORT, company, party; rank, degree

SORT, suit, fit; select

SOUSE, ear

SOUSED ("Devil is an Ass"), fol. read "sou't," which Dyce interprets as "a variety of the spelling of shu'd: to shu is to scare a bird away." (See his Webster, p. 350)

SOWTER, cobbler

SPAGYRICA, chemistry according to the teachings of Paracelsus

SPAR, bar

SPEAK, make known, proclaim

SPECULATION, power of sight

SPED, to have fared well, prospered

SPEECE, species

SPIGHT, anger, rancour

SPINNER, spider

SPINSTRY, lewd person

SPITTLE, hospital, lazar-house

SPLEEN, considered the seat of the emotions
SPLEEN, caprice, humour, mood
SPRUNT, spruce
SPURGE, foam
SPUR-RYAL, gold coin worth 15s.
SQUIRE, square, measure; " by the —," exactly
STAGGERING, wavering, hesitating
STAIN, disparagement, disgrace
STALE, decoy, or cover, stalking-horse
STALE, make cheap, common
STALK, approach stealthily or under cover
STALL, forestall
STANDARD, suit
STAPLE, market, emporium
STARK, downright
STARTING-HOLES, loopholes of escape
STATE, dignity; canopied chair of state; estate
STATUMINATE, support vines by poles or stakes; used by Pliny (Gifford)
STAY, gag
STAY, await; detain
STICKLER, second or umpire
STIGMATISE, mark, brand
STILL, continual(ly), constant(ly)
STINKARD, stinking fellow
STINT, stop
STIPTIC, astringent
STOCCATA, thrust in fencing
STOCK-FISH, salted and dried fish
STOMACH, pride, valour
STOMACH, resent
STOOP, swoop down as a hawk
STOP, fill, stuff
STOPPLE, stopper
STOTE, stoat, weasel
STOUP, stoop, swoop=bow
STRAIGHT, straightway
STRAMAZOUN (Ital. stramazzone), a down blow, as opposed to the thrust
STRANGE, like a stranger, unfamiliar
STRANGENESS, distance of behaviour
STREIGHTS, OR BERMUDAS, labyrinth of alleys and courts in the Strand
STRIGONIUM, Grau in Hungary, taken from the Turks in 1597
STRIKE, balance (accounts)
STRINGHALT, disease of horses
STROKER, smoother, flatterer
STROOK, p.p. of " strike "
STRUMMEL-PATCHED, strummel is glossed in dialect dicts. as "a long, loose and dishevelled head of hair "
STUDIES, studious efforts
STYLE, title; pointed instrument used for writing on wax tablets
SUBTLE, fine, delicate, thin; smooth, soft
SUBTLETY (SUBTILITY), subtle device
SUBURB, connected with loose living
SUCCUBÆ, demons in form of women
SUCK, extract money from
SUFFERANCE, suffering
SUMMED, term of falconry: with full-grown plumage
SUPER-NEGULUM, topers turned the cup bottom up when it was empty
SUPERSTITIOUS, over-scrupulous
SUPPLE, to make pliant

SURBATE, make sore with walking
SURCEASE, cease
SUR-REVERENCE, save your reverence
SURVISE, peruse
SUSCITABILITY, excitability
SUSPECT, suspicion
SUSPEND, suspect
SUSPENDED, held over for the present
SUTLER, victualler
SWAD, clown, boor
SWATH BANDS, swaddling clothes
SWINGE, beat

TABERD, emblazoned mantle or tunic worn by knights and heralds
TABLE(S), " pair of —," tablets, note-book
TABOR, small drum
TABRET, tabor
TAFFETA, silk; " tuft-taffeta," a more costly silken fabric
TAINT, " — a staff," break a lance at tilting in an unscientific or dishonourable manner
TAKE IN, capture, subdue
TAKE ME WITH YOU, let me understand you
TAKE UP, obtain on credit, borrow
TALENT, sum or weight of Greek currency
TALL, stout, brave
TANKARD-BEARERS, men employed to fetch water from the conduits
TARLETON, celebrated comedian and jester
TARTAROUS, like a Tartar
TAVERN-TOKEN, " to swallow a —," get drunk
TELL, count
TELL-TROTH, truth-teller
TEMPER, modify, soften
TENDER, show regard, care for cherish; manifest
TENT, " take —," take heed
TERSE, swept and polished
TERTIA, " that portion of an army levied out of one particular district or division of a country " (Gifford)
TESTON, tester, coin worth 6d.
THIRDBOROUGH, constable
THREAD, quality
THREAVES, droves
THREE-FARTHINGS, piece of silver current under Elizabeth
THREE-PILED, of finest quality, exaggerated
THRIFTILY, carefully
THRUMS, ends of the weaver's warp; coarse yarn made from
THUMB-RING, familiar spirits were supposed capable of being carried about in various ornaments or parts of dress
TIBICINE, player on the tibia, or pipe
TICK-TACK, game similar to backgammon
TIGHTLY, promptly
TIM, (?) expressive of a climax of nonentity
TIMELESS, untimely, unseasonable
TINCTURE, an essential or spiritual principle supposed by alchemists to be transfusible into material things; an imparted characteristic or tendency
TINK, tinkle

TIPPET, "turn —," change behaviour or way of life

TIPSTAFF, staff tipped with metal

TIRE, head-dress

TIRE, feed ravenously, like a bird of prey

TITILLATION, that which tickles the senses, as a perfume

TOD, fox

TOILED, worn out, harassed

TOKEN, piece of base metal used in place of very small coin, when this was scarce

TONNELS, nostrils

TOP, "parish —," large top kept in villages for amusement and exercise in frosty weather when people were out of work

TOTER, tooter, player on a wind instrument

TOUSE, pull, rend

TOWARD, docile, apt; on the way to; as regards; present, at hand

TOY, whim; trick; term of contempt

TRACT, attraction

TRAIN, allure, entice

TRANSITORY, transmittable

TRANSLATE, transform

TRAY-TRIP, game at dice (success depended on throwing a three) (Nares)

TREACHOUR (TRECHER), traitor

TREEN, wooden

TRENCHER, serving-man who carved or served food

TRENDLE-TAID, trundle-tail, curly-tailed

TRICK (TRICKING), term of heraldry: to draw outline of coat of arms, etc., without blazoning

TRIG, a sprue, dandified man

TRILL, trickle

TRILLIBUB, tripe, any worthless, trifling thing

TRIPOLY, "come from —," able to perform feats of agility, a "jest nominal," depending on the first part of the word (Gifford)

TRITE, worn, shabby

TRIVIA, three-faced goddess (Hecate)

TROJAN, familiar term for an equal or inferior; thief

TROLL, sing loudly

TROMP, trump, deceive

TROPE, figure of speech

TROW, think, believe, wonder

TROWLE, troll

TROWSES, breeches, drawers

TRUCHMAN, interpreter

TRUNDLE, JOHN, well-known printer

TRUNDLE, roll, go rolling along

TRUNDLING CHEATS, term among gipsies and beggars for carts or coaches (Gifford)

TRUNK, speaking-tube

TRUSS, tie the tagged laces that fastened the breeches to the doublet

TUBICINE, trumpeter

TUCKET (Ital. toccato), introductory flourish on the trumpet

TUITION, guardianship

TUMBLER, a particular kind of dog so called from the mode of his hunting

TUMBREL-SLOP, loose, baggy breeches

TURD, excrement

TUSK, gnash the teeth (Century Dict.)

TWIRE, peep, twinkle

TWOPENNY ROOM, gallery

TYRING-HOUSE, attiring-room

ULENSPIEGEL. See Howleglass

UMBRATILE, like or pertaining to a shadow

UMBRE, brown dye

UNBATED, unabated

UNBORED, (?) excessively bored

UNCARNATE, not fleshly, or of flesh

UNCOUTH, strange, unusual

UNDERTAKER, "one who undertook by his influence in the House of Commons to carry things agreeably to his Majesty's wishes" (Whalley); one who becomes surety for

UNEQUAL, unjust

UNEXCEPTED, no objection taken at

UNFEARED, unaffrighted

UNHAPPILY, unfortunately

UNICORN'S HORN, supposed antidote to poison

UNKIND(LY), unnatural(ly)

UNMANNED, untamed (term in falconry)

UNQUIT, undischarged

UNREADY, undressed

UNRUDE, rude to an extreme

UNSEASONED, unseasonable, unripe

UNSEELED, a hawk's eyes were "seeled" by sewing the eyelids together with fine thread

UNTIMELY, unseasonably

UNVALUABLE, invaluable

UPBRAID, make a matter of reproach

UPSEE, heavy kind of Dutch beer (Halliwell); "— Dutch," in the Dutch fashion

UPTAILS ALL, refrain of a popular song

URGE, allege as accomplice, instigator

URSHIN, URCHIN, hedgehog

USE, interest on money; part of sermon dealing with the practical application of doctrine

USE, be in the habit of, accustomed to; put out to interest

USQUEBAUGH, whisky

USURE, usury

UTTER, put in circulation, make to pass current; put forth for sale

VAIL, bow, do homage

VAILS, tips, gratuities

VALL. See Vail

VALLIES (Fr. valise), portmanteau, bag

VAPOUR(S) (n. and v.), used affectedly, like "humour," in many senses, often very vaguely, and freely ridiculed by Jonson; humour, disposition, whims, brag(ging), hector(ing), etc.

VARLET, bailiff, or serjeant-at-mace

VAUT, vault

VEER (naut.), pay out

VEGETAL, vegetable; person full of life and vigour

VELLUTE, velvet

VELVET CUSTARD. Cf. "Taming of the Shrew," iv. 3, 82, "custard coffin," coffin being the raised crust over a pie

VENT, vend, sell; give outlet to; scent snuff up

VENUE, bout (fencing term)

VERDUGO (Span.), hangman, executioner

VERGE, " in the —," within a certain distance of the court

VEX, agitate, torment

VICE, the buffoon of old moralities; some kind of machinery for moving a puppet (Gifford)

VIE AND REVIE, to hazard a certain sum, and to cover it with a larger one

VINCENT AGAINST YORK, two heralds-at-arms

VINDICATE, avenge

VIRGE, wand, rod

VIRGINAL, old form of piano

VIRTUE, valour

VIVELY, in lifelike manner, livelily

VIZARD, mask

VOGUE, rumour, gossip

VOICE, vote

VOID, leave, quit

VOLARY, cage, aviary

VOLLEY, " at —," " o' the volée," at random (from a term of tennis)

VORLOFFE, furlough

WADLOE, keeper of the Devil Tavern, where Jonson and his friends met in the *Apollo* room (Whalley)

WAIGHTS, waits, night musicians, "band of musical watchmen " (Webster), or old form of " hautboys "

WANNION, " vengeance," " plague " (Nares)

WARD, a famous pirate

WARD, guard in fencing

WATCHET, pale, sky blue

WEAL, welfare

WEED, garment

WEFT, waif

WEIGHTS, " to the gold —," to every minute particular

WELKIN, sky

WELL-SPOKEN, of fair speech

WELL-TORNED, turned and polished, as on a wheel

WELT, hem, border of fur

WHÊR, whether

WHETSTONE, GEORGE, an author who lived 1544 (?) to 1587 (?)

WHIFF, a smoke, or drink; " taking the —," inhaling the tobacco smoke or some such accomplishment

WHIGH-HIES, neighings, whinnyings

WHIMSY, whim, " humour "

WHINILING, (?) whining, weakly

WHIT, (?) a mere jot

WHITEMEAT, food made of milk or eggs

WICKED, bad, clumsy

WICKER, pliant, agile

WILDING, esp. fruit of wild apple or crab tree (Webster)

WINE, " I have the — for you," Prov.: I have the perquisites (of the office) which you are to share (Cunningham)

WINNY, " same as old word *wonne*, to stay, etc." (Whalley)

WISE-WOMAN, fortune-teller

WISH, recommend

WISS (WUSSE), " I —," certainly, of a truth

WITHOUT, beyond

WITTY, cunning, ingenious, clever

WOOD, collection, lot

WOODCOCK, term of contempt

WOOLSACK (" — pies "), name of tavern

WORT, unfermented beer

WOUNDY, great, extreme

WREAK, revenge

WROUGHT, wrought upon

WUSSE, interjection. (*See* Wiss)

YEANLING, lamb, kid

ZANY, an inferior clown, who attended upon the chief fool and mimicked his tricks

EVERYMAN'S LIBRARY: A Selected List

BIOGRAPHY

ESSAYS AND CRITICISM

FICTION

3